Pro Novell
Open Enterprise Server

SANDER VAN VUGT

Apress®

Pro Novell Open Enterprise Server

Copyright © 2005 by Sander van Vugt

ISBN (pbk): 1-59059-483-5

Printed and bound in the United States of America 9 8 7 6 5 4 3 2 1

Lead Editor: Chris Mills
Technical Reviewer: Rob Bastiaansen
Editorial Board: Steve Anglin, Dan Appleman, Ewan Buckingham, Gary Cornell, Tony Davis, Jason Gilmore, Jonathan Hassell, Chris Mills, Dominic Shakeshaft, Jim Sumser
Associate Publisher: Grace Wong
Project Manager: Kylie Johnston
Copy Edit Manager: Nicole LeClerc
Copy Editor: Mike McGee
Production Manager: Kari Brooks-Copony
Production Editor: Katie Stence
Compositors: Susan Glinert and Wordstop Technologies Pvt. Ltd., Chennai
Proofreader: Linda Seifert
Indexer: Michael Brinkman
Artist: April Milne
Interior Designer: Van Winkle Design Group
Cover Designer: Kurt Krames
Manufacturing Manager: Tom Debolski

Distributed to the book trade in the United States by Springer-Verlag New York, Inc., 233 Spring Street, 6th Floor, New York, NY 10013, and outside the United States by Springer-Verlag GmbH & Co. KG, Tiergartenstr. 17, 69112 Heidelberg, Germany.

In the United States: phone 1-800-SPRINGER, fax 201-348-4505, e-mail orders@springer-ny.com, or visit http://www.springer-ny.com. Outside the United States: fax +49 6221 345229, e-mail orders@springer.de, or visit http://www.springer.de.

For information on translations, please contact Apress directly at 2560 Ninth Street, Suite 219, Berkeley, CA 94710. Phone 510-549-5930, fax 510-549-5939, e-mail info@apress.com, or visit http://www.apress.com.

The source code for this book is available to readers at http://www.apress.com in the Downloads section.

This book is dedicated to Florence.

Contents at a Glance

PART 1 ▪▪▪ Getting Started

PART 2 ▪▪▪ Core Services

PART 3 ▪▪▪ Open Enterprise Server Web-Based Services

PART 4 ▪▪▪ Advanced Services

Contents

PART 1 ■■■ Getting Started

PART 2 ▪▪▪ Core Services

PART 3 ■■■ Open Enterprise Server Web-Based Services

PART 4   ▪▪▪ Advanced Services

About the Author

SANDER VAN VUGT is an independent trainer and consultant, living in the Netherlands and working throughout the EMEA area. He specializes in Linux and Novell systems, and has worked with both for over ten years. Besides being a trainer, he is also an author, having written more than 20 books and hundreds of technical articles. He is a Master Certified Novell Instructor (MCNI) and holds LPIC-1 and -2 certificates, as well as all important Novell certificates. You can reach the author via his web site at www.sandervanvugt.nl.

About the Technical Reviewer

ROB BASTIAANSEN is an independent consultant and trainer. Rob has a strong focus on NetWare, Clustering Services, eDirectory, and ZENworks. He delivers Advanced Technical Training for Novell in EMEA regarding these topics. Rob is also a technical writer, and writes for several IT magazines where he lives in the Netherlands. VMware is another of the areas in which Rob works as a consultant and trainer. In 2004, he wrote and published his first book: *Rob's Guide to Using VMware*. In 2005, he published *The NetWare Toolbox*. He is a Master Certified Novell Instructor and holds all the major Novell certifications, including Certified Linux Engineer.

Acknowledgments

Although my name is the only one printed on the cover of this book, writing a book is a team effort, and I want to thank everyone who was part of the team for all their efforts. First, I'd like to thank Rob Bastiaansen. He was not only an excellent technical editor, but he also tipped off Apress that I'd be capable of writing this book! Next, I want to thank editor Chris Mills, who approved the concept's Table of Contents and guided me through the process offering a lot of critical questions and answers. His devotion and hard work definitely made it a better book. Next, I want to thank Kylie Johnston, the project manager, who, with patience and kindness, helped me complete the book in a timely manner. Last but not least, I want to thank Mike McGee, who had the difficult task of transforming my manuscripts into easy-to-read English.

Introduction

This book is about Novell Open Enterprise Server. With Open Enterprise Server, Novell launched a new generation of server operating system, following a 20-year long tradition with NetWare. Open Enterprise Server is unique in the industry due to its two versions: one for Linux and another for NetWare. This book is meant as a guide to Open Enterprise Server, familiarizing administrators with this new server platform and helping them integrate it into their network system. This book covers both versions of Open Enterprise Server, helping readers integrate both versions of Open Enterprise Server, along with Windows and Linux PCs, into their network.

Who This Book Is For

This book is written for three different groups of people. First and foremost, it is written for existing NetWare administrators who need to integrate Open Enterprise Server into their network. For them, the book contains in-depth knowledge of how Open Enterprise Server is structured and where the most important parts of its configuration are stored. Secondly, the book is written for Linux administrators who want to familiarize themselves with what Open Enterprise Server can offer their networks. Finally, the book is written for anyone who wants to become an Open Enterprise Server administrator, because it does not only provide in-depth details about some advanced topics, but covers introductions to the basics as well. Most importantly, this book is intended to be an indispensable reference guide for anyone administrating an Open Enterprise Server.

How This Book Is Structured

The book is divided into four parts, with a total of 20 chapters.

Part 1—Getting Started

In the first part, which consists of seven chapters, Open Enterprise Server is introduced. Here, the reader learns how to install Open Enterprise Server, understand its underlying operating system, and receives an introduction to those management tools used to administer it.

- Chapter 1: Introduction to Open Enterprise Server

  In this chapter, Open Enterprise Server is introduced. A description is given as to how Novell moved from the NetWare platform to Open Enterprise Server. It also contains descriptions of the most important components of Open Enterprise Server.

- Chapter 2: Installing Open Enterprise Server

In this chapter, the reader is taught how to install both versions of Open Enterprise Server. This chapter concerns new installations (upgrades are covered in Chapter 3). Here, the reader also learns how to install Open Enterprise Server to an existing network environment.

- Chapter 3: Upgrading to Open Enterprise Server

No matter what network operating system you are currently using, with this chapter you can upgrade or migrate it to Open Enterprise Server. Not only is upgrading from NetWare or SUSE Linux covered, but there is also a section about the migration of a Windows Active Directory environment to Open Enterprise Server.

- Chapter 4: Introduction to SUSE Linux Enterprise Server

If you are a NetWare administrator who has never worked with Linux before, this is probably the best chapter to start with. Here, SUSE Linux Enterprise Server, the operating system used in OES - Linux, is introduced. You'll learn how to manage it both from a graphical user interface and from the command line.

- Chapter 5: Introduction to the NetWare Kernel

For Linux administrators that want to get familiar with Open Enterprise Server, this chapter is very helpful. An introduction to the NetWare operating system used in OES - NetWare is provided.

- Chapter 6: Connecting to Open Enterprise Server

Now that you've learned about both operating systems for use with Open Enterprise Server, you have to connect to OES. There are various ways to do so, and this chapter teaches you a bit about each of them, in particular the Novell Client software, which can be installed on either a Windows, Linux, or Macintosh workstation to connect to OES.

- Chapter 7: Open Enterprise Server Management Utilities

Several utilities are available to manage OES, of which iManager is the most important. In this chapter, the reader learns which utilities can be used for particular management tasks. It also includes information on how to configure the management utilities, should any additional configuration be required.

Part 2—Core Services

In the second part of the book, the Open Enterprise Server core services are introduced. Here, the reader will find an introduction to eDirectory, user management, and perhaps most importantly, File Access and File Storage protocols. The latter are two areas in which OES proves to be a very exciting and unique server platform.

- Chapter 8: eDirectory Management

eDirectory is the core directory service in Open Enterprise Server. In this chapter, you'll learn everything needed to manage eDirectory in your network environment. Though lengthy, the chapter offers an overview of eDirectory composition, design, and troubleshooting. Also, the role of the LDAP server in an eDirectory environment is clearly outlined.

- Chapter 9: Managing the User Environment

No network is complete without user accounts—although according to some, the ideal network is a network without users. In this chapter, you learn how to create users and configure their environment. Also included is a description of how to manage Linux users from eDirectory.

- Chapter 10: File Access

One of the strongest aspects of Open Enterprise Server is its file access options. This chapter explains how to configure file access protocols, such as NFS, Samba, and NCP. Also included is a description of the iFolder server and NetStorage utilities, which make accessing files even easier.

- Chapter 11: Configuring Volumes

Novell Storage Services is a robust volume type that can be used on either the NetWare version of Open Enterprise Server (OES - NetWare) or its Linux counterpart (OES - Linux). In this chapter, you learn how to configure NSS on both versions of Open Enterprise Server. You also learn how to work with traditional volumes.

- Chapter 12: Managing Security

Security is a key issue in every network environment. This chapter outlines how to use file access rights and eDirectory rights to secure information on your network.

- Chapter 13: OES Software Management

In Open Enterprise Server (OES), software can be installed. In this chapter, you get an overview of all the methods that can be used to install software. The traditional software installation program that can be used from the GUI on OES - NetWare is covered, but you also find out how to use RPM and ZENworks Linux Management to install software on OES.

- Chapter 14: Networking Open Enterprise Server

OES offers support for many network protocols. This chapter teaches you about services related to the management of these protocols. Included is information about the migration from IPX to IP, plus you learn how to set up Service Location Protocol (SLP) for the dynamic location of services. Also included are sections about setting up OES as a DNS or DHCP server.

- Chapter 15: Managing iPrint

In OES, iPrint is the default system used for printing. This printing protocol, which is based on the IPP standard, allows users to access printers from their web browser. Of course, iPrint is also integrated tightly with the printing environment used on either Linux or Windows workstations.

Part 3—Open Enterprise Server Web-Based Services

In the third part of the book, the reader learns how to take advantage of the web-based portions of Open Enterprise Server. The Apache and Tomcat servers are covered here, as well as the user portal Virtual Office. Also, some advanced services are covered, such as Nsure Identity Manager, Novell Clustering Services, and Novell's Health Manager, which is based upon the OpenWBEM standard.

- Chapter 16: The Apache Web Server

Because many services in OES are web-based, the Apache web server acts as a core service in OES. In this chapter, you learn how to manage the Apache web server and Tomcat servlet engine in an OES environment.

- Chapter 17: Using Virtual Office

There are two important ways that users can access information from Open Enterprise Server. One of these is the Novell client software (which is covered in Chapter 6). The other is Virtual Office, which provides a web-based environment that users can use to access any information they need from the network.

Part 4—Advanced Services

At the end of this book, you'll find some information on some of the advanced services that come with Open Enterprise Server. Two of these services, Novell Clustering Services and Nsure Identity manager, are very useful add-ons to Open Enterprise Server which are not a part of the core OS itself. Lastly, you can read about the OpenWBEM platform which is a brand new management standard implemented in Open Enterprise Server.

- Chapter 18: Nsure Identity Manager

Nsure Identity Manager is another key Novell product, which allows administrators to synchronize data from any application to any other application where eDirectory functions as a meta-Directory. With Open Enterprise Server, you get a version to synchronize data between eDirectory and the Microsoft environment for free.

- Chapter 19: Introduction to Novell Clustering Services

Novell Clustering Services allows administrators to build a high-availability cluster. In Open Enterprise Server, licenses for two cluster nodes are included. In this chapter, you learn how to build a cluster with nodes on either version of OES, where resources can be migrated from one of these nodes to the other, no matter what version of OES is used on that node.

- Chapter 20: Using OpenWBEM for Server Health Monitoring

Novell Health Monitoring is probably not the most significant new feature in Open Enterprise Server. The underlying OpenWBEM platform, however, is significant, because it has the potential to be the new standard for managing network services. In this last chapter, you learn how Server Health Monitoring and the underlying OpenWBEM platform can be used in a network environment.

Prerequisites

To get the most out of this book, the reader should have the NetWare and/or Linux version of Open Enterprise Server at hand. If needed, a free evaluation copy can be downloaded from http://download.novell.com.

Contacting the Author

The author of this book can be reached at mail@sandervanvugt.nl. He also has an Internet site: www.sandervanvugt.nl.

PART 1

###

Getting Started

In the first part of this book, you'll learn everything necessary to get started with Novell Open Enterprise Server. First, you'll find out exactly what Open Enterprise Server is and where it's positioned in the Novell tradition of NetWare. Next, you'll learn how to install and migrate to Open Enterprise Server, and discover all the underlying operating systems it can be used with. Finally, you'll be instructed how to connect to Open Enterprise Server and what management tools are available to manage it.

CHAPTER 1

■ ■ ■

Introduction to Open Enterprise Server

Since the early 1980s, Novell has offered a network operating system that can be used in a LAN environment. This operating system is known as NetWare, which is an operating system of its own, offering its own kernel, shell, tool set, and utilities. One of the major benefits of NetWare is that it provides exceptionally fast file and print services. It also allows administrators to manage user access to files and other resources on a NetWare server in a very efficient manner. Unfortunately, the NetWare market share has been decreasing for several years now, due mainly to competition from Microsoft products such as Windows NT Server, Windows 2000 Server, and Windows Server 2003.

However, Novell offers more than just NetWare. One of the most important products Novell developed in the early 1990s was eDirectory, formerly known as NDS. This is a directory service that allows administrators to store information about network users and resources in one hierarchical directory service. eDirectory will be introduced in depth in Chapter 8 of this book. After Banyan Vines, Novell was the first company to have significant success with its directory service. In the early 1990s, it was certainly the best directory service around, and to many users it still is.

Since eDirectory was one of the strongest products Novell had to offer, Novell made it available for other operating systems as well. Nowadays, eDirectory runs on Windows servers, different UNIX flavors, and also Linux. The competition from Microsoft's Active Directory is formidable, and although eDirectory is generally considered the better directory service, Active Directory also offers enough functionality for most users. Along with some additional components, eDirectory comes together to form OES, the new generation of Novell server products, which is gaining ground against Microsoft's products because of its Linux roots. This chapter discusses how the evolution from NetWare to Linux took place and what the strong points of OES are.

From NetWare to Linux

Although NetWare offers a very robust server platform, there's one major reason why NetWare has lost so much market share these last years: It's not an application server. Although some major databases do run on NetWare, and several products have been introduced to make NetWare a platform on which applications can run and be offered to users in the network, most software companies that develop applications develop them for Windows, not NetWare. For that reason, companies have been introducing Windows application servers on a very large scale. Even on the most pro-Novell networks, at least one or two Windows application servers are used to offer access to mission-critical applications that only run on Windows.

Since the late 1990s, available options have expanded beyond NetWare and Windows due to the rise of Linux. The Linux operating system, which started in 1992, evolved from a cheap educational alternative for UNIX to a serious operating system that's used to offer important services in both a LAN and Internet environment.

Because Linux became so successful, and because Novell was aware there wasn't much future in the NetWare platform, in early 2003 the company decided to focus on the Linux platform. This shift implicated that all Novell services had to be modified so they could also be used on Linux. Instead of the producer of a great network operating system, Novell wanted to become the producer of a great network operating system and of great network services that run on any platform. The first proof of this new concept was Novell Nterprise Linux Services (NNLS), which was launched in late 2003. In this proof-of-concept product, Novell demonstrated that many of its most important services could run on Linux. The NNLS suite was developed for installation on both Red Hat Enterprise Server and the SUSE Linux Enterprise Server.

Novell, however, wanted more than just a bunch of tools that run on the most important professional Linux platforms, it wanted to change the offering to one where customers could choose between the NetWare and Linux operating systems, both of them running Novell services like eDirectory and others. To offer this option in the best possible way, Novell needed a Linux distribution. For this reason, Novell bought SUSE Linux in late 2003 and continued development of the Novell Linux services, in particular, for SUSE Linux Enterprise Server (SLES) 9, the latest server version of SUSE Linux. This development resulted in what is now OES - Linux— in fact, it's just a customized version of SLES 9 with all the Novell services integrated into it.

Two Platforms

Although Novell has made a commitment to Linux for its future strategy, the company is still working on NetWare as well. Therefore, Open Enterprise Server comes in two versions, developed for both platforms: OES - Linux and OES - NetWare. Both share the same services (although some less-important services such as SLP v2, the eDirectory-integrated DNS and DHCP server, and others are yet to be implemented on OES - Linux). At the services level, it's thus not important what operating system is used.

Currently, customers can install both OES - Linux and OES - NetWare. As will be discussed in Chapter 5, the NetWare platform has also undergone some changes. Think, for example, of Linux features such as the bash-shell or RPM package management that are now integrated into the NetWare operating system.

When using OES - NetWare, the administrator can choose between two different options. Since OES - NetWare is basically a new support pack on Netware 6.5, one of the ways to install it is as Netware 6.5 support pack 3. If installed this way, most OES additions to NetWare 6.5 are installed, there are, however, a few changes with OES - NetWare. The most important of these differences is listed next:

- OES includes iManager 2.5

- OES includes Virtual Office 1.5

- In OES, the QuickFinder web search server is used.

As for the rest of their features, OES - NetWare and NetWare 6.5 are identical. Why bother installing NetWare 6.5 if a newer version of NetWare is available in OES - NetWare? The advantage of NetWare 6.5 SP 3 is that it allows the administrator to perform an upgrade that is less radical. You just have to install a new support pack instead of an entire different operating system.

The Future of NetWare

Open Enterprise Server is all about choice: the customer can choose his favorite platform and he can even choose the way he wants to install OES - NetWare: as a new operating system, or as a support pack on NetWare 6.5. There are however customers that have some serious concerns about the future of NetWare. Is OES the first step in abandoning NetWare, just as how the IPX protocol was eventually exchanged for IP? With the launch of OES in spring 2005, Novell guaranteed: "As long as we have a considerable amount of customers that want NetWare, we will continue working on NetWare." The company would drive important customers straight into the hands of the competition, should it abandon NetWare entirely. So, as long as customers want NetWare, they'll get NetWare. There is, however, some doubt that in the long term Novell will focus on its great services—and the primary platform of these services will be Linux. There will certainly be a transition period where networks run NetWare and Linux side by side, but there's little chance that in ten years' time NetWare will still be developed.

Open Enterprise Server Major Components

Open Enterprise Server (OES) offers a lot of software components, all of them together providing a very complete network server. All these components run on both OES - NetWare and OES - Linux. The most important components are listed next, and subsequent sections of this chapter offer an introduction to them.

- eDirectory

- Management Tools

- Integrated Linux User Management

- OES Security

- File Storage and File Access

- Software Management

- Network Services

- Printing

- The Web Based Application Platform

- Virtual Office

- Nsure Identity Manager

- Novell Clustering Services

eDirectory

As stated earlier in this chapter, eDirectory is the most important service offered by Novell. Everything in the Novell environment is integrated in eDirectory, and other platforms such as Microsoft Windows servers and workstations can even be managed from eDirectory. Chapter 8 provides in-depth knowledge of eDirectory.

Management Tools

The primary management tool in Open Enterprise Server is iManager. This web-based administration tool allows administrators to manage most services running on both versions of OES. Think, for example, of eDirectory management, printer management, and management of Nsure Identity Manager, which can be used to synchronize user data across different platforms. iManager, however, is not the only management tool available. Two other web-based management tools are Remote Manager and iMonitor. With Remote Manager, the administrator can manage a lot of server parameters, and from iMonitor advanced eDirectory management and monitoring can be performed. If you'd rather work with one of the older management tools, there are possibilities for that as well. ConsoleOne, for instance, can still be employed, and sometimes NetWare Administrator can even be used to manage certain parts of OES. Be aware that iManager cannot always serve as the only management tool in your network. It may be necessary to use ConsoleOne to manage older Novell products like ZENworks, GroupWise, and others. Be aware that these older tools lack the necessary snap-ins that allow you to manage the most recent additions to OES. More information about OES management tools is provided in Chapter 7.

User Management

When using OES - Linux, you not only have to deal with users in an eDirectory environment, you must manage local Linux user accounts as well. The latter is provided by Linux User Management (LUM): this component of OES - Linux allows you to manage all user accounts from one eDirectory environment. More information about user management is provided in Chapter 9.

OES Security

One of the most important reasons to use OES is its enhanced security model. Whereas Linux only has two real rights (or three if you consider execute also a right), Novell has eight different file system rights and more than ten attributes that can be used to secure access to files and directories. Besides that, Novell's eDirectory offers also advanced security options. For most Linux administrators, this is one of the most valuable additions to the current functions of their servers, even apart from the advanced options to assign different kinds of trustees to the files, directories, and eDirectory objects in an OES environment. Security is covered in Chapter 12.

File Storage and File Access

Linux offers many file systems to store data on a hard drive. All are POSIX-compliant and therefore inode-based. At the file system level, Novell adds Novell Storage Services (NSS) to this collection of file systems. NSS is a very robust file system that allows you to work with billions of files on one of the dynamic volumes created in an NSS partition. NSS also offers the option to work with the advanced Novell rights. On OES - Linux, you can configure an NSS volume as easily as configuring an ext3 or Reiser volume. As for accessing files, many options exist. One of these is the old Novell Core Protocol that has existed in NetWare for about two decades and still works fine to grant access to volumes on OES for users that have the Novell client installed on their workstation. NCP not only offers access no matter what volume type you use, it also offers you the option to use Novell rights while accessing any of these volumes. In this scenario, the rights are simply managed at the share level. Besides NCP, other important file access protocols are supported, such as NFS, Samba, and even Apple Filing Protocol. This way, OES provides users with options to access their files in most any way they wish. Chapters 10 and 11 cover file storage and file access in depth.

iFolder

One of the most innovative ways to work with files in an Open Enterprise Server environment is offered by iFolder. With iFolder, a user can install a small client program on her workstation. From this client program, she can mark one directory as the iFolder directory. The contents of this directory are automatically synchronized with the iFolder server whenever and wherever a user connects with the server. In this way, iFolder helps users work with the most recent versions of their files and to never lose a file again because is the system wasn't synchronized to the server. For environments where the user does not have her own computer available, she can choose to work with a browser to access files in her iFolder. iFolder is discussed in Chapter 11.

Software Management

For the installation of software and the management of installed software, Novell now uses the open-source Red Hat Package Manager on both OES platforms. This allows administrators to develop a standard for managing software platforms no matter what platform they use. On OES - NetWare, RPM can be used to install software. The old graphical Novell install utility can also still be used. For the most advanced way to manage software on servers and workstations, the Novell ZENworks suite can be deployed. You can read more about these services in Chapter 13.

Network Services

An entirely different part of Open Enterprise Server, are the Network Services. Of course, all standard Linux network services are present on OES - Linux, but OES - NetWare has some interesting extras. One of these is the option to integrate the DNS and DHCP configurations in eDirectory, which allows for optimal fault tolerance of these fundamental network services. Another important network service is the Service Location Protocol (SLP), which allows for dynamic maintenance of lists of available services on the network. SLP is supported on OES - NetWare as well as OES - Linux. More information about these services is provided in Chapter 14.

Printing

Novell has always been innovative with regards to network printing. For many years, the company has provided the robust system of queue-based printing, which looks a lot like the UNIX lpd-based printing environment. Of more recent date is Novell Distributed Printing Services (NDPS), which allows printers to be configured automatically and printer drivers to be downloaded to users' workstations automatically. Other advanced options, such as bi-directional communication between printers and workstations are also available. In OES, Novell has implemented an Internet-aware version of NDPS known as iPrint. iPrint gives URL-based access to printers. Thus, a user can choose his printer from a map displayed in a web page. When the user clicks in this map on the printer icon, it installs the printer on his workstation. Next, he clicks the printer icon, which installs the printer driver on his workstation automatically, no matter what his operating system. iPrint is covered in Chapter 15.

The Web-Based Application Platform

Linux is already an excellent application server, but to increase the number of applications supported by OES, Novell offers some web-based components as well. First up is the Apache web server, which is used as a generic web server to provide access to all web-based components of OES. Next is the Tomcat servlet engine, which allows you to run web applications on the server. Tomcat is used for most internal administration interfaces. Think of it as like iManager, except that it can be used as a web platform for custom applications as well. More information about these important servers is provided in Chapter 16.

Virtual Office

One of the most interesting applications that can run on the Tomcat servlet engine is Virtual Office. Virtual Office offers users a platform to access all important resources from both their Novell network and from a browser interface, thus providing an ideal solution for accessing services anywhere. Virtual Office provides a perfect alternative to an environment in which users need the Novell client installed on their workstations. Here, even though no client may be installed, it allows them access to anything they need from the browser. The Novell client can, of course, still be used as well. Besides the Windows client, there's even a Novell client for Linux now. Both are covered in Chapter 6. If, however, a customer chooses not to work with this Novell client, Virtual Office is a perfect alternative. One part of Virtual Office is especially notable: the ability for a user to work with virtual teams. The nice part about these virtual teams is that the user can create his own virtual team and share files, messages, and information with other members. All the administrator has to do to make this possible is install Virtual Office. Thus, Virtual Office makes it easy to create an environment for a group of users that wish to work together and share information on the network.

Nsure Identity Manager

Nowadays, most networks are of a mixed nature. Not only is Novell eDirectory used, but Microsoft's Active Directory and other applications are employed. However, someone must administer each of these applications. To prevent instances where different people do the same job on different applications, Novell uses Nsure Identity Manager. This application allows you to synchronize identities across the network. For example, if a user is created in eDirectory, Identity Manager automatically synchronizes it to all connected applications. eDirectory doesn't have to be the starting point when creating users: user accounts can be synchronized from any application to eDirectory, which is used as a meta directory in this scenario. From there, it can be synchronized to any other application. Nsure Identity Manager works with various drivers, offering support for over 30 different applications, thus synchronizing data from any application to any other application. Complementary with OES are drivers that allow you to synchronize data from Windows NT and Active Directory. It also comes with password synchronization, which helps you synchronize passwords between, for example, eDirectory and Active Directory. Nsure Identity Manager is discussed in Chapter 18.

Novell Clustering Services

Another important Novell service that's included free-of-charge is Novell Clustering Services (NCS). NCS allows you to build cluster solutions for nodes running either OES - Linux or OES - NetWare. For example, you can cluster-enable an NSS volume that's assigned to an OES - NetWare node as its primary node, so should it fail, it automatically fails over to an OES - Linux node. Other NetWare and Linux nodes can also be clustered with NCS. In addition, NCS offers support for up to 32 nodes, and with OES you get a two-node license for free. Chapter 19 has more on NCS.

Summary

With Open Enterprise Server, Novell offers a very versatile server platform running many services on either the NetWare or Linux operating systems. Amongst the most important of these services are the file services and the directory service eDirectory. In the next chapter, you'll read about how to install Open Enterprise Server.

## CHAPTER 2

Installing Open Enterprise Server

Like any other operating system, you need to install Open Enterprise Server before it can be used. However, there are some things to consider before attempting the install—the first of which is the differences between the installation of OES - Linux and that of OES - NetWare. The former uses YaST as its primary installation program, while the latter employs the NetWare installer. Next, you must decide how to install it. It's possible to install from the installation CDs, but a network installation is possible as well. In this chapter, you'll learn how to install both editions of OES.

■**Note** The installation of OES on an existing Linux or NetWare machine is not covered in this chapter because it's actually a migration rather than an installation. You can read more about these in the next chapter.

Preparing for Installation

Before starting the actual installation, you must prepare your tree for it. This preparation consists of two parts: the first part—preparing your tree—is necessary because the structure of the eDirectory defined in the eDirectory schema of your old tree has to be modified before installing OES. The schema of your old tree must be ready for the new objects that are installed with OES in the tree. To prepare the old tree for that, run the Deployment Manager from the OES - NetWare installation CD. Besides running Deployment Manager, you also need to be sure that your computer meets all the requirements.

■**Caution** You must run deployment manager before installing your first OES server in an existing tree, whether you're installing OES - NetWare or OES - Linux. Unfortunately, the deployment manager is not on the OES - Linux installation CDs. You can only find it on the first CD of OES - NetWare.

Running Deployment Manager

This section explains how to prepare an existing tree for OES by using the Deployment Manager. You'll need a Windows workstation with the Novell client installed on it to perform this procedure. For more information on how to install the Novell client, consult Chapter 6 of this book.

Note In this section, you'll learn how to prepare an existing tree for OES installation. If, however, your tree is up-to-date regarding support packs and uses a recent version of eDirectory, in most cases it won't be necessary to perform these steps. Nevertheless, it's recommended you read this entire procedure to determine if any action is required.

---

1. Insert the OES - NetWare CD labeled "Operating System" in the CD drive of a workstation. The NetWare Deployment Manager is started automatically. If not, start it manually by running NWDeploy.exe from the root of the CD. This starts the deployment manager from a browser.

Tip Instead of running Deployment Manager from the browser (which is the default), you can start the program file NWDeployNoBrowser.exe from the root of the OES - NetWare Operating System CD. This starts Deployment Manager as a Java application.

---

2. From the Deployment Manager browser window, click Network Preparation ➤ Overview. Here you can read the procedure that will be performed by using Deployment Manager. This procedure will also be described in this chapter.

3. Click the link Back Up Data. Here you'll find a description on how to back up existing NetWare 5 or 6 servers. It's strongly recommended that you perform a back up before attempting to install anything.

4. After reading the information about backup, click Search Tree For eDirectory/NDS Versions. This step checks all servers in your current tree to see if the schema is compatible with the eDirectory version you're going to install with OES. If this is not the case, you can update it in most cases to a compatible version from this screen. Click View And Update NDS to continue.

5. A Java application now starts, as shown in Figure 2-1. From this application, click the browse button and browse to the tree you want to scan. Select it and click OK to continue.

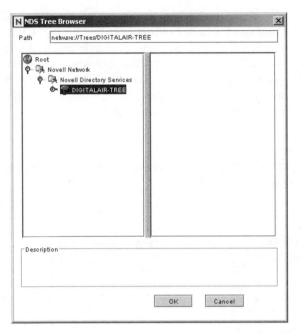

Figure 2-1. *From this screen, browse to the tree you want to prepare for OES installation.*

6. Make sure that the Include Subordinate Containers option is selected and click Next to continue. This will display an overview of all servers that were found and will tell you if the core Directory service on these servers needs an update. Currently, the name used for the Directory service is eDirectory, but be aware that the tool will refer to it as NDS. If servers are found that require an update, check the Update NDS box for these servers and carry out the procedure. After the procedure has been completed, close the application and return to the Deployment Manager main screen.

7. Now from Deployment Manager, select Network Preparation ➤ Prepare for New eDirectory. By doing this, you can extend the core schema on the network where you want to install OES. This step is not required if you're already running eDirectory on either NetWare or Linux. Click Extend The Core Schema to start the application with which to extend the schema.

8. Browse to the tree you want to extend the schema for and click Next to continue. An overview of all servers will now be displayed. Select the server on which you want to extend the schema and click Next to proceed. This prepares the server for OES installation. After the schema has been extended, click Exit to close the application.

Tip To extend the schema, you need access to a server that has a writable replica. Make sure the server you select for schema extension does have a writable replica before continuing.

---

9. Before starting the installation of OES, be sure that the current tree is healthy and there are no critical eDirectory or time synchronization errors. To do this, run the Server Health utility. You can start this utility by selecting Network Preparation ➤ Prepare A Server For Upgrade. Then, enter the name of the server and click Next to continue and perform the health check. This will require you to log in on the server. The utility next displays an overview of all critical components and tells you if any action is required, as shown in Figure 2-2. Make sure your tree is healthy before continuing!

Note This step may require some action on the server you're working on. If the procedure does not move forward, take a look at the server and press Enter if required.

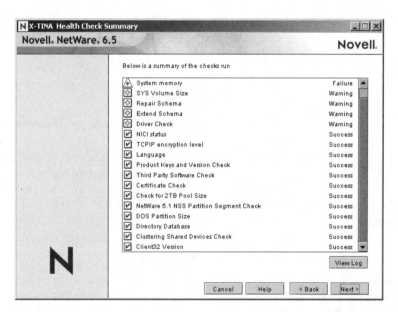

Figure 2-2. *The Health Check Summary shows you if all the requirements to install OES in an existing tree have been met. Make sure to correct any errors before proceeding!*

10. All other steps as listed in Deployment Manager are not often required. Read them and see if they apply to your situation. If they do, complete all required procedures before continuing the installation of the first OES server in your network. After the tree has been prepared properly, close the Deployment Manager and proceed with the installation of the first OES server in your tree.

Minimum System Requirements

To install OES, make sure your computer meets the following minimum requirements.

- A server-class PC with a Pentium III running at 700MHz or better. AMD is also supported. OES, however, is currently not supported on any other architecture.

- 512MB of RAM minimum; 1GB recommended.

- Super VGA or better display adapter.

- For OES - NetWare only: a DOS partition with 200MB of usable disk space minimum. 1GB of disk space available for volume SYS:. A minimum disk space of 500MB for the DOS partition and 4GB for the volume SYS: is recommended. If the DOS partition is not present on a server hard disk, the installation program will allow you to create one. This is described in the following section.

- For OES - Linux: 2GB of available disk space minimum; 4GB recommended.

- One network interface card.

- A bootable CD drive.

- A mouse is not required, but strongly recommended.

Installing OES - NetWare

Now it's time to learn how to install OES - NetWare. There's a reason I've chosen to begin with OES - NetWare instead of OES - Linux: if you were working in a real network environment, you'd have to install OES - NetWare before OES - Linux as well. This is because OES - NetWare needs some licensing objects in the tree it's installed in. If these licensing objects are missing, you can't join OES - NetWare to the desired tree. With the installation of OES - Linux, however, these licensing objects are not installed automatically. For that reason, you can't install OES - NetWare in a tree where no other versions of NetWare are already available. So if you want to install a mixed network, first install OES - NetWare. Only after that can you install OES - Linux.

1. Insert the OES - NetWare installation CD in the CD drive and reboot your computer. Make sure it boots from the CD. This loads the installation program automatically.

■Tip When OES is installed, it displays the Novell NetWare 6.5 logo screen. If you prefer seeing what happens on the console, use Alt+Esc to switch from that screen to the console. This lets you see any error messages that occur.

---

2. Select the language you want to install, as shown in Figure 2-3, and then press Enter to continue.

Selecte this line to install in English
Sélectionner cette ligne pour installer en français
Diese Zeile für deutsche Installation auswählen
Seleccione esta línea para instalarlo en español
Selecione esta linha para instalar em Português
Selezionare questa riga per installare in italiano
Select this line to install in Russian

Figure 2-3. *OES - NetWare can be installed in six different languages.*

3. For your keyboard to work properly, make sure the correct country, code page, and keyboard settings are selected in the next screen. If they are, press Enter to continue. If they aren't, use the Tab and Arrow keys to select the item you want to modify and then press Enter to continue.

4. Read the License Agreement. If you accept all statements in this agreement, press F10 to continue. Repeat the same procedure for the next screen where the license agreement for the JReport utility is displayed.

5. On the next screen, shown in Figure 2-4, choose what type of installation to perform. OES can be installed two ways: manually or by default. If you select Default, the installation process automatically detects drivers and installs the OES NetWare server with the following default settings:

    • 100MB DOS partition (unless you've already created a larger one).

    • 4GB (4000MB) volume SYS:—any remaining disk space will be left as free space.

    • LAN and disk drivers auto-discovered and loaded.

    • Video mode: Super VGA Plug N Play.

    • Mouse: Auto-discovered and loaded.

6. If you want full control over the installation process, select Manual to start a manual installation. In this section, you can read about the Manual installation. If you prefer performing a default installation, you'll notice that some steps described here aren't displayed on your computer screen. Next, select Continue and press Enter.

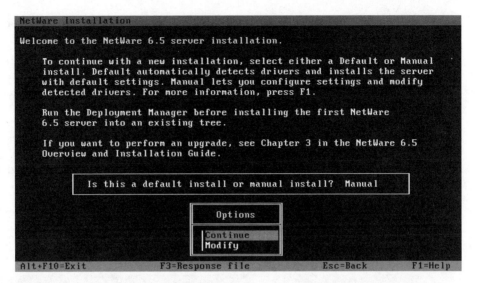

```
NetWare Installation

Welcome to the NetWare 6.5 server installation.

    To continue with a new installation, select either a Default or Manual
    install. Default automatically detects drivers and installs the server
    with default settings. Manual lets you configure settings and modify
    detected drivers. For more information, press F1.

    Run the Deployment Manager before installing the first NetWare
    6.5 server into an existing tree.

    If you want to perform an upgrade, see Chapter 3 in the NetWare 6.5
    Overview and Installation Guide.

     ┌─────────────────────────────────────────────────────────────┐
     │  Is this a default install or manual install?  Manual        │
     └─────────────────────────────────────────────────────────────┘

                    ┌─────────────────────────────┐
                    │          Options            │
                    │  ┌────────────────────────┐ │
                    │  │Continue                │ │
                    │  │Modify                  │ │
                    │  └────────────────────────┘ │
                    └─────────────────────────────┘

Alt+F10=Exit          F3=Response file          Esc=Back          F1=Help
```

Figure 2-4. *For full control over the installation process, select the Manual installation.*

7. In the next screen, select the DOS partition you want to use for booting the server and press Enter to continue. If no DOS partition is present, select Modify, and then choose the available free space where you want to create the DOS partition. Accept the default value of 500MB for the DOS partition and press Enter to continue. Select Continue and press Enter.

8. An overview of all current settings for the server should appear, as shown in Figure 2-5. A list of available settings is listed next. Make a selection, choose Continue and then press Enter.

• *Server ID Number*: Enter the IPX ID you want to use for this server. This parameter is only needed if IPX is used on your server. Upon installation, it's needed to detect if IPX is present on your network. If no IPX is needed, this number is removed automatically from the AUTOEXEC.NCF startup file that's processed automatically when you boot up.

• *Load server at reboot*: Select YES to start your server automatically when it reboots. If you select No, you'll have to start it manually by entering the **SERVER.EXE** command at the DOS prompt.

- *Boot OS*: Select DOS to make sure that DOS is booted when booting your server. This is necessary; otherwise, you can't start the SERVER.EXE that starts your server.

- *Allow unsupported drivers*: Select No to make sure only supported drivers for the network card and other hardware are used on your server. Working with unsupported drivers may crash your server, so they're not recommended. It's better to use hardware that's certified for NetWare; most server grade hardware is.

- *Server SET parameters*: Here you can specify SET parameters that are absolutely necessary for your server's hardware. If this is required, it will be indicated in the manual of your hardware. If you don't have such a requirement, leave it on the default settings and continue.

- *Video*: The default value of Super VGA Plug N Play automatically detects the best settings for the graphical display on your server. In the rare case that this doesn't work, you can manually select a Super VGA setting for your monitor.

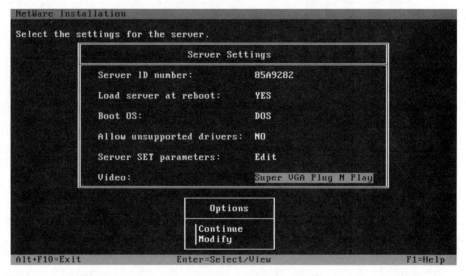

Figure 2-5. *If your server needs tuning before installation, enter all the required parameters here.*

9. Some files will be copied now. This takes a few minutes. When finished, you'll see a screen where you can add specific hardware support modules for your server. In most cases, they're added automatically if needed. If you must add some modules manually, select Modify to add them. Then choose Continue and press Enter.

10. A list of HotPlug support modules and storage adapters necessary for your server will appear, as shown in Figure 2-6. In most cases, all required modules are added automatically; however, use Modify to add modules by hand if necessary and then select Continue and press Enter to proceed.

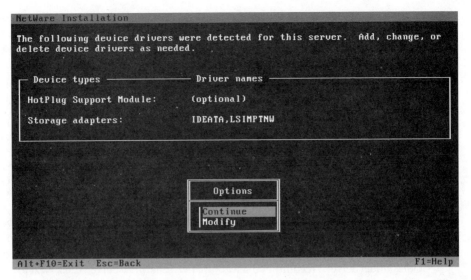

Figure 2-6. *If any hardware support modules are needed, they're selected automatically in most situations.*

11. Next, the drivers for the storage devices are detected. Press Enter to continue or modify the selection to add drivers by hand.

12. In most situations, a list of all drivers that would work with your network board is presented, as shown in Figure 2-7. Select the most appropriate driver for your network card and press Enter twice to continue.

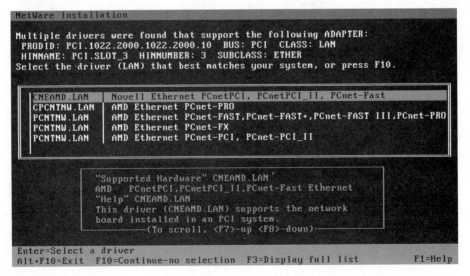

Figure 2-7. *In most cases, you have to manually select the most appropriate driver for your network card.*

13. If you have more than 4GB of available space on your hard drive, the installer will suggest that you use it all to create a SYS: volume. This is the volume where the installer places all the important operating system files. If less than 4GB of disk space is available, the installer claims it all for installation of the SYS: volume. Select Create to continue. It's not advised to use Create Manually Later because you'll need a SYS volume to put your files on.

14. The NSS Management Utility should appear. Here you can create additional volumes (more on this in Chapter 11). You don't need to install additional volumes at this point, just press Enter to continue the installation.

15. Another set of files is now copied to your server. When this is finished, the graphical part of the installation starts automatically. This can take a few minutes.

16. After the graphical part of the installation launches, you must choose whether you want to install Open Enterprise Server or NetWare 6.5 Support Pack 3. If you choose to install OES, you can benefit from the latest versions of iManager, Virtual Office, and the QuickFinder Server. I recommend selecting Open Enterprise Server. Click Next to proceed.

17. Now you must specify what you want to install, as shown in Figure 2-8. If you want to install OES as a special purpose server, make a selection from one of the preconfigured servers listed on the screen. For a multipurpose server installation, select Customized NetWare Server and click Next to continue. In this procedure, you can read how to install a customized NetWare server.

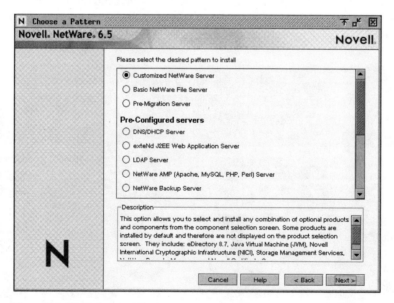

Figure 2-8. *To make installation easier, you can choose from a set of preconfigured servers.*

18. Next, choose from a list of services you want to install, as shown in Figure 2-9. All of these servers can be installed separately after initial installation. At this point, it's best to select only the Novell iManager 2.5 option and Apache2 Web Server And Tomcat 4 Servlet Container option. These are needed for the proper web-based management of your server. Even if you already have iManager in your tree, it's recommended you install it anyway, because OES is the first Novell operating system that used iManager 2.5 and this version is much faster than its predecessors. After selecting the required services, click Next to continue.

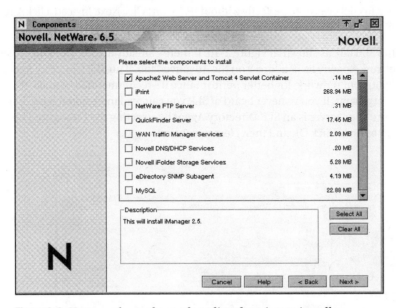

Figure 2-9. *You can choose from a long list of services to install.*

19. You'll now see a list of all products you've selected for installation. Verify that this really is what you want to install. If it is, click Copy Files to continue. If you need to make modifications, click the Back button to make the required modifications.

20. After a few moments, you'll be asked to insert the second installation CD-ROM. Insert it. You don't have to click OK; the installation procedure automatically continues after the CD has been mounted. Wait a few minutes for the files to be copied.

21. Once all the required files are copied, you must configure your newly installed server. This configuration consists of an eDirectory installation and the configuration of all services you've installed.

22. After all the files are copied, enter a name for your newly installed server. Click Next to continue.

■Tip On most of the screens that appear in these steps, you'll notice an Advanced button. Use this button to make advanced settings for the selected topic. These settings will not be discussed here since most are described later throughout the book.

23. Select IP and enter the IP address settings you want to use for this server. Select IPX only if you have both IP *and* IPX in your network and you need it on this server. Normally, you can run OES - NetWare perfectly without IPX. Don't click Next. Instead, click Advanced to configure the Service Location Protocol settings for this server.

24. Click the SLP tab, as shown in Figure 2-10. If there's already an SLP Directory Agent in this network, specify its IP address on the Advanced tab. If no SLP Directory Agent is yet present on your network, for better performance it's recommended to make this server a Directory Agent. If you've never heard of SLP, you can read more about it in Chapter 14. Make sure your server is an SLP Directory Agent by selecting the Configure This Server As A DA option. Click OK and then Next to continue.

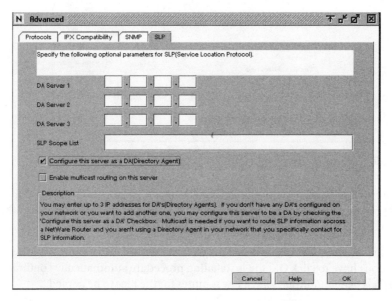

Figure 2-10. *For better performance of your network, configure your server as an SLP Directory Agent.*

25. Now specify the DNS host name of your server, and the name of the DNS server. Click Next to continue.

■**Caution** You'll need your own DNS server on your network since some OES services rely upon it. Chapter 14 explains how to set up this DNS server.

---

26. Specify the time zone you're in. If your area uses daylight savings time, select the Allow System To Adjust For Daylight Savings Time option and click Next to continue.

27. Next, specify whether or not you want to install this server in a new eDirectory tree, as shown in Figure 2-11. This procedure describes how to install this server as the first server in a new Directory tree, so select the Create A New eDirectory Tree option and click Next to continue.

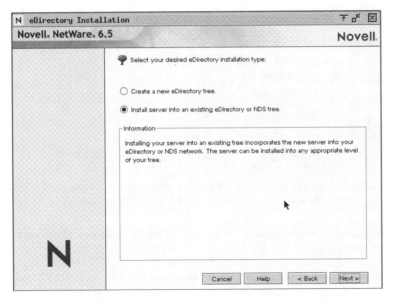

Figure 2-11. *Specify whether you want to install your server in a new eDirectory tree or not.*

■**Caution** Since this is one of the most important choices you have to make, be sure to choose correctly. It's possible to change this setting afterwards, but since many services depend on the eDirectory configuration, it can be difficult to make these services work afterwards.

---

28. On the next screen, shown in Figure 2-12, enter the name of the new tree and the context where you want to install the server in. If you don't know what to use for these values, read Chapter 8 of the book first. Or just enter the name of your company followed by - TREE as the tree name, and the name of your company as the context you want to install the server in if you're installing a test environment. Normally, you would need to do some planning before entering any value here. This is because the tree name cannot be changed after installation. Provide a context for your admin user and his password as well. Click Next to continue.

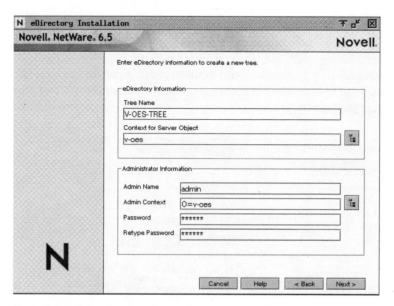

Figure 2-12. *Make sure you choose the proper tree name and the name for the container you want to install the server in, because they're hard to change later.*

29. Review the eDirectory information you've just assigned to your new eDirectory tree and click Next to continue.

30. Now enter the license information for your server (see Figure 2-13). On a purchased server, the license should be on the license diskette, or might already be installed in your tree. If you're installing this server as a test server, use the browse button to browse to the directory license on your OES CD. Both CDs will work. With this license, test OES for a limited period. The licensing option will also create the required licenses as objects in eDirectory. Don't select the option Install Without Licenses since you'll need licenses to do everything with your server. After selecting the license, click Next to proceed.

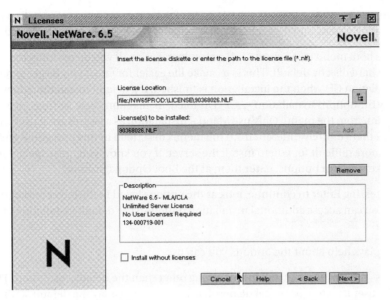

Figure 2-13. *You'll need licenses in your tree if you want to do anything useful with your newly installed server.*

31. Next, select the context where the license certificates have to be created as objects in your eDirectory tree. The default container will do fine in most situations. Click Next to continue.

32. Next, specify the ports used by the LDAP server (installed by default on your OES server). Accept the default port settings unless you have a very good reason not to, and then click Next to continue.

33. Now you can select all the NMAS Login Methods you need on this server. If you use advanced login mechanisms, such as smart cards, select your vendor here. In all other cases, leave the default selected and click Next to continue.

34. Based upon the information you've just entered, the installation of your server should now be finalized and your tree complete. This can take a few moments as well. Click Yes to restart your server now. After it restarts, it will be ready for use immediately.

Installing OES - Linux

Now that you've installed OES - NetWare, it's time to install your first OES - Linux server. Again, you don't have to install OES - NetWare to be able to install OES - Linux, but be aware that you cannot install OES - NetWare in a tree where only OES - Linux servers are available. The following steps explain how to perform an installation of OES - Linux.

1. Insert the OES - Linux 1 CD into the CD drive of the server on which you want to install the operating system, and then reboot your computer. Make sure it will boot from the CD.

2. From the boot menu (see Figure 2-14), select Installation. If you do nothing, it will boot from the hard disk by default. This is to make life easier for you if you forget to remove the installation CD when the installation is finished. If a default installation doesn't work, try the options Installation - ACPI Disabled, Installation - Safe Settings, or Manual Installation from the menu. Only use Manual Installation as a last resort. It uses a menu structure that's entirely different from the menus described in this procedure and will make it more difficult for you to install the server. If you know you must specify some specific kernel boot options, enter them at the Boot Options prompt.

3. Before pressing Enter to continue, look at the options listed in the lower part of the screen. You can access additional installation options if the default installation options don't work:

   • *F1*: Displays help about the options you can use.

   • *F2*: Press this button to install in something other than the default resolution. This may be useful if your graphical display hardware can't display the default settings.

■**Tip** You'll need the F2 key if you want to install OES - Linux in a VMware virtual machine. In a VMware machine, it's best to install in text mode since this is the only mode in which all screens are displayed correctly.

   • *F3*: Specify the source of the installation. By default, the installer will look for installation files on the CD-ROM; from this menu, you can select Hard Disk as well as other network locations.

   • *F4*: Use this button to specify the language you want to install in. Later in the installation procedure, you'll be given another chance to choose your installation language.

   • *F5*: Specify the amount of information you want to see upon the installation. By default, the installation will be performed silently. For more information, choose Native or Verbose. Verbose shows you the most information during the installation. It's recommended you use this option if for any reason a default installation fails.

   • *F6*: Press this button if you have a floppy with drivers you need to install.

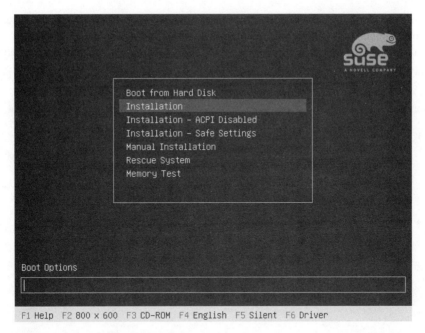

Figure 2-14. *If the default installation options don't work, you can use the installation menu to install OES - Linux a different way.*

4. After pressing Enter, the Linux kernel loads. When the kernel initializes hardware, a SUSE logo appears. If you want to see exactly what happens, press F2 for more details. It should tell you if your kernel was able to initialize all the hardware properly.

5. A window with the license agreement should appear. Click I Agree to agree to the license agreement.

6. Next, select the language you want to install in. Many languages are available, but in this book I'll discuss installation in English (after all, most of you probably wouldn't understand my native language, Dutch). Click Accept to continue.

7. If you're installing on a computer where a different Linux version was already installed, you must now choose what you want to do. In this case, select New Installation to remove the existing operating system and install OES. If you want to upgrade an existing installation of SUSE Linux Enterprise Server, abort the procedure and read Chapter 3 for more details. Press OK to continue.

8. The Installation Settings screen should appear (see Figure 2-15). From this screen, you'll specify everything that has to be done upon the installation. The installer will make a default selection for you. I recommend reading everything on this screen in order to make the best choice for your server. Details about this screen are provided next.

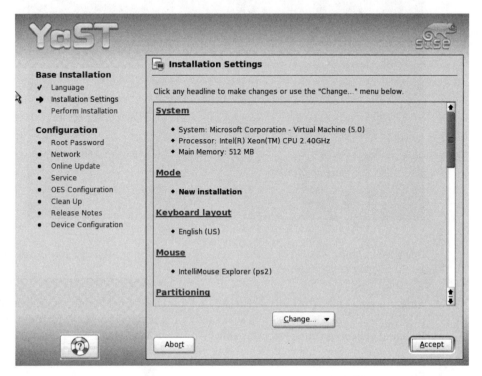

Figure 2-15. *From the installation settings screen, you must select what to install and how to install it.*

- *System*: Here you'll see information the installer detected about your computer. Click the link if these settings are not correct to restart hardware detection.

- *Mode*: Select the installation mode here. For new servers, it should read New Installation. For any other type of installation, consult Chapter 3 of this book.

- *Keyboard layout*: Use this setting to select the proper keyboard layout for your computer.

- *Mouse*: Use this link to specify the type of mouse you're using.

- *Partitioning*: Here you can indicate what type of partitions you want to use on your server. By default, all available disk space will be claimed for installation of the server. If an existing Windows installation was detected, it will be shrunk to make place for your OES installation. Click this link to get access to a custom partitioner utility. The menu it displays has three options. Use Create Custom Partition Setup for complete freedom of the partitioning of your computer's hard drive, or Base Partition Setup to modify the proposed settings. In step 8 of the procedure, you'll learn how to modify the partitioning of your hard drive.

Tip If you just have one hard disk in your server and want to configure NSS volumes as well as normal Linux volumes on it, you must configure the EVMS volume manager here. Novell strongly recommends you configure NSS on a separate hard disk, however. If, say for testing purposes, you want to do it anyway, see Chapter 11 for more information.

- *Software*: Here you can specify what you want to install. Everything necessary to work with Open Enterprise Server is selected by default. If some software component is not selected by default, you can always install it later. If you need to add or remove software components from your installation, click the software link to get access to the YaST software installation screen. You can find more details about this screen in Chapter 13 of this book, so it's not explained any further in this chapter.

- *Booting*: Use this link to modify the settings of the boot loader. You normally only want to do that on a multiboot system (which isn't very common for a server).

- *Time zone*: Use this option to specify the time zone you're in. If you don't live in the UTC - 8 time zone, change it; otherwise, it will be set to USA/Pacific time.

- *Language*: This is your last chance to modify the language the server will be installed in.

- *Default Runlevel*: This option specifies how the server boots. The default runlevel 5 starts your server with its graphical display. This is the recommended setting for OES, but you'll need the graphical environment from time to time to manage it.

9. To change the partitioning for your server, click the link Partitioning. Next, select Create Custom Partition Setup for maximum flexibility in defining the layout of the partition scheme on your server. From the next screen, select Custom Partitioning --For Experts and click Next to continue. This loads the partitioning utility (see Figure 2-16). This option is recommended only if you're familiar with the concepts of hard disk partitions. If you're not, use the automatic partitioning utility. This keeps you from causing errors in the partition scheme of your server.

10. If you're familiar with the partitioning of hard disks, you can delete the current root partition on your hard disk. This is the biggest partition displayed in the window, and shows a / in the mount column. Now you can create new partitions with the boundaries that are optimized for your server. In creating these new partitions, you can take advantage of advanced options, like the Linux file system you want to use. In most scenarios, however,

it's recommended to leave the partitions with the default Reiser file system. If you want to use NSS, read Chapter 11 for more information about the way you can create NSS partitions. Normally, you create them on an additional hard disk, so you don't need to leave any free space for NSS volumes here. When finished creating partitions, click Next to continue.

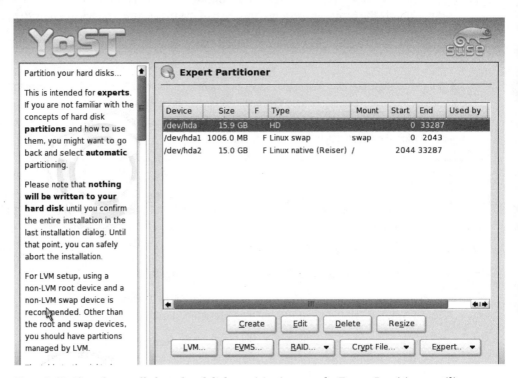

Figure 2-16. *If you know all about hard disk partitioning, use the Expert Partitioner utility to modify the partition layout of your hard drive.*

11. When you've made all the appropriate settings from the Installation Settings screen, click Accept to proceed with the installation. A pop-up window next appears, asking if you're sure you want to start the installation. Until now, no modifications have been made to your computer. Click Yes, Install to start the installation. This creates the new partitions on your computer and commits all other choices made so far. Required files will be copied now from CD1 to the disk of your server.

12. Insert new CDs when asked for. Be aware that the numbering of the CDs is odd: the installer will first ask for a maximum of three CDs called Open Enterprise Server CD 1, 2, and 3. When the necessary files are copied from these CDs, it will start asking for SUSE Linux Enterprise Server 9 CD 2 and so on. The CD label shows exactly which CD you must insert.

13. When all the files have been copied to your server, you're prompted for the password of the user root. Enter the same password twice and press Next to continue. Be careful about the password you select here since root is the administrator of your server. If you want to specify anything other than the default MD5 password encryption algorithm, click Expert options and select the algorithm you want to use.

14. Now you have to specify the network configuration, as shown in Figure 2-17. All network interfaces will be detected automatically and configured as much as possible. To use your server in a LAN environment, the only important option is the option Network Interfaces. Here you can configure the network cards in your computer. As a default, the network card in your server will be detected, but it will not be configured, so you must click Network Interfaces to modify the properties of your network card.

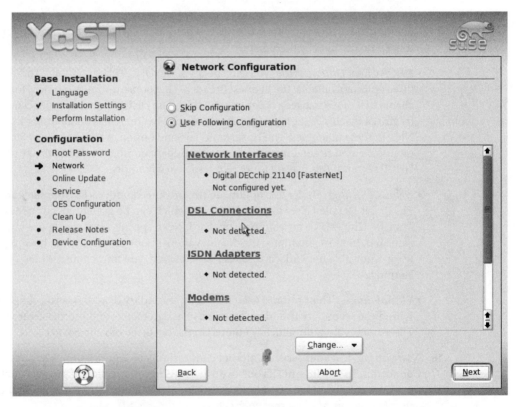

Figure 2-17. *By default, your network card will be detected, but it will not be configured.*

15. Click the network card that's detected and select Configure. This opens a dialogue where you can enter the IP address assignments for this server. Enter a static IP address and next specify the host name and name server, as well as the default router that should be used by this server. Most services used on OES need a static IP address. Thus, it isn't an option to install OES with a dynamic IP address. As for the name server: it's strongly recommended to use a DNS server in your network, some services rely upon it. iFolder for example won't work without it, so specify the IP address of the server you want to assign as the name server and don't forget to configure it. You can read more about name server configuration in Chapter 14. From this screen, it's possible to specify advanced options for the configuration of your network card as well. A list of available advanced options is shown next. After specifying all required information, click Next, Finish, and Next to continue.

- *Hardware Details*: Use this option to specify hardware options for the driver of your network board. In most cases, all required parameters will be detected automatically. If not, you can specify them here.

- *DHCP Client Options*: Here you can specify some DHCP client options. There are three options available: the Request Broadcast Response option is required for mobile clients that move between different networks. The DHCP client identifier can be used by virtual machines (as machines installed in VMware) to use an identifier for the NICs in these machines. The Host Name To Send option, which has the default value of Auto, is used to send the host name of the client computer automatically to the DHCP server. If this feature is not required, leave it empty.

- *Detailed Settings*: Under this option are two advanced options for your network card. The first is Detailed Network Card Settings, which can be used to specify a Maximum Transfer Unit (MTU) for your network card. Next, specify when the device must be activated. In most situations, the default value At Boot Time is fine. If, however, you use a removable network card, like a PCMCIA card, you may choose When Hotplugged.

- *Virtual Aliases*: This option is used to specify secondary IP addresses for the server. With these secondary IP addresses, you can assign names to these aliases as well. These names are automatically entered in the hosts file of your server.

16. Now you can test your server's Internet connection (see Figure 2-18). Select Yes, Test Connection To The Internet if you have a live Internet connection. If you also qualify for the automatic download of updates, these updates will be downloaded automatically. Select Next to test the Internet connection and download updates.

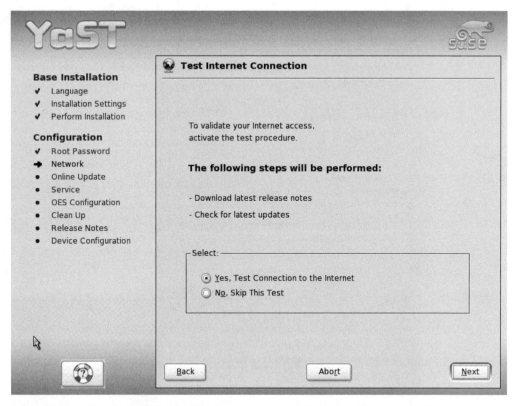

Figure 2-18. *To be sure that the latest updates are installed, test the connection to the Internet and download and install available updates immediately.*

17. If Online Updates are available, download them with YaST Online Update. It's recommended to do so directly, because with these updates you'll have a better server. Select Yes, Run Online Update Now and click OK to continue. Follow the onscreen directions to complete this procedure.

18. After downloading and installing the updates, a Certificate Authority and server certificates are installed (see Figure 2-19). You only need to install a new Certificate Authority if there are currently no CAs available in the tree. If you're installing into a network where a CA and certificates already exist, you can import the CA and certificate into your current installation. Read Chapter 9 for more details about this procedure. The OpenLDAP Server which is a default part of OES will not be installed. This is because eDirectory will be installed later and this Directory service can do anything that OpenLDAP does.

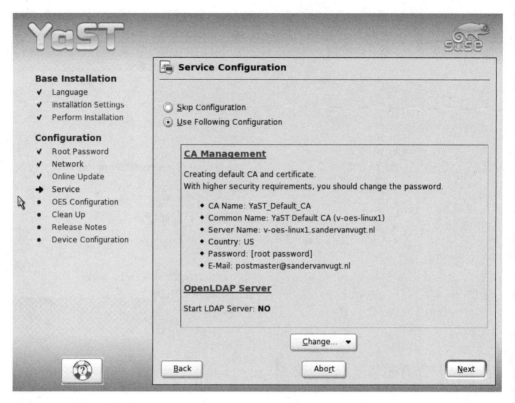

Figure 2-19. *If no CA exists in your network already, you can create a new one here.*

19. Next, specify whether you want to configure Open Enterprise Server now or later. If you want to, you can just leave the installation here and configure all OES components like eDirectory and others from SUSE's YaST later. Since it's useful to have at least eDirectory configured, in this procedure you'll learn how to configure the services that are selected by default. Select Configure Now and click Next to continue.

20. Specify whether you want to install in a new tree or an existing tree. If creating a new tree, you only have to enter the name of the tree. If installing in an existing tree, you must specify the name of the administrative user admin and his password as well. Enter the required information and click Next to continue. The installer now searches the network for trees with an identical name. This can take a few moments. When creating a new tree, enter the name and password of the admin user you want to create for this tree. This admin name has to be a fully distinguished name that reflects the container where the user object has to be created. It also must include the object types. An FDN looks like CN=admin.O=OES. For more information about this naming scheme, consult Chapter 8. Click Next to continue.

21. The screen shown in Figure 2-20 should appear. Enter the context where you want to install the server and the default port assignments. By default, the server will be installed in the same context as your admin user. If you have no good design reasons to choose another context, you can leave it like that. The ports are good with their default values as well. Accept all settings and click Next to continue.

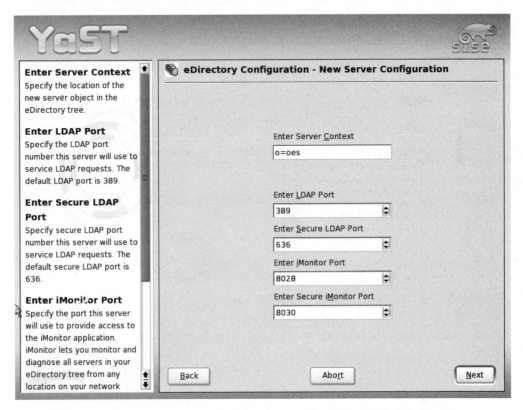

Figure 2-20. *The port addresses for LDAP and iMonitor are best left at their default values.*

22. Now enter the information required for time synchronization and SLP (see Figure 2-21). If this is the first server on your network, enter the IP address of an NTP time server on the Internet. If an Internet connection is not available, you can specify to use the internal clock of your server. This is, however, not recommended. If other servers are already installed in your network, this server automatically gets its time from the first server you installed in the tree. As for the Service Location Protocol (SLP) that allows your server to find other network services on the network (see Chapter 14), the default setting is to not use SLP. This is fine in a small network, but in a network with more than three servers it's recommended you use an SLP Directory Agent. Since these are currently not supported

on OES - Linux, you must configure them on OES - NetWare. After specifying the IP address of the Directory Agent, enter the default scope, which is conveniently named Default. This is fine if no scopes are configured. If scopes are configured, you should enter the name of the scope you want to use here. Only if there's no possibility of using an SLP Directory Agent should you select Use Multicast To Access SLP. In large networks, however, this is not recommended. In smaller networks, it won't cause too many problems. The reason for this is that it generates some network traffic. Unfortunately, it's your sole option if you only have OES - Linux in your network, because currently it's not possible to run a Directory Agent on Linux. After entering all the required information, click Next to continue. eDirectory will now be configured and started. This will take a few moments.

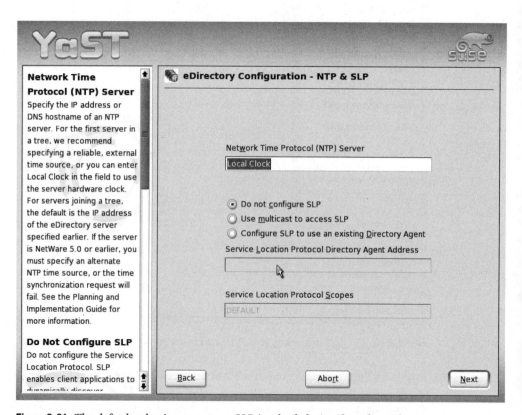

Figure 2-21. *The default selection to not use SLP is a bad choice if you have three or more servers.*

23. When eDirectory is started, you can configure all services that depend on it. These services are displayed in a summary screen that shows you what's being installed before the installation actually starts. (See Figure 2-22.) The default configuration is very simple: if you perform a default installation, the default settings will work for all services. Later in this book, you'll learn how to tune these services. Services that require additional information are not selected by default. Therefore, just leave all values as they are and click Next to continue. This installs and configures all selected modules, so it can take a few moments to complete.

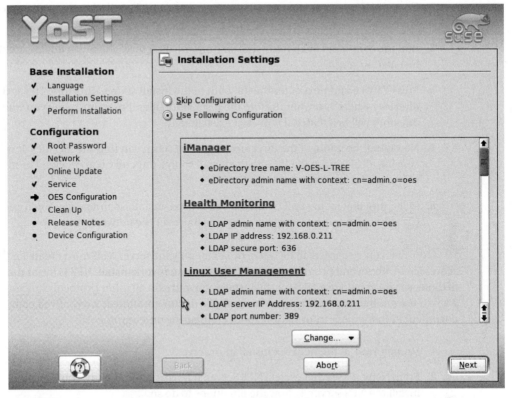

Figure 2-22. *The services that are installed in a default installation don't require additional configuration.*

24. Read the release notes with last-minute instructions about OES and click Next to continue.

25. You'll now get the opportunity to install additional hardware. All required hardware should be functioning now, so from this screen you can click Next to continue.

26. All required information has now been entered. Click Finish to complete the installation. Once your server boots, it's ready for use.

Performing an OES Network Installation

If you need to install many OES - Linux servers, you can perform a network install. This scenario needs two different servers: the SUSE Linux server that acts as the YaST network installation server, and the server that will become the new OES - Linux server. It also helps if you have a DHCP server on the network: this can provide your OES - Linux server with an initial IP address to contact the network installation server. The following procedure describes how you can prepare for a network installation:

1. Download the netInstall.sh script file on the server you want to use as the YaST installation server. You can download this file from http://www.novell.com/documentation/oes/script/netInstall.sh.

2. Copy the ISO images you want to use for the network installation to the directory of your choice.

3. Run the command **bash netInstall.sh** from the directory where you downloaded the installation script.

4. Press Y twice and next enter the full path to the install source directory. This is the directory where you want to store the installation files. Enter any name you want; the directory will be created if it doesn't exist already.

5. Now enter the name of the directory where the script can find the ISO files. It will start copying all files from the ISOs to the install source directory you provided in step 4 of this procedure.

6. Make sure that create a CD from the oes-linux-1-install.iso image file. You'll need this CD to boot from the server you want to install over the network.

Now that you've copied all ISOs to a directory on your server, you must create an NFS share. There are several protocols you can use to do a network install. NFS is by far the fastest of these, so you should use NFS for the installation and skip all other protocol choices. If you want to use another protocol anyway, consult the documentation at www.novell.com/documentation for more information about configuring other protocols.

1. Launch YaST at the network installation server.

2. From Network Services, select NFS Server. If not installed already, you'll be prompted to install the NFS server. Follow the directions to do so.

3. On the NFS server configuration screen, select Start NFS Server and click Next.

4. In the Top Directories Section, add the directory that you've copied the ISOs to, as shown in Figure 2-23. Accept all defaults and click Finish to finalize the installation.

■**Caution** To perform an NFS installation, your Network installation server must be reachable by its name. This only works if you've properly configured DNS for name resolving, and are using DHCP to distribute the IP address of the DNS name server to the clients.

Your Network Server is now prepared the way it should be prepared. Insert the OES Enterprise Server CD 1 in the drive of the new server you want to install. From the boot menu, select Installation and press F3 to specify that you want to perform an NFS installation. Next, specify the name of the server and the installation path and select OK to continue. Press Enter to continue. The rest of the installation procedure works exactly as described earlier.

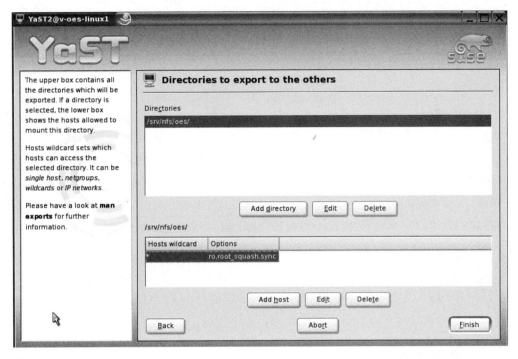

Figure 2-23. *To perform an NFS-based installation, you must configure the NFS server.*

Summary

In this chapter, you learned how to install both versions of OES. One of the most important things to remember is that you should always install OES - NetWare first and then install OES - Linux if you want to create a mixed tree. When installing OES - Linux, it's also possible to perform a network installation. To do so, download the netinstall.sh script file from the Novell web site. The next chapter covers how to upgrade various servers to OES.

■ ■ ■

## CHAPTER 3

Upgrading to Open Enterprise Server

Although a new server platform can be a very good reason to start all over again and design your network and services from scratch, in many companies the infrastructure is so complex that this isn't really an option. In these cases, the current versions of the server platform need to be upgraded to the next version. Fortunately, Novell offers many options to upgrade or migrate to Open Enterprise server.

Before starting, let's first talk about terminology. When discussing the transition from one version of an operating system to another, often a distinction is made between an upgrade and a migration. Of these, an upgrade is a situation where you're working on the same server but no data is copied from the server to a new server. A classic example of this in a Novell environment is the upgrade where the server is brought down, the installation CD for the new operating system is inserted, and an upgrade is started that converts all old files on the server to the latest version. In a migration procedure, however, data is copied over the network. Typically during migration, the old and new servers are operational simultaneously. To get data from the old server to its newer counterpart, data is copied across the network. In this procedure, a workstation is used to modify the data before it's copied across the network.

■**Note** In this chapter, it's assumed that an OES - compatible tree already exists. This means that the Deployment Manager has been used to prepare an existing tree for OES installation, or that an OES server is already installed. More information on this can be found in Chapter 2.

Upgrade/Migration Paths to Open Enterprise Server

Different methods are available for upgrading from any server to Open Enterprise Server. Which option to choose depends on the server platform you're currently using and the OES version you want to migrate to. To upgrade to OES, the following paths are supported.

- From an old version of NetWare to OES - NetWare

- From an old version of NetWare to OES - Linux

- From an old version of SUSE Linux to OES - Linux

- From Windows to OES - NetWare

- From Windows to OES - Linux

To perform any kind of upgrade, you must choose one of the available upgrade methods listed next.

- *Local Upgrade*: The advantage of a local upgrade is that it takes place on the same server, therefore it's also referred to as an in-place upgrade. It transfers the new operating system files to your existing server. In the in-place upgrade, the operating system CD is mounted as a volume on the current server and from there the installation utility is started. As an alternative, the Down-server upgrade can be used. In this scenario, the old server is brought down and boots from the new operating system CD. From the new operating system CD, the Upgrade option is selected to upgrade to the new version. Local upgrades do have one major disadvantage: if anything goes wrong, the rollback path is much more complex and takes longer, because an in-place upgrade actually replaces files on the original server.

- *Remote Upgrade*: The remote upgrade allows an administrator to upgrade a server, without the need to be present at the server console. In fact, a Remote Upgrade really is an in-place upgrade performed remotely. This method is supported for OES - NetWare only. If you want to perform a remote upgrade, you should make sure the target server has a DOS partition of at least 500MB, with 200MB of free space available. If these conditions are met, from a Windows workstation you can launch Deployment Manager or iManager to perform a remote upgrade of a server. Once the remote upgrade is finished, the old server will run OES - NetWare.

- *Hardware Upgrade (a.k.a., Migration)*: If you want to not only upgrade the software running on your server, but the hardware as well, you can choose the hardware upgrade method. The Migration Wizard is necessary to perform this type upgrade. In this scenario, the file system and eDirectory database are copied from the old server to the newly installed OES server. After the files and eDirectory information from the source server are migrated, the source server is automatically brought down. The destination server reboots, and after rebooting, takes the identity of the source server. Before using the Migration Wizard, you must first install OES - NetWare under a temporary name in a temporary eDirectory tree. This tree contains one server only in a basic installation of OES - NetWare and no additional products installed. The major advantage of a migration is that the roll back path needed to restore the system to its original state is simpler and faster. A disadvantage is that a new server is needed to perform a migration. The hardware upgrade is not supported on OES - Linux.

- *Consolidation*: The server consolidation utility is the most flexible way to migrate data from old servers to new servers. It can be used to copy data from NetWare or Windows to OES - Linux or OES - NetWare. With the server consolidation utility, you don't migrate everything from one server to another server, you merely copy users, data, and permissions from the source server to the target server. When using this utility, the new server does not take the identity of the old server—after performing the migration, you can bring down the old server manually. If you want to migrate a Windows server to Open Enterprise Server, this is your best option.

Tip With upgrades and migrations, your server keeps the same identity so all mappings and other references remain intact and work seamlessly after the upgrade.

- *Data Volume Transfer*: If you want to upgrade NetWare 6.5 to OES - Linux, you have the option to transfer NSS data volumes from OES - NetWare to OES - Linux. This is because the same NSS code is used on both servers. This way, you can take a disk with NSS from the OES - NetWare server and mount it on the OES - Linux server. See Chapter 11 for more information about NSS.

- *Nsure Identity Manager*: If no other upgrade method is available, you can always use Nsure Identity Manager to synchronize identities from any application to OES. The advantage is that if the right driver is supported, virtually any operating system can be synchronized this way. It is, however, only a synchronization of identities and is not a complete migration, because this method does not offer any option to migrate data volumes and rights as well. More information about Nsure Identity Manager can be found in Chapter 18.

In this chapter, the most common of these scenarios is discussed. A complete overview of all upgrade options is listed next in Table 3-1.

Table 3-1. *Upgrade/Migration Paths to Open Enterprise Server*

Migration Method	Destination OES - NetWare	Destination OES - Linux
From NetWare 4.11 or 4.2 SP9 with Minimum NDS Version 6.21		
Local/Remote Upgrade	Not supported	Not supported
Hardware Upgrade	Migration Wizard 6.5	Not supported
Consolidation	Supported, but IPX is required on the target server.	Not supported directly. Indirectly via OES - NetWare will work.

Table 3-1. *Continued*

Migration Method	Destination OES - NetWare	Destination OES - Linux
From NetWare 5.0 SP6a with NSS and Minimum NDS Version 7.62c or 8.85c		
Local/Remote Upgrade	Not supported	Not supported
Hardware Upgrade	Migration Wizard 6.5	Not supported
Consolidation	Server Consolidation Utility 4.0	Not supported, but indirectly via OES - NetWare will work.
From NetWare 5.1 SP7 or Later with Minimum NDS 7.62c or 8.85c		
Local Upgrade	In-place upgrade using NetWare 6.5 SP3 install overlay method	Not supported
Remote Upgrade	Across the wire with Deployment Manager or iManager	Not supported
Hardware Upgrade	Migration wizard 8.0	Not supported
Consolidation	Server Consolidation Utility 4.0	Server Consolidation Utility 4.0 if NSS volumes are present.
NetWare 6.0 SP4 or Later with Minimum eDirectory 8.6.2		
Local Upgrade	In-place upgrade using the NetWare 6.5 SP3 install overlay method	Not supported
Remote Upgrade	Across the wire with Deployment Manager or iManager	Not supported
Hardware Upgrade	Migration Wizard 8.0	Not supported
Consolidation	Server Consolidation Utility 4.0	Server Consolidation Utility 4.0 to NSS volumes only
NetWare 6.5 with Minimum eDirectory 8.7.x		
Local Upgrade	In-place upgrade using the NetWare 6.5 SP3 install overlay method	Not supported
Remote Upgrade	Across the wire using Deployment Manager or iManager	Not supported
Hardware Upgrade	Migration Wizard 8.0	Not supported
Consolidation	Server Consolidation Utility 4.0	Server Consolidation Utility 4.0 to NSS volumes
Data Volume Transfer	Not applicable	Install OES - Linux and mount existing NSS volumes on it

Migration Method	Destination OES - NetWare	Destination OES - Linux
SUSE Linux Enterprise Server 9		
Local Upgrade	Not supported	YaST with Open Enterprise Server selected
Remote Upgrade	Not supported	Not supported
Hardware Upgrade	Not supported	Not supported
Consolidation	Not supported	Not supported
Upgrade from any other version of Linux	Not supported	Not supported
Windows NT Domains and Windows Active Directory (One Domain at a Time)		
Local Upgrade	Not supported	Not supported
Remote Upgrade	Not supported	Not supported
Hardware Upgrade	Not supported	Not supported
Consolidation	Server Consolidation Utility 4.0 to copy file system data, users/ groups, permissions, and file ownership	Server Consolidation Utility 4.0 to copy file system data, users/ groups, permissions, and file ownership

■**Note** Two versions of the Migration Wizard can be used to migrate to OES - NetWare. Migration Wizard version 6.5, which can be downloaded from the Web, supports upgrades from NetWare 3.2 and NetWare 4.x to OES - NetWare. For all NetWare versions since 5.0, Migration Wizard 8.0, which is on the OES - NetWare Operating System CD, can be used.

Performing the Upgrade

As can be seen in Table 3-1, many upgrade options are available. It's not possible to cover all of them in the space available here, but in the following sections you can read about the most common types of upgrades. An example of each of the four most important upgrade methods is discussed. The data volume transfer will not be discussed here, however, since NSS is covered in depth in Chapter 11. If you're interested in using Nsure Identity Manager as an upgrade method, read Chapter 18. In this chapter, the following upgrade paths are explored:

- *Local Upgrade*: Upgrading SLES 9 to OES - Linux

- *Remote Upgrade*: Upgrading NetWare 6 to OES - NetWare

- *Migration*: Using the Migration Wizard to Upgrade NetWare 5.1 to OES - NetWare

- *Server Consolidation*: Migrating Windows Server 2003 to OES - Linux

Local Upgrade: Upgrading SLES 9 to OES - Linux

If you're currently running SUSE Linux Enterprise Server 9 and you want to upgrade it to OES - Linux, the Local Upgrade with YaST is your only option. Before starting the upgrade though, you need to perform a few steps first.

- The SLES server must have a static IP address.

- DNS must return the system's DNS name when presented with the system's IP address. This requires reversed DNS to be configured properly. Use the command **nslookup** to validate this if such is the case. If, for example, you need to verify this for the server with IP address 192.168.0.11, use **nslookup 192.168.0.11**. In the answer, you'll see if reversed DNS is set up properly. See Chapter 14 for more on DNS configuration.

- The server must have a server certificate that has been generated and exported as a common server certificate. To check this or add a certificate, use the following procedure:

    1. Start YaST and enter the root password if so required.

    2. Click Security and Users ➤ CA Management. This brings you to the screen shown in Figure 3-1.

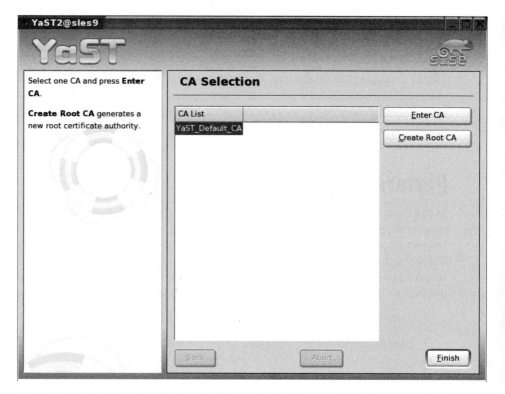

Figure 3-1. *After installing SLES, a Certificate Authority will be presented by default.*

3. If no CAs are currently configured on this server, create one by clicking Create Root CA. If a CA is listed, select it and click Enter CA. In the latter case, enter the CA password; most times this is the same password as the password of user root.

4. If no certificate is present yet, click Certificates ➤ Add and select the option Server Certificate (see Figure 3-2).

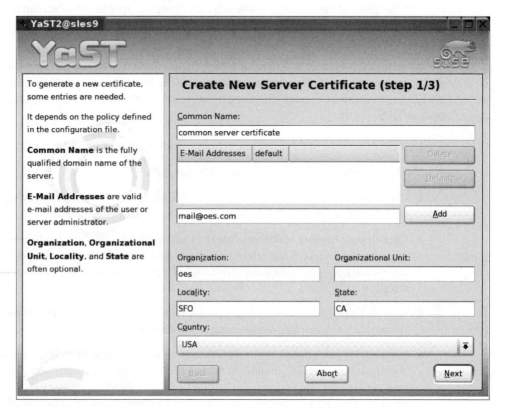

Figure 3-2. *In the forms for the server certificate, you must enter contact details for your organization.*

5. Fill out the forms required for a server certificate. In the first of these forms you must enter contact details for your organization and a name for the certificate. As the name, use the DNS name of the server where you're creating it. In the second form, provide a password for the certificate and enter the details for encryption. A password is required, which needs to be entered when using the private key associated to this certificate. Next, a summary of all entered details is shown. Complete the procedure by clicking Create. The server certificate is now created and listed in the certificate list.

6. Select the certificate you just created.

7. Click the Export button, and then select the Export As Common Server Certificate option. Now enter the password of the certificate to complete the procedure.

- If OpenLDAP is configured on your SLES server, you must export all data from the LDAP directory before proceeding. Use LDIF to perform this data export. Next, install eDirectory on the server. After installing eDirectory, data from the OpenLDAP server can be imported in eDirectory. More details about the use of LDIF to import and export data is provided in Chapter 8.

When all the preparation is done and each requirement is met, you can start the upgrade of SLES to OES - Linux. The procedure for this upgrade is described next, including a description of a CD-based upgrade. Consult Chapter 2 for more information about a network-based installation of OES - Linux.

1. Bring down your SLES server and reboot it from Open Enterprise Server CD 1.

2. From the boot menu on the CD, select Installation.

3. Click I Agree on the License Agreement screen and select the language you want to use for installation. Then, select Update An Existing System and click OK.

4. Click Update Option. Make sure that the Update With Installation On New Software And Features Based On The Selection option is marked, and select Novell Open Enterprise Server. Click Accept to continue. When asked if you really want to reset your detailed selection, click Yes.

5. Now click Accept followed by Yes, Update. This starts the update of the server. Follow the prompts to complete the file copy on your server.

6. When all files are copied, the server is ready to be configured as an OES - Linux server. You must start this configuration manually from YaST. First of all, from Network Services, select eDirectory. This starts the eDirectory configuration program (see Figure 3-3). The procedure you must apply to configure eDirectory is very similar (if not identical) to the procedure described in Chapter 2 of this book. Therefore, I won't cover it here in detail.

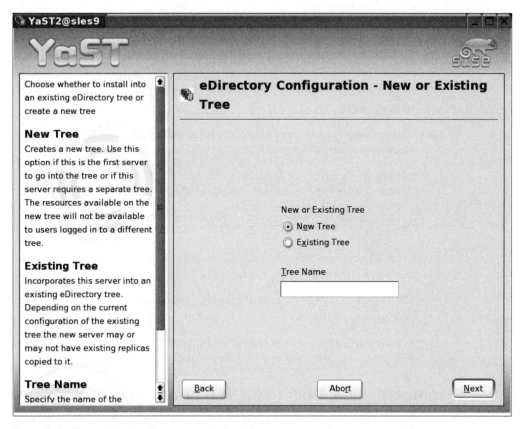

Figure 3-3. *After upgrading SLES to OES, the first step is to perform an eDirectory installation.*

7. After installing eDirectory, all other services related to eDirectory can be configured. The following is a list of these services with a short description.

• *Linux User Management*: This option allows you to manage Linux user accounts in eDirectory. See Chapter 9 for more details.

• *NCP Server*: This service allows you to create NCP shares so that files on OES - Linux can be accessed by users working with the Novell client. See Chapter 10 for more information about NCP.

• *NetStorage*: Use this service to enable web-based access to files on OES - Linux. See Chapter 10 for more details.

• *Novell Health Monitor*: This service can be used to monitor the health of your OES - server from iManager. See Chapter 7 for more information.

• *Novell Quick Finder*: Use this service to enable your server as an indexing server for searching web pages, both within your site and on the Internet. See Chapter 16 for more details.

- *Novell Samba*: The Novell Samba server allows Windows users to access files on an OES - Linux server that are shared by the Novell Samba server. Read Chapter 10 for more details.

- *Virtual Office*: This service allows you to configure a portal page for eDirectory users. From this portal page, users can get access to most services they need. See Chapter 17 for more details.

- *eGuide*: eGuide can be used as a white pages solution for users to locate information about co-workers. Consult Chapter 17 for more details.

- *iManager*: This is the web-based administration tool used to manage OES. You need it on at least one server in the network. Read Chapter 7 for more details about it.

- *iFolder 2.x*: This tool can be used for file synchronization. See Chapter 10 for more information.

- *iPrint*: This is the solution to print documents in a Novell environment. Chapter 15 has more on the subject.

- *NSS*: Novell Storage Services is a very robust file system. See Chapter 11 for more information.

- *NCS*: Novell Cluster Services can be used to cluster resources on OES - Linux as well as OES - NetWare. See Chapter 19 for more details.

Remote Upgrade: Upgrading NetWare 6 to OES - NetWare

One of the most flexible ways to upgrade an existing NetWare server to OES - NetWare is by performing a remote upgrade. This section explains how to perform a Remote Upgrade with iManager. Before starting the upgrade, make sure the following minimum requirements have been met:

- The target server is installed with one of the latest support packs. For NetWare 6.0, the oldest you could use would be SP4.

- The eDirectory tree is healthy. (Read Chapter 8 for more about health checks.)

- You have a SYS volume of at least 4GB.

- The DOS partition of your server is at least 500MB, of which 200MB is free.

When all these conditions have been met, you can begin the remote upgrade procedure.

1. Start iManager. Make sure you connect to an OES - NetWare server, otherwise the version of iManager you use will not show the required Install And Upgrade option.

2. From Install And Upgrade, select Upgrade To NetWare 6.5 (you should now see the screen shown in Figure 3-4). Next, click the link Upgrade A Server Remotely to start the upgrade.

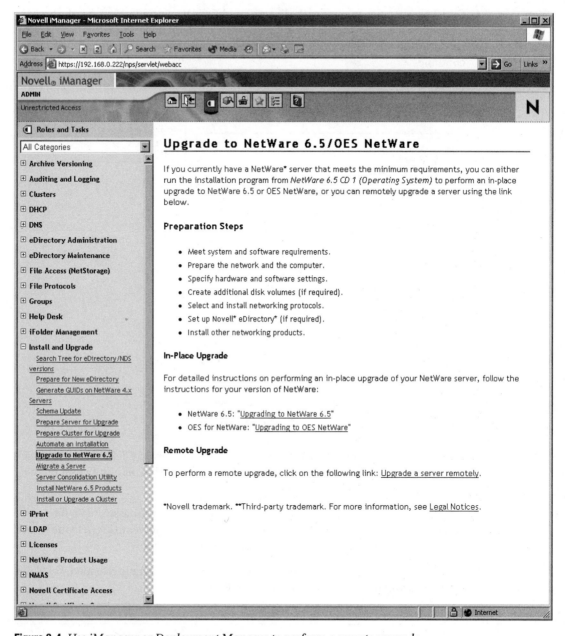

Figure 3-4. *Use iManager or Deployment Manager to perform a remote upgrade.*

3. Browse to the location where the OES - NetWare Operating System CD is available. You could insert it in the CD drive of your local workstation, but it will be considerably faster if you use another server to mount the CD. After entering the full path to the installation CD, click OK to continue.

4. Click I Accept twice to agree to the license conditions to continue. Next, use the browser (see Figure 3-5) to locate the target server you want to upgrade. From this browser, you can locate all the NetWare servers in your tree. Select the target server and click OK to continue.

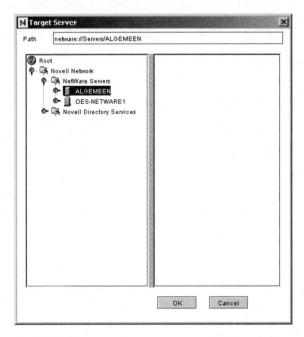

Figure 3-5. *Browse to the server you want to upgrade.*

5. Now enter all credentials required to log in to the target server. Click OK and then click Next to continue. You'll be prompted to enter the password of the admin user on the target tree again. Do this and click OK.

6. After logging in to the target server twice, you must provide the password on the source server as well. This password is needed for the destination server to log in to the source server and pull all files needed for the upgrade across the wire.

7. On the target server, everything necessary to perform the upgrade is loaded. You'll see the progress on the console of the target server.

■**Note** Under some conditions, you may get an error message related to the Certificate Server diagnostics at this point. If this is the case, refer to the file SYS:/etc/certserv/repair.log. Here, you'll find a report of all the errors encountered. One of these errors might be that the SSL Certificates in use by the NetWare 6 server will expire soon! For a complete list of all error codes and their solutions, consult TID 10089099 in the Knowledge-base on http://support.novell.com. It's strongly recommended to fix any errors before you start the upgrade, they might prevent OES - NetWare from being installed correctly.

---

8. When all preparatory steps have been completed, a summary screen appears (see Figure 3-6). On this screen, you can tell if all conditions have been met to start the remote upgrade. If you see anything besides the term Success, make sure you really want to continue. If needed, click View Log to get more information about errors or warnings displayed in the Health Check Summary window. If you're sure that all conditions have been met, click Next to continue.

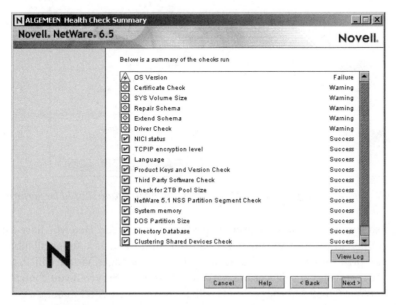

Figure 3-6. *Make sure there are no unresolved critical conditions before continuing the remote upgrade.*

9. The screen shown in Figure 3-7 should appear. Here, you can specify several options for the upgrade. The following options are available:

- *Backup the server boot directory files*: This option allows you to make a backup of all files on the server's DOS partition. Do not select the option if you don't have a DOS partition that is at least 500MB. If you want to make a backup of the old server boot directory, you can specify its backup location as well.

- *Reboot the system after file copy completes*: In most situations, this option can be selected. It reboots the server automatically after the upgrade; thus, allowing you to start using it immediately.

- *Allow unsupported drivers*: This option makes sure that only supported drivers are upgraded. This ensures that the server remains stable. Unsupported drivers stay untouched. If an upgrade of these drivers is required, you may do so manually.

- *Specify the upgrade type*: Select Default for an upgrade where a minimum amount of user intervention is required. If you want to be able to specify options while performing the upgrade (perhaps you want to choose extra protocols), select a Manual upgrade.

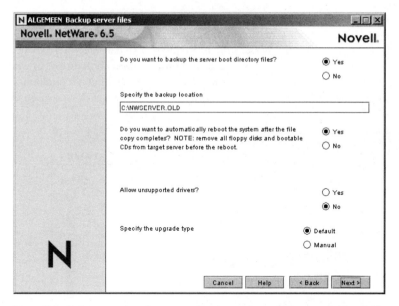

Figure 3-7. *Before starting the upgrade, choose how the upgrade should be performed.*

10. In the next step, specify how you want to perform the upgrade. Here you have a choice between Open Enterprise Server, or NetWare 6.5 Support Pack 3. An installation of Open Enterprise Server installs the latest versions of iManager, Virtual Office, and the QuickFinder server that replaces the NetWare Web Search Server. If you choose to install NetWare 6.5 SP 3, these products will not be installed. After making a choice, click Next to continue.

11. The product screen where you can select all the products you want to use on your new server should appear. Select all the products required and click Next to continue. An overview of your selection is provided now. Click Copy Files to start copying files. This starts the actual upgrade and makes the process irreversible. It can take a while for the entire procedure to complete, but you can view the progress of the upgrade on the screen of your server. When it finishes, the server reboots automatically and is then ready for use.

Note If new versions of the drivers have been installed while performing the upgrade, user interaction may be required to select the right drivers.

Across the Wire Migration: Using the Migration Wizard to Migrate NetWare 5.1 to OES - NetWare

You've already learned about two options for upgrading your server if you want to stay with the same server hardware. However, often while performing an upgrade, you'll find that not only is the server software upgraded, but the hardware is replaced as well. In that case, the option to move all relevant data from the old server to the new server is very welcome. Novell provides this functionality with the Migration Wizard. Two versions of this program are relevant: if you want to upgrade NetWare 3.x or 4.x to OES - NetWare, version 6.5 of this wizard is required. It can be downloaded from the Novell web site at download.novell.com. If, however, you want to upgrade NetWare 5.0 or later or if you want to migrate Windows to NetWare, version 8 of the Migration Wizard is needed. You can find this version of the program on the OES - NetWare Operating System CD. The Migration Wizard is a very versatile tool, but it has one drawback: only upgrades to OES - NetWare are supported.

The Migration Wizard is used to perform a one-on-one migration: the source server is migrated to a newly installed target server. After successful migration, the target server takes the identity of the source server and the original source server is brought down.

Installing Migration Wizard on a Workstation

To use the Migration Wizard, you must install it on a workstation. Currently Windows 2000 with SP 2 or later and Windows XP Professional Edition are supported. On this workstation, version 4.9 with Support Pack 2 or later of the Novell Client software must be installed. To check the current version of your client, right-click the red N in the task bar of your computer. Then, click Novell Client Properties ➤ Client. Here you can see the current version of your client software. If this version doesn't meet the requirements, install a later version before you proceed. In Chapter 6, you can read more about installation of the Novell client software. Before you can successfully use the Migration Wizard on the workstation, however, some settings must be made in the Novell Client software:

1. Right-click the red N in the task bar of your computer and select Novell Client Properties ➤ Advanced Settings ➤ File Caching. Make sure this parameter is set to Off.

2. From the same Advanced Settings menu, select Use UTF8 Encoding And NCPs and also set this parameter to Off.

3. Reboot your workstation. This must be done before you can use these parameters.

Now you can install the Migration Wizard on your workstation. The program is located in the OES - NetWare Operating System CD in the directory products/migration utilities. In this directory, you'll find installation files for both the Migration Wizard and the Server Consolidation utility. Double-click the MIGRTWZD.EXE program to launch the installation of the Migration Wizard (see Figure 3-8). You can select all defaults when installing the Migration Wizard on your workstation.

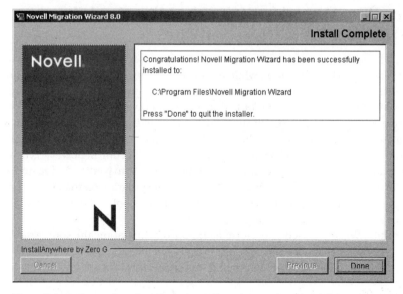

Figure 3-8. *Before using the Migration Wizard, you must install it on a workstation.*

Preparing the Source Server

Now that the migration wizard is installed, make sure the source server meets all the necessary requirements. To be certain, do all of the following:

- Shut down any applications, products, or services running on the server to be migrated.

- Perform a health check on the source server. You can do this by running DSREPAIR.NLM and selecting the following three options:

  - Unattended Full Repair

  - Time Synchronization

  - Report Synchronization Status

- Make a backup of eDirectory and all data on the server.

- Remove unnecessary applications and files

- Install the latest support pack for the source server

Preparing the Target Server

After the source server has been prepared, you must set up the destination server. This is a fresh installation of an OES - NetWare server (see Chapter 2 for more information on how to perform this installation). During the installation, make sure you do the following:

- Make sure the volumes you create on the target server have enough room for the source server's data. If compression is used on the source server, make sure that on the target server you have enough free space to store the uncompressed files.

- From the installation window, select the Pre-Migration Server option (see Figure 3-9).

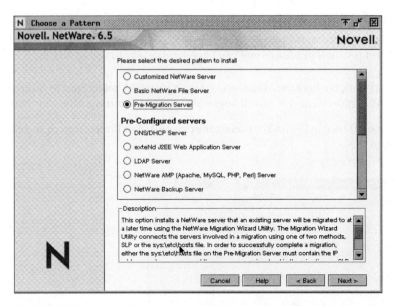

Figure 3-9. *To prepare the target server for migration, select the pre-migration pattern.*

- Create the server as a temporary server with an IP address that is different from the IP address of the target server. Also choose a temporary eDirectory tree name. If you want the target server to use the same IP address as the source server, you can change it after the migration has successfully completed.

- Do not enable the Universal Password before the migration completes.

Performing the Migration

When all prerequisites have been met, you can start the migration procedure. To complete the migration, the following tasks must be completed.

1. Start the Migration Wizard and create a project file.

2. Model the migration project.

3. Verify the migration project.

4. Copy the file system data.

5. Edit the configuration files.

6. Begin the NDS/eDirectory migration.

7. Finish the NDS/eDirectory migration.

8. Perform any post-migration tasks.

Starting the Migration Wizard and Creating a Project File

The first phase of the migration is where you start the Migration Wizard and create a migration project. This project is stored in a file so you can have an easy way to restart it later.

1. On the workstation where the Migration Wizard is installed, select Start ➤ All Programs ➤ Novell Migration Wizard ➤ Novell Migration Wizard to start the Migration Wizard.

2. On the screen shown in Figure 3-10, select the Create A New Project option and click OK to continue.

Figure 3-10. *All settings you enter into the Migration Wizard, such as the Create A New Project option, are saved to a project file so they can be opened again if needed.*

3. To be sure you work with the most recent version of the Migration Wizard, click Check Latest Updates to download the latest updates from the Internet. After verifying that no more new updates are available, click Next to continue.

4. Enter a name for the project filename and specify a location. Afterward, click Next to continue.

5. Next, connect to the source server. This is the NetWare server you want to migrate data from. If necessary, click the Login button to make a connection and log in to the source server. After logging in, click Next to continue (see Figure 3-11). From the source tree you're now connected to, select the NetWare source server. Make sure you have administrative rights to this server.

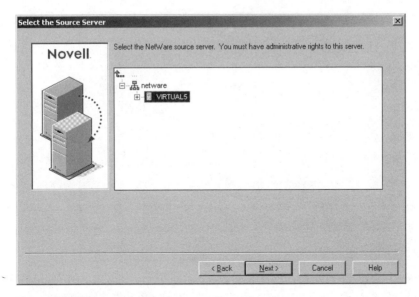

Figure 3-11. *To create the migration project, you must connect to the source server and the target server first.*

6. Next, log in to the target server. After logging in successfully, you'll see the name of the temporary tree you've installed. Click Next to continue and select the target server.

7. Click Create to create the project file. This allows you easy access to the same settings the next time you run the Migration Wizard.

Now that the basic settings for your migration project are saved, it's time to go on to the next stage of the Migration Wizard. In the next section, you'll learn how to model your migration project.

Modeling the Migration Project

In the Migration Wizard, you'll now see the modeling window with the old server in the left pane and the new server in the right pane. At this stage, you must select the volumes or directories you want to copy from the old server to the new server. At this stage, you're only modeling, so no changes will yet be made. You also won't be copying any eDirectory objects yet. That will happen at a later phase of the migration project.

1. In the Migration Wizard main window, you'll see the Getting Started Migrating From NetWare 5 Or 6 screen (see Figure 3-12). This screen tells you what to do in the migration process. Click Close, and to prevent this screen from popping up every time you start a new migration, deselect the option Always Show This Window.

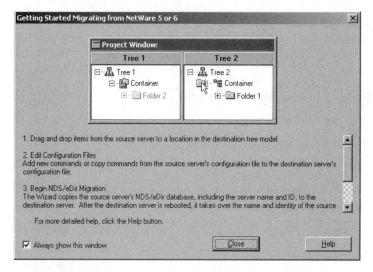

Figure 3-12. *In the first step of the actual migration process, you must drag and drop volumes and directories from the source server to the destination server.*

■**Tip** Normally, you just want to migrate datavolumes, not the SYS volume. By default, all system directories from the SYS volume on the source server will be migrated to the directory SYS.MIG on the target server.

---

2. Drag all directories you want to migrate to the location you select on the target server. Instead of directories, you can drag and drop entire volumes this way.

3. If so required, after dragging them to the target server, you can rename particular directories. Just right-click them and select Rename from the menu. It's also possible to create a new directory. All you have to do is right-click somewhere in the target server pane and from the menu select New. Then enter the name of the new directory you want to create.

4. If you drag a folder from the source server onto a folder with the same name on the destination server, the Duplicate Directory Encountered window appears. Here you can indicate what to do when duplicate directories are encountered. Your options are shown next.

- *Don't Copy the Directory*: This option ensures that already-existing directories are not overwritten.

- *Merge Directory Contents*: This merges the contents of the source server with the contents of the duplicate directory on the target server.

- *Rename*: This allows you to enter a new name for the directory on the target server.

Verifying the Migration Project

Now that you've modeled what you want to do, you must verify the migration project. In this verification, the Migration Wizard checks if there are any problems that might hinder a successful migration. Since this is just a check, no data will yet be copied.

1. In the menu bar of the Migration Wizard, select Project ➤ Verify And Migrate Project.

2. The Verification Wizard will run automatically and inform you of any problems it finds. If problems such as insufficient rights or disk space limitations are encountered, you must resolve them by hand before continuing. Next, copy the file system data (as described in the following section).

■**Tip** To minimize the chance of trustee rights getting lost, make a backup of all the trustees on the source server and put the backup file on the target server. If for any reason, there is an error while copying trustee assignments from the source server to the target server, you can restore them from this file. Select Project ➤ Backup Trustees from the Migration Wizard to start backing up all trustee rights on the source server.

Copying File System Data

Now it's time to copy files from the source server to the target server.

1. In the Project View dialog box (see Figure 3-13), click the Copy File System Data button.

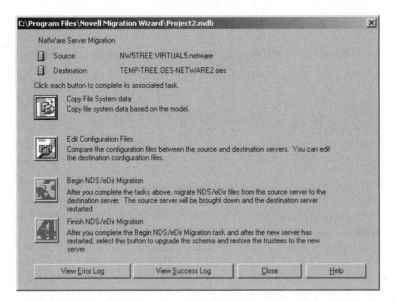

Figure 3-13. *Click the Copy File System Data button to start copying data from the source to the target server.*

2. In the Dropped Folders window (as shown in Figure 3-14), you can see an overview of all the work to be done. Verify this is what you want, and then click Next to continue.

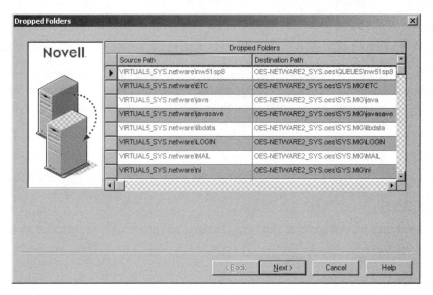

Figure 3-14. *From this screen, verify that everything is going to be performed the right way, then click Next to continue.*

3. An overview appears of all the new folders that the process will create. Click Next to continue.

4. Now, you must specify what to do if on the target server a file with the same name as on the source server is found. You have three different options:

• Don't copy over existing files

• Copy the source file if it is newer

• Always copy the source file

By default, a file will only be copied if the source file is newer than the target file. Change this default value if required and then click Next to continue.

5. Next, specify what to do with users that are currently logged in (see Figure 3-15). It's strongly recommended from this screen to select the option Disable Login. Then, click the Broadcast Logout Message button and enter a message you would like to broadcast to all users still logged in. Wait a few minutes and then, from MONITOR.NLM ➤ Connections on the source's Server Console, terminate every open user connection by selecting it and pressing the Delete button. This closes any open files so they will copy properly. Click Next to proceed.

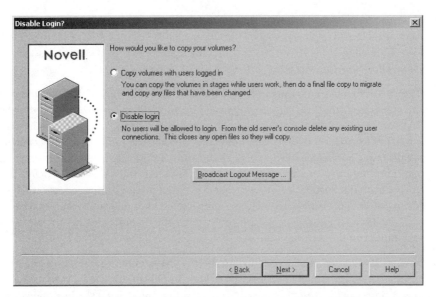

Figure 3-15. *Disable any logins before you start copying files and delete all open user connections. That way you'll be sure that open files will be copied as well.*

6. In the next window, specify a File Date Filter. Normally, you just want to copy all files. However, it's also possible to select files based upon the access date, modified date, or creation date. If so required, specify the dates you want to filter on (using the screen shown in Figure 3-16) and click Next to continue.

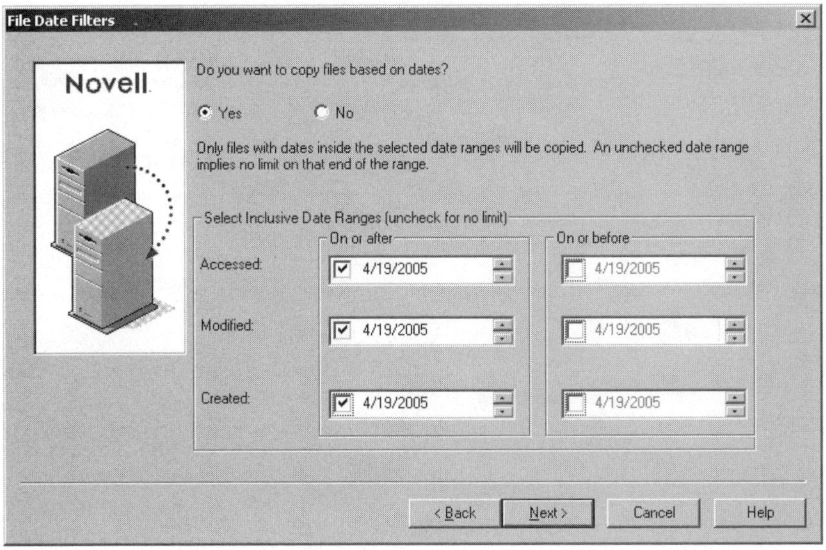

Figure 3-16. *If so required, you can copy files based on a selected date range.*

7. If on the source there are server files stored that you want to exclude, you can enter a wildcard selection string to specify files that will not be copied. For example, use *.mp3 to exclude all MP3 files from being copied from the source server to the target server. Then, click Next to proceed.

8. If you want to make sure the target server will be an exact copy of the source server, you can now specify that you want to delete all files and folders from the destination servers that don't exist on the source servers. This option can be useful if a user deletes one or more files from the source server after you've defined the migration project and started the file copy, but before the actual file copy ends. To prevent these files from being put back automatically after the migration, you can specify that you want to delete files and folders from the destination servers that don't exist on the source servers. It's, however, much better to prevent all users from being logged in on the source server while you're working on the migration project. If you so wish, the default value not to delete any files and folders on the destination server can be selected. Press Next to continue.

9. Now (as shown in Figure 3-17) you can specify if you want the Migration Wizard to compare files and folders between the source and destination servers to make sure everything copied correctly. Since this is a resource-intensive task, the default selection is not to compare files. If, however, you want to be sure everything is copied correctly, select Yes and then specify how to compare the files. By default, they will be compared based upon file information such as names, dates, size, attributes, trustees, and owners. If you want to make sure nothing went wrong, specify that a byte-by-byte comparison must be performed. If you do this, however, it will take considerably longer for the process to complete. I recommend you do a basic comparison based upon names, dates, and so on of the files. After selecting what you want to do, click Next to continue.

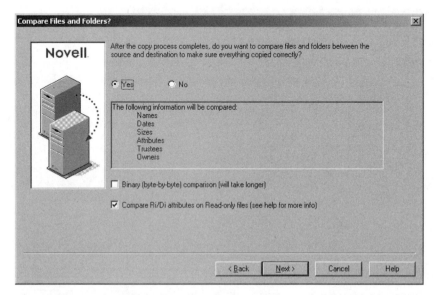

Figure 3-17. *To ensure everything went well, you can specify that (after copying the files) the files on the source and on the destination server must be compared.*

10. Next, select the volumes in which to store the trustee backup files. By default, the SYS volume is used for this purpose, which is fine if you have a minimum of a gigabyte of free disk space on the volume. Click Next to continue.

11. Once again you must enter passwords for the source and destination tree. These passwords are needed for both servers to connect to each other. To make this connection, the SMS engine (which is also employed when making a backup) is used. A message will appear when the Migration Wizard is ready to continue. From this screen, click Proceed to start. When a message pops up saying that a trustee backup will be made as well, click Yes to create the trustee backup. If, however, you're sure you currently have a good backup of all trustee assignments, click No to skip creating the trustee backup file. The process now starts, as shown in Figure 3-18. The window then displays how long it will approximately take to complete the procedure. Wait until the procedure has completed before continuing with the next step.

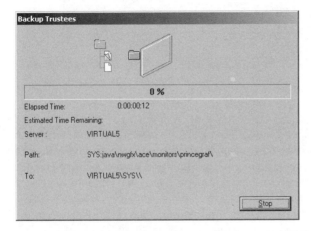

Figure 3-18. *Wait until the entire procedure completes before continuing.*

12. Once file copy procedure completes, click Done to finish. You'll be returned to the main screen of the Migration Wizard, as shown in Figure 3-19. On this screen, notice that the option Begin NDS/eDir Migration is now available. The following section explains what to do next.

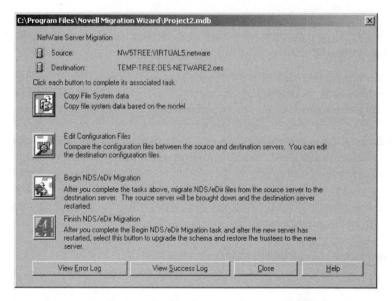

Figure 3-19. *When the file copy finishes, you'll return to the Migration Wizard's main screen.*

Editing Configuration Files

Upon the file system copy, file server configuration files are copied as well. If configuration files from the old server are copied to the new server, it may be necessary to make some changes to them to reflect the new environment correctly. The Migration Wizard helps you do that. If you need to make the changes, perform the following steps. If not, skip on to the next section.

1. From the Migration Wizard, click Edit Configuration Files. This displays a list of all configuration files on the target server, as shown in Figure 3-20.

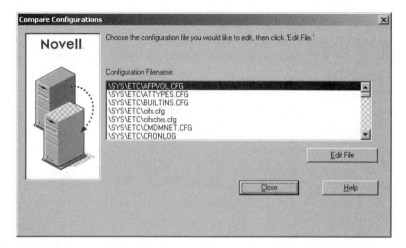

Figure 3-20. *The Migration Wizard shows a list of all configuration files found on the target server.*

2. From the list of configuration files, select a file and click Edit File. This opens a window in which you can see the file as it was on the old server, compared to the same file as it is now on the target server. Copy and paste any lines from the old server to the new server and when finished, click Save & Close to continue.

3. Edit all configuration files as required, and when finished, quit the Compare Configurations window by clicking Close.

Beginning NDS/eDirectory Migration

After making the required changes to the configuration files, go on to the next step in the Migration Wizard: the migration of eDirectory objects from the old server to the new server. In this step, the server is brought down and the destination server is restarted. After restarting, the destination server takes the identity of the source server. Before migrating eDirectory from the old server to the new server, make sure the following requirements are met:

- All data has migrated successfully.

- There are no critical errors.

- eDirectory on all the servers is healthy.

1. From the Migration Wizard main screen, select Begin NDS/eDir Migration. Then, click Next to proceed.

2. If the target server is the first OES - NetWare server in the source tree, the schema of the source tree must be updated to allow for all new objects to be created. In the Update Schema screen, select Yes. This allows the schema to be updated. Then, click Next to proceed.

3. A screen now appears saying it's important that eDirectory be in good health before continuing. If you're sure you've already performed a minimal health check, as described at the beginning of this procedure, select Yes and click Next to proceed.

■**Caution** An attempt to migrate eDirectory from an unhealthy tree may result in very serious problems with eDirectory. Never continue if you're not sure eDirectory is completely healthy!

---

4. To ensure that the server certificate allows PKI encryption to be used (see Chapter 12) and that it works properly on the destination server, you now need to copy the NICI configuration files from the source server to the target server. By using this process, there is a theoretical risk that the files will be intercepted by a cracker. To be absolutely sure they can't be stolen in transit, copy and move them using a diskette. Read the Migration Wizard manual for more details about this procedure. If your servers are both on the same LAN, it's generally no problem to copy the NICI configuration files over the network. Select Automatically to copy the NICI configuration over the network and then click Next to continue.

5. If user connections to the source server still exist, delete them now. The only user connection still allowed is your own connection. Click Next to continue.

6. Enter the passwords for the source and the destination trees and click Next to continue. If any errors were encountered, you'll see them on a screen like that shown in Figure 3-21. Resolve all critical errors before proceeding and then click Next to continue.

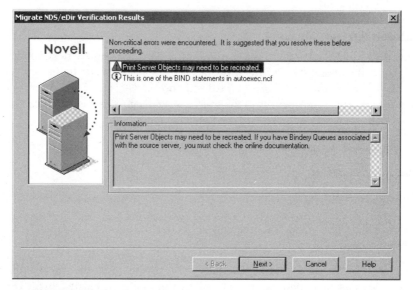

Figure 3-21. *Resolve any critical errors before continuing.*

7. Now the step-by-step migration starts. In this procedure, the migration is broken down into different steps so if it fails, you know exactly where it occurred. The following steps are performed.

   • Configuration files on the target server are modified.

   • eDirectory is backed up on the source server and the backup files are copied to the target server.

   • The source server is brought down.

   • The temporary eDirectory tree is removed from the target server and all client connections are terminated.

   • eDirectory is upgraded on the target server.

   • The target server is rebooted.

8. Click Next to start the step-by-step migration. If any of the steps fails, an error message will appear indicating what's wrong and what you need to do to resolve the problem. It may happen that you must restart the entire procedure to resolve the error. If this is the case, it will be clearly indicated. At the end of the procedure, the source server is brought down and eDirectory is reconfigured on the target server. When it's rebooted, the server is migrated. A message now appears indicating the eDirectory migration has concluded.

Finishing NDS/eDirectory Migration

After the eDirectory migration has completed, you must re-establish contact with the server. Once this is done, from the Migration Wizard select the fourth step down, Finish NDS/eDir Migration.

1. The Migration Wizard now gives an overview of the tasks that have to be performed to complete the migration. These steps are listed next.

2. Make sure your server time is synchronized. You can verify this from the DSREPAIR utility on the server. On the DSREPAIR main screen, select Time Synchronization. This will show if time is properly synchronized (see Figure 3-22). In case you have problems with time synchronization, read Chapter 8 of this book where an overview of the steps needed to synchronize time is given.

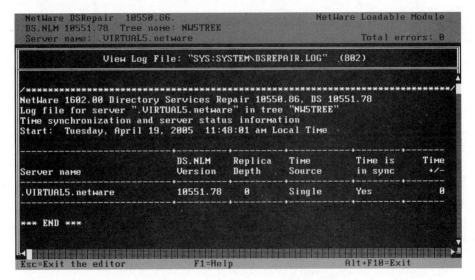

Figure 3-22. *From DSREPAIR, check that time is synchronized to the network.*

3. Also from DSREPAIR on the Server Console, check that eDirectory is properly synchronized. You can verify this by selecting Report Synchronization Status from the DSREPAIR main menu.

4. When these steps have been performed and everything is OK, click Next to continue. You're now prompted to log in to the target server. Since the target server has taken the identity of the source server, use the credentials you used to log in to the source server to make contact with the target server. Next, click Continue twice. The migration process is now completed on your new server. In this procedure, the trustee assignments to files are restored.

5. If everything finishes without error, a success message appears, as shown in Figure 3-23. Click Done on the success message window and close the Migration Wizard. The migration is now complete.

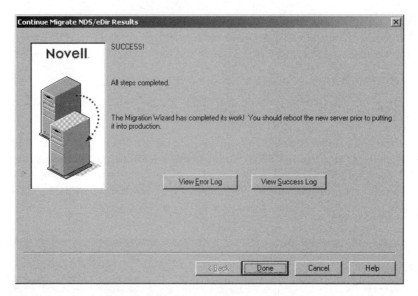

Figure 3-23. *Once the migration has completed successfully, this window appears.*

■**Tip** All steps performed in the migration are carefully recorded. You can access both an error log and a success log at any stage of the migration.

Performing Post-Migration Tasks

The automatic migration has now completed. This doesn't mean, however, that your work is done. To finalize the migration, make sure you do the following:

1. On the target server, run DSREPAIR ➤ Unattended Full Repair.

2. Verify manually that all user information has migrated successfully.

3. Run DSREPAIR ➤ Time Synchronization and verify that time is properly synchronized.

4. Use the **config** command on the target server to check that the right IP address is used.

5. Install the latest support pack on the target server if so required. If you've installed the migration target with the overlay CD where the latest support pack is already installed, you don't need to install it again here.

6. Reinstall any server applications. Upon installation of a migration target, no applications are installed automatically, so you need to install them by hand once the migration is completed.

Finished? Then you're done, and you now have a new working server.

Server Consolidation: Migrating from Windows Server 2003 to OES - Linux

The most flexible of all migration tools is the Server Consolidation utility. This utility is developed as a tool to migrate information from several servers to one server. The Server Consolidation utility in its OES version is the only tool that supports both OES - NetWare and OES - Linux as targets. Also, besides NetWare as a source operating system, Windows NT, Windows 2000, and Windows Server 2003 can be migrated as well.

In this scenario, you'll learn how to migrate information from Windows Server 2003 to Open Enterprise Server. With the Server Consolidation utility, you can select a Windows domain as a source and copy all file system data along with users, groups, and ownership to an OES server. At this time, you can only copy information from one Active Directory domain at a time.

To migrate data from Windows Server 2003 to OES, several steps must be performed:

- Install the Server Consolidation utility

- Perform prerequisite tasks

- Create a consolidation project

- Run the consolidation

- Perform post-consolidation tasks

■Note The Server Consolidation utility assumes that you already have an OES - Linux or an OES - NetWare server that is completely configured. For example, before starting the migration process from the Server Consolidation utility, you need to create eDirectory containers in which you want to put new users, and generate volumes on which you want to place files migrated from the Windows server.

Performing Prerequisite Tasks

Before starting the actual migration, it's important to plan it. Several issues have to be addressed before you can begin. Make sure you have answers to the following questions before starting.

- Which Windows users are accessing which files and where are these files located?

- Where on the OES server must the Windows users and files be migrated to?

- Which Windows users and groups need to be migrated?

- Are there any naming conflicts?

- Are there any applications in use that do not run on the OES server?

- Will any domain trusts be broken upon execution of the migration?

- Will a template object (see Chapter 9) be used to perform the migration?

Next, some prerequisites (listed next) have to be met to perform the migration.

- If you want to use a template object (see Chapter 8), create it before you start the migration. The use of a Template object will allow required eDirectory attributes to be added to migrated users automatically.

- The workstation where you want to install the Server Consolidation utility must be known to the domain. On Windows XP Professional, use the following procedure to perform this registration.

  1. Right-click My Computer and then click Properties.

  2. Select the Computername tab.

  3. Click Network Identification. This starts the Network Identification Wizard. Complete the wizard and fill in all required information to join the domain.

  4. Reboot the workstation. Now you can install the Server Consolidation utility.

■**Tip** If you install the Server Consolidation utility on your Windows server, you don't need to join the domain first but can start installing the utility straight away. Also, the files are copied directly from the source Windows server to the target server, which is much faster than via a workstation.

Installing the Server Consolidation Utility

Before starting a server consolidation, you must install the utility on a workstation or server. The necessary steps are outlined in the following procedure:

1. Make sure the Novell client is installed on the workstation where you want to use the Server Consolidation utility. If it's not installed yet, download the latest version of the Novell client from http://download.novell.com and install it on the workstation. Read Chapter 6 for more information about the Novell client.

2. Insert the OES - NetWare Operating System CD in the CD drive of the workstation.

3. From Product\Migration_Utilities, double-click the NWSC.EXE program file. This starts the installation program for the Server Consolidation utility.

4. Accept all defaults to perform a default installation.

Creating a Consolidation Project

Now that you've installed the Server Consolidation utility, it's time to start. The procedure listed next explains how to start a new server consolidation project.

1. From the workstation where you installed the Server Consolidation utility, select Start ➤ All Programs ➤ Novell Server Consolidation Utility ➤ Novell Server Consolidation Utility. This starts the consolidation utility. As you can see in Figure 3-24, it looks a lot like the Migration Wizard.

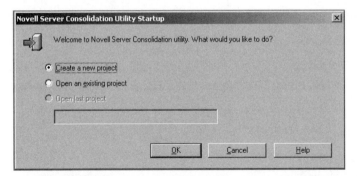

Figure 3-24. *The Server Consolidation utility looks a lot like the Migration Wizard.*

2. Select Create A New Project and click OK. Next, as shown in Figure 3-25, select Microsoft Windows Domain as the source type for the project and click OK.

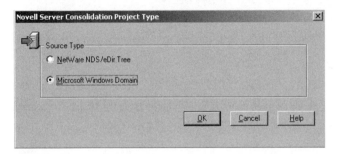

Figure 3-25. *You can choose to start the consolidation project from an eDirectory or a Windows environment.*

3. On the next screen, you have an opportunity to consult the online documentation or to check if any updates are available. Do this if so required. After that, click Next to continue.

4. Provide a filename for the project and click Next to continue. This allows you to get easy access to the configuration settings you've entered if you must stop the project and restart it later.

5. Now, connect to the right source NT domain (a Windows 200x Active Directory is seen as a domain as well) and to the destination eDirectory tree (see Figure 3-26). By default, you'll connect to the Active Directory that the workstation is joined to, so you must connect to the eDirectory tree manually. Use the Login button to connect to your eDirectory tree and then click Next to continue.

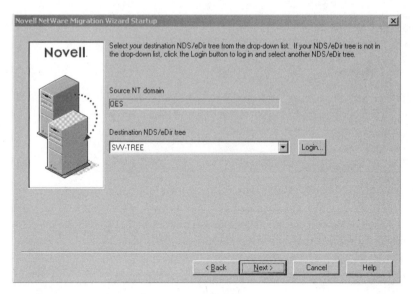

Figure 3-26. *To start the migration from Windows to eDirectory, you must log in on both systems.*

Tip Need to migrate from a different domain than the domain that's listed by default? Then register your workstation to this different domain as described in the beginning of this section.

---

6. The utility asks if you want to match up users. If you decide to do so, the target eDirectory tree will be searched for users with the same name and if these users are found, you can manually decide what to do with them. It's recommended to always select Yes to this option so you can decide manually what to do with users that appear to have the same account (further on in this procedure you'll see what happens if this is the case). Click Next to continue.

7. Click Create to create and save the project file. If you've decided not to match up users from eDirectory with users from the Windows environment, this part of the procedure is now finished. If you have decided to match up users, browse to the eDirectory container where you want to search for existing users and click Next to continue.

8. You'll now see a list of all users that appear to match (as in Figure 3-27). The system compares users based on different criteria. Even if something appears to be a match, it may not be, so you should always verify manually if it really is. If you don't want to merge data from both accounts, click the name óf each user that falsely appears to be a match and from the drop-down list select Don't Merge. If you do want the accounts to be merged, you don't have to do anything. Just click Finish to continue.

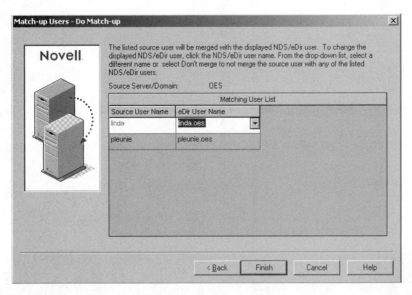

Figure 3-27. *If the same user exists in both the Windows and the eDirectory environment, you can merge user accounts automatically.*

Based upon the information you've entered so far, you should now see the Server Consolidation Utility project window with the Windows domain you've selected in the left-hand window, and the destination eDirectory tree in the right-hand window (as shown in Figure 3-28). In this screen, you can model the project—the modeling is performed offline, so anything you do here doesn't actually change your Windows environment. In reality, nothing is changed until you actually start the migration.

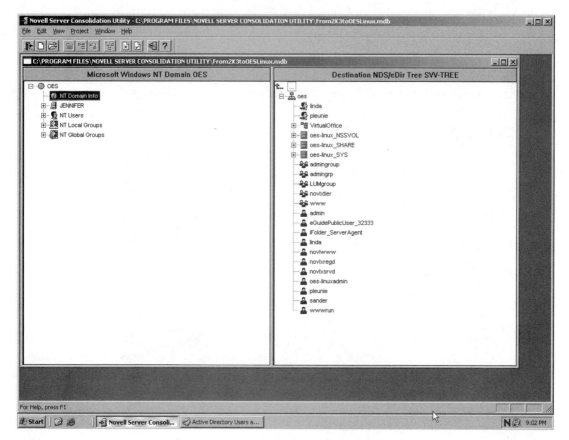

Figure 3-28. *From the project window, you can drag Windows domain objects to a position in your eDirectory environment.*

Use the following tips to help model your new environment:

- If you've chosen to search for matches between users in the domain and users in eDirectory, every match found for which you've indicated that you want to merge the related object is already present in the eDirectory environment. In Figure 3-28, these are user objects linda and pleunie.

- The remainder of the migration is not performed automatically, for the simple reason that you, as an administrator, have to indicate where to migrate the information to. For example, it's possible to create a separate container for the newly created objects that come from the Windows environment, but it's also possible to merge all the Windows objects into existing containers.

- To move objects from the Windows environment to the Novell environment, just drag and drop. You'll see that all objects marked for migration are indicated on both sides with a red arrow underneath them.

- If on second thought you decide you don't want to move a given object after all, right-click the object as it appears in the eDirectory environment and from the menu select Back Out Dropped Object.

- You can find Windows shared folders under the NT Server object (which is used for Windows 2000 and 2003 servers as well). To migrate them to the eDirectory environment, put them under an existing eDirectory volume. This assumes that you've already created all the volumes needed in the OES environment. More information about the creation of volumes can be found in Chapters 11 and 12.

- If you need to create a new folder on a Novell volume, right-click the volume object in the eDirectory pane and from the menu select New Folder. Next, enter the name of the folder you want to create.

- The same goes for any new eDirectory container objects: if you need a new container object, right-click one of the current container objects in your tree and from the menu, select New Organizational Unit.

- The Windows group Everyone will be translated to the container into which you drop the NT Domain Info object.

- Don't forget to migrate the NT Domain Info object as well. This object contains general information about the domain, such as policy packages and permissions for the group Everyone. It's essential not to miss this information!

Running the Consolidation

Now that everything is modeled the way you want it, it's time to run the consolidation process. Be sure this is really what you want, because once it's started, a running consolidation cannot be stopped!

1. From the menu bar in the Server Consolidation utility, select Project ➤ Verify And Migrate Project. This starts the Novell Server Consolidation Verification Wizard which checks if all conditions have been met so the server consolidation can start (see Figure 3-29).

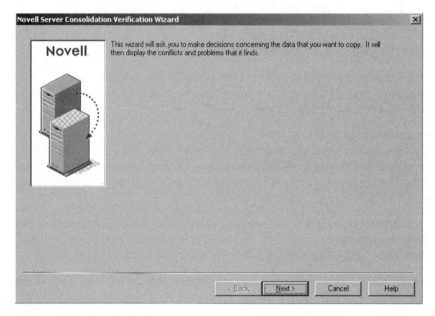

Figure 3-29. *Before starting the actual process, the Server Consolidation Verification Wizard will run.*

2. Click Next to proceed. You'll now see an overview of all users in the Windows Domain and the name of the eDirectory container where they'll be dropped. Of course, this is will all occur according to the modeling you performed while creating the project. Click Next to continue.

3. An overview appears of all the shared folders you've selected to migrate from the Windows environment to the eDirectory environment. Click Next to continue.

4. In eDirectory, a template object can be used to set generic parameters for users. If you want to use a template object for the migration, it should already exist at this point (if necessary, read Chapter 9 for more information on creating template objects). If a template is available, select it now, as shown in Figure 3-30. If you don't want to apply the template to the new users migrated from the Windows environment, deselect Add Template Properties To New Users. In either case, click Next to continue after making your choice.

5. Now you need to specify what to do when files are found on the destination server which have the same name as files on the source server. In this situation, you can choose from the following options:

• Don't copy over existing files.

• Copy the source file if it is newer.

• Always copy the source file.

In most situations, it makes sense to use the default selection, Copy The Source File If It's Newer. After making your choice, click Next to continue.

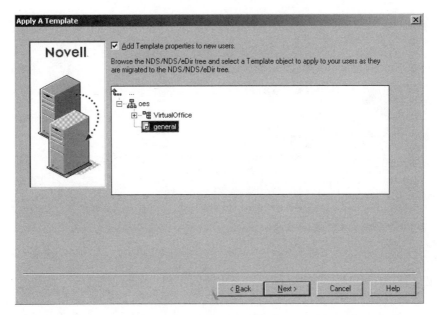

Figure 3-30. *To apply uniform settings to the users imported from the Windows environment, apply an eDirectory template object.*

6. You must now specify what to do with passwords for users that are migrated from the Windows environment (as shown in Figure 3-31). This is because Windows passwords cannot be migrated with this tool. There are three options to handle user passwords. In all cases, the user can log in just once with this password. After this, he must change it using one of the following methods.

- *Assign the same password to all users*: In this scenario, you must enter a new password that is the same for all the users that are imported. This is the default scenario and, although not very secure, it makes sense to use this option because users have to change the password immediately. To make it easier for you, use blank passwords as the new password for imported users.

- *Assign a random password to all users*: This option assigns a random password to all new users. This password is then written to a file named *YourProjectName*_OUT.TXT.

- *Read passwords from a file*: In this situation, as an administrator you must create a file called *YourProjectname*_OUT.TXT in which you must write the new password for all users. In this file, each line contains one Windows username and password, separated by a comma. For example, if you're migrating user Linda with password Alex and user Helga with password Kees, they should appear as follows in the text file:

```
Linda, @fb53g
Helga, qc5612b
```

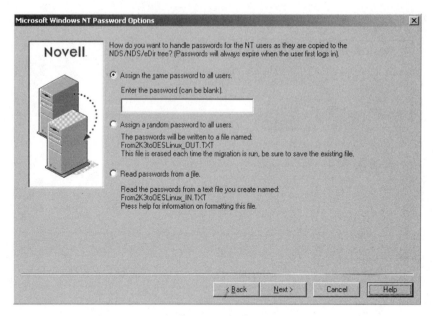

Figure 3-31. *Before starting the migration, you must specify what to do with existing user passwords.*

7. More options need to be specified (see Figure 3-32). The following is a list.

   • *Copy file permissions*: Use this option to copy file permissions from the Windows environment to the eDirectory environment. It's selected by default.

   • *Copy the 'Everyone' permissions*: This option copies the permissions assigned to the Windows Group Everyone to the container object in eDirectory where the Domain info object is dropped.

   • *Erase info from PDC registry*: Each time you run this server consolidation after the first attempt, you need to select this option to make sure the registry of the Windows domain is cleaned properly.

8. Click Next to continue. You should now be presented with the screen shown in Figure 3-33. Only if you're copying users to OES - Linux is it recommended to also make these users Linux-enabled (LUM) users (see Chapter 9 for more details). By default, all new users are made LUM users as well, because this helps to set permissions properly at the Linux file system level. If LUM is already enabled on your OES - Linux server, you must specify the location where the Server Consolidation utility can find existing LUM groups. If no LUM groups are present yet, browse to the container where LUM groups can be created automatically.

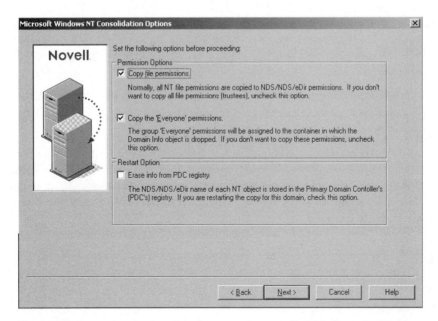

Figure 3-32. *In most scenarios, it makes sense to copy all rights from the Windows environment to the eDirectory environment.*

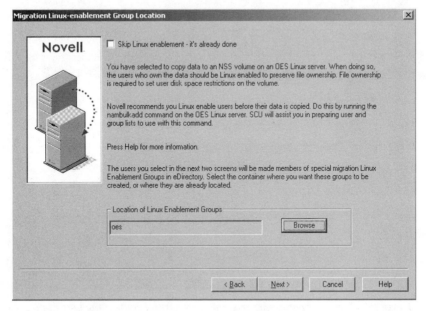

Figure 3-33. *To manage new user accounts properly at the Linux file system, they need to be Linux-enabled.*

9. If you want to make new users LUM users automatically, you can now specify a list of containers. All users in the containers listed here (and in all subordinate containers) will be Linux-enabled. Use the Add button to add containers to this list. Then, click Next to continue.

10. If in addition to the users in the containers you've just selected you need to make individual users LUM users as well, use the Add button to select these users. Click Next to continue.

11. All required information is entered now. Click Next to start a verification of your project. The first screen you'll see is a list of users that have the same username in both the Windows and the eDirectory environment (see Figure 3-34). Select Merge to merge these user accounts, or choose Don't Migrate if you don't want to migrate them. Then, click Next to continue.

■**Note** If in the project modeling phase of the server consolidation process you also specified that you want to check for users with the same name on both sides of the migration path, you must again specify what to do with these users.

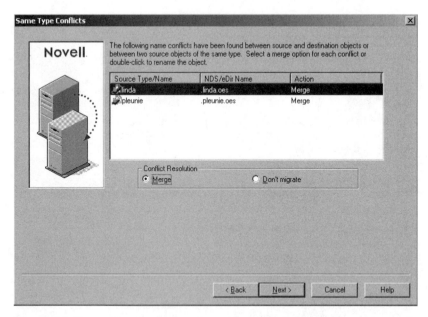

Figure 3-34. *The verification process shows if users with the same username exist on both sides.*

12. A list now appears of all the users from the Windows environment that you've chosen not to migrate. If this list is OK with you, click Next to continue. Otherwise, you must start all over again and return to the project window to drag and drop these objects. In the next screen, the same will happen for local groups you've selected not to migrate. After that, you'll also see a listing of global groups you've selected not to migrate.

13. If no further errors were found, click Proceed to start the copy phase in which objects and data are copied from the Windows environment to the eDirectory environment.

14. After the copy process has finished, you'll see a message indicating that the process has completed. Review both the error and success logs to assess what's happened. You can do this by clicking the corresponding button. If you're happy with the copy process, click Close to finish. Now close the Server Consolidation utility. You're finished.

Performing Post-Consolidation Tasks

Now that all information has been copied from the Windows environment to the OES server, you need to perform a few post-consolidation tasks. Mainly, this involves verifying that everything happened correctly, but some additional tasks are required as well, as in the following:

- Make sure all Windows users and groups are copied to the right place in eDirectory.

- Verify that the volume was migrated correctly and check that permissions are properly set. (See Chapter 12 for more information about permissions.)

- Set up the iPrint print environment for the new users.

- Make sure that home directories have been created properly at the location you designated.

- If you've chosen to generate random passwords for the new users, distribute these passwords to your users so they can log in to the OES server.

Summary

In this chapter, you learned how to perform an upgrade and a migration from Linux, NetWare, and Windows to either OES - Linux or OES - NetWare. To perform the upgrade, several tools can be used. Not every tool can be used in every scenario, however. An in-place upgrade can only be performed when upgrading to the same operating system. This kind of upgrade is supported from NetWare to OES - NetWare and from SUSE Linux Enterprise Server 9 to OES - Linux. If you're installing OES - NetWare on new hardware and you want to modify the data before it's copied from the old server to the new one, the Migration Wizard is the best tool to use. Most flexible of all, however, is the Server Consolidation utility, which can be used to copy data from multiple old servers to a new OES server. With this tool, even upgrades from Windows are supported.

In the next chapter, you'll become familiar with the Linux operating system used behind OES - Linux.

CHAPTER 4

■ ■ ■

Introduction to SUSE Linux Enterprise Server

In Chapter 1, you learned that Open Enterprise Server can run on two different operating systems. This book, however, focuses on Open Enterprise Server Linux Edition, and since many of you may be long-time NetWare users, this chapter provides an introduction to the Linux operating system in addition to discussing OES - Linux.

Logging In

If you are working on a NetWare server, life is easy. There is no need for authentication. You can begin work without taking any special precautionary measures. On a Linux server, however, this is not the case. You have to tell the system who you are before you can go any further. The first thing you see after your server has successfully booted is a login prompt. At this prompt, you specify who you are. If you like, you can also choose the graphical environment you want to work in. There's no need to make it any more difficult than that. Simply work in the KDE environment, which is loaded by default.

Linux User Accounts

In order to log in to your system, you need a valid user account. Though you're the administrator of your server, it's not practical to always log in as an administrative user. You're more likely to make mistakes this way. Logged in as administrator, the Linux operating system typically won't ask if you're sure you want to perform a certain action. If you've given it a command and pressed the Enter key, it does just as asked. So, to protect yourself, it's a good idea to log in as a normal user and only become the administrative user root when needed.

The Graphical Login Prompt

As mentioned earlier, after the system boots up, the graphical login prompt is displayed. The window also shows all the users currently present on the system. Click one of the usernames, enter the password, and click the Login button to finish.

You can do more than just login at the login window. If you open the menu, you can also specify additional tasks, as shown in Figure 4-1. For example, you can choose a Window Manager you want to work from. By default, Open Enterprise Server uses the KDE Window Manager, but if for any reason you don't like KDE, you can choose something else by selecting the option Session Type. From the KDE login manager, you can select this option by clicking the Menu button. The exact possibilities depend on what you have installed. You might, for example, want to use the Gnome Window Manager, but if that Window Manager isn't installed, it won't appear as an option.

Figure 4-1. *From the login menu, you can specify what Window Manager to work with.*

More options are available from this menu. For instance, you could choose to restart the graphical environment of your server by selecting the option Restart X Server, or shut down or reboot your entire server by choosing the Shutdown option.

Working with Virtual Consoles

What if your graphical environment is inhibited and the login screen doesn't appear on bootup? In such cases, it's good to know that you can also work from six virtual consoles, accessed by pressing the Ctrl+Alt+F1 thru F6 keys. These text-based consoles come in handy if your graphical environment is impaired or if you want to perform operations while logged in as another user on your server.

The text-based virtual consoles can be activated whenever needed. To return to the graphical environment when finished, simply press Ctrl+Alt+F7.

When working with more than one virtual console, you may get confused about which console you're actually working on. If this happens, check the login prompt at the top of the screen. The console you're using should be identified by letters like tty2, as shown in Figure 4-2. tty2 means that this is the second terminal (virtual console) attached to your computer, which you activated by pressing the Ctrl+Alt+F2 key combination.

```
Welcome to SUSE LINUX Enterprise Server 9 (i586) - Kernel 2.6.5-7.97-smp (tty2).

linux login: _
```

Figure 4-2. *When you activate a virtual console, you see an indication of the active virtual console.*

You can also determine which tty is active while you are working. If you get confused about your identity, type the command **who am i** and the screen will display the identifying tty code. (Note: Don't confuse **who am i** with **whoami**. The latter will display your login name and nothing else.)

Getting Administrative Access

As noted earlier, it's good practice to log in as a normal user, not as an administrative user. But what if you need administrative access to perform some task? In that case, type the command **su** from a text-based console. As shown in Figure 4-3, this prompts you for the password of the user root. Once entered, you are temporarily root and can perform any task using the system administrator account. Finished as root? Type **exit** to return to your earlier environment.

You can also get root privileges from within the graphical environment. When starting a tool that normally needs root access, you'll be prompted for root's password. Once entered, you'll have root privileges for that program only. In any other programs, you'll have the permissions of your normal user account.

One aspect of su to be careful of is that it doesn't overwrite the environment variables of the previous root user. This can lead to problems, especially when you try to start a graphical program from your su console window in a graphical session. To prevent this, on SUSE Linux type **sux** instead. This command ensures all environment variables are correctly set, and prevents you from getting error messages when, say, trying to start graphical programs from a console window.

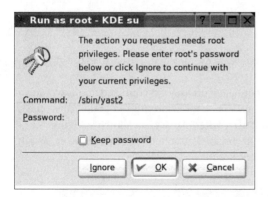

Figure 4-3. *When you start an administrative tool as an ordinary user, you are prompted for the password of the user root.*

This is one way to change to root from a text-based console. In Open Enterprise Server, you'll find yourself working with the GUI most of the time. In this interface, it is also possible to run one program as the user root, and be logged in as any other user simultaneously. To do so, follow these steps.

1. Use the keys Alt+F2 from the KDE interface to open the Run Command window.

2. Click Options (see Figure 4-4) and select Run As A Different User. Specify the name and password of the user account you want to use.

3. Type the name of the program you'd like to run. You will now have root access from this program only.

Figure 4-4. *From the KDE graphical interface, you can use Alt+F2 to perform commands as another user.*

You can also switch your current user ID another way. From the Novell menu, select the option Switch User. This opens a new login screen in which you can authenticate as a different user—for example, as the user root. This isn't recommended, however, because if you switch to a new session as user root, you'll again have root access to all system components, which is just what we wanted to avoid.

The Graphical User Interface and the Console

By default, your server starts with a graphical user interface. This is useful if you're new to Linux and don't like console-based interfaces, or if you want to work directly from the server console to manage your network. If, however, your server is in a locked-down server room and you rarely sit behind it to work on it, this graphical interface is merely a waste of valuable system resources. So why not change the way your server boots and let it boot each time with a console-based interface? To do this, you have to change the runlevel of your server.

The Concept of Runlevels

Linux server can be booted in many different ways. One method is by setting the runlevel in the configuration file /etc/inittab, as shown in Figure 4-5.

The runlevel is the state your system starts in. Using the runlevel, you can determine which programs are started automatically and which aren't. When using Windows, this is similar to starting Windows in safe mode, safe mode with networking, and so on. On a Linux system, this same concept is called a runlevel.

Normally, seven runlevels are defined:

- *runlevel 0*: This is the runlevel that is activated when you shut down your system.

- *runlevel 1*: On Open Enterprise Server, this is single-user mode. Only the most essential services are started and you have only one virtual console to log in from.

- *runlevel 2*: This is local multiuser without network services. You could use this runlevel if you have a problem with some network services and want to test them extensively.

- *runlevel 3*: In runlevel 3, your system is fully functional. You can do anything you like, have network services available, and have six different virtual consoles, but the graphical user interface isn't started automatically. This is a good runlevel to set as default on a Linux system used as a server.

- *runlevel 4*: This runlevel is not in use currently.

- *runlevel 5*: This is the default runlevel you get after performing a default installation of Open Enterprise Server. In fact, runlevel 5 is the same as runlevel 3, except that a graphical login prompt is generated automatically. In Open Enterprise Server, the KDE Display Manager (KDM) is used for that.

- *runlevel 6*: When you activate runlevel 6, your computer reboots.

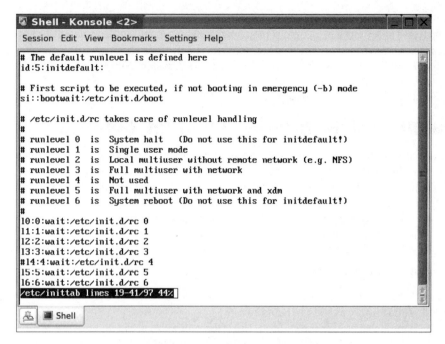

Figure 4-5. *The runlevels on your server are defined in /etc/inittab.*

Now that you are familiar with the concept of runlevels, you might ask yourself if these runlevels are manageable. In fact, they are. When a certain runlevel is activated, the system starts all services in the directory used by that runlevel. In /etc/inittab, you'll find the exact definition of that directory. For the default runlevel 5, for example, the directory /etc/init.d/ rc5.d is used. In this directory, your system finds symbolic links (UNIX's way of creating a shortcut) to scripts that are used to start services in your runlevel. Symbolic links to scripts also exist, which are used to stop these same services if you leave your runlevel for another runlevel.

So, in short, all you need to define your runlevel are symbolic links to the services you want to start automatically. Of course, you'll need a decent script to start these services in the first place. If you're a Linux guru, you can configure it all by hand with commands like **ln –s /etc/ init.d/sbm /etc/init.d/rc5.d/S35smb** (this command is normally used to start the Samba server). If this frightens you, you can also use the runlevel editor integrated in the system management tool *YaST* to do it from a graphical interface, as shown in Figure 4-6. Additional services can also be started automatically in a runlevel by using the command **chkconfig**. If, for example, you want to activate the smb script automatically in runlevel 3 each time your computer boots up, use **chkconfig smb 3**.

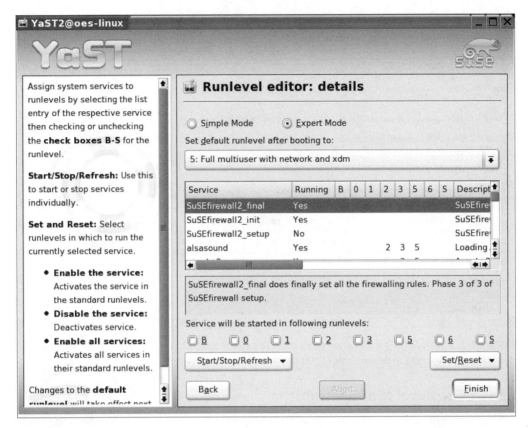

Figure 4-6. *You can set up everything that must be started from your runlevels in the YaST runlevel editor.*

Tip Are you a shell scripting guru who isn't afraid to make his own scripts? In that case, you can write your own shell scripts for any service you want to start automatically when your system boots. One such script is shown in Figure 4-7. All you really need is a script that executes a command and listens at least to the parameters "start" and "stop" so it can be started automatically.

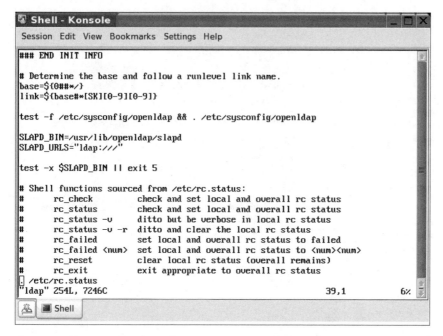

Figure 4-7. *If you aren't afraid of some shell script programming, you can write your own scripts to start your services automatically from any runlevel.*

Basic Runlevel Management

With regards to runlevels, there are some basic runlevel management tasks you might be interested in. First, let's discuss how you can change your default runlevel. Then you'll see how to optimize your runlevel so only those services you want automatically started will be.

Changing the Default Runlevel

Usually, you can change the behavior of your Linux server in two ways. One is the graphical way, while the other is the hard way in which you edit some text-files directly. Since this isn't a book about Linux server management, but a book about Novell's Open Enterprise Server, let's discuss the graphical way of managing things. Thus, next you'll learn how to set the default runlevel from YaST. YaST stands for Yet another Setup Tool and is the default management utility for SUSE Linux.

1. Start YaST by clicking the icon on your desktop.

Tip Want to use YaST from a console environment? No problem! First make sure you are root by using the **su** command, and then type the command **yast** from your console. The ncurses version of YaST is then started, as shown in Figure 4-8. You'll find it has the exact same options, they're just not graphical.

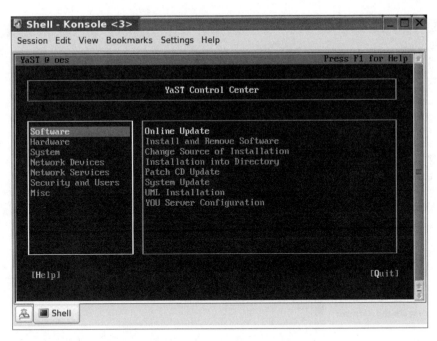

Figure 4-8. *A text-based version of YaST is also available.*

2. Enter the root password and click OK.

3. Activate System and browse to runlevel editor. The runlevel editor is now started in Simple Mode. Working in Simple Mode isn't recommended because it doesn't give you many options.

4. Select Expert Mode and click Finish. A screen like that in Figure 4-9 should appear.

5. Find the Set Default Runlevel After Booting To: field and select Full Multiuser With Network.

6. Click Finish to save your changes. This writes the new setting to the configuration file /etc/inittab. The next time you start your server, it will start automatically in runlevel 3.

■**Caution** You can change the runlevel directly from /etc/inittab. Just use your favorite editor and locate the line id:5:initdefault. The 5 in this line specifies the default runlevel. Want to change it to runlevel 3? Easy! Just change the 5 into a 3. This method is not recommended, however. Most configuration files on your Open Enterprise Server are managed by YaST. YaST uses a structure of files (the suseconfig files) in which settings that do relate to your original configuration files are kept. If you do change the original configuration file, but you don't change the corresponding suseconfig-setting, it will break your configuration. Read the later sections in this chapter on YaST for more information.

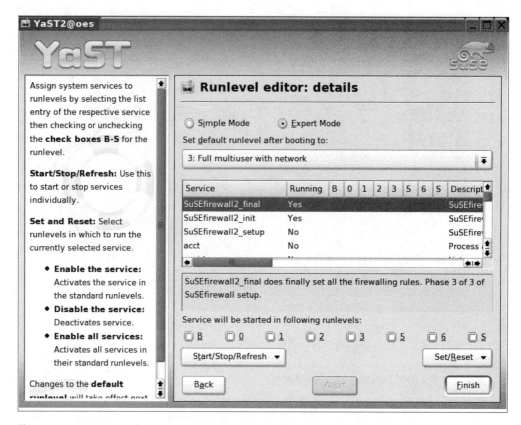

Figure 4-9. *You can easily select a new runlevel from YaST.*

Starting the GUI from the Console

If you've chosen to start your server in runlevel 3 by default, only a bash shell is started automatically. There might, however, come a time when you need a graphical display. In this aspect, Linux is just like NetWare. Start the graphical user interface with the command **startx**. This enables the GUI on tty7. Finished your work in the graphical interface and want to remove all related components from your server's memory? Select the Novell menu and click Logout. This closes the graphical environment and returns you to your text-based console.

Managing OES - Linux with YaST

One of the most important tools in OES - Linux is YaST, because it can be used to manage the Linux environment—working with YaST makes it often unnecessary to use complex commands from the OES - Linux console. The YaST management interface is organized into different categories. In the side bar on the left half of the screen, you see the name of the specific management category. The following categories are available:

- *Software*: Here you'll find all the options to install and manage software packages on your server.

- *Hardware*: Use this option to configure specific hardware. For example, you can use it to install a printer, specify settings for your sound card, or even configure a joystick!

- *System*: This option contains all the services necessary for your operating system in general. For example, choose an option to configure how it boots, or select the language you want to work in. On OES - Linux, you can also find tools to configure important Novell services, such as Clustering Services and NSS.

- *Network Devices*: Here you can find everything necessary to connect your server to the network. Not only can you use the program to configure the network board in your server, there are options to configure modems or DSL interfaces as well.

- *Network Services*: With this option, you can configure a part of the network services. For network services that are not integrated into eDirectory, use the programs available here to perform a basic configuration. For services integrated in eDirectory, use the programs under this option to install the services and indicate where in eDirectory they should be created. These programs aren't advanced management tools, however: you can use them to initialize the service, but the management itself should be performed from iManager or Remote Manager.

Note Especially for some of the network services, the options that can be managed from YaST are rather limited. To manage advanced options as well, it's a good strategy to start the configuration of a given service from YaST, and finish it by editing the configuration files by hand to in order to modify advanced parameters.

- *Security and Users*: Here you can find the option to create local Linux users and manage security settings. Notice there is a VPN option as well, which allows you access to an easy interface to initiate a VPN connection. There is also an option to manage the Certificate Authority for your SLES machine. In an OES environment, however, it's more logical to use the corporate CA installed in eDirectory and import server certificates signed by this CA. You can read more about this subject in Chapter 12.

- *Misc*: This option contains some useful programs, such as an interface to the system log where all system errors are recorded, and CD Creator, which helps you burn CDs.

On OES - Linux, YaST is the main configuration tool. It's the recommended way to configure Linux-related settings for your server. To do its work, YaST makes modifications to the configuration files used by the related Linux services. YaST also uses many variables. These variables allow YaST to manage your system in a coherent fashion—for example, the variable NETWORK_INTERFACE defines the name of the network interface. These variables are typically defined in configuration files under /etc/sysconfig and are called from the specific configuration files themselves. The use of these variables allows you to manage all important information for your system at one specific location, instead of through lots of different files. As an administrator, you should be aware of this mechanism, because you can seriously mess up the configuration of your system if you edit the server's configuration files by hand without understanding exactly how they relate to the variables defined in /etc/sysconfig. If you understand how it all works, editing configuration files by hand is fine. If you're not sure, use YaST to configure your server.

Finding Your Way in the File System

Now that you know how your system uses the concept of runlevels, it's time to get more familiar with the structure used in the file system on your server. Nowadays, it's still very important to know your way around the file system. Therefore, let's next discuss the most important directories created by default on your system and explore how to perform some essential tasks in this directory structure.

Default Directories

If this is your first introduction to Linux, you might be surprised by the way the file system is organized. In this section, you can read about the default directories used by almost any Linux system.

In order to grasp how Linux file systems are organized, you must first understand that within the system structure a clear distinction is made between files that are accessible for ordinary users and files that are accessible for the system administrator. If these are program files, you'll find the former in a directory called bin (binary) and the latter in a directory called sbin (system binaries). Each directory lies at a different level.

Apart from that, you need to understand that on a Linux server it's quite normal to work with more than one partition (as in NetWare). The file system structure on any Linux system begins with the root partition. It's here you'll find the root directory.

Tip Don't confuse the root directory with the directory /root. The root directory (/) is the starting point of your file system under which you'll find all other directories. The directory /root is one of these directories. /root is the home directory for the user root, the administrator of your system.

Now it is possible to separate the contents from different directories from this root partition. The reason why you want to do this is obvious: if you have separated, for example, the directory /home (in which you'll find user home directories) from the rest of the directory structure, it's impossible for a user who accidentally has too many rights to fill up the entire file system.

Although it's good to work with more than one partition, it also implies a certain risk. For example, if one of the partitions is damaged, it will be impossible to mount it when you start your server. For this reason, program files are available on many levels. Most of the utilities needed to maintain and repair your system are in the root partition. Less critical programs and utilities can be found one level deeper—for example, under /usr.

Open Enterprise Server has the following default directories:

- *bin*: This holds binaries accessible to all users. These are essential binaries that must be available at all times, even if there is a problem with other partitions on your system. For that reason, the directory /bin is always on the root partition. In it, you will find essential utilities and commands like /bin/bash (the shell), cp (used to copy files), and many more.

- *sbin*: Contains binaries for the system administrator. These critical binaries must always be available in case you need to repair your system. This directory holds commands and utilities that should never fall into the hands of your users, like the general system management tool yast2 or the partitioning tool fdisk.

- *boot*: The directory boot contains your secondary boot loader. A boot loader consists of two parts. The first part is installed in the Master Boot Record and—depending on your configuration—in the boot sector of an active partition. The second part, the so-called secondary boot loader, is located in the directory /boot. This directory is critical to the functioning of your system, so stay clear of it. Under normal circumstances, there is absolutely no need to modify anything in this directory.

- *dev*: On a Linux system, all hardware you work with corresponds to a file on your system. If you want to address the hardware, you have to address the corresponding file. All these device files are contained in the directory /dev. For example, a device called /dev/fd0 could refer to a floppy drive that might be present in your system. Whether you have a floppy drive or not isn't the issue; you will always have a device /dev/fd0. Devices that only create a device file if the corresponding device really exists on your system, haven't made it to default Linux installations so far. One property of these device files is the so-called major and minor numbers. Using the command **ls –l**, you can find these numbers by looking at the properties of the file. These major and minor numbers are an indication to the kernel what device it actually is. Apart from the major and minor numbers, all devices are of a certain type. The most common types are block and character devices. Whether a device is a block or a character device is indicated by a "b" or a "c" in the properties of the device file. This can also be determined by using the command **ls –l**. An example is shown in Figure 4-10.

Tip One of the nice things about Linux is its flexibility. I once lost my device /dev/hdc, which I needed to address my CD-ROM drive. I found out from another Linux system that the associated major and minor were 22 and 0. With this information, you can use the command **mknod** to create your own devices. In this case, I used **mknod /dev/hdc b 22 0** to restore access to my CD-ROM drive. You can even use **mknod** to create entirely new devices.

- *etc*: Most services running on Linux use an ASCII text file to store all necessary configurations. These text files are kept in the directory /etc, as shown in Figure 4-11. In this directory are important configuration files like /etc/passwd which contains the database of local Linux users. You'll also find configuration files here for all other important services, like httpd.conf, which stores the configuration of your Apache web server. /etc also holds many subdirectories. If a service uses more than one configuration file, it normally creates a subdirectory in which all these files are stored. Almost all configuration files of OES - Linux are installed somewhere under /etc/novell.

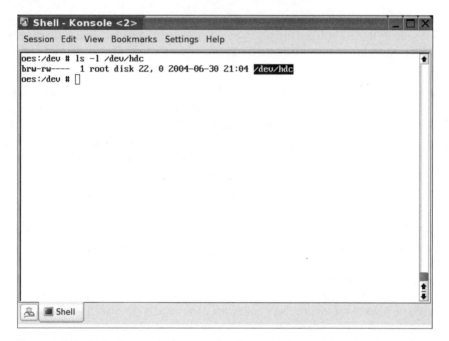

Figure 4-10. *A device has special properties that help the kernel understand what it's used for.*

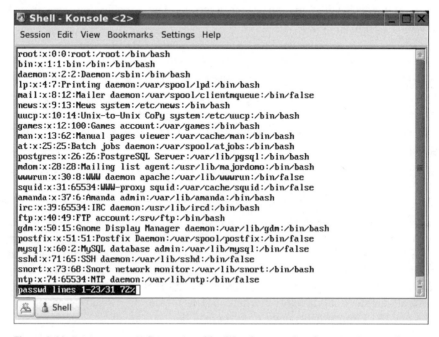

Figure 4-11. *Important configuration files like the user database /etc/passwd are stored in /etc or one of its subdirectories.*

- *home*: On any server, there must be a place for the user home directories. In UNIX, the directory /home is used for this purpose. In most cases, to prevent a user from accidentally filling up the entire file system, a separated partition is created for this directory.

- *lib*: Many programs used in a Linux environment share some of their code. This shared code is stored in different library files. All the libraries needed by binaries in a subdirectory of your file system root are contained in the directory /lib. Other important modules can be found in this directory as well, like the driver modules used by the kernel of your server and the security modules used by the PAM (Pluggable Authentication Modules) mechanism.

■Tip Want to know which modules are used by a certain binary? Type **ldd**. For example, find out which libraries are used by /bin/bash by typing **ldd /bin/bash**. It will show that all the libraries it uses are in /lib, as shown in Figure 4-12.

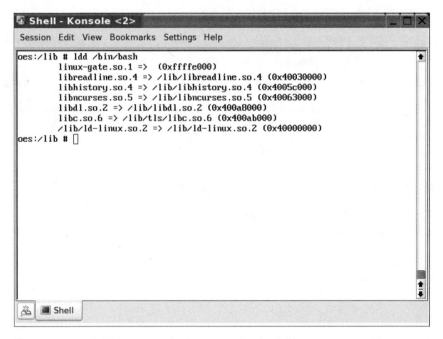

Figure 4-12. *With ldd, you can find out exactly which libraries are used by a certain command.*

- *media*: On a Linux system, to access files that are not on the hard disk of your computer, you need to mount the medium they are on. When you mount, for example, a CD-ROM, you connect it to some directory on your file system. This must be a directory that exists before you start mounting anything. Most Linux distributions use the directory /mnt for this purpose. SUSE Linux, on the other hand, uses /media to mount foreign file systems.

This directory is automatically created when you install Open Enterprise Server on your computer.

- *mnt*: See media.

- *usr*: The directory /usr is probably the largest directory on your system. In it you will find almost all the user-accessible files. Because there are so many files in this directory, it has its own framework of subdirectories, as shown in Figure 4-13. Included is /usr/bin, in which most programs are stored; /usr/X11R6, where your graphical user environment resides; and /usr/src, where you can put the source files of the open-source programs you use. Because it contains so many files, it's quite normal to give /usr its own partition.

■Tip Want to find out how much space a directory occupies on your hard disk? Use **du –h**. It shows you the disk usage of a specified directory. The normal output of this command is in blocks; the parameter –h presents the output in a human readable form. For example, type **du –h /usr** to find out exactly how much space is occupied by /usr.

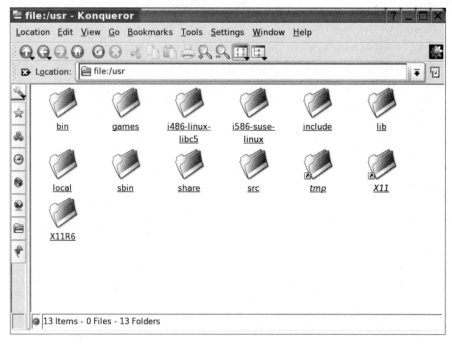

Figure 4-13. *Because there are so many files in it, /usr has its own subdirectory structure.*

- *opt*: /usr contains a lot of binaries, many of which are small software packages. Normally, large software installations (like office suites and other sizable programs) are stored in /opt. For example, in Open Enterprise Server you'll find the KDE graphical interface and the Mozilla browser in this directory, while the directory /opt/novell holds most components of Open Enterprise Server.

- *proc*: The directory /proc is a bit odd. This is because it doesn't really exist on the hard disk of your computer. /proc is an interface to the memory of your server. An advanced administrator can use it to tune the working of his server. You can also find a lot of information about your server in the files in this directory. Try, for example, the command **cat /proc/cpuinfo** (you must be root to do so). This command shows you a lot of information about the processor(s) in your server, as you can see in Figure 4-14.

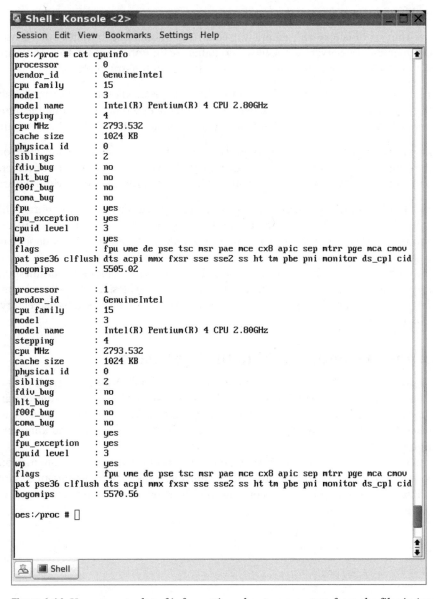

Figure 4-14. *You can get a lot of information about your system from the files in /proc.*

- *root*: Normal users have their home directories in /home. A system administrator is not a normal user; in a UNIX environment, she is therefore respectfully called superuser. Since this user may have some important tools in her home directory, this directory is not in /home with those of other users. Instead, the user root uses /root as her home directory. There is a good reason for this: on many servers the directory /home is on a separate partition. If for any reason you can no longer access this partition, at least user root still has access to her home directory in which she has probably stored some important files.

- *srv*: The /srv directory isn't generally used on other Linux distributions, but it is used on Open Enterprise Server. All the files it contains are for important services. For example, it's used to store your entire web server and ftp server file structures.

- *sys*: /sys is also a non-standard directory which can be used to store information about the state of your system. It's used like /proc, with the difference being that the information in /sys is kept on the hard disk of your server so it's still available after rebooting.

- *tmp*: As the name suggests, /tmp is used for temporary stuff. This is the only directory on the entire system which every user can write to. To write to this directory, however, is a bad idea, since its contents can be wiped clean by any process or user without warning.

- *var*: The last directory on any Linux server is /var. This directory mostly contains files created by your server, the content of which can grow very fast. For this reason, it's a good idea to keep /var on a separate partition. The exact contents of /var depend on what's installed on your system. In most cases, you'll find the directory /var/spool where print jobs are spooled before being processed by your server. Another important subdirectory of /var is the directory log which contains several log files. In a Novell environment, this directory is particular important because the database files used by eDirectory are stored in /var/nds.

Performing Essential Tasks in the File System

Now that you know which directories are important on your server, the next step is to find out how to manage the files in these directories. The easiest way to do this is by means of a graphical file manager like KDE's Konqueror, shown in Figure 4-15. You don't need a book to learn its intricacies, just click the house icon in the menu bar of the KDE desktop and Konqueror starts automatically.

If you really want to manage your server, there is only one way to do it—from the console with one of the many commands available. This section discusses the most important commands you need to manage your Linux file system. If you've worked with DOS in the past, you won't find it too difficult.

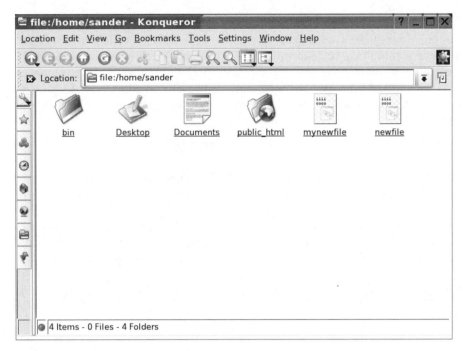

Figure 4-15. *Working with KDE's Konqueror is easy and intuitive.*

Listing Files

The first thing you need to know when working with Linux is how to get an overview of the files on your system. For all you DOS lovers out there, you'll be pleased to know that on most Linux distributions you can use **dir** to show a listing of your files. This is not the best way to get a file listing, however. Using **ls** is recommended instead. One of the most frequently used options with this command is –l, which shows you all the important properties of your files.

  ls does have one drawback, unfortunately. If, for example, you use **ls –l /etc/d*** to show all files in /etc/ that start with the letter *d*, the command will not only show you the name of directories that start with a *d*, but will also show their contents. If you only want to see the name of the concerned directory, add –d to the mix. Thus, you should instead use **ls –ld /etc/d***.

■Tip Linux commands come with many options. Use the **man** command to get an overview and explanation of all the available options. You can read more about man and other ways to find information about the commands you use in the section "Getting Help" later in this chapter.

Copying Files

Once you've found out what files are on your system, you'd probably like to do something with them—for example, copy them. To do so, use **cp**. This command also comes with many options. Two of special interest are **–p** and **–r**. Use **–r** to copy recursively—that is, to copy a directory and everything in it. If you want to preserve all the attributes of the files, use **–p** (preserve). So, to copy everything in /etc to your home directory while preserving all their attributes, use **cp –pr /etc ~**. The ~ refers to the home directory of the current user.

Creating Links

When copying a file, you make a copy of that file and create a new one with exactly the same contents. From that moment on, any modifications made to the original file are not applied to the copy.

There is another way to make the contents of a file available from several places on your server. This method is called linking. A link is nothing more than a pointer to the real file, so any changes to the original file will, of course, appear in the same when you open the file through the link.

There are two types of links. The first is called the *symbolic link*; the second is the *hard link*. A symbolic link really is a pointer to a file. This means that if you remove the file it points to, it will no longer work. A hard link, on the other hand, is a copy of the administrative information about the file. This means that with a hard link, you have two entries to the data that make up the file. In a hard link, there's no difference between the original file and the link you've made to it. If you remove the original, the hard link will still work. It is just a second entry in the administrative information of the file system to make your data accessible.

■**Note** On a Linux system, an *inode table* is used to get access to the information in a file. An inode contains all the information necessary to access the file. The most important information in this regard is in which blocks the data of the file is written. If you create a file, the first thing that happens is that an entry is generated in the directory where you create the file. This entry is needed so you can later find your file by name. This file name points to the inode used by the file. It's in this inode that all the other administrative information of the file is kept. It also contains information on the blocks the file is currently using. If you create a hard link, a second name is generated for the file which points to the same inode as the original file. If you try to remove the original file, the file system notices that there is still another name connected to the inode concerned, so it leaves the inode and the blocks of the file intact. The only thing it removes is the name of the original file and not the datablocks.

In some situations, you may prefer to use hard links. The major advantage is that they are faster than symbolic links, because they are on the same medium. If you want to create a link that points to a file on another medium, the only option is to create a symbolic link.

To create a link, use the command **ln**. **ln** works a lot like **cp**: as its first argument, the name of the original file is specified; as its second argument, the name of the link that must be created is mentioned. If, for example, you want to create a link for /etc/hosts to ~/computers, use **ln /etc/hosts ~/computers**. This creates a hard link. If you need a symbolic link, use the option **–s**. The command **ln –s /etc/passwd ~/users** creates a symbolic link.

Renaming and Moving Files

Technically there is no difference between the renaming and the moving of a file. This is because in both cases, the location of the blocks in which the content of the file is stored doesn't change as long as the file stays on the same partition. The only thing that does change is the name of the file. Thus, looking for a specialized rename utility will prove fruitless. For both purposes, use **mv**. It's easy. The first argument you give this command is the name of the original file; the second argument is the name of its new location. As with all other commands that work with files, you can use a wildcard as well. If, for instance, you want to move everything from ~/rubbish to /dev/null (the null device on your system), use **mv ~/rubbish/* /dev/null**.

Deleting Files

Sometimes it makes sense to do some house-cleaning on your server. For example, now and then you may want to move all the files in /tmp by hand. To do so, use **rm**. This command normally only removes files from the current directory, not from any underlying subdirectories. If you want it to remove a complete directory structure, use the option **–r** (discussed earlier in the "Copying Files" section). If you want **rm** to just do its work and not complain about anything, use **–f** as well. This forces the removal of all files without asking for confirmation. If instead you want to remove the entire content of the /tmp directory as well as the directory itself, use **rm –rf /tmp/***. This removes the directory, but this isn't necessarily a good idea given it's a system-created directory. If you only want to remove the content of the directory, but not the directory itself, first activate the directory and then use **rm –rf ***.

■Caution It probably won't surprise you that **rm** is one of the most dangerous commands you can use on a Linux system. If, for example, you want to wipe the directory /wipeme, including all its contents, and you accidentally type **rm –rf / wipeme** instead of **rm –rf /wipeme**, rm will erase the entire content of your hard disk. Therefore, be extremely careful when using this command.

Working with Directories

Up to now, only commands used for working with files have been covered, but there are also commands for use with directories. These will prove relatively simple, especially if you've worked with DOS before. The first is **cd**, which stands for change directory. Let's say you're in /usr/bin and want to activate /home. Just use **cd /home**. Need to create a directory? Use **mkdir**. Linux **mkdir** is even better than DOS md, because in Linux you can use **mkdir –p /some/new/directory**, which not only creates the specified directory but any necessary parent directories needed if they don't already exist. Lastly, there's **rmdir**, which is a special command that only removes empty directories.

Viewing Files

Sometimes you just need to see the contents of a file. Two great utilities help you just do that. The first is **less**. If, for example, you want to see the contents of /etc/hosts to see some mappings between IP addresses and host names, use **less /etc/hosts**. This opens the viewer less in which you can scroll up and down the file. Finished viewing your file? Type **q** to quit using less.

less is just one method of viewing files—a method which is often too complicated. If you need to see the content of a very small ASCII text file, you can use **cat** as well. This command just dumps the content of the file on your screen without any possibility of scrolling back or forth through it. If this isn't enough, the command **tail** will show you just the last lines of a file. **tail** is useful for monitoring what happens in log files. If you're testing something on your system, use **tail –f /var/log/messages** in another console screen on your desktop. This shows you immediately if any error is generated during your tests. The option **–f** is a useful addition to **tail**. It not only shows you the last ten lines of the specified file, but keeps the file open. The result is that you know immediately if a new line is added to it.

Getting Help

On an average Linux system, there are hundreds of commands available to perform any task. Most of these commands have a lot of options. It's not rare to find a command with more than 30 options! For us normal human beings it's impossible to learn them all, so a good help system is essential. Open Enterprise Server knows different ways of getting information on how to use a command.

The System Programmer's Manual

The first way to get more information about a command is by using **man**. **man** stands for "the system programmer's manual." In the early days of computing, every computer system came with several user guides. A UNIX system had nine of these manuals, each focusing on a specific aspect of the operating system:

1. Executable programs or shell commands

2. System calls (functions provided by the kernel)

3. Library calls (functions within program libraries)

4. Special files (especially the devices in /dev)

5. File formats and conventions (like /etc/passwd)

6. Games

7. Miscellaneous

8. System administration commands (usually only for root)

9. Kernel routines (non-standard)

Not surprisingly, even in the early days of UNIX, people didn't like having to browse through endless user manuals. That's why the guides were later presented electronically on the hard disks of every Linux and UNIX computer.

Once you've decided which command to look up information on, you can use the name of the command as the argument to the command **man**. For example, if you want to know more about the **passwd** command (for setting a user's password), simply type **man passwd**. The system then displays everything you ever wanted to know (and more) about the selected command. Sample output from the **man** command is shown in Figure 4-16.

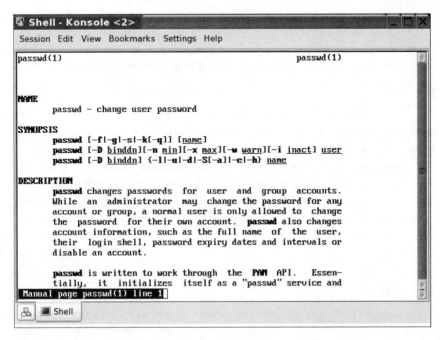

Figure 4-16. *With man, you can get extensive information about most commands available on your server.*

Man pages can be extremely comprehensive. For a simple command like **passwd**, you'll be presented with 158 lines (about 3 pages of printed text). Some of the biggest man entries can fill up an entire book. The man page for the oft-used bash shell, for example, totals 5268 lines (or about a hundred printed pages). Because man pages can be so extensive, you probably won't read them in their entirety. Fortunately, it's easy to glean information from the man pages. If you know what you're looking for, you can use **/string** to locate the information by keyword.

Imagine, for example, that you're in the man page of the bash shell and you want to know how to set a search path. Just use the command **/path** from within the man page, and it will instantly take you to the first instance of the word. Want to search again using the same string? Press **n** and man shows you the next occurrence.

■**Tip** Most commands are documented with man. Some commands are not, because they are documented in the **info** system. Thus, the number of commands is rather limited. If you ever want to learn more about the system, use the command **info info** to call up more information on its usage.

There is one thing you should be aware of when working with **man**. If you use it to get information about the usage of the command **passwd**, it starts looking in the first section of the man pages (the section that describes normal commands). When it finds something, it displays it, and stops searching. Some items, however, appear in more than one section. Besides the command **passwd**, which is described in section one, there is also the configuration file /etc/passwd, outlined in section five.

If you want to be sure that **man** displays all existing entries on the item you're looking for, use **man –a**. The option –a tells man to keep searching and to only stop after it's scanned every section. If you know beforehand which section holds a certain item, you can tell **man** to look in that section by specifying the section number—thus, typing **man -5 passwd** will only show you the man page for /etc/passwd.

■**Tip** Sometimes you know what you want, but you just don't know what command you need to get it. Let's say you want to know how to set your password, but you've never heard of the **passwd** command. In that case, use **man –k**. The option **–k** is used to specify a keyword. **man –k password** looks for the keyword **password** in the description of all man pages and shows you a list of all the pages where the keyword password appears. If the list of commands returned is too long, try to perform a search for a keyword in the result. You can use the **grep** command for that, as in **man –k password | grep change**. This limits the results to entries that cover changing passwords.

Command --help

Because man pages are so extensive, it isn't always the best way to find the information you need. If, for example, you just want to know what parameter you have to use with your command to perform a certain task, you can use the option --**help** with many commands. This option shows a short summary of the selected command. Well, short by comparison… Many times, the information is still too much to fit on one screen. In such cases, you can pipe it easily to **less** to see it screen by screen. For instance, you could use **ls --help | less** to browse the information generated for this command screen by screen. This shows you a short summary of the selected command. The summary always starts with a short message about usage and then alphabetically displays all the available options.

```
Usage: /bin/ls [OPTION]... [FILE]...
List information about the FILEs (the curent directory by default).
Sort entries alphabetically if non of -cftuSUX nor -sort.

Mandatory arguments to long options are mandatory for short options too.
        -a, --all              do not hide entries starting with .
        -A, --almost-all    do not list implied . and ..
        ...
```

In the preceding example (taken from the first lines of output of **ls –help**), the top line is the usage line. In this line, it shows you can use [OPTION]… Available options are listed beneath it. After [OPTION]… you'll notice three dots. This means you can use one option, but more are available as well. The fact that [OPTION] is set in brackets, means that the usage of options is, well, optional. You can use them, but you don't have to. After the options, you can specify the name of one or more files. Again, [FILE] is set in brackets to let you know you can use one or more filenames.

Online Resources

Apart from the options available electronically on your system, there are also many online resources. The most useful of these is www.tldp.org (see Figure 4-17). This is the home site of The Linux Documentation Project. On this site, you'll find just about any kind of open-source documentation ever written. Most of the information is available in several languages in addition to English.

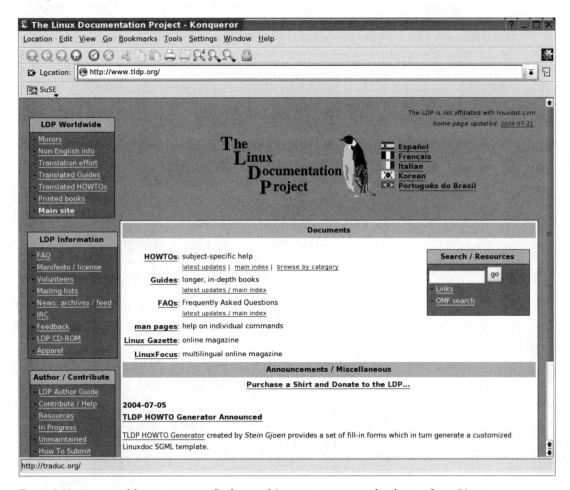

Figure 4-17. *At www.tldp.org, you can find everything you ever wanted to know about Linux.*

tldp.org is divided into many sections that carry various kinds of documents. In the HOWTO area are extensive descriptions of complex tasks that can be performed on your Linux system. For example, there's a 4mb-Laptop HOWTO that explains how to install Linux on a laptop with only 4MB of RAM available, or a MultiOS HOWTO that outlines how you can use Linux alongside other operating systems on your computer. Many other useful HOWTOs are available, but I'd recommend always noting the date the HOWTO was written before reading it. Some have since become obsolete.

The Guides on tldp.org are also very useful and include longer documents and books. Most of the books are also available in print, but as Linux is all about open source, you can download them here for free as well.

Besides these two categories, much more is available at www.tldp.org and definitely worth a look.

The SUSE HelpCenter

A great deal of SUSE Linux–specific information can be found at the SUSE HelpCenter (see Figure 4-18). This tool is located in the Novell menu on your server. Though the HelpCenter isn't a complete source of information, it does have many useful features, such as the integrated SLES Adminguide where you'll find extensive information about many programs used in SUSE Linux Enterprise Server. The HelpCenter is particularly useful if you want a clear explanation of how to perform a particular task on your system.

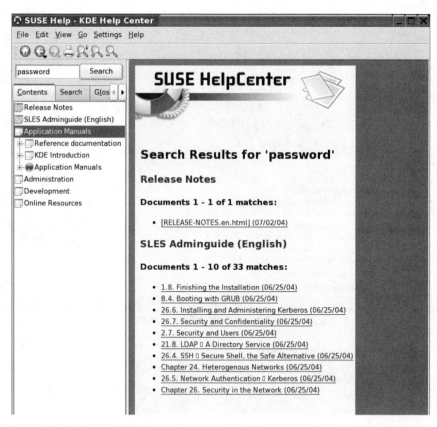

Figure 4-18. *In the SUSE HelpCenter, you can easily access information about tasks specific to your Open Enterprise Server.*

Editing Text Files

Although in Open Enterprise Server you want to do most configuration work from Novell's excellent iManager and YaST, if you really need to get down to your system, you'll have to edit some text configuration files. In order to do so, you need a decent editor. Since Open Enterprise Server is Linux, many different editors are available. I've chosen some favorite editors to discuss in this section. First, let's take it easy and use the nice graphical editor Kate. Afterward, I'll show you the real way of working with text files and discuss the venerable editor vi.

Tip This chapter actually doesn't discuss vi. Instead, it focuses on its user-friendly version: vi improved (vim). vim has features for use with the various flavors of UNIX that you won't find in many versions of vi. There are even some UNIX versions of vi in which the arrow keys on your keyboard don't work and you have to use the commands **h**, **j**, **k**, and **l** instead!

Editing Text Files with Kate

One user-friendly way to edit your text file is to use the graphical editor Kate, shown in Figure 4-19. Kate can be found under Novell ➤ Utilities ➤ Editor on a default installation. Working with Kate is so easy we don't need to waste much time here on it. Just enter your text and work with it the same way you would any other graphical editor. It even has some basic typesetting features included in the Tools menu, and you can check your ASCII file for proper spelling.

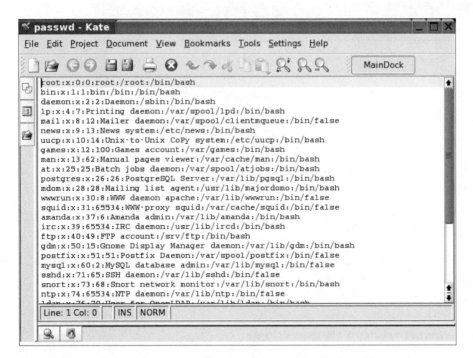

Figure 4-19. *Working with Kate is as easy as working with Windows Notepad.*

Introduction to vim

One day, you may find yourself working on a text-only console. If this happens, no fancy editors like Kate will be available to help in editing your configuration files. In such cases, you need vim, the user-friendly version of the classical UNIX editor vi. (Since it's referred to as vi in most instances, I'll refer to it as vi in the rest of this book as well. After all, you still start it with the **vi** command.)

Many bad things have been said about vi. Unfortunately, most of it will seem true if you're new to the Linux operating system. If, however, you want to work with the most versatile ASCII editor available, vi is probably your best choice. Luckily, you can find it on almost every Linux and UNIX-based server out there, and you don't need much to use it, just a modem connection from a text-based console. In this section, I discuss some of the most common vi commands.

Entering Text and Saving Files with vi

For people who have never worked with vi before, one of its most difficult aspects is that it has two different modes. When first starting, it brings you up in command mode. But don't start typing anything, command mode is for commands only. Thus, the first command you need will help you open up the input mode. As with many things in Linux, there are several ways to enter input mode from command mode. Some commands in vi consist of only one character. In this case, for instance, you can use **i** (insert), **a** (append), or **o** (open new line) to enter input mode. To help you along, vi tells you when it's in input mode, as can be seen in Figure 4-20.

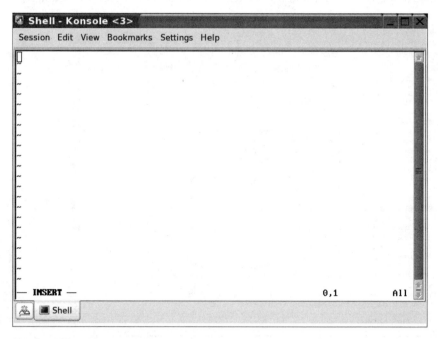

Figure 4-20. *vi shows you when you're in input mode.*

Once in input mode, you can start entering text. From here on, it works pretty much like any other editor. It only starts getting interesting when you want to save what you've typed in so far. At this point, you need to change from insert mode to command mode by pressing the

Esc key. The next step is to save your work. The needed command starts with a colon followed by the destination on the disk you want to save the file to, and usually the preferred name of the file. The complete command might look something like **:w mynewfile**. If another file with the same name exists, vi will complain. However, if you're sure what you're doing is correct (and that your file's contents are different), you can silence vi by using an exclamation mark, as in the command **:w! mynewfile**.

■**Tip** There's no such thing as vi automatically saving the files you're working on. You must do this by hand using the **w** command, as described in the previous paragraph.

Employing the write commands just mentioned, vi writes your file. Remember, Linux is a type of UNIX operating system and does just what you ask it to do, nothing more. If you want to save your file and close vi as well, you need to add something else to the command, such as **:wq**. To prevent vi from complaining, use an exclamation mark. This brings you back to your console where you can go on with your work. To quit vi without saving your changes, use the **:q!** command.

Deleting Text from a File with vi

When working on a text file in vi, you may want to delete characters, words, or lines from it. As you've probably guessed, vi has lots of commands to let you do this. Some can be used to delete the current character (**x**), the current line (**dd**), or the rest of the word, starting at the current position of the cursor (**dw**).

Besides these easy commands, you can also delete an entire selection. If, for example, you want to delete everything from line 9 thru line 15, type **:9,15d**. But how do you know which line numbers you want to work with? Easy, use **:se number** in command mode to display line numbers. Figure 4-21 shows the result of this command. Don't want to see line numbers any more? Just use **:se nonumber** and go on with your work.

In fact the delete command (like any other commands that delete text) doesn't really delete anything, it just places the text in a buffer from which you can restore it easily. One way to do so, is with the command **u** that stands for undo. Another way is to put the cursor somewhere else in your document and paste the selection at the new position of the cursor.

■**Tip** Even if you are an experienced vi user, sometimes things happen that are impossible to understand. For instance, you may press the wrong key without knowing it and copy your file's contents about six hundred times. In most situations, **u** helps you restore the original file prior to pressing this unfortunate key sequence. If **u** doesn't help, you can always use **:q!** in command mode. This quits vi immediately. Yes, all the changes you've made to the file will be lost, but at least you still have the original file.

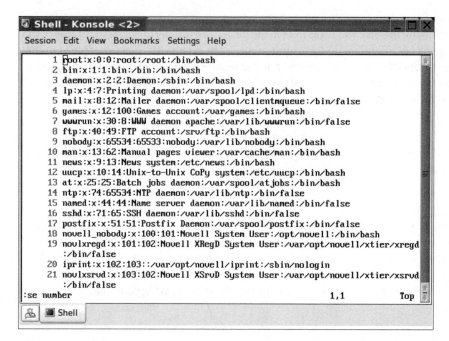

Figure 4-21. *To make working with vi easier, you can show line numbers in vi.*

Cutting, Copying, and Pasting Text with vi

You've just read about deleting text with vi. In fact, when you delete text with vi, you don't really delete anything; you just put the text in a buffer from which it can easily be restored with the command **u**. Instead of restoring it at the exact same position, you can also paste it somewhere else in your document. It's not difficult to do so. First, enter command mode, then put the cursor at the position where you want to paste your text, and finally use the command **p** to paste in your selection.

Instead of cutting and pasting your selection, you can, of course, also make a copy of some of the text in your file. This is only slightly different than deleting text; instead of **d**, you just use **y**. If, for example, you want to copy lines 12 thru 16, use **:12-16y** and paste it anywhere you like. (See Table 4-1 for vi's most powerful commands.)

Table 4-1. *The Most Important vi Commands*

Command	Use
i	Activate input mode and insert the cursor at the current position
a	Enter input mode and append the cursor to the current position
o	Enter input mode and open a new line

Command	Use
Esc	Enter command mode from input mode
x	Delete the current character from command mode
dd	Delete the current line
dw	Delete from the current position of the cursor to the start of the next word
y	Yank (copy) the current selection
p	Paste everything in the buffer
:w	Write the file
:q!	Quit vi and don't complain about anything
:wq	Write the file and quit vi without complaint
/word	Search for "word" in the current file
n	Repeat the last search

Mounting Devices

On a DOS computer, you just have to insert a floppy or CD-ROM in your system and you're immediately able to access it. In Linux, it doesn't always work that way, however. True, if you're working in the graphical interface, it will mount a CD you insert automatically, but this functionality is limited. Floppy disks, for example, are not mounted automatically, and neither is your CD mounted automatically when your graphical environment is not active. For this reason, you must know how to mount your devices manually.

In order to mount a device, the first thing to do is use the **mount** command. Second, you must specify what exactly you want to mount. Third, you have to indicate where you want to mount it. That sounds easy, but it doesn't always work out that way. The use of different options and device names can make the execution of a simple mount rather difficult. If you're lucky, however, and your server is well-configured, mounting a diskette can be as easy as typing **mount /dev/floppy**.

Device Names

In order to make the mount, start by telling what it is you want to mount. To do so, you need the name of a device. Each piece of hardware has a specific device file that must be addressed if you want to access the hardware. Some of the most important device files are outlined in Table 4-2.

Table 4-2. *Device Files*

Device File	Usage
/dev/fd0	Refers to the first diskette drive in your system.
/dev/fd1	Can be used to refer to a second diskette drive in your computer.
/dev/cdrom	Is actually a symbolic link that points to the device used as your CD-ROM drive. Using this, you can create symbolic links to your DVD drive, CD burner, and so on.
/dev/hda	Points to the master IDE device on IDE interface 0. In an IDE-based system, this normally is your hard disk.
/dev/hdc	The master IDE device on IDE interface 1. In many computers, this is your CD-ROM or DVD drive.
/dev/hda1	The first partition on hda.
/dev/sda	The first SCSI-drive in your computer.
/dev/sdc	Often used to mount a USB stick, but can also refer to any third hard drive in the system. It all depends on what other devices are present in your computer.

■Note Since the names of USB sticks vary according to the system you're using, it's recommended to use the automount feature from the graphical user interface. Make sure the graphical user interface is active and insert the USB stick you want to use in your computer. This will automatically mount the USB device. Next, use the **mount** command to find out where exactly it's mounted.

The Type of File System

On a Windows system, it's easy to access files on any device. This is because Windows only supports a few file systems. Linux, however, supports almost any kind of file system you can imagine. For this reason, you always have to specify what kind of file system is used on the device you are trying to mount. This can be a file system for local devices, but it can also be a network file system for a mount of a directory on a remote file server. In many cases, **mount** can guess the file system used on a certain device. To prevent mistakes, it's always better to specify the file system that should be used. You can find an overview of some of the most often used file systems in Table 4-3.

Table 4-3. *Most Popular File Systems*

File System Type	Usage
minix	This is a minimal and old Linux file system. It can be used on installation media and floppy disks.
ext2	ext2 has been the default Linux file system for a long time. Presently, on most servers, a journaling file system is used instead.

File System Type	Usage
ext3	ext3 is ext2 with journaling built in. It is fully backwards compatible with ext2, but because of the journaling system it is also a bit slower.
ReiserFS	Like ext3, ReiserFS is a journaling file system. It comes from a completely new design and is therefore faster and more robust than ext3. It's the default file system in all current SUSE products.
msdos	The msdos file system can be used to mount DOS diskettes, but is hardly used anymore.
vfat	vfat is the file system needed for all FAT-based media that support long names. This file system has made msdos redundant.
ntfs	The ntfs file system is needed to access information on any Windows volume formatted with NTFS.
iso9660	This file system is needed to access information on a CD-ROM drive.
swap	This is a special file system used to work with swap partitions.
nfs	NFS is a network file system. It's used to mount NFS shares made available by a remote NFS server.
smbfs	Like NFS, smbfs is a network file system. It's used to mount Samba shares from a remote Samba server or Windows server or workstation.
nss	The default file system needed to create a volume that can be mounted in Novell eDirectory. You can read more about configuration of this file system in Chapter 11 of this book.

Performing the Mount

If you know the device you want to mount, and you also know the file system type that has to be used, you only need one more thing: the directory on which you want to connect the mount. On Open Enterprise Server, the directory /media was created for this purpose. In this directory, you'll find subdirectories for removable media like floppies and CD-ROMs. If there are any other devices you want to mount regularly, you can create a special directory for them under media. Of course, there are no laws that oblige you to mount your devices on a directory under /media. In fact, you can even mount them on an existing directory that already has files in it. You might find that impractical, however. Alternatively, on a system where multiple partitions are used, it's absolutely normal to mount a partition on your hard disk in a directory like /usr.

Once you know everything you need to perform the mount, you can simply begin by typing a command like **mount /dev/hdc /media/cdrom**. This command activates the master IDE-device on the secondary IDE-interface and connects it to the directory /media/cdrom. No special options are needed.

A more complicated example involves mounting an ISO-image. Using the command **mount –t iso9660 –o loop /image.iso /media/isofile**, the content of the ISO-image file image.iso is mounted in the directory /media/isofile. To clearly specify what had to happen, some options were added. The first of these is **–t iso9660**, which specifies the file system to be used for the medium. The second option is **–o loop**. These options were used, because the **mount** command expects a block device to be mounted. In this case, however, the contents of a file are mounted, not a device. Thus, to specify that this file should be mounted just like a device, **–o loop** is used. The rest of the command should be clear.

■**Note**   OK, it doesn't really have anything to do with Open Enterprise Server management, but it's nice to know anyway. If you have mounted the ISO-file of a CD-ROM on your file system this way, you might as well add some changes to it. Once the file is mounted, you can add and delete from the file in any manner you like. Finished your modifications? Then unmount the device with the **umount** command. This saves the changes to the ISO-file, which you can then write to your CD burner with using your CD-burning software—as in the case of K3b, which is included in Open Enterprise Server.

The last example of an advanced mount to be presented here is **mount –t smbfs –o username=sander,password=secret //Julia/ifolder /media/smb**. This is a very practical mount that I'm using to make my shared iFolder directory on my Windows laptop available from my Linux server. This is a Windows mount, so I need the file system type smbfs (**-t smbfs**). Now, since it is a mount to my laptop that is from somewhere else in the network, my laptop also wants to know who is trying to access my files. This is what the **–o username=sander, password=secret** part of the command is used for. As a result of this command, I'm able to access all the files on my Windows workstation on my Linux server.

■**Caution**   The awful truth is that I'm a lazy person. That's why I included the password in the preceding example on the **mount** command. You should be aware that this is bad practice! By default, the last 500 commands used by every user are logged to the history mechanism (try the **history** command to get some idea of this). When a user specifies his password in clear-text like this, any cracker can easily find it by reviewing his history file. Thus, it's much better to just forget the **password=secret** portion. This causes a prompt to show up on which you can specify your password. This way, your precious password isn't stored in any log file, nor can anyone looking over your shoulder see it.

Unmounting Devices

Maybe you're used to computer systems where you can just remove a device when you're finished working with it. On Linux, it doesn't work this way! If you try to remove a CD-ROM from a drive when it's still mounted, you won't even be able to open the CD-ROM drive! Before removing a mounted device from your system, always unmount it first by using the **umount** command. Be careful though: the command is **umount**, not **unmount**. Proper use of **umount** causes all changes to be saved so you don't lose any information.

Sometimes, it's impossible to unmount a device. Perhaps when you try, the system returns the error "device busy." This means that some files on the device are still in use, maybe because you're still in the directory on which the device was mounted?

■**Tip** umounting a CD-ROM or DVD and then pushing the button on the drive to open it and take out your disc is a lot of work. Fortunately, someone came up with the **eject** command. If no files are in use on the disc, this is the fastest way to unmount any CD or DVD and automatically open the drive. The only thing you have to do is take out the disc and put it back in its case.

Automating the Mount

When a Linux-based server is started, some mounts have to be performed automatically. For example, think about the root file system and other partitions necessary to work with your server. To make mounting as easy as possible, some default settings are provided in the configuration file /etc/fstab. Listing 4-1 shows an example of this file.

Listing 4-1. *Example /etc/fstab*

```
/dev/sda2   /         reiserfs   acl,user_xattr  1 1
/dev/sda1   swap        swap        pri=42          0 0
devpts     /dev/pts devpts    mode=0620,gid=5 0 0
proc       /proc     proc       defaults       0 0
usbfs      /proc    /bus/usb   usbfs nouauto   0 0
sysfs      /sys           sysfs noauto        0 0
/dev/cdrom /media/cdrom subfs fs=cdfss,ro,procuid,nosuid,nodev,exec 0 0
/dev/fd0   /media/floppy subfs fs=floppyfss,procuid,nodev,nosuid,sync 0 0
//julia/ifolder   /media/smb smbfs      username=sander,password=secret 0 0
```

In the preceding example, some devices are defined with their default mount point. The first goal of the settings in /etc/fstab, is to mount some devices automatically. This is what happens in the lines /dev/sda2 to proc. In these lines, four devices that are essential to the operation of your server are specified. In the first line, note the specifications for the root file system which is on /dev/sda2. The location where this file system must be mounted automatically is specified in the second column: /. In the third column, the options that have to be used while performing the mount are specified, while in the last two columns more options are specified. This section won't dive into detail about all the options; it's just important to explain the main idea of this line: by specifying some device with its default mount-point and all options that are needed to activate the device, the mount will be performed automatically while booting the system.

Likewise, you could define a new line that automatically mounts the device /dev/hda2 by using default options on the directory /var. Therefore, the following line must be added to /etc/fstab:

```
/dev/sda2        /var default 0 0
```

This line carries out the mount automatically while the system is booted.

The second kind of mount you'll find in /etc/fstab is for some system devices. These are the lines that start with devpts, proc, usbfs, and sysfs. Don't worry about them for now; they're added to fstab automatically and you shouldn't touch them.

Following the system devices is a specification for the cdrecorder, /dev/cdrecorder, and the floppy drive, /dev/fd0. These specifications will not mount the devices automatically. They just make mounting these devices easier. If, for example, you use the command **mount /dev/fd0** without specifying the location where the device has to be mounted, mount will look in /etc/fstab to see if it can find more information like a default mount point and options that have to be used. If these are present in fstab, the **mount** command will perform the mount without complaining.

Finally, in the last line is a mount to an SMB-share that is performed automatically every time the system boots. This is not done in a secure way (the password is mentioned in clear-text), but it helps the lazy administrator of the system so he doesn't have to perform the mount manually each time he needs it.

Startup Procedures

You're already familiar with the working of runlevels, but before your system can enter its default runlevel, a few more things have to be taken care of. Note the schematic overview of the boot procedure in Figure 4-22. To continue, let's explore the start of the boot-procedure of your Open Enterprise Server. This is useful, because if something goes wrong, you can do some troubleshooting here.

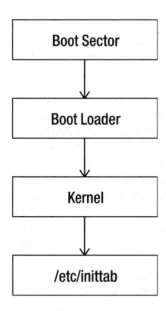

Figure 4-22. *In the system boot procedure, the boot loader decides what has to be loaded next.*

The Boot Loader Grub

The boot loader plays a major role in the boot procedure for your server, and is typically called from some boot sector on your computer. This can be a boot sector on a floppy drive, but in most cases it's the Master Boot Record (MBR) on the hard drive of your computer. The easiest way to specify where the boot loader has to be installed on Open Enterprise Server is with the systems management tool YaST, as shown in Figure 4-23. Of course, if you'd prefer, you can also hack it directly into the configuration file /etc/grub.conf.

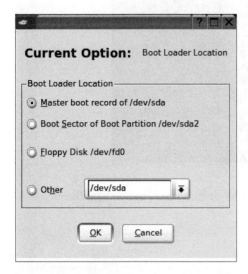

Figure 4-23. *In YaST, it's very easy to specify where the boot loader should be installed.*

As an administrator you should have some knowledge of Grub in case your system is broken. If, for example, you accidentally specify runlevel 6 as your default runlevel or something else happens that prevents your server from booting normally in its default runlevel, it's good to know that at the boot loader prompt, you can specify some options. You can think of options as like kernel modules that have to be loaded first to properly use a new piece of hardware. Similarly, the runlevel also has to be entered.

If you want to specify some options on system boot, you have to intervene when the system boots. The first thing that appears after the POST completes successfully is the Grub menu, as shown in Figure 4-24. You can specify various boot options here. First, make sure the Linux option is selected on the menu. Second, in boot options, specify any additional information you want to communicate to the kernel. If, for example, your server refuses to boot in its normal runlevel, you can specify a 1 to tell it to boot in the single-user runlevel. From there, you can repair the boot procedure on your server (you probably need to change something in /etc/inittab in this case), reboot, and it should all work normally.

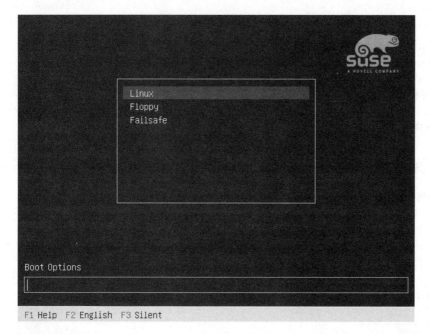

Figure 4-24. *On the Grub menu, you can specify any non-default kernel option you like.*

Process Management

Everything you do and any server that is started on a Linux server is activated as a process. Most of the time, these processes behave well. Sometimes you'll have problems with your processes, however. If that happens, you may be forced to terminate the process. In this section, you'll learn how to monitor process activity and, if necessary, terminate a misbehaving process.

Viewing Process Activity

If your system is acting slowly, the best thing you can do is generate an overview of all process activity. The best utility to use for this is top. This tool shows you an overview of your topmost active processes, as shown in Figure 4-25. It immediately tells you which process is generating the top CPU-load and also displays useful statistics about memory usage on your computer.

top is nice, but sometimes it's just not good enough. The main reason is that it shows only a list of the most active processes. If you need an overview of the activity of some process that isn't in the top-list of active processes, use **ps**. This command has lots of options that show you process activity; you'll discover almost every Linux administrator has his own preferred options. Remember that you should run **ps** as root, if you don't, you'll just see a list of the processes you've started and nothing more.

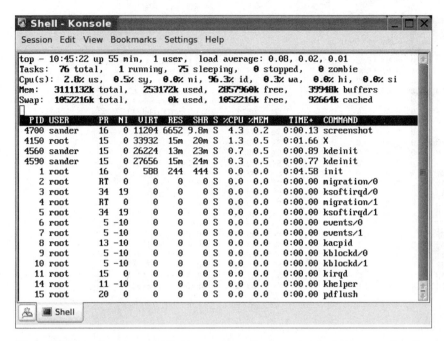

Figure 4-25. *top shows an excellent summary of your system's status as well as the most active processes.*

One of the best ways to get an overview of process activity on your system is by using **ps aux** (see Figure 4-26). This displays a list of all processes currently active on your server, and includes a lot of information about each process. The following columns in Table 4-4 are most interesting.

Table 4-4. *Information Displayed with ps*

Column	Meaning
USER	Name of the user that owns the process.
PID	The process identification number (PID). This is a unique identifier for each process active on your system.
%CPU	The relative CPU load.
%MEM	The amount of memory used by the process.
tty	The terminal the process is started on. If a ? is shown, it refers to a daemon-process that isn't connected to any terminal
STAT	Shows the status of your processes.
START	Displays the time the process started.
COMMAND	The name of the process. Will often display the name of the command used to start the process.

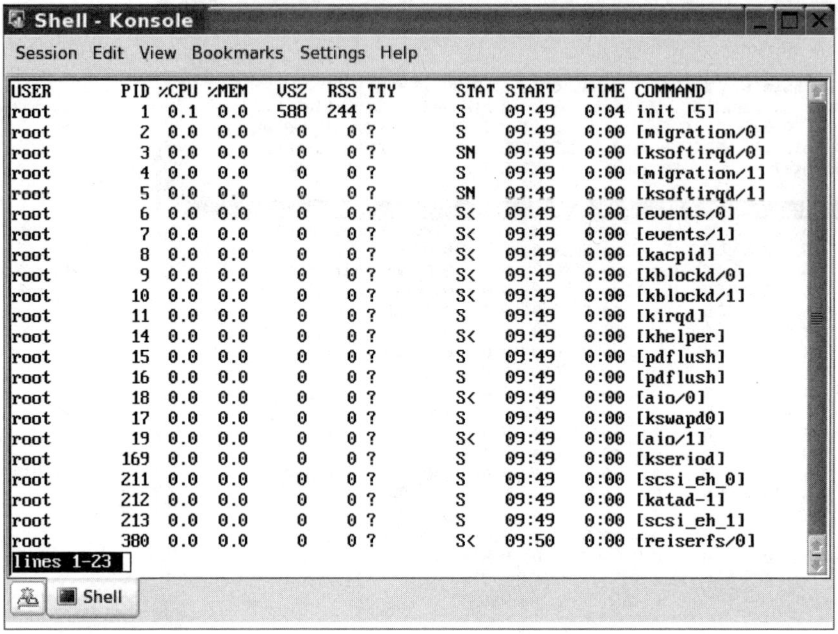

```
 Shell - Konsole                                                    _ □ X

 Session  Edit  View  Bookmarks  Settings  Help

USER        PID %CPU %MEM   VSZ  RSS TTY      STAT START   TIME COMMAND
root          1  0.1  0.0   588  244 ?        S    09:49   0:04 init [5]
root          2  0.0  0.0     0    0 ?        S    09:49   0:00 [migration/0]
root          3  0.0  0.0     0    0 ?        SN   09:49   0:00 [ksoftirqd/0]
root          4  0.0  0.0     0    0 ?        S    09:49   0:00 [migration/1]
root          5  0.0  0.0     0    0 ?        SN   09:49   0:00 [ksoftirqd/1]
root          6  0.0  0.0     0    0 ?        S<   09:49   0:00 [events/0]
root          7  0.0  0.0     0    0 ?        S<   09:49   0:00 [events/1]
root          8  0.0  0.0     0    0 ?        S<   09:49   0:00 [kacpid]
root          9  0.0  0.0     0    0 ?        S<   09:49   0:00 [kblockd/0]
root         10  0.0  0.0     0    0 ?        S<   09:49   0:00 [kblockd/1]
root         11  0.0  0.0     0    0 ?        S    09:49   0:00 [kirqd]
root         14  0.0  0.0     0    0 ?        S<   09:49   0:00 [khelper]
root         15  0.0  0.0     0    0 ?        S    09:49   0:00 [pdflush]
root         16  0.0  0.0     0    0 ?        S    09:49   0:00 [pdflush]
root         18  0.0  0.0     0    0 ?        S<   09:49   0:00 [aio/0]
root         17  0.0  0.0     0    0 ?        S    09:49   0:00 [kswapd0]
root         19  0.0  0.0     0    0 ?        S<   09:49   0:00 [aio/1]
root        169  0.0  0.0     0    0 ?        S    09:49   0:00 [kseriod]
root        211  0.0  0.0     0    0 ?        S    09:49   0:00 [scsi_eh_0]
root        212  0.0  0.0     0    0 ?        S    09:49   0:00 [katad-1]
root        213  0.0  0.0     0    0 ?        S    09:49   0:00 [scsi_eh_1]
root        380  0.0  0.0     0    0 ?        S<   09:50   0:00 [reiserfs/0]
lines 1-23

 🖳 ■ Shell
```

Figure 4-26. *ps aux offers a great deal of information about all active processes.*

On an active server, the amount of information displayed by **ps** can be overwhelming. Since most of the time **ps** is used to display information about a specific process, you can pipe the output of the command to the output-filtering tool **grep**. If, for example, you use **ps aux | grep ndsd**, the output of **ps** will be filtered with **grep** and only the lines in which the string ndsd appears will be displayed. This can make working with **ps** a lot easier.

Terminating Processes

Sometimes a process will act badly. In that case, you may need to terminate it. Normally, you will also start by trying to terminate the process in a nice way. If, for example, your ndsd processes are started with **/etc/init.d/ndsd start**, you should try to stop them with **/etc/init.d/ndsd stop** first. If that doesn't work, use **kill** or **killall** to terminate the process.

The **kill** command is written to terminate a process based on its PID. You could, for example, kill the process with ID 836 by using **kill 836**. Of course, you first have to use **ps** to find out the PID of the process you want to kill. The command **kill 836** will ask the process nicely to terminate its activity and, if necessary, will save any data not saved yet. Most times this works perfectly, but sometimes it doesn't.

If a process can't be stopped the nice way, you can be more insistent by sending the signal SIGKILL. Once done, the process is terminated, no matter what. This is not the best way to stop a process, however. If SIGKILL is employed, the process won't be able to save its data. Even worse, the kernel might get confused about the status of the process, leading to an unstable system. If you must kill a process with SIGKILL, use **kill** with the option **-9**. The command **kill -9 836**, for example, will send SIGKILL to the specified process.

Sometimes in terminating a process, you may discover the process wasn't activated just once, but tens or hundreds of times. This occasionally happens for processes like ndsd (your eDirectory daemons) and httpd (your Apache web server). If that's the case, it's undoable to terminate them all with their specific PID. In such situations, use **killall**. With this command you'll kill processes by name rather than PID. For example, **killall ndsd** kills all ndsd processes. Of course, you can also send some signals to the processes. For instance, **killall –SIGKILL ndsd** kills your eDirectory daemons the hard way (not recommended!). Another useful signal is **SIGHUP**. This stops the process and immediately starts it again. It's very useful if you've made a change to a configuration file that can only be detected when the process is started again.

To clarify things a bit, let's explore how you can locate the PID of some process and then restart it by sending it the **SIGHUP** signal.

1. If you need to find the PID for your Samba server, the first thing to do is use **ps aux | grep smbd**. This command generates a listing of all processes, filters only the lines that have smbd (the Samba daemon), and displays them.

```
oes # ps aux | grep smbd
root 4621 0.0 0.3 9029 3212 ? Ss 08:48 0:00 /usr/sbin/smbd
root 11919 0.0 0.0 1696 644 pts/50 S+ 12:39 0:00 grep smb
```

2. Notice that most times, a command like **ps aux | grep smbd** shows you two lines. The first line is the one that matters: it displays information about the Samba daemon. The second line is the result of the command itself; here it's **grep smb**. You can safely ignore this line.

3. From the output of **ps aux | grep smbd**, you have learned that the process ID of the Samba daemon is 4621. Thus, the next step is to restart this process by sending it the **SIGHUP** signal. Use **kill –SIGHUP 4621** to do so.

Working with Linux Permissions

It's very important to know how Linux permissions are applied. Although in Open Enterprise Server all management of users and files is performed from the Novell management tools, let's take a look at the classic method for handling permissions on a Linux system. This is useful knowledge if you ever need to do any serious troubleshooting on your Open Enterprise Server or configure it to exchange information with other Linux-based systems.

Note As compared to the advanced possibilities Novell offers to work with permissions, users, and groups, the use of Linux permissions is rather limited. Refer to Chapter 9 for more information about the way permissions are handled in a Novell environment. Be aware, however, that these permissions can only be applied if you're using NSS (see Chapter 11) as the file system or NCP (see Chapter 10 as well) as the file access protocol.

Linux Users and Groups

The basic element needed to work with permissions on a Linux system is the Linux user. In the most elementary way, this user is defined in the ASCII text file /etc/passwd (see Listing 4-2). A long time ago (for some brands of UNIX not so long ago) encrypted passwords were stored in this file. The problem with this is that every user has the right to open /etc/passwd and view its contents. Because this is a serious threat to the security of your system, on a modern Linux system the information on the user account is kept in /etc/passwd, while the encrypted password is stored safely in /etc/shadow, which is only accessible by root.

Listing 4-2. *Local Users Are Defined in /etc/passwd*

```
root:x:0:0:root:/root:/bin/bash
bin:x:1:1:/bin:/bin/bash
daemon:x:2:2:Daemon:/sbin:/bin/bash
...
squid:x:31:65534:WWW-proxy squid:/var/cache/squid:/bin/false
...
sander:x:500:100:sander:/home/sander:/bin/bash
```

On each line in /etc/passwd a user is defined. In these lines, the following fields are used:

- *Username*: Each user needs a unique username. This name can be no longer than eight characters. In /etc/passwd, not only are normal end-users defined but some system-accounts are created, such as the administrative user root and other accounts like bin, daemon, and many more that are needed to run various processes.

- *Password*: The second field in /etc/passwd is reserved for the encrypted user password, because on modern Linux distributions the x in this field is used to refer to the encrypted password stored in /etc/shadow. If for some reason the x is removed from this field, however, the password will be stored local.

- *User identification*: On a Linux system, every user needs a unique user identification number (UID). Normally, the first UID used for a normal user is 500, while the last UID that can be used for a normal user is 65533. The user root always uses UID 0. It's very important that UIDs remain unique on your server.

- *Primary group*: On a UNIX system, every user must be a member of at least one group. This is the primary group. In this field, you'll find the group identification number (GID). It's possible to make a UNIX user member of more than one group, but the system isn't made for that, so it's awkward to make a user a member of more than one group. The groups are defined in the file /etc/group and it's very common to have all the users be members of the same group.

- *Description*: This field is used to describe the user. Compare this field to the full name field for an eDirectory user.

- *Home Directory*: This specifies the directory that acts as the user's home directory. Normally, this should be a directory on the local Linux system of which the user is owner.

- *Shell*: For each user a shell must be defined. This is the command interpreter that starts when a user logs in to the system from a non-graphical session. For normal users, the shell /bin/bash is used. The shell /bin/false is often used for system accounts. This is because it's impossible to log in with this shell.

As mentioned, on a modern Linux distribution you'll always find an /etc/shadow besides /etc/passwd. The main purpose of this file is to store encrypted passwords so no one besides root can use them. There really are only two fields that are important in /etc/shadow, and these are the first two fields. The first field contains the name of the considered user, while the second field holds the encrypted password. If this second field is filled with an asterisk or an exclamation mark, the user concerned can't log in from a shell. This is often the case with system accounts, which are chiefly used to provide system processes with those permissions necessary for them to function.

Tip In Open Enterprise Server, most user management is done through Novell's browser-based tool iManager. It's also possible to just create a local user with Linux utilities, however. The most important utility used for this purpose is **useradd**. Enter **useradd alex** and immediately you'll find the user alex that was created locally on your system. The need to create local users on OES - Linux is limited, though. It's much easier to create users in eDirectory and make them LUM users as well. This way they're automatically available on all known Linux workstations. You can read more about LUM in Chapter 9 of this book.

File Ownership

If a user is known on your local system, you can give him permissions to your local files. In order to understand permissions in a UNIX environment, you have to understand the concept of ownership. Every file and directory on a Linux file system has a user and a group that are owners of that file or directory. These two are important from a permissions perspective. Technically, if you are not the owner and you are not a member of the group that is an owner, then you automatically belong to "others." For each Linux file and directory, these three entities (user, group, and others) are granted permissions by default. Sometimes the granted permissions are null for the group owner and others, which is good for security, but most of the time the owner, the group owner, as well as others, get read-access to files by default. (No, in Linux there is no such thing as full control for everyone). You can display both the user and group owners of each file with **ls –l**, as shown in Figure 4-27. On a normal server system, user root and group root are owners of most of the files.

Since the user and group who are owner of your files are very important for the security of your system, you'll have to know how to make someone owner. The command used for that, is **chown**. You can also use **chown** to make a group owner of a file. If you'd like to make user linda owner of the file schedule that is in the current directory, use **chown linda schedule**. If you'd like to assign the group users as group-owner of this same file, use **chown :users schedule**. Since this is Linux—and in Linux you can often perform tasks in many ways—you can also use **chgrp users schedule** to create a group owner. Once you've decided who the owner of your files is, the next thing to do is assign these owners some permissions.

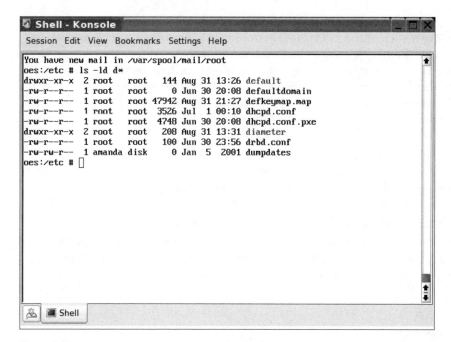

Figure 4-27. *On a Linux system, you can display both the user and group owners of each file via the ls –l command.*

Linux Permissions

In a Linux environment, there is a possibility to work with three different permissions. The effect of the use of these permissions is different if applied to files or directories. The first permission is read (r). This permission gives a user the possibility to browse the content of a file or directory. Ordinary users have the read permission on a lot of files on a Linux system, because this permission is often granted to others.

The second permission is write (w). If applied to files, this permission allows a user to modify the content of an existing file. If it is applied to directories, it allows the user to create and delete files in the designated directory. The last permission is a rather strange one: execute (x). Applied to files, this permission makes a file executable so you can run it as a program. If applied to a directory, it allows a user to browse to subdirectories in this directory. (See Table 4-5.)

Tip If you're used to rights in a Novell environment, then you're familiar with the concept of inheritance. The effect of inheritance is that a right applied to a high level (for example, on a directory), applies to everything underneath it. In a Linux environment, inheritance is not an issue. The only thing that counts in determining whether a user has permissions or not, is the following question: Is the user an owner of the file? If not, is he a member of a group that is owner of the file? If not, what are the permissions granted to others?

■**Caution** If you are using an NSS volume on OES - Linux, or if you are working with NCP to make shares to directories on the Linux system, Linux permissions will have to interact with the Novell rights applied to that volume. The solution chosen for this in OES is simple: disregard the permissions at the Linux level and work with the Novell permissions instead. A detailed description of these permissions is covered in Chapter 12 of this book.

Table 4-5. *Basic Permissions Summarized*

Permission	Files	Directories
Read	Browse the content of a file.	Browse the content of a directory with **ls**.
Write	Change the content of a file.	Create files. Remove a file. Move files. Delete files.
Execute	Start a program file.	Use **cd** to activate a subdirectory of the current directory.

Apart from the three basic permissions, some advanced permissions can also be applied. The first is Set User ID (SUIDs). When this permission is applied to a program file, it allows the program file to run with the rights of the owner of the file. This permission is useful if applied to /bin/passwd, because it permits a user to change his password in the file /etc/shadow that is only writable for root. SUID can, however, be a disaster if not applied in the right way. This is because it can create a backdoor for hackers. Imagine the rather strange situation in which SUID is applied to the default shell /bin/bash. Since root is the owner of /bin/bash, it gives root-permissions to every user that uses /bin/bash. Of course, a clever hacker will never apply SUID to /bin/bash as a backdoor. He will instead apply it to some program file that isn't used very often.

SGID (set group ID, S) is the second of the advanced permissions. It is basically the same as SUID, with the sole difference that it gives a program the rights of the group that is owner of the program when it is executed. Both SUID and SGID can be useful for your operating system. I advise you never to apply them for yourselves.

The last of the three special permissions is the sticky bit (t). If applied to a directory, the meaning should be that a user can only remove files from this directory if he is the owner of the file, or has specific write permissions. This feature however is not implemented in most Linux file systems and for that reason it makes no sense to apply the sticky bit to directories.

Assigning Permissions with chmod

If you want to apply Linux permissions from the command line, use the **chmod** command. This command can be used in two modes: the absolute mode and the relative mode. If applied in absolute mode, the permissions you want to apply are written as numbers. If you prefer the relative mode, the permission is denoted by its abbreviation. Most experienced Linux administrators prefer absolute mode, since it's clearer what happens. Use of relative mode can, however, be practical once in a while.

As mentioned, numbers are used in absolute mode to refer to permissions. This should be a four-digit number: the first digit refers to the special permissions, the second refers to the permissions of the owner of the file, the third refers to the permissions of the group-owner of the file, and the fourth refers to the permissions of other. Alternatively, you can also use a three-digit number. If that's the case, the digits refer to owner, group, and others, respectively.

To know what number you have to use in absolute mode, you have to know the value used to represent a permission. This is shown in Table 4-6.

Table 4-6. *Permissions and Their Values in Absolute Mode*

Value	Permission
4	Read or SUID
2	Write or SGID
1	Execute or sticky bit

With these values combined, you can set the permissions you need. Imagine that you want to give read, write, and execute to the user, read and write to the group, and nothing to others. No special permissions are applied. Thus, the first digit you use is a 0, because you're not using any special permissions. The second digit should be the result of the sum 4+2+1. This is because the user gets read (which has the value 4), write (which has the value 2), and execute (which has the value 1). So in the end you have to give 7 to the user. The group, meanwhile, only gets read and write; that's 4+2, which makes 6. Others don't get anything, which means you can work with 0. In the end, the permissions will be mentioned as 0760, or, alternatively, could be mentioned as 760, since you're not using any of the special permissions. To apply these permissions to ~/file, use **chmod 760 ~/file**.

Working in absolute mode is one thing; you can, however, also work in relative mode. In that case, you have to use an abbreviation for each permission:

- *r*: Read

- *w*: Write

- *x*: Execute

- *s*: SUID

- *S*: SGID

- *t*: Sticky bit

Next, you'll need to specify to whom you are giving the permissions:

- *u*: User
- *o*: Others

- *g*: Group
- *a*: All

Finally, you need to specify what exactly you want to do:

- =: Set and forget about all permissions that have been set before.

- +: Add to the existing permissions.

- -: Remove from the current permissions.

With all this information, you can create nice commands like **chmod u=rw,g+x,o-r ~/file**. This may make you understand why most administrators prefer working with **chmod** in absolute mode. The only time relative mode is useful is when you want to apply a permission to a file that is valid for everyone. You could use, for example, **chmod +x ~/bin/myprogram** to make the program you have just written executable.

As an administrator, you certainly want to check the permissions that are set to your files and directories from time to time. You can do so with **ls –l**, which shows all permissions listed in relative mode. This could appear in a line like

```
-rw-r--r-- 1 root root 1674 Aug 31 13:54 passwd
```

The first character in this output line from **ls –l** is used to indicate what kind of file it is you're looking at. You could find, for example, **d** to indicate that it's a directory. Digits 2, 3, and 4 are used to specify the permissions of the owner of the file. Digits 5, 6, and 7 specify the permissions of the group owner, while digits 8, 9, and 10 indicate the permissions for others. This means that the owner has read and write, while the group owner has read as well as others. The permission executable is not applied to anyone on this file.

In the output of **ls –l**, just nine characters are reserved to specify the permissions applied to the file. This means that there is no space reserved for the special permissions. If special permissions are applied, you can see that at the position of the execute permission, as shown in Table 4-7.

Table 4-7. *Various ls –l Output*

ls –l Output	Meaning
---s------	SUID and execute for user
---S------	SUID
------s---	SGID and execute for group
------S---	SGID
---------t	Sticky bit and execute for others
---------T	Sticky bit

You can find an example of these special permissions when you ask a long listing for /usr/bin/passwd, the binary that can be used to change a user's password:

```
-rwsr-xr-x
```

As you can see, on this executable, SUID is applied, as well as execute for the owner of the file.

Of course, you can also set and view permissions from a graphical file manager such as KDE's Konqueror, which is a lot easier for Linux newbies (as shown in Figure 4-28).

Figure 4-28. *Permissions can be set from the graphical interface as well.*

Setting Default Permissions with umask

You can use **chmod** to specify the permissions that should be used on existing files. There also is a command that specifies what permissions must be used on new files. This is the **umask** command. If you just enter **umask** in a shell prompt, you'll see the default umask as used on your system. The values used in the **umask** are a bit confusing. They have almost the opposite meaning of the values used by **chmod** in absolute mode. Table 4-8 displays a summary of all **umask** values.

Table 4-8. *umask Values and Their Meanings*

Value in umask	Default Permissions Applied to Files	Default Permissions Applied to Directories
0	Read and write	All
1	Read and write	All
2	Read	Read and execute
3	Read	Read
4	Write	Write and execute
5	Write	Write and execute
6	Nothing	Execute
7	Nothing	Execute

On most Linux systems, the default **umask** is set to 022, which does apply the read permission to others on all new files created. If you consider this an insecure situation, you can change the default **umask** to 027. The problem with **umask** is that it is not just a command. It is an environment variable that has to be set every time a user logs in to the system. In order to do so, you have to change the umask-value specified in the "login-script" for your system: /etc/profile (shown in Figure 4-29). Be careful when making changes to this file, because it's a complex shell script and even a minor mistake can cause severe problems.

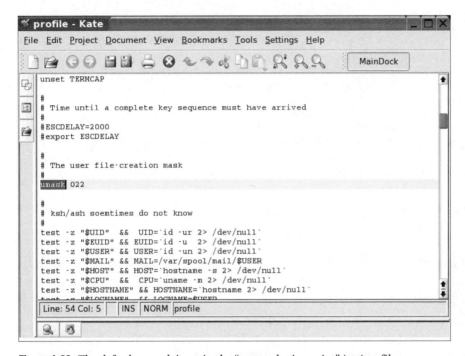

Figure 4-29. *The default umask is set in the "system login-script" /etc/profile.*

■**Caution** The configuration file /etc/profile is managed by YaST. Any changes you make to this file can get lost the next time you open YaST and do some configuration of your system. If you want to add things to this file, you should use /etc/profile.local instead so they are processed for all users logging in to the system.

Finding Things

Although there is an excellent Find Files tool included in the KDE-interface of Open Enterprise Server (see Figure 4-30), at the end of this chapter I'll talk a little about finding things from the command line.

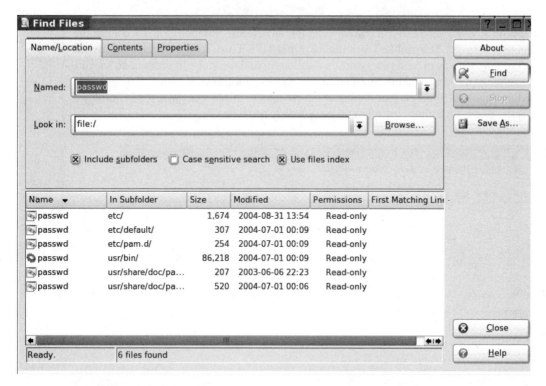

Figure 4-30. *The KDE graphical interface includes a very user-friendly tool to find files and text in files.*

Finding Files

Two important utilities help find files. The first is **find**. This powerful utility can be used to search for files based on any property of the file itself. Of course, you can use it to just find a file with the name *somefile*, but one nice feature of **find** is that you can also use it to find all files greater than 10 kilobytes in size that were created by user paul on September 19 and delete them automatically. There is just one disadvantage to **find.** Because it is this powerful, it is also slow. It may, for instance, take a few minutes before find has located the file you're looking for. The alternative is **locate**. This utility works on a database that must be created and updated and that contains the complete names of all files on your system. The advantage? It's much faster, but it coughs up a lot less than **find**.

find

find is not a utility you get used to by just reading a few lines from a lovely book like this one. The only way to get used to **find** is by trying it, doing new things with it, and then trying it again. The following shows some examples of the power of **find**. For complete information on the topic, consult the man page of **find**.

```
find / -name "passwd"
```

This example is easy: it looks for any file with the name "passwd" and displays it. The slash in the command is used to specify the directory in which find should begin looking—in this case, it starts from the root of the file system.

```
find / -user "linda" -type d
```

Here, **find** looks for all files created by user linda, which are of the type "directory".

```
find / -perm "4000"
```

This is an important one. It locates all files on your system that have the sticky bit set. It's not a bad idea to use this command regularly as a security check of your system.

```
find / -user "paul" -exec rm -rf {} \; &
```

Here we have my personal favorite. It looks for all files of which user paul is the owner. If it finds any, it executes the command **rm –rf** on them. Since this command can take a while to complete, an ampersand is placed behind it, which makes it a background job.

locate

The **locate** tool is much simpler than **find**. It looks for a string in a database in which all file-names are marked. If you want to make good use of **locate**, this database should be updated regularly. Normally, it's done automatically once a day. If you can't wait that long (for example, because you've just installed a large software suite and want to locate some files in it), use **updatedb** to update the database manually. After that, it's not difficult. Use **locate host** to show all lines in the file that match the pattern "host". Yes, it not only finds the file /etc/host, but also directories like /etc/ghostscript. Though **locate** is not the most sophisticated tool around, it can be quite useful.

Finding Text

It may also happen that you need to find some text. With the **grep** utility, you can find the requested text almost anywhere. Previously, the command **ps aux | grep something** was discussed which looked for the pattern "something" in the output of **ps aux**. **grep**, however, can also be used to look in the content of files. It'd be awfully convenient to use **grep mysecretpasswd /etc** to look in all the files in /etc to see if your password is stored there.

The disadvantage of **grep** is that, by default, it only looks in the current directory and not in subdirectories. Luckily, it's easy to change this behavior: just use the option **–r** to include subdirectories.

Summary

You should know enough about Linux now to perform most important Linux-related tasks. Don't forget, however, that this was just a short introduction to a very rich and sophisticated operating system. Now, let's forget about Linux for a while and discuss in the next chapter how you can connect to Open Enterprise Server from any workstation.

CHAPTER 5

■■■

Introduction to the NetWare Kernel

In the previous chapter, you read about SUSE Linux Enterprise Server, which is used as the operating system in OES - Linux. In this chapter, you'll learn more about NetWare, the operating system used in OES - NetWare, and be introduced to the kernel and console interface of this operating system.

Components of the NetWare Operating System

Like any other operating system, NetWare consists of three major components. At the heart of the operating system, there's the kernel. This is the part that manages the dataflow from the services running on NetWare to the hardware. In order to recognize the hardware available in the server, NetWare uses drivers that can be loaded and unloaded as needed. In addition to the kernel are the services, such as the different processes running on top of NetWare.

Drivers

The bottom layer of the operating system, are the drivers. In NetWare, all drivers are available as modules—the so-called NLMs (NetWare Loadable Modules). These drivers make it possible to use the different hardware components connected to the server. NLMs are only loaded when needed: they aren't part of the kernel itself. There is, however, no mechanism that loads the drivers dynamically if needed; thus, the administrator needs to create configuration files that instruct the system to load these drivers upon startup. Normally, this is done in STARTUP.NCF and AUTOEXEC.NCF (discussed in later sections of this chapter).

NetWare uses two different kinds of drivers: drivers for network interface cards and drivers for hard disks and other storage devices. These drivers can be identified by their extensions. Drivers for the network card always have the extension .LAN. For instance, you might have a driver called 3C90X.LAN that's used to communicate with 3COM network cards in your server.

Apart from the LAN drivers, drivers are also needed for your server's storage devices. These come in two different types, the first of which is the Host Adapter Module (HAM). This particular driver is used to communicate with the controller to which your storage device is connected—such as SCSI controllers or IDE interfaces in your computer. Second are the Custom Device Modules (with the extension CDM), which communicate with the storage devices themselves.

Kernel

The kernel is the heart of the operating system and provides all the fundamental services of the operating system, like the handling of interrupt requests and I/O. The NetWare kernel organizes several processes, dividing them into threads that can be handled by the scheduler and thus divided amongst all the processors available on the server. This functionality is known as Symmetric Multi Processing (SMP).

Services and Applications

The last part of the NetWare operating system is the services and applications provided by the server. A NetWare server furnishes many different services on the network, which are implemented as NetWare Loadable Modules (NLMs). More advanced applications use modern application server frameworks like the exteNd application server. Some of the most important services on NetWare are

- *Directory services*: These services, implemented by the NLM DS.NLM, make sure that eDirectory can do its work. They locate the eDirectory database and give access to database records to users, servers, and services.

- *DNS/DHCP services*: The DHCP service provides all the workstations in a network with the configuration needed to connect with the network. A special feature of the Novell DHCP service (implemented in DHCPSRVR.NLM) is that it saves its information in eDirectory. The advantage is that the DHCP data can be replicated across the network and that other DHCP servers can access this data. The DNS service takes care that names of computers can easily be translated into IP addresses. On NetWare, the module NAMED.NLM provides this service.

- *Web services*: Like on the Linux platform, the well-known Apache web server is used to provide http service to the network. This server is not only needed to give access to HTML documents on a NetWare server, but Apache is also integral to the management of many other network services—for instance, all web-based management programs like iManager and iMonitor need it to perform their tasks.

- *iFolder services*: iFolder is the service that synchronizes files between the user's workstation and the iFolder process running on a server.

- *Novell Storage Services (NSS)*: This is the default file storage system on NetWare. It lets you save files on a fast journaling file system.

Managing NetWare from the Console

There are many different ways to manage your NetWare server. The easiest is to work directly from the server console. This is the black screen on the server where you type commands to instruct it as to what it needs to do. The server console is very particular to NetWare. It is its own shell and doesn't resemble those of other operating systems such as Linux and DOS. Because of its simple appearance, some consider the NetWare console primitive; however, if you know your NetWare commands, it's a very powerful management interface. (See Figure 5-1.)

Figure 5-1. *The OES - NetWare console doesn't look like much, but it provides a powerful interface to manage your server.*

The second way to manage your NetWare server is through one of the many NLM utilities available. For example, MONITOR.NLM can be used to monitor the health of your server, while INETCFG.NLM helps you manage the properties of your server's protocols.

The third way to manage your server is with the graphical user interface (GUI). Based on the X Windowing System, it offers configuration utilities that can be used for several purposes. For instance, the Install utility helps install new software, and ConsoleOne can be used to manage eDirectory information directly from your server. The GUI on the server, however, is rather basic and doesn't offer complete management capabilities for your server.

As a last option to manage a server, the remote management utilities can be used. For OES, many programs are available to perform remote management. The browser-based Remote Manager is by far the most versatile tool. It gives GUI-based access to all parameters of your server, and offers you the ability to access the console screen of your server from a remote workstation.

Introduction to the Console

In general, you can do two things from the server console: enter commands to perform certain tasks, and load NLMs to add new functionality to your server. One of these NLMs, by the way, is NWCONFIG.NLM (see Figure 5-2), which can be used to configure various parts of your server.

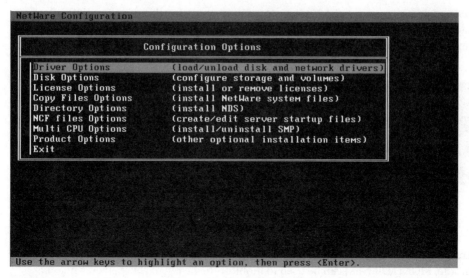

Figure 5-2. *NWCONFIG is one of the many NLM utilities available for server management.*

You can load an NLM just by typing its name. If, for example, you want to load MONITOR.NLM, just type the command **monitor** on the server console. This loads the module. In the case of MONITOR.NLM, you'll see a new screen in which the NLM displays its output. Some modules, however, do not show a new screen, but just get loaded. In order to unload an NLM, use the **unload** command followed by the name of the NLM. For example, you can unload MONITOR.NLM by issuing the command **unload monitor**. If the NLM in question displays its own screen, in many cases you can use the Esc key to exit the screen.

After loading an NLM like MONITOR.NLM, you'll find that the normal console screen of your server is no longer available. In this case, you can use some key combinations to switch between the different screens active on your server:

- *Ctrl+Esc*: Use these keys to get a listing of all screens currently active on your server. Enter the number of one of the screens to activate it. (See Figure 5-3.)

- *Alt+Esc*: Use Alt+Esc to browse through the different screens on your server.

- *Ctrl+Alt+Esc*: Only use these keys if you have problems on your server and it isn't operating normally. They will display a small menu where you can choose from three different actions to safely shut down a frozen server—in this regard, the option **Down the File Server** is particularly useful. The option **Spawn new command line process** is useful as well: it will give you a new command line that can be used to continue working on the server, even if some particular screen has hung.

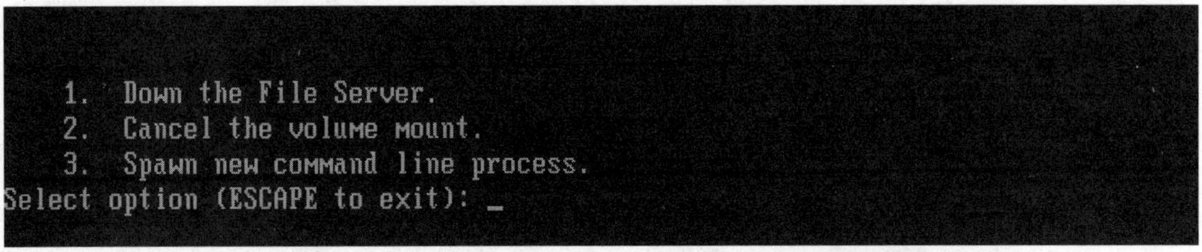

```
 1.  Down the File Server.
 2.  Cancel the volume mount.
 3.  Spawn new command line process.
Select option (ESCAPE to exit): _
```

Figure 5-3. *If your server appears frozen, Ctrl+Alt+Esc provides a menu to shut it down properly.*

Shutting Down the Server

When a server is operational, normally a lot of files are open. Some of these are user files that have been saved in cache, but haven't been saved to the hard disk of your server yet. This makes the server faster because it doesn't have to write all the files immediately, but it can also cause some problems. For example, if you lose power on your server, all these files will be lost. For this reason, you should always shut down the server properly. To do this, the following three commands can be used.

- *down*: Use **down** if you want to shut down your server. For example, this command must be used to turn off your server before replacing any non-hot-pluggable hardware. After issuing the command **down**, you'll be returned to a DOS-prompt. It's then safe to switch off your server.

- *reset server*: Use this command to reboot your server. This command performs a cold reboot of the server and has the same effect as pushing the reset button on a computer. The computer will restart with a power on self test (POST). If you use **reset server**, you can be sure that all the information in your server's RAM will be cleared.

- *restart server*: Use **restart server** to reload the server kernel SERVER.EXE. This command will also shut down your server and reboot it, but the memory of the server will not be cleared completely. You can save some time by using **restart server** instead of **reset server**, but, in general, it's more thorough to use **reset server**.

Starting Up the Server

When problems arise with your server, sometimes it's useful to have some insight as to just what happens when the server boots up. The following list outlines the internal processes of your server during startup.

1. After being switched on, the computer performs a power on self test and makes sure all the necessary hardware is present.

2. The Master Boot Record on a hard disk is used to start the operating system on your server. On OES - NetWare, DOS is used for booting the server. (See Figure 5-4.)

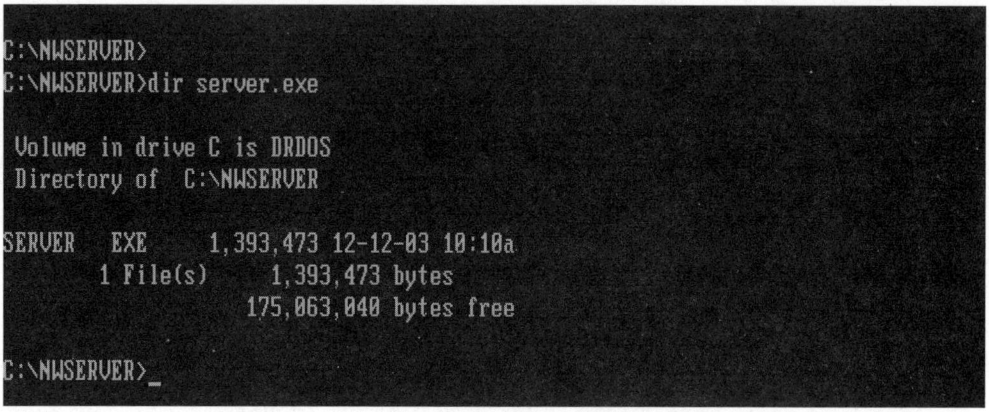

```
C:\NWSERVER>
C:\NWSERVER>dir server.exe

 Volume in drive C is DRDOS
 Directory of  C:\NWSERVER

SERVER   EXE     1,393,473 12-12-03 10:10a
        1 File(s)      1,393,473 bytes
                     175,063,040 bytes free

C:\NWSERVER>_
```

Figure 5-4. *OES - NetWare still uses DOS to boot the server.*

3. From the DOS file C:\AUTOEXEC.BAT, the command **c:\nwserver\server.exe** is executed. This
    starts the NetWare kernel and puts DOS in the background. DOS will not be used while the
    NetWare kernel is operational; you will only see it when you shut down the kernel.

4. When SERVER.EXE is activated, it scans the configuration file C:\NWSERVER\
    STARTUP.NCF. From this file, SERVER.EXE finds information about the hardware it
    has to use in starting the server. For example, here it finds information about the
    drivers that have to be loaded for the storage devices. This file also contains special
    commands that can be used to specify how the memory of the server should be used.
    You can edit this configuration file from a DOS prompt with an editor. It's also possible
    to edit it after the NetWare kernel has finished loading.

5. Once SERVER.EXE has been loaded, DOS will disappear into the background and the
    NetWare kernel will become active. The file SYS:SYSTEM\AUTOEXEC.NCF is then read
    to find out how NetWare should operate. It lists all the NLMs that have to be loaded
    while starting the server.

It's possible to influence the boot procedure of the server by employing one of the
following measures.

• Press F5 or F8 when the text "Starting DOS" displays on your screen. These keys interrupt
  the boot procedure and get you to the DOS prompt so you can load the server manually.

• From the DOS prompt, type **SERVER –NS** to start the server without using STARTUP.NCF.
  This allows you to load all necessary drivers manually.

• From the DOS prompt, type **SERVER –NA** to start the server without processing the
  AUTOEXEC.NCF configuration file.

• From the DOS prompt, type **SERVER –NL** to boot the server without displaying the
  Novell logo on startup. This allows you to see exactly what happens on system boot.

• Type **SERVER –NDB** to boot the server without opening the eDirectory database. This is
  useful if you need to do maintenance of the eDirectory database on your server.

startup.ncf

The first configuration file that's processed while booting your server is C:\NWSERVER\ STARTUP.NCF. In this file, the drivers are specified that need to be loaded while starting the server. You can edit it from the server console with **edit c:startup.ncf**. It displays information like the following:

```
######## End PSM Drivers ########
LOAD IDEHD.CDM
LOAD IDECD.CDM
######## End CDM Drivers ########
LOAD IDEATE.HAM SLOT=10005
######## End HAM Drivers ########
```

All lines starting with # in the preceding example are not interpreted by the SERVER.EXE; # is used as a remark sign. First, the drivers for the storage devices in use on this server are specified. IDEHD.CDM is used for the IDE hard disk in this system, while IDECD.CDM is used to communicate with the system's optical drive. Notice that this driver is also used to communicate with a DVD drive. After loading drivers for the individual storage devices with LOAD IDEATE.HAM, a driver for the IDE interfaces is loaded. The parameter **SLOT=10005** is used to specify the hardware address of the device.

autoexec.ncf

One of the most important configuration files on your server is AUTOEXEC.NCF. In this file, lines are included to load everything needed for your server to start functioning. The following are defined in SYS:SYSTEM\AUTOEXEC.NCF:

- Definition of the time zone

- Name of the server

- Definition of a default location in eDirectory where utilities should look for objects if they aren't aware of the hierarchical structure of eDirectory, the so-called BINDERY CONTEXT

- Definition of the Server ID which is used to get a unique server identifier on the network

- The search path that can be used by the server when it is trying to locate a command or NLM

- Commands to initialize the network card

- Protocol settings for the network card

- Commands to mount available NetWare volumes

- Commands to call other batch files that can be recognized by their extension .NCF

- Commands to load NLMs

- Comment lines to specify what exactly happens at a given line

To give you an impression of everything that happens, I've included some of the most important lines in AUTOEXEC.NCF on OES - NetWare. Some comments are included to specify what exactly happens in these lines:

```
# Specify a default container
Set Bindery Context = digitalair
# time settings
SET Daylight Savings Time Offset = 1:00:00
SET Start of Daylight Savings Time = (MARCH SUNDAY LAST 2:00:00 AM)
SET End Of Daylight Savings Time = (OCTOBER SUNDAY LAST 3:00:00 AM)
SET Time Zone = CET=1CEST

# Note:The Time zone information mentioned above
# should always precede the SERVER name.

# search path settings for the NetWare kernel
SEARCH ADD SYS:\JAVA\BIN
SEARCH ADD SYS:\JAVA\NWGFX\BIN
SEARCH ADD SYS:\JAVA\NJCLV2\BIN
# WARNING!!
FILE SERVER NAME DA2
#WARNING!!
# If you change the name of this server, you must update
# the server name in all the licenses that are assigned
# to it using iManager

# load the traditional loggin mechanism for NetWare
LOAD CONLOG -MAXIMUM=100
#activate the network card and related protocols
LOAD TCPIP
LOAD CE100B.LAN SLOT=3 FRAME=ETHERNET_II NAME=CE100B_1_EII
BIND IP CE100B_1_EII addr=192.168.0.11 mask=255.255.255.0 gate=192.168.0.1
MOUNT ALL
IPMINIT.NCF

# make the server manageable for Zen for Servers
SYS:\SYSTEM\NMA\NMA5.NCF
# start the Btrieve database that is needed for some internal services
BSTART.NCF
# load support for web-based management tools
# and necessary encryption
Load nile.nlm
Load httpstk.nlm /SSL /keyfile:"SSL CertificateIP"
LOAD PORTAL.NLM
LOAD NDSIMON.NLM
LOAD NICISDI.XLM
LOAD SASDFM.XLM
# -- Added by CIFS Install
```

```
CIFSSTRT.NCF
# -- End of CIFS Install
….
#RCONAG6.NLM is required by RConsoleJ
# support for legacy RConsoleJ remote control
LOAD RCONAG6 novell 2034 16800 2036
# start the GUI
STARTX
```

The NetWare Registry

When the server starts up, it reads its configuration from several settings. You can get an overview of these settings from MONITOR.NLM by choosing the Server Parameters option. Using these settings, an administrator can define how the server handles available memory, what parameters should be applied to the Directory services running on the server, and many other things. These settings are stored in the NetWare registry, which is read upon the loading of the server. To access an overview of all current settings in the NetWare registry, use the command **display environment**.

When you make a change to one of the settings, whether through MONITOR.NLM, Remote Manager, or any other way, this change is applied to the NetWare registry. (See Figure 5-5.) You can view all changes with the **display modified environment** command, which makes it much easier to find changes amongst the hundreds of settings used by your server. Perhaps you realize something is wrong with the settings on your server and you just want to return to the original environment. In that case, you can use the **reset environment** command to return the NetWare registry to its default settings.

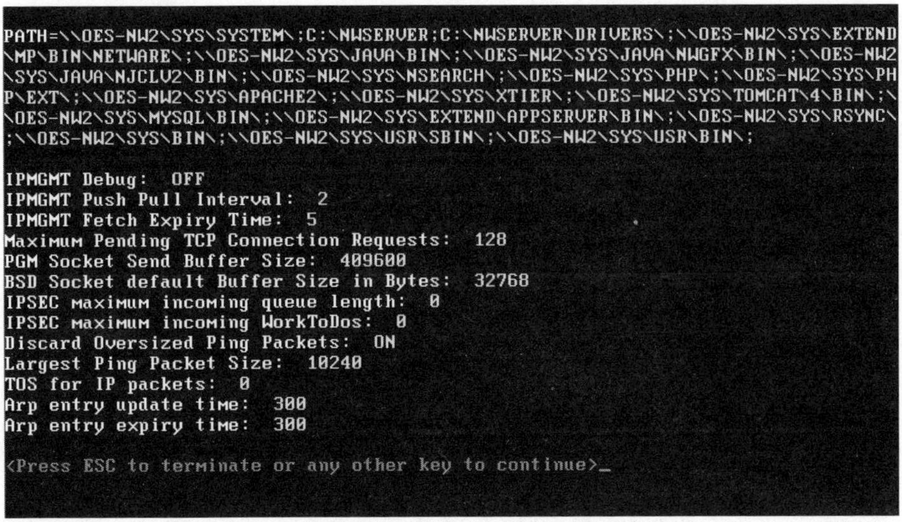

```
PATH=\\OES-NW2\SYS\SYSTEM\;C:\NWSERVER;C:\NWSERVER\DRIVERS\;\\OES-NW2\SYS\EXTEND
\MP\BIN\NETWARE\;\\OES-NW2\SYS\JAVA\BIN\;\\OES-NW2\SYS\JAVA\NWGFX\BIN\;\\OES-NW2
\SYS\JAVA\NJCLU2\BIN\;\\OES-NW2\SYS\NSEARCH\;\\OES-NW2\SYS\PHP\;\\OES-NW2\SYS\PH
P\EXT\;\\OES-NW2\SYS\APACHE2\;\\OES-NW2\SYS\XTIER\;\\OES-NW2\SYS\TOMCAT\4\BIN\;\
\OES-NW2\SYS\MYSQL\BIN\;\\OES-NW2\SYS\EXTEND\APPSERVER\BIN\;\\OES-NW2\SYS\RSYNC\
;\\OES-NW2\SYS\BIN\;\\OES-NW2\SYS\USR\SBIN\;\\OES-NW2\SYS\USR\BIN\;

IPMGMT Debug:  OFF
IPMGMT Push Pull Interval:  2
IPMGMT Fetch Expiry Time:  5
Maximum Pending TCP Connection Requests:  128
PGM Socket Send Buffer Size:  409600
BSD Socket default Buffer Size in Bytes:  32768
IPSEC maximum incoming queue length:  0
IPSEC maximum incoming WorkToDos:  0
Discard Oversized Ping Packets:  ON
Largest Ping Packet Size:  10240
TOS for IP packets:  0
Arp entry update time:  300
Arp entry expiry time:  300

<Press ESC to terminate or any other key to continue>_
```

Figure 5-5. *The server settings are kept in the NetWare registry.*

Console Commands

If you need to work from the server console—and sooner or later you will have to—you need to know some commands that can be used on the console. In most cases, these are external commands that refer to a file stored somewhere on your server. Your server uses a search path to find these commands. You can query the current search path by using the **SEARCH** command on the console of your server. (See Figure 5-6.)

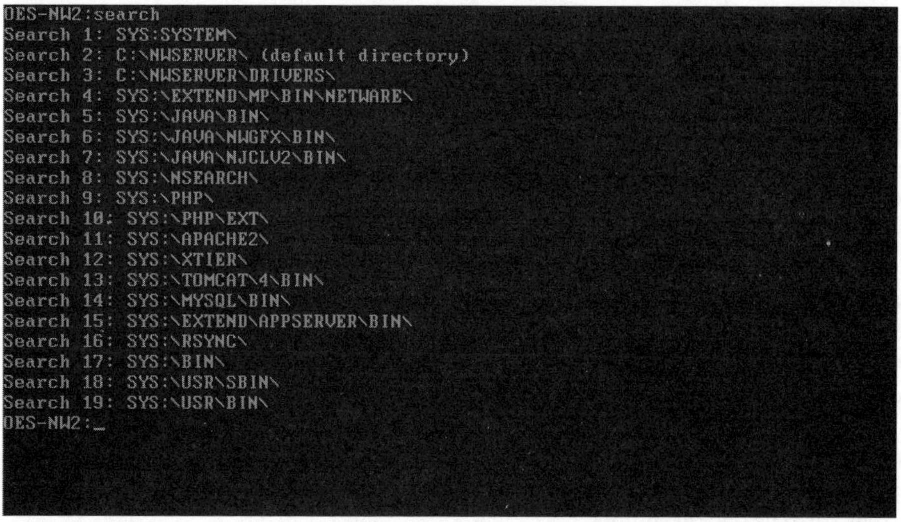

```
OES-NW2:search
Search 1: SYS:SYSTEM\
Search 2: C:\NWSERVER\ (default directory)
Search 3: C:\NWSERVER\DRIVERS\
Search 4: SYS:\EXTEND\MP\BIN\NETWARE\
Search 5: SYS:\JAVA\BIN\
Search 6: SYS:\JAVA\NWGFX\BIN\
Search 7: SYS:\JAVA\NJCLV2\BIN\
Search 8: SYS:\NSEARCH\
Search 9: SYS:\PHP\
Search 10: SYS:\PHP\EXT\
Search 11: SYS:\APACHE2\
Search 12: SYS:\XTIER\
Search 13: SYS:\TOMCAT\4\BIN\
Search 14: SYS:\MYSQL\BIN\
Search 15: SYS:\EXTEND\APPSERVER\BIN\
Search 16: SYS:\RSYNC\
Search 17: SYS:\BIN\
Search 18: SYS:\USR\SBIN\
Search 19: SYS:\USR\BIN\
OES-NW2:_
```

Figure 5-6. *You can use SEARCH to get an overview of all search paths in use on the server.*

It is also possible to add your own search paths. Use **SEARCH ADD**, followed by the complete path to the directory you want to include in the search path. The previous example of AUTOEXEC.NCF displays some examples of this command. Table 5-1 offers examples of some common console commands.

Table 5-1. *Common NetWare Commands*

Command	Description
BIND	Is used to bind information about a protocol to a network board. For example, **BIND IP CNEAMD_1_EII addr=192.168.0.102 mask=255.255.255.0 gate=192.168.0.1** can be used to specify the IP configuration for network board CNEADM_1_EII.
BROADCAST	This command can be used to send a message to all users who currently have a connection to the server.
CONFIG	Displays information about your server's configuration. You can use it to display the IP address in use, or the name of the current eDirectory tree and context.
DISMOUNT	Use **DISMOUNT** to deactivate a volume that is currently active. You should only perform this command if you are sure that there are no files in use on the volume.

Command	Description
DISPLAY SERVERS	Can be used in an IPX environment to display a list of all servers using IPX. In Open Enterprise Server, IPX normally isn't used.
DISPLAY SLP SERVICES	Gives an overview of all services available on your network. This command displays a list of all servers in the network as well.
DOWN	Use this command to shut down your server.
INETCFG	Loads the NLM that can be used to configure the protocols on your server.
LIST DEVICES	Gives an overview of all storage devices currently in use on your server.
SCAN FOR NEW DEVICES	Looks for new storage devices on your server. Use this command to initialize devices that haven't been initialized properly to the operating system before.
MEMORY	Displays the total amount of RAM available on your server.
MODULES	Shows a list of all NLMs currently loaded on your server.
HELP	Displays a list of all commands that can be used on the server console. Use this command to display usage information for the selected command.
MOUNT	Use this command to activate a volume. Normally, this is done automatically from AUTOEXEC.NCF with the command **mount** all. A volume can be mounted manually by using **mount** *volumename:*. Don't forget the colon after the name of the volume, or else the command won't work.
PROTOCOL	Displays a list of all protocols in use on your server.
RESET SERVER	Can be used to perform a cold restart of your server.
RESTART SERVER	Use this command to reload the NetWare kernel.
SEARCH	Displays a list of the current search path in use on your server.
SPEED	Displays the relative speed of your server's CPU.
TIME	Displays the time and date on your server. Also shows if the time is properly synchronized with the time on other servers.
VERSION	Displays the NetWare version in use, the support pack currently installed, and for how many users a connection license is installed.
VOLUMES	Shows a list of all volumes currently mounted.

Creating Batch Files

If you are using the Bash-shell on OES - Linux or OES - NetWare, you can write Bash shell scripts. It is possible as well to write simple shell scripts for the NetWare shell. There are no advanced possibilities to work with; a NetWare shell script is just a list of commands that have to be performed sequentially. You are already familiar with two default shell scripts on a NetWare server: STARTUP.NCF and AUTOEXEC.NCF. If you want to create your own shell script, just create a file with the extension .NCF and put all necessary commands in it. If you want to create your own NetWare shell scripts, you must obey two rules:

- All NetWare shell scripts must have the extension .NCF.
- You can only use commands that are understood by the NetWare kernel. These are commands like those listed previously. Don't try to use any Linux or DOS commands, or commands which can only be issued from a NetWare client that has a connection to a NetWare server.

To create your own shell scripts, you can use EDIT.NLM on the console of your server. Alternatively, the Edit AUTOEXEC.NCF File and Edit STARTUP.NCF File options from NWCONFIG.NLM can be used. (See Figure 5-7.)

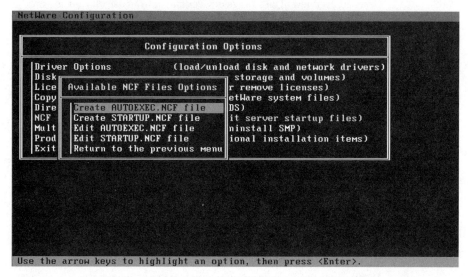

Figure 5-7. *You can edit STARTUP.NCF and AUTOEXEC.NCF from NWCONFIG.NLM.*

Alternatives to the NetWare Console

If you are working on OES - NetWare and you don't like the NetWare console, some alternatives are available.

NSNSHELL

The first alternative to using the NetWare console is the NSNSHELL. With NSNSHELL, you can open a DOS-like shell that offers more possibilities, especially regarding file management. The number of commands that can be used is limited, but that doesn't make the tool less useful. As an example, the following explains how to copy an NLM from a floppy disk to the directory SYS:SYSTEM on your server.

1. Use the command **nsninit** to initialize support for the Novell scripting environment.

2. Type **nsnshell** to start the Novell Script for NetWare shell environment. This is, in fact, a basic environment—meaning that all scripts available are written in basic.

3. Use the command **cd \Nsn\UTIL**. Here, you'll find many basic scripts with the same names as your favorite DOS commands.

4. To copy the file NW5-IDLE.NLM from a diskette to the directory SYS:SYSTEM on your server, use the command **copy a:\nw5-idle.nlm sys:\system\nw5-idle.nlm**.

Still not convinced that the NSNSHELL is useful? Just start it and try some of the following programs.

- *userlist*: Displays a list of all current connections to your server.

- *screen*: Displays all active screens one after another in a loop.

- *netmon*: Shows a list of critical parameters on your server like activity in the file system and CPU utilization.

- *phaser*: No comments, just try it!

- *wordgame*: A word-guessing game that's included with your server software! (See Figure 5-8.)

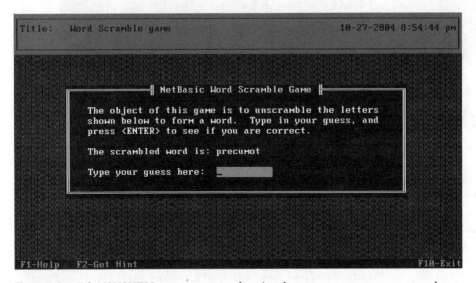

Figure 5-8. *With NSNSHELL, you can even play simple games on your server console.*

The Linux Bash Shell

As an alternative to the DOS-like shell that can be called from the NSNSHELL environment, OES - Netware includes the popular Linux bash shell as well. You can start it with the command **bash**. (See Figure 5-9.) Don't expect much from it, however. You certainly won't find a complete Linux environment. You will, however, find the most important Linux commands (programmed as NLMs) in the directory /bin. For these commands, even default Linux man functionality is available. So if you ever find yourself wondering what a particular command is for, just type it using the format **man** *command*.

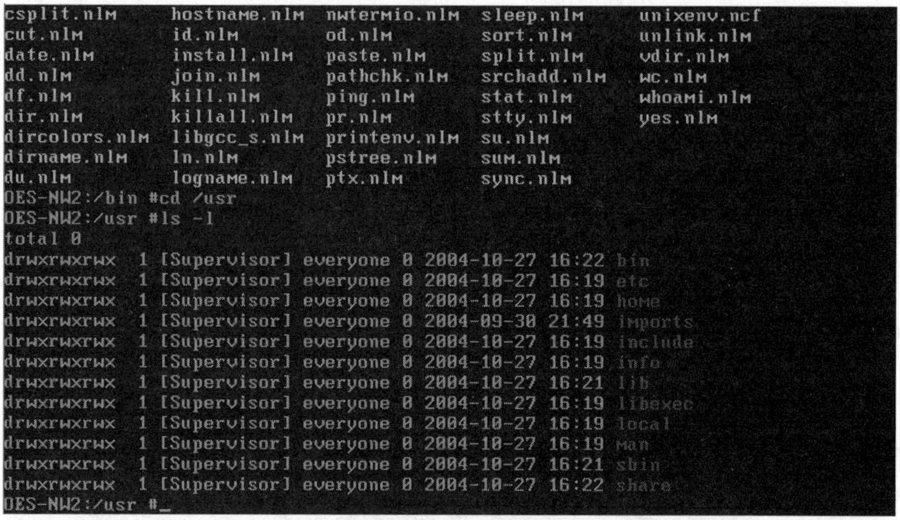

```
csplit.nlm       hostname.nlm    nwtermio.nlm    sleep.nlm       unixenv.ncf
cut.nlm          id.nlm          od.nlm          sort.nlm        unlink.nlm
date.nlm         install.nlm     paste.nlm       split.nlm       vdir.nlm
dd.nlm           join.nlm        pathchk.nlm     srchadd.nlm     wc.nlm
df.nlm           kill.nlm        ping.nlm        stat.nlm        whoami.nlm
dir.nlm          killall.nlm     pr.nlm          stty.nlm        yes.nlm
dircolors.nlm    libgcc_s.nlm    printenv.nlm    su.nlm
dirname.nlm      ln.nlm          pstree.nlm      sum.nlm
du.nlm           logname.nlm     ptx.nlm         sync.nlm
OES-NW2:/bin #cd /usr
OES-NW2:/usr #ls -l
total 0
drwxrwxrwx  1 [Supervisor] everyone 0 2004-10-27 16:22 bin
drwxrwxrwx  1 [Supervisor] everyone 0 2004-10-27 16:19 etc
drwxrwxrwx  1 [Supervisor] everyone 0 2004-10-27 16:19 home
drwxrwxrwx  1 [Supervisor] everyone 0 2004-09-30 21:49 imports
drwxrwxrwx  1 [Supervisor] everyone 0 2004-10-27 16:19 include
drwxrwxrwx  1 [Supervisor] everyone 0 2004-10-27 16:19 info
drwxrwxrwx  1 [Supervisor] everyone 0 2004-10-27 16:21 lib
drwxrwxrwx  1 [Supervisor] everyone 0 2004-10-27 16:19 libexec
drwxrwxrwx  1 [Supervisor] everyone 0 2004-10-27 16:19 local
drwxrwxrwx  1 [Supervisor] everyone 0 2004-10-27 16:19 man
drwxrwxrwx  1 [Supervisor] everyone 0 2004-10-27 16:21 sbin
drwxrwxrwx  1 [Supervisor] everyone 0 2004-10-27 16:22 share
OES-NW2:/usr #_
```

Figure 5-9. *OES - NetWare has a complete bash shell environment.*

Working from the Graphical User Interface

NetWare is managed traditionally from the console interface. Since NetWare 5.0, however, it also comes with a graphical user interface (GUI). This GUI is built on the X Windowing System, which is also the engine behind the graphical interface used on UNIX and Linux systems. Novell added a Java stack to the GUI since most of the programs that can be started from the GUI need Java, too. From the default GUI, it is possible to start several programs that have been provided with the GUI. (See Figure 5-10.)

After a default installation, the GUI is started automatically from AUTOEXEC.NCF when the command **startx** is added. If it isn't started automatically, you can always start it manually by issuing the command **startx**. If you ever need to unload it, use the **unload java** command.

Figure 5-10. *Many tasks can be performed from the NetWare GUI environment.*

The most important tools that can be used from the GUI are in the Novell menu, which you'll find at the bottom left of the interface. The taskbar also contains buttons that provide shortcuts to items in the Novell menu. The exact contents of the Novell menu depend on what exactly you have installed on your server. For instance, the exteNd Application Server option is only present if you have installed the application server as well. On top of the menu, you'll find two very useful programs: the server version of the management program ConsoleOne, and the Install utility, which can be used to install products and updates on your server.

ConsoleOne

One of the most useful programs you can start from the GUI on the server is ConsoleOne. Before it was replaced by iManager, ConsoleOne was the default management utility in earlier versions of NetWare. This utility is still present on the server. You can't completely manage your network with it, however, because some important snap-ins are missing, but it is possible to perform many network management tasks from it. (See Figure 5-11.) Before you can use this program on your server, you must authenticate the following:

1. Start ConsoleOne from the Novell menu.

2. Click NDS under My World. Next, select Authenticate from the File menu.

3. Enter your login name, password, tree, and context to authenticate.

4. Click Login. You will now be authenticated to your tree. You will find all trees you are authenticated on under NDS. Just click the tree name to see a list of all objects that exist immediately under the tree. If you want to manage one of these objects, click it with the right mouse button. This gives you a menu from which you can select any action you like.

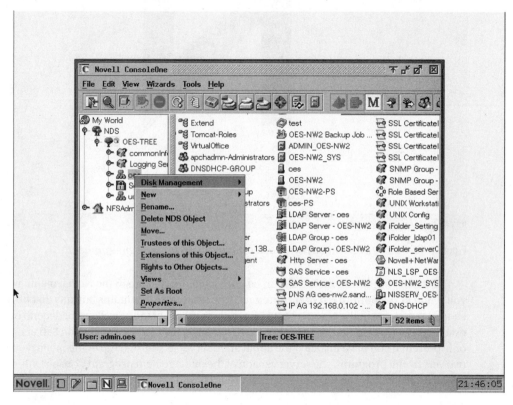

Figure 5-11. *In ConsoleOne, you can perform various basic network management tasks.*

■**Tip** ConsoleOne can be sluggish on the server. This is because it's rather resource-intensive and if your server has limited resources, it can slow things to a crawl. In such cases, it's recommended you don't use it. Instead, use iManager on a workstation to perform the necessary network management tasks.

Install

The other important tool you'll find in the Novell menu is the Install utility. Use it if you need to install additional products on your server, or if you want to install the latest support pack. When you activate this utility, it shows you a list of all products currently installed. You can use **Add** to add anything to that list. (See Figure 5-12.)

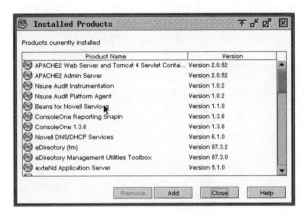

Figure 5-12. *The Install utility displays a list of all products currently installed on your server.*

If, for example, you want to install the latest support pack on your server, you need to perform the following procedure.

1. Activate the Install module from the Novell menu on your server.

2. Insert the installation medium for the product you want to install, and click Add.

3. You will now see a window in which you can specify where to install the product. On the medium, browse to the install script or response file. They will be recognized automatically by the installer.

4. Click OK after locating the install file. This starts the installation procedure for the product you have selected. The next procedure will be different, depending on the selections you have made.

Utilities

From the GUI console, you can access other important utilities as well. You'll find them in the menu option Utilities in the Novell menu.

Console Log

The utility Console Log can be used to access the log files created on your server by CONLOG.NLM. This nice little utility shows you a log of all important messages that have appeared on your OES - NetWare server. Your NetWare server has two screens that display log messages: the Console screen and the Logger screen. You'll find options to activate the log for both of these screens in the Screens menu of the Console Log Window. Not impressed by the power of CONLOG.NLM? Then I have good news for you. There is also a SYSLOGD.NLM file for NetWare which can be configured to do more extensive logging on the network. Unfortunately, you can't monitor this information with the Console Log utility. (See Figure 5-13.)

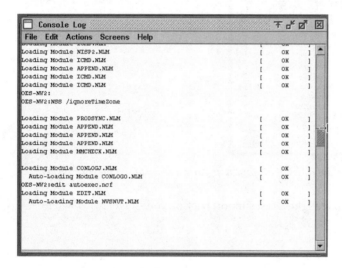

Figure 5-13. *The Console Log utility gives access to the information that is logged by CONLOG.NLM.*

Editor

Like Linux, NetWare contains many ASCII text files in which the configuration of programs is defined. On the server console, you can use EDIT.NLM to edit them; there is a graphical equivalent for EDIT.NLM from the GUI. This utility is self-explanatory. If you've ever worked with an editor before, you'll have no problem with it. (See Figure 5-14.)

Figure 5-14. *The OES - NetWare GUI comes with a simple and intuitive ASCII editor.*

Tip So you don't like fancy editors, preferring instead the basic thing? Good news for you! vim, the improved version of vi, is also available on OES - NetWare! You can start it by typing **vi** from the Bash shell environment.

File Browser

When managing your server, quite often you'll feel the need to do some simple file administration. With the File Browser utility you can manage files on NetWare volumes and on the DOS partition or floppy drive of your server as well! (See Figure 5-15.) Right-click a file displayed with the file manager and you'll instantly see all the options available for that file. It's not the most advanced file management utility around, but it is enough to perform basic file management tasks, such as removing, replacing, or renaming a file. It even gives you the possibility to modify the file's attributes.

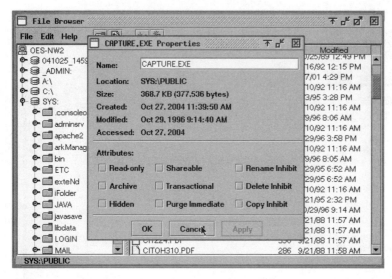

Figure 5-15. *With File Browser, you can perform basic file management tasks.*

NetWare Remote Manager

One of the most powerful management utilities available for both editions of Open Enterprise Server is Remote Manager. This browser-based utility can be used to perform management tasks on many settings of your server. More in-depth information about this tool can be found in Chapter 7. After you start it on your server, it will probably generate a security alert about the certificate used. Since this is a local connection, click Always to accept the certificate for all future connections. Next, you'll see a login prompt.

After logging in successfully, you'll have access to Remote Manager. Take special notice of the upper-left corner. Here you'll see an icon symbolizing your file server. If it's healthy, it'll display a green traffic light. If, however, there's a problem with the server, a red stop-signlike light will display. Click the stop sign to find out what's wrong with your server. It should give you an overview of all important parameters, with a green sign next to each parameter that's okay, and a red sign next to those where something is wrong. (See Figure 5-16.) You'll also have the opportunity to modify the parameter directly; just click it to configure its new settings.

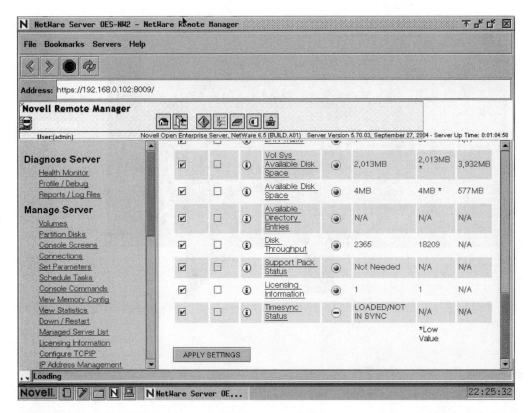

Figure 5-16. *With Remote Manager, you'll quickly see which parameters are misconfigured on your server.*

Server Console

From the GUI environment, use the key combination Alt+Esc to activate your console screen. If, however, you're working in the GUI, it can be very cumbersome to switch between screens all the time. For this reason, there is the Server Console utility. It opens a NetWare console window on your GUI that lets you easily switch between the different screens active on your server. (See Figure 5-17.)

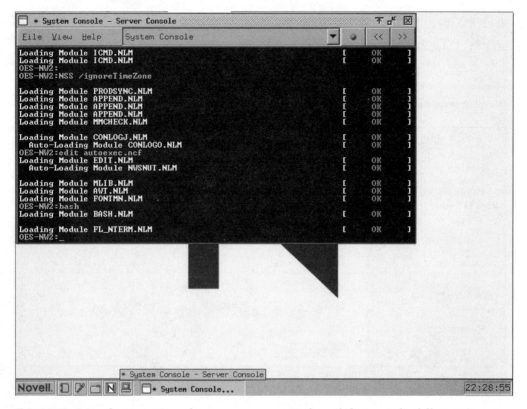

Figure 5-17. *From the Server Console screen, you can switch easily between the different screens that are active on your server.*

Settings

In the Settings menu in your GUI, you'll find options that control the appearance of your server. You can change any aspect of the GUI, such as the active background, hardware settings, and the contents of the Novell menu. If you don't like the default background of your server, change it with the Background option. Using this option, you can designate any BMP, JPG, or GIF image to be used as the background for your server. To do so, follow these steps:

1. Save your favorite graphics file in a format that is supported by your server. (Just want to be sure that it works? Then save it as an 8-bit file with a low resolution.)

2. Copy the file to some location on your server.

3. From the Novell menu, choose Settings ➤ Background. Then click the Background Image tab.

4. Use the Browse button to browse to the location where you saved your image.

5. Select the image and click Test to see if you like it. If you do like it, click OK to save and apply the new background.

Another important item you'll find in the Settings menu, is the option to change the properties of your graphics card and monitor. These settings can be found in Settings ➤ GUI Environment. Here you'll find five tabs on which to tune your graphical environment. (See Figure 5-18.)

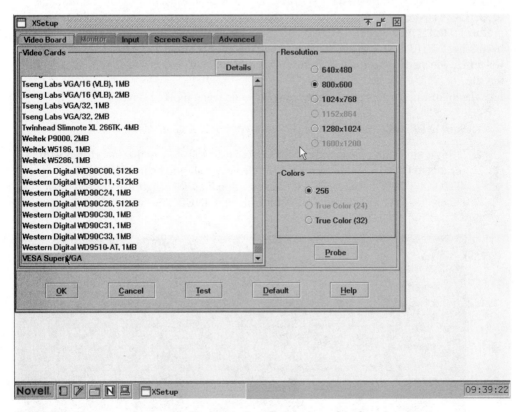

Figure 5-18. *It's easy to change the display settings for your graphical environment.*

Some Important Management Programs

Your OES - NetWare server has a lot of graphical management possibilities whether from the server itself or remotely from a browser-based program. On the server console are some useful classic NetWare management tools. They're powerful and fast and can be found on any NetWare version after NetWare 4.0. This section introduces the most famous blue-screen management tools: INETCFG.NLM, which can be used to make all possible protocol settings for your server; MONITOR.NLM, useful in tuning server parameters; and DSREPAIR.NLM, an invaluable aid in troubleshooting the eDirectory database on your server.

INETCFG

If you want to configure advanced protocol settings on OES - NetWare, INETCFG.NLM is the place to be. Even for a simple task like changing your IP address, it is recommended to use INETCFG. The reason for this is simple: with INETCFG you have all the relevant settings at hand.

When you start work with INETCFG.NLM, the first thing it does is remove all protocol settings from AUTOEXEC.NCF and import them into INETCFG. You should be aware of that, because it also implies that you can't make any changes to your protocol settings after you work with INETCFG for the first time. INETCFG writes all settings to the configuration file SYS:ETC\NETINFO.CFG. Remember this name: if you ever have any serious problems with protocol settings managed by INETCFG, simply remove this file and re-create it automatically by running INETCFG.NLM again. Also, never edit this configuration file by hand. INETCFG.NLM will notice you've done so and will make it impossible to load your protocol settings again from this file.

The following is a short demo of what you can do using INETCFG.NLM:

1. Start INETCFG.NLM from your OES - NetWare server's console.

2. If this is your first time working with INETCFG, it will tell you that all settings with regards to LAN drivers, protocol, or remote access should be transferred from AUTOEXEC.NCF to the INETCFG configuration files. (See Figure 5-19.) You must choose Yes to be able to continue your work with INETCFG.

Figure 5-19. *Before starting work with INETCFG, all protocol settings must be transferred from AUTOEXEC.NCF to INETCFG configuration files.*

3. After transferring your settings to INETCFG, restart your server. Choose Yes to exit INETCFG and restart your server.

4. When your server has finished reloading, activate INETCFG again. It will ask you if you want to use fast setup, or work with the standard method. Using the standard method is best. It gives you a better overview of all available options. (See Figure 5-20.)

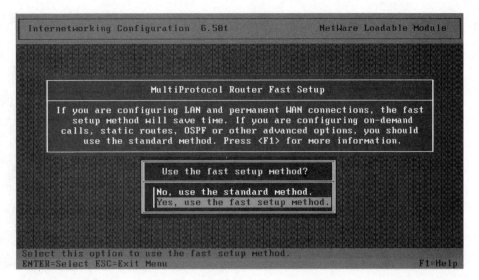

Figure 5-20. *If asked how you want to use INETCFG, choose the standard setup method.*

5. You'll now see a menu in which you can manage all properties of your network interfaces. INETCFG can be used to configure local network interfaces as well as WAN-interfaces. For management of local interfaces, the following options are most interesting:

   • Boards

   • Protocols

   • Bindings

   The Reinitialize System option is also indispensable. To activate these changes, you must select it each time you make changes to the INETCFG configuration.

6. In the Boards menu is a list of all network interfaces in your server. You can use this option if you want to install a new network board. You can also use it to temporarily change the status of a network card: if you want to disable a network card temporarily, just press the Tab key. You can also edit the properties of the network card from this menu, say, if you need to change the speed or duplex mode of the network card.

7. The next interesting submenu is Protocols. Here you specify what protocols you want to use. Normally, you'll find that only TCP/IP is enabled. If, for backward compatibility, you need to enable another protocol like IPX, you can do it here. After selecting a protocol and pressing Enter, a menu with advanced protocol settings will be displayed. If you select TCP/IP and press Enter, you'll see a list of all TCP/IP properties. (See Figure 5-21.) In this list, you can specify how your server will be routing, which DNS server should be used for name resolving, and many other tasks.

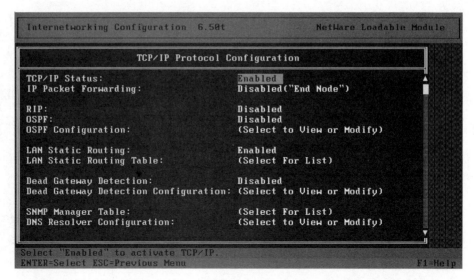

```
Internetworking Configuration  6.50t                    NetWare Loadable Module

                        TCP/IP Protocol Configuration

TCP/IP Status:                          Enabled
IP Packet Forwarding:                   Disabled("End Node")

RIP:                                    Disabled
OSPF:                                   Disabled
OSPF Configuration:                     (Select to View or Modify)

LAN Static Routing:                     Enabled
LAN Static Routing Table:               (Select For List)

Dead Gateway Detection:                 Disabled
Dead Gateway Detection Configuration:   (Select to View or Modify)

SNMP Manager Table:                     (Select For List)
DNS Resolver Configuration:             (Select to View or Modify)


Select "Enabled" to activate TCP/IP.
ENTER=Select ESC=Previous Menu                                       F1=Help
```

Figure 5-21. *In the Protocols menu, you'll be able to specify advanced TCP/IP options.*

8. The next important item is the Bindings option. Here, you'll find the binding of protocols to your network card. This is the place to go if you want to change the IP address used by one of your network cards. In the properties of a network card, you'll also find advanced options, such as the option to enable Network Address Translation (NAT) on one of the interfaces.

9. When you've finished making changes in TCP/IP, you need to apply them. To do this, select the Reinitialize System option from the Internetworking Configuration menu. This activates the changes immediately.

Monitor

With the coming of web-based administration utilities like Remote Manager, MONITOR.NLM has become less important than it used to be. Because it still exists and is a good tool for monitoring the health of your server, it's necessary to discuss some of the options it offers. After starting MONITOR.NLM, it immediately presents you with a slew of information, which, through interpretation, gives you a clear picture of your server's well-being at a particular moment. (See Figure 5-22.) For example, it displays the load on your server's CPU as well as details on how its memory is currently utilized. In the different MONITOR menus, options are available to fine-tune your server's behavior.

To interpret MONITOR.NLM the proper way, you need to be familiar with the inner workings of your server. It's not the goal of this book to cover this. In fact, there are other and better books that can help. Instead, the focus of this discussion will be the most important parameters that can be tuned from MONITOR.NLM, such as the following:

- Original cache buffers

- Total cache buffers

- Packet receive buffers

- Current service processes

If you know how these parameters are used, you can fine-tune the health of your server.

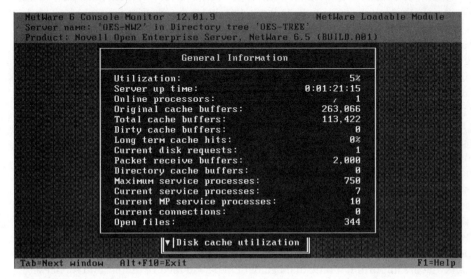

```
NetWare 6 Console Monitor  12.01.9              NetWare Loadable Module
Server name: 'OES-NW2' in Directory tree 'OES-TREE'
Product: Novell Open Enterprise Server, NetWare 6.5 (BUILD.A01)

                        ┌──────────────────────────────────┐
                        │        General Information        │
                        │                                   │
                        │  Utilization:                 5%  │
                        │  Server up time:        0:01:21:15│
                        │  Online processors:          / 1  │
                        │  Original cache buffers:  263,066 │
                        │  Total cache buffers:     113,422 │
                        │  Dirty cache buffers:          0  │
                        │  Long term cache hits:        0%  │
                        │  Current disk requests:        1  │
                        │  Packet receive buffers:   2,000  │
                        │  Directory cache buffers:      0  │
                        │  Maximum service processes:  750  │
                        │  Current service processes:    7  │
                        │  Current MP service processes: 10 │
                        │  Current connections:          0  │
                        │  Open files:                 344  │
                        └──────────────────────────────────┘
                        ║▼│Disk cache utilization ║
Tab=Next window   Alt+F10=Exit                              F1=Help
```

Figure 5-22. *Use MONITOR.NLM to check the health of your server and fine-tune its behavior.*

Original Cache Buffers and Total Cache Buffers

One of the important tasks of a server is to save frequently used data in RAM. This process is called caching. The advantage of caching is that data can be used directly from your server's RAM and doesn't have to be copied from your server's hard drive first. Since RAM on a server is much faster than the speed of a hard drive, the speed of a server can be increased enormously if an efficient caching algorithm is used. The MONITOR parameters Original Cache Buffers and Total Cache Buffers give an indication of the availability of cache buffers on your server.

First, there is the parameter Original Cache Buffers, which indicates how much cache was available just after the server was started and the NetWare kernel was loaded. With the parameter Total Cache Buffers, you can see how much memory is still available for caching at this moment. The available memory can be used for several different things: it can be used to cache files, but it can also be used to provide memory that is needed to load new NLMs on your server. To determine whether or not your server has enough available memory, use these two general rules:

- If less than 20 percent of the total memory is available for caching, more memory needs to be added.

- On an average server, about 50 percent of the server's RAM must be available for caching. The exact amount of memory available for caching, however, depends on server usage.

Packet Receive Buffers and Service Processes

Two parameters closely related to each other are the settings for packet receive buffers and service processes. A packet receive buffer is a buffer in your server's RAM that is reserved for incoming packets. These buffers are very important: they are the waiting room for those packets entering via your server. You must always have enough of these buffers, but you should also take care never to have too much of them, because a server that has too many unused packet receive buffers is wasting precious resources.

At the moment a packet comes in on the network card of a server, there must be a packet receive buffer available. If there isn't, the incoming packet is dropped and must be sent again. If this happens too much, it can lead to congestion on the network. If, on the other hand, you have too many allocated packet receive buffers, these unused buffers can't be used for the caching of files, and that's bad as well.

Closely related to the packet receive buffers are the service processes. These handle all incoming packets from the packet receive buffers. It may be clear that if you haven't enough service processes, packets are waiting too long in the packet receive buffers. It may, however, appear that there is no possibility to allocate new service processes, because your server is overloaded. Every service process needs time on the server's CPU to do its work, and if this CPU's utilization is up to 100 percent, there's no more room for new service processes. In short, it's a chain you have to monitor. In order for these two parameters to work efficiently for your server, you as an administrator must set the minimum and maximum value for these options. The minimum value determines how many must always be available, while the maximum value is used to specify the maximum amount that can be allocated automatically. If you have a problem with these two parameters, adjust the minimum and maximum setting for a better server performance. To do so, use the SET parameters. Table 5-2 offers an overview of five SET parameters that are important for the management of packet receive buffers and services processes. You can set these parameters by hand from the server console, as well as set them from Remote Manager or MONITOR.NLM.

Table 5-2. *Common Set Parameters*

Parameter	Modify if
SET MINIMUM SERVICE PROCESSES	It appears that the server always uses a large number of service processes. Set the minimum amount of service processes to 50% of the average number of service processes in use. The advantage of a higher amount of service processes is that they don't have to be allocated dynamically, which saves server resources.
SET MAXIMUM SERVICE PROCESS	If the CPU is not overloaded, but the packet receive buffers on your server are filling up quickly.
SET MINIMUM PACKET RECEIVE BUFFERS	The average number of package receive buffers is much higher than the minimum assigned with this parameter.

Parameter	Modify if
SET MAXIMUM PACKET RECEIVE BUFFERS	The number of packet receive buffers allocated is the same or almost the same as the maximum number of packet receive buffers allocated with this parameter, leaving some service processes still available.
SET MAXIMUM PHYSICAL RECEIVE PACKET SIZE	This parameter should be set to 1514 if your server is on an Ethernet network.

It is easy to modify these parameters. If you just enter the complete set parameter on the server console, it shows you in yellow the current value assigned to the parameter. It also displays the minimum and maximum value for the parameter. Now, choose a value that's reasonable for your server. If, for example, you want to raise the minimum amount of service processes, just type **set minimum service processes = 200**. The new setting will be written to the NetWare registry, and in this case, will be available immediately. Since the setting is also written to the NetWare registry, it loads automatically after your server restarts.

You'll also notice that some parameters aren't effective immediately. Some settings can only be applied when your server is booting. This is true for the setting **set maximum physical receive packet size**. This parameter specifies how large a packet receive buffer must be. Since it's a physical block in memory, a packet receive buffer can only be set on system startup. In the default parameter, Novell sets a size for the biggest possible packet that can arrive on a LAN. These are Token Ring packets that can have a maximum size of 4224 bytes. On an Ethernet network, however, no packets larger than 1514 bytes can be sent. With the default setting, about 2.5KB is wasted for each allocated packet receive buffer. With a minimum of 2000 packet receive buffers, this means about 5MB of RAM is wasted this way. It's easy to modify your server environment to change this. You can, however, only change it in STARTUP.NCF, as described in the following steps.

1. On your server's console, enter the command **edit c:startup.ncf**.

2. Append the line **set maximum physical receive packet size = 1514**.

3. Press Esc to close EDIT.NLM. Select Yes to save your changes. The next time you restart your server, the setting will be applied automatically.

DSREPAIR

The last utility to discuss is DSREPAIR.NLM. With this NLM, you can repair almost any aspect of the eDirectory database on your server in case you are having problems. The most important thing you should know about this program is that it's dangerous. Never just try the options in this program; you may only make your problems much worse. (See Figure 5-23.) In order to use DSREPAIR the right way, you should be fluent in eDirectory troubleshooting. It has three options that can be used without harm:

- Unattended full repair

- Time synchronization

- Report synchronization status

■**Tip** This chapter includes only a short introduction on the things you can do with DSREPAIR. More about the working of eDirectory and how to repair it using the advanced browser-based utility iMonitor can be found in Chapter 8 of this book.

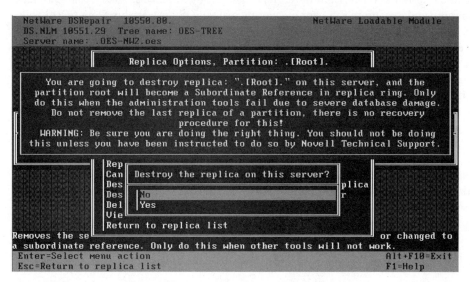

Figure 5-23. *If not used properly, DSREPAIR.NLM can prove deadly to your eDirectory database.*

The first option that can be used without harm is Report Synchronization Status. This option offers an overview of the current synchronization status of your database. (See Figure 5-24.) With it, you can check if all servers in the network are capable to communicate changes the proper way amongst each other. If there is something wrong, in many cases an error code will be displayed. If nothing is wrong, the report will show this as well. If you get an error message, you can try to find the meaning of it in the knowledgebase at support.novell.com. It's recommended you don't experiment with this option by yourself. Instead, see an expert on eDirectory and ask how he can help you resolve this problem.

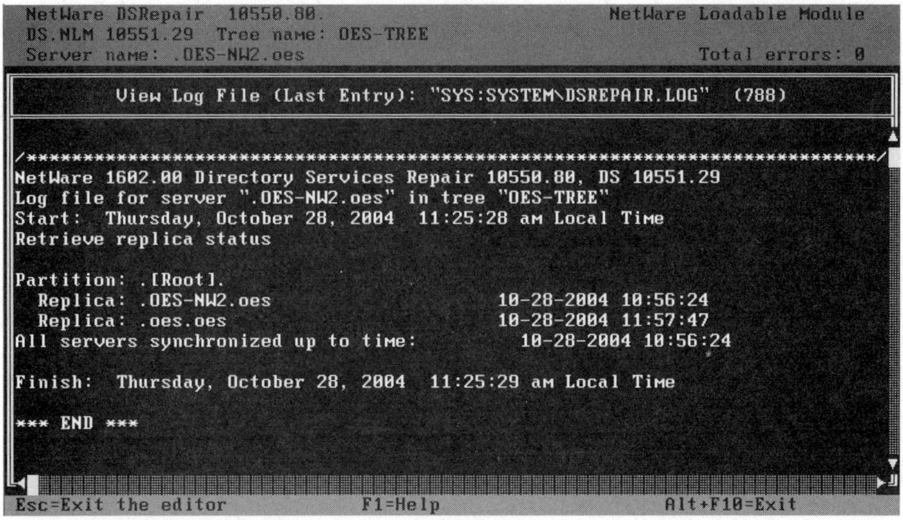

```
NetWare DSRepair  10550.80.                     NetWare Loadable Module
DS.NLM 10551.29  Tree name: OES-TREE
Server name: .OES-NW2.oes                            Total errors: 0
╔══════════════════════════════════════════════════════════════════════╗
║        View Log File (Last Entry): "SYS:SYSTEM\DSREPAIR.LOG"   (788)  ║
╠══════════════════════════════════════════════════════════════════════╣
║                                                                       ▲
║/*********************************************************************/  
║NetWare 1602.00 Directory Services Repair 10550.80, DS 10551.29        
║Log file for server ".OES-NW2.oes" in tree "OES-TREE"                  
║Start:   Thursday, October 28, 2004  11:25:28 am Local Time            
║Retrieve replica status                                                
║                                                                       
║Partition: .[Root].                                                    
║  Replica: .OES-NW2.oes              10-28-2004 10:56:24               
║  Replica: .oes.oes                  10-28-2004 11:57:47               
║All servers synchronized up to time:         10-28-2004 10:56:24       
║                                                                       
║Finish:  Thursday, October 28, 2004  11:25:29 am Local Time            
║                                                                       
║*** END ***                                                            ▼
Esc=Exit the editor          F1=Help              Alt+F10=Exit
```

Figure 5-24. *With DSREPAIR, you can generate a quick overview of all current errors in your eDirectory database.*

The second important option is Time Synchronization. This option let's you verify that the time is properly synchronized amongst the servers in your network. The important thing to look for with this option is whether in the **Time is in sync** column you see Yes behind each server. For proper eDirectory synchronization, it's important that all servers share a common time. (See Figure 5-25.) If for any reason the time on your server is not synchronized, you can try the command **set timesync restart flag = on** on the console of your server. This non-destructive command lets the server try to synchronize its time immediately.

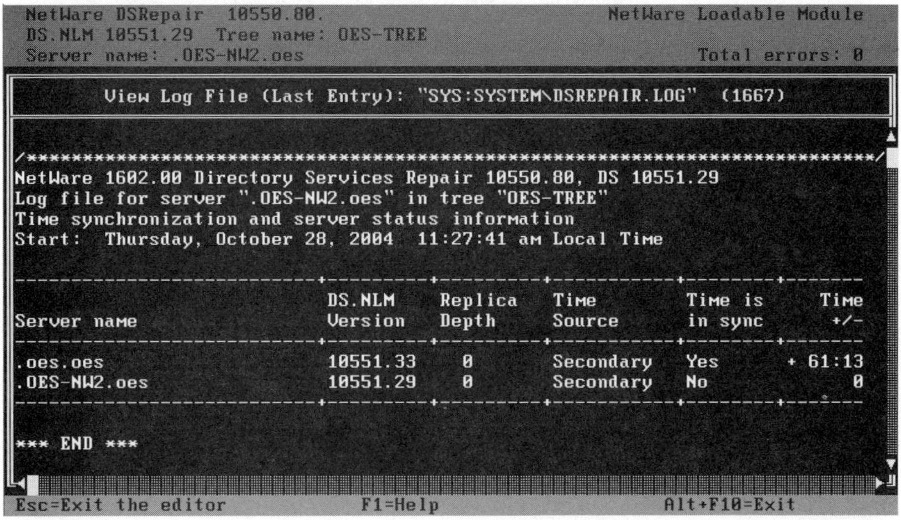

```
NetWare DSRepair  10550.80.                     NetWare Loadable Module
DS.NLM 10551.29  Tree name: OES-TREE
Server name: .OES-NW2.oes                            Total errors: 0
╔══════════════════════════════════════════════════════════════════════╗
║        View Log File (Last Entry): "SYS:SYSTEM\DSREPAIR.LOG"  (1667)  ║
╠══════════════════════════════════════════════════════════════════════╣
║                                                                       ▲
║/*********************************************************************/  
║NetWare 1602.00 Directory Services Repair 10550.80, DS 10551.29        
║Log file for server ".OES-NW2.oes" in tree "OES-TREE"                  
║Time synchronization and server status information                     
║Start:   Thursday, October 28, 2004  11:27:41 am Local Time            
║                                                                       
║------------------------+--------+--------+---------+---------+--------
║                        | DS.NLM |Replica | Time    | Time is | Time  
║Server name             |Version | Depth  | Source  | in sync | +/-   
║------------------------+--------+--------+---------+---------+--------
║.oes.oes                |10551.33|   0    |Secondary| Yes     | + 61:13
║.OES-NW2.oes            |10551.29|   0    |Secondary| No      |   0   
║------------------------+--------+--------+---------+---------+--------
║                                                                       
║*** END ***                                                            ▼
Esc=Exit the editor          F1=Help              Alt+F10=Exit
```

Figure 5-25. *For proper eDirectory synchronization, it's important that the time is synchronized on the network.*

If the DSREPAIR report option shows you that there is a problem with the local database, there is exactly one option you can try without harm to repair the problems. This is the **Unattended Full Repair** option found in the DSREPAIR main menu. This option attempts to repair everything that is wrong with the database and that can be repaired automatically. This option is non-destructive. It's best, however, to use this option only when there isn't too much activity on your network and when no more than a few users are logged in because it will temporarily lock the database so it can no longer be accessed by users. Chapter 8, which discusses eDirectory, offers more in-depth information on the subject.

Summary

This chapter discussed the NetWare console and its management possibilities. Several options were covered, such as traditional tools like MONITOR.NLM and other NLM modules, and also some new and more advanced tools like the Linux Bash shell on NetWare. In the next chapter, you'll read about the different ways a client can get connected to Open Enterprise Server.

CHAPTER 6

■■■

Connecting to Open Enterprise Server

Open Enterprise Server gives you freedom–freedom to use the server platform you want, but also freedom to connect to that server platform any way you wish. This chapter offers an overview of all the methods that can be used to connect to Open Enterprise Server, but most of it's dedicated to teaching you how to use the Novell Client software to connect to OES. Other methods for connecting to OES are discussed in their own separate chapters.

Making a Connection Any Way You Want It

In the early days of NetWare, there was only one way to access a NetWare server, and that was by installing Novell Client on the local operating system, which made the local operating system aware of the network. With Windows 95 and later, Microsoft furnished a client for NetWare networks as well. This client provided about the same functionality, but it was not able to communicate with more advanced services on the Novell server such as ZENworks or NDPS printing. As a result, the Novell Client software has always been considered the better choice of the two.

The necessity of using Novell Client hasn't always been appreciated by everyone. The first reason is because Novell Client is rather huge (it requires about 30MB to be installed) and there was a time when it required updating frequently. In addition, you couldn't use Novell Client to access the network from every available PC. Because of this, Novell developed some other methods for accessing the network, such as the following.

- Native File Access Protocols

- Web-based access

- Client programs for specific services

The following sections introduce and explain all four connection methods.

Native File Access Protocols

With NetWare 6.0, Novell implemented Native File Access protocols (NFAPs). These protocols implement a native protocol stack for Apple, Windows, and UNIX clients by means of an AFP server, the Samba server in a NetWare version, and an NFS server. On all these servers running on NetWare 6.0 and later, users can log in with their eDirectory username, using the file access protocols that are native to their local workstation. However, because the password used in a Native File Access scenario is a password encrypted in the Windows, Apple, or UNIX way, this password encryption is not compatible with the eDirectory password. For that reason, Novell originally implemented the "simple password," which was replaced in NetWare 6.5 by the universal password. Native File Access is useful if a user only requires file access. However, for access to other advanced Novell services such as, say, ZENworks, Native File Access isn't an appropriate solution. Chapter 10 has more on Native File Access Protocols. The different passwords that can be used in a Novell environment are handled in Chapter 9.

Web-Based Access

In a world where users need to work from everywhere, the concept of a client installed on the local computer is not ideal. What if a user wants to access his data on the network using a computer in an Internet café or in a hotel lobby? There's no chance of installing a client on that computer! For situations like this, Novell developed Virtual Office. Virtual Office is a complete user environment where users can access all important resources from a web portal. Files are used via the NetStorage component or iFolder, printers are accessed with iPrint, access to the user's mail box can be integrated, and there's even an option to run applications from the Virtual Office environment if Novell ZENworks is integrated. Besides all that, the user has the option to create his own virtual teams in order to work with co-workers in the most efficient way available. (Chapter 17 has more on Virtual Office.)

Specific Client Programs

Some of the services used in an Open Enterprise Server environment have their own client application that must be installed. The file synchronization server iFolder, for example, has its own lightweight client that must be available from the local workstation; iPrint also has a client that needs to be installed on the local workstation in order to access printers with iPrint and install their drivers locally on the workstation. You can read more about iFolder and its client in Chapter 10; iPrint and its client are covered in Chapter 15.

Novell Client

Lastly, Novell Client can be used as a native way to access resources on the Novell network. Originally, Novell Client was developed to contact the NCP server (see Chapter 10) to access resources on the Novell network. In the latest client versions however, Novell Client can be used to authenticate to the Novell network. Once this authentication has been completed, it can be used to access any shared files on the network, even if these files are shared by means of one of the Native File Access protocols used on either OES - Linux or OES - NetWare. Novell Client is available for three client platforms: Windows, Macintosh, and Linux. More details about the use and configuration of Novell Client can be found in the next section.

■Note At the time of writing, Novell Client for Linux was still in its earliest development phase. For that reason, most examples in this chapter will be based upon Novell Client for Windows. If it's known that something is handled differently in Client for Linux, I'll note this as we go.

Using Novell Client

You can download the latest version of Novell Client from http://download.novell.com. This section explains how to install Novell Client, while those following discuss how to manage and use it.

Installing Novell Client

The following options are available after downloading the Novell Client files.

- Run **setupnw** locally on the workstation to perform a local installation of Novell Client.

- Run **setupnw /u** to run an unattended installation of the Novell Client software. To use this type of installation, an unattended file must be created with the nciman utility.

- Run **setupnw /acu** from a login script to automatically upgrade Client if so required. The /acu utility compares the current version of Client with the new Client version that's available. To automate client installation, the /acu option can be combined with the /u option.

- Run setupsp.exe to install a support pack to your current Novell Client version.

- Use setupip.exe to perform an installation of Novell Client from a web server. The administrator can use the writeip.exe utility to generate a setupip.exe file for his users.

- To update Novell Client, run the Client Update Agent, cuagent.exe, from a login script, or do so manually from the Red N in the task bar of the computer where Client is installed. This is an alternative to the /acu option, where the update is performed automatically.

Of these options, the two used most often are the unattended installation, combined with the /acu switch, and the manual installation on a workstation (the first and third bullets from the previous list). The advantage of using an unattended installation is that it allows you to install the Client software automatically on your users' computers. The other options are employed only rarely. Therefore, they're not covered in this chapter. For more information about these options, consult the documentation at http://www.novell.com/documentation/oes.

Manual Installation

The following steps outline how to install Novell Client by hand.

1. From your browser, go to http://download.novell.com (see Figure 6-1) and from the Most Popular links section select the item Novell Client. If the Novell Client software for your platform isn't listed here, use the Search feature to find it, and then download it.

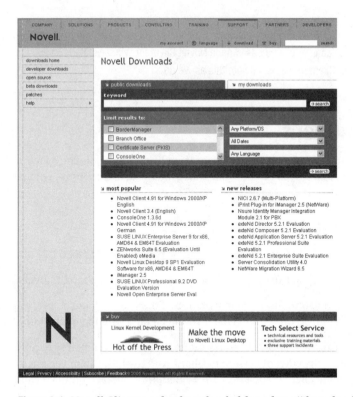

Figure 6-1. *Novell Client can be downloaded from http://download.novell.com.*

■**Note** You can choose from four different versions of Novell Client, as shown in the following list (version numbers may have been altered since this was written).

- *Novell Client 4.91 for Windows 2000/XP*: Use this version for Windows 2000 professional and XP platforms.

- *Novell Client 3.4*: Use this version for Windows 9*x* and ME.

- *Novell Client for Macintosh*: Use this client if you're using an Apple computer.

- *Novell Client for Linux*: Use this client to access OES from Novell Linux Desktop (NLD). Other Linux versions may work as well, but are not supported.

---

2. Click the link for the platform that you want to install Client for. From the File Download dialog box, click Save to save the Client installation file to your local computer.

Tip It's best to save the Client installation file to a location on the network. This helps you install Client on other computers, and is also great if you need to run an unattended client installation. For this purpose, you should create a directory "client" in the directory SYS:\PUBLIC on your server. Of course, you can only do that if you currently have a way to access files on your server.

3. After downloading the Client installation file, click Open to open it and start the installation. The extraction program on your local operating system should now start. Select the location where you want to extract the files, and then click Unzip to start the extraction. Next, close the extraction program and access the folder where you just extracted the Client installation files to. Browse to the subdirectory where the Client installation files for your platform are extracted, and then double-click the installation file you need. On Windows, this is the file setupnw. This starts the installation program.

4. Click Yes to accept the license agreement. Now select the type of installation you want to perform, as in Figure 6-2. In most scenarios, a Typical Installation is fine, but in this example the Custom Installation is used because it allows you to go work with additional options. So, after selecting Custom Installation, click Next to continue.

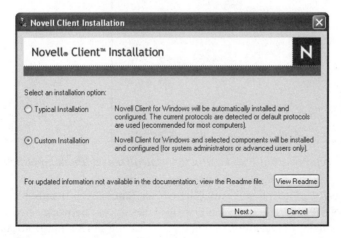

Figure 6-2. *To install the Client software, you can choose between the typical and custom installation types.*

5. Now you need to select the components you want to install. The option Novell Client For Windows (or any other platform that you install Client to) needs to be selected. If you want to be able to use bi-directional communication between your workstation and NDPS printers in use on your network, select Novell Distributed Print Services as well; this client component, however, is not needed for iPrint. Then, click Next to continue.

6. Next, choose any additional products you want to install. The following products are available for selection (see Figure 6-3):

- *Novell Modular Authentication Services (NMAS)*: Select this option to use other kinds of authentication than the default eDirectory authentication. You'll also need this if you want to use the Universal Password. (Chapter 9 has more about NMAS.) It's recommended you always install this component.

- *Novell International Cryptographic Infrastructure (NICI)*: This component is selected automatically if you're installing the NMAS client. It's also a good idea to install it if you don't use NMAS, because it provides the cryptographic algorithms needed for many tasks in an OES environment.

- *NetIdentity Agent*: The NetIdentity agent works with eDirectory authentication to provide background authentication to Windows web-based applications that require eDirectory authentication, such as iPrint, Novell Portal Services, eGuide, ZENworks, NetStorage, and iManager. Since it can make life a whole lot easier for you, it's better you install this component as well.

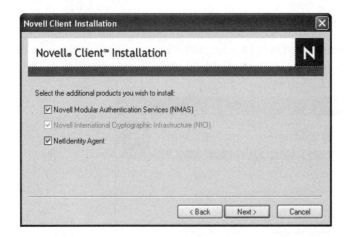

Figure 6-3. *For maximum flexibility, it's useful to install all the additional products.*

7. Now you can select the protocols you want Client to use. Since OES is IP only, it's recommended you choose IP only. If IPX services are still in use on your network, select either IP With IPX Compatibility or the option IP And IPX. (See Chapter 14 for more information on protocol selections.) Click Next to continue.

8. Select NDS in order to make a connection with NDS networks during login, as shown in Figure 6-4. The Bindery option is relevant for NetWare 3 networks only, so you don't need it. Click Next to continue. Now you must specify everything that's needed. Click Finish to finish the installation. The client files are now copied to the workstation.

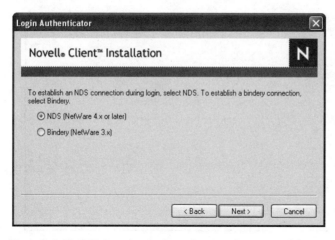

Figure 6-4. *The NDS option is the only one relevant on this screen since a Bindery connection is used only for connecting to NetWare 3.*

9. After copying all client files to the workstation, click Reboot to reboot the workstation, and then start logging in to the network.

Unattended Installation

If as an administrator you need to install Novell Client on a large number of workstations in your network, the unattended installation option may be useful. With this type of installation, a configuration file is read to apply settings automatically. As a result, Client can be installed from a login script (see Chapter 9), or any other mechanism such as ZENworks (see Chapter 13 for a brief description), and then run without any user interaction. To make the system even more perfect, the /acu (automatic Client update) switch can also be used. If the Client installation program setupnw is run from a login script with the /acu switch, it automatically checks to see if the user still has the most recent version of the Client software on his workstation. If the user doesn't, it updates the workstation automatically. To use the unattended installation, as an administrator you need to create an unattended file with the nciman utility. This section explains how to create the unattended file and how to perform an unattended installation.

1. Log in as administrator to your server. In SYS:public, create the Client folder and copy Novell Client files to that folder.

2. From the client*yourplatform*\\admin directory, run the nciman utility to create the unattended file. This starts the Novell Client Install Manager, as shown in Figure 6-5.

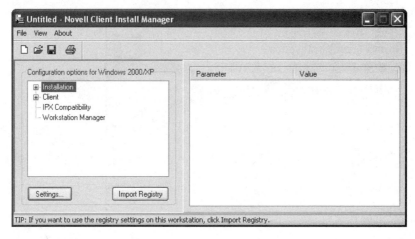

Figure 6-5. *From the Novell Client Install Manager, you can create an unattended file in order to perform an automatic installation or update of the Novell Client software on workstations in your network.*

3. The easiest way to enter settings for use in the unattended file is to use this utility on a workstation that has all the settings you need. In such cases, click the Import Registry button to import local settings to the utility. This automatically imports all settings in use on the local workstation. You can manually configure everything as well. Under the Installation option, you can find all the settings that determine what exactly has to be installed. Under the Client option, you have access to all advanced configuration options. (These advanced configuration options are covered in the next section.)

4. To change installation settings, click any item from Installation—for example, the Setup item. Next, click the Settings button. This opens a window in which you can specify all the installation options (see Figure 6-6). These options are used to outline exactly what has to happen upon installation of Client. All options from the previous section are covered in this. Some advanced options are available as well, like the option to specify how the workstation should be rebooted after installation of the Client files. From this window, make any modifications you need to and then click OK to apply them.

5. To set other Client options, select Client and then choose any feature under it. Next, you'll see an overview of the settings that are currently applied. Click the Settings button to open a window where you can modify all of these settings, as shown in Figure 6-7. The most important of these are covered in the next section. After instituting all the required settings, click OK to close the settings window as well.

6. When you're finished with the settings, from the Novell Client Install Manager, select File ➤ Save and save the settings to a file. Save this file as \public\client*yourplatform*\ unattend.txt—for example, \public\client\winnt\i386\unattend.exe (this is the default file name for an unattended file). You can use another name for this file, but in that case you must specify the filename when calling it from the **setupnw** command, as in the following: **setupnw /u=myfile.txt**.

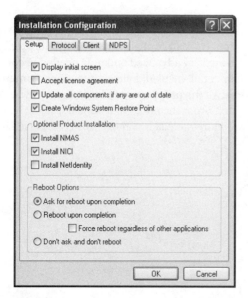

Figure 6-6. *In the Installation Configuration window, you can specify exactly what must happen upon installation of the Novell Client software.*

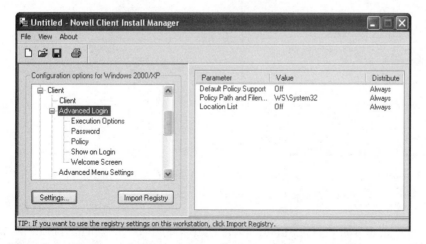

Figure 6-7. *All advanced settings for Novell Client can be modified before installation.*

7. Now that you've made all the settings available, you must set up the network installation of Novell Client. Three methods are available to do this, as shown next.

• Run the installation from a login script (see Chapter 9 for more on using login scripts).

• Use ZENworks to distribute the new client.

• Start the installation from a workstation with the command *yourserver***sys****public**\ **client***yourplatform***setupnw /u**.

Configuring Novell Client

When Novell Client is installed on a workstation, you can configure almost all of its properties. Many properties are available, some of which are very advanced and only needed in specific situations. Therefore, I won't cover them all in detail. Instead, following sections, contain descriptions of the most important properties. All the properties can be accessed if you right-click the red N in the taskbar on your computer. From the menu that appears, select Novell Client Properties to display the dialog box in Figure 6-8. Each of these tabs is discussed in a separate section that follows.

Figure 6-8. *Many properties are used to configure the Novell Client software.*

Client

The Client tab shows some generic information. The important options on this tab are as follows:

- *First Network Drive*: This is the first local drive letter used for mappings to network drives. The default value for this drive letter is F, which is fine for most corporate desktops, but may pose a problem if more than four local drives are already available.

- *Preferred Server*: This is the server that Client automatically tries to connect to. As an alternative, you can use the preferred tree setting. This setting is only used to make it easier for you; if you want to log in to another server or tree, from the Novell Login screen click the Advanced button, then specify any server or tree you want to log in to on the NDS tab (see Figure 6-9). If, however, as an administrator you have chosen not to make the Advanced Login option available to your end users, be sure the right default tree and server are entered here.

- *Tree and Name Context*: Here a list of trees and contexts that the user recently logged in to is shown.

Figure 6-9. *From the Advanced options in Novell Client, the user can specify what server or tree to log in to.*

Location Profiles

If you're working on a laptop, and frequently connecting to other Novell networks where different settings must be used from Novell Client, you can save these settings to a location profile (see Figure 6-10). By default, there's just one location profile called Default. If you want to add a new location profile, first specify all settings to be used in that profile. These settings can be entered from the tabs under the Novell Client Configuration options (again, see Figure 6-10). Then, on the Location Profiles tab enter the name for the new location profile and click Add to add it to the list of profiles.

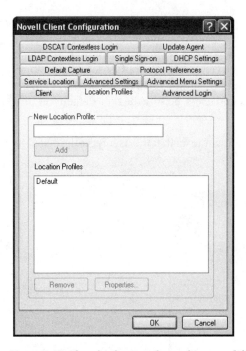

Figure 6-10. *If you're frequently working on different Novell networks, you can save settings for each of these networks by using the location profile.*

Advanced Login

On the Advanced Login tab, several options can be used to specify how a user can use Novell Client. For a description of each available option, highlight the option with the mouse to see a description or that particular option as shown in Figure 6-11. A short description of some of the most useful options is given next.

- *Advanced button*: This setting determines if a user sees the Advanced button in the login window in order for her to specify settings like the tree she wants to log herself into.

- *Bitmap filename*: By default, the Novell logo is displayed in the Novell Client window. If you want to change it to anything else, use this option to indicate the BMP file that should be used. Any BMP file can be used, as long as it's in the Windows NT/2000/XP directory.

- *Caption*: You can use this option to display text shown in the welcome screen title.

- *Context box*: This specifies whether the context box is displayed on the login dialog. You can safely set this option to Off if a contextless login (see the section "LDAP Contextless Login" later in this chapter) is used.

- *Initial Novell login*: Use this option if you don't want to start Novell Client automatically when the workstation is started.

- *Policy path and filename*: If you want to work with Windows policies for the Windows login part of the authentication procedure, specify the path to the Windows policies here.

- *Windows password synchronization*: If enabled, when the user changes his Novell password, the Windows password needed for local login on the Windows machine is synchronized as well.

- *Workstation only*: In a restricted environment, set this parameter to off to disallow a user to log on to his workstation without logging in to the Novell network.

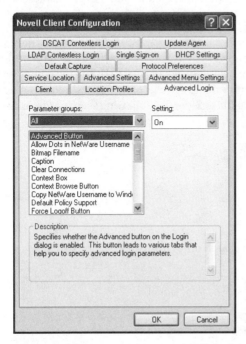

Figure 6-11. *With the Advanced Login option, you can specify how Novell Client is utilized by users.*

Service Location

On the Service Location tab, you can specify how your client should be configured for use of the Service Location Protocol. These settings are discussed in Chapter 14.

Advanced Settings

On the Advanced Settings tab, you can specify which advanced settings are used by Client. Settings such as timeout values specifying how much time should pass before Client stops trying to contact a server are set here. Typically, you only need to set these parameters in specific situations so as to optimize performance in a specific scenario. Therefore, they are not covered in depth here.

Advanced Menu Settings

The advanced menu settings are used to specify what elements should appear in the Novell Client components, and what elements shouldn't. For example, use the option Change Password if you want to enable the interface where a user can change his password. In a similar fashion, any other element of Novell Client can be enabled or disabled.

Default Capture

If queue-based printing is used, a default capture to a printer can be set on this page. Queue-based printing is not supported in an OES environment; therefore, you don't need these settings.

Protocol Preferences

On the Protocol Preferences tab, as shown in Figure 6-12, you can specify the default protocols you want to use. In an OES environment, the default protocol is set to IP and the component of naming is selected. Next, in the Protocol Components Settings part of this window, name resolution is defined. By default, when searching for services, the following search order is used.

1. NDS

2. The local host file

3. DNS

4. SLP

If required, you can change this default search order from here.

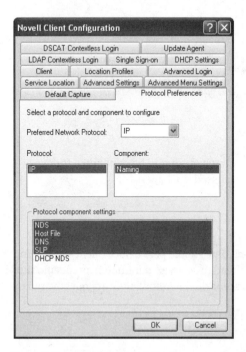

Figure 6-12. *On the Protocol Preferences tab, you can define the default protocol to be used and also how the name resolution should be handled.*

LDAP Contextless Login

The LDAP Contextless login feature, as well as the LDAP treeless login feature, can be used to log in to the network without needing to identify the context or even the tree that the user must log in to. This feature makes life much easier for both users and administrators. For the user, this feature is useful because it allows him to only enter his username and nothing more. For the administrator, it's a useful feature because containers of users can be changed in a tree or even the treename can be changed without the need to notify all users about what happened. The LDAP Contextless Login feature, with the optional extension of the LDAP treeless login feature, allows users to look up their user information in eDirectory based upon either their username or their e-mail address. You can use LDAP contextless login in any network running eDirectory 8.5 or later and the LDAP server. Since both conditions are met in an OES environment, the LDAP Contextless Login feature can be used. You should however make sure that the LDAP server object in your tree is configured properly with enough rights to search the LDAP tree. More information about this requirement can be found in Chapter 9.

After you've set up the LDAP objects properly (as described in Chapter 9), you can enter the required properties on the LDAP Contextless Login tab of the Novell Client software, as shown in Figure 6-13.

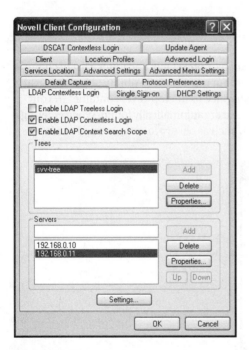

Figure 6-13. *If you don't want your users to specify a context when they log in, select the Enable LDAP Contextless Login option.*

1. To enable treeless login, select Enable LDAP Treeless Login. This automatically selects LDAP Contextless login as well.

2. If you're using LDAP Treeless Login, enter the names of the trees where you want to search for the user object. If you're only using LDAP Contextless login, enter the name or address of the servers where the LDAP service is set up, and click Add to add these servers to the list.

3. When adding an LDAP server to the list, a window appears in which you must set up the communication parameters for the LDAP server. The easiest way to connect to the LDAP server is over the unsecured LDAP port 389. If, however, you want to make an encrypted connection to the LDAP server, select Encrypted Data (SSL) and specify the location on your workstation where the SSL certificate used by the LDAP server is exported to. You can read more about exporting SSL certificates in Chapter 12.

4. If you want to specify a list of contexts to search, select the Enable LDAP Context Search Scope option. Next, choose the tree designated to be searched and click Properties. In the window that appears (see Figure 6-14), you can choose between the following two options:

   • Search Context and Subtree

   • Search Context Only

5. To minimize searches in your tree, select Search Context Only and enter a list of contexts that should be searched for user information. For maximum flexibility, select the Search Context And Subtree option and enter a reference to the top-level container in your tree. All users in all containers under that context are automatically found. When entering a context, use its LDAP name for the context, such as `ou=sfo,o=oes,` instead of `sfo.oes`.

Figure 6-14. *On the Context Search Scope tab, you must enter the names of the container objects that should be searched.*

6. Click OK to close the Context Search Scope window and then click OK to close the LDAP Contextless Login window. The settings are now applied. The next time the user logs in, he only has to enter his username. The LDAP Contextless Login feature does the rest.

Single Sign-On

Single Sign-on is a Novell product that allows a user to log in once and then get access to many services on the network. This product is not a part of OES and is therefore not covered in this book.

DHCP Settings

If a DHCP server is configured to deliver OES-related items to workstations where Novell Client is installed, you can overwrite settings distributed by this DHCP server on the DHCP Settings tab. By default, Client automatically works with settings distributed by a DHCP server. If it's not what you want, establish the default location in order to get the settings from this tab.

DSCAT Contextless Login

In NetWare 5.x, the DSCAT contextless login service allowed for contextless login on the network. In OES, LDAP is used for contextless login, so the DSCAT Contextless Login feature has become obsolete.

Update Agent

The Automatic Update Agent can be configured to check on a regular basis if a more recent version of the Client software is available. To use this feature, as shown in Figure 6-15, several options must be specified:

- *Enable Automatic Update Agent*: Use this feature to specify that Client should check regularly as to whether updates to the Client software are available. If this option is enabled, also specify the interval Client should use to check for new software.

- *Update Location*: Here you specify where the workstation should search when looking for a new version of the Client software. Typically, this would be a directory on the network.

- *Previous Install Location*: Here the location of the last client update is noted automatically. There's no need to manage this setting.

- *Latest Client Configuration Settings File*: If you want the update mechanism to use an unattended file like the one described earlier in this chapter to apply settings to Client automatically, you can refer to the name of this unattended file here.

- *Administrator Rights*: Check this box if you want to perform the update with administrator rights on the workstation. It's best to always leave this option selected.

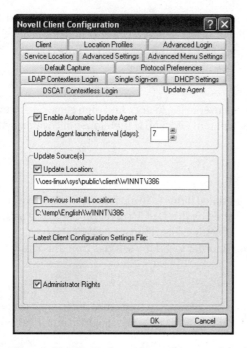

Figure 6-15. *The Update Agent allows workstations to update their Client software automatically.*

Using Novell Client

When the administrator of the network has configured Novell Client the right way, the user can access client components in different parts of her workstation, no matter if she uses a Linux workstation or a Windows workstation. The client software is integrated into the following parts of the local workstation.

- The red N in the taskbar of your computer (see Figure 6-16)

- In the menu used to start applications on your computer

- In the file browser on the local computer

Figure 6-16. *On the Gnome desktop, Novell Client also delivers a quick-menu that can be accessed by right-clicking the red N.*

Accessing Novell Client from the Taskbar

Most of the functionality of Novell Client is hidden under the red N in the taskbar of your computer. From this menu, many options can be chosen. A summary of the possibilities is shown next.

Tip If you don't like your users to change these settings by themselves, it's good to know that as an administrator you can disable the option for users to modify them.

- *NetWare Login*: Use this option to log in to a server or an eDirectory tree. It shows the login window where you can enter your user credentials.

- *NetWare Connections*: As shown in Figure 6-17, this option gives an overview of all current connections that exist. It displays the name of the trees a user is connected to, and shows the name of all servers on which the user has files open as well. From this screen, it's possible to set one particular connection as the primary connection, which can be useful when connections to more than one tree exist, or when it's necessary to detach from an existing connection.

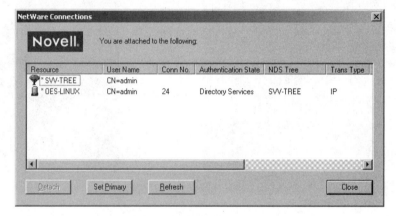

Figure 6-17. *All current connections can be managed from the NetWare Connections window.*

- *NetWare Logout*: This allows a user to log out from OES.

- *Novell Map Network Drive (NetWare Mount Directory)*: This helps a user make a mapping (Windows) or mount (Linux) to a shared directory on the network.

- *Novell Capture Printer Port and Novell End Capture*: These options exist in Novell Client for Windows to allow users to connect to legacy queue-based printers.

- *NetWare Utilities*: This option gives access to several utilities that can be used for simple management tasks on the local workstation. The following tasks are available:

  - *NetWare Copy*: Copy files from one location on your OES server to another location on the server without losing special Novell rights and attributes attached to these files.

  - *Send Message*: Allows you to send messages to other users.

- *Trustee Rights*: This gives access to a utility that can be used to manage file system rights on an OES server. (See Chapter 12 for more on this subject.)

- *Inherited Rights*: With this option, a user can set inherited rights filters to directories where he has the Access Control right. (See Chapter 12 for more details.)

- *Object Properties*: Provides a simple browser to look up information in eDirectory, as shown in Figure 6-18.

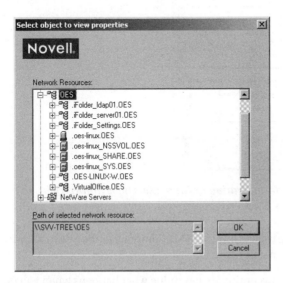

Figure 6-18. *The object properties utility allows users to browse to eDirectory resources on the network.*

- *Salvage*: Allows users to salvage files they accidentally deleted from their own home directory or other locations where they have write rights on the server.

- *Purge*: Allows users to purge deleted files from the server. This only applies to files to which the user has write rights.

- *User Administration*: From this option, users have access to limited properties in eDirectory. Here, they can manage some of their own properties. For example, a user can change her password from this option, or have a look at the user account restrictions that apply to her account. Figure 6-19 shows an example of these options, where the user can enter her own mailing information, provided that the admin user of the network hasn't limited this possibility by applying eDirectory rights.

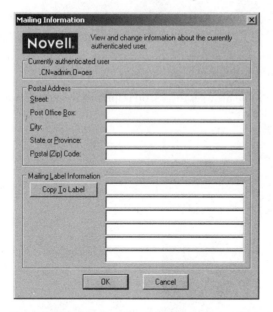

Figure 6-19. *From the User Administration utilities, users have limited rights to manage their own properties.*

- *Browse to*: This option can be used to browse to My Computer or the Network Environment to get access to all mounted network drives.

- *Configure System Tray*: Use this option to determine what happens when you double-click the System tray. By default, this opens My Network Places. Pressing the Shift key and double-clicking opens the Novell Map Network Drive utility. All other options available from the menu that appears when you right-click the red N can be used as well.

- *Update Novell Client*: A user can launch this icon to manually perform an update to Novell Client on his computer.

- *Novell Client Help*: This item gives access to help texts about Novell Client.

- *Novell Client Properties*: Use this to configure options regarding Novell Client, as described in the preceding section.

Accessing Novell Client from the Application Menu

If on Windows you open the Start menu and select All Program Files, you'll notice that an item that gives access to Novell Client is also added. From this submenu, two options are available.

- *Novell Login*: This gives access to the login program. A user can use this option to establish a connection to a given server.

- *Novell Send Message*: Use this option to send instant messages to other users that are currently logged in to the network.

Accessing Novell Client from the Local File Browser

The last place where you'll see the Novell Client software nicely integrated is in a local file browser such as Windows Explorer. If you right-click a drive that's mapped to a location on any Novell server, a menu appears displaying the options that are available, as shown in Figure 6-20. All of these are options available from the menu that appears when you right-click the red N in the taskbar of your computer.

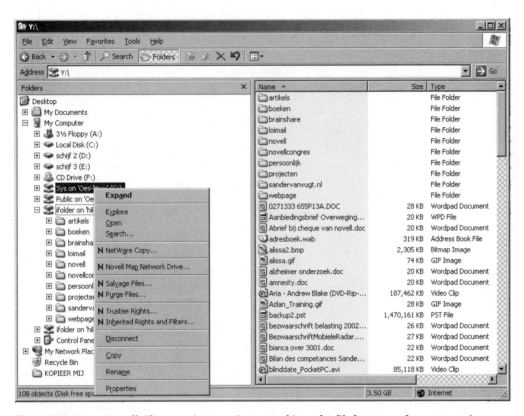

Figure 6-20. *Some Novell Client options are integrated into the file browser of your operating system as well.*

Summary

There are many ways to access an Open Enterprise Server. OES has a complete web-based work environment with Virtual Office, and some service-specific client programs exist as well. The preferred way for many users, however, is still to connect to OES with Novell Client. In an OES environment, a client for Windows, Linux, and even Macintosh is available. In this chapter, you learned how to install and use this client software. In the next chapter, the utilities used to manage an OES environment are explored.

CHAPTER 7

■ ■ ■

Open Enterprise Server Management Utilities

Novell has a rich history in the development of different management utilities. Netadmin was the very first tool that could be used to manage an eDirectory environment. This utility, however, was a curses-based non-graphical utility, so it was followed soon by Netware Administrator, a graphical utility that could run from a Windows environment. The biggest shortcoming of this utility, though, was that it could only run from a Windows environment. When Novell wanted to become more platform independent with the release of NetWare 5.0, it realized the software needed a new management utility. ConsoleOne is its name. It's a Java-based utility and is available in versions for Windows, NetWare, and Linux.

With NetWare 6.0, Novell started focusing on the browser as the starting point for network management and so iManager was launched. This utility can run from any browser and needs both an Apache web server and the Tomcat application server to manage a network.

In Open Enterprise Server, the following management tools are available:

- *iManager*: iManager is the most important management utility and can perform most day-to-day management tasks. For additional, more specialized tasks, other utilities are available.

- *Remote Manager*: The other important utility is Remote Manager, which can be used to manage several server parameters from a browser. Whereas iManager is the tool to administer your entire eDirectory from, Remote Manager was developed to manage specific parameters on a server.

- *iMonitor*: With regards to management of your eDirectory environment, there is iMonitor. This utility runs also from a browser and helps you manage all available eDirectory parameters. This utility will be covered extensively in Chapter 8 of this book which is about eDirectory management.

- *OpenSSH*: Apart from these browser-based utilities, it is also possible to manage your server remotely. Although not the only utility available, the Open Secure Shell (OpenSSH) software is the most common environment in which to manage OES NetWare and OES Linux.

- *YaST*: Specific to the OES - Linux environment is YaST, which can be used to manage most parameters on an OES - Linux server.

- *ConsoleOne*: Apart from the preceding utilities, some legacy tools still exist, like ConsoleOne. Also, if you really want to, and you use OES - NetWare, even the old Windows-only tool, NetWare Administrator, will work.

Using iManager

Novell iManager is the administration tool for your network. It can be run from any browser on any platform and almost all aspects of network management can be performed with it. iManager is based on the Novell extend Director standard edition software. This software provides the portal on which iManager can be reached. iManager also provides support for plug-ins that make management of third-party software possible. Some of these plug-ins are provided with other Novell software, while additional vendors also offer iManager plug-ins.

One of the key features of iManager is Role Based Services (RBS). RBS allows the administrator to define different administrative roles on the network. Specific tasks are assigned to each of these roles. There is, for example, a specific task "Help Desk User" to which all roles are assigned that are commonly needed by someone who works at the help desk.

Getting Familiar with iManager

The first thing you'll need to access iManager is a supported web browser. The following are supported:

- Microsoft Internet Explorer 6 SP1 or later

- Mozilla 1.7 or later

- Mozilla Firefox 0.9.2 or later

- Epiphany 1.2.6

You can access iManager from other browsers, but complete functionality using them is not guaranteed.

To access Novell iManager, do the following:

1. From a supported web browser, type the following link: **http://yourserver/nps**. Use http://192.168.0.100/nps to access iManager on the server with IP address 192.168.0.100.

2. If you get a security alert (like the one in Figure 7-1), read it and decide if you can connect safely with this server. In many cases, a security alert is generated because the certificate used for the secure connection is signed by the Certificate Authority running on your Open Enterprise Server and your browser is not yet familiar with this Certificate Authority. Click Yes if you want to proceed, in spite of the error message. You can read more about certificates used in an OES environment in Chapter 12 of this book.

3. Provide the username, password, and IP address of a server that has a replica of the eDirectory database to access iManager.

Figure 7-1. *In most cases, the security alert can be disregarded.*

You should now have access to iManager. In the left column will be a list of all the roles and tasks you're authorized to view. If you're logged in with an administrative account such as admin, you'll see all tasks and roles defined on your server. If you've logged in with a more limited account, you'll just see the roles and tasks assigned to that account. On top of the screen will be buttons that can help you navigate to some specific iManager tasks. Take special notice of the button View Objects. If you click here, it opens a sidebar in which you can browse through your eDirectory tree, as shown in Figure 7-2.

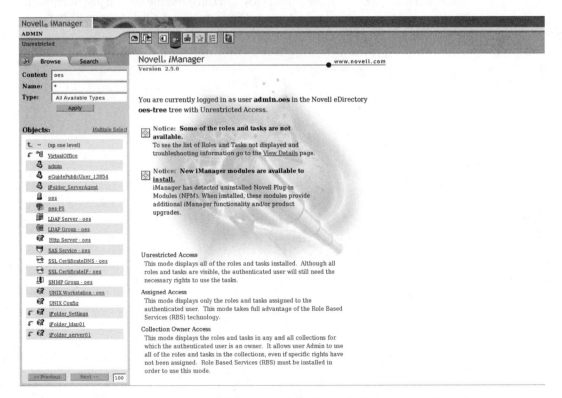

Figure 7-2. *For a graphical overview of the contents of your tree, click the button View Objects.*

Tip iManager takes advantage of the features offered by your browser. If you're using another browser than the one described here, the features may look different.

You'll find the most important part of iManager under the Roles And Tasks button. Here you'll see an overview of all roles and tasks granted to your user account. All management abilities (the tasks) are grouped together in a set of roles. This is to make it easier for you to grant a certain set of roles to a user account. This implies, however, that some options will be shown several times. If, for example, you want to create a new user, the most obvious place to look is in Users ➤ Create User. You can also create a new user object by selecting eDirectory Administration ➤ Create Object. iManager gives you the flexibility to handle tasks just the way you want. To demonstrate, the following details show how to create a user object in eDirectory with iManager.

1. Start iManager and authenticate to your server.

2. Select eDirectory Administration ➤ Create Object.

3. In the list of available object classes, scroll to the User object and click OK. The screen shown in Figure 7-3 is displayed.

4. All required options are marked with an asterisk. Enter the desired username, last name, and context in the appropriate fields. You can enter the context just by typing it. It's also possible to browse to the desired eDirectory object. Click the magnifying glass to open the browser. This opens a new window.

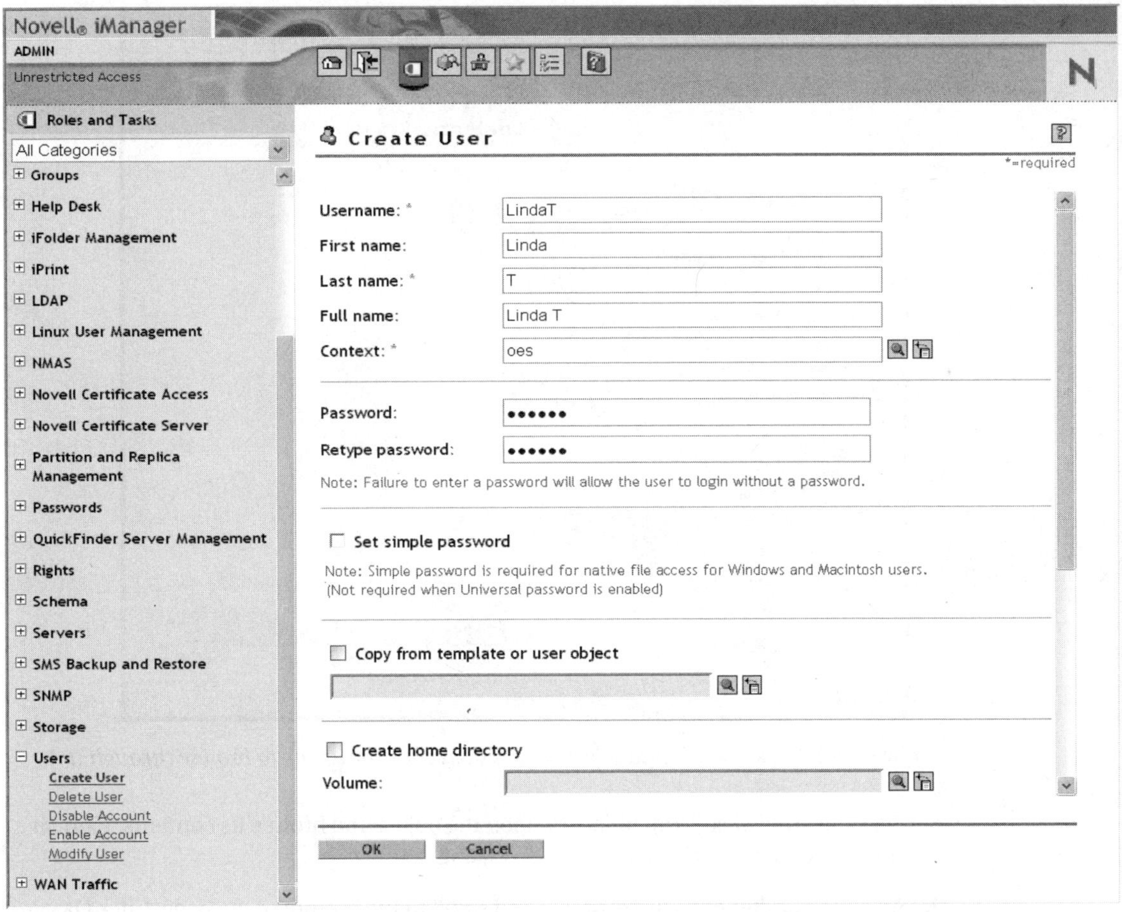

Figure 7-3. *The options marked with an asterisk are required options to create the object.*

5. Click Browse to browse using the interface shown in Figure 7-4. A list of objects should be displayed that exist under the context specified by the Look In option.

Tip Next to the Browse button is the History button. When you click this button, a history of recently used objects for this property is displayed. Just click any of the objects to use them.

Figure 7-4. *Click an object to select it, and then click the arrow to browse through it.*

6. Click the arrow next to an object to open the object and browse its contents. Find an object you want? Click its name to start using it.

7. Specify any other options you'd like and scroll to the bottom of the page. Click OK.

8. The new object is created. Click OK to finish.

Tip Differences exist between OES - Linux and OES - NetWare. If you're running OES - Linux, after creating a user object, options will display that allow you to create the LUM user object. This object is needed to authenticate locally on the Linux computer as the user you've just created. More about this option can be found in Chapter 9.

---

iManager Configuration

After this short introduction to iManager, it's time to describe its configuration. iManager configuration consists of two main parts: the setup of Role Based Services and the configuration of iManager plug-ins.

■Tip Upon installation of OES, iManager is installed automatically. For this reason, in a network with 30 servers, you'll end up with 30 copies of iManager installed on all your servers. This isn't necessary and only consumes precious resources. In most cases, it's more than enough to install iManager on one or two servers in the network.

Setting Up Role-Based Services

One of the biggest advantages of iManager is its ability to work with roles. With these roles, you can assign specific responsibilities to users. Before this can happen though, the administrator has to set up RBS and define the roles available on the network. Multiple roles can be assigned to a single user, but it's also possible to assign the same role to multiple users. For the convenience of the network administrator, a number of default roles already exist in iManager. These allow the user to easily delegate the management of specific parts of the network to one or more users. A specific set of tasks is assigned to each of these roles. There is, for example, a role Users with the tasks Create User, Delete User, Disable Account, Enable Account, and Modify User associated with it. Because a number of default tasks and assigned roles already exist in eDirectory, the setup of RBS is optional. If in your network everyone can work with complete administrative rights, you don't need it. However, if you want to grant rights to certain users to perform specific tasks, RBS can be a great help.

■Tip The next section includes information that requires knowledge of the working of eDirectory. If you're unfamiliar with eDirectory, you can find all the necessary details in Chapter 8 of this book.

Initialize RBS

Before you can use Role Based Services, it must be set up. For this, use the iManager configuration wizard. If you choose not to configure RBS, no problem. In that case, all iManager modules will be displayed after you log in. This is fine in a network where you're the only administrator, or when all administrators have full rights to use every module available. If, however, you want to differentiate between administrative tasks, you must set up RBS. To do so, perform the following steps:

1. In iManager, select the button **Configure** in the upper part of the iManager window.

2. Select Role Based Services and then choose RBS Configuration to view the screen shown in Figure 7-5. You should now be able to tell if RBS has been set up or not. If it's set up, the contents of the existing RBS collections will be displayed. If it hasn't been set up, click Configure iManager to configure RBS.

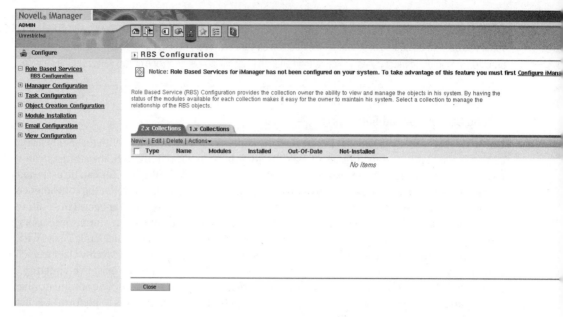

Figure 7-5. *Before using RBS, it must be set up.*

3. After clicking Configure iManager, the iManager Configuration Wizard starts. Click Next to proceed to the screen shown in Figure 7-6.

4. The first step in the configuration of RBS is setting up an RBS collection. In order to create it, you have to give it a name and specify the container in which it must be placed. By default, the RBS collection gets the name Role Based Service 2. This is not because there is already another Role Based Service collection, but because the RBS collection you created is for iManager version 2.x, which is not compatible with previous versions. Click Next after specifying all necessary details.

5. A list of all iManager modules not yet installed should appear, as shown in Figure 7-7. By default, all these modules are selected so they can be applied in the iManager configuration. The first thing you need to do to set up these modules is to apply a scope. A scope is a container in which members of a role can perform tasks. If you make the scope an inheritable scope, selected tasks can also be applied in all subcontainers of the selected container. It's possible to select the eDirectory tree as a scope to include everything within your network.

6. You have finished the RBS configuration. Click Start to apply your settings to eDirectory. All selected modules are installed now and you can start working with them. Click Close to close the wizard.

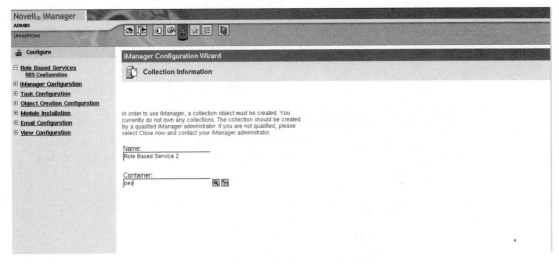

Figure 7-6. *To set up RBS, RBS collection information must be entered.*

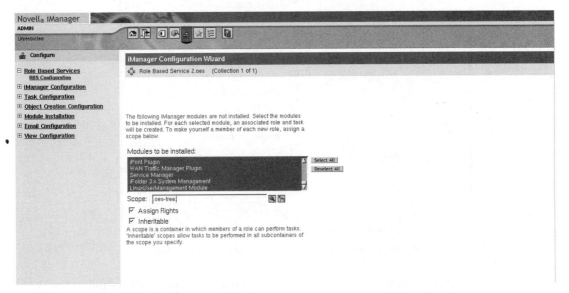

Figure 7-7. *An essential part of RBS configuration is specifying the scope of the modules.*

RBS Objects in eDirectory

After RBS has been set up in your tree, an entire subtree of eDirectory objects will have been created (as demonstrated in Figure 7-8). These objects can be found under your Role Based Service container. You'll first notice various modules and roles. In a module, you can find tasks and in a role you'll find a scope object. Beneath that will be a list of the objects. Be aware that normally there's no need to work directly with the objects. This is because RBS can be managed from the normal iManager setup interface. The different objects are as follows.

- *rbsCollection*: This is the container object in eDirectory which houses all RBS objects. In an eDirectory tree, more than one rbsCollection object can be used. An rbsCollection has an owner (normally the user that created the rbsCollection). The owner of the rbsCollection has all management rights to it. The rbsCollection object contains rbsModules and rbsRoles.

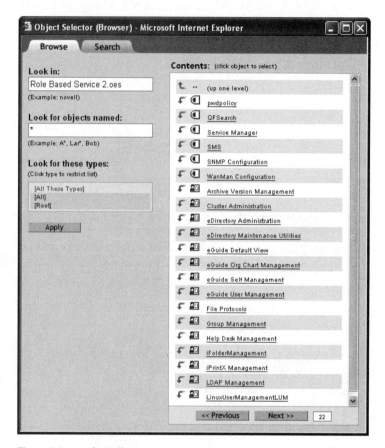

Figure 7-8. *An rbsCollection contains rbsModules and rbsRoles.*

- *rbsModule*: An rbsModule is also a container object. It holds rbsTasks and rbsBooks objects that specify the exact possibilities of tasks in RBS. An rbsModule typically carries the name of the product that the module manages. For example, the RBS module Cluster Administration is used to group tasks needed to manage a cluster.

- *rbsRole*: An rbsRole specifies the tasks that its members are authorized to perform. In order to define a role, you have to specify its name as well as the tasks associated with it. You do this from the iManager configuration option. This results in rbsRole objects created in eDirectory. Role members can be users, groups, organizations, or organizational units. They are associated with a role for a specific scope of the tree. The rbsTask and rbsBook objects are associated with these roles to specify what exactly the role consists of.

- *rbsTask*: An rbsTask is a leaf object that holds a specific function that can be performed in RBS.

- *rbsScope*: This leaf object is found under the rbsModule. The rbsScope is used for ACL assignments instead of making assignments for each User object. Because of this, the user is given a security level equivalent to the object. An rbsScope represents the context in the tree where a role will be performed. rbsScope objects are associated with rbsRole objects. This object is dynamically created when needed and is also dynamically removed when it's no longer required.

Configuring iManager Roles

With the proper knowledge of RBS, it's possible to assign RBS roles to specific eDirectory objects. This creates a specific management interface for certain users after they have authenticated successfully to iManager.

1. Start iManager and authenticate as admin-user. Choose the Configure tab.

2. Select Role Based Services ➤ RBS Configuration. A list of all available RBS Collections will be displayed. Select the default RBS Collection on the 2.x Collections tab. This displays a list of all available RBS Roles on the Role tab, as shown in Figure 7-9. Select the role you want to make a specific assignment for.

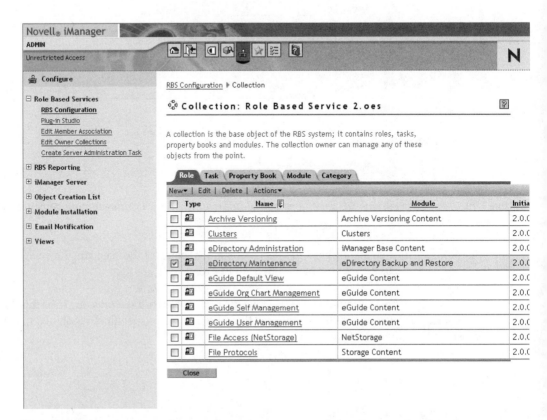

Figure 7-9. *Before you can assign members to one or more roles, you must select the roles.*

3. From the Actions menu, select Member Association. This opens a new window, shown in Figure 7-10, which lets you specify an assigned member and the scope that can be used by this member. You'll also see a list of eDirectory accounts that are currently assigned as a member.

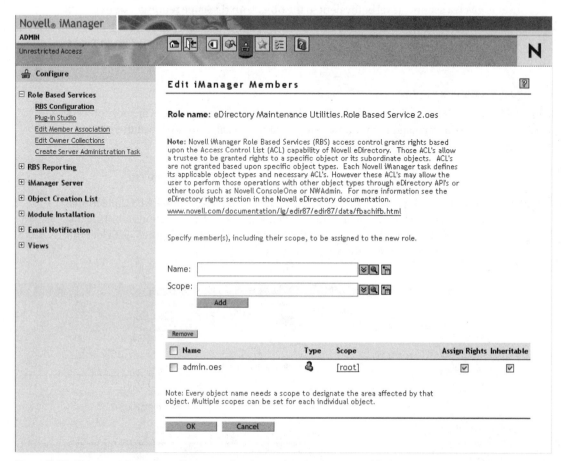

Figure 7-10. *Users can be assigned as a member to a role to create a specific iManager management console for the user in question.*

4. Use the magnifying glass to select a user and a scope for the user, and then click Add to add the user to the list of members for this role.

You have now assigned a user to a specific role. To verify if it works, log in as this user account in iManager. You'll see that only the roles the user is specifically assigned to are displayed, as shown in Figure 7-11.

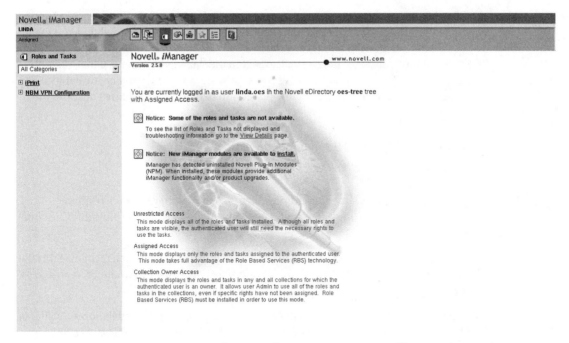

Figure 7-11. *By assigning a user as a member to a role, you can create a specific management view for one or more users in your tree.*

Caution You've just assigned a user as a member to a specific role. At an eDirectory level, this means that the user needs some eDirectory rights to a certain scope in eDirectory. You should be aware that, at an eDirectory rights level, there is no way to differentiate between the right to create a user or a printer object in a given container. If, for example, you assign a user as a member to the iPrint role, this user will have the right to create printer objects. This is fine as long as the user only uses iManager to perform his tasks. If, however, the user ever gets his hands on another management tool, like ConsoleOne, he'll find that he is not only able to create printers, but any object in the specified container. In some cases, the user concerned will even have supervisory rights to this container, but you'll be warned of these excessive rights in the Roles overview.

Configuring iManager Plug-Ins

iManager ships with all necessary core plug-ins needed to manage every aspect of Open Enterprise Server. Many other Novell products include specific plug-ins. Normally, these plug-ins are installed automatically when you install the considered product. It's also possible to download the products separately after the product installation. The particular procedure needed after downloading the products varies depending on whether or not RBS is already configured. You can find iManager plug-ins on the Novell Product Downloads web site at http://download.novell.com/pages/PublicSearch.jsp?filter=category&filterselection=180.

After installation of the plug-ins, extra work has to be performed. This is because plug-ins are not replicated automatically between servers. It's therefore recommended that you install the necessary plug-ins on each iManager server.

If RBS is not configured, the plug-in will appear in the iManager contents panel, regardless of your access rights. If, however, RBS is configured, the new plug-in won't be available until you upgrade your RBS collection. The following section details the procedures necessary to install plug-ins.

Plug-in Installation When RBS Is Not Configured

If you haven't configured RBS, follow these steps to install plug-ins:

1. Activate the link http://download.novell.com/pages/PublicSearch.jsp?filter=category&filterselection=180 to get an overview of all the available plug-ins. Click one to download it.

2. The name of the file you've chosen to download is displayed. You can recognize this file by its npm extension. Download the file and save it to a location where you can access it later.

3. Activate iManager, log in, and select Configure. Choose Module Installation ➤ Available Novell Plug-in Modules. This displays a list of plug-ins already installed, as shown in Figure 7-12.

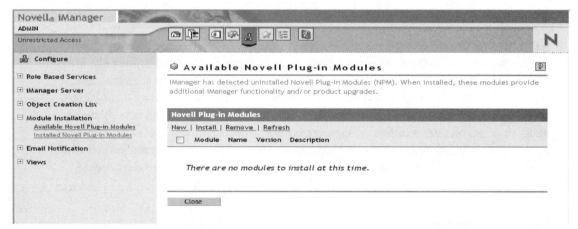

Figure 7-12. *Under Available Novell Plug-in Modules you'll find a list of installed plug-ins.*

4. Click New and browse to the plug-in file you downloaded in step 2 of this procedure. Click OK to install the plug-in. Its name will appear in the overview.

5. Select the module by clicking the box to the left of its name and then click Install.

6. It's now necessary to stop Tomcat. On OES - NetWare, enter **TC4STOP** at the server console. On OES - Linux, issue the command **/etc/init.d/novell-tomcat4 stop**. Wait at least one minute to allow all related services to shut down.

7. After a minute, start Tomcat again. At the OES - NetWare console, enter **TOMCAT4** to restart the service. At the OES - Linux console, use **/etc/init.d/novell-tomcat4 start** to start the service again.

8. The new role will appear on the roles and task page.

Tip It takes a while before Tomcat finishes loading all the necessary components. After restarting Tomcat, give the software a few minutes before trying to reconnect. If you reconnect too soon, you could get an Internal Server Error message. Normally, it can take up to two minutes before everything is loaded.

Plug-in Installation When RBS Is Already Configured

If you've already configured RBS, you need to upgrade the RBS collection after installing a new module. This makes the procedure slightly different. The first steps are the same as in the previous procedure, except that after step 6 the following steps have to be performed:

1. In iManager, select Configure.

2. Select Role Based Services ➤ RBS Configuration. This shows the RBS Collection installed on your server. You'll notice a difference between the two parameters Modules and Installed as you can see in Figure 7-13. There is probably one more module under Modules. Under Not-Installed, of course, the various modules not yet installed will appear. You can see these modules when you click on the number in the column **Not Installed**.

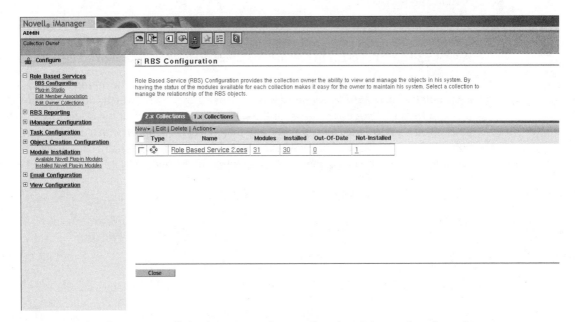

Figure 7-13. *If in the Not-Installed column any other number than 0 is mentioned, you have iManager modules that still need to be installed.*

3. Click the link under Not-Installed. This displays all modules not currently installed. Select the check box next to the name of the module and click Install to install it, as shown in Figure 7-14.

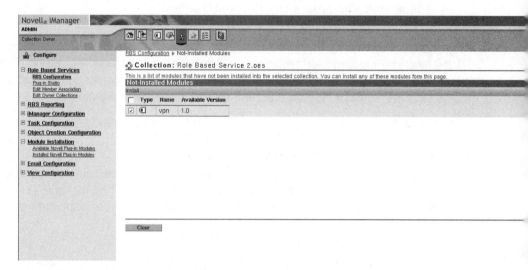

Figure 7-14. *Click the check box next to the name of the module and then click Install to install it.*

4. Once the module is installed, you'll see a message indicating that installation of the module was successful.

5. You must now assign users to the new role. Choose Role Based Services ➤ RBS Configuration and then select the RBS Collection in which you installed the role. Choose the Role tab and click the check box next to the role you just installed (as shown in Figure 7-15).

6. With the role you want to assign selected, click Actions and select the option Member Associations. This opens a new window (shown in Figure 7-16) in which you can specify members and the scope to be used for the selected role. First, select the eDirectory objects you want to assign as a member, and then select the scope in which the specified object will have rights to perform its various management tasks. Finally, click Add to add the specified objects as members of the role, and then click OK.

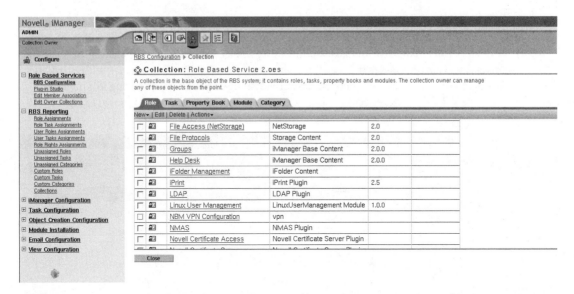

Figure 7-15. *Before a role can be used, it must be assigned to one or more eDirectory objects.*

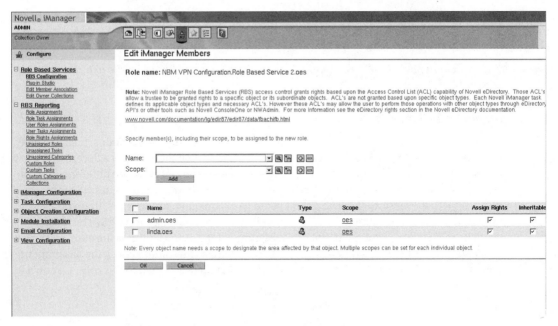

Figure 7-16. *For each role, you'll see a list of assigned users that can use the role to perform management tasks.*

7. If you activate the window Roles and Tasks, you'll see the roles from the module you just installed.

Plug-in Studio

If you really want to improve your iManager experience, you can use Plug-in Studio. Plug-in Studio lets you create custom tasks and property books. In creating these custom tasks, you can use all available classes that exist in eDirectory. It's even possible to work with Auxiliary classes to create your own tasks. You can activate Plug-in Studio by choosing iManager ➤ Configure ➤ Role Based Services ➤ Plug-in Studio. This displays the screen shown in Figure 7-17.

Figure 7-17. *If the default possibilities aren't enough for you, you can use Plug-in Studio to build your own custom tasks and property pages.*

Generating RBS Reports

RBS is very powerful, but since the configuration is saved at different locations, it can also be very confusing when presented with an overview of all the possibilities. To get a decent overview, use a feature called RBS Reporting in iManager 2.5. Here, you can generate different kinds of reports to verify that you configured everything the way it should be configured. This can be useful if there is ever something you can't get to work. Imagine, for example, that you just imported a new module, but it doesn't appear in the roles and tasks overview. The reason could be that you've forgotten to make an assignment for this role. If this is the case, just select RBS Reporting ➤ Role Assignments. Next, choose the role you want to check the assignments for in the list. This immediately presents a list of all members assigned to this role, as shown in Figure 7-18.

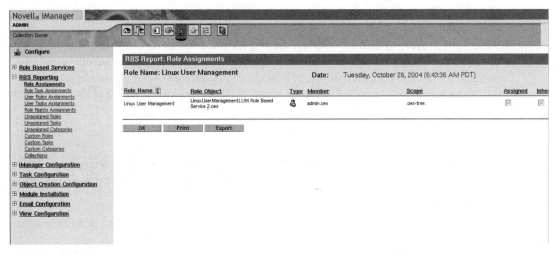

Figure 7-18. *RBS Reporting is a nifty tool for checking if everything is configured properly.*

Mobile iManager

You can start iManager from a server where iManager is installed. If you want a more flexible and most of all faster version of iManager, Mobile iManager can be used instead. This standalone version of iManager is not on the OES installation CDs, but can be downloaded from http://download.novell.com. After downloading and installing it to a workstation, you can start it from that workstation, without the need to download anything from the server.

1. Open your browser and access http://download.novell.com.

2. In the Search field, enter the keyword **imanager** and click the Search button.

3. From the list of results, click the link iManager. Next, select the version of Mobile iManager for the platform where you want to install it and click Download. Follow the prompts to download Mobile iManager.

4. After downloading the archive file, extract it to a directory on your workstation. This is all you need to do to install it. After extraction of all files, you can start Mobile iManager by executing the file imanager/bin/iManager from the directory where you extracted all Mobile iManager files.

5. You now have access to the standalone version of iManager. This version is configured with a minimum of roles and tasks. If you want to have more management abilities from Mobile iManager, you need to step up the plug-ins as described earlier in this chapter.

Using Remote Manager

There are two ways to manage a server: directly from the server console, and with Remote Manager. Novell Remote Manager (NoRM) is a browser-based interface that allows you to manage lots of server properties. One of its main characteristics is that it is server-based and not eDirectory-based; thus, you can use it to access one server and modify specific parameters on the same server.

■**Note** Remote Manager does not need the Apache web server, it runs on its own mini web server called httpstk. This mini web server is available on both OES - NetWare and OES - Linux and it allows you to use Remote Manager, even if Apache is down.

Linux Utilities

MONITOR.NLM has existed in NetWare for a very long time, and it's still available for OES - NetWare. If, however, you're using Linux, there's no such thing as MONITOR.NLM. The reason for this is obvious: Linux is an entirely different operating system compared to NetWare and it can't be monitored with NetWare's traditional MONITOR.NLM. There are, however, many specific Linux tools that can monitor components of the Linux operating system. Most of them are command-line utilities. A brief overview of them is provided next.

- *lsof*: This command generates a list of open files on your system. It can also be used to generate a list of all files in use by a particular process. If, for example, you want to see a list of all files opened by the process with PID 100, use the command **lsof -p 100**.

- *fuser*: With this command, you can generate a list of users using one or more specific files. For example, use **fuser –v /mnt/*** to see a list of all users currently accessing files in the directory /mnt.

- *stat*: Use **stat** to display details of the properties of a file. The command shows you properties like size, file type, inode number, links, and many more.

- *top*: Displays a list of the most active processes on a server.

- *ps*: Is used to show a list of active processes. **ps** comes with many options, which can be used to determine what should be displayed.

- *pstree*: Shows a list of all processes and the parent process they originated from.

- *w*: With the powerful **w** command, you can get a list of all users logged on to the system and watch what they're doing at any specific moment.

- *free*: This utility examines RAM usage. It displays the amount of RAM currently available, and also gives details about the usage of cache memory and swap.

- *dmesg*: Displays the kernel ring buffer. This is a buffer in which messages generated by the kernel are kept.

- *mount*: Shows you all file systems currently active (or "mounted," in Linux-speak).

- *df*: This command shows how much space is available on the devices in your file system.

- *du*: **du** is used to show "disk usage." For example, enter **du –sh** ~ to get a short (-s) human-readable (-h) list of the space used by the files in your home directory.

- *procinfo*: Shows a short list in which the most important information from the Linux file system /proc is displayed, like that shown in Figure 7-19. This file system is used by the kernel to provide an interface to the memory currently utilized by your system. It also offers an overview of important usage statistics.

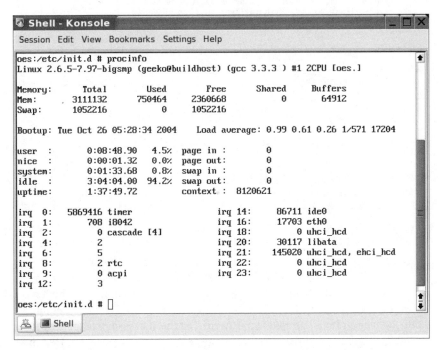

Figure 7-19. *The command procinfo displays the most important information on the /proc file system.*

- *lspci*: This command lists the PCI resources. You can use it to find out which devices are connected to the PCI bus. Use it with the option –v and it offers more detailed information about the memory addresses used by the PCI devices.

- *strace*: Okay, for most people it's a bit too much, but with **strace** you can enable a trace of all system calls for a process currently running. For example, use **strace ls** to find out just exactly what the **ls** command is doing.

- ***ldd***: Gives an overview of libraries required by the command specified, as shown in Figure 7-20. A library is a file that contains code which can be shared by different Linux utilities (meaning you could compare a Linux library with a Windows DLL). If, for example, you want to find out what libraries are used by the program file /bin/ls, use **ldd /bin/ls**. It can be very useful when troubleshooting problem commands.

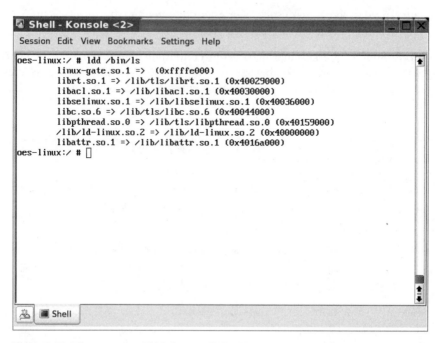

Figure 7-20. *The command ldd shows all the libraries used by a particular binary.*

It's great that there are so many Linux commands that can be used to monitor what your server is doing, but it's not really a unified way to monitor the performance of your computer. For this reason, Novell created Remote Manager. This browser-based utility (which has existed since NetWare 5.1) has been ported to the Linux platform as well. You can access Remote Manager on HTTP port 8008 or on HTTP port 8009. Be aware that the successor to Remote Manager is already available in Open Enterprise Server. This successor is called the Server Health Monitor (see Figure 7-21). This is an entirely new management platform based on the OpenWEBM standard. Chapter 20 covers the Server Health Monitor in more detail. You can start Server Health Monitor from iManager by selecting Servers ➤ Monitor Servers.

Figure 7-21. *In the future, the Server Health Monitor is likely to replace Remote Manager.*

Introduction to Remote Manager Server Management

To start Remote Manager, access it on HTTP port 8008 of your server. After entering your user-name and password, you'll gain access to the Remote Manager interface, as shown in Figure 7-22. This interface is divided into different task groups: all available task groups are shown in the bar on the left, while in the main window is an overview of the tasks assigned to a task group. After logging in to Remote Manager, you'll see an overview of available volumes: from this interface, you can manage files and volumes on your server. For example, it's possible to mount or dismount a volume from the Remote Manager interface. Methods of managing the file system from Remote Manager are discussed extensively in other chapters of this book.

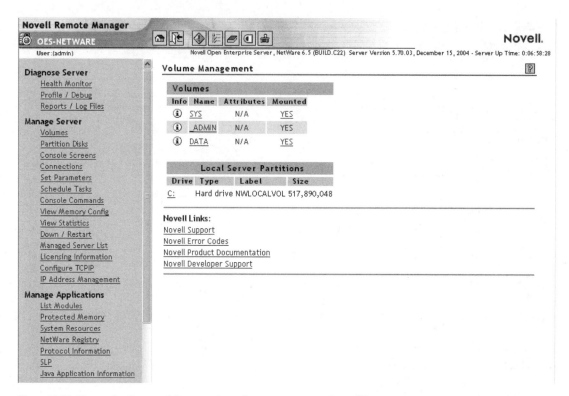

Figure 7-22. *From the Remote Manager interface, you can perform file system management.*

One of the nicest items integrated in Remote Manager is the Health Monitor, shown in Figure 7-23. The Health Monitor offers an instant view of your server's current condition. Is everything in order? If so, only green items are displayed. If you're approaching a critical value, the item will be marked in orange, and if the situation is absolutely critical, it will appear in red. You can access the Health Monitor from the Health Monitor button at the top of the Remote Manager screen. Even when you're not in the Health Monitor, you can view the current status of your server. In the upper-left corner of the Remote Manager window is a traffic light. The color of the traffic light indicates whether there is a problem or not.

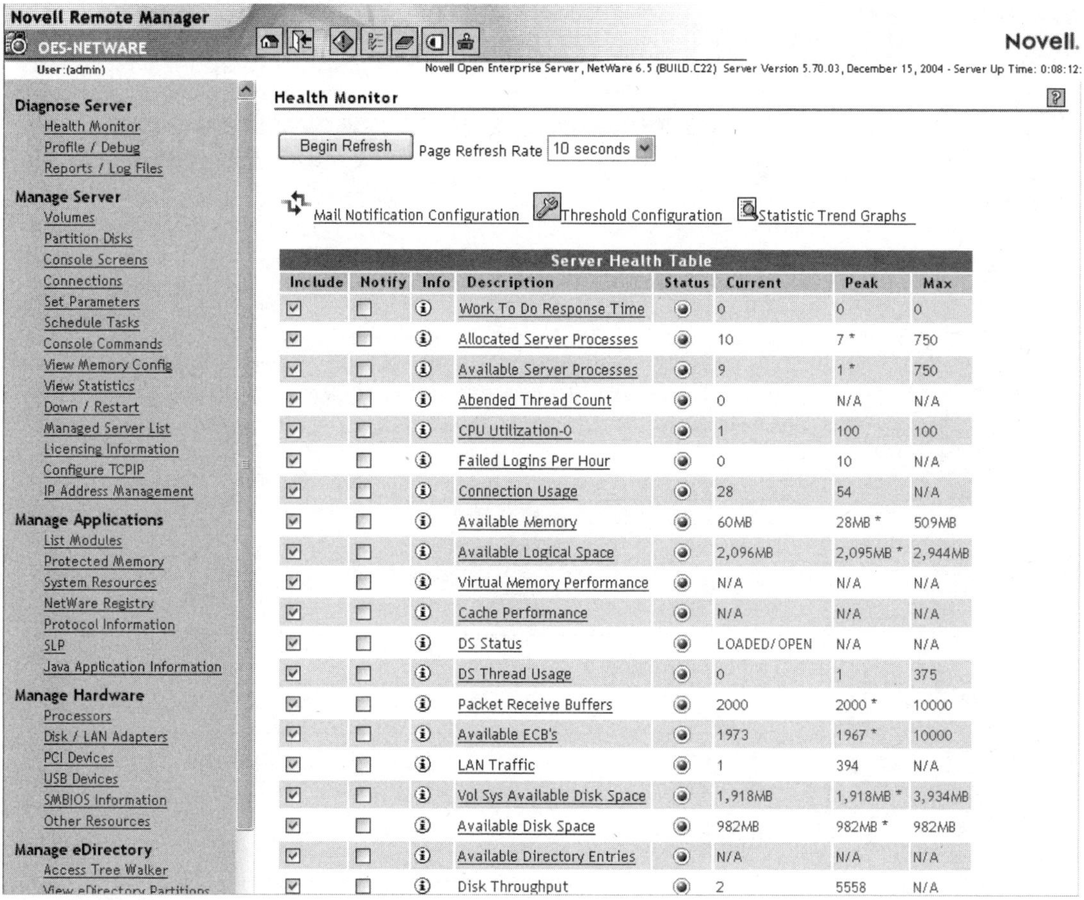

Figure 7-23. *The Health Monitor offers an instant view of your server's current condition.*

From the Health Monitor interface, you have several options to specify what should happen if anything is wrong on your server. Use the Notify option to be alerted if anything is wrong with a parameter; the e-mail address from an administrator can be set with the Mail Notification Configuration parameter. From this screen, it's also possible to view trend graphs, as shown in Figure 7-24. The fact that a parameter is marked critical at that moment doesn't mean anything by itself. If, however, the parameter has been listed as critical for the last few weeks, there might be something seriously wrong with your network.

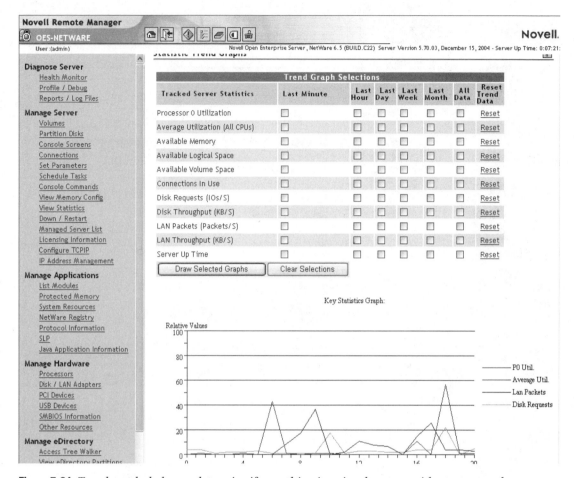

Figure 7-24. *Trend graphs help you determine if something is seriously wrong with your network.*

Using YaST

YaST has been the default configuration tool for SUSE Linux for a long time. In OES - Linux, it's still used to manage some components of Open Enterprise Server. More importantly, however, YaST can manage all the "local" aspects of SUSE Linux (you learned about this in Chapter 4). In OES - Linux, click the icon on the desktop to start YaST. A YaST front options screen will appear, as shown in Figure 7-25. By clicking Network Services, you're given limited management capabilities for Novell services like iManager, eGuide, eDirectory, and many more running on SUSE Linux.

Figure 7-25. *Basic management of some Novell services can be performed with YaST.*

You should not expect too much from YaST with regards to management of Novell services. YaST isn't for configuring Novell services, it's used to configure the way these services are installed on your OES - Linux server. To manage all local aspects of your OES - Linux server, YaST is the tool. Chapter 4 has more information on YaST.

Using OpenSSH

If you're used to working with Linux, you're probably already familiar with Secure Shell (SSH). For Linux, this is the most secure way to get a remote console connection to a server. The Open SSH version of Secure Shell has also been ported to the NetWare platform, starting with NetWare 6.5. In this section, you'll learn how Secure Shell can be used to establish a remote connection to a server.

Using OpenSSH on NetWare

Before you can use OpenSSH on NetWare, the product must be installed on the server. In many cases, this is done during the installation of your server. It's also possible to install it after installing NetWare by performing the following steps.

1. Insert the NetWare CD into the drive of the server where you want to install OpenSSH.

2. Start the NetWare GUI by entering **startx** at the console prompt.

3. Select Novell, choose Install, and then click Add next.

4. In the Path To Install From dialog, browse to your CD and select the file POSTINST.NI. Click OK twice.

5. Specify Open Enterprise Server 1.0 as the installation type and click Next.

6. On the Install Components screen, select OpenSSH from the list and click Next.

7. Follow the remaining screen prompts to complete the installation.

8. Click Reset Apache to complete the installation.

Before users can access files on OES - NetWare using OpenSSH, some additional configuration has to be done: the OpenSSH server must be started and some parameters installed. You can do this by manually loading sshd.nlm at the server console, and editing the configuration file sys:etc\ssh\sshd_config on your server. You can also designate these settings from the OES - NetWare Administration interface that you'll find on HTTPS port 2200 of your server. I'll explain how to do this next.

■**Tip** Normally, the SSHD configuration is stored in the configuration file sys:etc\ssh\sshd_config. Alternatively, it can also be stored in eDirectory. The advantage of this is that other servers in the eDirectory tree can also use the information for their SSHD configuration. Another advantage is that this way it's stored in a fault-tolerant database. To specify if you want to store relevant information in the configuration file, or in eDirectory, click the Administration Mode button in OpenSSH Manager. This opens an interface in which you can specify where the SSHD configuration should be saved, as shown in Figure 7-26. If you choose to save it in eDirectory, a corresponding eDirectory object will be created.

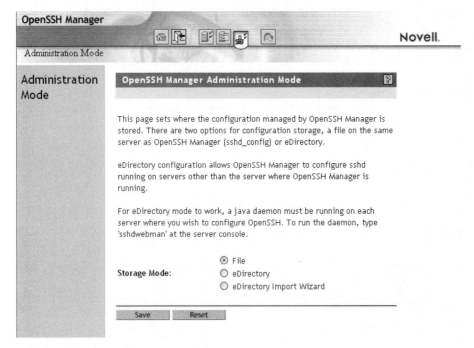

Figure 7-26. *The SSHD configuration can be saved in a configuration file or in eDirectory.*

1. Open a browser and access your server on HTTPS port 2200.

2. Select Open Source, choose OpenSSH, and click OpenSSH Simple Administration. This opens the web interface that lets you manage the OpenSSH service on the selected server (as shown in Figure 7-27).

3. Click Start Server to start OpenSSH on your server.

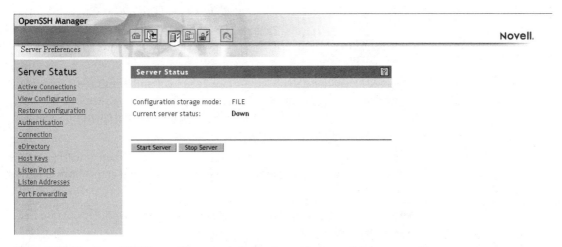

Figure 7-27. *The OpenSSH Server Manager interface provides everything you need to manage your OpenSSH server.*

4. Click View Configuration to view the current configuration, as shown in Figure 7-28. You'll now get web-based access to all SSH parameters kept in the configuration file sys:etc\ssh\sshd_config. The most important options are mentioned next.

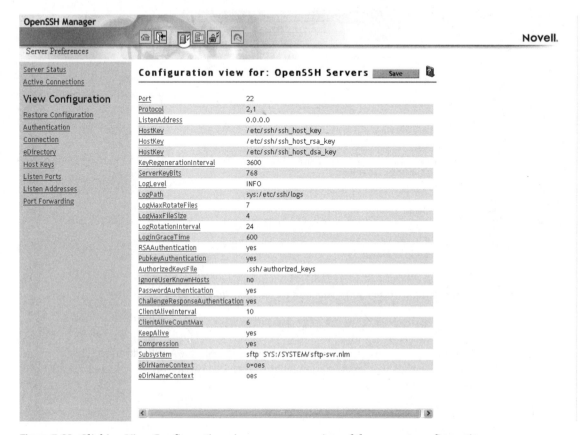

Figure 7-28. *Clicking View Configuration gives you an overview of the current configuration.*

- *Port*: Specifies on which port the OpenSSH server listens. In most cases, you can leave this on the default: port 22.

- *Protocol*: OpenSSH provides default support for versions 1 and 2 of the SSH protocol. Version 1 provides backward compatibility for older clients that only support the less-secure SSH version 1. For security reasons, it's better to upgrade the clients to version 2 and disable version 1 support on the server.

- *ListenAddress*: Specifies the address SSHD should listen on. By default, it will listen for incoming connections on all interfaces. For security reasons, you can choose to limit this to only some interfaces.

- *HostKey*: Specifies the file in which the OpenSSH hostkeys are saved. This parameter can be left on the default value.

- *LogLevel*: Use this option to specify what information should be written to the log file. By default, this is information with a status of informational and above.

- *LogPath*: Denotes the file where log information should be saved.

- *RSAAuthentication*: This is an SSH version 1 option to specify that logins using RSA keys are allowed. This option was replaced in version 2 by the PubKeyAuthentication option.

- *PasswordAuthentication*: Specifies whether or not authentication with a password is allowed. For a secure configuration where only keys are allowed for authentication, you should turn this off.

- *ChallengeResponseAuthentication*: Specifies whether challenge response authentication is allowed.

- *eDirNameContext*: Specifies the context in eDirectory with which the SSH server looks for user accounts to try and authenticate.

Using OpenSSH on Linux

If you're familiar with the way OpenSSH must be configured on NetWare, you're in luck because you can configure it the same way on Linux. The entire SSH configuration is stored in the well-documented configuration file /etc/ssh/sshd_config. This file contains the same options that can be configured from the OpenSSH Manager interface. (This is true for the OES - Linux server as well.) After configuring these options, you just have to tell SSHD to start using them. You do this by restarting the daemon-process with the command **/etc/init.d/sshd restart**. If you don't change anything to your OpenSSH configuration, you can start using it right out of the box. The next section explains how to access OpenSSH from the client.

Using the SSH Client to Make a Secure Connection

A few issues must be resolved before using the OpenSSH server. First, you must decide what software to use on your client computer. This is easy if you work with Linux, because a command-line SSH client is included by default. If, however, you work from Windows, you'll have to download something from the Internet. Next, you need to specify how you want to connect to your SSH server. Once this is decided, you can start using the different client parts of SSH: ssh, sftp, and scp.

Choosing the Right Client

If you're working with Linux, things are easy. An SSH client is included with every Linux distribution, you'll always find a client that can be used from the command line, and sometimes even a graphical client is included. Windows, however, doesn't include an SSH client. To remedy this, choose one of the many clients that can be downloaded for free from the Internet. One of these clients is PuTTY, which can be downloaded from www.chiark.greenend.org.uk/~sgtatham/putty/download.html and other locations. It's recommended that you search using Google to find the location nearest your site and download it from there. Different files are included with PuTTY. The file you need is called putty.exe. Besides this, other files are available, such as PSCP, the putty secure copy client, and PSFTP, the putty Secure FTP client.

After downloading PuTTY, you can execute it immediately (see Figure 7-29). Specify the name or IP address of the host you want to make an SSH connection to, choose SSH for the protocol, and click Open.

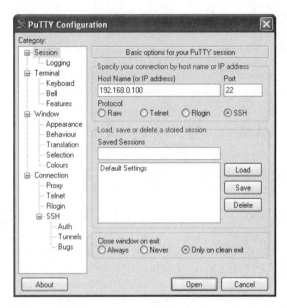

Figure 7-29. *It's very easy to make an SSH connection from PuTTY.*

If this is the first time making a connection to the remote host, you'll get a message that there is no way to verify that the server is the computer you think it is. If you're sure this computer *is* the computer you think it is, click Yes to continue and save the host-key in PuTTY's registry. Next, you'll see the login-prompt where you can specify the username and password for log in. Once this is finished, you're connected and you can work on the remote host as if you were sitting in front of your home console (see Figure 7-30).

If you're working on Linux, things are a lot easier. An SSH client is always included on almost any Linux distribution. If you'd like to use a graphical SSH client because of the some-times more advanced management options, simply download it from the Internet. For instance, there's a free UNIX version of PuTTY that can be compiled on Linux from the source files. Many people don't feel the need for such a client though, because SSH is really about terminal access to another computer and it doesn't make any difference if this terminal is displayed in a window or not.

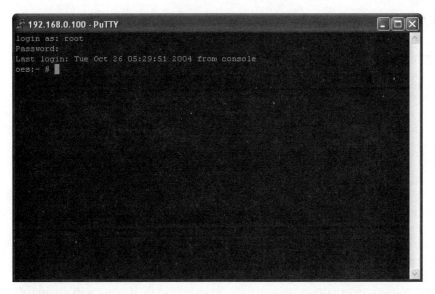

Figure 7-30. *Once connected, you can work on the remote host as if sitting in front of your home console.*

Configuring Authentication

Several ways exist to configure how authentication is handled in an SSH environment. Most of the time, usernames and passwords are used, but it's also possible to log in using RSA or DSA keys. This option is supported by default on the SSH server, whether you're using NetWare or Linux. In a Linux configuration, a user must complete the following procedure if he wants to log in using a DSA key.

1. Use the command **ssh-keygen –t dsa** to generate a DSA key pair. This creates a private key in the user's home directory under .ssh/id_dsa. The public key is then saved in the file .ssh/id_dsa_pub. The keys can be protected with an optional passphrase as well.

2. To authenticate with the user's keys, the public key in the file id_dsa_pub must be copied to the user's home directory on the remote server. On this server, the key must be stored in .ssh/authorized_keys in the user's home directory. To ensure secure transport of these keys, some additional encryption must be used.

3. Once the public key is present at the remote server, it can be used to create a challenge that's sent to the user who is trying to authenticate. This user must then access his private key to send back the right response. Once this is done, the user will be authenticated without providing a password.

While key-based authentication functions are okay in a Linux-only environment, this feature hasn't been implemented yet in an Open Enterprise Server environment.

ssh, scp, and sftp

SSH is not just about secure logins on a remote machine. When the SSH daemon is active, you can use the commands **scp** and **sftp** as well. **scp** is used to securely copy a file from one location to another, while sftp is considered a secure alternative for the legacy FTP daemon.

ssh

The **ssh** command is used to connect to an SSH server. The syntax is easy:

```
ssh [user@]host command
```

For example, if user franck wants to make an ssh connection to a certain host, execute one command, and immediately return to the local host he is working on, he could use the command **ssh franck@somehost ls**. This executes the command that is specified on the remote host, after which the user continues working on his local console. This way of working with SSH is very functional if you create script files for execution on the remote host.

This isn't the only way a user can work on a remote host. Alternatively, she can just log in to the remote host. If she uses the command **ssh somehost**, the SSH client utility will try to authenticate with the same username as the user that's logged in locally. It then opens a terminal session in which the user can work until she employs the **exit** command to terminate her SSH session.

scp

The **scp** command is used to copy files securely over the network. You can use it to copy files between any two hosts running the SSH server SSHD. The syntax is very similar to the syntax of a normal copy command, the only exception being that certain features have been added to enable communication with remote hosts:

```
scp localfile user@remoteserver/remotefilename
```

Notice that localfile, as used here, can be any file. You can even use it to specify the name of a remote file to be copied. For instance, with **scp alex@somehost/home/alex/nice-document franck@someotherhost/home/franck/alex-his-document**, a user could log in to the first host as user alex and copy a file to a second host on which he needs the credentials of user franck. For administrators working with Windows, WinSCP can be used. WinSCP can be downloaded from winscp.sourceforge.net/eng/download.php.

sftp

The last command in the ssh bundle is **sftp**. This is a secure alternative to the traditional ftp command-line client. The syntax is also the same as these clients:

```
sftp username@remoteserver
```

For example, to connect as user admin to a remote OES - NetWare server with the IP address 192.168.0.101, use **sftp admin@192.168.0.101**. Next, an interactive FTP prompt will appear. Use standard FTP commands to navigate the server's directories and transfer files to and from it. The following are some very common FTP commands:

- *bye*: Exits the sftp session

- *cd*: Changes the directory of the SFTP server

- *lcd*: Changes the local directory on the server where the FTP-client is used

- *get* **filename**: Retrieves the specified file you name and copies it to the current directory on the local computer

- *put* **filename:** Copies the specified file from the current local directory to the current directory on the remote server

- *ls*: Displays a list of contents of the current directory at the SFTP server

Using Legacy Tools

Although they're no longer formally supported, some legacy tools can still be used to manage Open Enterprise Server. The first of these tools is ConsoleOne, which has been the default Novell Management platform for the last five years. This Java-based tool has one major advantage over iManager: it provides a hierarchical graphical overview of your eDirectory tree. ConsoleOne is not installed by default, but you can download and install it from the Internet. The following steps describe how to install ConsoleOne on OES - Linux. If you use OES - NetWare, there's no need to download it because it's already present in sys:public\management.

Tip If you have a Windows workstation on which the latest version of ConsoleOne is already installed, there's no need to install it again. Just run it and authenticate on the eDirectory tree you want to manage.

---

1. Open download.novell.com in your browser and start a search for the product ConsoleOne on the platform Linux. This displays the most recent version of ConsoleOne available. Download it. Since the file is about 50MB, it may take a while.

2. Open a console and extract the downloaded file with **tar –zxvf c1_136c-linux.tar.gz**. Be careful, the version number used in this command may have changed!

3. The previous command created a directory with the name Linux in it. Change to this directory and use the command **./c1-install**. Be sure to include the leading ./ to the command. The current directory is not in the source path, so without the ./, the shell won't be able to recognize the command. The installation script should start now.

4. Select the language you want to install. Next, specify the snap-ins you want to install. If you don't know which ones to choose, just install all the available snap-ins.

5. When asked if you want to install the Java Runtime Environment, choose n if it's already present on your server, or choose y to install it.

6. You might get an error message at this point, indicating that the wrong version of eDirectory is installed. The error message will tell you which version of eDirectory is needed to run ConsoleOne as well as the version you currently have installed. Note the version already installed. Next, open the script cl install with an ASCII text editor such as vi. Locate the line nds_version and make sure the value given to this option is the same as the eDirectory version you're currently using. The install script should run without problems now.

7. Once the installation is finished, execute **/usr/ConsoleOne/bin/ConsoleOne** to run ConsoleOne.

8. Once ConsoleOne is started, select File ➤ Authenticate to authenticate in the dialog box shown in Figure 7-31. Because you aren't using any client, you won't be authenticated by default. Provide your login name, password, tree, and context to log in successfully.

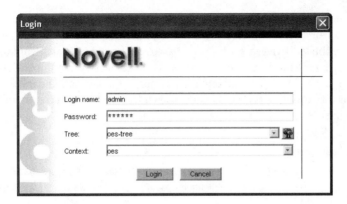

Figure 7-31. *Before you can manage your network with ConsoleOne, you have to authenticate.*

9. After successful authentication, you'll have access to the ConsoleOne management interface, shown in Figure 7-32. Also notice that some objects are marked with a question mark. These are unmanageable objects. Since ConsoleOne is deprecated, you'll find quite a few of these objects. You can, however, still manage the more common objects like users and groups without problems with ConsoleOne. Occasionally, you might even find that ConsoleOne is the only tool available to manage a certain program.

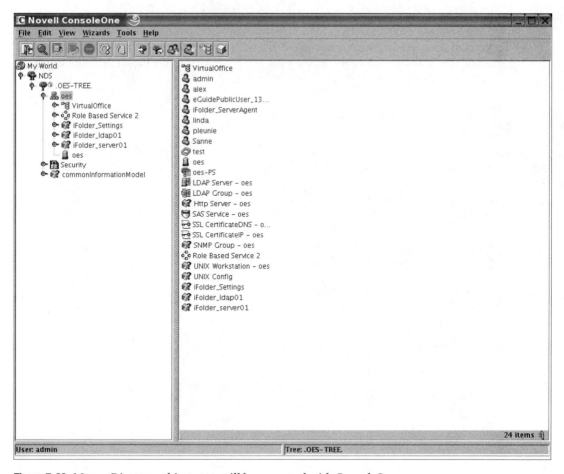

Figure 7-32. *Many eDirectory objects can still be managed with ConsoleOne.*

Summary

In this chapter, you learned about the tools that can be used to manage Open Enterprise Server, the most important of which is iManager. This browser-based tool is created to manage and configure eDirectory in your network. One advantage to it is that Role Based Services can be used. By employing Role Based Services, it's possible to provide customized views for specific administrative users where they will only see those components that they're allowed to manage. Another important tool discussed was Novell Remote Manager, which was created to manage your server and those items specific to it. You can use it to monitor performance issues as well as manage the file system. Also covered was iMonitor, which is used to monitor the performance of eDirectory in particular. Lastly, you learned about Secure Shell which is used to manage a server remotely.

Apart from these four tools, other tools can be used to manage OES, the most important of which is the Java-based ConsoleOne. The biggest advantage of this tool is that it runs on Windows, Linux, and the OES - NetWare server console. It is, however, no longer supported, so you shouldn't use it anymore. In the next chapter, you'll learn about the most important thing these tools manage on your OES network: eDirectory.

PART 2

■■■

Core Services

Up to now in this book, you've read about things you needed to know to get you going with Open Enterprise Server. In the book's second part, the core services of OES are discussed. These are the services that people buy OES for. First, you'll learn about the most important of the core services: eDirectory. After that, you'll read how eDirectory is used to implement important services like user management, file services, security, and print services on OES.

CHAPTER 8

■ ■ ■

eDirectory Management

The most important service on any Novell network is eDirectory. This has been so ever since the early days of NetWare 4.0, back when eDirectory was still called NetWare Directory Service (NDS). eDirectory is the network's central database, where almost anything of importance is stored—for example, information on printers and users. This chapter introduces you to the workings of eDirectory, explaining what eDirectory consists of, how the hierarchical structure is organized, and how it should be deployed in a large network environment.

eDirectory Basics

eDirectory is the most fundamental service in a Novell network. It contains network information of every kind. Resources like servers, volumes, and many others are installed in eDirectory, as well as information on the users allowed to utilize these resources. Apart from that, structural elements are created in eDirectory to organize the network in a hierarchical fashion. This section explains what eDirectory is and from what components it's composed.

Note In this book, I make a difference between a Directory and a directory. If I talk about a Directory (capital D), I'm referring to the Directory Service that's used as the central database in which almost all information about the network is kept. When using the term directory, I'm citing a place in the file system where files are kept.

What Is eDirectory

eDirectory is a Directory Service. Though it's not the only Directory Service in the world, it's the center of the universe in a Novell network. A Directory Service is more than just the database containing all the information about the network. It has different roles for different users, as outlined in the following points:

- For the Administrator, it's the management tool to manage all resources and users in the network.

- For users, it's the tool that can be used to locate all objects in the network.

- For everyone, it's the central database needed to authenticate to the network.

As the central repository of all information in the network, eDirectory has some specific functions, including the following:

- The integration of incompatible systems.

- Providing access to network resources to users in the network.

- The centralization of network management.

- Establishing trust relations between users and resources that are defined in the Directory.

- Relating the information about an enterprise with the information about the network. This is accomplished using some of the structural elements of eDirectory that can be designed to reflect the way an enterprise is organized. For example, if an organization has offices in different locations, you can reflect these different locations in Organizational Unit objects created in eDirectory.

- Providing information to network users and administrators.

eDirectory is the central repository for just about everything in the network. Fundamental Novell services cannot function without it. Not only are users stored in eDirectory, all Novell network services are stored as well. Important services like printing, Novell Clustering Services (NCS), and Nsure Identity Manager cannot function without eDirectory. In fact, OES NetWare isn't even usable if eDirectory is not present.

eDirectory Components

The eDirectory database is composed of a hierarchical structure in which you can find information about all network resources and users. This structure can best be compared to the structure of the file system on a client computer. In the file system, there are directories that function as a container to keep all the files that belong together; there are also container objects, which are containers that keep all the eDirectory leaf objects together.

On top of the eDirectory tree is the tree object. In earlier days, this was called the root of the Directory structure (the tree). Under the tree object are several container objects. There must be at least one container object directly under the tree (in recent versions of eDirectory there's always more than one of these containers). This is because, besides the container of the type *Organization*, there's always a container called Security in which some objects are kept that are related to the security of the network. Within a container object, you can find other container objects or leaf objects. These leaf objects are the objects that really matter since these are the network resources and users that a network is built for.

Object Classes

eDirectory is composed entirely of objects, also known as classes. These classes can be divided into three different categories:

- Network resources

- Structural classes

- Users and related classes

The most important class type is known as network resources. These are the hardware devices and services you've built a network for. Then there are the users who want to get access to these network resources. To grant a user access to a network resource, a user account has to be created. Normally, each user has their own user account, but in many cases there are users who have the same needs. Take accountants, for instance, who might all need access to the same accountancy application. You can make it easier to grant these users access by working with groups in which all similar users are grouped together. To do so, you could create an "accountants" group to refer to whenever dealing with the accountant's permissions. Be aware, too, that a user can be a member of more than one group simultaneously. (Chapter 9 has more on group management.)

eDirectory is a very scalable Directory. In fact, you can group millions of objects into one Directory structure. Indeed, the Directory has been tested with as many as 100 million objects in one tree! To make searching in the Directory easier in such cases, eDirectory works with structural classes: the so-called container objects.

■**Tip** A container object is also called a "structural class," which is the formal LDAP terminology. This book, however, will stick to the more informal "container object."

Container objects are used to group users and other objects that share something in common. For example, if in an enterprise, these objects exist in different locations, it's useful to create a container object for each of those locations. In such a container, you could create a second level of containers for each of the departments in these containers. For instance, you could create a container named sales.sfo.svv to group all sales users in the location San Francisco in the organization called svv together. Grouping users together is not the only reason to create container objects. You could instead create a container called workstations.rtd.svv to make management of workstations in the location Rotterdam easier.

Each of these object classes has characteristics, known in eDirectory as attributes (and referred to as properties in other systems). With these attributes, you define exactly what the possibilities of a class are. As an example, take the user class, which is an object in eDirectory that represents an employee of a company that wants to use resources on the network. To do so, the user needs to log in to the network, and to make that happen, the object class user has an attribute of *login name* in which the login name of the specified user is defined. For each object class, exactly what attributes can be used is defined in the eDirectory schema. With the schema editor, it's even possible to create your own object classes and attributes: if you need a refrigerator as an object in eDirectory with the attribute number of bottles of beer, that's all possible. You can read more about these possibilities in the section on managing the schema called "The eDirectory Schema," later in this chapter.

Attributes associated to a class have at least one value. These values can be managed with a management program like iManager (see Figure 8-1). An attribute has one or more values (if more than one, they are called multivalued attributes). Think about a telephone number, for instance. Most people have more than one telephone number where they can be reached. Therefore, the telephone number attribute is multivalued. Another example is group membership, where a user can be a member of more than one group at a time. If an attribute is multivalued, this is defined in the schema.

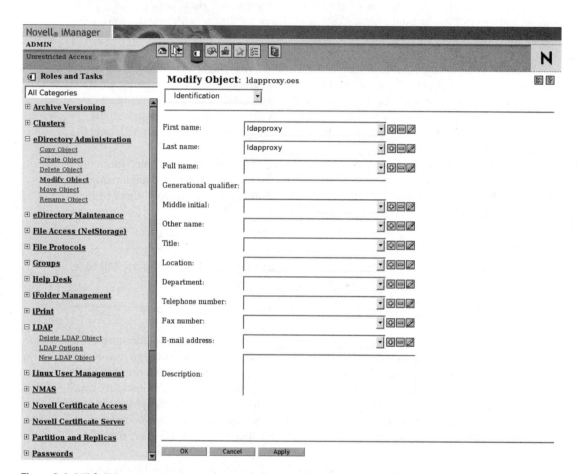

Figure 8-1. *With iManager, you can access and change many properties of the user object.*

Hierarchical Structure

eDirectory is a hierarchical Directory structure. At its top, you'll find the tree object, which is the most important object in the eDirectory structure. Your eDirectory can't exist without the tree object, whose importance is comparable to the root directory of a file system. The tree object is created upon installation of the first server in eDirectory. Give some thought as to the name of the tree before entering it since it's practically impossible to change it afterwards.

The tree object is the highest object in the eDirectory hierarchy. Directly under the tree you can create container objects with ConsoleOne or iManager such as special purpose containers, the Country container object, and the Organization. Apart from that, you can create an alias object as well. The alias isn't a real object though; it's actually a pointer to another object some-where in the tree. Table 8-1 lists some important container objects that can be used in eDirectory.

Table 8-1. *Important Container Objects*

Container Object	Description	Place in eDirectory
Security	Used for some special-purpose security-related objects, like the Certificate Authority (see Chapter 11) and NMAS login methods (Chapter 6).	Only directly under the tree object.
Organization	Used to represent an organization in the eDirectory hierarchy. This container object exists in every eDirectory tree and can contain leaf objects as well as other container objects.	Can exist directly under the tree object, or in the country object.
Country	Used for X.500-compatibility. This object is used to represent two-character ISO country codes, like UK, NL, JP, and so on. A country object can only contain an organization object. Because of its limited flexibility, use of this object is not recommended.	Only directly under the tree object.
Organizational Unit	Used to bring structure in an eDirectory tree. You can compare it to map objects in a file system tree. Use of organizational unit objects is optional, but strongly recommended in almost all cases. In the section "eDirectory Tree Design" later in this chapter, you can read more about the use of this object.	Can be created in an Organization object or in an Organizational object.
License Container	Special purpose container created to store OES licenses.	Can be created in Organization or Organizational Unit objects.
RBS Container	Special purpose container, used for setup of iManager Role Based Services.	Can be created in Organization or Organizational Unit objects.
Domain	Used to represent DNS domains in an eDirectory environment. This object exists mainly for reason of X.500 compatibility and is not used often.	Can be created anywhere in the Directory tree.
Locality	Used to represent a specific location in eDirectory. Instead of using a locality, often a general organizational unit object is employed for this. Localities are not commonly used.	Can be created in the Organization or under Organizational Unit objects.

One important aspect of the tree object is that you can use it to grant rights to others. If a user has the eDirectory Supervisory right to the tree, he automatically inherits supervisory rights to everything beneath it by default. If a group has Browse rights to the tree, members of the group can browse everything beneath it. Rights to the tree object can also be used the other way around: if you grant the tree object Create rights to a certain container, every user defined in the tree can create objects in this container. You can read more about eDirectory security in Chapter 12.

Directly under the tree object are container objects, which are used to create a logical structure in the eDirectory tree. Container objects have two possible functions. First, they can be utilized as special-purpose container objects that are created automatically upon installation of special products in eDirectory. For example, if you install the Identity Manager Starter Pack, it creates a special-purpose container for Identity Manager with all related classes in it.

For you as the administrator of eDirectory, the functional container objects are the most important. They are used to group users and other objects in the tree. Normally, the structure of these containers must be designed for optimal performance. You can read more about this design later in the chapter in the section "eDirectory Tree Design."

The most important objects in an eDirectory tree are the leaf objects. There are many varieties, most of which will be covered later in this book. As a little sample, a few are described in the Table 8-2.

Table 8-2. *Some Important Leaf Objects*

Leaf Class	Description
Alias	Used to point to other objects at another location in the tree. Use these objects for greater accessibility.
Application	Represents an application in the network. These objects can be used to automatically display icons for applications on a user's desktop which the user has rights to.
Directory Map	A pointer to a directory in the file system on a server. Used as a uniform way to refer to locations in the file system.
Group	Used to group users with a common need together. This leaf object is often employed to grant rights to groups of users.
LDAP Server	Represents an LDAP Server object in the tree. The LDAP Server is a default object in the tree because many applications need it to get access to services on the network.
LDAP Group	Used to group LDAP Servers together. All servers that are appointed to an LDAP Group share the same properties defined at group level.
License Certificate	Contains information about the license installed on your network. In this license certificate, the operating system can read, for example, how many users have rights to access resources on the network.
Organizational Role	Used to define a role in an organization. A role has occupants, which are similar to members of a group. You could, for instance, create an Organization Role with the name "helpdesk" and make all users that work at the helpdesk member of this role.
Print Queue	Indicates a directory in the file system where print jobs are spooled before they are actually printed.
Profile	A login script that can be used by a group of users.
Volume	Represents a volume in the file system on a server. On a volume, you'll find files that can be used by the users of the server.

Naming Conventions

You can probably tell by now that an eDirectory structure can be rather complex. It's even possible for two users in your worldwide tree to have the same login name (although it's better to avoid this). If this happens, it's important you use efficient naming to specify which object exactly you want to use.

Caution You can create objects with the same name, like two users called Liz, at totally different locations in the tree (as shown in Figure 8-2), but it's best not to. It can be extremely confusing for applications that can't properly handle your tree's structure.

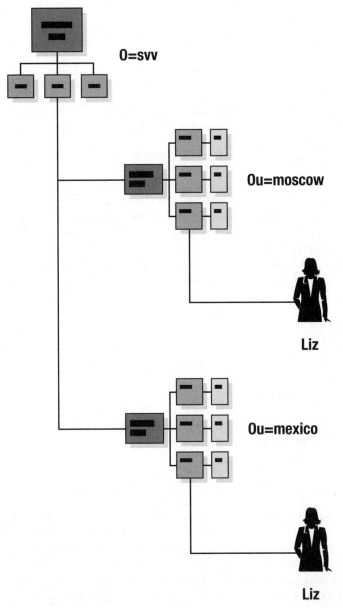

O=svv

Ou=moscow

Liz

Ou=mexico

Liz

Figure 8-2. *Users with the same name can exist at different locations in the Directory tree.*

Distinguished Names

Notice the user Liz in Figure 8-2. She exists at two different locations in the Directory tree. If the user wants to log in, there might be confusion about which account to use. For example, imagine that Liz just gives her username at the login prompt and nothing else. How could the operating system possibly know what user account to use? To avoid such situations, a distinguished name can be used. This allows you to specify exactly which user you wish to authenticate. The distinguished names for Liz are

- .liz.berlin.svv

- .liz.moscow.svv

Tip For example purposes, the preceding scenario was made overly complicated. In real life, the network administrator would take precautionary measures to prevent such a situation arising. It wouldn't be a good idea to expect a user to remember a distinguished name.

If a distinguished name is used, there can be no confusion. This is because in a distinguished name you indicate exactly what object should be used. A distinguished name normally starts with a leading period, which tells the operating system that the following name should be related to the tree level of the Directory.

A distinguished name can be written in two ways: typeful and typeless. In the example .liz.berlin.svv, a typeless distinguished name is used. This name can be made typeful by indicating the exact type. In typeful distinguished names, the following types can be used.

- Organization: O

- Organizational Unit: OU

- Country: C

- Domain: DC

In a typeful distinguished name, all leaf objects get CN as a type indicator. For our user Liz in the previous example, the typeful distinguished names are

- cn=liz.ou=berlin.o=svv

- cn=liz.ou=moscow.o=svv

Typeful distinguished names can be full distinguished names with or without the leading period. They can also be relative, meaning that in the preceding example cn=liz.ou=sfo is a typeful relative distinguished name if your current context is o=svv. To make it even more confusing, there's also an LDAP version of the distinguished name. In LDAP, you always have to use typeful distinguished names. As a separator between the different elements of the distinguished name, a comma must be used instead of a period. The distinguished names for user Liz in LDAP are

- cn=liz,ou=berlin,o=svv

- cn=liz,ou=moscow,o=svv

Obey the following rules when you're working with distinguished names.

- A typeless distinguished name always starts with a period.

- A typeful distinguished name can start with a leading period, but doesn't need to.

- In a distinguished name, you start with the name of the leaf object and work up to the name of the top-level container the object is in.

- In an eDirectory distinguished name, you use dots to separate the elements of the distinguished name from each other.

- In an LDAP distinguished name, commas have to be used to separate the different elements of the distinguished name.

Relative Distinguished Names

In contrast to the distinguished name, there's the relative distinguished name. This is a short name that is related to the current position in eDirectory. This position is called the current context of a user in eDirectory. Users from a Windows workstation can use the **cx** command to find out their current context. If, for example, the current context of Liz is set to berlin.svv, there's no need for Liz to provide her complete name. It's best not to use relative distinguished names, however, since it can be pretty confusing. If you always use distinguished names, you never have to think about your current position in the eDirectory tree and that can avoid mistakes.

Using eDirectory for Authentication

eDirectory is not only the place where information about your network is kept, it's also the central service used for network authentication. This is the process by which a user's credentials are verified in order to see if she has permission to use the services she's trying to access. Upon authentication, the following procedure is applied.

1. The user enters her username and password at the login prompt. In this procedure a credential and a signature are composed. The credential is a data structure that contains all relevant information about the user. In this credential, you'll find, for example, the login name, password, login time, and network address of the user. The credential is encrypted with the user's private key. The result of this encryption is called the signature.

2. The user requests access to some service on the network.

3. After the user has contacted the network service, a random number is sent to the user. This random number is encrypted with the user's public key, which is publicly available from eDirectory.

4. Now the user proves her identity by decrypting the packet sent in step 3 with her private key. The result of this decryption is the proof. It really is a proof because only the user herself can decrypt the package that has been encrypted with her public key since the public and private key are related to each other.

5. The user sends back the random number which was provided to her in step 3, as well as the proof and the credential to the service.

   The service checks if the proof is valid. If this is the case, the service sends back an acknowledgement to the user. If it's not valid, access to the resource is denied.

6. If successful, the user gets access to the service she wants to use.

The eDirectory Database

eDirectory consists of two parts: the service and the database. The service is a process running on a server that gives access to the database. In this section, you'll read how this service can be started and how the database is physically organized.

Structure of the Database

Depending on the OES version you're using, you'll find the eDirectory database on different locations on your server. On OES - Linux, you can find the eDirectory database in the directory /var/nds/dib. On OES - NetWare, the eDirectory database is hidden in the directory SYS:_NETWARE. This directory is specially protected; you can't just access it as a normal user.

■Tip What, you can't see the database? There's no such thing as "you can't." Here's how to see the contents of the _netware directory on your server. First, start the Bash shell with the **bash** command. If you try a plain **ls –l** command, it won't show you the directory _netware, but if you use **cd _netware**, it pops up instantly.

On OES - Linux, you'll find some additional configuration files as well. The most important of them is /etc/nds.conf, which stores critical information needed to access the Directory properly.

The eDirectory database itself consists of several files which together make the FLAIM database that's used by the Directory Service (as shown in Figure 8-3). In this database, log files are used to back out and roll forward transactions in case of a system failure. The primary file is nds.db. This is the control file for the entire database and includes the roll-back log which is used to abort incomplete transactions. If a roll-forward is needed, it's created automatically in the nds*.log files. Transactions recorded in these files can be replayed automatically after a system crash.

The data itself is in the file nds.01, which has a maximum size of 4GB. When the eDirectory database grows larger than 4GB, the system automatically creates a second file in which to store the database that's given the name nds.02 (and so on if more files are needed). In these files, the actual records of the database are stored. Some index files are stored as well to speed up searching in the database.

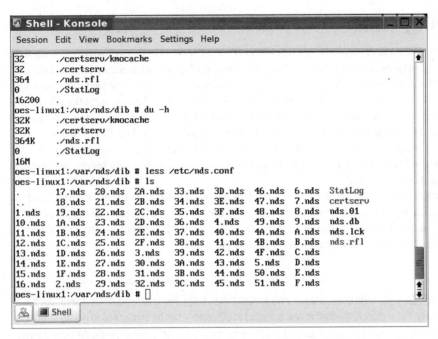

```
32       ./certserv/kmocache
32       ./certserv
364      ./nds.rfl
0        ./StatLog
16200    .
oes-linux1:/var/nds/dib # du -h
32K      ./certserv/kmocache
32K      ./certserv
364K     ./nds.rfl
0        ./StatLog
16M      .
oes-linux1:/var/nds/dib # less /etc/nds.conf
oes-linux1:/var/nds/dib # ls
.        17.nds  20.nds  2A.nds  33.nds  3D.nds  46.nds  6.nds  StatLog
..       18.nds  21.nds  2B.nds  34.nds  3E.nds  47.nds  7.nds  certserv
1.nds    19.nds  22.nds  2C.nds  35.nds  3F.nds  48.nds  8.nds  nds.01
10.nds   1A.nds  23.nds  2D.nds  36.nds  4.nds   49.nds  9.nds  nds.db
11.nds   1B.nds  24.nds  2E.nds  37.nds  40.nds  4A.nds  A.nds  nds.lck
12.nds   1C.nds  25.nds  2F.nds  38.nds  41.nds  4B.nds  B.nds  nds.rfl
13.nds   1D.nds  26.nds  3.nds   39.nds  42.nds  4F.nds  C.nds
14.nds   1E.nds  27.nds  30.nds  3A.nds  43.nds  5.nds   D.nds
15.nds   1F.nds  28.nds  31.nds  3B.nds  44.nds  50.nds  E.nds
16.nds   2.nds   29.nds  32.nds  3C.nds  45.nds  51.nds  F.nds
oes-linux1:/var/nds/dib # []
```

Figure 8-3. *The eDirectory database is stored in several files, which together compose the FLAIM database.*

The last part of the eDirectory database is the stream files. These are the files that start with a hexadecimal number and end with the extension .nds. Normally, you'll find quite a lot of them. Stream files are used to store attributes of the type Stream, like login scripts and print job configurations in the database. These attributes are not stored in the actual database, because that would be inefficient.

Starting and Stopping the Service

We have just looked at the eDirectory database stored in the files on your server's hard drive. There's another part to eDirectory too—the service that makes these files accessible: the eDirectory service, or the nds service (eDirectory was called nds in the old days). As an administrator, it's important to know how to stop and start this service. If you're administrator of an OES - NetWare server, you have to deal with DS.NLM. You can unload it by using **unload ds.nlm** at the server console, and you can load it again by just issuing the command **ds**.

On OES - Linux, the directory service is started with the program file /usr/sbin/ndsd. Of course, you can stop it like any other process with **kill**, but there's a nicer way of doing so. The startup script /etc/init.d/ndsd manages the automatic starting of ndsd from your default runlevel. You can also use this script to stop and start the service manually. For instance, use **/etc/init.d/ndsd stop** to stop the service, **/etc/init.d/ndsd start** to start it, or **/etc/init.d/ndsd restart** to stop and start the service.

Though the commands just listed can be used to stop and start the eDirectory service, you'll find you rarely need to restart the Directory service this way. They're really used more as troubleshooting tools. You can read more about this in the section "eDirectory Troubleshooting" at the end of this chapter.

Managing Time

For eDirectory to function properly, it's important that all servers in the network agree on the time that's used. This is because the synchronization of changes in eDirectory is based on timestamps. When determining if anything needs to be changed, servers in the network compare timestamps in objects in the Directory. Based on these timestamps, synchronization does or does not take place. If the difference in time on servers that need to synchronize is too big, there's a risk that a change won't be recognized and won't get changed on the network. This could result, for example, in a password change on one server that doesn't get through to another server. In such cases, the user would need his new password on one server, yet require his old password on the other.

In OES, there are two mechanisms that can be used to synchronize time. The first (and default) mechanism is based on the Network Time Protocol (NTP). The second employs the legacy Timesync mechanism. If you're running OES - Linux, NTP is the only option. If OES - NetWare is used, you can choose between NTP and Timesync.

Tip It's possible to make time configuration very complicated, but if you follow the default settings, it's actually rather easy. For instance, the first server installed in eDirectory can be configured to get its time from a trustworthy Internet NTP time source. This server will be the time provider in the network. All other servers are then automatically configured to get their time from this server. I recommend using this default setup since it works well. Only use the information that follows to tune your own NTP time server if somehow this information doesn't work for you.

The Relationship Between eDirectory and Time Synchronization

Though time synchronization is not a function offered by eDirectory, it is largely dependent upon it. Whenever a change to an object is made, timestamps in this object are changed. When a server initializes a synchronization with another server, it compares these timestamps with its own timestamps. If time is not properly synchronized on the network, this can lead to problems.

Time synchronization is a critical service in eDirectory because the information in eDirectory is scattered through different replicas. Since no replica has a leading role in synchronization, eDirectory must rely on another mechanism: a proper time synchronization. If all servers share the same time, information can be properly synchronized in the network.

NTP

Network Time Protocol (NTP) is an Internet standard for time synchronization, and only runs on the TCP/IP stack, which shouldn't be a problem in an OES environment. NTP doesn't use real local time for time synchronization. Instead, it works with UTC time. This is Universal Time Coordinated, which can be calculated for every server in the network. In NTP, the concept of stratum is used to decide with which server on the Internet it's synchronized. Stratum 1 is a clock with the highest level of accuracy. Normally, this stratum is used for atomic clocks on the Internet and other clocks that are absolutely reliable. A server that synchronizes with a stratum 1 clock becomes a stratum 2 time provider because it gets its time from the most reliable time source on the network. If another server synchronizes with this stratum 2 server, it becomes a stratum 3 server, and so on. The advantage of using NTP over other proprietary protocols like Novell's timesync is that NTP is available for all platforms and can be used by all major operating systems. Linux natively supports it and NetWare's timesync can be made compatible with NTP. Since NetWare 6.5, timesync is no longer the preferred way to synchronize time. All NetWare versions since NetWare 6.5 support NTP services as well. These NTP services are provided on the OES - NetWare platform with XNTPD.NLM, which is basically the same service used on OES - Linux.

Tip Two different versions of NTP can be deployed: version 2 and version 3. The problem is that both versions are not completely compatible. To ensure compatibility, it's best to use version 3 NTP servers on all the servers in the network. OES - NetWare and OES - Linux both use NTP version 3 with the XNTPD implementation.

The configuration of the xntpd service is rather similar on OES - NetWare and OES - Linux. In both cases, time synchronization is started with the xntpd service and in both cases the configuration of the time server is maintained in the configuration file ntpd.conf which is found in the directory, and so on. The most important part of a proper NTP synchronization is the configuration file ntp.conf. An example of this file is discussed next.

Proper Time Synchronization with NTP

One of the major characteristics of a pair of servers that want to synchronize time in an NTP-environment is that only a maximum time difference is allowed. This difference is 1000 seconds, or about 16 minutes. If the difference between two servers is more than 1000 seconds, the other server is declared "insane" and your server refuses to communicate with it. As a proper preparation for NTP time synchronization, you should make sure that no difference greater than 1000 seconds exists.

To reduce the difference in time between two servers, it's recommended to use the ntpdate utility before you start synchronizing anything. With ntpdate, you can perform a one-time synchronization with a time server on the Internet. ntpdate uses only one argument: the name of the server you want to synchronize with. If, for example, you want to synchronize time with the server with IP address 10.0.0.1, issue the command **ntpdate 10.0.0.1**. It's best to use this command to edit ntp.cnf before you start configuring NTP.

Tip You can use a private NTP timeserver in your network. It's also possible to use one of the public NTP timeservers available on the Internet. You can find a complete list of these servers at www.ntp.org.

Modifying ntp.conf for Proper Time Synchronization

Once the time is more or less synchronized between the time server and your server, you can start the configuration of your time server. Both OES versions have an example ntp.conf which, once edited, will work on your server. You can start the configuration using the following small amount of code:

```
server 127.127.1.0
fudge 127.127.1.0 stratum 10
server 10.0.0.1
```

In this example, two things will happen: by default, the server will try to communicate with NTP server 10.0.0.1 on the Internet. If that works, all is well. If it doesn't work, the line server 127.127.1.0 defines that this server will be its own NTP server. In that case, there has to be a stratum as well: the stratum is defined as stratum 10. This is a rather secure definition; the self-declared stratum is so low that any other Internet NTP server that's reachable takes over the job as soon as it's available. The keyword fudge (the fudge factor) allows an NTP time server to run as its own time provider when no external NTP time server is available.

Another important issue for proper NTP time synchronization is the possibility to work with restrictions. Some NTP implementations are open by nature; others are not. If you don't want your NTP server to be open to everyone, include some restrictions in the configuration file. In the following example, the first line is the most important: it tells the NTP server to totally ignore all servers not mentioned specifically in one of the lines mentioned next:

```
restrict default noquery notrust nomotify
restrict 127.0.0.1
restrict 192.168.0.0 mask 255.255.255.0
```

In this example, only the local host and servers whose IP address starts with 192.168.0.0/24 are accepted as NTP clients of this server; all other servers are rejected. If your server is connected to the Internet, consider protecting it in a similar way.

Starting the NTP Service

Once the NTP configuration file is created, the NTP service can be started. From OES - NetWare, issue the **xntpd.nlm** command to start it, or from OES - Linux, use the xntpd process. The former can be started just by entering **xntpd** on the console, while the latter can be started with **/etc/init.d/xntp start**. It's best to include this script in your default runlevel so it begins automatically when your server is started.

Timesync

Timesync is the legacy way to synchronize time on a Novell network. This synchronization method is developed for use in an IPX network and is no longer recommended for an OES environment. The only important thing to know is that a timesync environment can work together perfectly with an NTP environment.

To set up a timesync environment to work with NTP, a configuration of a timesync reference server communicating with primary and secondary servers is recommended. Normally, the reference server gets its time from a hardware clock. In a mixed timesync/NTP network, the reference server must be configured to get its time from an NTP timeserver. This can be accomplished by creating a configured list. These settings can be entered from MONITOR.NLM ➤ Server Parameters ➤ Time. In an easier configuration, the timesync server can be configured as a secondary server. If, however, you're using OES - NetWare as a time client in an NTP environment, instead of configuring with timesync, it's best to configure as an NTP client. The following lines of code show the settings that must be used to configure a timesync server as client to an NTP server.

```
TIMESYNC Configured Sources              On
TIMESYNC Time Sources          ip-address-of-time-provider:123;
TIMESYNC Type    SECONDARY
```

eDirectory Management

If you work in a small- to medium-sized environment, the eDirectory database will not be too big and will still be manageable. If you work in a large environment, or if your company has several remote sites, it's no longer ideal to put all eDirectory information in one large undivided database. In that case, it makes sense to work with more than one eDirectory partition. If you do nothing, you'll just have one partition named [Root], or the root partition. Other reasons to create further partitions in an eDirectory tree include the following:

- There are too many objects and you want to make eDirectory more manageable.

- You work with remote sites and have rather slow WAN links.

- For security reasons, you want to separate users.

- You want to split up a special purpose container to make the objects in it available every-where in the tree.

- You want to work with decentralized eDirectory management in which each administrator is responsible for a branch of eDirectory.

Now the information in an eDirectory partition is stored in a replica. This is a copy of the physical database stored in SYS:_NETWARE on OES - NetWare or in /var/nds/dib on OES - Linux. The first replica on an eDirectory partition is the master replica. It's very unwise to work with just one replica for a partition. Instead, you should make at least two replicas of each partition for fault-tolerance purposes. That way, if a server goes down, you don't lose all your eDirectory information. It's strongly recommended you have at least three replicas for each partition.

Managing Partitions

eDirectory partitions are managed from iManager. Partitions can be created, merged, and moved. It's not possible to delete a partition. Instead of deleting it, you'll merge it with its parent partition. Before you start any partition or replica operation, be sure you've met the basic conditions:

- The eDirectory tree is healthy and there are no critical errors.

- Time is synchronized.

- You're performing the operation during times where the network and server load is low.

Creating Partitions

The following procedure outlines how new partitions can be split off from an existing partition.

1. Start iManager from your web browser on the URL https://ip-address/nps/iManager.html and log in with an administrative account.

2. Select Roles And Tasks ➤ Partitions And Replicas. A list of options appears. Select Create Partition.

3. Browse to the container you want to be the root of the new partition. A container object must always be used as the top of a partition. It's not possible to divide the contents of one container over more than one partition if no underlying containers are used. Click OK after selecting the container.

4. It will take a few moments for the operation to complete. Don't start any other activity during this time. If you do, you could severely damage your tree. Once the partition is created, a completion message appears. You may now repeat the task or click OK to stop creating partitions.

5. Select View Partition Information from the iManager Partitions And Replicas menu to get an overview of the current situation (as shown in Figure 8-4). You'll now be able to browse to one of your partitions to display information about it.

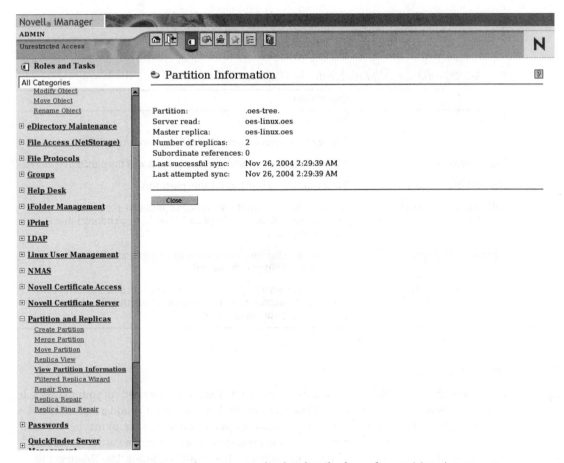

Figure 8-4. *Select View Partition Information to display details about the partitions in your tree.*

The option View Partition Information displays the following information (shown in Table 8-3) about the partition.

Table 8-3. *Information Displayed with View Partition Information*

Value	Description
Partition	Name of the partition
Server read	Name of the server where the information is read from
Master replica	Name of the server where the master replica of the partition is stored
Number of replicas	Total number of replicas for this partition
Subordinate references	Number of subordinate reference replicas (see the section "Subordinate Reference Replicas" later in this chapter) that exist for this partition
Last successful sync	The last time the information between replicas of this partition were successfully synchronized
Last attempted sync	The last time an attempt was made to synchronize information between the partitions of this replica. This value should be similar to that of Last successful sync.

Moving Partitions

If you have an existing eDirectory environment that no longer fits the needs of your network, it may be necessary to move partitions. For example, perhaps you want to add a regional level between the Organization level of your tree and the level of your locations, or maybe you need to move a container and its contents. If so, then you should use the Move Partition option, since there's no other option to move a container with its entire contents. Use iManager to move partitions, as shown in the following steps.

1. Start iManager, log in, and select Partitions And Replicas ➤ Move Partition to be presented with the screen shown in Figure 8-5.

2. Choose the object you want to move and then in the Move To field specify where you want to move your partition to.

3. After a move, there's always a possibility that a user or applications will look for the information at the old location (which, of course, no longer exists). Select the Create An Alias In Place Of Moved Object option so these requests can be resolved. Click OK to start the move.

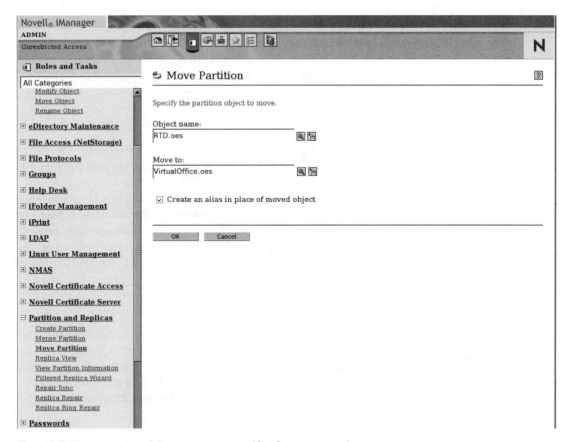

Figure 8-5. *To move a partition, you must specify where to move it.*

Merging Partitions

In some situations, you'll find after creating a partition that it's no longer needed. In that case, you can choose to merge the partition with its parent. This can be useful, for example, after closing a remote office whose partition was separated: before you can remove all objects from the container related to that office (including the container itself), you must merge the partition back into its parent partition. This can also be done from iManager on the Partition And Replicas screen.

1. Start iManager, log in and select Partitions and Replicas ➤ Merge Partition.

2. Select the partition which you want to have merge with its parent and click OK. The merge is performed immediately. It can take a while before the process completes. If you want the process to occur in the background, click Close to close the progress screen.

3. Wait for the message that the merge has completed successfully before attempting any other operation on eDirectory.

Managing Replicas

The information in eDirectory is physically stored in replicas. A minimum of three replicas is created automatically when the first three servers are installed in a partition. Sometimes it will be necessary to add or delete some replicas manually. Before you can judge how to do that, you need to be aware of the different replica types that can be used.

Replica Types

There are five different replica types that can be used in an eDirectory environment. Only three of these replica types are created automatically: the Master, the Read/Write, and the Subordinate Reference replica. The first replica of a given partition is always the master replica. After a second and third server are added to the same partition, read/write replicas are placed on these servers automatically. If needed subordinate reference replicas are added automatically, they are added to a server with a replica of a parent partition but not a child partition. Subordinate reference replicas are then needed in order to find replicas of the child partitions, because there is no pointer in the replicas of a parent partition to existing replicas of those child partitions. All other replica types must be added manually.

Master Replica

The first replica that's automatically created for a partition is the master replica. It's called this because it has a leading role in some operations. The master replica must be accessible if you want to add or delete servers, replicas, or partitions in eDirectory. It's not really needed to create users and other more common objects. These can be created from any read/write replica as well and can be synchronized from read/write replicas to other replicas. This is called multi master replication.

Read/Write Replica

All replicas created after the initial creation of the master replica become read/write replicas automatically. For a fault-tolerant network environment, it's recommended you have at least two read/write replicas. This is because a read/write replica is a full copy of the data in the master replica. The process of replica synchronization takes care that all information between the replicas is consistent: if a new object is added to a master or a read/write replica, in a few seconds it's synchronized to all other replicas on the same network. The nice thing about replica synchronization is that it doesn't really matter in which replica a new object is created since it's replicated to all other replicas anyway. Because of replica synchronization, you'll always have an up-to-date backup of the critical information in your eDirectory tree if you have at least one read/write replica.

On the other hand, you should be careful not to create too many read/write replicas. This is because information still needs to be synchronized between the different replicas in the tree. If there are too many replicas, it takes too much performance away from your servers and networks to keep everything up-to-date. It's therefore recommended not to have more than eight replicas for each partition.

For your daily work as an administrator, it's not important to work directly on the master replica or on a read/write replica. If, for example, you're adding a user to the tree, eDirectory adds it to the nearest replica (it doesn't matter if this is a master or a read/write replica).

The network can even survive if the master replica is offline for a while since changes will be synchronized automatically to it once it comes back online.

Read-Only Replica

The read-only replica is comparable to a read/write replica. The major difference is that read-only replicas can't be changed. This makes them less useful compared to read/write replicas. Though they're synchronized to other replicas in the network, they can't even be used to login in to. This is because every time a user logs in to the network, the last login time property must be changed in eDirectory. Therefore, read-only replicas are considered rather useless, thus read/write replicas are recommended instead.

Filtered Replica

A filter replica is a replica that doesn't contain all of the information in the particular partition. In a filtered replica, the administrator can specify exactly what objects and properties need to be present and what can be missed. A filtered replica can be very useful in getting only a selected amount of information present at a certain server. This can be useful if, say, eGuide is used to provide users with only selected information from eDirectory. Though a filtered replica does participate in replica synchronization in order to receive new objects in a partition, this isn't a complete backup of the information in a partition since not all objects and properties are included. A filtered replica is defined as a property of the server object, and the replica filter is only valid on the server where the filter is defined.

Subordinate Reference Replica

A subordinate reference replica isn't really a replica. Instead it's a pointer for information that isn't present locally on a server. The general rule for the occurrence of a subordinate reference replica is that it's created automatically if a server has a replica of a parent partition but no replica of a child partition. Imagine a simple tree that consists of o=oes, ou=rtd.o=oes, and ou=sfo.o=oes. Server1 has a replica of the root partition but no replica of the partition ou=sfo.o=oes. In that case, a subordinate reference replica of the ou=sfo partition is created automatically. It's needed for server1 to indicate where it can find real replicas for the partition ou=sfo.o=oes. As such, the subordinate reference replica doesn't contain many real objects: it only contains information about the top-level container object of the subordinate container and a replica list that indicates on which servers real replicas can be found. As an administrator, you don't have to think about the creation of subordinate reference replicas at all, because they are created automatically. You just have to be aware of their existence. Besides that, it's recommended you try and avoid the occurrence of subordinate reference replicas in your tree design as much as possible.

Managing Replicas

When you install the first server in a tree, a root partition is created automatically. The master replica of this partition is then automatically created on this first server. Upon creation of the second and third servers in the tree, read/write replicas are added automatically as well. Anything else has to be created manually. In this section you'll learn how to manage replicas in the tree.

Creating and Deleting Replicas

Like all partition tasks, replicas are also managed from iManager.

1. Start iManager on https://your ip address/nps/imanager.html and select Roles And Tasks ➤ Partitions And Replicas ➤ Replica View.

2. Replica management can be performed server-centric or partition-centric. Select the partition or server whose replicas you want to manage, and then click OK. This gives you the screen shown in Figure 8-6. This example describes how to manage replicas from the partition view.

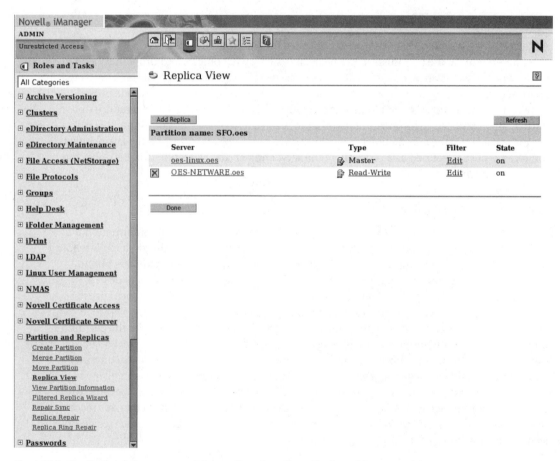

Figure 8-6. *Replicas can be managed from a list of replicas displayed for a partition.*

3. If there are still servers in the tree that don't have a replica of the selected partition, click Add Replica to add a replica for this partition.

4. To change the replica type for a replica that is not the master, click the replica type. A list of all available replica types are now displayed, as shown in Figure 8-7. Note that it's not possible to change the replica type of the master replica. It is possible though to change a replica that is not the master into the master replica. This changes the type of the master replica automatically.

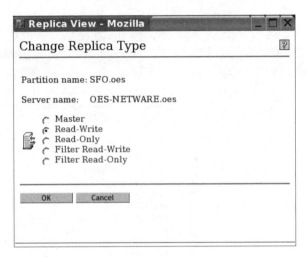

Figure 8-7. *It's easy to change a replica type. Just select the desired new type from a list.*

5. If you want to delete a replica from a server, click the red crosses in front of all replicas that are not the master replica for a server. The state of the replica will temporarily change to Dying. It may be necessary to click the Refresh button to refresh the browser view. Notice in some cases that after the deletion of a replica a subordinate reference replica will be created automatically.

6. Click Done when you've finished making changes to the replica list.

Creating Filtered Replicas

A special wizard that can be started from iManager is available for the creation of filtered replicas.

1. Start iManager, log in, and select Roles And Tasks ➤ Partition And Replicas ➤ Filtered Replica Wizard.

2. Browse to the server on which you want to configure a filtered replica. It's only possible to place filtered replicas on servers that have no other copy of the replica yet. Click Next after selecting the server.

3. Click Define The Filter Set to start specifying what classes and attributes you want included in the filtered replica.

4. If you want to be able to log in from the filtered replica, select the check box Enable Local Login.

5. Click The Filter Is Empty to start creating the filter. An Edit Filter Dialog is displayed, as shown in Figure 8-8. In this dialog, you can select all the classes and attributes you want to include in the filter. Click OK when you're finished.

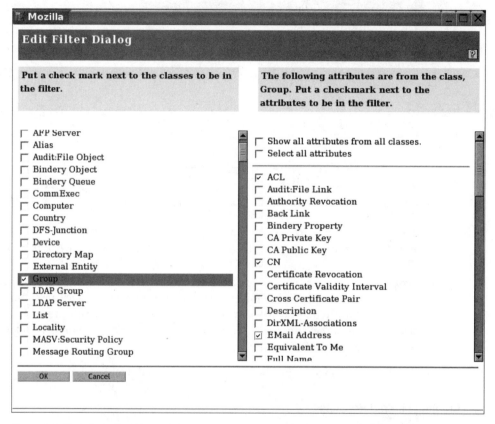

Figure 8-8. *Use the Edit Filter Dialog screen to specify which classes and attributes you want to include in the filter.*

6. Check the current settings for your filter in the overview window (see Figure 8-9) and click OK if you're satisfied. Then, click Next.

7. A filtered replica isn't related to any partition automatically. In this step, you must assign a partition scope. A replica of the root partition can be selected to include objects from the entire tree, but it's also possible to choose a specific child partition for which to create the filtered replica. Click Next after defining the partition scope for your filtered replica.

8. Click Finish to complete the creation of the filtered replica.

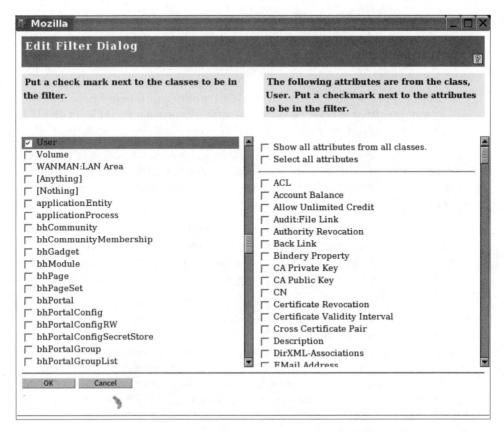

Figure 8-9. *If you're satisfied with all the settings in the filtered replica, click OK to save them.*

Linux eDirectory Management Tools

In an OES environment, eDirectory can be managed from iMonitor and iManager. Some Linux command-line utilities are also available though. The following list presents a short overview of the commands and their usage. This overview is not complete, so read the main pages for further details.

- *ldapconfig*: Lets you modify, view, and refresh the attributes of LDAP server and Group objects. This is a complex utility that can be used to query all LDAP attributes in eDirectory. If, for example, you want to view the value of an attribute in the LDAP attribute list, enter the following command: **ldapconfig –t yourtreename –w** *yourpassword* **–a useraccount –v "Require TLS for simple binds with password", "searchTimeLimit"**.

- *ndsbackup*: This creates eDirectory object archives and adds or extracts eDirectory objects. You must log in as a user with administrative rights to eDirectory to be able to make backups with ndsbackup. The working of the command is more or less comparable to the working of the **tar** command. If, for example, you want to back up the contents of o=oes, use **ndsbackup cvf ndsbackupfile .o=oes**. A complete backup of the entire tree can be made with **ndsbackup cvf ndsbackupfile [Root]**. If later you need to restore the backup created with ndsbackup, use **ndsbackup xvf ndsbackupfile**.

- *ndsconfig*: Used to configure eDirectory. This is a very powerful utility. You can use it to configure a new tree, to add a server into an existing tree, or to remove a server from the eDirectory tree. If, for example, you want to add your server to the eDirectory tree oes-tree, use **ndsconfig add –t oes-tree –n o=oes –a cn=admin.o=oes**. It's also possible to remove a server from the Directory tree. To do so, use **ndsconfig rm –a cn=admin.o=oes**. Apart from adding a server to a tree or removing it from a tree, **ndsconfig** can also be used to configure some specific eDirectory modules. If you want to configure the HTTP module, use **ndsconfig add –t oes-tree –n o=oes –a cn=admin.o=oes –m http**.

- *ndsd*: The eDirectory daemon. This daemon is started from the default runlevel when the system boots up. To do its work, it reads the configuration file /etc/nds.conf, creates the file /var/nds/ndsd.pid with process information, and starts providing the eDirectory service to the network.

- *ndslogin*: Can be used to diagnose eDirectory authentication. This utility is not a Novell client for Linux. It's simply a troubleshooting tool to verify that eDirectory login is working properly. If login is successful, it displays a message indicating the success. For example, use **ndslogin –t oes-tree admin.oes** to see if the specified tree can be reached.

- *ndsmerge*: A utility for merging two eDirectory trees. Merging trees is heavy work for the eDirectory process. Before attempting a merge, be sure both trees are functioning properly and that both are synchronized to the same time source. Verify that the schema is synchronized as well before attempting a merge. If needed, use **ndsrepair –S –Ad** to import the schema from the remote tree before attempting the merge. After you've verified that all conditions are met, use **ndsmerge –m target-tree target-admin source-admin** from the source tree. For example, if you want to merge NW-TREE into OES-TREE, this command must be used on a server that has a replica (master replica of root is strongly recommended) in NW-TREE.

- *ndsrepair*: A very powerful utility for repairing and correcting problems with the Novell eDirectory database. Because this utility is very complex and very powerful as well, its use is only recommended for advanced eDirectory administrators. Most tasks that can be carried out with ndsrepair can be performed from the browser-based iMonitor utility as well. For example, use **ndsrepair –U** to perform an unattended full repair of the Directory on your server. This optimizes the local database without further user assistance. Another useful command is **ndsrepair –T**, which checks the time synchronization on the local network.

- *ndssch*: A utility that can be used to extend the eDirectory schema. The eDirectory schema is modular and can be extended with extra schema files. These schema files add new records to the database. If you have such a schema file, use **ndssch –t treename adminname schemafile** to extend the schema of your tree.

- *ndssnmp*: The SNMP services module for eDirectory. This service enables SNMP monitoring of eDirectory services. You'll need it to monitor eDirectory with a management program like Zen for Servers. It's best to load it from your default runlevel on an eDirectory server that needs to be monitored permanently. It can also be loaded manually with **/usr/bin/ndssnmp –l** and unloaded with **/usr/bin/ndssnmp –u**.

- *ndssnmpconfig*: This utility can be used to enable and disable eDirectory SNMP traps, set time intervals for traps, or list all present traps. The command works with a complex shell interface on its own. Read the man page for more details.

- *ndsstat*: A utility that displays eDirectory information related to a certain server (see Figure 8-10). Just enter **ndsstat** to get details about eDirectory on the local server, or **ndsstat –h servername** to get information about eDirectory on a remote server.

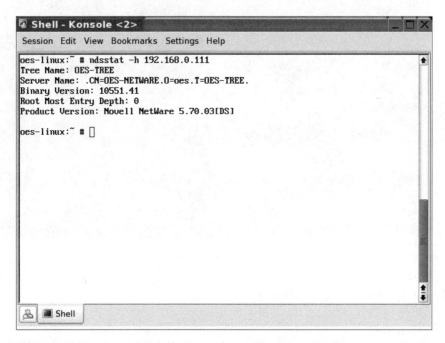

Figure 8-10. *ndsstat can be used to get information about eDirectory on another server or the local server.*

- *ndstrace*: A tool to display eDirectory traffic debug messages (see Figure 8-11). This is an advanced utility that can be used to display and filter all kinds of eDirectory debug messages. When you start it for the first time, it displays a list of options that can be used to filter ndstrace output. Each of these options can be enabled from the ndstrace user interface with **ndstrace [+|-] option**. If, for example, you want to display all change cache messages, use **ndstrace +chng**. To disable it again, use **ndstrace –chng**. Based upon the default selection, the utility starts displaying information all by itself. Particularly interesting are the error codes (displayed in red). These indicate if eDirectory is still healthy or not. ndstrace can also be started from the browser-based tool iMonitor. In fact, it's somewhat easier this way.

- *nldap*: The LDAP services daemon used by eDirectory. This daemon should run on all eDirectory servers that you want to use to enable LDAP access to eDirectory.

- *nmasinst*: A utility that can be used to add and configure NMAS login methods. To add NMAS functionality to eDirectory, use **nmasinst –i**. This extends the schema, configures NMAS, and creates NMAS objects in eDirectory.

Figure 8-11. *The utility ndstrace can be used to monitor eDirectory health.*

eDirectory Tree Design

By this point, you probably realize that installing a network based on eDirectory involves more than just putting in the installation CD and following the onscreen instructions. To implement eDirectory the right way, you need to design the eDirectory tree properly—a properly designed tree simply runs better. For that reason, the basics of eDirectory tree design are discussed next.

Designing a Small- to Medium-Sized Tree

How you design your eDirectory tree depends on the size of the network it will be used in. If your OES server supports a small company with one location and about 20 users, you hardly need to do anything regarding the tree's design. Just one container object could be enough. Simply put all the objects you're creating into this single container object. It's definitely the easiest way.

However, if your network is going to grow fast, a single container tree might present some problems later. If in a few years a single container tree in a network with 20 users will likely turn into a multisite network with over 2000 users, you'll need more than a single container tree.

To avoid problems at a later stage, it may be useful to start with a robust design right from the beginning. Thus, it's best to begin by creating containers for special purposes in your tree. In many cases, it's very useful to create an organizational unit in which you put your user objects, make another in which you put the printer objects, use another one for the workstation objects, and so on (as illustrated in Figure 8-12). This makes your tree more versatile should it grow larger at a later stage.

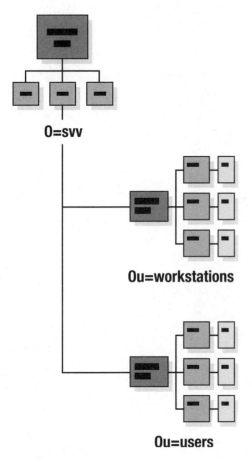

Figure 8-12. *In a small network, it makes sense to create a container for the different types of network objects.*

Designing a Medium Tree

How you design a tree for a medium-sized company depends on the way the company is organized. Is it a company with multiple sites? If so, it's best to create a container object for each of the locations (as in Figure 8-13). This makes decentralized management by local administrators much easier. If, however, network management is centralized and fast WAN links are used, it's not really necessary to create a container object for each of the locations.

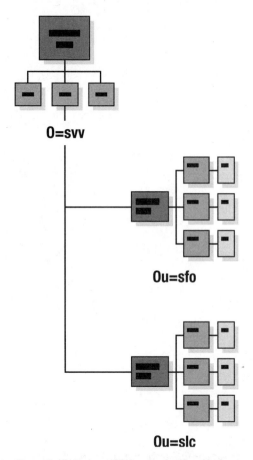

O=svv

Ou=sfo

Ou=slc

Figure 8-13. *In a medium-sized network that consists of different locations, it often makes sense to create an OU for each of these locations.*

If on the other hand you're designing a tree for a medium-sized company where all people work at the same site, the departmental approach might work for you. If your enterprise, for example, consists of several different entities, it makes sense to create an OU for each of these entities. This would work for an IT company that has different branches for training, services, and product distribution. In that case, it's natural to make a container object for each of these branches. If, however, within a large company all people are working with the same products and the same resources, it's often less useful to make such a distinction. If everyone in a company is involved in the distribution of network routers, but some of the employees are in sales, others are in marketing, some are administrative staff, and so on, it doesn't make sense to create an OU for each of these groups, especially if they aren't all working with the same data and applications located on the same fileservers.

Despite the preceding tips, the proper design of an eDirectory tree tends to vary from case to case. Sometimes it will make sense to create a separate container for the sales staff in a company and sometimes you're better off making an eDirectory group for these sales people. The distinction isn't always clear. There is, however, one important question you should always ask before deciding to make an OU for a group of users: Is this a rather isolated group in which all people work with more or less the same resources? If the answer to this question is yes, it often makes sense to create an OU. If, on the other hand, it isn't an isolated group but is instead a group where its members work together with the employees of other departments using the same vnetwork resources, it often makes more sense to create an eDirectory group object. If, however, you have a container object that holds all the objects you want to add to a group, it's preferred to use the container object for rights assignment.

Designing a Large Tree

The larger the network, the more complex your design will be. In a large network, there are many factors to consider, each of which plays a part in the final design of the network. I'll end this portion of the chapter with the following hints about the design of large networks.

- Does your network have additional locations? Make an OU for each of the locations.

- Are there many network locations? If so, it might help to add an additional layer of OUs, where, between the organization and the actual locations, an OU is added for each of the geographical locations.

- Does the network consist of different locations and low-capacity WAN connections? If it does, consider making a separate tree for each of the networks behind a slow WAN connection.

- Do you have one huge head office and many smaller locations? Consider a combined approach in which you make functional OUs for each of the major departments in the company and an OU for each of the separate locations (as illustrated in Figure 8-14).

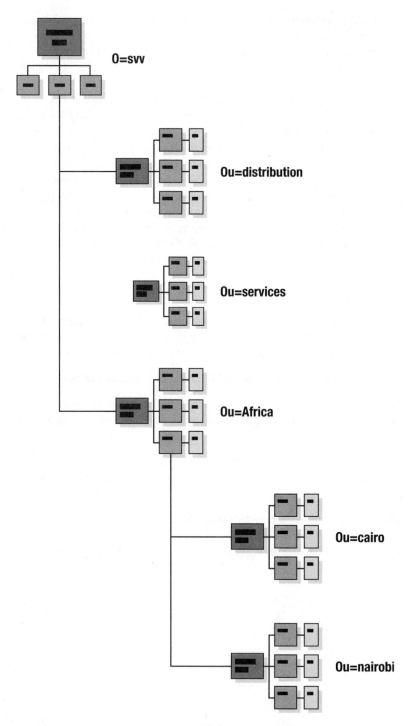

O=svv

Ou=distribution

Ou=services

Ou=Africa

Ou=cairo

Ou=nairobi

Figure 8-14. *In a large network, it's often better to go for a combined approach.*

Scalability and Fault Tolerance

In the previous sections, one important technical argument in the creation and design of the Directory tree was omitted: replica placement and partitioning. You can't make a proper design of a tree if you just look at the organization. You must also think about how your network resources are deployed. In your eDirectory design, you should consider the way replicas and partitions are deployed in order to achieve maximum flexibility.

To optimize the traffic flow and the fault tolerance of your network, consider the following tips:

- To optimize WAN traffic, create a partition for each geographical location.

- Partition key containers as well and place a replica of this partition on the child partitions of the partition.

- For fault tolerance, create at least two, or possibly three, replicas for each partition.

- Avoid creating partitions that span WAN links since it might lead to a decrease in performance.

Accessing Resources

One final important factor in the design of an eDirectory tree is the placement of replicas with regards to the access of resources. The following two factors should be considered.

- For network administration purposes, it's advisable to place the master replica near the network administrator. If your WAN links are fast enough and you've centralized network management at one site, consider placing the master replicas of all partitions on a dedicated replica server at the administrator's site.

- For usability, place a replica with the information users require near the user. This way, you avoid the need for the user to cross slow WAN links each time he needs information.

The eDirectory Schema

The structure of the database is defined in the eDirectory schema. As an administrator, you'll sometimes have to perform eDirectory schema management tasks. For example, if you're installing an additional product, the schema may be extended to make it possible to work with the newly created objects in your eDirectory tree. In this section, you'll get a short introduction to working with the schema.

Function of the Schema

The eDirectory schema defines the structure of the eDirectory database. You can't create a class before the class is defined in the schema. In this class definition, you define where the class can be created, and what attributes the class can have. Of course, these attributes are defined in the schema as well.

All settings in the schema are saved in the schema partition. This is a special hidden partition that exists on each server in the eDirectory tree. If extensions to the schema are made, these have to be synchronized to all other servers that have a copy of the schema partition. A special schema synchronization process takes care of that. If the schema is not synchronized properly, it may result in problems while working with eDirectory classes.

Schema Structure

The schema is defined in a hierarchical structure such as eDirectory. Different kinds of classes exist within the schema. Some are called superclasses, while others are referred to as effective classes. The purpose of a superclass is to define things that are common to several different classes in eDirectory; thus, a superclass is a class that other classes in the schema can inherit from. In addition, a class can inherit from more than one superclass. For example, there's a superclass Top. Some attributes associated to this class have to be associated to all other classes in eDirectory as well. Instead of defining these attributes for each separate class in eDirectory, simply specify that the class should inherit from Top. In this case, Top is the so-called superclass and all attributes associated to Top are inherited by all objects that have Top as their superclass.

Another type of class is the effective classes. These are the real objects you'll find in eDirectory, like users, printers, and so on. Most effective classes have superclasses they inherit their properties from. They also have containment rules. These are the definitions where a specific object can be created in eDirectory, as shown in Figure 8-15. Ever tried to create a user directly under the tree object, or tried to create a country object in an organization? Then you realize this isn't possible. That's because a containment rule is in force. A containment rule defines where exactly in eDirectory a certain class type can be created.

The last important part of the schema is the auxiliary class. This is a collection of attributes associated to some objects but not to all objects of the same type. You'll find an example of this in Linux User Management, covered later in this book. If LUM is enabled for a certain user, the user needs a new set of attributes. These attributes are only required for LUM users, not for all users in the eDirectory tree. The solution is to work with an auxiliary class. Only users that are LUM users have the auxiliary class associated to their user objects. Normal users don't have this auxiliary class.

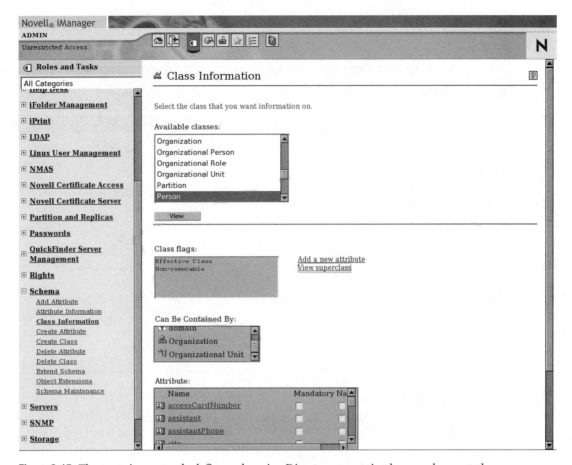

Figure 8-15. *The containment rule defines where in eDirectory a certain class can be created.*

Managing the Schema

As I said earlier, you may have to perform schema management from time to time, which involves numerous tasks. For instance, you may run into cases where it's necessary to extend the schema. Most times, however, this occurs automatically upon installation of the new product that needs the schema extension. Or perhaps it may be necessary to modify some parts of the schema. This section offers examples of both.

Extending the Schema

A schema can be extended in several ways. One option is to work with a schema file, which is sometimes provided with an application that needs a schema extension. In this situation, you directly extend the schema by adding a file in which the extensions are defined to the schema. Another option is that schema data is imported from another server. The latter is especially useful when you're preparing to merge two eDirectory trees. To avoid problems while performing the merge, it's good practice to update the schema before starting the merge. The following steps show how the schema from another server can be imported to the local server.

1. Start iManager, log in, and select Roles And Tasks ➤ Schema ➤ Extend Schema. This shows all the options available for schema extension in the ICE Wizard (see Figure 8-16).

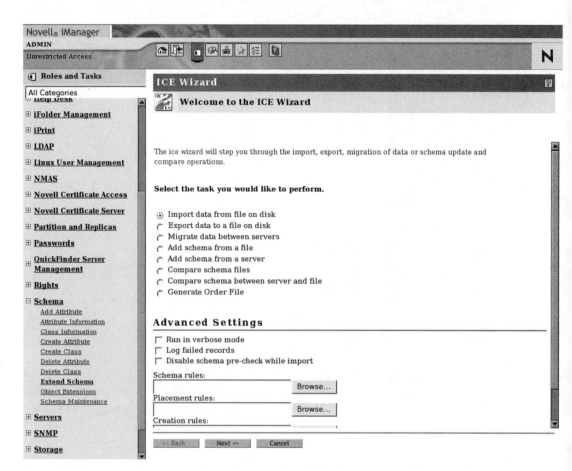

Figure 8-16. *Several options are available for extending the local schema on a server.*

2. Let's import a schema from another tree. Since this involves some risks, it's best to start by exporting the current schema to a file on disk. If anything goes wrong, the data from the original schema can always be imported later.

■Caution Exporting data from the local schema to a file on disk is not a good backup. Instead, it's best to create a real backup before starting schema operations like this. On OES - Linux, use **ndsbackup cvf schemabackupfile Schema** to make a backup of the schema. On OES - NetWare, use **sbcon** on the server console to create a backup of the schema.

---

3. Select the Export Data To A File On Disk option and click Next to continue. This starts the ICE Wizard to export the schema to an LDIF file.

4. Enter all necessary information to authenticate on the remote server. In order to export the schema, you need a secure authenticated login to this remote server. Authenticate as an administrative user to export your schema to a file and follow the rest of the procedure.

5. After exporting your local schema to a file, activate Extend Schema again from iManager. Select Add Schema From A Server from the menu and click Next.

6. Enter all necessary information to authenticate against the remote server. Note that, in this case, LDIF is used as well, so the options are very similar to the options from the previous procedure. Click Next to continue. This imports the server on the local tree.

Modifying the Schema

Another interesting schema management task is to modify the existing schema by hand. It's possible to add any new object you like and to add properties to an existing object as well. The following example shows how an existing class can be provided with an additional attribute.

1. From iManager, select Roles And Tasks ➤ Schema, and then choose Create Attribute.

2. Enter the attribute name and the optional ASN1 ID. The ASN1 ID can be used for management of the attribute if it has a unique ID in the ASN1 hierarchy. If the attribute is for local eDirectory use only, the ASN1 ID can be omitted. Click Next.

3. Select the syntax type that has to be used for the attribute. If, for example, you want to create an attribute called *shoesize*, you could give it the syntax type Numeric String. What syntax type you need is determined by the use of the attribute. Click Next to continue.

4. Specify attribute flags to be used. If, for example, the attribute is very important and you want it to be synchronized immediately if anything changes, select the option Synchronize Immediately. Click Next to continue.

5. Have a look at the summary screen shown in Figure 8-17. Is everything okay with it? If so, then click Finish to create the attribute in the schema. Click OK next to close the Attribute Creation Wizard.

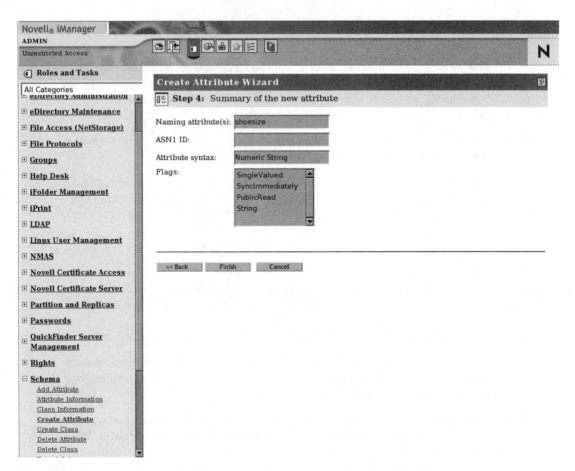

Figure 8-17. *The schema manager allows you to create your own classes and attributes.*

In the previous procedure, you created an attribute. That's great, but it's only useful to create attributes if you associate them to a class as well. The next procedure demonstrates how this is done.

1. From iManager, choose Roles And Tasks ➤ Schema, and then select Add Attribute to add an attribute to a selected class.

2. From the list of available classes, select the one you want to associate the attribute to. Both effective classes and superclasses are available. If you want the attribute to be used by more than one class, you can associate it to a superclass. Since you created the attribute *shoesize* in the earlier procedure, I'll show you now how this attribute can be associated to a user object. After selecting the desired class, click OK to continue.

3. Now you'll be presented with the screen shown in Figure 8-18. Browse through the list of Available Optional Attributes. The attribute you created in the previous step should be present in this list. Select the attribute and click the arrow to add it to the list of optional attributes. Click OK to add the attribute.

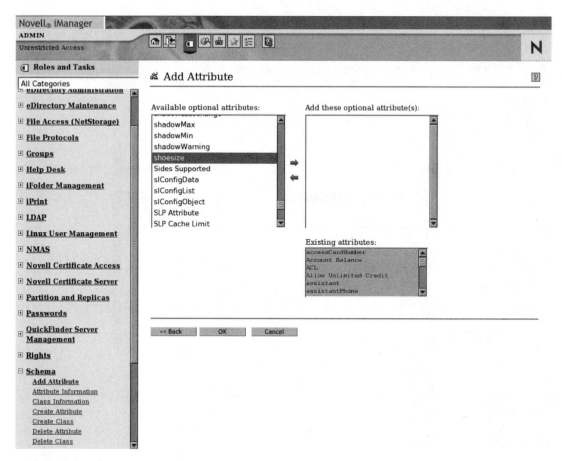

Figure 8-18. *You can add the attribute you created earlier to any class you like.*

4. Now the added attribute can be managed. From iManager, select eDirectory Administration ➤ Modify Object, and select one of the objects you added the attribute to.

5. From the drop-down list, select General ➤ Other. You'll find the newly created attribute in the list of unvalued attributes, as shown in Figure 8-19. Select it and click the blue arrow to add it to the list of valued attributes.

6. Select the attribute from the list of valued attributes and click Edit. You'll now see a window in which a value can be given to the attribute. Enter a value and click OK to save it.

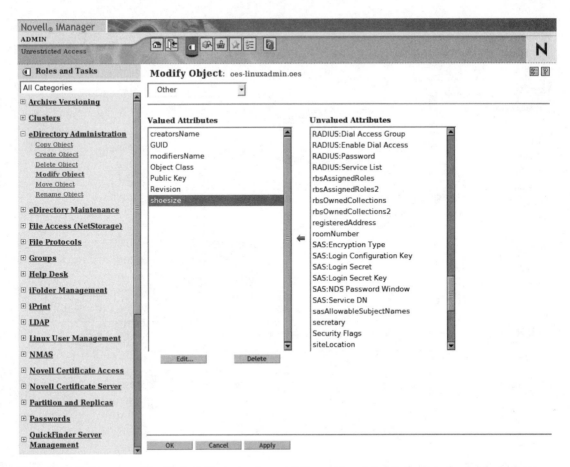

Figure 8-19. *Before a newly added attribute can be used, it must be added to the list of valued attributes.*

eDirectory and LDAP

Historically, in order to acquire information from eDirectory, a computer with the Novell client installed had to issue an NCP call. NCP is the proprietary Novell protocol to get information from eDirectory. To use NCP, a user had to install the Novell client software. We discussed the Novell client in more detail in Chapter 6. Chapter 10 will discuss NCP.

In a heterogeneous network where more network operating systems are working together, it can be a disadvantage if special client software has to be used. As a universal method for accessing information from an X.500-compatible Directory Service, LDAP can be used.

LDAP (Lightweight Directory Access Protocol) was developed to get information from a X.500-compatible Directory Service. Since most important modern Directory Services are compatible with X.500, LDAP can be used instead as an alternative to the proprietary NCP client.

Apart from being a way to get information from a Directory, LDAP can also be used as a network service. This is what happens if, for example, SUSE Linux Enterprise Server 9 is installed in a network: on the server, authentication is handled by the OpenLDAP service that allows users to authenticate to the LDAP server. In an Open Enterprise Server environment, this OpenLDAP server is not used; eDirectory is used instead.

Why LDAP

There are two good reasons to use LDAP in a network environment. First, there's the client perspective: every browser natively supports LDAP. This means you don't have to install anything extra on your client to get information from an LDAP-compatible Directory Service.

Second, it's a universal standard. All major Directory Services offer LDAP support. Some Directories are completely open to any LDAP request, while other Directories are only partially open. Most important Directories, however, can be accessed with any LDAP client. One of the major reasons that many services in Open Enterprise Server can be accessed with LDAP is because no special client is needed for it: in most cases, a browser with LDAP support is enough.

The use of LDAP makes the coexistence of different Directory Services on the same network easier to manage. LDAP not only can be used as a client protocol to get information from, and into, the Directory, but also as a protocol to exchange information between the Directories. There's even an LDAP specification to get information into the Directory: the LDIF format.

Managing LDAP

eDirectory is not the same as an LDAP Directory. For instance, eDirectory is accessible by LDAP, and you can get information from eDirectory with any LDAP client, but you can't get it out there by just communicating directly with the NDS service. In order to get LDAP-compatible information from eDirectory, two special objects are used: the LDAP server object and the LDAP group object. These objects are needed to translate between the native eDirectory format and the LDAP format. Be aware that there are some differences in naming between eDirectory and LDAP, as well as in the schema itself. To translate between these differences, Novell uses two LDAP-specific objects in eDirectory: the LDAP server and the LDAP group object.

Differences Between eDirectory and LDAP

Although eDirectory and LDAP are both derivatives from the same X.500 standard, differences exist.

eDirectory and LDAP sometimes use different terminology to describe things. To avoid confusion, this section begins with a short overview of some important differences between LDAP and eDirectory terms.

First, there's the LDAP entry, which refers to a record in the database. In an eDirectory environment, this is often called an object, although eDirectory terminology is changing.

Second, LDAP uses the term attributes, which refer to the fields of the records in the database. (eDirectory instead calls these properties.) For example, each user entry has a password attribute. This is not the actual password itself, but the possibility of having a password.

The third item might be the most confusing if you're a long-term eDirectory user. In an LDAP environment, a naming context is a branch of the Directory tree, while in an eDirectory environment, this is referred to as a partition.

Lastly, there's a difference when it comes to naming objects in the tree. In an eDirectory environment, you can work with typeful and typeless names, like cn=admin.o=svv, .admin.svv, or admin.svv. In an LDAP environment, the naming convention is easier: everything is typeful: meaning there's just cn=admin,o=svv. Take special notice of the dot used in eDirectory to separate the different components of a distinguished name. In LDAP, it's a comma. Thus, .admin.svv in eDirectory becomes cn=admin,o=svv in LDAP.

LDAP Server

Two objects in an eDirectory environment make eDirectory accessible for LDAP clients: the LDAP group and the LDAP server. The LDAP server is a module running on at least one eDirectory server in the network that translates between LDAP calls made by a client and eDirectory calls. The LDAP server consists of two parts: the server process and the server object. In the eDirectory LDAP server object, translation from LDAP to eDirectory is arranged, the server itself is the process running on your eDirectory server and listening to incoming LDAP calls.

The LDAP group object contains information that can be shared among multiple LDAP servers. This object represents a group of LDAP servers.

The LDAP server module used on each platform is

- *NetWare*: NLDAP.NLM

- *Linux*: /usr/sbin/nldap

Upon startup, the LDAP server reads its configuration from eDirectory. Whenever changes are made to the LDAP server configuration, the server should be forced to read these changes. The special refresh button is used for this.

In order to manage the LDAP server configuration, iManager is used, as the following steps illustrate.

1. Start iManager and log in.

2. Under Roles And Tasks, select LDAP, and then LDAP Options.

3. Click the View LDAP Servers tab (see Figure 8-20) and select the LDAP server you want to manage.

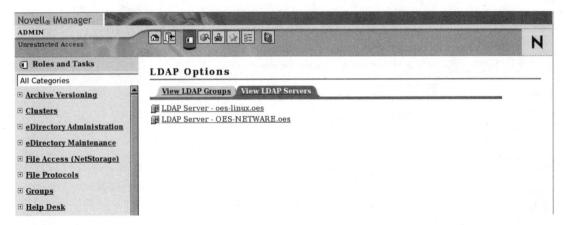

Figure 8-20. *The LDAP server can be managed from iManager.*

Many properties for the LDAP server can be managed. Under General ➤ Information, you'll find the associations for the LDAP server. First, note the non-changeable value Host Server. This parameter indicates which eDirectory server object the LDAP server is running on. Second, you'll find the name of the eDirectory group of which the LDAP server is a member. Each LDAP server is a member of one LDAP group in order to make management of the properties of the LDAP server easier.

On the next tab, specify in what way the connection between the LDAP server and eDirectory is established. Here, you specify what certificates have to be used and on what ports the LDAP server is accessible. The default, unsecure port (also called the clear-text port) is 389, while the default secure (encrypted) port is 636. Later in this chapter in the section "Enabling Secure LDAP Communications," it's discussed how these settings can be used to establish a secure connection between the LDAP Server and eDirectory.

A search for objects can be performed in different ways. The major difference is between the persistent search and the non-persistent search. In a normal search, the LDAP server searches for objects and stops searching after producing a result. To expose eDirectory events to applications dynamically, a persistent search can be used. This is a search operation that keeps going after the initial set of matching entries is returned. In a normal search, at the end of the search operation, the server sends a SearchResultDone message to the client. In a persistent search, the search operation maintains a connection so the client can be updated each time an entry in the search result changes. For LDAP applications to work dynamically with data from eDirectory, the persistent search is enabled by default. If necessary, this feature can be disabled from the Searches tab (see Figure 8-21) where you'll find other options specifying how a search should be performed. Most of these options regulate the maximum number of results given. Take special note of the option Include Filtered Replicas In Search. This is switched off by default, so you have to enable it if you want filtered replicas to be searched as well.

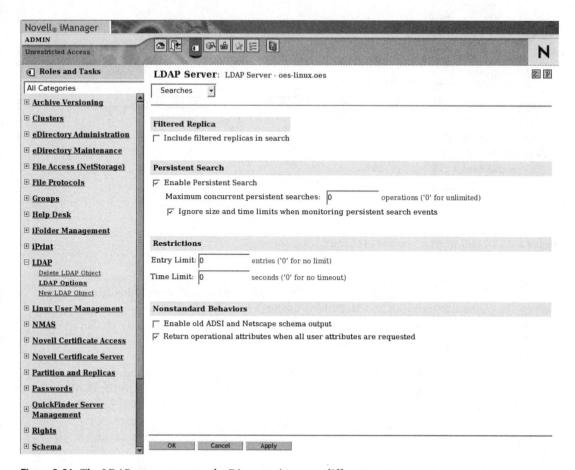

Figure 8-21. *The LDAP server can search eDirectory in many different ways.*

The next interesting tab is the Tracing screen (see Figure 8-22). In this screen, you can specify what information will be displayed on a dstrace screen. By default, only critical error messages and non-critical error messages are displayed, but you can modify this as needed. For connection troubleshooting, the Connection Information option is particularly useful and displays information about establishing connections.

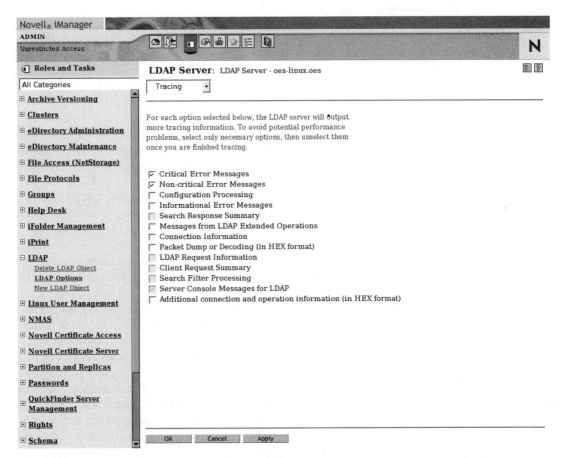

Figure 8-22. *The tracing options determine what information about LDAP are shown in the dstrace screen.*

In most situations, an eDirectory tree is serviced completely by the eDirectory service. Large deployments, however, often need a directory tree that uses LDAP server software from different vendors. This is called a global federated tree. If eDirectory is part of such a global federated tree, the LDAP server included in eDirectory has the capacity to communicate with a superior DSA in that tree. For these referrals to work, the URL for a Directory Service in the upper part of the tree must be specified. You can do this with a URL—for example, ldap://ldap.sandervanvugt.nl:389. In this URL, you first specify ldap:// to indicate that the LDAP protocol has to be used, then you indicate the name of the server you want to address, and finally you specify on which port to communicate with this server. Should referrals be used, a client can be instructed by the LDAP server to use another LDAP server instead. A referral is a pointer to information on another server. If this other server that's pointed to doesn't have the required information either, the process can be repeated by that server by using a referral that exists on that server. If referrals *are* needed, you can specify the server you want to refer to on the Referrals tab.

■**Caution** In order for configuration changes to be applied, the LDAP server must be refreshed. Select the Refresh or Apply button to save and apply all changes you've made.

The LDAP Group

Many settings in the LDAP environment are set on the LDAP server object. There are, however, some global settings. For these, you can use the LDAP group object. Some settings that can be applied on the LDAP server can be applied to the LDAP group as well; most of them are unique settings that define how the translation from LDAP to eDirectory (and vice versa) should be performed. You can get to the LDAP group object by choosing LDAP ➤ LDAP Overview as well.

On the Information tab, you'll find a list of all LDAP server objects that are presently members of the LDAP group. In most scenarios, you just need one LDAP group and you can make all LDAP servers members of this unique group. On this same tab, you'll also find the Authentication Options. You can specify the name of an LDAP Proxy user here. This is the name of a user that has rights to view some specific objects in eDirectory; use this option to fine-tune your LDAP configuration.

The second set of options is used to configure how referrals are handled. These options exist on the LDAP server object as well. If referral options are configured on the LDAP group object as well as on the LDAP server object, the options on the server object will be applied.

The last two parts of the LDAP group configuration are the Attribute Map (see Figure 8-23) and the Class Map (see Figure 8-24). These options exist because the eDirectory and LDAP schemas are incompatible. You'll find mappings for all default classes and attributes on these tabs. If you've installed non-default schema extensions on your tree, a manual mapping can be made using these tabs by clicking the plus (+) symbol. If a mapping does not exist, the LDAP server searches the schema dynamically to find a corresponding class or attribute. For regular searches on specific classes and attributes, always add your mappings.

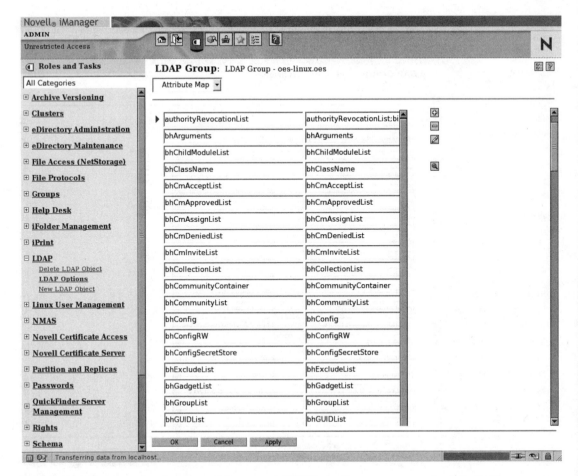

Figure 8-23. *Most mappings between eDirectory and LDAP attributes are present by default. If necessary, they can also be created manually.*

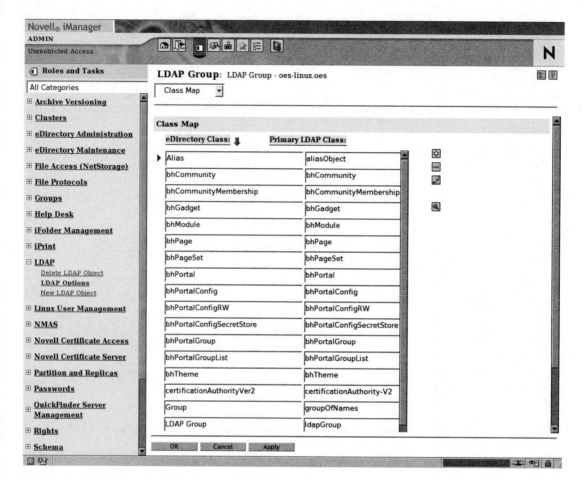

Figure 8-24. *A default mapping list between LDAP and eDirectory classes is already present on the LDAP group object.*

Enabling Secure LDAP Communications

All LDAP clients need user credentials to connect to eDirectory. This bind can be accomplished as one of the following types of users:

- [Public] user (anonymous bind)
- Proxy user

Tip A bind is the process in which a user connects to a service. In this case, the user is the LDAP client and the service is eDirectory.

What kind of bind the user authenticates with affects the amount of information shown to the user. If an anonymous bind is made with the credentials of the [Public] user, a user of the LDAP service will only see limited information, since [Public] has limited rights in eDirectory. All users connected to eDirectory, also via LDAP, are security equivalent to the [public]-trustee. Also, if not logged in, these are also the rights for anonymous LDAP searches. The rights for [public] are discussed in Chapter 12. If on the contrary you want to set up the LDAP service in a way that access is given to specific information in the Directory, you should work with the LDAP proxy user and grant additional rights to this user.

Another scenario is where the user needs to change information from within an LDAP client. In this case, the user must be able to log in to eDirectory from his LDAP client. The problem with this scenario is that LDAP will send passwords unencrypted to the eDirectory server. This is no problem if the LDAP server and the eDirectory server are on the same box. If they aren't, LDAP has to be configured with TLS for a secure connection between the LDAP server and eDirectory.

[Public] User

In an anonymous bind using the credentials of the public user, no username and password are specified. The LDAP client only has access to those properties which the [Public] user has access to. By default, the [Public] user has browse rights to most parts of the Directory tree. This allows the LDAP client to see that some objects exist, but it will block access to most of the properties. This kind of connection is the default. If you want the LDAP client to see more information, consider configuring a proxy user. You might think that changing the rights of the [Public] user is a valid alternative, but it isn't recommended since it will grant everyone access to your tree and thus be very dangerous. Because of the limitations, Novell recommends working with a proxy user instead.

Proxy User

If you configure the LDAP server to work with a proxy user, this is considered an anonymous bind as well. The only purpose of the proxy user is to grant more rights to the LDAP client so more than the default information can be seen. This proxy user should be a secure account in eDirectory which has only enough rights granted to it for the user to do his work and nothing more. The following procedure shows you how to configure LDAP with a proxy user.

1. Create an eDirectory user account with no password.

2. Disallow this user to change his password.

3. Give the user all eDirectory rights that you want to be available from the LDAP client interface.

4. Associate this user account to the LDAP group object, as shown in Figure 8-25.

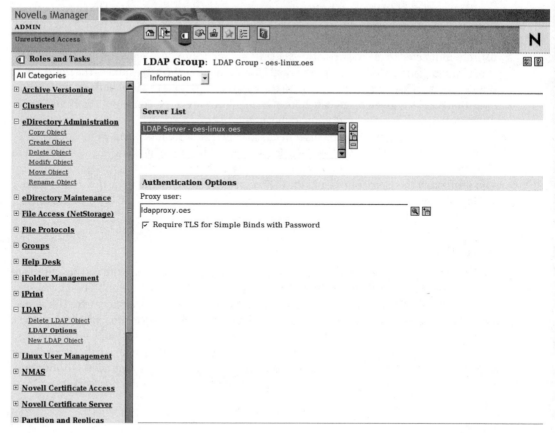

Figure 8-25. *For access to the eDirectory database, the LDAP group object can be configured to use a proxy user.*

5. Don't forget to refresh your LDAP server.

Secure Connections Between the LDAP Server and eDirectory

The LDAP Server is available on two different ports. It listens on port 389 for non-encrypted binds, but it's also available on port 636, where it listens for encrypted connections. Before an encrypted connection can be established, the following steps should be taken.

1. The LDAP server must be configured for TLS.

2. The client has to be configured for TLS.

3. Certificates must be exchanged between eDirectory and the LDAP client.

In the first step, you must verify that your LDAP server can work with TLS. The required options can be found on the LDAP group object. Ensure that on the LDAP group object under General ➤ Information the option Require TLS For Simple Binds With Password is enabled. Normally, it's enabled by default.

Next, you must configure your server to use TLS. Upon establishing a TLS connection, a handshake occurs. The server and client exchange data is in this handshake. To establish that the server is legitimate, it always sends the server's certificate to the client. This way, the client can verify that it's indeed working with the expected server. There's also an option to work with mutual authentication. In this scenario, the server sends a certificate and the client sends back a certificate. Once this exchange of certificates is finished, the identity of both is established and they can communicate securely.

■Tip To make sure that no clients are trying to log in with a clear-text password, always disable access to port 389 from the LDAP server object. If you leave the port open, the authentication fails but unfortunately the password has already been sent across the wire. Disabling the clear-text port prevents the client from setting up a TCP connection in the first place, thus stopping the user from sending his password as clear-text.

With regards to the Client Certificate, there are three different possibilities. In the default option, a Client Certificate is not requested. In such a scenario, it doesn't matter if the client sends a certificate—a secure connection is established anyway. If a client certificate is requested, the server asks for a client certificate upon establishing the connection with the client. If the client doesn't send a certificate, the server maintains the connection anyway. If the client sends a certificate that can't be validated, the connection between client and server is terminated. The last option is to specify that a client certificate is required. If the client doesn't provide a certificate, or if the certificate can't be validated, the connection is terminated.

In the default setting, the server uses a certificate, but the client doesn't. This server certificate is automatically provided during eDirectory installation as a part of the Public Key Infrastructure (PKI). The SSL CertificateDNS is automatically associated with the LDAP server. There's also an SSL CertificateIP, which will work as well.

Without doing anything extra on the client, you can make a secure connection to the LDAP server immediately. This displays an error message on the client that the certificate couldn't be validated. If you want the client to trust your LDAP server without further questions, the certificate from the server must be imported into the client. The way that the client imports a certificate is different for each application used. If, for example, you've imported a certificate for Internet Explorer, that certificate can't be used automatically by the ICE utility.

If you want the clients to trust your server automatically, it's a good idea to export the Trusted Root to the client. This can be done automatically while accepting the certificate server on the client. As a result, a file is created. Next, you can import this file in the client application. This ensures that the client trusts the certificate authority that signed the certificate you're using while establishing a secure connection with the LDAP server.

To realize a secure connection between the LDAP server and eDirectory, the following procedure can be implemented. It shows how a secure connection between a client and an LDAP server can be established. It also covers how Internet Explorer can be configured to use the Trusted Root certificate of the Certificate Authority that signed the certificate used by the LDAP server. Be aware that this is just one example; different procedures must be followed for other LDAP applications.

1. Start iManager and select the LDAP server object.

2. Select the Connections screen (see Figure 8-26). Choose SSL CertificateDNS at the Server Certificate option. Next, select the option Require TLS For All Operations on the same tab.

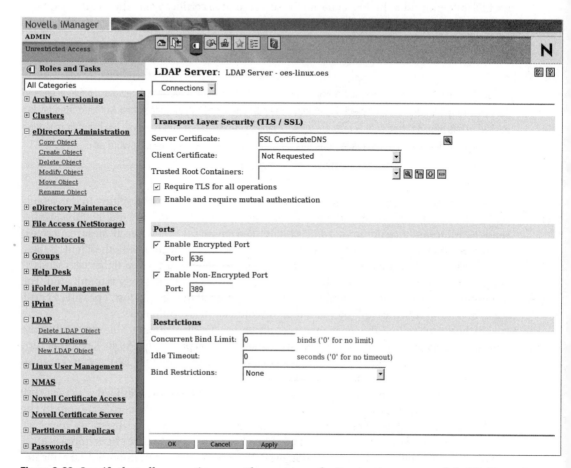

Figure 8-26. *Specify that all connections must be secure on the Connections screen of the LDAP server object.*

3. Click Apply to apply your changes to the LDAP server.

4. To make an automatic secure connection from within the client application, it's useful to import the certificate. Select eDirectory Administration and click Modify Object next. Browse to the SSL CertificateDNS for your server object and select it. Click OK to open its properties.

5. Click Certificates and select the Trusted Root Certificate (see Figure 8-27). Click Export to export this certificate to the workstation you're currently working on.

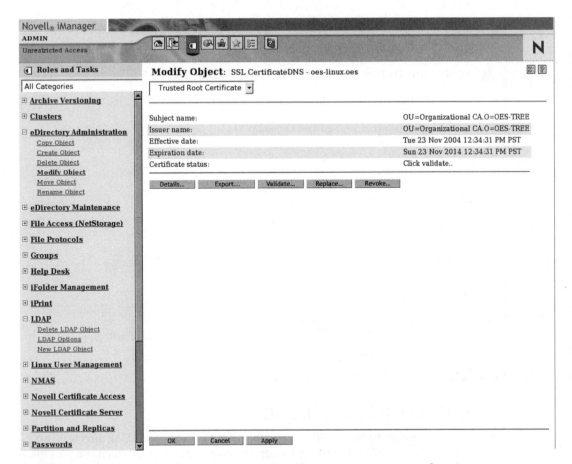

Figure 8-27. *Export the trusted root certificate to all workstations you want to make a secure connection from.*

6. The Export Certificate Wizard is started now. On the first screen (see Figure 8-28), it's very important to mention that you don't want to export the private key with the certificate. This is because the private key is supposed to be private and you want to keep it as secure as possible.

7. Now you need to specify in what format the certificate must be saved. Choose the file in binary DER format for optimal compatibility and click Next.

8. Click the option Save The Exported Certificate To A File to save the certificate. Choose Save to save it to the hard disk of your computer, or choose Open to open and install it immediately from your browser. In this example, I'll cover how to install the certificate directly into your browser.

9. Click Install Certificate to install the certificate. This starts the Certificate Import Wizard for your browser. Accept all default values to install the certificate.

Figure 8-28. *Don't export the private key!*

Importing LDAP Data with LDIF

LDAP Data Interchange Format (LDIF) is used to present data from an LDAP directory in a readable format as a text file. An LDIF file holds various records, each of which contains information about an object. The records are separated from each other by a blank line. LDIF can be used to export data from an LDAP Directory, but it can also be used to add or modify data from the Directory. In an LDIF file, several operations can be used that relate directly to those specified in the LDAP protocol. The following operations are available:

- Add

- Delete

- modrdn

- modify

Novell also provides a utility to manipulate data in the LDIF format: the Novell Import/ Convert/Export utility (ICE). This utility can be used on the command line, but it's also integrated into iManager. In order to use LDIF files, you must create them yourself or use LDIF files exported from another system. Exporting is also something that ICE can do.

Add

Four important operations can be used from an LDIF file. The first of them is Add, which is used with the changetype value to add information to eDirectory. Listing 8-1 shows an example of this operation. Take special notice of the multivalued attributes; they're specified once for each value that has to be added to the attribute. Also, don't forget the first line: version: 1. This mandatory line specifies the version of the protocol to be used.

Listing 8-1. *The Add Operation*

```
version: 1
#add a new user
dn: cn=Betty Schoot,ou=users,o=svv
changetype: add
objectclass: inetorgperson
sn: Schoot
telephonenumber: 23456
telephonenumber: 912345
title: Manager

dn: cn=Andreas Ollenburg,ou=users,o=svv
changetype: add
objectclass: inetorgperson
sn: Ollenburg
telephonenumber: +49123123456
title: Winner of the Open Road Challenge
```

One thing to be careful of is that if you want to create some new users in a container object that doesn't exist yet, the creation of the objects will fail. Of course, you can avoid this by first creating the container object you need. Do this manually with iManager. It's also possible to add a new container object with an entry in your LDIF file.

```
version: 1
changetype: add
dn: ou=users, o=svv
objectclass : organizationalunit
```

Delete

Of course, you can do more than just add information with LDIF. It's also possible to delete a range of information with the Delete operation. Not much is needed to work with delete: just specify the distinguished name of the object involved and then use changetype delete to delete them from the Directory, as shown in Listing 8-2.

Listing 8-2. *The Delete Operation*

```
version: 1
#delete some former collegues

dn: cn=Frans Kevenaar,ou=users,o=svv
changetype: delete
```

```
dn: cn=Paul Avontuur,ou=users,o=svv
changetype : delete

dn : cn=Jeroen van Osta,ou=users,o=svv
changetype: delete
```

modrdn

It's also possible to change the relative distinguished name of an object with modrdn. An illustration of modrdn is shown in Listing 8-3.

Listing 8-3. *The modrdn Operation*

```
version: 1
# modify the name of a user object
dn: cn=Christina Anderson,ou=users,o=svv
changetype: modrdn
newrdn: Christina Jones
deleteoldrdn: 1
```

modify

modrdn is the required action for modifying the name of an object in your directory. However, if you need to modify the value of certain attributes, use modify. An example is shown in Listing 8-4.

Listing 8-4. *The modify Operation*

```
version: 1
dn: cn=Christina Jones,ou=users,o=svv
changetype: modify
-
delete : description
-
replace: facsimiletelephonenumber
facsimiletelephonenumber: +43 123454321
-

dn: cn=Andreas Ollenburg,ou=users,o=svv
changetype: modify
-
replace: title
title: Winner of the Open Road Challenge
-
add: loginshell
loginshell: /bin/tcsh
```

As you can tell from the last example, modify is a very general action that can be used in an LDIF file to remove, replace, or add information. If modify is used to add information that already exists, the LDIF procedure simply adds it again. This way, you can easily create a multi-valued attribute.

Tip The most difficult part in creating an LDIF file is using the correct syntax. This can be very hard, especially if you want to work with advanced features like superclasses and ACLs. There is, however, a good way to learn everything you need about LDIF syntax: export some objects from your current eDirectory. In the resulting output, you'll see exactly how certain eDirectory features are specified in an LDIF file.

The Import Conversion Export Wizard

The Import Conversion Export (ICE) utility is available in two different flavors: one which can be used as a command-line utility and the other which can be used from iManager. It allows you to do the following:

- Import data from an LDIF, delimited text file, schema file, or LOAD file in eDirectory.

- Export data from eDirectory to an LDIF file.

- Migrate data between servers that support the universal LDIF format.

Tip This chapter describes how to import and export with ICE from iManager. There's also a command-line available called ice on NetWare, Linux, and Windows. This command-line utility is more powerful because it offers more command-line options.

Importing eDirectory Objects with ICE

The following procedure explains how to import data from an LDIF file into eDirectory.

1. In Novell iManager, select Import Convert Export Wizard (see Figure 8-29) from eDirectory Maintenance.

2. Select the option Import Data From File On Disk. Then, under Advanced Settings, choose Run In Verbose Mode. This shows you more extensive information on what's happening. Click Next.

3. Under File type, specify what type of file you want to import. Next, browse to the location where you saved your LDIF file. In Advanced Settings, deselect Exit On Error and select Run In Verbose Mode. This shows you what happens while the import procedure is underway. Another interesting option is Add Records Without Change Type. This option just adds records if no change type is provided. Click Next to continue.

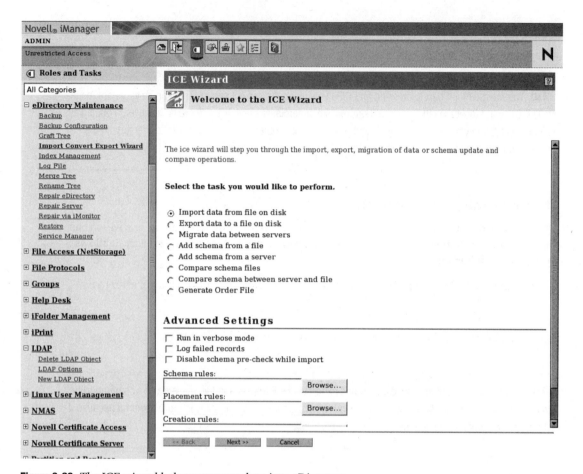

Figure 8-29. *The ICE wizard helps you move data into eDirectory.*

4. Next, you must specify where the data has to be imported to. Specify the name or IP address for your server and the port you want to connect to. In a secure configuration, you'll also need to specify that a connection has to be made to port 636 and the location in which the DER file with the exported certificate of your LDAP server can be found. Next, specify the credentials you want to use to log in with. Since this is an import action, you can't do an anonymous login (you could, however, do an export with an anonymous login). Under Advanced Settings, select Allow Forward References as well. This option makes sure that placeholders are created for objects that are referred to during an import. These objects are created later in the LDIF import—for example, when creating users and groups with cross references for memberships from the same file. The options should now look like those shown in Figure 8-30. Click Next.

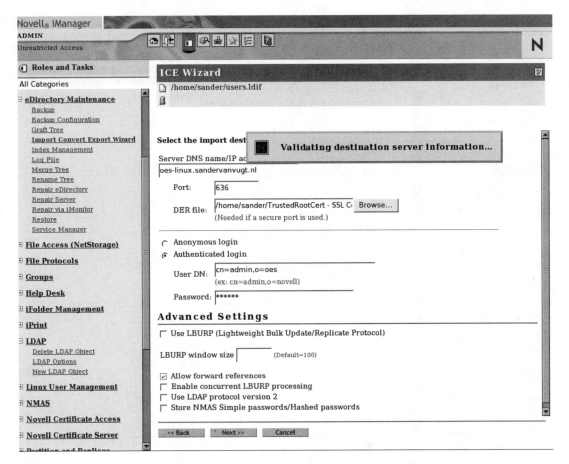

Figure 8-30. *To import data into eDirectory, a secure connection must be used.*

5. The software shows you the command used to import the data from your LDIF. For troubleshooting purposes, you can analyze whether all the necessary components are present in this command. Click Finish to start the actual import. After a while, you'll see the result screen (shown in Figure 8-31), which tells you if everything went well. If an error occurred, the screen instead offers valuable hints on what to do next.

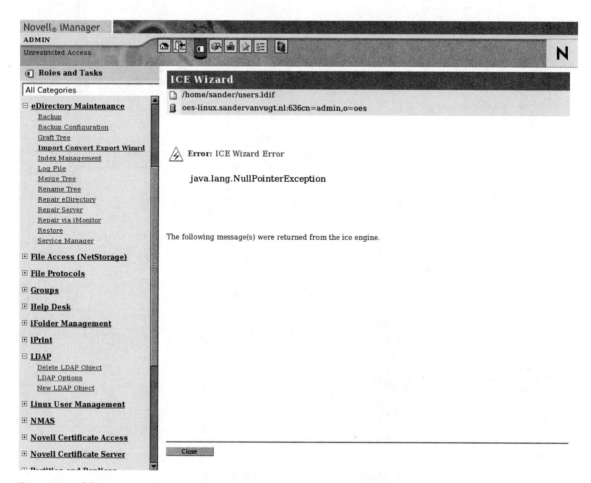

Figure 8-31. *If there was an error in the process, the results screen will tell you.*

Exporting eDirectory Information with ICE

In the preceding section, you read about the way information can be imported with ICE. It's even easier to export information from your current eDirectory environment. This can be useful in exporting sections of your tree or in moving objects from one tree to another tree if both trees use the same schema.

1. Start iManager and select eDirectory Maintenance ➤ Import Convert Export Wizard.

2. Select the option Export Data To A File On Disk to export information from eDirectory to a file on the hard drive of your computer. Click Next.

3. Specify the name or IP address of the server you wish to export from and specify everything else you need to make a secure connection to your LDAP server. In the Authenticated Login options, specify the name of the user you want to perform the export. Be aware that you'll only be able to export the information this user account has rights to.

4. Specify the export search criteria. At the very least, you need to specify the Base DN. This is the container that you want to start the export from. You should also specify how deep you want to go into the eDirectory tree while performing the export. The default setting is One Level; this includes all immediate children of the base object with everything inside. Use Sub Tree if you want to include everything under the selected container, or Base if you don't want to include any child containers. Use the Filter option and Include Attributes option to specify exactly what you want to include in your LDIF export as seen in Figure 8-32. Click Next to continue.

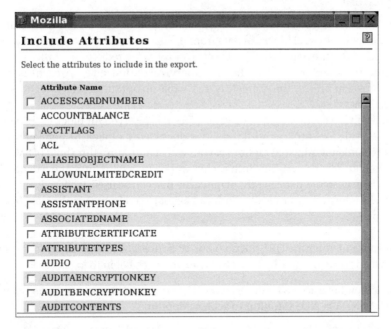

Figure 8-32. *You can create extensive filters to specify exactly what must be included in the LDIF export.*

5. Specify what file type you want to export the information to. By default, the information is written in the LDIF format; you can write to a delimited text file as well. Click Next after specifying the file type to be generated.

6. Click Finish to perform the actual export. Depending on the size of your tree, it may take a while until the process has finished completely.

7. In the Completion screen, select what you wish to do with the result. Be aware that nothing has been saved so far! In order to save your LDIF export, select Download Export File and specify the name and location of the file you want to export. Click Close.

Improving eDirectory Performance

To improve eDirectory performance, you can configure the eDirectory cache. Indexes are another performance issue. If indexes are applied the right way, search times can be increased dramatically.

Managing Cache

With eDirectory 8.5 or later, you can specify a block cache limit and an entry cache limit. The block cache caches only physical blocks of data from the database. The entry cache is used to cache logical entries from the database. The use of an entry cache reduces the processing time needed to place entries from the block cache in memory. An optimized entry cache is most useful for operations that browse the eDirectory tree, while an optimized block cache is useful for update operations.

If a server doesn't have a replica, a fixed value of 8MB is reserved for block cache and another 8MB is set aside for entry cache. If the server does have a replica, 51 percent of available memory is dynamically adjusted for both caches with a minimum threshold of 8MB and a maximum threshold of 24MB available. Both caches work with a hard limit and a dynamical limit. A hard limit is an absolute value in MBs of the cache that can be used, while a dynamic limit is a limit that can be adjusted dynamically. Both can be managed from iMonitor, as shown in the following steps.

1. Start Mozilla and enter the URL https://your-IP-address:8030/nds. Enter the typeful distinguished name of the administrative user and click Login to log in.

2. You should now have access to the DHost HTTP Server running on your Open Enterprise Server. Click NDS ➤ NDS iMonitor to access iMonitor.

3. Select Agent Configuration and then click the link Database Cache. This displays the screen shown in Figure 8-33. Under Database Cache Configuration, specify all the options that have to be used for your database cache. You can find the necessary statistics regarding database cache usage under the Database Cache option.

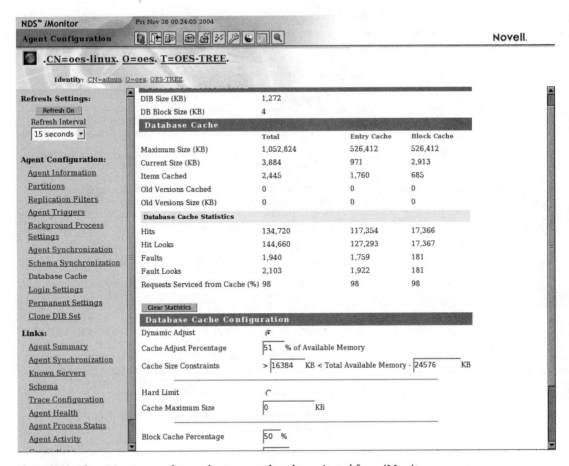

Figure 8-33. *The eDirectory cache can be managed and monitored from iMonitor.*

In the database cache statistics, you can monitor database cache usage. Some of the options are particularly important. Table 8-4 lists the important cache parameters.

Table 8-4. *Important Cache Parameters*

Information	Description
Maximum Size	The maximum amount of memory in kilobytes available for caching.
Current Size	The current size in kilobytes of the cache. If the current size is almost as big as the maximum size, you should consider increasing the maximum size.
Requests Services from Cache	The percentage of requests that could be resolved from the cache. If this percentage falls beneath 90 percent, you should consider increasing the maximum cache size on your server. The bottom line in these kinds of cases is that you should add more RAM to your server.

In most situations, the default values work fine. Sometimes, however, the defaults need to be adjusted. In such incidents, you can choose from the following options shown in Table 8-5.

Table 8-5. *Database Cache Configuration Parameters*

Option	Description
Dynamic Adjust	Default value. Specifies that the cache size will be adjusted dynamically to the value specified in Cache Adjust Percentage.
Cache Adjust Percentage	The maximum amount of memory that can be used for the eDirectory cache.
Cache Size Constraints	Can be used to specify a minimum amount of memory in KB that should always be allocated for eDirectory caching and a maximum amount of memory in KB that should always remain available for other purposes.
Hard Limit	Can optionally be used to specify an exact amount of system memory to be used for cache.
Cache Maximum Size	Used to specify the maximum size of memory used for cache if a hard limit's used.
Block Cache Percentage	This value specifies the part of the reserved cache memory that can be used for the block cache. The other half is automatically reserved for the entry cache. On most servers, the default values will work fine. If a server is used mostly for eDirectory lookup (perhaps because there's a Virtual Office server running on it), it makes sense to reserve more memory for entry cache at the expense of available memory for block cache.
Cache Adjust Interval	Specifies how often the cache size is adjusted if a dynamic cache is used.
Cache Cleanup Interval	Controls how often unused values are removed from cache.
Cache Settings Permanent	Use this option and click the Submit button to make the settings made through iMonitor permanent.

Managing Indexes

Another feature that can be used to improve the client experience when working with eDirectory is eDirectory indexes. Default indexes are created to increase the performance of a large tree. Indexes can also be created manually to increase performance on a particular property. An index is a server property and not a global available eDirectory property. If an index is created for a specific attribute, a user that addresses a server that keeps the index can get information faster from eDirectory if that particular server is addressed. Some default indexes are provided with eDirectory. You can find them on the Index Management tab on a selected server object. Indexes are created per server. Some of these are system indexes, which are critical indexes that should never be modified. Four different types of indexes are available, as shown in the following list.

- *Operational*: These are indexes that must always be present. You cannot modify or delete them because they are critical for eDirectory search operations. Operational indexes are created automatically on the `Aliased Object Name` attribute to increase the search for aliases, the `Obituary` attribute to increase the deletion of objects in eDirectory, and on Global Unique ID (GUID) to increase the search for objects in eDirectory based on their global unique ID.

- *Auto Added*: If certain attributes are used, eDirectory adds this index type automatically. They can be modified or deleted, but for optimal eDirectory performance this is not recommended. Auto Added indexes can exist for different attributes, depending on the objects that occur in your tree. Some of these attributes include a user's `Given Name` and `Surname`.

- *System*: These are indexes that must be present on the system as well to run the system. They cannot be modified or erased. Indexes of the type system exist on different attributes— for example, on the `member` attribute to localize group membership and on the `Equivalent To Me` attribute to enhance searches for rights in the Directory.

- *User*: The User type index is the only index that can be added with the Index Manager from iManager. This is a user created index that can be used to increase performance if certain attributes are used very often in the Directory.

Sometimes it makes sense to create an extra index manually. Imagine a server that serves as eGuide server: if users look up mail addresses regularly from eGuide, the process can be speeded up if you create an index for the *eMail* attribute.

■Caution Only create an index if you're really sure you need it. Indexes do improve search performance, but they also add to directory update time.

Indexes can be created from Novell iManager by performing the following steps:

1. Start your browser and access iManager at https://yourserver/nps.

2. Click the Roles And Tasks button and then select eDirectory Maintenance ➤ Index Management (see Figure 8-34).

3. Select the server on which you want to create the index. A list of already existing indexes for that server is displayed.

4. From the drop-down list, select Modify Indexes and then choose Create to bring up the dialog shown in Figure 8-35.

5. Specify the name of the index. If no name is specified, the name of the attribute is used automatically for the index name. Next, select an attribute.

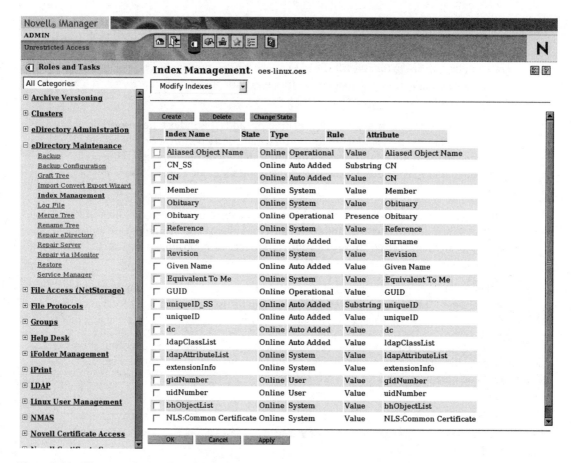

Figure 8-34. *All servers have a list of default indexes.*

6. Select the index rule. You can choose from three different options. Use Value to match the entire value or only the first part of the value of an attribute. Substring is used to match on a subset of the attribute value string, no matter where it appears in the string. Meanwhile, Presence only requires the presence of an attribute and no specific value. In most cases, Value is the most useful choice.

7. Click OK to update the index table and then click Apply to create the index on your server.

■**Tip** Indexes can be created, modified, and deleted. Instead of deleting an index you don't need temporarily, you might consider taking it offline. In iManager, choose eDirectory Management ➤ Index Management, then select the index you want to take offline and click Change State. This allows you to take an index temporarily offline. You can only do this with non-critical indexes; it's not possible to take a System index offline, for example.

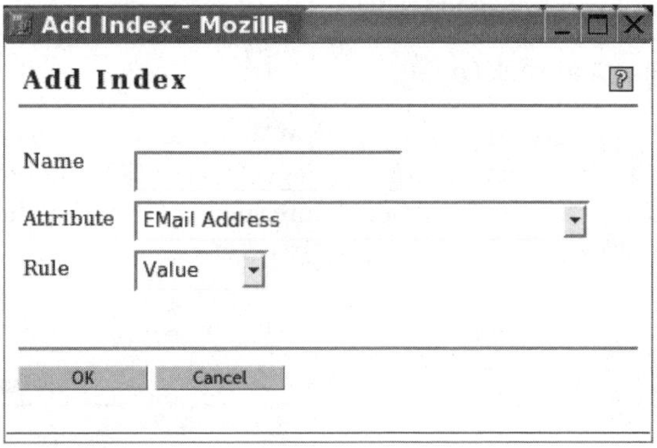

Figure 8-35. *Most indexes work with the Value rule.*

Troubleshooting eDirectory

In the early days of NetWare Directory Service (NDS), troubleshooting was the most important skill an administrator could have. Changes were synchronized across replicas in the Directory and for lots of reasons they often went wrong. If you were among the users of the NetWare 4.0 versions, you probably still have nightmares about it. Nowadays, eDirectory is a very stable Directory Service and problems occur less often. Nevertheless, sooner or later you'll encounter some difficulty with your Directory Service.

Thus, the goal of this last section is to provide you with a basic introduction to eDirectory troubleshooting. I'll cover some of the most common problems encountered and explain how to resolve them.

Performing a Basic Health Check

Sooner or later you'll encounter problems working with eDirectory. However, a lot of these problems can be reduced in frequency if you regularly perform a basic health check of your tree. The goal of a basic health check is to see if there's anything wrong in eDirectory currently. In a basic health check, some of the most critical components of eDirectory are checked:

- The current version of the Directory Service

- Time synchronization

- Last successful synchronization

- Fault tolerance of the tree

A basic health check should always be performed before undertaking any critical action in eDirectory, like adding a server, removing a replica, and so on. The best tool to perform a basic health check is iMonitor. The following procedure outlines how a basic health check can be performed.

1. Start iMonitor at https://your ip address:8030/nds.

2. Enter your distinguished name and click Login.

3. Under Links, click Known Servers. This shows you a list of all servers in your tree, as displayed in Figure 8-36. Click the server you want to manage. Make sure the name of this server appears in the upper-left corner of the screen before you start checking the health of eDirectory on that server.

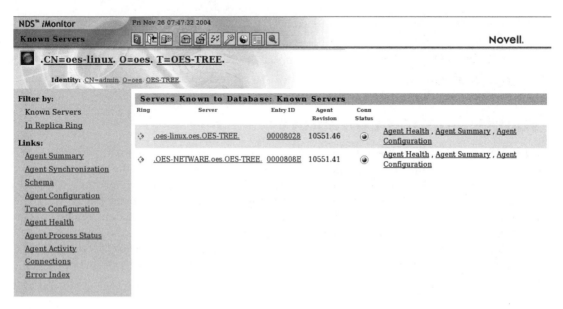

Figure 8-36. *Before you start working with iMonitor, be sure you're looking at the server you want to manage.*

4. Click Agent Configuration under Links (see Figure 8-37). This shows you a list of all relevant information for this server. Take special notice of the parameters Time Synchronized and Agent Build Number. You need the agent build number because it's the eDirectory version you're using. It should be the same version on other servers. Make sure time is properly synchronized before you start any process on your Directory.

Tip In iMonitor, click the Reports button and select Report Config. Next, click the Run Report button in front of the Server Information report that has the scope Treewide. This report allows you to easily access the same information for all servers in your Directory tree.

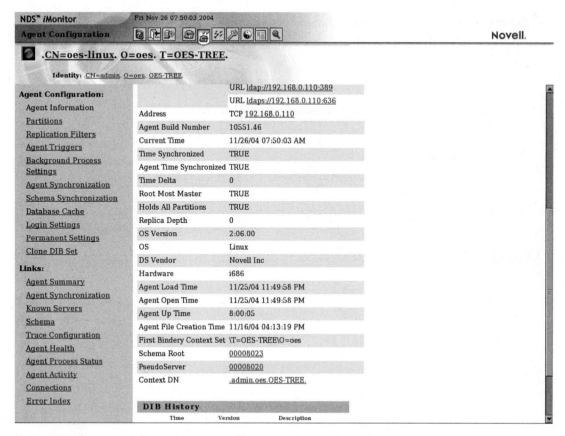

Figure 8-37. *The Agent Information screen offers an overview of some important parameters.*

5. Under Links, select Agent Synchronization. This shows you an overview of the current synchronization status of your server. The important thing to look for is whether there are any errors.

6. The best way to manage any errors is to click Continuity. This displays an overview of all servers that have a replica of the partition involved in the error, as shown in Figure 8-38. If there's an error, you'll see an error code. Click this error code for more details on what's wrong.

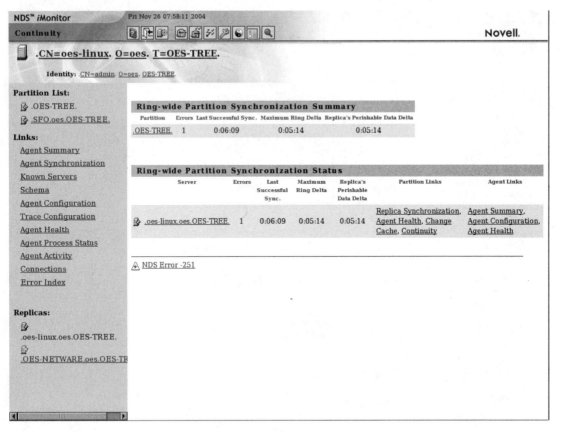

Figure 8-38. *On the Continuity screen, you get an overview of all current errors and the codes associated to them.*

7. You've seen some of the steps needed to perform a basic health check. Another efficient method of seeing whether anything is wrong is by looking at the agent health report. Click the Reports button in the button bar at the top of the iMonitor screen.

8. Now select Report Config under Reports (see Figure 8-39). This presents a list of items for which you can display a report.

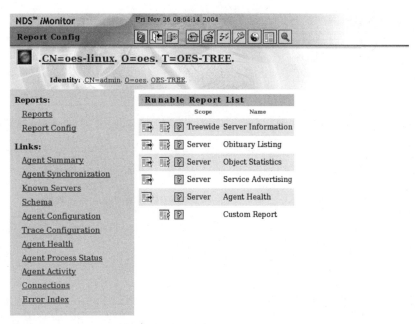

Figure 8-39. *iMonitor offers you the ability to run reports about several important eDirectory items.*

9. Click the link next to Agent Health. This calls up a summary of the health of this server. In the report, you'll see several items that you can click. If you only see green buttons, there's no need to click any further because everything's okay. If you see anything other than a green button, it may be best to click the link next to the button to display the error related to the selected item.

10. Another very useful report is the treewide Server Information report (see Figure 8-40). Select this option to find out the health status of all known servers on your network.

Tip If you're running health reports from iMonitor, the most important thing to look out for are error codes. Every single event that can happen in eDirectory is associated to an error code. The good thing with error codes in iMonitor is that you can just click them. This displays an explanation of the error, a list of possible causes, and a list of actions you can take to resolve the error.

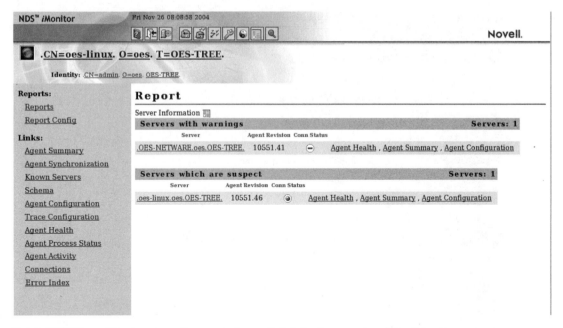

Figure 8-40. *If anything is wrong, it appears immediately in the reports run by iMonitor.*

Resolving Some Common Issues

Troubleshooting eDirectory is an art, and if you don't know precisely what you're doing, you can get stuck easily. In case of doubt, the best idea is to hire a specialist who has plenty of experience resolving eDirectory troubles.Don't start using DSREPAIR options following TIDs from support.novell.com if you're not sure what you're doing. You could break more than you're fixing.

There are, however, some things you can do without risking your entire tree. In the last section of this chapter, I summarize the four most important tasks you need to know while troubleshooting eDirectory problems.

Unattended Full Repair

eDirectory is a database that consists of replicas scattered around many servers in your network. These replicas are always synchronizing. In this synchronization process, things can go wrong, which can lead to obscure errors in your eDirectory database. These kinds of errors often appear when you run a health report from iMonitor. One of the most common things to do is run an unattended full repair against your local eDirectory database. This tries to repair your local eDirectory database automatically without doing any harm to your system.

If you ever decide to perform eDirectory maintenance tasks, like running an unattended full repair, be sure to do it in the evening or on the weekend when no more than a few users are working. This is because many eDirectory maintenance tasks lock the database while executing, which can cause problems for users with an active connection.

There are many ways to run an unattended full repair. The following shows you how to do it from iManager, from OES - NetWare, and from OES - Linux.

- In iManager, select eDirectory Maintenance ➤ Repair eDirectory. In the Basic Repair Wizard that appears, select the server you want to run the repair on and click Next. Specify the username and password you need on this server and then select the kind of repair you wish to run (see Figure 8-41). Selected your favorite action? Click Start to begin with it. After a minute or two, your database will be repaired.

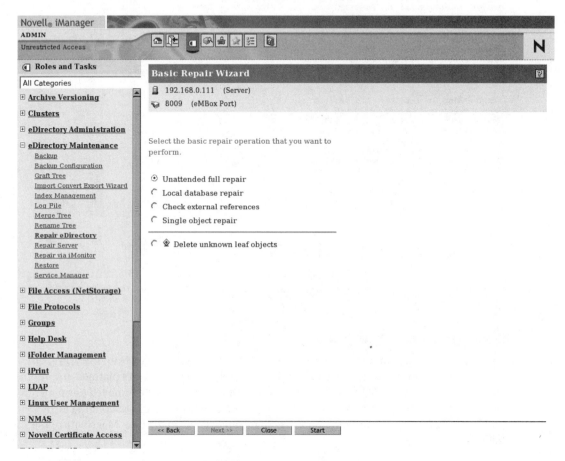

Figure 8-41. *You can run an unattended full repair straight from iManager.*

- On the OES - NetWare console, there's the famous DSREPAIR.NLM. This module has been around for four generations of NetWare now and it's still an excellent tool to manage Directory services on the local server. Start it from the console, select the option Unattended Full Repair option and press Enter. DSREPAIR now locks the database and starts the automated repair. You'll get a notice about the number of errors that have been found in the repair.

- Using **ndsrepair –U** (see Figure 8-42), open the OES - Linux console. This command automatically scans the eDirectory database in the server and repairs anything that can be repaired, without any intervention by the administrator.

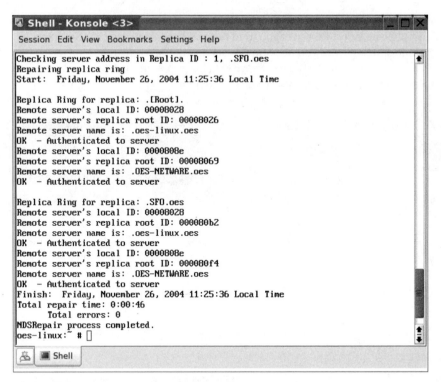

Figure 8-42. *The ndsrepair utility automatically repairs the eDirectory database on an OES - Linux system.*

Removing a Server from the Tree

A server that plays an important role in a network can't just be removed from the eDirectory tree. If it's temporarily down, it normally isn't a big problem if you haven't planned any important eDirectory tasks during that time. If, however, the server has to be removed permanently from the tree, the proper procedure has to be applied to remove it without creating further problems. First, you must prepare the server to be removed from the tree. Make sure of the following before continuing.

- If the server is a time provider, have another server assume the role temporarily.

- If the server has master replicas of some partitions, give the master replica assignment to another server in the network.

- Make sure eDirectory is healthy.

- Make sure there are no mission-critical applications running on the server.

- Disconnect any users if they are still connected.

If all conditions have been met, you can continue removing the server from the tree. The procedure is different depending on the operating system. On OES - Linux, a server can be removed with **ndsconfig rm –a admin-name**. On OES – NetWare, you must perform the correct procedure from NWCONFIG.NLM.

1. Start NWCONFIG.NLM from the console and select Directory Options ➤ Remove Directory Services From This Server.

2. Read the warning and press Enter to continue.

3. Answer Yes to the question Remove Directory Services.

4. Log in as an administrative account with enough permissions to remove Directory Services from the tree and follow the rest of the prompts. If no fatal conditions are encountered, eDirectory is removed properly from this server.

After you've removed eDirectory with NWCONFIG or **ndsconfig**, there's still more to do. You'll find that in eDirectory some objects that refer to the server still exist. You must clean them up manually before the server can be removed properly.

In the procedure previously described, NWCONFIG only does its work if all conditions have been met to remove the server properly from the tree. If any conditions haven't been met, the server can't be removed this way. This happens, for example, if the server isn't able to communicate with other servers in the network. In this case, you can use NWCONFIG – DSREMOVE. This option forces eDirectory from the server, even if it can't be done properly. Be aware though that, in this case, references on other servers to this server can't be removed properly. Thus, it may be necessary to remove them by hand later.

Removing a Server after a Crash

The previous procedure described how a server can be removed from the tree properly. If, however, the server perished in a fire or something else destroyed it completely, you obviously can't start it again to properly remove it from the tree. In such a case, you still must make sure the server is removed from the tree so other servers don't try to contact it. Use the following procedure to remove a server from eDirectory after a crash.

1. From iManager, select Roles And Tasks ➤ Partitions And Replicas ➤ Replica Ring Repair.

2. Select Server Object In eDirectory and browse to the server object that needs to be removed from the replica ring. Click Next to continue.

3. Authenticate to the selected server and click Next to continue.

4. A list of available options is displayed. Click Advanced. This displays the option Remove This Server From The Replica Ring. Select this option and click Start to continue.

5. Wait until the procedure has been completed. The server is then removed from the replica ring.

Troubleshooting Communications Problems

Amongst the most notorious of all eDirectory error codes is error -625: transport failure. You'll see this error if a server fails to communicate with one or more servers in the eDirectory tree. The good thing is that these errors aren't often caused by eDirectory. Most times they're due to external factors like a disconnected network cable. You'll find that if you resolve this external issue, the communication problem takes care of itself. Some common causes of communication problems are

- *Hardware failure*: The server is down, a router is broken, a cable is disconnected, and so on.

- *Misconfigured transport protocols*: You won't see these kinds of communication failures occur spontaneously. Usually they happen after an administrator has been working on the protocol configuration of the server. Check to see if the correct gateways are configured, the right protocols are enabled, and that there are no errors in the IP address binding to the network board.

- Misconfigured SLP: Servers use the Service Location Protocol (SLP) to find each other. If SLP isn't configured the right way, servers won't be able to locate each other. This often results in error code -634. (Chapter 10 has more on SLP configurations.)

- *Slow WAN connections*: If you try to synchronize eDirectory over a slow and overloaded WAN connection, servers will timeout and generate a communication error. In the meantime, you'll still able to ping the other server. You can find out if communication errors are due to slow network connections by using a network traffic analyzer.

- *Locked or disabled database*: If you've started an eDirectory maintenance task on the other server, the server will not be able to communicate with other servers in the network. This often results in error code -663. In many cases, a message that the eDirectory database has been locked can also be found in the server's log files. In many cases, this problem resolves itself: when the eDirectory maintenance task completes, the database is unlocked automatically.

- *High server utilization*: It can also happen that a communications failure isn't caused by a communications link that isn't performing well but by high server utilization. If your server has a constant processor load of 90 percent or higher, it will soon be incapable of replying to eDirectory traffic from other servers. In this case, solving the high utilization problem will solve the communication problem as well.

Managing Synthetic Time

The last subject in this chapter concerns the issue of synthetic time. This occurs if anywhere in the replica an object is found with a future timestamp. This might happen after a serious problem in time synchronization. It can also happen more or less spontaneously—for example, if someone moved the time of the server into the future and then back again because of a mistake when changing the server's time. The solution to synthetic time is easy: do nothing! Synthetic time is annoying because your server beeps every two minutes, but it's not critical. Replica synchronization can still go on—the only problem is that the server continues beeping every two minutes. On OES – NetWare, there's a perfect solution for that problem: use **set sound bell for alerts = off** on the server's console. The problem is automatically resolved if your server's local clock catches up with future timestamps in the database. You can find the culprit object(s) with the search option and iMonitor, and search for timestamps in the future by performing the following steps:

1. Start iMonitor and click the Search button.

2. On the Search screen, click Advanced. This displays the screen shown in Figure 8-43 with the advanced search options.

3. In Scope Options, select the base object you want to start the search from. Use the drop-down list to start the search at the partition level. At Relative Scope, select Subtree to search everything under the specified scope.

4. Under Entry Filters, select Timestamp. In the drop-down list, you can choose between Modification Timestamp and Creation Timestamp. You need them both, but you must choose them one by one. At Comparison, select the > sign to search for timestamps after a specified date. Now specify the current time and click Search. This causes all objects that have a timestamp in the future to be displayed.

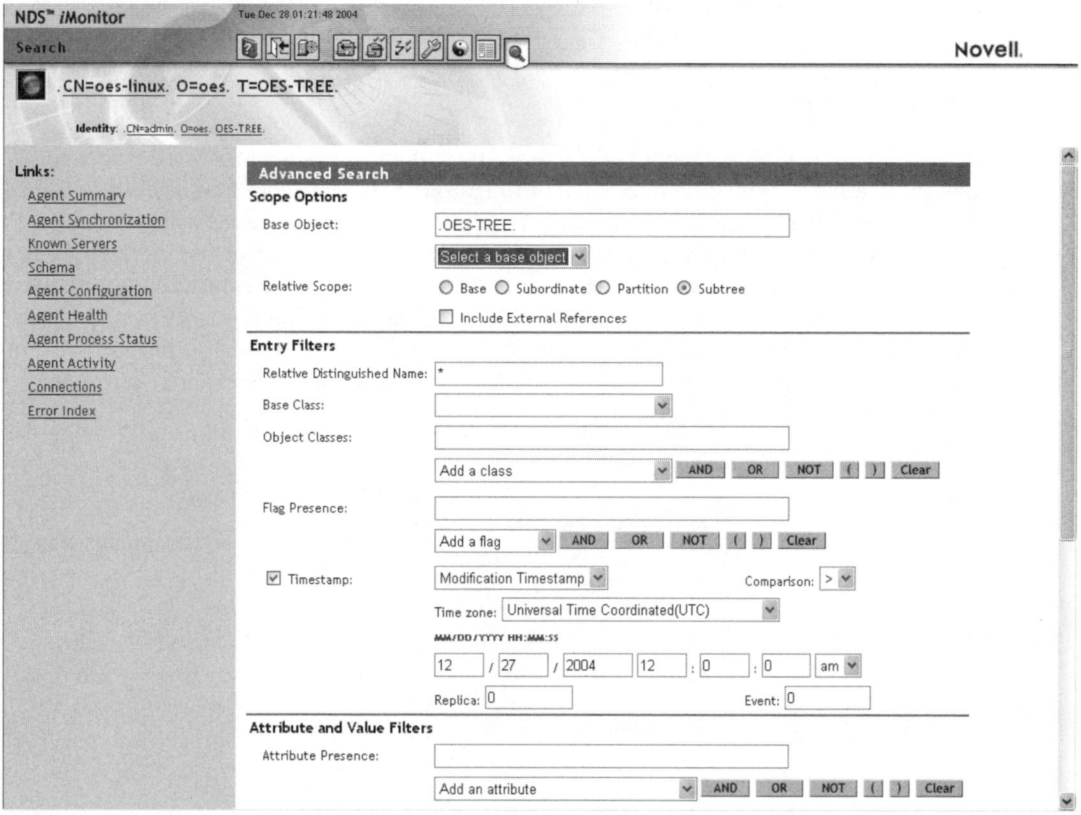

Figure 8-43. *With iMonitor, you can search for all objects that have a timestamp in the future.*

The first thing to do after you've discovered synthetic time somewhere in the tree is to make sure that all servers synchronize their time correctly and that they all catch up to the correct local time. The correct local time can be set with the **set time** command. The section "NTP" earlier in the chapter explains how to synchronize time properly with an NTP timeserver.

If synthetic time becomes a problem because the server is still beeping after six months, there's an advanced solution in DSREPAIR.NLM that can be used on the OES - NetWare console. The solution is called Repair All Timestamps And Declare A New Epoch. You'll see this option only if you load DSREPAIR.NLM with the switch –A. It's best not to use this option though since it generates an enormous load on the server, clears all timestamps from the replicas concerned, and synchronizes all timestamps from the master replica. If for any reason you need to repair timestamps on the network, first make sure that all servers are communicating and synchronizing without problems. Then use the option Repair All Timestamps And Declare A New Epoch on the server with the master replica of this partition. After the timestamps have been repaired, all Read/Write replicas are replaced by new replicas, and all objects are sent from the Master replica to all other replicas.

Summary

In this chapter, you learned about eDirectory. The structure of eDirectory was introduced, as well as the way an eDirectory tree should be organized. You read about how eDirectory can be explained with the native Novell Directory Access Protocol NCP, as well as with the standard LDAP protocol, which can be used from many applications. If a default eDirectory tree doesn't fit your needs, it can be extended by managing the schema. In the schema, additions to the database structure can be made. It's also possible to tune eDirectory performance by optimizing the database cache or by creating indexes. Finally, some common problems that can occur in an eDirectory environment were covered. In the next chapter, you'll read about user management in an eDirectory environment.

CHAPTER 9

■■■

Managing the User Environment

Anetwork with just network resources in it is useless. Networks are made for users that access these resources. In this chapter, you'll learn about management of the user environment. First on the docket is how to create users in eDirectory and how to create a default environment for them where they get secure access to the network resources they need. Following sections cover how Linux User Management can be integrated into eDirectory, usage of the universal password, and how to create a login script which defines default settings for your users.

eDirectory User Management

In an OES environment, all users need a user account, through which they are assigned specific permissions that allow them to access network resources and save personal files in a home directory that no one else can access.

During the installation of Open Enterprise Server, only one user account is created: Admin. This is an administrative account that has, by default, all rights to the entire eDirectory tree. Some specific user accounts that are needed by some network services may also exist, but that depends on the services installed in your tree. To make the network accessible to the users in your company, you'll need to create user accounts for all employees. It's good practice to create one account per user and to not have any users share accounts. User accounts can be created in several ways, including the following:

- Through iManager

- By using a template object to create user accounts with default settings

- By importing users with LDIF (described in Chapter 8)

Creating User Accounts with iManager

To create a user account, you can use many generic tools provided with Open Enterprise Server, such as iManager and ConsoleOne, and in an OES - NetWare environment, NetWare Administrator. Since iManager is the default management tool for OES, the following section explains how to use it to create user accounts.

Creating a User Account with Basic Settings

Creating a user account is very straightforward. In this section, you'll learn how a user account with basic settings can be created (some advanced settings are covered later in this chapter).

1. Start your browser and enter the URL **https://*yourserver*/nps** to access iManager.

2. Enter the username of a user with administrative permissions on your network (typically this is the admin user) and then enter the user's password. Also, enter the IP address of a server with an eDirectory replica or the name of the tree you want to log in to and next click Login. The iManager main screen displays.

3. In Roles And Tasks, select Users ➤ Create User. This displays the screen in which you can enter all the necessary properties for user accounts in your network (see Figure 9-1).

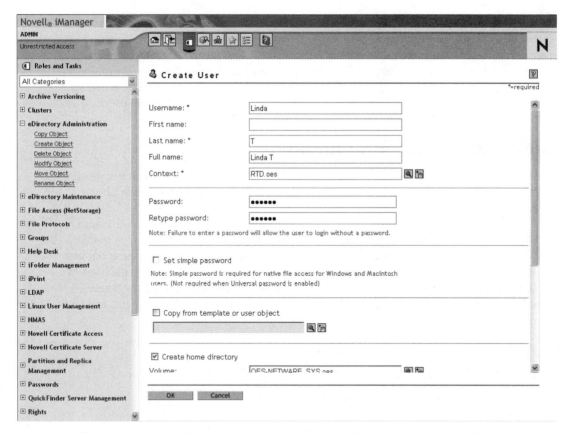

Figure 9-1. *All options marked with a red asterisk are mandatory. They must be completed before you can create the user object.*

4. Some properties are optional, while some are mandatory. These required properties all have a red asterisk. You must provide a value for all these properties otherwise the user object cannot be created. The first mandatory property is the username. Although not mandatory, it's strongly recommended you use a unique username for each user. As you

learned in Chapter 8, it's possible to have two users with the same name as long as they're in different containers. Nevertheless, all LDAP-based applications will have a problem with that, so you should avoid it.

Tip If you just started to implement an eDirectory environment, it's recommended you develop a naming strategy for your network. In this naming strategy, you should define how eDirectory objects are named by default. You should also try to define how exceptions are handled. If, for example, your naming strategy defines that all usernames have the first name initial at the beginning of the username, followed by the entire last name, also define how to handle a situation where you have two users with the same family name and first initial—for example, if you need to create an account for Julia Jones as well as Jessica Jones. To prevent IT support staff from each having their own strategy for newly created users, it's strongly recommended to define a company-wide naming strategy before creating the first user account in the network.

---

5. Enter the last name of the user. This is a mandatory property so you must enter a value for the last name.

6. Enter the context in which the user must be created. Use the magnifying glass to browse for the default context, or type the context where the user must be created manually.

Tip Normally, the context in which you want to create users should already exist at this point. If it doesn't, create it in iManager by choosing Roles And Tasks ➤ eDirectory Administration ➤ Create Object before creating any users in your network.

---

7. All properties necessary to create the user object are present now, so click Create to add the user object. Don't do this right now; instead, add some more useful properties beforehand. The first of these is the password. Passwords should be at least five characters in length and be a mix of letters, numbers, and special characters, thus making the passwords harder to crack—for example, n0v3ll% is a much better password than simply novell. There is no need to use upper and lowercase since the default user password isn't case-sensitive. The section "Universal Password," later in the chapter, explains how the universal password can be used to work with more advanced passwords. Enter the initial password you want to use for the user twice.

8. Apart from the default eDirectory password, it's possible to work with a simple password. This simple password is needed for native file access for Windows and Macintosh users. Because it has limited security though, it's best not to use it; use the universal password instead.

9. Very useful is the option to create a home directory. This is a directory on an NSS or traditional NetWare volume where a user can store his pcersonal files. The home directory is not accessible to other users; the only user that can access files in a user's home directory (apart from the user himself, of course) is admin. Before creating home

directories for individual users, be sure the required volume is present as an object in eDirectory. On OES - NetWare, it's present by default; on OES - Linux, you have to add it manually. First, create an NSS volume for this purpose. On this volume, create a parent directory in which you put the home directories for all users in the network. Since user home directories can fill up rapidly, do not put them on the volume SYS; instead, create a dedicated volume for them.

■Caution If you want to work with user home directories, create them while creating the user object. This way the necessary eDirectory property gets its value automatically, the home directory is created, and the user gets the necessary rights automatically. It's cumbersome to do this manually later since you must modify settings at different locations.

---

10. All the other options can be overlooked for now. If you want to deploy eGuide (see Chapter 17) in your network so that users can look up information about each other automatically, it's recommended you fill in the naming options like title, location, department, telephone, fax-number, and e-mail address as well. Click OK when you're finished creating the user in eDirectory. You'll see a success message. Click OK to continue.

11. If you have OES - Linux in your network, you'll be prompted to enter the Linux User Management (LUM) settings at this point. LUM is covered later in this chapter in the section "Linux User Management."

Modifying Login Security Settings

In the previous section, you learned how to create a user account with some basic settings. Generally, these settings are secure, but Novell provides some advanced properties to fine-tune security related to logging in and use of user accounts. That's what this section is for.

■Note In this section, you'll learn about login security, which is the security related to logging in to the network and its usage. This is not the only possibility to handle security in an OES environment. There is also file system security, which handles access to files and directories on your server, and eDirectory security which handles management possibilities in eDirectory. Chapter 12 has more information on these subjects.

---

1. Start iManager, then in Roles And Tasks select Users and choose Modify User. Verify that the option Select A Single Object is chosen and use the magnifying glass to browse to the user object you want to modify. Afterward, click OK to start working on the object. You'll see different tabs on which you can specify all settings related to the selected user object. (See Figure 9-2.)

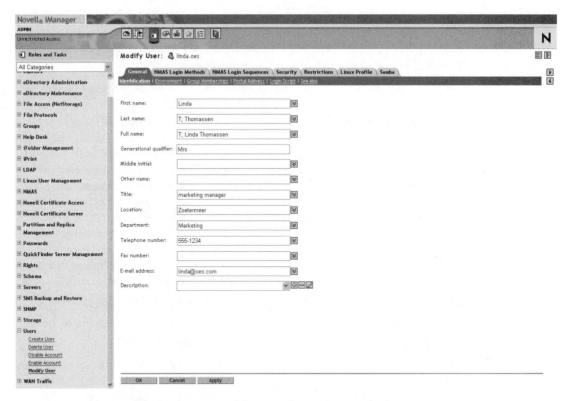

Figure 9-2. *You can modify the properties of the user object via several tabs.*

2. Select the tab Restrictions and then choose Password Restrictions. On this tab, you can specify how settings for the default eDirectory password are handled. Settings of the advanced universal password are covered later in the chapter in the section "Universal Password."

3. On the tab with password restrictions, several settings can be made with regard to the password:

   • *Allow user to change password*: It's recommended that this option be selected at all times. It allows a user to manage his own password. If it's not selected, it'll mean a lot more work for your IT department.

   • *Require a password*: Since a password is the most important way to protect your user accounts, this option should always be selected. By default, however, it's not selected. After selecting it, specify a minimal password length as well. It's recommended never to work with passwords shorter than five characters.

■**Tip** Normal users should always have a password. There can, however, be exceptions to this rule: user accounts created for usage of public computers don't need a password since they should have very limited rights on the system. Also, some system accounts don't need a password.

- *Force periodic password changes*: After a certain time, passwords will become less secret than they originally were since users will eventually tell other users what their passwords are. For this reason, Novell provides an option to force periodic password changes. By default, the password must be changed every 40 days. In general, this is a reasonable amount of days for a forced password change (although many users will think it's way too short!). Be aware that if you force users to change their password too often, they won't take it seriously anymore and will choose passwords that are easy to guess—for example, they may choose their previous password except with a 1 on the end. After selecting Force Periodic Password Changes, the Date Password Expires option becomes available as well. This lists when the current password will expire. If a password is set by an administrator, the password expiration date is automatically set to the present day. This forces the user to enter a new password the first time he logs in.

- *Require unique passwords*: This option forces a user to choose a password he hasn't previously used. eDirectory remembers the last 20 passwords used.

- *Limit grace login*: A grace login is when a user is allowed use of his old password even though she should have already specified a new password. By default, a user has six grace logins. When the password expiration date occurs, the user gets a message stating that she should change her password, and if she wants to change it now (see Figure 9-3). In the last grace login, the user gets a message that she must enter her new password now, followed by a prompt to enter her new passwords. The feature of grace logins is useful, but can be confusing for end users since it doesn't force them to change the password immediately. For this reason, many system administrators set the number of grace logins allowed to one. This way, the user logs in once with her old password, but then must change it immediately.

Figure 9-3. *When a user password expires, the user is asked if he wants to change it.*

- *Set password*: This is an important option for help-desk employees, letting them reset the password for a user.

4. The next set of restrictions is under Login Restrictions (see Figure 9-4). With these
   options, the usability of an account can be influenced. After a user has left the company, or
   if it's unclear whether a user is still working for the company, use the Account Disabled
   option. This disables any attempted logins for the user account; if, however, the user
   suddenly comes back and needs to log in again, you're just one click away from reenabling
   his account. On the same tab is the Account Has Expiration Date option. Use this if you
   already know the date the employee will leave the company. Specify it here and the
   account will be disabled automatically on that day. Finally, there is the Limit Concurrent
   Connections option. Using this, you can avoid the situation where a user is logged in
   more than once to the network. By default, there is no limitation. Setting a limitation to
   this parameter is recommended to prevent a user from being logged in at several workstations simultaneously. This is especially useful if there are only a limited number of
   licenses available on the network. Because under certain conditions it can take a few
   minutes before every server on the network knows that a user is logged out, limiting the
   number of times a user can be logged in to two is recommended so they don't find they've
   been locked out. Another important piece of information on the tab is the Last Login
   Time. The value displayed changes every time the user logs in to the network again.

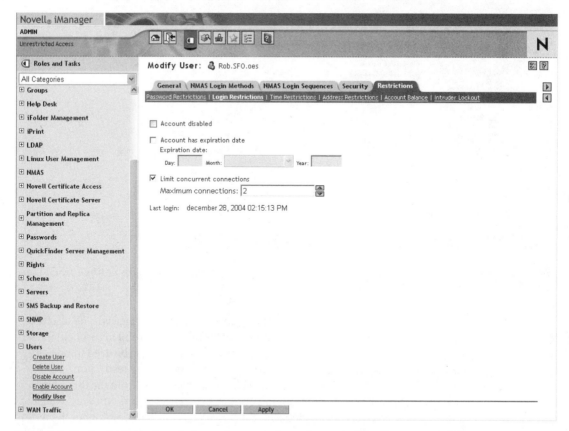

Figure 9-4. *Under the login Restrictions tab, you can see when a user last logged in to the network*

5. Another important limitation that can be applied to user accounts is the login time restriction (see Figure 9-5). With this option, you can limit the times users can be logged in to the network. With a login time restriction, you can make it impossible for users to log in to the network or use network resources at times they shouldn't be logged in to the network. This can be useful if your company is closed on the weekend. On the other hand, it can be impractical if a user needs to work after normal office hours. You can set a login time restriction by Shift-clicking anywhere in the matrix of available login times.

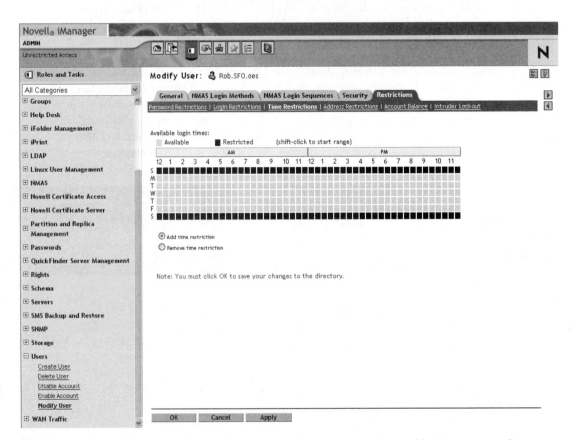

Figure 9-5. *With a proper login time restriction, you can prevent unauthorized logins at times when users shouldn't be logged in.*

6. Apart from restricting users from logging in during certain time periods, it's also possible to restrict logins from certain addresses. This feature is useful for users that need some special security, like the company's accountant. It can also be used to prevent remote login from unknown addresses. To set a network address restriction, click the plus (+) sign. A pop-up window appears where you can choose from the different available address types. All current (and even less current) address types are available. Enter the desired address and then click Add to add it to the list of addresses the user is allowed to log in from.

Tip If you want to limit logins for a certain user to all addresses in one network, just enter a network address as the address restriction. If, for example, 192.168.0.0 is entered as the address restriction, this allows the user to log in from all nodes in that network.

7. Address restrictions are the last important restrictions related to login security that will be discussed. Click OK to save and apply the new settings to eDirectory.

Activating Intruder Detection

One of the greatest security threats comes from users who try to crack the accounts of other users by guessing passwords. Far too often, this is rather easy, because many users employ passwords that are easily guessed, such as the names of their spouse, children, pets, or favorite football players. As an added safeguard, intruder detection can be used. Intruder detection is a setting that has to be done at a container level. It works for all users directly under that container, but cannot be inherited. If, for example, intruder detection is set for o=oes, it will be applied to cn=admin.o=oes, but will not be applied to cn=rob.ou=sfo.o=oes. This means you must apply intruder detection to all individual containers in your directory tree where you want it applied. Once it has been applied, it works for all users in the considered container and locks the account of any user who tries to log in with the wrong password too many times. If that happens, as an administrator you must reset the account after it has been locked.

Tip Intruder detection can be a blessing, but it can be dangerous as well. Imagine what would happen if someone tries to guess the password of your admin user! You can prevent admin from being locked by intruder detection by just not disabling intruder detection on this container. On the other hand, this makes it easier to crack the admin account. It's therefore recommended to use intruder detection even on the container where admin is, but hide a backup admin somewhere in the tree. Chapter 12 explains how a backup admin can be created using eDirectory rights.

1. Start iManager and from Roles And Tasks select eDirectory Administration ➤ Modify Object. Next, browse to the container you want to set intruder detection for, select it and click OK.

2. Select the General tab and click Intruder Detection (see Figure 9-6). Choose the Detect Intruders option to activate the mechanism.

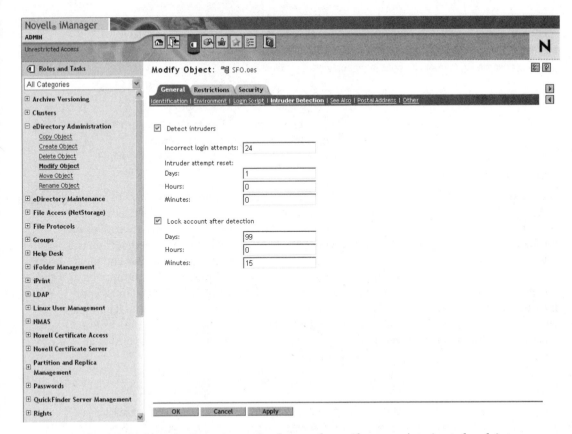

Figure 9-6. *Selecting the Intruder Detection option lets you know if someone's trying to break into a user account.*

3. Select the number of incorrect login attempts and the intruder attempt reset interval. The default value will look for seven incorrect login attempts within 30 minutes. This allows an intruder to try to log in more than 300 times with the wrong password in a 24-hour period! For a more restricted setting, I recommend limiting the number of incorrect login attempts to four in a 24-hour period. This lets a user make a few mistakes while entering his password, but also nicely limits an intruder who tries to log in repeatedly with the wrong password.

4. Select the Lock Account After Detection option and an account will be locked after a user has logged in with the wrong password too many times. You'll see that the default lockout period is just 15 minutes! After that, the intruder can start all over again! Many administrators prefer to set this to a much longer period, like 99 days. This way an administrator will always know if a user has tried to log in too many times with the wrong password. Click OK to save and apply the settings.

■Note You can see it on the user object if intruder detection has locked an account. You can also find this in your server's log files. Since all admins should regularly check these files, it's hard to miss an intruder detection event.

Now that you've set intruder detection to a container, it will be applied to all users in that container. If someone tries to break into a user account, the next time a user logs in with his valid password, a message will appear stating that someone tried to log in to his account with an invalid password and that his account is locked (as shown in Figure 9-7). As an administrator, you can now unlock his account.

Figure 9-7. *When intruder detection has locked out an account, the user gets a message indicating what happened.*

1. Start iManager, select Roles And Tasks ➤ Modify User and choose the user whose account has been locked out by intruder detection.

2. Select Restrictions ➤ Intruder Lockout. On this tab, you'll see the option Locked By Intruder selected. Deselect this option to allow the regular user to log in again.

3. Some important information helps you identify the person trying to break in to the other user's account—for instance, the parameter Intruder Address contains the IP address of the intruder's computer. If you combine this with the parameter mentioned at Login Intruder Reset, you'll know exactly what time and from which computer the intruder tried to log in to the other user's account. (See Figure 9-8.)

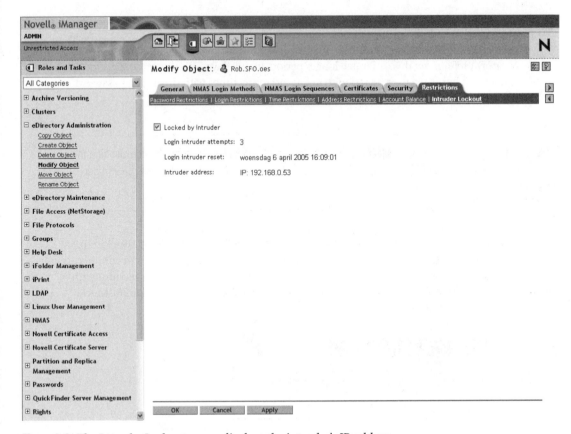

Figure 9-8. *The Intruder Lockout screen displays the intruder's IP address.*

Working with Multiple User Accounts

Of course it's nice that you can select one user object at a time to modify its properties. In many cases, however, it's necessary to select more than one user object to modify a property—maybe you want to implement a new and stricter security policy for your organization or perhaps the telephone number for an entire department has changed. Working with more than one object at the same time is easy; the only thing you need to do is assure that all objects are of the same class to avoid errors.

1. From iManager, select Roles And Tasks ➤ eDirectory Administration ➤ Modify Object.

2. In the Modify Object window, choose Select Multiple Objects (see Figure 9-9). Now use the magnifying glass to locate the objects you want to modify and add them to the object list.

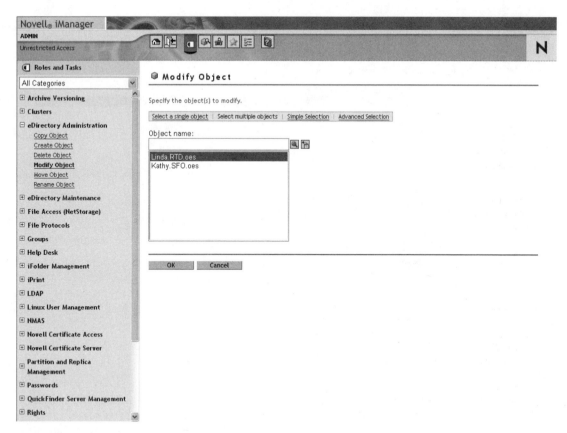

Figure 9-9. *With Select Multiple Objects, it's easy to compose a list of objects in which you want to change a common property.*

3. Click OK after you've finished composing the list of objects. This displays a window in which you can enter new values for common properties. Notice that not all properties are present: some can only be changed on individual user objects.

4. If you're changing properties on multiple objects, there's always a risk that the property concerned already has a value present. Behind every option you'll find a drop-down list in which you can specify what to do if a property already has a value (see Figure 9-10). The default setting for this drop-down list is Ignore. This is a rather useless but at the same time very safe option since it ignores all changes you make and saves the original values for the selected properties. Other options are Replace and Remove, which replaces the original value with the new one, and Add, which adds the new value to any existing value of that property.

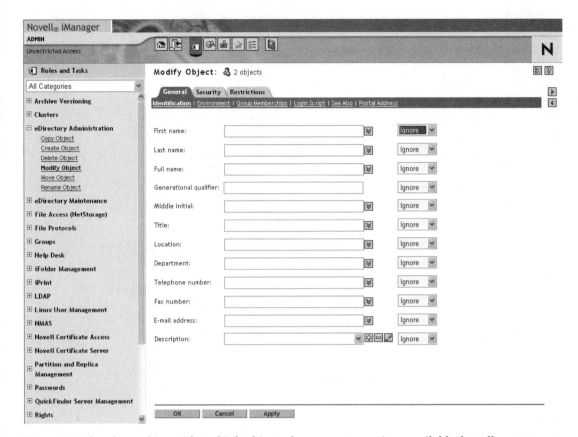

Figure 9-10. *If you're working with multiple objects, there are extra options available that allow you to specify what to do with the original values for the properties that are changed.*

Tip In previous versions of NetWare with NetWare Administrator, it was only possible to change multiple properties for user objects. In OES ConsoleOne and iManager, multiple values can be changed for any type of object.

Working with the Template Object

Creating a user can be a lot of work, especially if a value has to be provided for a lot of specific properties. To make creation of user objects easier, you can add default settings to the template object. This is an object in eDirectory that can be used upon creation of user objects; the user object inherits all settings that are applied to the template object. This way, creating users in eDirectory can be done a lot easier.

1. In iManager, select Roles And Tasks ➤ eDirectory Administration ➤ Create Object.

2. From the list of available object classes, select the Template object and click OK.

3. Provide a name for the template object and specify the context where you wish to create the template object. Click OK to continue.

4. A message displays stating the template was created successfully. In this screen, click Modify to get access to the properties of the template object, as shown in Figure 9-11. Now you can set all general settings for new users in your network. Click OK when finished.

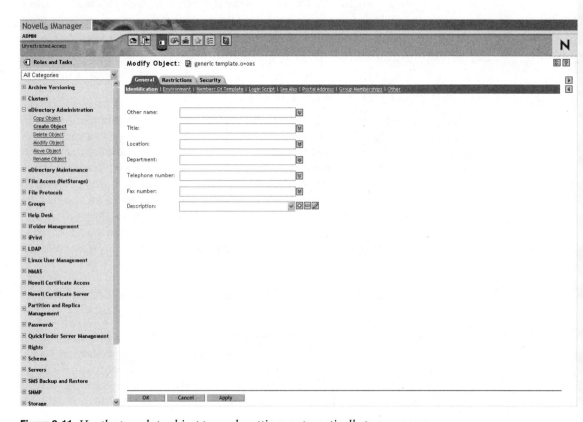

Figure 9-11. *Use the template object to apply settings automatically to new users.*

5. Now create a new user object. In the Create User screen, provide a value for all mandatory attributes. Next, select Copy From Template Or User Object. Click OK to create the user. All properties set for the template object are automatically applied to the user object.

Tip It's best to work with template objects to add some default properties to newly created users. It's also possible to refer to an existing user you want to copy all properties from. A template object is more clear, however, since it's a different object in eDirectory and it shows immediately what the purpose of this template object is.

Tip Users that are created via a template become a member of that template; thus, you can always check what users are created via the Template object. If you select the Template object and then choose Modify Properties On Multiple Objects, the properties will be modified for all the members of the Template.

Searching for Objects in iManager

If you're working with the Modify Object option from eDirectory Administration in iManager, you can use the magnifying glass to browse manually to the object you need. In a small tree where you know exactly what kind of object to look for, this isn't problematic because you know where to find the object in the tree. In a large tree, however, it can be difficult to locate objects. To make it easier for you, iManager provides two tools: Simple Selection and Advanced Selection. Both help you find an object in eDirectory and can be used to locate an object in the tree based on the name of the object, or on the value of a certain property. In Simple Selection, you can specify the property on which you want to base your search, while in the Advanced Selection option, several properties can be combined into a filter to find exactly what you need in the eDirectory tree.

1. From iManager, select eDirectory Administration, Modify Object, and click Simple Selection. This shows you the Simple Selection interface (see Figure 9-12).

2. By default, the property Common name is selected, which allows you to search for objects based on their name. In the second drop-down list, you can specify what exactly to look for. For instance, you can search for objects that start with "rob," which will bring up the users "rob" and "Robert." You can also select Equals, in which case only exact matches will be produced—in this example, only user "rob" would be found.

3. Click the triangle that's pointing to the right, next to the field where you entered the search string to start searching for objects that match your search criteria. Be aware that in a large eDirectory environment, it can take several minutes before the search finishes.

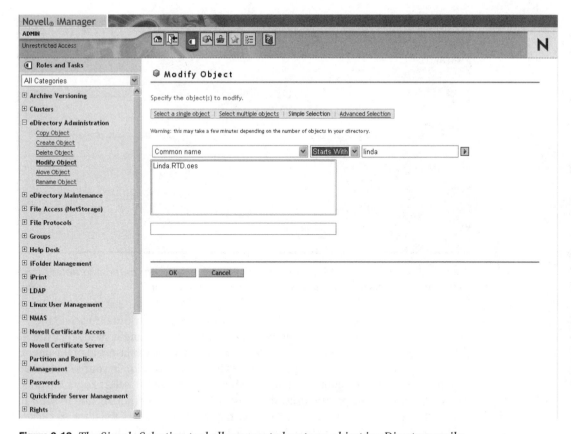

Figure 9-12. *The Simple Selection tool allows you to locate an object in eDirectory easily.*

Whereas the Simple Selection allows you to locate eDirectory objects based on quite a few criteria, you can also use Advanced Selection to work with advanced filters in which you specify where to look for objects and select complex filters for criteria with which you want to search. In the next example, you'll learn how to scan your eDirectory tree for user objects that have an unsafe password, and where someone has tried to log in with the wrong password more than once.

1. From iManager, select eDirectory Administration, choose Modify Object, and click Advanced Selection.

2. Select the object class User and optionally specify the container where you want to look for user objects. Specify also whether or not you want to scan sub-containers of this container.

3. Click the button next to the Filter option to open the Advanced Selection Criterion dialog box (see Figure 9-13) in which a filter can be defined. In this pop-up window, you can compose a filter based on multiple criteria.

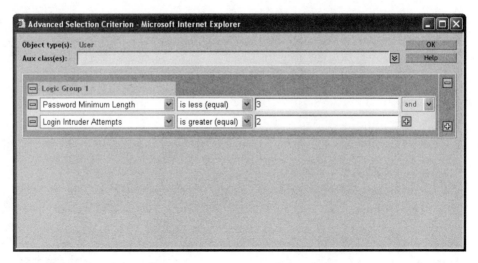

Figure 9-13. *In the Advanced Selection Criterion window, you can compose complex filters to search for objects in which a specific value is present (or not).*

4. Let's go through an example. Click the first drop-down list (Attribute) to select the attribute you want to search for. Choose Password Minimum Length. Next, click the second drop-down list (Operator) and select Is Less (Equal). In the last field of the query, specify the value 3. Now click the plus sign next to the first criterion in your search filter to add a new criterion to look for. In the Attribute drop-down list, select Login Intruder Attempts, then in the Operator drop-down list, select Is Greater (Equal), and in the last field of the query, enter the value 2. You have now finished creating the filter, so click OK to save it. This filter can be used to look for all user objects that have the minimum password length set to three characters and where at least two times an invalid password was entered upon login. Any users that appear in this output may have a security problem.

5. Click OK to start searching. A result will be displayed immediately after the search has finished. In a large network this may take a few minutes.

Linux User Management

But with Open Enterprise Server, Novell wants to provide an open environment to the world, where users can use the services of Open Enterprise Server, no matter what their operating system. With Novell Linux Desktop, Novell provides a good alternative for the Windows client. There is, however, one issue to be solved: management of local Linux users. When a user is connecting from a Linux workstation and he wants to be able to use local files and services on that workstation, he needs a local account on that workstation as well. This is just like a Windows 2000 Professional or Windows NT workstation where a user needs a local account to get access to local system resources. In OES - Linux, Novell Linux User Management (LUM) provides these local user accounts.

Linux User Management is installed only as a part of OES - Linux. It does not exist on OES - NetWare and has two main functions:

- LUM is used to handle local Linux authentication through eDirectory.

- LUM also allows you to create Linux user objects in eDirectory for Windows users who will access Samba file services on your OES Server.

Before you can understand how LUM is used in an OES - LUM environment, you'll need to learn about the PAM (Pluggable Authentication Modules) mechanism that's used to handle Linux authentication: once you understand the way PAM works, you'll also be able to understand how local Linux authentication can be handled remotely by modifying the PAM mechanism on the Linux workstation.

Tip So you know NetWare but don't know anything about the Linux side of OES? No problem. It's very easy to understand what PAM does—it does exactly the same thing as Novell NMAS. Both systems use modules to define how exactly authentication should take place.

PAM—Pluggable Authentication Module

On a Linux workstation, many services need authentication. The way this authentication is handled is in most cases defined by the PAM mechanism. PAM allows for flexible authentication. The basic functionality of PAM is simple: an application calls PAM to handle authentication and by using a PAM configuration file, PAM will use the proper mechanism. Many applications can use PAM. As an example, let's discuss how it's used by the login program.

PAM Explained

In the normal situation, on user login on a Linux workstation the local user database in the Linux files /etc/passwd and /etc/shadow is checked. In /etc/shadow, the encrypted password is recorded. Based on the settings in this database, the user will or won't get access. However, in order to log in to eDirectory, the PAM configuration file /etc/pam.d/login that's used for login needs to be modified, which is done automatically when installing OES - Linux. This is because Linux does not know about eDirectory. This problem is solved with PAM. The modified PAM configuration file (see Listing 9-1) includes a referral to the PAM modules that enable the Linux workstation to communicate with eDirectory. The module pam_nam.so is shown next.

Listing 9-1. *The PAM Configuration File*

```
auth       sufficient    /lib/security/pam_nam.so
account    sufficient    /lib/security/pam_nam.so
password   sufficient    /lib/security/pam_nam.so
session    optional      /lib/security/pam_nam.so
auth       requisite     pam_unix2.so
auth       required      pam_securetty.so
auth       required      pam_nologin.so
#auth      required      pam_homecheck.so
auth       required      pam_env.so
```

```
auth       required     pam_mail.so
account    required     pam_unix2.so
password   required     pam_pwcheck.so nullok
password   required     pam_unix2.so nullok use_first_pass use_authok
session    required     pam_unix2.so
session    required     pam_limits.so
```

In the authentication process, there are four different parts to take note of. In the first part, authentication is handled. In the preceding example file, these are the lines that start with the keyword auth. In the second part, the validity of the account and other account-related parameters are checked. This happens in the lines that start with account. In the third part, all settings relating to the password are verified. This happens in the lines that start with password. Last, settings relating to the establishment of a session with network resources are defined. This happens in the lines that start with session.

The procedure that will be followed upon completion of these four instances is defined by calling the different PAM modules. This happens in the last column of the example configuration file. There's also the pam_securetty module, which can be used to verify that the root user is not logging in to a Linux computer via an insecure terminal. (A terminal in Linux is referred to as a tty, which is where the name securetty comes from.) The keywords sufficient, optional, required, and requisite are used to define the importance of the conditions in a certain module being met. Except for the first four lines (which are added to the default PAM configuration file by the OES installer), conditions defined in all modules must be met since they are all defined as requisite or required. For example, it's necessary that the conditions as stated by the PAM module pam_unix2 are passed. Without going into detail, this means that authentication will fail if one of the conditions implied by the specified module is not met.

When OES - Linux is installed, four lines are added to the default PAM configuration. In the preceding example, these were the first four lines—but they don't have to be on the first positions of the file. These four lines offer an alternative for valid authentication by using the module pam_nam.so. This module specifies that eDirectory must be used to handle authentication. Passing these modules at the four instances of authentication is sufficient, but is not required. Sufficient in this context means that if the instance auth passes all conditions defined in pam_nam.so, this is enough for the auth part of authentication to succeed. The same applies for the account, password, and session parts of the authentication procedure. If this is the case, the local Linux authentication mechanism will no longer be used, since the user is authenticating against eDirectory in this case. In order for this to work, you need a valid user account that has all required Linux properties in eDirectory. You can read how to create such a user account later in this section.

The nice thing about this example PAM configuration file is that it will first check if eDirectory can be used to authenticate to the network. If this doesn't work, the default Linux login mechanism is used, as specified by pam_unix2.so. The workings of this default mechanism are defined from the fifth line on in the example configuration file.

Required Local Components

In order for PAM to work, some local components need to be present at the Linux workstation. These components can be installed locally on a Linux workstation by installing the OES LUM component. Upon installation of this service, four different components are installed on the Linux workstation:

- *pam_nam*: This is the PAM module used to redirect authentication of the Linux user to eDirectory. The exact working of pam_nam is defined in the configuration file /etc/nam.conf. The most important parameters in this file define where to find eDirectory and what context should be used for default authentication to the server. This happens on the first three lines of the example file in Listing 9-2. It shows the contents of this file after a default installation of OES - Linux. For more details about the file, consult its man page.

Listing 9-2. *Default /etc/nam.conf after Installation of OES - Linux*

```
base-name=o=oes
admin-fdn=cn=admin,o=oes
preferred-server=192.168.0.100
num-threads=5
schema=rfc2307
enable-persistent-cache=YES
user-hash-size=211
group-hash-size=211
persistent-cache-refresh-period=28800
persistent-cache-refresh-flag=all
create-home=yes
type-of-authentication=2
certificate-file-type=der
ldap-ssl-port=636
ldap-port=389
support-alias-name=no
support-outside-base-context=yes
```

- *nss_nam*: A module that is used to retrieve user and group information from eDirectory and make it available locally on the Linux workstation. This component works with the configuration file /etc/nsswitch.conf to search for information needed for verification of local credentials. The relevant entries in this file are "passwd: files nam" and "group: files nam". In these lines, the field files define that for verification of local rights to the workstation, the local Linux userdatabases /etc/passwd and /etc/shadow are always consulted first. This is useful, because it allows the local user root to do his work. After the local files are checked, the field nam defines that eDirectory will be checked next. For caching of Linux user information from eDirectory on the local workstation, a local process called namcd is used. Both pam_nam and the nss_nam modules use namcd to get Linux-related user information from eDirectory. You can specify the Linux workstations where namcd must be active by creating a Linux workstation object in eDirectory (more about this process in the next section).

■**Note** nam is short for Novell Account Management, an old product that could be used to authenticate Linux or UNIX users on eDirectory.

- *namconfig*: This command-line utility can be used to add or remove LUM from a specific eDirectory context and retrieve or set LUM configuration parameters. You also need namconfig if you want to configure an existing Linux workstation with LUM. For example, if you want to configure a local Linux workstation to use LUM, use the command **namconfig add –a cn=admin,o=oes –r ou=lum,o=oes –w ou=ws,ou=lum,o=oes –S** *YOURSERVER***:389 -1 636**. In this example, you authenticate to the server specified with –S as cn=admin,o=oes. This is a pure LDAP authentication that works over SSL-port 636. In order for this SSL connection to work, the unsecure port 389 must be enabled as well. In order to create the proper LUM workstation object, the partition root of the partition where the objects are created must be specified with the parameter –r; the exact container where the workstations must be created can be used with the option –w. In order to work over a secure SSL connection, an SSL certificate must be imported to the local machine. For this, use **namconfig k**. If this command is slightly modified, it can be applied to work over an unsecure connection as well: **namconfig add –a cn=admin,o=oes –r ou=lum,o=oes –w ou=ws,ou=lum,o=oes –S** *YOURSERVER***:389**. namconfig can be used for more than adding Linux workstations to the Directory. Consult its man page for more details.

- *Command-line utilities*: On the Linux workstation, LUM also provides some command-line utilities, which can be used to manage LUM users and groups. It's also possible to manage your LUM environment from iManager. Since this is a much more straightforward procedure, it's best to do it this way instead of using the command-line utilities. If you prefer the command-line utilities, the following are available, some of which refer to the creation and modification of LUM users and groups. This subject is covered in the next section.

  - *namconfig*: This utility is used to configure your LUM environment, say, by adding a Linux workstation to eDirectory.

  - *unix2edir*: Use **unix2edir** to export users from your local Linux workstation to eDirectory.

  - *namuseradd*: Use **namuseradd** to add LUM users to eDirectory.

  - *namusermod*: This command can be used to modify existing LUM accounts.

  - *namuserdel*: Use **namuserdel** to delete LUM accounts from eDirectory.

  - *namuserlist*: This useful command is good for troubleshooting. It displays a list of all LUM users known to your server in a given container. For example, use **namuserlist – x o=oes** to display a list of all LUM-enabled users in the specified container.

  - *namgroupadd*: Use **namgroupadd** to add a LUM group to eDirectory.

  - *namgroupmod*: Use **namgroupmod** to modify LUM groups.

  - *namgroupdel*: Use **namgroupdel** to remove LUM groups from eDirectory.

  - *namgrouplist*: This utility can be used like **namuserlist** to display a list of all known LUM groups in a given container.

- *ndslogin*: Use **ndslogin** for eDirectory troubleshooting—for instance, to test if login to eDirectory works. Be aware that this is no full-scale Linux client since it will not execute any login scripts and therefore does not support some of the vital services provided by your OES server.

In an environment where you want to replace all Windows workstations with Linux workstations, one of the most important tasks is to use **namconfig** to import the workstation into eDirectory. This is performed automatically upon installation of the LUM component on OES - Linux. If you want to install a Linux workstation manually into eDirectory, after having installed the LUM software from the OES - Linux installation CDs on a workstation, you can import the workstation in eDirectory using the following procedure:

■**Caution** Currently, there is no LUM component that can be installed directly on the Novell Linux Desktop. It is possible to install all required packages manually on the Novell Linux Desktop, but this method is not officially supported. Use the following procedure at your own risk. In order to apply the procedure outlined next, the following RPM packages must be installed on your Linux workstation: NOVLAM, libldapsdk.so.0, libldapssl.so.0, libldapx.so.0, NLDAPbase, and NLDAPsdk. Currently, Novell is working on a full-scale client for the Linux-platform. This replaces the need to configure LUM manually on a Linux workstation.

---

1. From a console prompt, issue the command **namconfig –k** to import the necessary SSL key from eDirectory to your workstation. You'll be prompted to enter the admin password to continue.

2. You'll get a message that the certificate file has been updated successfully. Now you can use **namconfig** to add your workstation to eDirectory.

3. If, for example, you want to add your Linux workstation to the container ou=ws, ou=lum,o=oes by using a connection to the secure LDAP port on your eDirectory server, use **namconfig add –a cn=admin,o=oes r ou=lum,o=oes –w ou=ws,ou=lum, o=oes –S** *YOURSERVER***:389 -l 636**. You'll be prompted for the admin password now. Enter it to add your Linux workstation to eDirectory.

■**Tip** This section covered how you log in to eDirectory from a Linux workstation. To be more precise, it explained how the login procedure for a Linux workstation can be redirected to an OES server containing eDirectory. This is not the only option in which a Linux workstation can communicate with an OES server. From a Linux workstation, you can also use the ndslogin utility to perform a complete login to eDirectory. Support for eDirectory by this utility is limited though, since not all functionality is supported. Another method is to use one of the many client components available from different OES utilities like iFolder and iPrint. These give access to the related service only. The Novell client for Linux can be used to access NCP-based services running on Netware. Chapter 6 has more information on how to connect a Linux workstation to OES.

Enabling LUM Users

In the preceding section, you learned how the login process on a Linux workstation can be redirected to log in against eDirectory. The most critical component of this, however, hasn't been covered so far: the LUM user. In this section, you'll learn how to create a LUM user. In this instance, let's assume that the LUM services have already been installed on at least one Linux workstation in the network. By default, this will be the case, since it's installed on OES - Linux automatically.

Note LUM is not installed with OES - NetWare. If you want to connect Linux workstations with OES - NetWare, you need Linux client software. See Chapter 6 for more information.

To create a working LUM environment in eDirectory, a few steps have to be completed. First, you need to create a LUM group. This is because a Linux user cannot exist if he is not a member of at least one Linux group. Therefore, you start the procedure for creating a LUM user with the creation of a Linux group. This Linux group is connected to a Linux workstation object, which was installed in eDirectory during the installation of LUM on the workstation (explained in the previous section). If these conditions have been met, LUM users can be created. They can be created as new users. It's also possible to convert an existing eDirectory user to a LUM user.

When you've created a LUM user, the software automatically asks if you want to create a Samba user as well. These two are related: a LUM user is needed for access to the local file system if a user from another computer wants to access shares offered by the Samba server. You can read more about the Samba server and other ways to access files in Chapter 10 of this book. In order to create LUM users, follow these steps:

1. Start iManager, log in as administrator and from Roles And Tasks select Groups ➤ Create Group to give you the screen shown in Figure 9-14.

2. Specify the name and the context where you want to create the group and click OK.

3. Now you have to make the new group a LUM group as well. You do this by assigning it to at least one Linux workstation. The group will be known on this Linux workstation and will be cached by the namcd daemon on that workstation (as well as all users that are members of this group). If you want the LUM group to be known on all Linux workstations in your tree, associate it to the Linux config object. This object is created automatically when LUM is installed in the tree. Associate the LUM Group object to at least one Linux workstation object (as shown in Figure 9-15) and click OK to continue. You'll see a message that the group has been created successfully.

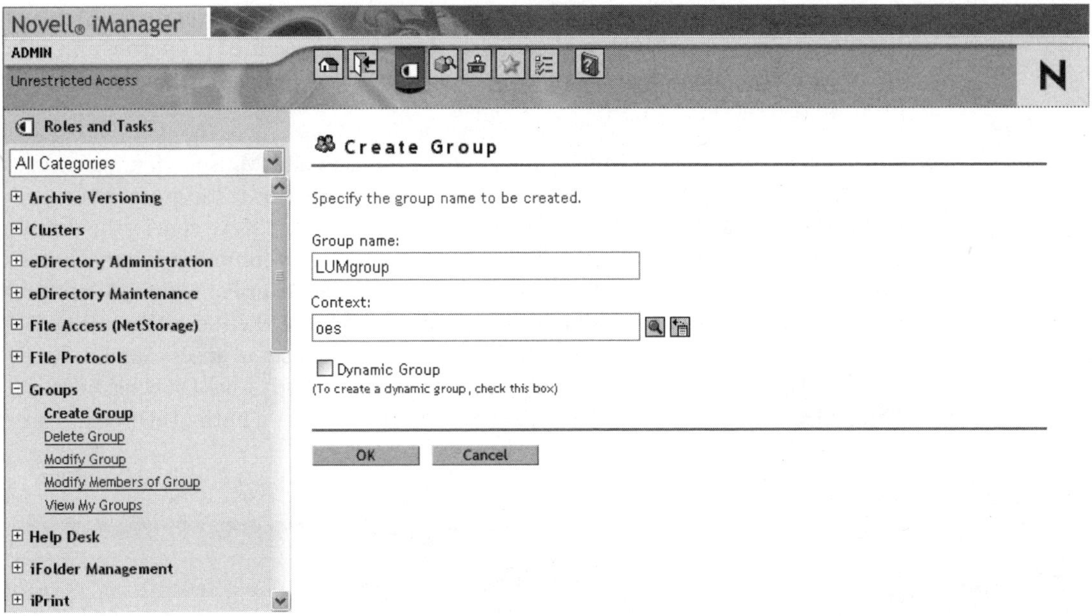

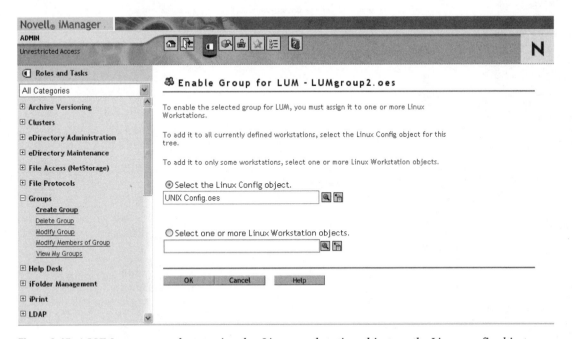

Figure 9-14. *To create a LUM group, start creating a normal group.*

Figure 9-15. *A LUM group must be associated to Linux workstation objects or the Linux config object.*

4. Now that the LUM Group object is created, you can create a LUM user. From iManager Roles And Tasks, select Users ➤ Create User. Enter all the required properties and click OK to continue. Click OK again once you see the message indicating that the user has been created successfully.

5. You'll now see a screen in which you can make the user a LUM user. First, you must specify the primary group for this user (see Figure 9-16). This is the group object required for all users that are defined on a Linux workstation. Next, specify the default shell type the LUM user will use when working on the Linux computer. In most cases, the default shell /bin/bash is fine. Check **Also Enable This User For LDAP (eDirectory) Authentication To Samba** to allow this user account to be authenticated on the OES - Linux Samba server as well. You need this if you want the user to access Samba shares on the server (Chapter 10 has more about Samba configuration). Click OK when finished. This adds some auxiliary classes to the user object that turns a normal eDirectory user into a LUM user.

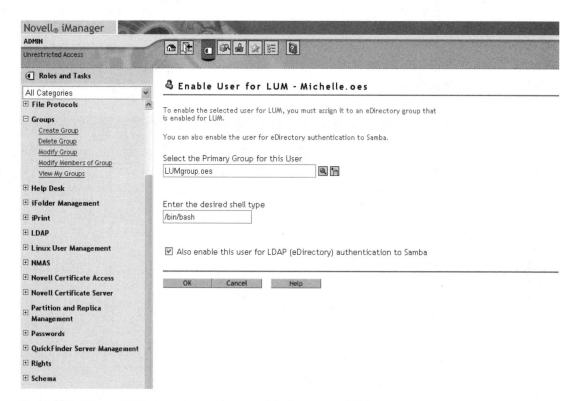

Figure 9-16. *Select a LUM group for your user and he becomes a LUM user.*

In this section, you learned how to create an eDirectory user that is also a LUM user. It's also possible to convert existing eDirectory groups or user objects to LUM groups and users when they are already present in eDirectory. Under iManager Roles And Tasks, select Linux User Management to find more options to help you do that.

Tip The purpose of LUM is that the LUM users are made available at the local Linux workstation. For this, the namcd service is used. namcd is short for Novell Account Manager Cache Daemon, which is the daemon that caches LUM-enabled accounts from eDirectory at the local workstation. In some situations, you can have problems viewing LUM users directly on the Linux workstation. If this is the case, I recommend restarting the namcd by using the command **/etc/init.d/namcd restart** as root.

Modifying the Linux Config and Linux Workstation Objects

LUM groups are associated to a Linux workstation object and each Linux workstation object is associated to a Linux config object. On these objects, you can do some minimal configuration as well. You can edit their properties from iManager Roles And Tasks ➤ Linux User Management. Here you'll find the two options Modify Linux/Unix Config Object and Modify Linux Workstation Object. It can be useful to change the default settings for these objects to ensure they do not conflict with local settings on the Linux Workstations associated to these objects. An example of this is the option to change the range of UID numbers that can be assigned by LUM so you can prevent a UID from being handed out more than once.

The Linux config object has just one property page (see Figure 9-17). On this page, you'll find the Linux Workstation Contexts option. These are the contexts in eDirectory where Linux workstation objects reside. It's not possible to modify the value of this setting from iManager, if you want to do so, you'll need **namconfig,** which has been described in the preceding section. Other interesting options include those related to the PosixGidNumber and PosixUidNumber; these refer to the unique IDs that must be assigned to users and groups in a UNIX environment. With these options, you can specify what numbers are available for that purpose.

Even fewer options are available for the Linux workstation object: only group membership can be managed from this object. It's possible to add and remove Linux groups associated to the selected Linux workstation object from its property page.

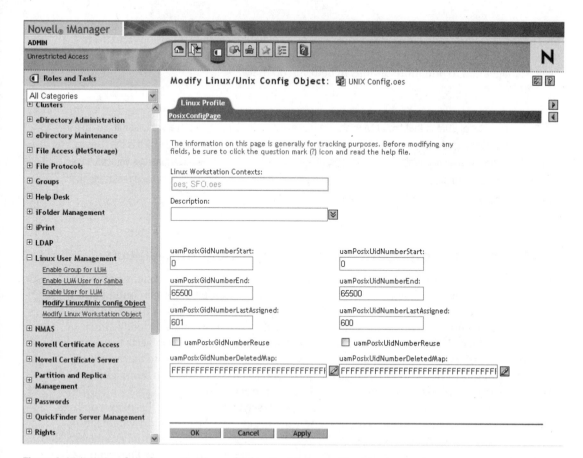

Figure 9-17. *Minimal configuration is applied to the Linux config object.*

Universal Password

A few services in an OES environment can use passwords. Unfortunately, these passwords are not synchronized properly and sometimes are even insecure. For this reason, in OES you can use the Universal Password. The Universal Password is like a special storage container to which passwords from other services can be synchronized. This allows for a much more secure mechanism of working with passwords than is the case for all the normal passwords stored in eDirectory. There are, however, some cryptographic implications; you have to make sure your entire network environment is ready to use the universal password. To prepare your network, all servers that have to work with the universal password need to be members of an SDI domain. Besides, if the Novell client software is used to connect to Novell services, you must make sure that at least version 4.9 of this software is installed. This allows the servers to work with encryption keys to securely communicate the universal password.

Universal passwords address three problems in particular:

- Management of multiple types of password authentication methods from disparate systems in a heterogeneous network environment

- Password policy enforcement across multiple authentication systems

- Security issues in the simple password

All options to manage universal passwords are present by default. However, because of the implications for cryptography in some mixed network environments, the universal password is not enabled by default. To enable a universal password for a selected user, you first have to set a password policy and then assign the universal password to that user. From then on (in most cases), the passwords will be synchronized to the universal password.

Creating an SDI Container

Before the universal password can be implemented in an OES - NetWare environment, an SDI domain must be present. You don't have to configure anything for this to work on OES - Linux, it will work automatically. With SDIDIAG.NLM on the OES - NetWare console, you can check if the SDI domain presently exists and what servers are added to it. The SDI domain is created from the OES installation procedure. OES - NetWare and OES - Linux are added by default, older servers can be added manually. The following procedure describes how the current state of the SDI container can be monitored:

1. On the OES - NetWare server console, type **SDIDIAG**.

2. Accept the default server and tree name and log in as an administrative user. This will bring you to the SDI console.

3. Type **check** to verify the status of the SDI Domain. This command provides you with an overview of all servers that are currently members of the domain, as shown in Listing 9-3.

   Listing 9-3. *Result of the SDI Status Check*

```
SDIDIAG > check
*** [Key Consistency Check - BEGIN] ***
  [Checking SDI Domain]
    SDI Check Domain Configuration…
      SDI Domain Key Server .oes-linux.oes.OES-TREE.
       - Configuration is good.
    *** SDI Check Domain Configuration is [GOOD]
    SDI Check Domain Keys…
      SDI Domain Key Server .oes-netware.oes.OES-TREE.
      - Configuration is good
    *** SDI Check Domain Configuration is [GOOD]

  [Checking SDI Domain: GOOD]
    *** No Problems Found ***

*** [Key Consistency Check - END] ***
```

If a server is not currently present in the SDI domain, you can add it manually by following these steps:

1. Load SDIDIAG at the server console.

2. Authenticate as user with administrative rights.

3. On the SDI Console, enter the command **AS –s** *<Full-server-name>* to add this server. For example, to add server .oes-netware.oes.OES-TREE to the SDI domain, use **AS –S .oes-netware.oes.OES-TREE**.

4. The server is now a member of the SDI domain and can exchange keys with other servers necessary to work with the universal password.

Assigning a Universal Password to Users

After SDI has been set up, you can use the following procedure to implement a universal password for selected users.

1. Start iManager and select Roles And Tasks ➤ Passwords. Here you'll find all options related to universal passwords.

2. Before a universal password can be assigned to a user account, a password policy has to be defined. Select Password Policies to manage password policies. In the Password Policy List, you'll see a Sample Password Policy. This policy can be modified, but it's better to create an entirely new password policy by clicking New. Do this now.

3. A wizard starts to help you properly format the password policy. First, enter the policy name. If you work with different policies for different departments, it's recommended to reflect the name of the department in the name of the policy. You can also specify a description for this policy and a message that's displayed when the user has to change her password. To make it easier to create a password policy, it's a good idea to select the option Create A New Password Policy Based On The Default settings. This creates a working policy immediately, all you have to do is change the default settings. If you choose to work from the default settings, an overview of these settings appears in the next screen and the password policy is created. If you choose not to work with the default settings, the wizard continues. This procedure shows you how to set the policies manually. Click Next to continue.

4. On the next screen, the wizard asks if you want to enable the universal password. Select Yes. Now click View Options to display choices as to how the universal password should be used. Here you can choose from the following:

    • *Remove the NDS password when setting the Universal Password*: This option enables just the universal password and removes the NDS password of users. Since many utilities still work with the NDS password, in most situations it's recommended not to select this option.

    • *Synchronize NDS password when setting the Universal Password*: This option makes sure changes from the NDS password are synchronized to the universal password and vice versa. Its enabled by default.

    • *Synchronize Simple Password when setting Universal Password*: This option synchronizes the Simple Password with the Universal Password. Enable this option if you use the Native File Access protocols (see Chapter 10) to access files on the network which are running on NetWare 6.0. In most situations, this option is not needed.

- *Allow user agent to retrieve password*: This option, which is selected by default, enables a user to retrieve his password from the password self-service web page when it's lost. It's enabled by default.

- *Allow admin to retrieve passwords*: If this is needed, you can use this option for admin to retrieve user passwords when they are lost. By default, this option is not selected to protect the user's privacy.

- *Synchronize Distribution Password when setting Universal Password*: This option is needed if a universal password is used in an Identity Manager environment. Consult Chapter 18 for more details about Identity Manager. Because problems with password synchronization can occur when this option is not set in an Identity Manager environment, it's selected by default.

- *Verify whether existing passwords comply with the password policy*: This option checks all existing passwords to see if they apply with the universal password policy. The check happens on login. If an existing password does not comply, the user is required to change it.

5. On the next screen (shown in Figure 9-18), you can define the rules for the password policies. There are quite a few rules to specify exactly what conditions must be met to work with safe passwords. Available rules are divided into different categories. A description of the available categories is listed next. Make your choice from the available options and click Next to continue.

- *Change Password*: Here you specify whether the user can change the password, and if he changes his password, whether or not the new password must be unique.

- *Password Lifetime*: Specify the minimum amount of days before the password can be changed, and the maximum amount of time the user can use his password with these options.

- *Password Length*: Use these options to specify the minimum and maximum length of new passwords.

- *Repeating Characters*: Here you can specify the minimum number of unique characters that must exist in the password, as well as the maximum number of times a character can be used, and repeated, in the password.

- *Case Sensitive*: With these options, you can specify the minimum and maximum number of upper- and lowercase letters in the password.

- *Numeric Characters*: Use these options to specify if, and how, numeric characters can be used in the password.

- *Special Characters*: Use these options to specify if and how special characters can be used in the password.

- *Password Exclusions*: Use this option to define a list of passwords that are not allowed.

Caution It's possible to set the most restrictive password policy. Your users will not be happy with it, though, and it may result in Post-it notes on the screens of their computers with passwords scribbled on them. Not exactly good for security. I recommend using a restrictive password policy only in situations where it's really needed. In normal situations, the default policy will do fine.

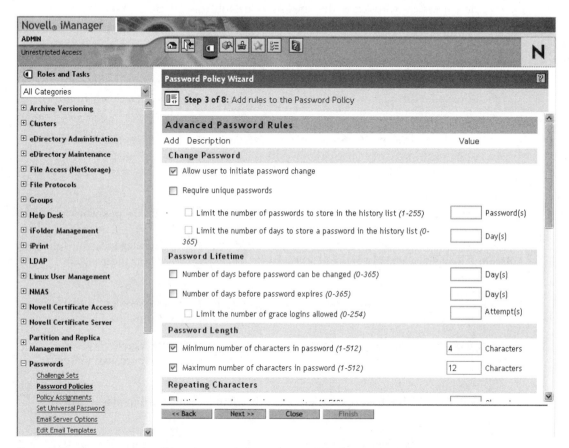

Figure 9-18. *In a password policy, many options can be combined to assure only secure passwords are used on the network.*

6. In the next list, you can enable self-service options for users who forget a password. If you choose to work with this feature, you must specify what conditions have to be met before a user can change his passwords with this feature. Be aware that this feature makes the password usage in your network less secure. If security is an important issue in your network, don't use this option. For the purposes of this example, it will be enabled, however. Click Next to continue.

7. With the installation of a universal password, a self-management page is provided. The key component to password self-management is a challenge set. In this challenge set, some questions are asked. The user must provide the right answer to these questions beforehand or else they can't be used for password recovery. Users can specify these answers when entering a new password. Some questions such as "What is your mother's maiden name?" are present by default. You can modify the challenge set by adding your own questions. Use the plus sign (+) for this purpose. Click Next to continue.

8. Next, select an action that has to be performed when a user has forgotten his password. Different options are available, from very secure to less secure. By default, the option Show Hint On Page is selected. This displays a hint that will hopefully help the user remember his original password. Make your selection and click Next to continue.

Note The option for a user to ask for a hint when he has forgotten his password sounds nice, but it only works from a limited amount of web applications. Several important client programs don't offer this feature, such as the Novell client users typically utilize to log in to their network.

---

9. Now you must assign the password policy. A policy can be assigned to almost anything: a user, a group, a container, or an entire organization. In most situations, it works best to assign the policy to the entire company. Select the object you want to assign the policy to and click Next to continue.

10. A summary of the new policy is displayed. Verify that all options are the way you want them and click Finish to finalize the policy.

11. Now that the policy is created, assign it to a user. Select the options Policy Assignments from the Passwords option, choose the user you want to assign the policy to, and click OK to continue.

12. Now that the policy is assigned to a user, set the universal password for that user. Choose the Set Universal Password option (see Figure 9-19), select the user you want to assign the password to, and click OK. This shows a summary of the rules from the policy that is applied to that user. Also enter the new password for this user. To do so, enter the new password twice and click OK to save it.

13. The universal password is now assigned to the selected user. Repeat this procedure for all other users in the network that need the universal password.

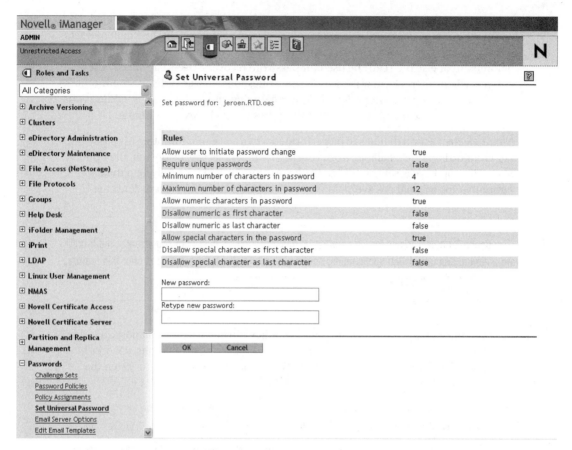

Figure 9-19. *When setting a universal password for a user, a short summary of current password settings is displayed.*

Working with Login Scripts

Upon logging in, it's useful if some default settings can be passed to a user. These are settings like connections to network drives (mappings), but you can also think of other things like messages that need to be displayed to users. These settings can be provided from the login script, but be aware that the login script is only processed if the user logs in from the Novell client on either Windows or Linux. On Open Enterprise Server, four different login scripts are available:

- *Container login script*: This login script is a property of a container object, and the commands in the login script are executed for all users in that container. A container login script cannot be inherited. For example, if a container login script is set for ou=sfo.o=oes, the login script will not be executed for .alyssa.sales.sfo.oes.

Tip You can create a hierarchy for login scripts with the **include** command. This command can be used to include other login scripts, such as parent login scripts or login script commands that are written in separate files. The include feature even allows you to create a company-wide login script if required.

- *Profile login script*: In eDirectory, it's possible to create a profile object. The login script property is the most important property of this profile object. This object can be associated to individual users and in this way behaves a bit like a group login script. In order for a profile login script to be useable, users associated to it need special eDirectory rights to the login script property of the profile login script. A user can be assigned to a single profile login script only.

- *User login script*: A user login script is a login script that is associated as a property to a user object. It will only be executed for that user object. Since it's a lot of work to manage login scripts for all individual users in the network, it's not recommended to work with user login scripts.

- *Default login script*: The default login script is included in the login program file. It contains some essential commands that are always needed when a user logs in, such as a mapped drive to the default volume on the OES server. It's recommended you create "real" login scripts for your users so the default login script is not executed.

With all these different types of login scripts, it may look hard to decide which login script should be used in your network environment. Most administrators try to include everything they need in the container login script. In most cases this isn't a problem, because even in a container, login script commands can be included that are only executed for a limited amount of users by using statements like **if member of**, which checks if a user is a member of a given group and executes the related command only if he is. If a specific group of users needs settings from a login script, a profile login script can be created. Because it's difficult to manage user login scripts for individual users, try to avoid using user login scripts at all times.

Order of Execution

With all these different login scripts floating about, it's important for an administrator to know when they should be executed in relation to one another. In all cases, the system first determines whether there is a container login script that can be executed. If it exists for the default container where the user resides, the container login script is executed. Next, the login procedure checks if there is a profile login script associated to the user. If it exists, it will be executed. After that, the login procedure executes the user login script associated to the user. If a user login script exists for the user, no more login scripts are processed after its execution. If no user login script exists, the default login script is executed instead. This can be undesirable, because if the default login script commands are executed they may conflict with the commands to be executed from the other login scripts. To prevent the default login script from being executed, the statement **no_default** can be included in one of the other login scripts.

Mappings

One of the most important things that happen from a login script, is the creation of mappings to drives on the network. Two different kinds of mappings can be created: the drive mapping which is just a connection to some location on the network and the search mapping which adds a network location to the search path of the local user. These mappings only apply to workstations that have the Novell client installed, or to users using the NetStorage product to get web-based access to files.

An example of a command to create a drive mapping is **map k:=.oes-linux-data.sfo. oes:groups**. In this drive mapping, the drive letter k: is assigned to a location on the network. This creates the drive k: on the user's workstation, which gives access to the network location. If the Novell client is installed on a Linux workstation, it creates a mount point to this drive in the user's home directory. A link to this mount point will also be accessible from the user's desktop. The network location in the preceding example is the directory groups on the volume oes-linux-data, which exists as an object in the eDirectory container sfo.oes. Notice that following the distinguished name of the volume is a colon; the colon separates the name of the volume from the name of the directory on the volume that is referred to. In this example, I've referred to the eDirectory name of the volume, but you can also refer to the physical name of the volume or the UNC name. In the physical name of the volume, you first specify the name of the server, and then the name of the volume as it exists on that server. These two are separated by a slash and after the name of the volume is another colon. The UNC name of a volume looks like \\servername\volumename. Only in the UNC name does the name of the volume not have to be followed by a colon. The differences between the three ways of referring to a volume are illustrated in the following overview:

- eDirectory name: .oes-linux-data.sfo.oes:groups

- Physical name: oes-linux\data:groups

- UNC name: \\oes-linux\data\groups

You can also use search mappings. These are used to add a location in the file system on a server to the search path on your local workstation. The creation of search mappings is similar to the creation of drive mappings; the only difference is that instead of a drive letter, a combination between the letter *s* and a colon is used. An example of this is **map s1:=\\oes-netware\ sys\public**, which creates an entry in the search path of the local workstation to the directory public on the volume sys of the server called oes-netware. The combination s1: specifies at what exact position in the search path the search mapping should be added; in this case, it's on the very first position of the local search path. The advantage is that it takes only a minimum amount of time to find commands located in that directory. If a less frequently used directory is added to the search path, it makes sense not to put it on the first position in the search path. If you use s16:, you're sure it will always be added to the last position in the search path. The number 16 is also the largest number that can be used; s17: and higher are not recognized.

There is one important thing you should be aware of when working with search mappings: by default they overwrite existing settings in the search path on the local machine. To prevent this from happening, use the modifier INS (for insert) each time you create a search mapping—so, use **map ins s1:=\\oes-netware\sys\public** and not **map s1:=\\oes-netware\sys\public**.

There is one more thing you should be aware of. Imagine that you create a drive mapping to a certain location on the file system of your server with the command **map g:=oes-netware\ data:groups\sales**. This makes a drive g: available to the user. If from his workstation the user activates this drive, he'll see the prompt g:\groups\sales. If he's curious what is above the groups\sales directory and decides to move up in the file system by using a command like **cd **, it will rewrite the drive mapping. Since this can be very confusing, it's recommended to always create root mappings instead of normal drive mappings. In a root mapping, the user is prevented from navigating up into the file system. The command **map root g:\oes-netware\data:groups\ sales** also creates a drive g: on the workstation and redirects it to the directory groups\sales. The big difference is that the user only sees g:\ at the g: prompt, and has no way to move up in the file system; with a root mapping, a fake root directory has been created for the user. A root mapping can not only be created for drive mappings, you can also apply it to a search mapping. The command **map root ins s3:=oes-netware\sys:login**, for example, creates an entry to the directory login in the search path that appears as the root of the file system to the end user. To prevent confusion, it's recommended to always use root mappings instead of normal mappings.

Other options can be used when working with the map command. The following are some examples:

- *map n \\server\volume\directory*: Maps the next available free drive letter to the specified location.

- *map del k*: Deletes the mapping for the letter k: drive.

- *map*: Gives an overview of all current mappings on a workstation.

- *map l:=k*: Creates a drive l: which is the same as the drive mapping assigned to k:.

In the old days of DOS, it was quite common to create mappings from the command prompt. Nowadays, this is rarely done. The only place where mappings are still created is in the login scripts of the system. You'll see some examples of this later in the chapter. The **map** command by itself can still be useful (see Figure 9-20). If it's used at the DOS prompt, an overview of all mappings that currently exist will be displayed.

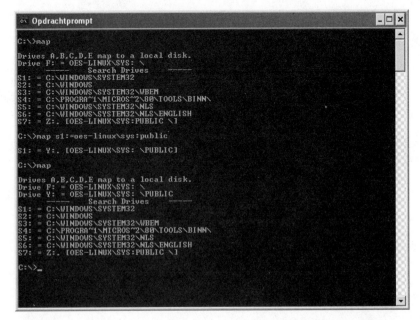

Figure 9-20. *On a workstation, you can use the map command to display an overview of current mappings.*

Working with Profile Login Scripts

If you want to make a login script and assign it to some specific group of users, you should work with a profile login script. There is, however, one difficulty associated with the profile login script: by default no one has the right to read the login script property of the profile object. You must solve this issue by applying the necessary eDirectory rights to this property. Chapter 11 has more on eDirectory security, so for now let's look at how to apply eDirectory security so users in your network can work with a profile login script.

1. Start iManager, log in, and from Roles And Tasks select eDirectory Administration.

2. Click Create Object and from the list of available objects, select Profile. Click OK.

3. Enter a name for the profile login script and specify the context where you want to create it. In the Login script box, enter the text **write "hello world"**. This provides you with a very simple login script. The dialog box should look like the one in Figure 9-21. Click OK when finished. This creates the profile object.

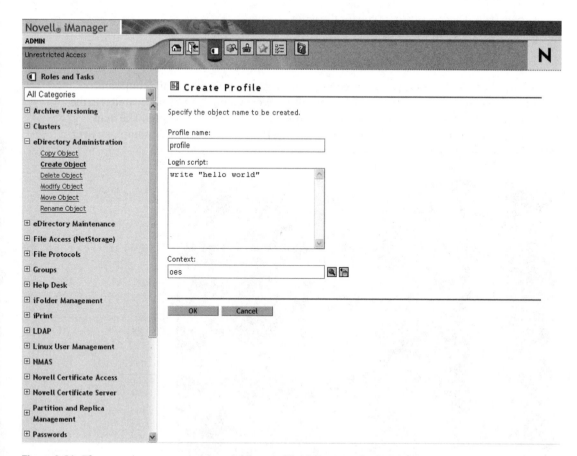

Figure 9-21. *The most important property of the profile object is its login script.*

4. Although you've created a profile object, no one yet has the permission to use it. To give the entire tree read-rights to the login script property of this object, from the iManager Roles And Tasks, select Rights, and then Modify Trustees.

5. Choose the profile object you just created and click OK.

6. In the Modify Trustees interface, select Add Trustee, and browse to your tree object (as shown in Figure 9-22). Select it and click OK to continue. This allows you to grant rights to all users in your network.

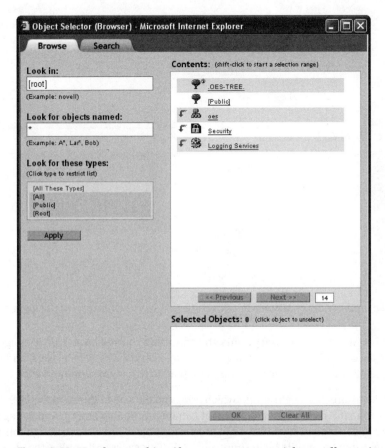

Figure 9-22. *Use the tree object if you want to grant rights to all users in your network.*

7. Click the Assigned Rights link to specify what rights must be granted to the selected trustee. In the overview of available rights, click Add Property, browse to the Login Script property, and click OK to add it. This adds the property to the list of granted rights. Automatically, the Compare and Read rights are selected, which is exactly what is needed for users to read the login script (as shown in Figure 9-23). Click Done to close this screen and then OK on the next screen. This saves the changes.

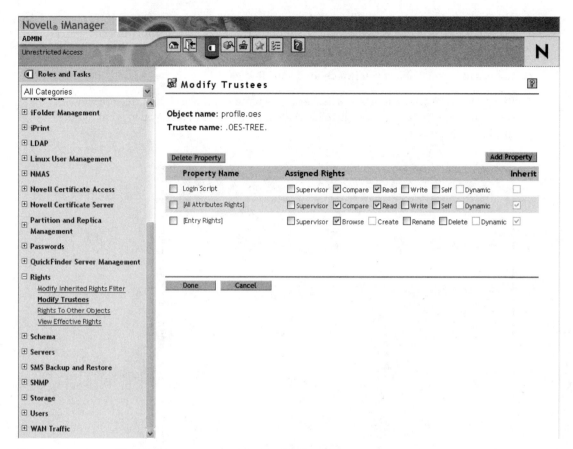

Figure 9-23. *After adding the property, users automatically get the necessary rights to read the login script.*

8. Now that you've set the necessary rights, the only thing you still have to do is assign the profile login script to a user. In iManager, from Roles And Tasks, select Users, and then Modify User. Browse to the user you want assigned to this login script and click OK.

9. On the General tab, click Login Script (which brings up the screen shown in Figure 9-24). This shows you the current user login script (which is probably empty) and a magnifying glass that can be used to browse to the profile object you want to assign this user to. After selecting the profile login script, click OK. This saves and applies the changes. The next time the user logs in, the profile login script is executed.

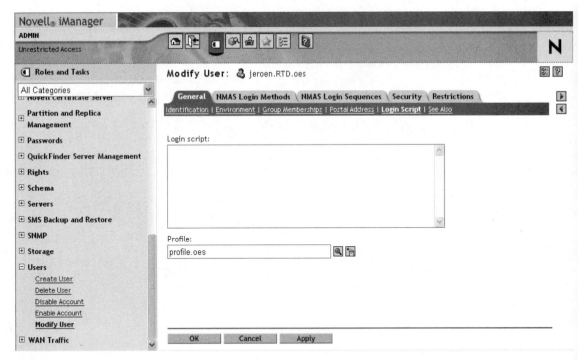

Figure 9-24. *On the Login Script screen, you can assign a profile login script to a user.*

Creating Your Own Login Scripts

In the preceding section, you discovered what must be done to create a profile login script. Creation of a container or a user login script is much easier: in iManager both containers as users have a property login script in which you can enter the login script commands directly.

Now that you know how where in eDirectory to add a login script, it's time to have a look at what can be included in a login script. Only the most important commands are covered here; there are a lot of commands that can be used in a login script, but I'll only discuss the ones you're likely to use in your day-to-day work. Let's look at an example login script (see Listing 9-4). The comments explain what each part of the script does. From this example, you should be able to build your own login scripts.

Listing 9-4. *Example Login Script*

```
REMARK This is an example of a container login script.
REMARK The script starts with a welcome message. I don't know why
REMARK but Novell seems to consider it important to say hi to its users.

WRITE "Good %GREETING_TIME, %LOGIN_NAME"

REMARK Next, we want to disable the possibility to suspend execution of the login
REMARK script
REMARK by hitting the Ctrl-Break or Crl-C keys.
```

```
BREAK OFF

*Now you see some commands to create search mappings
MAP ROOT S16:=\\OES-NETWARE\SYS\PUBLIC
IF MEMBER OF "SALES" THEN MAP INS S3:=OES-NETWARE\DATA:GROUPS\SALES
IF MEMBER OF "OPERATIONS" THEN MAP INS S3:=OES-NETWARE\DATA:GROUPS\OPERATIONS

;here a drive mapping to the user's home directory is created
MAP ROOT H:=%HOME_DIRECTORY

IF MEMBER OF ".IT.OES"
THEN
    INCLUDE OU=IT.O=OES
    WRITE "Good morning oh network supervisor!"
END

;some weekly events
;fire phasers makes some noise
IF NDAY_OF_WEEK = "2" AND HOUR24 < "10" THEN
    WRITE "WAKE UP!!!"
    WRITE "It's Monday again!"
    FIRE PHASERS 10
    PAUSE
ELSE
    WRITE "Have a good day!"
    PAUSE
END

*Do not execute the default login script
NO_DEFAULT

*Execute the external command nav.exe, start it in the background, ➡
*and go on with the login procedure.
@OES-NETWARE\SYS:APPS\NAV.EXE
```

Most commands in this login script are explained with the comment in the script itself. There are, however, some things that need a bit more explanation. First, is the way the comment is included. There are many ways to do so, but in this example, they are all mixed. REMARK, ;, and * are all valid ways to indicate that the next thing on this line should not be interpreted, but instead is just a comment to be read by a human. Next, you might have noticed that most of this login script is written in uppercase. The rule is that all variables need to be in uppercase, but the rest can be in either case.

Next you'll notice that there are three different ways to check if a certain condition has been met. In all three cases, IF is used. The first time, it all fits on one line. If someone is a member of the group sales, a mapping must be made to the sales directory on the server. You don't have to close the IF statement with an END if the condition that has to be met and the command that has to be executed fit on one line.

In the second IF statement, more then one command has to be executed if the condition is met. In that case, the condition IF MEMBER OF ".IT.OES" is stated on the first line, and on a separate line is the word THEN. Thus, each line is a command that must be executed. Finally, the IF loop is closed with the statement END on a separate line. Take note of the include statement used in this loop: include can be used to include some other login script. If the include statement refers to a file, the other login script is a text file with login script commands in it. If it refers to an eDirectory object, as in this example, it will execute the login script attached to that eDirectory object as well.

In the last IF statement (IF NDAY_OF_WEEK = "2"), you see a slight modification of the IF loop just discussed. In this case, the statement ELSE is introduced. If it's Monday, some commands are executed; in all other cases (ELSE), some other commands are executed.

The last thing you'll notice in this example is that some variables are used. These variables are internal to the login script, like GREETING_TIME and NDAY_OF_WEEK. Table 9-1 shows a list of some of the most common variables that can be used in login scripts.

Table 9-1. *Common Login Script Variables*

Variable	Explanation
GREETING_TIME	Can be used to determine if it's morning, afternoon, or evening.
LOGIN_NAME	Shows the name a user has logged in with.
STATION	Displays the connection number of a workstation.
HOMEDIRECTORY	Can be used to refer to a user's home directory. This variable works with the home directory property in eDirectory.
DAY	Shows the day number (1 to 31).
DAY_OF_WEEK	Displays the current day of the week.
NDAY_OF_WEEK	Shows the current numeric day of the week, where Sunday is day 1.
MONTH	Shows the month number (1 to 12)
MONTH_NAME	Shows the name of the current month.
SHORT_YEAR	Displays the last two digits of the current year.
HOUR24	Shows the current hour in a 24-hour notation.
MINUTE	Displays the current minute.
SECOND	Shows the current second.

In Table 9-2, you'll find an overview of the most common commands that can be used in login scripts, as well as a short message on the usage of these commands.

Table 9-2. *Common Login Script Commands*

Command	Explanation
#	The pound sign is used to call an external command. The login script waits for the external command to be finished before it continues.
@	Can be used to execute an external command as well. Contrary to the # sign, the login script executes the external command and in the meantime continues its execution.
attach	**Attach** is used to establish a connection with another server.
break	The command **break** specifies whether or not a user can terminate the execution of a login script. The default is **break off**.
context	**Context** can be used to set a user's current context in the tree.
display	The command **display** can be used to display the contents of a text file when the user logs in.
drive	The **drive** command can be used to set the default drive for users.
exit	Use **exit** to exit the execution of the login script. This command is useful in an if … then loop to exit the login script if a certain condition has been met.
fdisplay	The command **fdisplay** can be used to show the contents of a formatted text file, like a file that's created with a word processor.
fire phasers	This command can be used to play a sound. Here, the file phasers.wav is used. If you want to use another WAV file that contains a sound, use the name of the sound file as an argument. Instead of fire phasers, just **fire** can be used as well.
if … then	With **if … then,** a command is only executed if certain conditions have been met. A useful example of if … then is the IF MEMBER OF construction you've seen in the preceding example. This construction can be used to check if a user is a member of a given group.
include	The command **include** is used to execute a login script attached to another eDirectory object or to execute login script commands in a file given as an argument.
lastlogintime	Displays the last time the user logged in.
map	Map is used to assign drive letters to directories on the network.
no_default	Prevents execution of the default login script.
pause	The command **pause** creates a pause in the execution of the login script. The script will continue when the user hits a key.
profile	The **profile** command can be used to call a specific profile login script. This command can be used in combination with "**if member of**" to execute a profile login script for users that are members of a certain group.
remark	Use the **remark** command to include comments in the login script. Alternatively, **rem** or a colon can be used to indicate that something is a remark.
set	**set** can be used to define a variable on a workstation.

Command	Explanation
set_time	This command synchronizes the time on the workstation with the time on the server.
tree	The **tree** command can be used to attach to another eDirectory tree.
write	With **write** you can write a message to the screen of the user when the login script is executed. **Write** can be compared to the Linux/DOS command **echo**.

Summary

In this chapter, you learned how to manage the user's environment, which was broken down into the following topics:

- *Basic user management tasks*: Creating users and applying proper login security settings.

- *Linux User Management*: The way to integrate management of Linux Users in eDirectory. Authenticate Linux users against eDirectory and integrating a Linux workstation as a separate object in eDirectory were both covered.

- *The universal password*: Makes password management easier and, above all, more secure.

- *Login scripts*: How they can automate the creation of a user's environment on her workstation.

In the next chapter, you'll read about security in an OES environment.

CHAPTER 10

■ ■ ■

File Access

Although OES can be used for many purposes, the most important is still file access, just like so long ago on the NetWare platform. Users want to store files on their server and want to be able to access these files. Many ways exist for files to be accessed in OES. First, there is client-based file access to files stored on a volume. The main characteristic of this file access method is that access to files on the network is integrated into the client operating system. Think of the drive letters that can be applied to some location on the volume. While client-based access to files stored on a volume is the classic way to access files on OES, other solutions are available as well.

- *iFolder*: The service that makes it possible to immediately synchronize changes to files made in a local directory to the iFolder stored on a server.

- *NetStorage*: An interface that makes it possible to refer to files; no matter what access mechanism is used to access these files.

- *Samba*: The server that can be used to share files on OES - NetWare as well as OES - Linux so they can be accessed by Windows clients simply through their native Windows client interface.

- *FTP*: The classical File Transfer Protocol that can be used to transfer files to and from your server from a browser or an FTP-client program.

In this chapter, you'll be looking in detail at all the file access methods just listed.

Client-Based File Access

The classic way to access files stored on a NetWare server is by using the Novell client software on the client platform. Currently, there is a Novell client for both Windows and Linux. After installing the Novell client software, storage locations on the OES - Server are integrated into the client environment. The Windows client, for example, allows you to access locations on the OES server by using drive mappings, and the Linux client allows you to make mounts to certain locations in the file system. To use this Novell client software, you need the Novell NetWare Core Protocol (NCP) on both the server and the client. In an OES - NetWare environment, this is no problem since the NCP server is a part of the NetWare kernel. In the OES - Linux environment, the NCP server has to be installed separately since it's not a standard part of the Linux server environment. Chapter 6 offers detailed instructions on how the Novell client can be installed and configured on Linux and Windows workstations.

For client-based file access, something else is needed as well: on the OES server, you'll need a volume. Two different kinds of volumes can be used; the NSS volume and the NetWare traditional volume. The latter is only supported on OES - NetWare. In Chapter 11, you can find detailed information about the configuration of volume objects on OES.

iFolder

When I'm travelling, I always work on my laptop. I write a lot and travel a lot. As a result, many files change on my laptop almost every day. When I work at home, I prefer to work on my desktop computer—the screen is nicer, the processor is faster; it's just a better computer. Before iFolder though, I did have a problem: all the files that changed on my laptop had to somehow be made available on my desktop computer and vice versa. Given the fallibility of human beings, I occasionally would lose many of the files because I'd have a problem with one computer or another resulting in my files not being properly synchronized.

With iFolder, the situation was made much easier. Nowadays, on my laptop I have installed an iFolder client. It monitors the folder where I've stored my files, both on my laptop and desktop. If anything changes, the iFolder client notices it and synchronizes it immediately to the iFolder server the next time I'm connected. Since I run iFolder client on my laptop and desktop, new files on my laptop will appear automatically on my desktop and vice versa, as long as they're connected with the iFolder server. To connect with the iFolder server, I don't need to be on the LAN. The iFolder server can be contacted from anywhere—the LAN, the Internet. It doesn't matter as long as access is not blocked by the firewall. The nice thing is that the server, as well as the client, are supported on many platforms.

■**Note** Currently, iFolder 2.1 is used in OES. Novell is working on iFolder 3, but the software isn't stable enough yet, so it hasn't made it into Open Enterprise Server. iFolder 3 provides many more options, such as the possibility to work with more than one directory that's monitored with iFolder, or to share an iFolder amongst the different members of a group.

---

iFolder Benefits and Features

The use of iFolder provides many benefits, both to IT managers and end users. The major benefit for both is the possibility to access their data from anywhere. Some other benefits include the following:

- *Seamless Data Access*: iFolder helps a user access her data everywhere she goes. The only thing needed is an iFolder client which can be installed locally on the computer where the user works. The files can be accessed from a browser interface as well.

- *Data backup and Recovery*: Data is not only synchronized between user workstations, it's stored in a central directory on the server as well. iFolder clients don't communicate directly with one another; they communicate with the central data store and synchronize files there if anything is changed. Since the files are stored on the server as well, a network administrator can easily make backups of these user files.

- *Data Encryption*: There are two ways to store the iFolder data on the iFolder server: encrypted or as is. For increased security, use data encryption so files can't be read by others while they're transferred on the network or stored on the server. If you want maximum speed when working with iFolder and aren't too worried about data security (unwise), it's better not to use encryption.

- *Easier access for mobile users*: Without iFolder, a user needs a VPN connection to access data stored on a server securely. This is no longer needed when iFolder is used; iFolder uses authentication and encryption, so it provides a safe and easy way to access files stored on a central server for mobile users.

- *Cross platform support*: iFolder virtually runs on anything and that goes for the server as well as the client. There is an iFolder server that runs on NetWare since version 5.0, and an iFolder server for Linux and Windows. Thanks to LDAP communications, any central Directory server can be accessed. Novell eDirectory can be used; if iFolder is installed on Windows, Active Directory can be used as well. Unfortunately, Macintosh is not yet supported, but it should be in the next version of iFolder.

- *Easy management*: iFolder is created to make data and account management as simple as possible. Management can be performed from a simple web interface.

iFolder Architecture

iFolder itself consists of a few central components parts: the iFolder Server, the web-based and the normal client, the Apache server that iFolder runs on, and the LDAP server(s) that iFolder communicates with. You can see a global overview of the relation between these parts in Figure 10-1. From the user perspective, the first relevant component is the iFolder client. This is a Java application installed on the user's workstation. The user can also choose to use the Web-based client. From this client, the user accesses the iFolder server, which runs on top of the Apache server in an OES environment. If iFolder is deployed in a Windows environment, the iFolder server can be used on top of IIS as well. For all its settings, the iFolder server communicated with an LDAP server. This LDAP server doesn't need to be on the same server, but it does need to be present in the same tree. Two different kinds of settings are stored on the LDAP server: global settings and user settings. The global settings define the working of the iFolder server itself, in the user settings the properties of the user are specified.

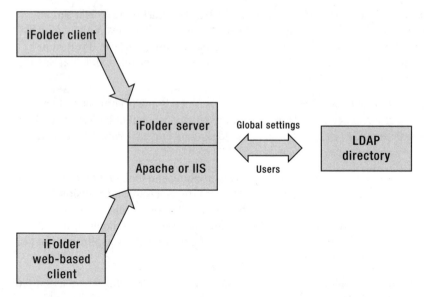

Figure 10-1. *In iFolder, the iFolder client, iFolder server, web server, and LDAP server work together to provide seamless access to files.*

To work with iFolder, a user authenticates from the client to the iFolder server by sending her encrypted username and password. Next, this information is used to verify that the user exists and the user object has been enabled as an iFolder user in the iFolder Management console. Before a user can begin to work with iFolder, the iFolder account must be initialized on the iFolder server. This happens the first time the user logs in to the iFolder server. After the first login, a user can start to add files to her iFolder directory and automatic synchronization of the files begins. Based on the synchronization preferences set on the client, the client periodically synchronizes changes to local files. This is a delta sync: not the entire changed file is synchronized, only those blocks that have really changed on the client's workstation. If the user later works from another computer, the updates made on the other computer are downloaded after the user has logged in. Only after the updates have been downloaded are new changes made from the client to the server. Since it's exceedingly rare that one user simultaneously works from two different locations on the same file, there is no such thing as a locking mechanism. Thus, the user can work on a file when he is not connected to the iFolder server. If it happens that different changes have been made to the same file, both versions will be moved to the conflict bin, where the user can manually merge the two versions of the file.

Installing, Managing, and Monitoring iFolder

It's possible to install the iFolder product upon installation of OES. Since there are a few iFolder-specific parameters that must be entered upon installation, let's discuss in this section how the product can be installed on OES - Linux. The situation is more or less the same for OES - NetWare. The only difference is that, instead of YaST, you use the NetWare installation utility to install it. You can read more about product installation on OES - NetWare in Chapter 13. After the section about iFolder installation, I'll explain how the iFolder server can be managed and monitored.

■**Caution** iFolder requires a working DNS server; otherwise, it's not possible to install it. It's also strongly recommended you give the iFolder server its own secondary IP address on your server. In DNS, you must create an A Resource Record and a PTR Resource Record as well. If you don't, you won't be able to configure iFolder. Chapter 14 has more about the configuration of a DNS server in OES - Linux.

iFolder Installation

iFolder can be installed on many platforms, including both versions of OES, but it's also possible to install it on a Windows server. This section explains how to install it on OES - Linux. For installation on OES - NetWare, the same information has to be provided, but instead of YaST, which is used in this procedure, the installation utility on the OES - NetWare console should be used. You can read more about this utility in Chapter 13.

Prerequisites

To install iFolder on OES, make sure that the following prerequisites are met.

- Apache must be installed (see Chapter 16).

- An SSL certificate must be available (see Chapter 12 and Chapter 16).

- eDirectory must be available on this server or another server in the network (see Chapter 8).

- DNS must be configured (see Chapter 14).

- You need proper rights to extend the schema of your iFolder server (see Chapter 12).

- Create a storage volume where iFolder data can be stored. If heavy use of the server is expected, it's recommended you use a separate volume or partition (see Chapter 11).

Installing iFolder on OES - Linux

The following steps outline how iFolder can be installed with YaST on OES - Linux.

1. Log in to OES - Linux and from the graphical console start YaST by clicking the YaST icon. Enter the password of the user root if required.

■**Tip** Don't like graphical consoles on your server? That's OK. There's an ncurses interface of YaST as well. From runlevel 3, just enter the command **yast2** on a text-based terminal and YaST will be started.

2. From Software, select Install And Remove Software.

3. From Network Services, click iFolder2.x. This initializes the iFolder 2.x Configuration screen.

4. If the iFolder software hasn't been installed yet, you'll get a prompt that the RPMS for iFolder needs to be installed. From this prompt, click Continue.

5. If prompted to insert a CD, insert it and click OK to continue.

6. Next, you'll be prompted for the LDAP Server Configuration (as shown in Figure 10-2). If the LDAP server is on the local server, enter the name and context of your admin user and his password. If LDAP is on a remote server, also enter the IP address of the remote server in the Directory Server field. If required, specify the LDAP port that should be used as well. Click Port Details to specify the LDAP server port addresses if required. Click Next to continue.

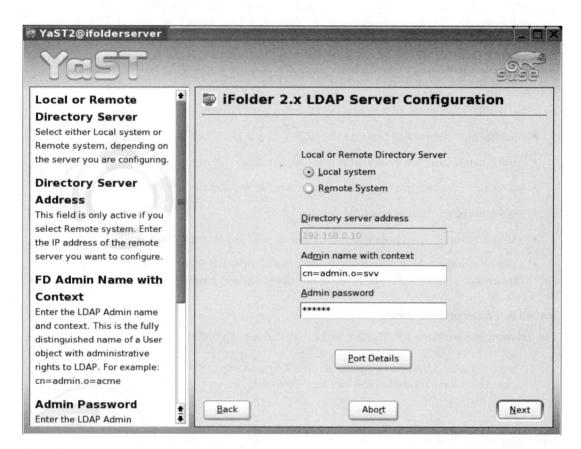

Figure 10-2. *Specify where the LDAP server can be contacted.*

7. Now you must specify on which address the iFolder server can be reached, as shown in Figure 10-3. If iFolder is the only web application on this server, the iFolder server can use the IP address of this server. If there are other web applications running on this server, the option iFolder 2 And Other Web Applications Will Run On This Server is selected automatically. In this instance, you must specify the IP address, netmask, and DNS hostname for the iFolder server. These secondary IP addresses are assigned automatically to the network card of your server, as shown in Figure 10-4. Another important setting you can select from this screen is iFolder 2.x User Data Path. Here, you specify the path where users can save their data. In selecting this path, you should be aware that every iFolder user is allowed 200MB of disk space to store his iFolder files. Therefore, make sure the volume or partition where you store the iFolder data has more than enough available disk space. If high usage is expected, consider placing the iFolder home directories on a separate disk system. After specifying all necessary parameters, click Next to continue.

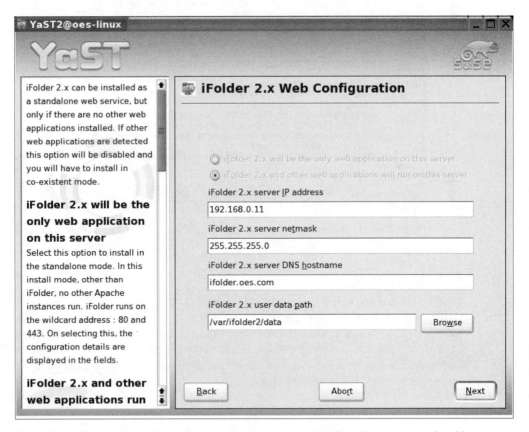

Figure 10-3. *If iFolder is not the only server running on the Apache web server, you should give iFolder its own IP address.*

8. Now, some iFolder administrators can be added. By default, your admin user is listed as an iFolder administrator. Click Add to add new iFolder administrators. All names you enter here should be names of existing eDirectory users as well. Click Next when finished.

9. The iFolder settings are now written to the configuration files. Before you can start using iFolder, the Apache server must be restarted. Click Yes to restart it now. When this has finished, iFolder is installed and ready for use.

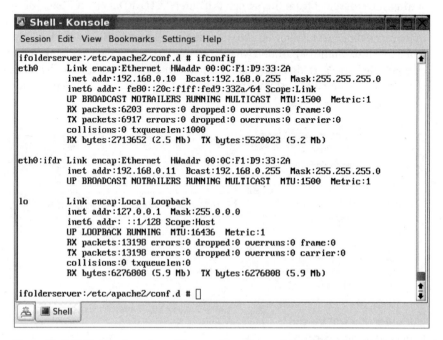

Figure 10-4. *If iFolder is assigned its own IP address, this address is added automatically to your network interface card.*

iFolder Management

After the iFolder server has been installed, two web interfaces are available: the iFolder Management console for administrators (see Figure 10-5) and the iFolder web site for end users. Novell NetStorage can also be used to provide access to data stored on the iFolder server.

Before users can start using iFolder, access to the iFolder server must be configured from the iFolder Management console. You can access the iFolder Management console from https://*yourserver*/iFolderServer/Admin.

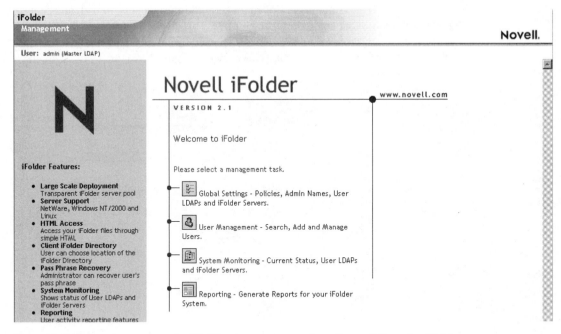

Figure 10-5. *Before you can use the iFolder server, you must configure it from the iFolder Management console.*

Configuring iFolder Global Settings

To prepare iFolder for your users, you must define the global iFolder settings. After that, you need to add iFolder users. These are users that are selected in the LDAP directory and enabled as iFolder users.

1. Start the iFolder Management interface at http://yourserver/iFolderServer/Admin. At the top of the screen (see Figure 10-6), you'll see a button bar that gives access to the most important management utilities iFolder has to offer. From left to right, these include the following:

   • *Home*: Takes you to the main iFolder Administration interface (as shown in Figure 10-5). From this interface, you can also access the most important iFolder management programs.

   • *Logout*: Logs you out from the iFolder Management interface.

   • *Global Settings*: Gives you access to global settings to determine how the iFolder server should behave.

   • *User Management*: Allows you to enable iFolder users and manage their properties.

   • *System Monitoring*: Enables you to monitor iFolder usage.

   • *Reporting*: Gives you access to a reporting interface.

   • *Help*: Displays the iFolder help screen.

2. Select Global Settings from the generic management interface. Log in with an account that has administrative permissions on your tree. This gives you access to the Global Settings screen. The General Info screen is displayed by default. This screen offers an overview of the current iFolder settings (as shown in Figure 10-6).

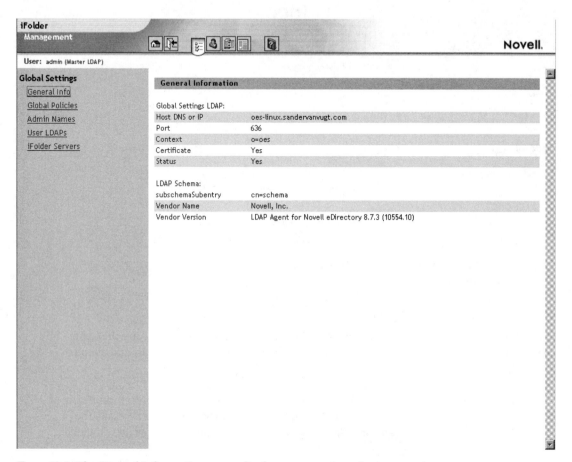

Figure 10-6. *The General Information screen displays an overview of current settings.*

3. Click the Global Policies link and select Client Policies (see Figure 10-7). This allows you to set the default behavior of your iFolder clients. These default settings can be over-written by setting policies for individual users. For almost all policies, you can select between three options. By selecting On, you enable a feature, but a client can overwrite it with his own settings from the client software. By selecting Enforced, you enforce the setting so that the client is no longer able to overwrite it from the client software. The option Hidden can be used to hide the policy and its default setting from the user. To avoid confusion, it's recommended if you want to enforce an option, you should make it hidden as well. That way the user won't notice the option is even available. You can set the values and behavior for the following client policies:

- *Encryption*: Specifies that iFolder data is encrypted when it's stored on the server and when it travels on the network. This policy applies only to newly created accounts; it's not possible to modify this policy for an existing iFolder account.

- *Save password*: Allows a user to save his password in the iFolder client software. This feature is off by default. The password is needed to authenticate against the iFolder server.

- *Save pass phrase*: Allows automatic entry of the user's encryption pass phrase upon login. The pass phrase is needed to access encrypted files on the iFolder server.

- *Recover Pass phrase*: Enables the iFolder administrator to recover a user's encryption pass phrase. This option implies that the administrator will also be able to access encrypted user files.

- *Automatic Sync*: Specifies that the iFolder client automatically syncs files between the iFolder directory on his workstation and the iFolder server.

- *Sync to Server Delay*: Specifies the time the iFolder client waits after a file in the local folder changes before it's synchronized.

- *Sync from Server Interval*: Sets the interval the client uses to check the iFolder server to see if there are new files that need to be synchronized.

- *Conflict Bin Space*: The conflict bin is used to help the inadvertent loss of user files. Each workstation has its own conflict bin on its local hard drive. In this bin, files are saved that cannot be synchronized due to a conflict with another copy of the same file that exists. In this case, the file is saved in the conflict bin so it can be synchronized manually. If a file exceeds the size of the conflict bin, it is purged immediately. It's thus best to increase the minimum size of the conflict bin to more than 25MB.

- *iFolder Location*: By default, the iFolder is saved in the user's My Documents directory on the local Windows workstation. Changes to this policy apply only to new instances of the iFolder client for existing accounts, or to new iFolder accounts. If this option is not enforced, upon installation of the iFolder client the user will have the option to change the default location for his folder.

After changing the client policy, click Update Client Policy to save and apply the changes.

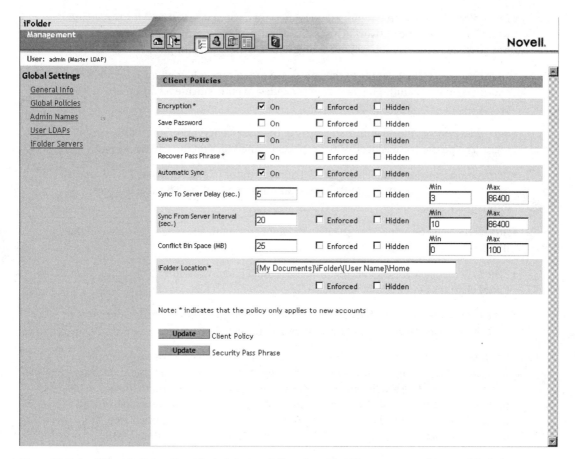

Figure 10-7. *In Client Policies, the administrator defines how the client communicates with the iFolder server.*

4. After you've set the Client Policies, select Server Policies from Global Policies. You're presented with three options that can be specified at the server level:

- Select the Initial Client Quota option to specify the amount of disk space available to clients

- Select the Session Timeout option to specify a session timeout interval. After this timeout, any open connection that is no longer in use will automatically be terminated.

- Activate the Debug Output option if you want debug output displayed. This option is particularly useful when troubleshooting.

5. Don't forget to click Update after you've modified your server's properties.

6. Next, you must specify the name(s) of the users that are allowed to administer the iFolder server. By default, the eDirectory user admin is used, but you can specify the names of other users as well. All these users must be in the same context where you installed the iFolder server. Click Update if you've made any changes.

7. In the next setting, specify the User LDAPs. This refers to objects stored in eDirectory that define the link between iFolder and the LDAP server. By default, you'll always find that one object is present; it has the default name iFolder_ldap01. If you select this object, you'll see its properties. In the properties, the name of the LDAP server is specified, as well as the port and whether or not a certificate has to be used. These are all default settings and cannot be changed. The only item you can change on this screen is the Context To Search. Here, you specify in what context the LDAP server has to look for eDirectory user objects that can be enabled as LDAP users. By default, just the container where iFolder is installed is selected, the Search Subcontexts option is not selected. If you want your entire eDirectory tree to be searched for user objects, make sure your Organization level object is added and the Search Subcontexts option is selected as well. In a large environment where multiple iFolder servers are deployed, this may affect performance negatively, however. If you're using iFolder in a large environment, add all individual contexts where this server has to look for eDirectory user accounts that can be enabled as iFolder users. Don't forget to click Update to save any changes you've made.

8. Next, click the User LDAPs link from the Global Settings menu. Now click the link that refers to your iFolder LDAP server (as shown in Figure 10-8). It's possible to refer to additional LDAP servers as well. This allows you to search for users in more than one LDAP tree.

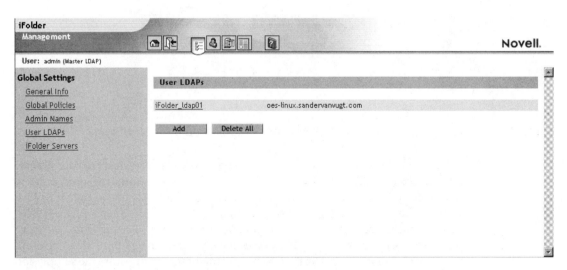

Figure 10-8. *Here you can specify all the LDAP servers which iFolder must search for users.*

9. To add a second LDAP server that should be searched, select User LDAPs and from the main User LDAPs interface, click Add. You're now shown a screen where you can provide all the required properties to indicate another LDAP server that can be used (see Figure 10-9). Just enter the LDAP server host name, port, certificates and other required properties to make communication with this LDAP server possible.

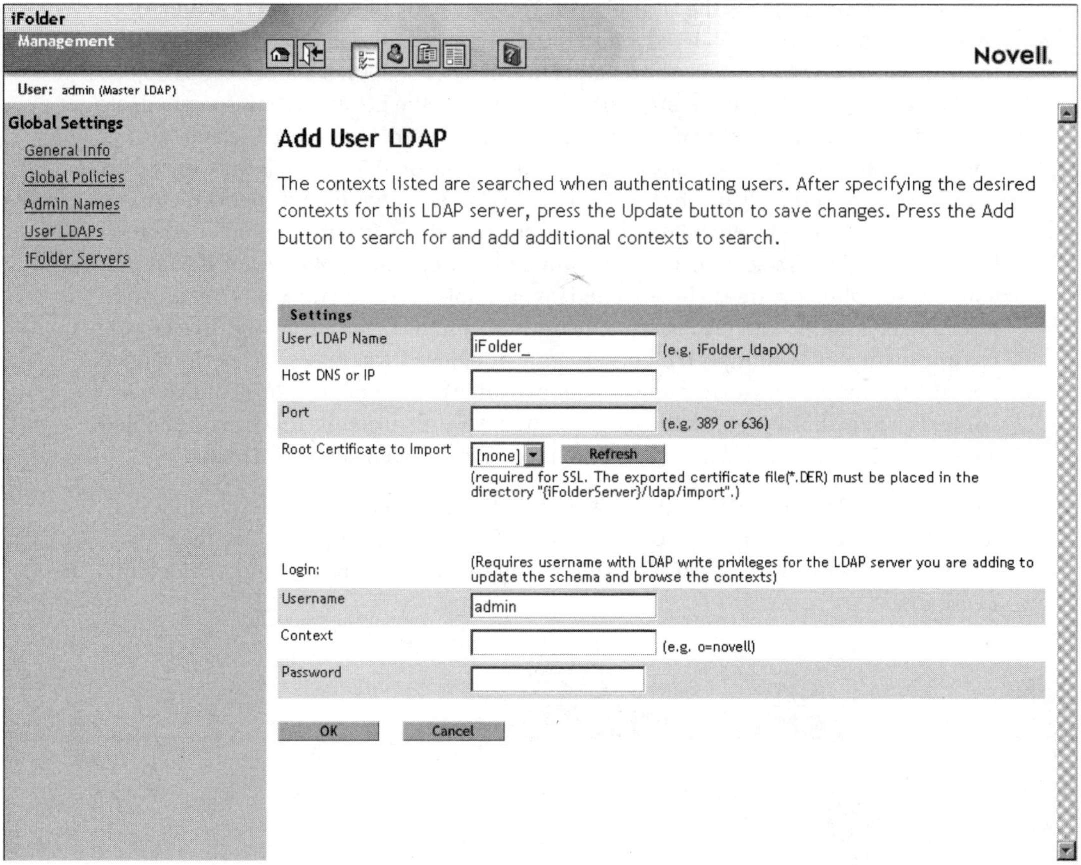

Figure 10-9. *If needed, iFolder can get its user information from more than one LDAP server.*

10. iFolder can be installed on an unlimited number of servers to create an iFolder system. In this scenario, the iFolder system is a collection of iFolder servers that the user connects to. To add another iFolder server to your iFolder system, you must first install the iFolder product on that server, as described at the beginning of this section. Then from the iFolder management interface, you can add it to your iFolder system by selecting Global Settings, then iFolder Servers, and then Add. In this screen, as shown in Figure 10-10, some properties have to be specified. The most significant of these properties are the settings for the public and private iFolder server names. If the DNS name or IP address of your iFolder server goes directly to the iFolder server without being routed by another device such as a router, switch, or firewall, you're only required to fill in the information beneath the public heading. If, however, your iFolder server can only be contacted through another device such as a Firewall that does port forwarding, you need to enter both the public host name and IP address as the name and address that must be used to access the server on the private network. In this case, the private settings allow the iFolder servers to communicate directly with each other within the iFolder system and the public settings allow you to access the iFolder server from outside the firewall as well. After adding an iFolder server to the network, you must also add a User LDAP server for this server. How to enter a User LDAP is described in step 7 of this procedure.

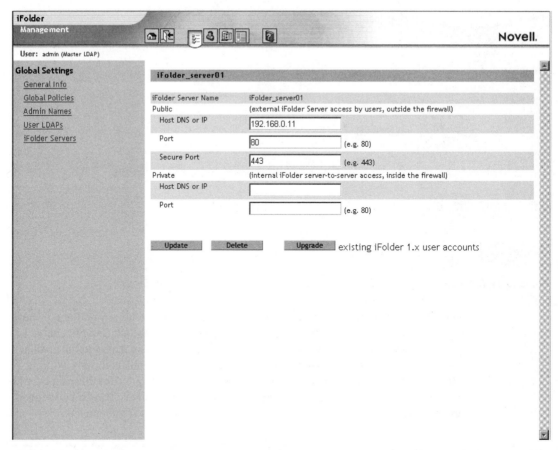

Figure 10-10. *To reach the iFolder server from both outside and inside the firewall, you must enter both a public and private address for the server.*

Enabling Users to Use iFolder

Now that you've configured all the global settings for your iFolder server, you must enable your users to use it. To do so, click the User Management button at the top of the iFolder Management screen.

1. Having entered all the data for your iFolder global settings, it's time to create and manage iFolder users. Click the User Management button in the button bar at the top of the screen to activate the iFolder User Management interface (see Figure 10-11). From this interface, you can use the Search feature to look for existing users. With this option, it's possible to search for existing users in the default iFolder context. For example, use * to display all current eDirectory users. Remember that you'll only find users from child containers of this container if you specified that child containers should be searched as well on the iFolder LDAP object.

Figure 10-11. *Before a user can use iFolder, you must enable the user as an iFolder user.*

2. From the list of users displayed after using the Search feature, click any of them to show their iFolder properties. By default, iFolder usage is disabled for all users. To enable it, click Enable and specify the iFolder server to be used by your user. This adds an auxiliary class with iFolder properties to the user and enables the user object to start working with iFolder. Before adding other iFolder users, specify a disk quota for this user as well (as shown in Figure 10-12). Click Update when you've finished specifying the user properties. Repeat this procedure for all users you want to enable as iFolder users.

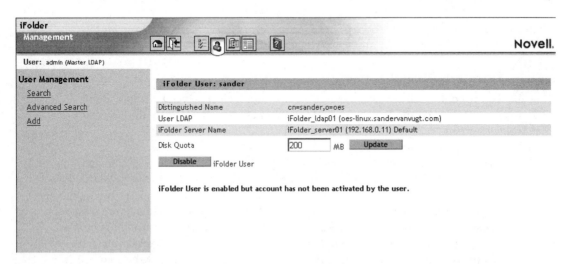

Figure 10-12. *One of the most important user settings to manage is the user's disk quota.*

3. In the previous step, you enabled an existing eDirectory user as an iFolder user. It's also possible to create new users from the iFolder User Management interface. To do so, click Add from the left-hand menu to display an interface where you can enter the properties for a user you want to create. After specifying the eDirectory container where you want to create the user (see Chapter 9 for more details), the user will be configured as an iFolder user automatically.

iFolder Monitoring

As the administrator of an iFolder system, you can perform some iFolder monitoring and tuning as well. A general monitoring screen is available from the iFolder management interface under the System Monitoring button that you'll find in the button bar of your browser (see Figure 10-13). On this screen, you'll find statistics about current iFolder usage and settings.

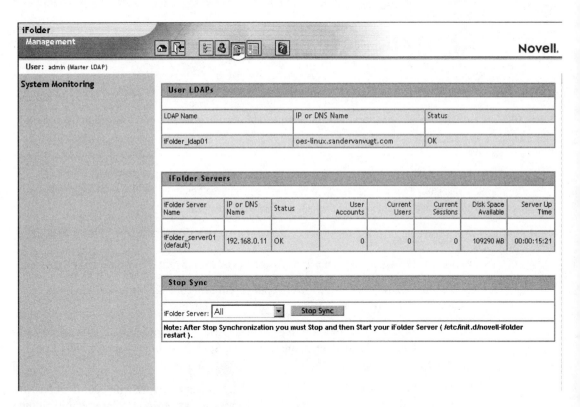

Figure 10-13. *iFolder offers some limited monitoring options.*

The monitoring options offered by the iFolder monitoring interface are rather limited. As an administrator, you'll often feel the need to monitor current iFolder usage for individual users on your network. This can be done from the iFolder User Manager interface which you can activate by clicking its corresponding button in the button bar at the top of the screen.

In the overview of users on your system (shown on this screen), all current iFolder users appear in yellow with a red I over their icon (as shown in Figure 10-14). If you click the name of a user that has already activated his iFolder account, you get access to the account settings of this user (as shown in Figure 10-15). From this screen, you can perform some important actions:

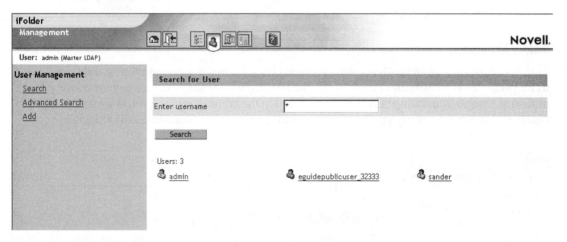

Figure 10-14. *From the User Management interface, some detailed per-user monitoring options are offered.*

Tip Notice that different options are displayed for users that have downloaded the iFolder client and activated their iFolder account compared to those users that haven't done so yet. If only limited options are shown for a selected user, make sure the user is an active iFolder user.

- *Remove iFolder User Data*: This option destroys all the current user's data on your system.

- *Recover the iFolder User Pass Phrase*: If policies are set that allow the administrator to recover the user's pass phrase, you can use this option just to do that.

- *Set user-specific policies*: It's possible to set generic iFolder policies on your server as you've read before. It's also possible to set user-specific policies if a user has some specific needs.

- *Increase the size of the user's iFolder*: By default, the user can work with 200MB of files in his iFolder. You'll find that very soon this isn't enough for the user. He'll start complaining and ask you for more disk space. Use this option to make friends and increase the available disk space in the user's iFolder.

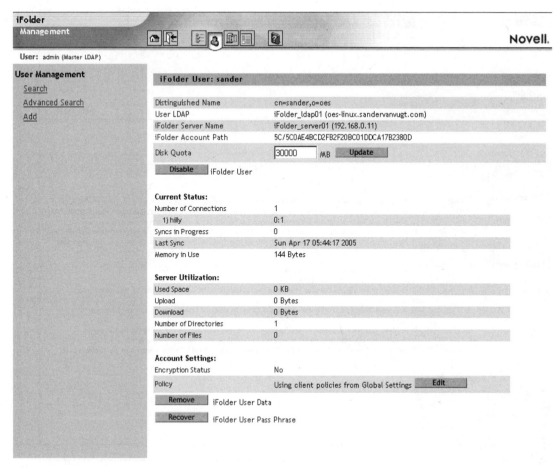

Figure 10-15. *Properties for individual users can be changed from the iFolder User Manager interface.*

Working with the iFolder Client

Now that you've configured iFolder at the server level, the rest of the configuration is up to the user. As an administrator, you can facilitate the usage of iFolder, but you can't force the user to use it if it's not company policy. To start using iFolder, the user first needs to navigate to https://*yourserver*/iFolder (shown in Figure 10-16). From here, they can use the browser-based client immediately by clicking the Login link. Working with this client is covered further on in this section. To use the desktop iFolder client, however, they need to download and install it (this is also done from this location). The following procedure explains how a user can install the iFolder Linux client on his workstation and start using iFolder. First, though, let's cover the installation of the iFolder client for Linux. After that, the iFolder client for Windows will be covered, and at the end of this section you'll learn how files can be accessed from the browser interface.

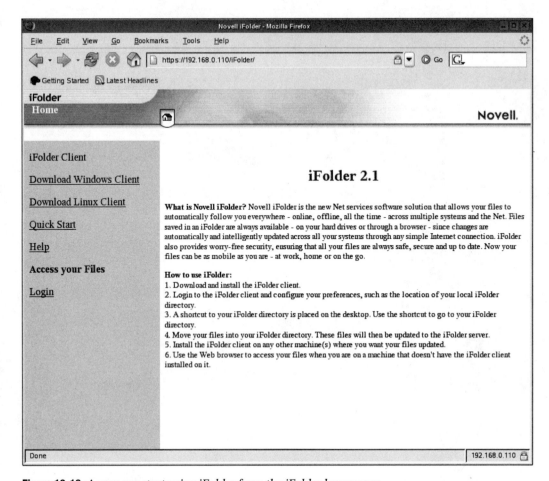

Figure 10-16. *A user can start using iFolder from the iFolder home page.*

Installing the iFolder Client for Linux

The following steps outline how to install the iFolder client.

1. Start your browser and access the iFolder user interface from https://*yourserver*/iFolder.

2. Select Download Linux Client. To access your iFolder files from the browser interface, select Login. Click Download Linux Client to start downloading the Linux client.

3. The iFolder RPM starts to download now. Click Save To Disk to save the RPM in your home directory.

■Note In this procedure, I describe the most common way to install the iFolder client on a Linux desktop. You should know that on some Linux desktops, the procedure can be performed much more quickly if you know how—for example, by calling YaST directly from the browser interface to install the RPM. This functionality is not available on all Linux desktops. Therefore, in this procedure you don't learn the quickest way to do it, but you do learn a method that will always work.

4. Open a Console window, activate the directory where you downloaded the Novell iFolder client, and enter the command **rpm –i novell-ifolder*** to install it on your system. This installs the iFolder client automatically to /opt/novell/ifolder.

■Tip Are you using the Novell Linux Desktop? If so, then life suddenly got much easier for you! The Novell iFolder client is installed as a part of the Novell Linux Desktop. You can start the iFolder client utility directly from /opt/novell/ifolder/bin/novell-ifolder-client. Alternatively, ZENworks Linux Management can also be used to roll out the iFolder client to Linux desktops in your organization.

5. Start the iFolder client by using the command **/opt/novell/ifolder/bin/novell-ifolder-client**. This opens the iFolder login dialog (shown in Figure 10-17). From this dialog, enter your username (not the complete distinguished name, but just the name of the leaf object), the iFolder user's password, and the name or address of the iFolder server. Confirm that the option Place A Shortcut To The iFolder On The Desktop is selected. This automatically creates a shortcut on your desktop through which a user can access iFolder. It makes life much easier in the future.

Figure 10-17. *The iFolder client can be used from Linux as well as Windows.*

6. A short wizard starts that helps you optimize your iFolder environment. In the first step in this wizard, you must specify where you want to create the iFolder directory. By default, it will be created in your user home directory. Click OK to continue.

7. Next, the client installation program asks if you want to start up the iFolder client automatically after logging in and if you want to encrypt files automatically (as shown in Figure 10-18). Select the options you want and click OK to continue.

Figure 10-18. *The Client Setup Wizard lets you specify whether you want to start the iFolder automatically on system startup and if you want to encrypt files.*

8. Enter a pass phrase and confirm it. If you're worried you might forget your pass phrase, you can also enter a hint here. Click OK to continue.

9. If it hasn't been disabled by the administrator of the server, you can next specify whether or not you want to enable pass phrase recovery. If it's enabled, the system administrator can recover it and the user can access his files again. If the option isn't enabled, the user will lose access to his encrypted files forever if he forgets his pass phrase. Click OK to continue.

10. The iFolder client is now installed on the user's computer. He can copy files to it, and after the synchronization interval these files will be synchronized immediately to the iFolder server. When the user clicks with the right mouse button on the iFolder icon in the task bar, he'll also have access to some self-management features (as shown in Figure 10-19). The most interesting of these is the Account Information option. The activity screen, as seen in Figure 10-19 is useful as well. This screen gives an overview of everything that happened in the users iFolder. Other preferences can be changed as well if allowed under system policy.

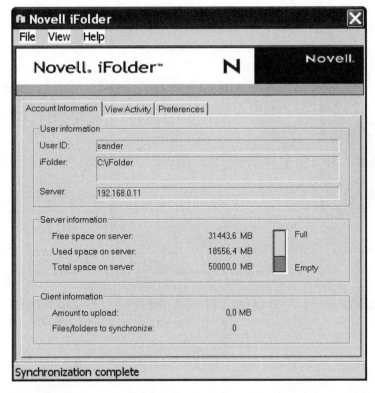

Figure 10-19. *From the iFolder View Activity screen, the user can see an overview of everything that happened in his iFolder.*

Installing the iFolder Client for Windows

An iFolder client for Windows is also available, and it can be installed using a method similar to the one you just read about.

1. Access the iFolder web page from your browser. Next, select Download Windows Client.

2. In the File Download window, click Open to start the installation of the Windows client immediately after downloading the files.

3. In the first screen of the iFolder Setup Wizard (see Figure 10-20), click Next to continue.

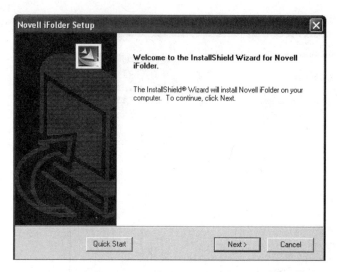

Figure 10-20. *On Windows, users can access a wizard to set up the iFolder client.*

4. Choose the language in which you want to display the license agreement and click Next to continue. Close the browser window with the license agreement and click Yes to continue.

5. Specify the folder where you want to install the iFolder Windows client and click Next to continue. The iFolder program files are copied to the hard drive of your computer now. When the wizard is complete, click Finish.

6. Now close the readme file which is opened automatically and select whether you want to restart your computer now or later. You must restart your computer before you can start using the iFolder client. Click Finish to complete the installation procedure.

7. After rebooting, an iFolder Welcome screen appears. Click Continue to proceed.

8. Log in with your iFolder username and password. Also, specify whether you want to place a shortcut on the desktop of your workstation to get easy access to the folder you've shared with iFolder.

9. After successfully logging in, the user can specify which directory he wants to share with iFolder—that is, if the general iFolder policy hasn't disabled this option. By default, a folder with the name iFolder is created in the user's home directory and shared automatically. Accept this or enter the name of the folder you want to share and click OK.

10. Now specify if you want to log in to iFolder automatically. This is fine for a computer that is always connected to the server. If this isn't the case, don't select this option. For maximum security, select Encrypt Files to ensure that files are encrypted when they're sent over the network. For maximum performance, make sure this option is not selected. Click OK to continue.

11. If you've chosen to use encryption, enter a pass phrase to protect the private key used for encryption. You can also specify a hint here in case you forget the pass phrase. For easier future access, select Remember Pass Phrase. This allows the pass phrase to be entered automatically if so desired. (Of course, this is a very bad security practice.)

12. Now specify whether pass phrase recovery should be enabled (as shown in Figure 10-21). Only if the user selects this option will the administrator be able to recover the pass phrase if any problems occur.

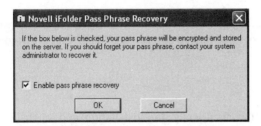

Figure 10-21. *If the user does not select the Enable Pass Phrase Recovery option, the administrator cannot recover lost pass phrases.*

13. Click OK to finish iFolder initialization. This enters an iFolder icon in the task bar of the computer and, if so selected, an icon to access the folder shared with iFolder on the desktop of the computer as well.

Accessing iFolder Files from the Web Interface

When a user works on her own computer, she has easy access to her file. If a user needs to access her files in the iFolder directory while away, she can use the browser interface, as described in the following:

1. From the iFolder web page, click Login.

2. At the login prompt, enter your username and password and click OK. This gives you access to your iFolder files from the NetStorage web interface. From this interface, select the File, Edit, and View menus to work with shared files.

■**Note** If NetStorage is not enabled, users will not get access to their iFolder directories from the NetStorage interface. NetStorage configuration is covered in the next section.

NetStorage

In an Open Enterprise Server environment, a user has many ways to access files. Files can be accessed from mapped drives if the Novell client is used, from the iFolder client interface or from a Samba shared drive on a Linux client machine, or by using WebDAV or Microsoft Web Folders on a Windows client machine on the network.

However, if a user is on the road and needs access to his files from a computer where no Novell client software is installed, a solution is needed. Never fear, however, for one is available in the form of NetStorage. NetStorage is the ideal solution to provide users with access to their files on the Web. A number of ways exist to access files shared with NetStorage:

- From Novell Virtual Office

- From Novell exteNd Director Standard Edition

- From the special NetStorage web site

You can read how to access the NetStorage web site in this section, but Novell Virtual Office is covered in Chapter 17. Because of its advanced nature, exteNd Director is not covered in this book.

Managing NetStorage

The nice thing about NetStorage is that it works directly after installation, and the installation is very straightforward. After a default installation of the NetStorage software on your server, you can access the NetStorage server directly on http://*yourserver*/netstorage (as shown in Figure 10-22). The only thing needed on the client computer is a connection with the NetStorage server. The default installation offers users only limited options, so you need to do some configuration before it can be put to optimal use.

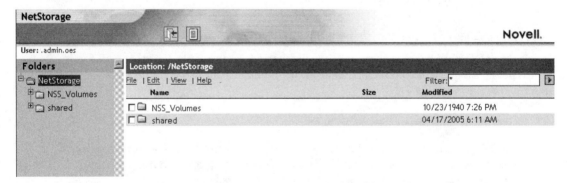

Figure 10-22. *The NetStorage web interface can be used directly after its installation.*

The most important task in NetStorage configuration is getting some useful data into it. After all, the main purpose of the software is to give a user Internet access to his files. In the default configuration, the user only gets access to some default locations, like a shared data directory, which is rather useless. To give the users access to something practical like his home directory and directories to which he has drive mappings, you must first facilitate it.

There are two ways to get access to files through NetStorage. If a login script exists for the user where drive mappings (see Chapter 9) are created, the user gets access from NetStorage to these mapped drives. The other option is to use NetStorage Location objects that point to locations in the file system. After you've created NetStorage Location objects in eDirectory, you must assign this Location object to your users so they can see it. The last part of this configuration is the NetStorage Provider. This is an object you normally don't have to configure. It provides you with access to different kinds of storage locations like NetWare Storage, WebDAV-based storage, and iFolder Storage. Later in this section, you'll learn how to configure all of these.

Defining Mappings for NetStorage

If NetStorage is deployed in an environment where drive mappings are used, all mappings created in login scripts are automatically applied to the user that logs in to the NetStorage site (see Figure 10-23). You can define drive mappings in login scripts from iManager (as shown in Figure 10-24). See Chapter 9 for more details about this procedure.

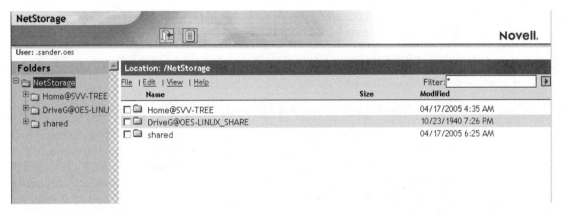

Figure 10-23. *Drive mappings are applied automatically to the NetStorage environment as well.*

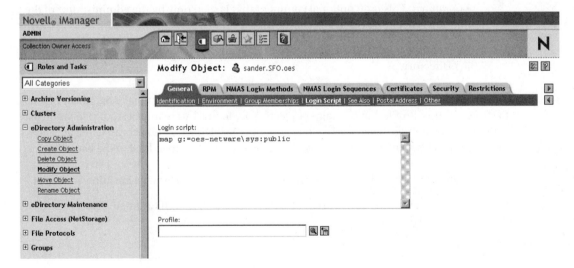

Figure 10-24. *You can create drive mappings in the login scripts processed when logging in to the network.*

Creating Storage Locations

If NetStorage is installed on OES - Linux, no default access to storage is provided, except for the default NetStorage shared folder. In order to manage NetStorage access to storage devices other than this default shared folder and mappings that users get from login scripts, storage locations and storage providers have to be configured. After installation of NetStorage, some storage providers are present by default to give you access to the different kinds of storage in your network; normally, they don't have to be configured. An important task for an administrator, however, is to provide access to locations in the file system by configuring storage locations.

1. Start your browser and access iManager on http://yourserver/nps/. Next, enter your admin username and password and log in.

2. From the left column, select File Access (NetStorage), and then New Storage Location. You'll be presented with the screen shown in Figure 10-25.

3. Enter the following required information to create the storage location:

   • *Object Name*: The label for the related object in eDirectory.

   • *Display Name*: The name the user will see in the NetStorage directory access list.

   • *Directory Location*: The location of a directory in the file system. The location of this directory must be specified in URL format. If in the URL the file system type is omitted, it's assumed that NCP must be used. You can use URLs to NCP, CIFS, or SSH shares in the file system. For example, both ncp://yourserver/yourvolume/*yourpath*; cifs://*yourserver*/yourcifsshare, and ssh://*yourserver*/home/*youruser* are all valid.

   • *Context*: The directory context where the storage location object resides.

   • *Comment*: This is an optional comment that is seen only by the administrator of the Storage Location object.

4. After entering all required attributes, click Create to create the Storage Location object in eDirectory.

After you've created one or more Storage Location objects, you must assign these objects to Users, Groups, Profiles, or Container objects. You do this by creating a storage location list with the Assign Storage Location To Object option. The eDirectory objects assigned get access to all directories provided by the Storage Location objects that are added to the list:

1. From iManager, select File Access (NetStorage) ➤ Assign Storage Location To Object.

2. Use the browser to browse to the eDirectory object you want to assign. Select this object and click OK.

3. Specify the Storage Location objects to be assigned to the selected eDirectory object. It's possible to add more than one Storage Location object; use the History button to get an overview of all objects currently assigned.

4. Click OK to finish assignment of Storage Location objects.

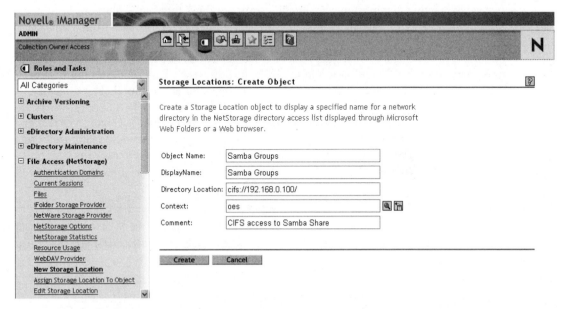

Figure 10-25. *With NetStorage Location objects, you can provide access to different kinds of shared directories on your servers.*

■**Note** The software is somewhat confusing. In eDirectory, three different things have to be present to work with NetStorage. First, there is the Storage Provider that provides access to different kinds of storage. These Storage Providers are default objects, which normally the administrator does not change. Second, is the Storage Location object, which makes the connection to some location in the file system. Last, a storage location list is created with the Assign Storage Location To Object option. The problem with this, however, is that the storage location list does not appear as a separate object in eDirectory. Instead, it is used to assign users to all different kinds of storage. On these objects, it appears as a separate property. After these three parts have been configured the proper way, a user needs local file system rights to the directory accessed with NetStorage. If, for example, a user is assigned access to a CIFS location on the file system, but he isn't granted any rights to this location, the storage location will appear in his user interface but he will not be able to do anything with it because he lacks the proper rights assignment. A later section in this chapter explains how to solve this problem for CIFS-based file access.

Using NetStorage

Once you've completed the basic NetStorage configuration on your server, the user can start accessing his NetStorage locations. In most situations, he will do this from Virtual Office (see Chapter 17). It's also possible to access NetStorage from its own separate web interface. This provides the user with a web-based alternative to the normal way local files are managed— instead of creating, editing, and viewing files from Windows Internet Explorer or SUSE's Konqueror on a user's local machine, the NetStorage interface is accessed from a browser instead, allowing the user to work with his files. From this interface, the user does have many options to work with files: new folders can be created, files can be deleted, renamed, uploaded, or purged, and so on. Some features, though, are not always available. For example, it's not possible to download and lock files from the NetStorage interface to your iFolder directory.

1. To access NetStorage from a workstation, start your browser or Microsoft Web Folders and specify the URL for NetStorage. On OES - Linux, you can access NetStorage from http://*yourserver*/netstorage, while on OES - NetWare you have to use http:// *yourserver*/oneNet/NetStorage.

Tip If you have persistent cookies enabled on your workstation, the date and time on the workstation being used to access NetStorage must be within 24 hours of the date and time on the server running NetStorage to avoid conflicts.

---

2. Enter your username and password. There is no need to work with a full eDirectory name like cn=eric.ou=azlan.o=com. Just enter the name of the user (eric, in this case) and it will work.

3. You now have access to your NetStorage environment, as shown in Figure 10-26. All important actions are in the File Menu. Use this menu to create, delete, rename, upload, download, download and lock, mail, purge, undelete, or archive files. From this menu, you can create new directories and modify properties of existing files as well.

Tip Which NetStorage elements you can see depends on the server you're on. Different things are available if you access NetStorage from OES - NetWare or OES - Linux. On OES - Linux, for example, you have access to a NetStorage shared directory which is accessible to everyone. This shared directory does not exist on OES - NetWare.

Be aware that some NetStorage tasks are not currently available from OES - Linux. You cannot view, salvage, or purge deleted files on Linux servers. These tasks are only functional on OES - NetWare.

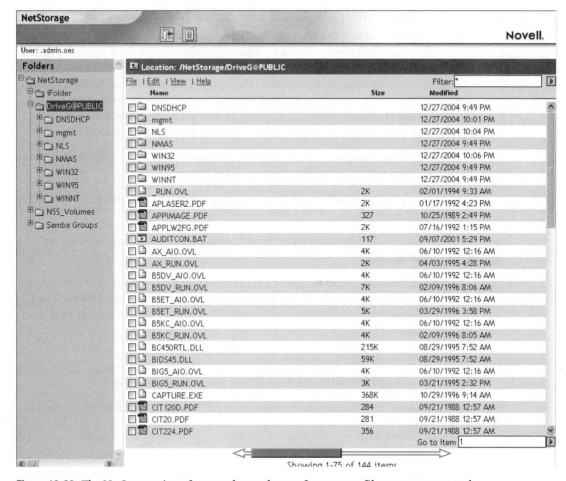

Figure 10-26. *The NetStorage interface can be used to perform many file management tasks.*

Advanced NetStorage Configuration

If you followed the previous procedure, your users can access their files from the NetStorage web page or from iFolder. It's also possible to configure NetStorage with some advanced options, such as the following:

- Working with authentication domains

- Displaying reports about NetStorage Activity

- Managing general NetStorage options

- Managing the storage provider objects

The following paragraphs offer more information about these tasks.

Working with Authentication Domains

An authentication domain is an eDirectory server that is used for authentication to the NetStorage environment. By default, the server on which NetStorage is installed is used for this purpose. As an administrator, you have the ability to specify other eDirectory servers to be used for this purpose in order to build in some fault tolerance. I recommend doing this in all cases—by default, only one eDirectory server is listed as an authentication domain, but for fault tolerance purposes, you should list at least two servers for this purpose. From the File Access ➤ Authentication Domains interface in iManager (see Figure 10-27), the following options are available:

- *Add Domain*: Use this option to add another eDirectory server. Use the server IP address or DNS name to add it. Users are authenticated to this server.

- *Make Primary*: Specify that the selected eDirectory server must be used as the first server for authentication.

- *Remove Domain*: Removes the server from the list of servers that can be used for authentication.

- *Add Context*: Use this option to specify a context list that the server must search through for authentication. By default, all containers below the specified context are specified as well, but to speed up searching you might prefer to add a list of the contexts your users are in.

- *Remove Context*: Removes a context.

- *Add Hosts*: Lets you list additional hosts for the authentication domain.

- *Change Priority*: Lets you specify the order in which you want the different contexts to be searched.

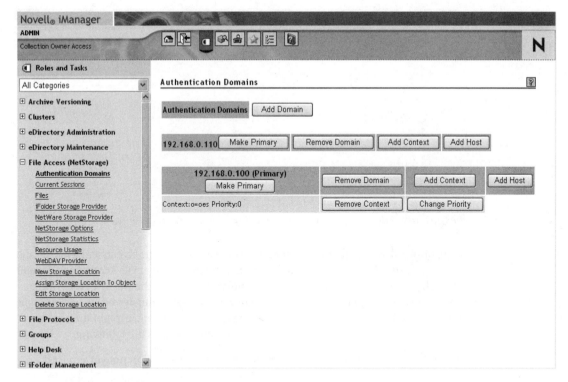

Figure 10-27. *From the Authentication Domains screen, you can specify which servers and contexts must be used to search for users that want to authenticate.*

Displaying Reports about NetStorage Activity

If you want a usage overview of your NetStorage environment, you can view a default report about the current sessions on your server. From this screen, you'll see a list of users that are currently connected and the number of requests serviced for these users. This information is useful to troubleshoot NetStorage usage. If, for example, a user is not able to perform some tasks from the NetStorage interface, from this screen you can get more information about the activity of the user account. The following information is available from this screen (see Figure 10-28).

- *Name*: The name of the user that is currently connected.

- *Id*: An internal ID for that user that is used within the NetStorage environment.

- *Address*: The IP address the user is connected from. For administrative accounts that currently don't have a connection to any files in the NetStorage environment, no IP address is listed.

- *Login Time*: The time the user logged in.

- *Request Serviced*: The number of actions the user has issued on the NetStorage environment. Be aware that every time a file is accessed, it will be listed here as a request that is serviced.

- *Last Request Time*: The time of the latest request.

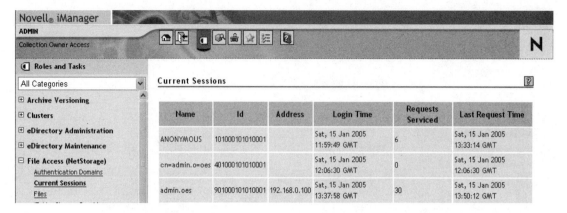

Figure 10-28. *Use the Current Sessions screen to get information about current activity.*

A second option that's useful for NetStorage troubleshooting is the screen with NetStorage statistics (see Figure 10-29). You can access this screen from the iManager File Access (NetStorage) interface as well. This screen offers an excellent general overview of the way the NetStorage server is working—for example, you can view the number of bytes transferred, as well as login failures and many other useful statistics. Most of the items shown here, explain themselves. Some options are of particular interest for the administrator, such as the following:

- *Outstanding Requests*: The number of requests that are issued but not yet serviced.

- *Login Failures:* The number of times a user tried to log in but failed.

- *Memory Allocation Failures*: The number of times the NetStorage application failed to allocate memory. Under normal conditions, this counter should show 0 as its failure.

- *IO Buffer Allocation Failures*: The number of times NetStorage failed to allocate an IO buffer. If this counter is set to anything other than 0, take a look to see if an update for your NetStorage software is available.

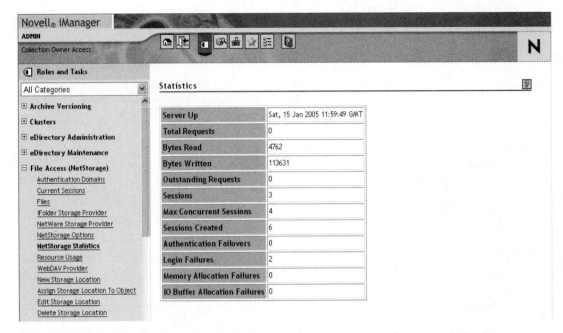

Figure 10-29. *The NetStorage Statistics screen offers an excellent overview of usage statistics since the moment the NetStorage server was up.*

The last option that provides information about the current use of NetStorage is Resource Usage (as shown in Figure 10-30). This option provides debugging information about the use of your NetStorage environment. The information provided here doesn't say much to most administrators, but if Novell Technical Support is helping you resolve a NetStorage issue, they may ask you for the parameters listed here.

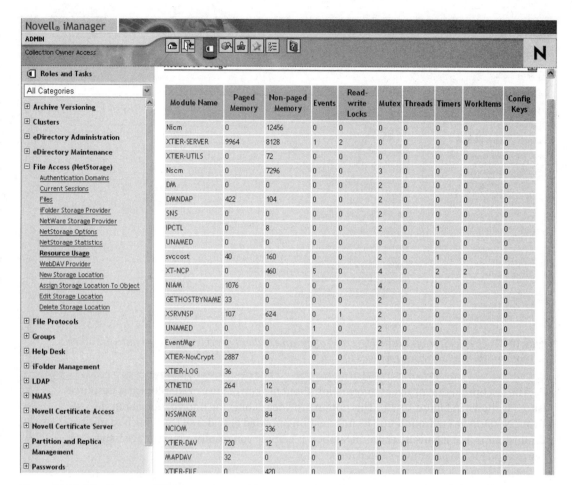

Figure 10-30. *The Resource Usage screen provides an overview of resource usage for all the different NetStorage components.*

Managing General NetStorage Options

Some general NetStorage options can also be used to fine-tune NetStorage performance. These options can all be accessed from the NetStorage Options option under iManager File Access (NetStorage), shown in Figure 10-31. The following options are available:

- *Proxy Username and Proxy Password*: This is the username and password of the administrator account used for NetStorage administration. By default, the eDirectory admin and password are used for this purpose. Note that if you change this username and password, you still need to specify a user with administration rights to all relevant parts of your eDirectory tree.

- *Location*: This is the location you want users to enter as part of the NetStorage URL in order to access NetStorage. By default, the value is set to the directory /oneNet. If you change this option, you must change it in the NetStorage configuration textfile xsrv.conf as well.

- *Certificate Name*: This is the name of the SSL Certificate used by NetStorage. By default, one of the certificates signed by the eDirectory CA is used. If, for example, you want to use a certificate signed by an external CA, you can specify the name of that certificate here.

- *Session Timeout*: The number of seconds of inactivity after which a user's NetStorage session will timeout and close automatically.

- *Janitor Interval*: The interval between Janitor settings that clean up the NetStorage environment. *Never* change this setting unless directed by Novell Technical Support.

- *Persistent Cookies*: A persistent cookie allows a user to connect again to the NetStorage server after he has closed his browser without authenticating again. This only works if the user wants to reestablish contact within the session timeout interval. This option is, however, very insecure if a user works from a workstation that is shared with other users, because another user who uses the machine after them could reestablish a session as the first user without entering any username or password. For this reason, it's best to leave the value of this parameter as 0 (persistent cookies disabled).

- *LDAP Port*: Allows you to change the LDAP port. This option is useful if another user is already using the same LDAP port.

- *Cookieless*: Some clients, such as the Apple WebDav client don't support the use of cookies. For this reason, it's possible to switch on cookieless authentication. You can turn off cookieless authentication by switching the default value of this parameter to 0.

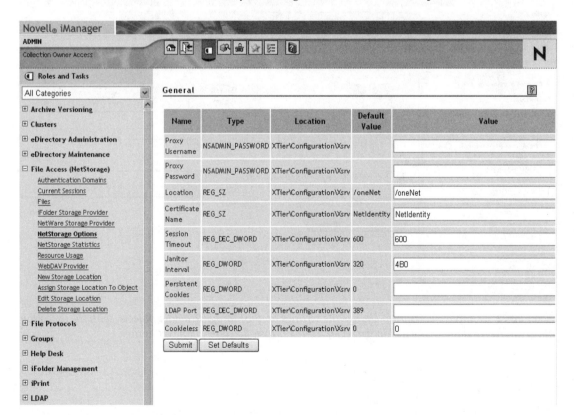

Figure 10-31. *You can fine-tune NetStorage performance by modifying some of its general parameters.*

Managing Storage Provider Objects

iManager offers the option of managing the Storage Providers in your network. In the File Access menu in iManager, options are available to manage settings for the NetWare Storage Provider and the iFolder Storage Provider. In most cases, however, it does not make sense to change settings for them, since the default configuration generally works well. If, however, you've installed iFolder later than NetStorage, you'll need to indicate on the Storage Provider object where the iFolder Server can be found. You can do this by following these steps:

1. From iManager, select File Access ➤ iFolder Storage Provider.

2. Make sure that at the iFolder Server option, the name or address of your iFolder server is specified (as shown in Figure 10-32).

3. Click Submit to submit any modifications.

The other options on both storage objects are rarely needed so you can leave their default values in place. For that reason, they will not be discussed here. Consult the online documentation at http://www.novell.com/documentation for more information about the available parameters.

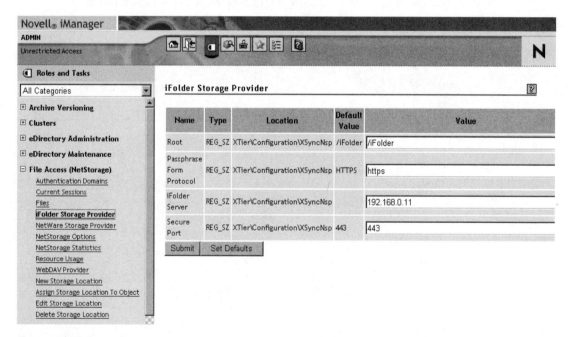

Figure 10-32. *It's rarely necessary to change the settings for the Storage Provider objects (with the exception of the address or name of the iFolder server) if iFolder is installed later than NetStorage.*

File Access Protocols

You've just learned how clientless access to files on OES - NetWare and OES - Linux can be configured by using NetStorage. Another way to access files on OES is by using one of the available file access protocols used with either OES - NetWare or OES Linux, a few of which are shown next.

- *Novell Core Protocol (NCP)*: This has been the default protocol in a NetWare environment to access files for over 20 years. On OES - NetWare, it's present as part of the kernel. On OES - Linux, it's available as an installation option to allow users using the Novell client software to access files on an OES - Linux server in the same manner they access files on an OES - NetWare server.

- *Common Internet File System (CIFS)*: Common Internet File System is the standardized version of the Server Message Blocks (SMB) protocol. This protocol is used in a Microsoft environment to access shared directories. On OES - Linux, CIFS is implemented in a Novell-modified version of the Samba server. On OES - Netware, CIFS can be installed as part of the NFAP package (see the next section). This protocol is important if you want to give access to files on OES without the need to install the Novell client software on all workstations.

- *Apple Filing Protocol (AFP)*: Apple Filing Protocol is the protocol used by Apple clients to access files on a shared directory on an Apple server. Since the release of Apple's OS X, however, which came out in the year 2001, Apple has adopted CIFS as their default file access protocol. For this reason, AFP is hardly needed anymore.

- *Network File System (NFS)*: NFS is the ancient UNIX way to share files. On OES - Linux, it's present by default, as on any other Linux server. On OES - NetWare, it can be installed as part of the NFAP software package.

The following sections describe how to configure file access protocols on OES - NetWare and OES - Linux. The following subjects will be covered:

- Using CIFS on OES - NetWare to grant native file access to Windows users

- Using CIFS on OES - NetWare to grant native file access to Apple users

- Using the Samba server on OES - Linux to grant native file access to Windows users

- Using the Novell Core Protocol (NCP) on OES - Linux to grant native file access to any workstation logging in with the Novell client.

Native File Access on OES - NetWare

On OES - NetWare, just one protocol is installed by default to access files: the Novell Core Protocol. This protocol allows workstations where the Novell client software is installed to access files on that server. To access files any other way on OES - NetWare, the protocols available from the Native File Access Package need to be installed.

Enabling Native File Access on OES - NetWare Using CIFS

On OES - NetWare, the native file access protocols are installed by default. All you have to do to start using them is configure them from iManager. The following shows ways in which some NCFs can be used to start and stop the native file access software.

- Use AFPSTRT to start the Apple Filing Protocol (AFP) Services.

- Use AFPSTOP to stop the AFP services.

- Use CIFSSTRT to start all CIFS services

- Use CIFSSTOP to stop all CIFS services.

Managing Native File Access from iManager

After installation, Native File Access services can be managed from iManager:

1. In iManager, from Roles And Tasks select File Protocols, and then choose CIFS/AFP (as shown in Figure 10-33).

2. In the Server field, browse to the OES - NetWare server for which you want to manage native file services. This interface does not support management of OES - Linux servers.

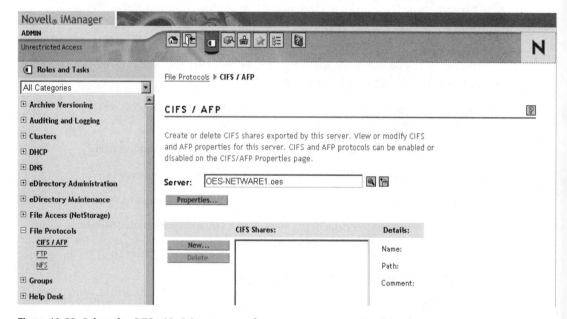

Figure 10-33. *Select the OES - NetWare server where you want to create CIFS shares.*

3. Click Properties to manage the properties of the server. As seen in Figure 10-34, on the Server tab you can specify which of the native file access protocols must be available. Some parameters can be specified as well. First, you can specify the NetBIOS name to be advertised for the virtual CIFS server. By default, this is the name of your server with

"-W" added; thus, our server OES-NETWARE would become OES-NETWARE-W. Next, a comment field can be added. This comment is visible to users that browse to your server. Finally, it's also possible to specify the address of a WINS server as if WINS is used in your network. Two options exist as well to specify whether OpLocks should be used and if Distributed File System (DFS) support is required. I recommend always using the OpLocks option. Only if you're going to work with Distributed File System (see Chapter 11), should the Distributed File System (DFS) Support option be enabled.

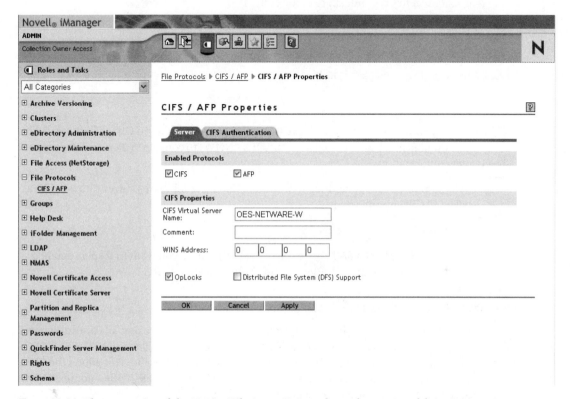

Figure 10-34. *The properties of the Native File Access Protocols can be managed from iManager.*

4. On the CIFS Authentication tab, specify how CIFS authentication should be handled. By default, user authentication happens locally. It's also possible to specify the name or address of a Windows NT 4–style primary domain controller (PDC) that handles all authentication requests.

■**Note** An important administrator task that enables Native File Access is allowing end users to work with their simple password. Chapter 9 has more about the simple password and its replacement of the universal password.

After the generic CIFS configuration has been handled, you can create CIFS shares:

1. In iManager, select File Protocols ➤ CIFS/AFP.

2. Under CIFS Shares, choose New. A dialog opens in which you can specify the properties of the CIFS shares you want to make available.

3. Enter the name, path, and an optional comment you want to use for the share, and then click Finish to save your share to the system.

Tip If no shares are defined, then all mounted volumes are displayed. Users will, of course, only have access to files that they're granted rights to.

Now that you've configured the Native File Access environment on OES - NetWare, there are some commands that can be used from the OES - NetWare console to display details about the current configuration:

- **CIFS INFO** displays operational information. You'll see all shares currently available, as well as all CIFS options in use.

- **CIFS SHARE** displays all active shares.

- **CIFS SHARE <SHARENAME>** (use the name of the share you want to display detailed information for) will display information about a specific share.

Specifying the Default Contexts for CIFS Users

Since the CIFS service is not eDirectory-aware, you need to make sure that all contexts where the software has to search for users are specified in the configuration file SYS:\ETC\CTXS.CFG. By default, the container where your server is installed is listed in this file. This allows the CIFS service to look in that container for users that want to log in using CIFS. If other contexts have to be searched as well, you also need to include them here.

Managing the CIFS Environment for Macintosh Users

If there are many Macintosh users on your network, you must manage their CIFS environment as well. First, Macintosh users must be able to work with a simple password. This means that a simple password must be set for each of them. This is a tedious task. If you want to create simple passwords for many Macintosh users without doing too much work, use the command **LOAD AFPTCP CLEARTEXT** on the server console. When this option is active, users can log in with their eDirectory name and password. After the eDirectory password is verified, a simple password is created automatically and stored in eDirectory. There is, however, one drawback: the eDirectory username and password are sent in clear-text over the network. This is bad, because anyone using a sniffer like the free program Ethereal, is then able to capture both the username and password. After most of your Macintosh users have logged in once, thus creating the simple password in eDirectory, you should switch off this option as soon as possible.

Next, specify the default contexts for your Macintosh users in the contexts file. This allows Macintosh users to log in without entering their complete distinguished name. You can enter a list of default contexts that should be searched for users in the file sys:\etc\ctxs.cfg. This lets a Macintosh user log in with just their username and password.

The Macintosh user can now access the files on the OES - NetWare server from his own desktop interface, as outlined in the following:

1. In Mac OS X, select Finder and then choose Go ➤ Connect to Server.

2. Enter the IP address or DNS name of the OES - NetWare server and click Connect.

3. Enter the username and password and click Connect. Now the user can select a volume to be mounted on the Mac OS X desktop.

4. Create an alias to the desired volume on the desktop; the advantage of using an alias is that aliases are retained after rebooting. Next, click the OES - NetWare server icon and select File ➤ Make Alias. This creates an alias icon on the desktop.

CIFS and Working with Domains

If you're running CIFS protocol services on OES - NetWare, you can work with domain users in few different ways:

- You can use OES - NetWare as a Windows NT 4–style PDC. (This is explained later in this section.)

- You can provide access to users from an existing NT domain by importing them into eDirectory.

- You can use Nsure Identity Manager 2.0 to connect OES - NetWare directly to a Windows domain.

We look at the first two possibilities in the following paragraphs. You can read more about Nsure Identity Manager 2.0 configuration in Chapter 18.

Configuring OES - NetWare as a PDC

Instead of working with a Microsoft PDC, it's possible as well to configure OES - NetWare as a PDC. This makes management of your network easier: you no longer need to maintain two separate databases because all users can be stored in eDirectory. There are, however, some features that aren't supported when using OES - NetWare as a CIFS PDC:

- There is no Microsoft Active Directory functionality.

- PDCs running on OES - NetWare cannot replicate with BDCs running on Windows.

- You cannot work with trusted domain relationships.

- Microsoft administration tools cannot be used for administration.

- Roaming profiles are not supported.

- Microsoft NTFS ACL mappings are not supported.

Looking at this list, it seems like there are many disadvantages to running an OES - NetWare PDC, but you should be aware that most of these disadvantages relate to the use of the traditional

Microsoft mechanisms for the domain environment. In truth, these aren't really disadvantages since eDirectory and its management tools offer at least as much flexibility as the tools and mechanisms from the Microsoft environment.

To make an OES - NetWare server a PDC, you must create a PDC on that server. You can only do this if the server is not a domain controller or a domain member in another domain already.

1. On the OES - NetWare console, enter the commands **cifs domain enable** and then **cifs domain create** to start the procedure to create the CIFS domain, as shown in Figure 10-35.

2. Enter the domain name of the new PDC and press Enter.

3. Enter the context where the PDC object will be created in eDirectory. You must enter the typeful or typeless distinguished name of the context where the domain is created: .sfo.oes will do; .ou=sfo.o=oes will work as well.

4. Enter the username of a user with sufficient rights to create objects in eDirectory.

5. Enter the password for this user and press Enter. You'll see a message stating that the domain has been successfully created.

```
V-OES-NETWARE1:cifs domain create
domainName> cifsdomain
context> v-oes
username> cn=admin.o=v-oes
password> ******
Domain cifsdomain successfully created.
V-OES-NETWARE1:_
```

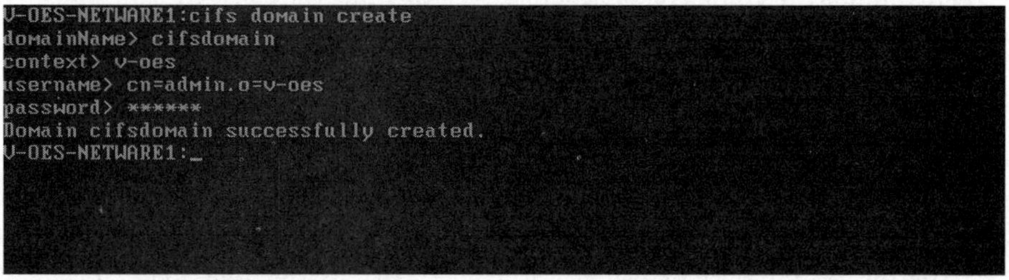

Figure 10-35. *The CIFS environment must be created from the OES - NetWare console.*

You now have a CIFS domain in eDirectory. Some objects are also created to enable you to manage the domain from your eDirectory management tools, as shown in Figure 10-36:

- *Domain Admins*: This group contains users that will have local administrator rights on any workstation or server that joins the domain.

- *Domain Controllers*: This is a group object of which all domain controllers configured in the domain will be a member.

- *Domain Groups*: This object is strictly for internal use. You should not perform any management tasks on it. All eDirectory groups used in the domain will be added automatically as members.

- *Domain Guests*: This group can be added to the local workstation guest group if desired to allow for guest access. No members are added automatically; you should do this manually if so required.

- *Domain Users*: All users that log in to the domain are automatically added to this group. This group is added to the local users group of each Windows workstation that joins the domain as well.

Apart from these default accounts, machine accounts will be added for all clients that join the domain as well. These accounts are contained by the domain object; eDirectory user objects of which the name starts with $ are used for these accounts. After the initial domain is created, other OES - NetWare servers can be added as members of the domain by issuing the command **CIFS DOMAIN JOIN** from the console of these servers. You can read more information about the configuration of CIFS Domains on OES - NetWare in the online documentation at http://www.novell.com/documentation/oes.

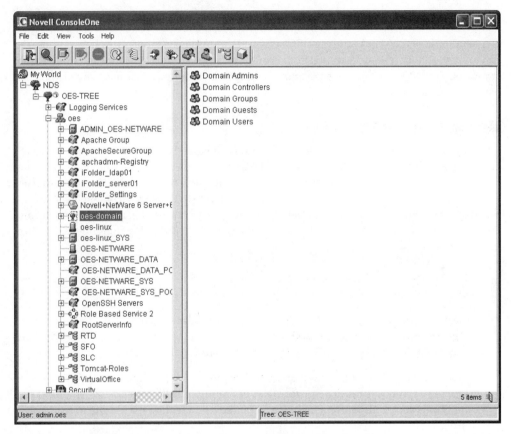

Figure 10-36. *After an OES - NetWare server is configured as a CIFS PDC, some objects are added to eDirectory.*

Importing Users from an Existing PDC

If you want to provide access from an existing NT domain, you can import users from that domain into eDirectory by performing the following steps.

1. In iManager, configure CIFS for domain authentication. You don't just specify that domain logins should be used; you also need to specify the name of the domain you want to use. Click OK to save and apply your changes.

2. Start Remote Manager from https://*yourserver*:8009 and enter your username and password to log in to Remote Manager.

3. In the left frame, select Manage eDirectory ➤ NFAP Import Users. You'll now have access to an interface where you can import NT domain users to eDirectory.

4. Browse to the eDirectory context where you want to import the NT Domain users. Once you've selected the container where you want to create the NT Domain users, click Start to begin importing them.

5. When the import is complete, click Done to clear the screen.

Natively Accessing OES - NetWare from Windows

After configuring OES - NetWare as a CIFS server, all traditional Windows mechanisms can be used to access its shares. For example, from Windows CP, select Start ➤ Search and then search for your OES - NetWare server. Your server should appear in a window. Click it to view all available shares on your server.

Creating NFS Shares on OES - NetWare

OES - NetWare also has a complete NFS protocol stack installed for native file access. The NFS server can be managed from iManager as well. OES - NetWare even allows you to integrate the NFS server on OES - NetWare with a traditional UNIX infrastructure, where NIS is used for user management. Fortunately, for access to information about UNIX users accessing the share, Directory Access can be configured as well. NFS is not used very often in a NetWare environment, so I won't describe it in depth. Instead, you'll learn in the following steps how to create a simple NFS share on OES - NetWare.

1. In iManager, select File Protocols and then choose NFS to access the options to configure OES - NetWare as an NFS server.

2. Next to the server field, use the magnifying glass to browse to the OES - NetWare server you want to configure for using NFS. This automatically starts the NFS services on your server: you'll see the status change from Stopped to Running.

3. Leave the Umask settings as they are. This sets the default UNIX rights on the NFS share and the default value is just fine for UNIX environments. It's the same default used on any Linux server that sets the rights to all for the user creating the file and to read for all other users.

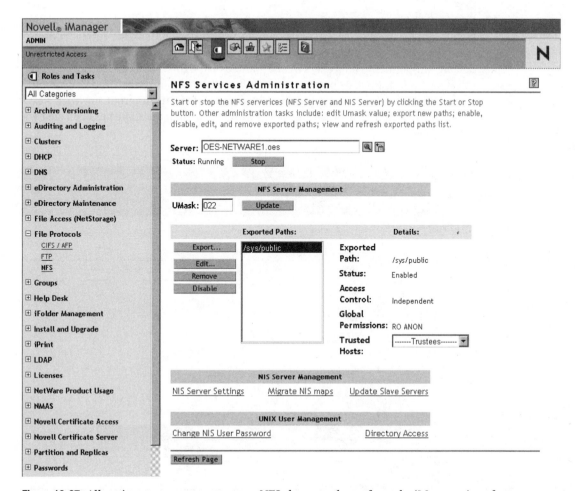

Figure 10-37. *All settings necessary to create an NFS share can be set from the iManager interface.*

4. Now click the Export button. This opens a dialog where you can specify the path you want to export, as shown in Figure 10-38.

5. In the Access Control window, select Independent. This allows UNIX users to use UNIX permissions on files they create and NetWare users to use NetWare permissions on the same files.

6. Next, set the Global Permissions the way you want. In most situations, the default is fine since it's the same default used on any UNIX system where all users have read access to the files.

7. Enter the IP addresses or DNS names of the host you want to grant access to this share. If you want to give access to an entire subnet, use an & to prepend the subnet address. Next, specify the kind of access you want to give users from these specified hosts. By default, only authenticated users will be granted read rights. For a less restrictive setup, select the options Root, Anonymous, and RW to allow anyone to read and write in the share. You shouldn't do this if your server is accessible from the Internet, however. Next, click OK to continue. A message displays informing you that the share has been created successfully.

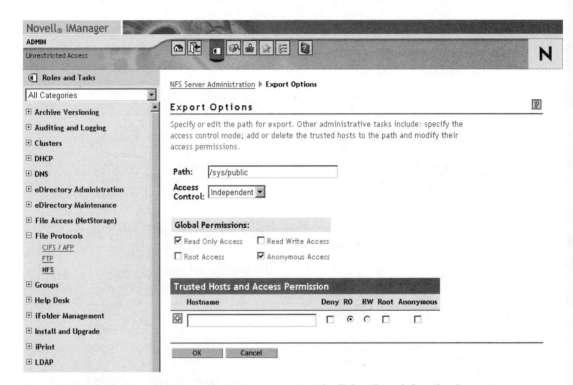

Figure 10-38. *On the Export Options screen, you must specify all details to define the share.*

8. From the NFS Services Administration screen, repeat this procedure to create new shares. When finished, click Directory Access to specify how UNIX users can authenticate from eDirectory.

9. On the screen Directory Access screen (see Figure 10-39), make sure that eDirectory is selected and specify the context where the NFS server should start searching for users that want to access the NFS shares. Next, click OK to continue. This prompts a message stating that the file etc/nfs.cfg has been successfully updated. Click Close to close this screen.

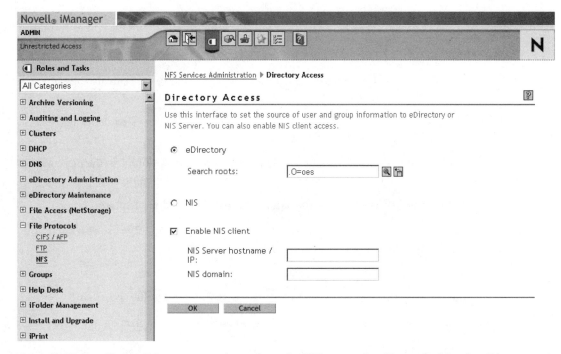

Figure 10-39. *Specify the eDirectory container where the NFS server should start looking for eDirectory users.*

Managing File Access Protocols on OES - Linux

Earlier, configuring native file access protocols on OES - NetWare was covered. In this area, Linux offers some advanced options as well. The following paragraphs, however, explain how to configure OES file access protocols on OES - Linux. First, I'll discuss the workings of the Novell version of the open-source Samba server that comes with OES - Linux. Then, I'll cover how NCP can be used to grant access to workstations that have the Novell client installed to volumes on OES - Linux.

Configuring the Samba Server on OES - Linux

In the preceding sections, you learned how Native File Access Services can be configured on OES - NetWare. In this section, the Linux side of the story is given its due. Since CIFS is the de facto standard to access files on the network and Samba is the best way to allow this CIFS access on a Linux machine, I'll focus on the configuration of the Samba server in an OES environment.

Samba is the most popular server to share files in a Linux environment. In OES - Linux, it's included as standard and can be used as a way to share files with users. Novell compiled Samba to enable LDAP authentication by default. These options enable user authentication against an LDAP server. The Novell version of the Samba server has the following characteristics:

- eDirectory users can be turned into Linux/Samba users very easily.

- Home directories are created automatically when the Linux/Samba user first logs in to a Linux box.

- Home directories of Samba users are automatically shared so they can also be accessed from a Windows client.

- In order to access files shared by the Samba server, users must authenticate against eDirectory. Secure LDAP is used for this authentication.

The purpose of the Samba server is to share files, folders, and printers on the network. Files and folders shared by the OES Samba server can be accessed in many ways:

- Windows users can navigate to the Samba share using Windows Explorer.

- Linux users can navigate to Samba shares using an smb-compatible browser such as Gnome Nautilus.

- Linux users can mount a Samba share locally on their computers.

- Linux users can access files in a Samba share with the client utility smbclient.

- Windows users can access files on the Samba server when they create a web folder.

- All users can access files on the Samba server from a browser if Novell NetStorage is installed and a storage location for the Samba server is created. In this case, files can be uploaded and downloaded but can't be modified directly.

Installation and Configuration

In most cases, the Samba server is installed automatically when OES - Linux is installed. If, however, this is not the case in your situation, you can install it afterwards from YaST. The following shows how to install and then configure Samba. If Samba is already Installed and you just need to configure it, proceed with the next section.

1. Start YaST, and enter the password of your root user if required.

2. Select Network Services ➤ Novell Samba. If asked if you want to continue configuration, choose Yes.

3. As the first step in the configuration, you must specify where the LDAP server used for authentication can be found. Choose between Local System if the LDAP server is available on the same server and Remote System if you will use an LDAP server running on another server. Next, enter the name of the Admin user and his password and, if required, the directory server address. If you're using something other then the default ports for LDAP, click Port Details and enter the ports needed. Then click Next to continue.

4. As shown in Figure 10-40, enter all the information that's required in the LDAP server directory and click Next to continue.

• *LDAP server Host*: The IP address or DNS name of your LDAP server.

• *Base context for Samba users*: The base container where the server should start looking for available Samba users. All child containers of this container will be searched as well.

• *eDirectory tree name*: The name of the eDirectory tree where the Samba users are stored.

• *Proxy user name with context*: The name of a user with sufficient rights to enter new information in eDirectory. By default, the admin user is used for this purpose, you could choose to use another user account for tighter security.

• *Proxy user password*: The password of the proxy user.

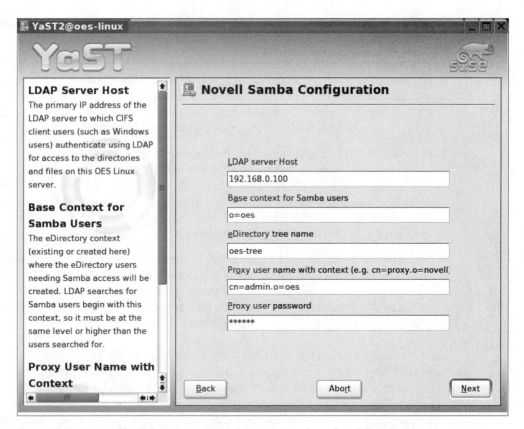

Figure 10-40. *Enter all information required to store Samba-related data in eDirectory.*

5. Settings are now stored and the installation is finished. You can now start using the Samba server.

Samba User Management

After the Samba server is installed, you must enable your eDirectory users to allow them to use it. It's possible to create entirely new eDirectory users that are also enabled as Samba users. Alternatively, it's also possible to convert existing eDirectory users so they become Samba users. In both cases, LUM is the keyword. (Chapter 9 has more about LUM user management.) The procedure to create a LUM user, who is also a Samba user, is detailed next.

1. Before you can create an eDirectory user, who is also a Samba and LUM user, you must create a LUM group object. This is necessary because Linux users must have a primary group. A Linux user that doesn't have such a group can't log in to the system. If you're using OES - Linux, the LUM group can be used as a primary group for your Linux users.

2. Open a browser and start iManager. Log in as a user that's assigned to all user management roles in iManager.

3. Select Groups ➤ Create Group and enter a name for the group and the context where you want to create it. Click OK twice when finished.

4. Next, specify the Linux workstations you want to add the LUM group to. On all workstations you select, the group will be available. If you have several workstations in your group, you can also refer to the Linux Config object to simultaneously refer to all Linux work-stations in your tree. Use the magnifying glass to browse for this object; you'll find the Linux Config object as UNIX Config. Click OK twice when finished.

5. Now that the LUM group is created, you're ready to start creating LUM users and specify that these users must also be created as Samba users. In order to create Samba users, use iManager and select Users ➤ Create User. Now enter all required properties for your eDirectory user. If you want to give the user a home directory on an NCP share or an NSS volume, specify the location of the home directory here. Click OK at the bottom of the page after specifying all required properties. Click OK once more.

6. On Linux, every user needs a primary group. Without a primary group, the user won't be able to log in to their Linux workstation. You can specify the group you just created as the primary group for your user now. Select the option Also Enable This User For LDAP (eDirectory) Authentication To Samba. This allows the user to authenticate on eDirectory when accessing a Samba share. Click OK when finished.

You have now created a LUM user who is also a Samba user. This means that everything necessary to authenticate on the Linux workstations in your network and on your Samba server is now present in eDirectory. Before continuing, log in once as the user you just created. Do this on the server where your Samba server is running. This creates a Linux home directory for the user. This home directory is automatically shared by your Samba server and allows you to easily test whether the Samba server is really sharing anything. To do so, perform the following steps.

1. From your OES - Linux server, press Ctrl+Alt+F2 to open a virtual console.

2. At the login prompt, enter the name and password of the LUM user you just created. A home directory is then created automatically. This home directory is shared automatically by the Samba server, so your user will be ready to access his home directory from a Samba share immediately!

Modify smb.conf to Configure the Samba Server

All access to your Samba server is defined in the configuration file smb.conf. You'll find this file at /etc/samba/smb.conf. Because it's well documented—the file includes working examples—all you have to do to activate them is remove the remark sign (#) at the start of the line. In most cases, it will start working right after you've saved your changes and restarted the Samba server.

The following are a few lines in smb.conf that are of particular interest. These lines are used to connect the Samba server to eDirectory.

```
netbios name = %h-W
passdb backend = NDS_ldapsam_compat:ldaps://192.168.0.10:636 smbpasswd
ldap addmin dn = cn=admin,o=oes
ldap suffix = o=oes
ldap idmap suffix = o=oes
ldap machine suffix = o=oes
ldap passwd sync = on
security = user
encrypt passwords = yes
use sendfile = no
```

In these lines, the NetBIOS name of your OES - Linux server is first set. This name is used to identify your server on the Windows network. The default is to set it to the current hostname (indicated by %h), with "-W" appended to it. In this way, the access to your LDAP server is defined. The line *passdb backend* tells you how to access the LDAP server. Next, the name of the admin object needed to write information in the LDAP directory is shown. After that, there are three lines—all containing the word suffix—that indicate where the information should be searched for in the LDAP directory. Then there is a line that tells you that the LDAP password (which is your eDirectory password) should be synchronized with the Samba password. This allows for password synchronization, even if the secure password is not enabled. Following this are the two lines *security = user* and *encrypt passwords = yes*, which are required to communicate user information to the LDAP server. Finally, there is the option *use sendfile = no*. This is required if you want to share directories on an NSS volume. If you don't need to share directories on NSS volumes, it's better to use *use sendfile = yes* for better performance. If you ever need to change any of these values (which you'll probably never have to do), you can find them in this file in the section [global].

Later in this configuration file, you'll find some examples of how to create a shared directory. This, however, is not as easy as just removing the pound signs at the beginning of the lines. For a user to get access to a shared directory, she has to have some rights to this directory. This is similar to the Windows environment where a user has sufficient access to a share, but no NTFS permissions to the shared files. That simply doesn't work.

Before we dive into this problem, there are some things you should know regarding permissions on a Linux system (also see Chapter 4 for more information). There are just three basic permissions: read, write, and execute (rwx). The execute permission makes files executable, so that leaves just two "real" permissions as compared to the eight rights you can assign when working on a NetWare volume.

To determine the permissions of a certain user, the file system checks first if this user is the owner of the specified file, and next, if the user is a member of the group that is owner of the file. If neither is true, the user automatically gets the permissions assigned to "others."

The user root can make a user owner of a file or directory by using the command **chown**, while **chgrp** is used to make a group owner of a file or directory. A user on a Linux system is always a member of one primary group. He can be a member of more groups, but normally users are members of just one.

You can see the permissions assigned to files and directories, as well as the user and group that is owner of these files and directories by using the command **ls -l**, as shown in Figure 10-41. Some additional permissions are available, such as SGID, SUID, and Sticky bit, but they only give a user basic access to certain files and folders.

Thus, the bottom line is, if you want a user to have access to some directory by means of a Samba share, you must also grant him permissions on the underlying Linux file system. In the next procedure, you can read how a new directory with the name "documents" is created and how user franck and group LUMgroup are made owner of this directory. To do this, you must assume this user and group are already created as LUM user and LUM group on your OES - Linux server. After the objects are assigned as owners of the directory, both the user and the group get all available rights to this directory.

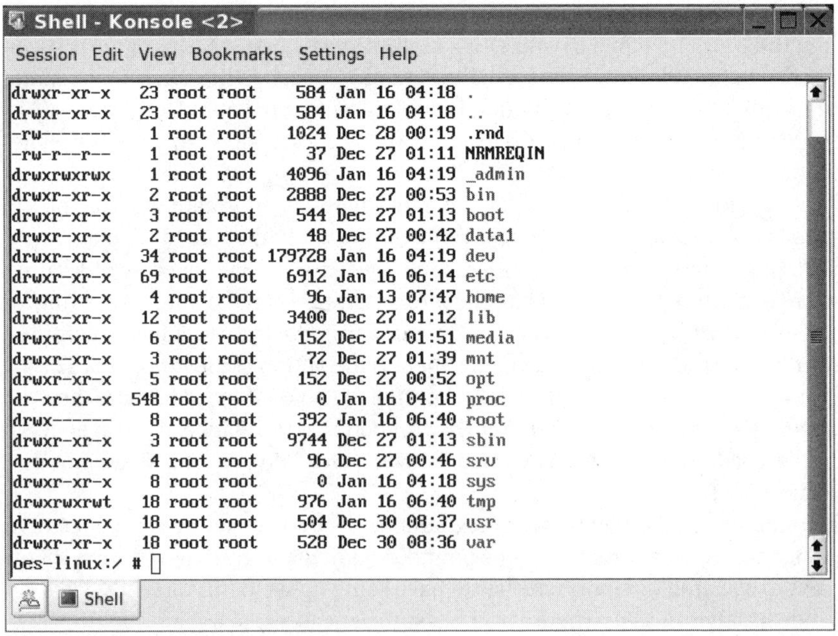

```
🗔 Shell - Konsole <2>                                            _ □ X
Session  Edit  View  Bookmarks  Settings  Help
drwxr-xr-x   23 root root    584 Jan 16 04:18 .
drwxr-xr-x   23 root root    584 Jan 16 04:18 ..
-rw-------    1 root root   1024 Dec 28 00:19 .rnd
-rw-r--r--    1 root root     37 Dec 27 01:11 NRMREQIN
drwxrwxrwx    1 root root   4096 Jan 16 04:19 _admin
drwxr-xr-x    2 root root   2888 Dec 27 00:53 bin
drwxr-xr-x    3 root root    544 Dec 27 01:13 boot
drwxr-xr-x    2 root root     48 Dec 27 00:42 data1
drwxr-xr-x   34 root root 179728 Jan 16 04:19 dev
drwxr-xr-x   69 root root   6912 Jan 16 06:14 etc
drwxr-xr-x    4 root root     96 Jan 13 07:47 home
drwxr-xr-x   12 root root   3400 Dec 27 01:12 lib
drwxr-xr-x    6 root root    152 Dec 27 01:51 media
drwxr-xr-x    3 root root     72 Dec 27 01:39 mnt
drwxr-xr-x    5 root root    152 Dec 27 00:52 opt
dr-xr-xr-x  548 root root      0 Jan 16 04:18 proc
drwx------    8 root root    392 Jan 16 06:40 root
drwxr-xr-x    3 root root   9744 Dec 27 01:13 sbin
drwxr-xr-x    4 root root     96 Dec 27 00:46 srv
drwxr-xr-x    8 root root      0 Jan 16 04:18 sys
drwxrwxrwt   18 root root    976 Jan 16 06:40 tmp
drwxr-xr-x   18 root root    504 Dec 30 08:37 usr
drwxr-xr-x   18 root root    528 Dec 30 08:36 var
oes-linux:/ # ▯
🖳 ▣ Shell
```

Figure 10-41. *Use the ls –l command to get information about permissions and owners of files in your file system.*

1. In order to create the directory from a console window, use the command **mkdir /share**.

2. Use **chown franck.LUMgroup /share** to make user franck and the group LUMgroup owners of this directory.

3. Use **chmod 770 /share** to give read, write, and execute permissions to user franck as well as the group LUMgroup. Now, the user franck, as well as any user who is a member of LUMgroup, has access to the directory /share on the local Linux file system.

4. Now that you've arranged the local access for your users, you can define the Samba share. Let's keep it easy here: if you add the following lines to /etc/samba/smb.conf, you'll make the share /share accessible and writable for everyone who is a member of LUMgroup.

```
[share]
            comment = User documents
            path = /share
            public = yes
            writable = yes
            printable = no
            write list = @LUMgroup
```

5. The last thing you need to do is restart the Samba server. Once this is done, your Samba share will be accessible for anyone who is a member of LUMgroup. You can restart your Samba server with the command **/etc/init.d/smb restart**. This command, however, starts the Samba server only once. If you want it to start automatically each time your server boots, use the **chkconfig** command to add it to your default runlevel. On OES-Linux, use **chkconfig smb 235** to instruct the service to be started automatically. On other distributions, check the man-pages help file for the exact syntax.

■Tip You've just learned how to create a Samba share by hacking the configuration file directly. There is, of course, also the easy way: in OES - Linux, you can use iManager to create shares on the Samba server (just like on OES - NetWare). Select File Protocols ➤ CIFS/AFP. This option allows you to create Samba shares from the browser interface. There is, however, one condition: you need at least one NSS volume on the server to create the share. Chapter 11 has more on this.

Accessing Samba Shares

Now that you've successfully created a Samba share, you can access it both from Windows and Linux computers. The easiest way to do this is by connecting from a Windows computer, as explained in the following steps.

1. Open Windows Explorer and select Tools ➤ Map Network Drive.

2. Enter a valid username and password if asked for. You'll see the mapped network drive opened in a new Window.

3. You can map network drives from Windows to the Samba server like you map network drives to Windows servers.

Besides mapping drives from Windows, you can also access shared Samba drives from a Linux computer. One way to access a shared Samba drive is with the use of the mount command. Since only root can make a mount, usage in this way is rather limited, but it's an easy way to test if a shared Samba drive is accessible at all. In order to make the mount, you must have some available mount point on your local Linux computer. If nothing else is already mounted on it, you can use the directory /mnt for this purpose. If, for example, you want to access the share documents on the server named oes-linux, you can use the **mount** command like so: **mount -t smbfs -o username=franck //oes-linux/documents /mnt.** After you provided a valid password for this share, you can access all files in it from the directory /mnt on which it's mounted. A more common way to access a Samba share from a Linux desktop is from one of the many network browser tools available on Linux workstations. These tools allow you to browse to a share on your network and integrate the share in your local file manager.

Creating NCP Shares on OES - Linux

If you're using OES - Linux in an environment where clients using the Novell client software want to access shared files, you need the NCP server. On OES - Linux, this server has two roles. First, it allows users to access files stored on NSS volumes (see Chapter 11). On the other hand, NCP can be used to create shares on any other type of volume as well—for example, on a Linux ext3 or Reiser volume. This has two advantages:

- Users using the Novell client can access the NCP shares.

- On each NCP share, the administrator can configure the advanced Novell rights (see Chapter 12) to grant access to files on the share.

When NCP shares are created, these rights are stored in an XML file in the root of the NCP share. You'll now learn how to create an NCP share:

1. Start Remote Manager on https://*yourserver*:8009 and log in as admin.

2. From Manage NCP Services, select View Server Information, as shown in Figure 10-42. This option displays information about current NCP usage on your server.

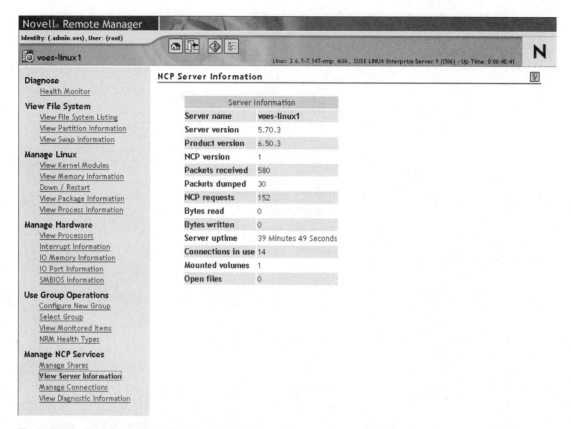

Figure 10-42. *Use Manage NCP Services from Remote Manager to get information about current NCP usage on your server.*

3. To create a new NCP share, after creating the directory you want to share on the Linux file system, select Manage NCP Services ➤ Manage Shares from Remote Manager. This displays the default share with the name SYS (see Figure 10-43). The share points to the directory /usr/novell/sys on your Linux file system. This share is needed because if a user connects to a server by using the Novell client, he must have a volume SYS to connect to. On that volume SYS, a directory "public" and a directory "login" should exist. This functionality is provided automatically through the share provided by NCP on the OES - Linux server.

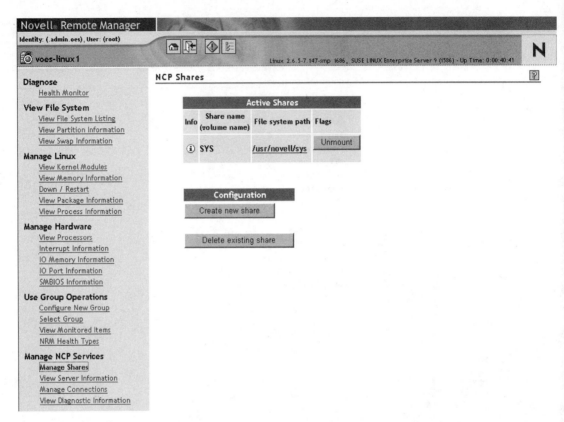

Figure 10-43. *To allow users to log in with the Novell client, a default share called SYS is present on all OES - Linux servers.*

4. To create a new share, click Create New Share. Enter a name for the share. This name will be available as a volume for the Novell clients that want to connect to it.

5. In the Path field, enter the name of the directory you want to share (unfortunately, no browse button is available). You must enter the name of the directory in its Linux format—for example, /share. Click OK to continue,

6. A summary of the share is now given. Click OK to create the share. The share is imme-diately added to the overview of active shares (see Figure 10-44). From this moment on, users can map a drive to it and access the new share.

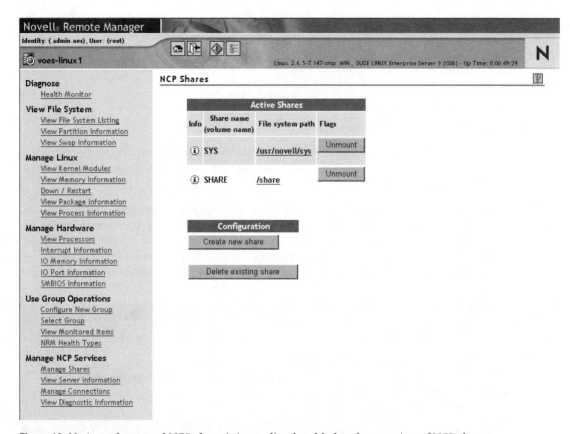

Figure 10-44. *A newly created NCP share is immediately added to the overview of NCP shares.*

■**Note** Unfortunately, it's not possible to manage the rights on your new share from iManager or Remote Manager. If you want to set rights, three options are available:

- As admin, make a drive mapping to the share on a workstation where the Novell client is installed and manage the rights on the share from the local file manager, such as Windows Explorer or Konqueror.

- Install ConsoleOne and access the NCP share from there. In ConsoleOne, you'll see the NCP share appearing as a volume on your server. Afterward, set its properties.

- Use the **rights** command from the OES - Linux console. (This command is only available if you've installed the NSS software components on your server.)

Chapter 12 has more information about setting file system rights.

Creating NFS Shares on OES - Linux

Like OES - NetWare, on OES - Linux it's also possible to create NFS shares. Since this is a traditional Linux service though, you won't create and manage it from iManager. Instead, this is done from SUSE YaST. Without going into detail about all the options, the next procedure explains how to create an NFS share on OES - Linux. Be aware that NFS is not a very secure protocol. It's recommended you instead use a protocol with more advanced options for user access management, such as Samba or NCP.

1. In YaST, select Network Services ➤ NFS Server.

2. Choose Start NFS Server and click Next.

3. In the next screen (see Figure 10-45), click Add Directory to specify a directory you want to export with NFS. You can use the Browse button to browse to the name of the directory you want to export.

4. A window appears where you can specify which hosts should get access to this directory. By default, an asterisk is used to specify that all hosts get access. You can modify this by entering a (partial) DNS name, an IP host address, or an IP network address. The default options used to get access are fine in most situations. If you want to enable remote hosts to write to the directory as well, change **ro** into **rw**. Click OK to save the modifications.

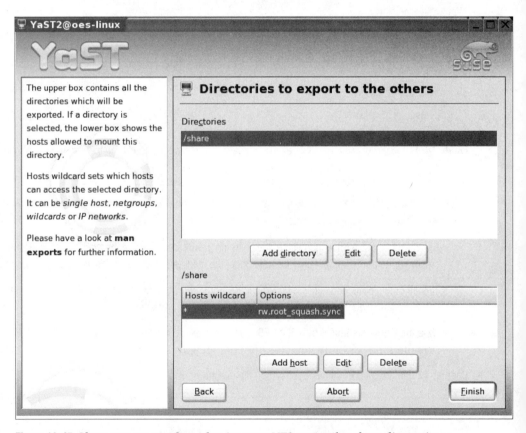

Figure 10-45. *If you want to use the rather insecure NFS protocol to share directories to other hosts, you can use SUSE's YaST.*

Planning Rights Management in an OES Environment

Open Enterprise Server offers the administrator a very flexible way to manage rights in his server environment. In the NSS file system, eight sophisticated rights are available to determine access for users. (Read more about these rights in Chapter 12.) These rights, however, are also available in the NCP file access protocol. The difficult thing about Open Enterprise Server, especially in its Linux version, is that different file access protocols and different file storage protocols can be used, each with its own set of rights. In OES - Linux, like on Microsoft Networks, you can set the rights at the file system itself (like on the NSS volume, or the Reiser volume). You can also set them at the share, like on the Samba share, the NFS share, or the NCP share. This can lead to very confusing situations.

To make rights management more transparent in an OES environment, the administrator should carefully plan where he wants to manage these rights. It doesn't make much sense setting all rights carefully at the volume level if you want to set them at the share level as well. The following rules help make rights management in an OES environment easier.

- If using OES - NetWare, use Novell rights as the NSS volume.

- If using OES - Linux, determine if you want to manage rights at the shares level or at the volumes level and stick with that.

- If you're using NSS or NCP—but not both of them—set rights at the NSS volume or the NCP share because these rights are more advanced than traditional UNIX rights.

- If you're using NSS, NCP is automatically used, and the only way to configure rights is at the NSS volume.

Consult Chapter 12 of this book for more detailed information about managing file system rights in an OES environment.

FTP

Many ways to access files on an OES - Server have been covered so far, but one option as yet untouched is one that uses an FTP server. Let's look at this option now. Though there's an FTP server for OES - Linux as well as for OES - NetWare, the configuration of these servers is quite different. Let's look at both next. For complete information, consult the online documentation at http://www.novell.com/documentation/oes.

In comparison to the other file access protocols discussed so far, FTP is a rather poor solution. This is especially true since it offers few options to secure access to the FTP server. Also, it's not possible to integrate FTP sites in a transparent way in the local file system, as is the case with NCP, Samba, or NFS. It is a good solution, however, when it comes to making files available for download since it's easy, transparent, and, most importantly, can be set up to run in its own environment so users can't get to other directories. In the next sections, you'll learn how to set up an FTP server on OES - NetWare and OES - Linux.

The OES - NetWare FTP Server

FTP on OES - NetWare is very useful since it provides a very basic way for users to access files on a server if no other option is available. Almost all client platforms have an FTP client as well, and by using the Novell FTP server you can grant access to files based on the eDirectory credentials of your users, so it's more secure than a normal FTP server. Besides, it's possible as well to establish a secured client session to the FTP server by using SSL/TLS. The following is a summary of all the advantages of the Novell FTP server. Notice that some of these are rather unique for the Novell FTP server.

- The ability to log in securely by using SSL/TLS

- Multiple instances of the FTP server on the same OES - NetWare server

- FTP access restrictions

- Intruder detection

- Access for authenticated users to other servers in the same eDirectory tree, even if on these servers the FTP process is not active

- The possibility to work with an anonymous user account

- Some special eDirectory-related commands that can be used from the FTP client

- Working with passive data ports, which makes it possible to connect even through a firewall

- The possibility to view details about active sessions

- Error reporting via SNMP

- A possibility to log errors to different kinds of files

- Multiprocessor-enabled

- Web-based administration with iManager

- The OES - NetWare FTP server is cluster-enabled for high performance and load balancing.

The Novell FTP server stores its information in the configuration file sys:etc\ftpserv.cfg. Of course, you can manage the settings in this file by hand, but an iManager interface is provided as well. The FTP Server Management interface is available from iManager Roles And Tasks ➤ File Protocols ➤ FTP. Before starting the procedure described next, make sure that the FTP server is installed using the Installation option on the OES - NetWare server console.

1. From the iManager FTP management interface, select the OES - NetWare server where you want to install the FTP server.

2. The configuration file that's installed by default is displayed. If you want to serve more than one FTP server from this OES - NetWare server, use the plus sign (+) to refer to the configuration files for these servers. This option is not covered in this book, refer to http://www.novell.com/documentation/oes for more information.

3. Click Start to start the FTP server. The management interface (as shown in Figure 10-46) now displays the Monitor Active FTP Sessions option. Use this option if you need to monitor who is currently using your FTP server. For further tuning of the FTP server, you should manually edit its configuration file sys:/etc/ftpserv.cfg.

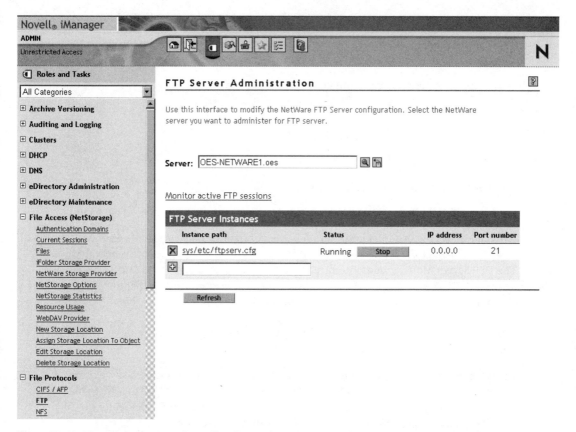

Figure 10-46. *The iManager interface offers limited options to configure the OES - NetWare FTP server.*

4. For tuning of the OES - NetWare FTP server, use an editor to edit the contents of its configuration file. This file is very well-documented and clearly indicates which options to use and which ones not to use. The following is a short overview of the most important of these.

- *DEFAULT_USER_HOME*: This parameter specifies the directory where the content is displayed when a user connects to the FTP server. By default, it refers to SYS:PUBLIC. You may want to change this to a directory where files are stored for the FTP server.

- *DEFAULT_FTP_CONTEXT*: Since the OES - NetWare FTP server integrates with eDirectory, you can use this parameter to specify which eDirectory context should be searched for the occurrence of FTP users. If nothing is specified, the context of the server is searched by default.

- *SEARCH_LIST*: If more than one container should be searched for users, specify a comma separated list of these containers at the SEARCH_LIST parameter.

The OES - Linux FTP Server

An FTP server is also available for OES - Linux: the Linux FTP server VSFtpd (the Very Secure FTP Server). Currently, administration of this server is not integrated into any of the Novell management utilities. All management has to be performed by hand by editing settings in the configuration file /etc/vsftpd.conf. Since this Linux FTP server has not been integrated with eDirectory yet, the only way to make it eDirectory-aware is by using the PAM configuration file /etc/pam.d/vsftpd. You can edit this file to also include the module pam_nam.so to authenticate to the network. This allows you to log in to the VSFtpd server by using your eDirectory credentials. More information about the setup of VSFtpd can be found in its documentation file or on the vsftpd.conf man page.

Summary

There are many ways to access files stored on OES - server, so you should be able to find a method suitable to your needs, whatever they may be. All the possibilities have been discussed in this chapter. First, you read about client-based access, which allows a user who has the Novell client software installed to access files on an OES server that runs NCP as well.

Discussion also centered on the very popular service, iFolder, which can be deployed to synchronize files between iFolder directories of a user that exist in more than one location. Even if a user normally only works from one location, iFolder can still be very useful since files are synchronized from the workstation to the server so they can be backed up by the latter. It's even possible to work with these files remotely from a web browser.

Another useful service that allows access to files is NetStorage. This interface provides one uniform way of accessing files, no matter where they're stored. NetStorage can work with files accessible from an iFolder directory, a Samba share, an NCP mapped directory or WebDAV.

After that, this chapter discussed the way native file access can be deployed. In an OES - NetWare environment, native file access methods exist for all major client platforms. In OES - Linux, files can also be made accessible for every client platform imaginable, but in this chapter you only learned how to configure OES - Linux as a Samba server since the OES - Linux Samba server integrates very nicely with eDirectory.

Last but not least, you read about deploying an FTP server in an OES environment.

In the next chapter, you'll learn about a very important system that sits behind file access in OES: the Novell Storage Services. This, along with other methods, works with volumes in an OES environment.

CHAPTER 11

■■■

Configuring Volumes

If you're working on a Windows or Linux system, you need to create a partition in order to store files. On OES, you must create partitions as well, since they're the starting point of any file system. In these partitions, however, volumes have to be created. If you're unfamiliar with the concept of volumes, you could describe them as some kind of logical entity within a partition. On OES - NetWare, the use of volumes is mandatory. It's not even possible to install OES - NetWare without at least creating a system volume called SYS. In OES - Linux, the use of volumes is optional. For storage of data files though, it's recommended to use volumes both on OES - NetWare and OES - Linux; on OES - Linux, this is suggested because Novell volumes offer advanced possibilities for management of file rights. Besides, NSS volumes are very fast and extremely flexible when used in a clustered environment. In this chapter, the following topics will be discussed.

- Traditional volumes versus NSS

- NSS architecture

- Creating traditional volumes on OES - NetWare

- Creating NSS volumes

- Working with volume attributes

- Maintaining volumes

- Implementing advanced NSS features

- Configuring iSCSI on NSS

Traditional Volumes vs. NSS

Since the early days of NetWare, Novell has used volumes for file storage. These volumes allow for more flexibility in a Novell file system and since a special Novell file system is used, the advanced Novell file system rights (as discussed in Chapter 9) can be implemented. There are, however, some drawbacks to the original volume design, one of the most important being that no journaling was available. It used to be that if you were on a NetWare 4.x server where the server crashed and files were damaged, upon server restart the notorious utility VREPAIR was started automatically. This utility checked the consistency of all tables on the volume and after that repaired any inconsistencies, something which took a long time. If you were lucky, the volume was repaired after no more than 15 minutes, but in some cases it took hours to repair a damaged volume. The bad thing was that the time to repair a volume increased as hard disk and volume size increased.

To remedy this, Novell Storage Services (NSS) was created, and shipped for the first time as part of NetWare 5.0 in 1998. NSS offers some major advantages compared to the old volume setup, but in rare cases it may still be necessary to use traditional volumes; this is the case when using Novell BorderManager Proxy Cache volumes. Therefore, in this chapter you'll learn how to create traditional volumes on OES - NetWare (traditional volumes are not supported on OES - Linux) and configure NSS volumes.

NSS provides the following benefits:

- NSS is a journaling file system. The advantage of a journaling file system becomes apparent in cases when the file system is shut down improperly and files are damaged. On a journaling file system, transactions on open files are logged. If the server crashes, upon restart the journal can be checked to find out which files were still open. These files can then easily be rolled back to their original version. For this reason, recovery on a journaling file system is much easier and quicker than recovering files on a traditional file system.

- Volumes can be created out of NSS pools. An NSS pool is a collection of free space taken from the available storage space on any supported device.

- Pool snapshots can be made. In a snapshot a "photo" is taken of the status of the file system at that moment. Based upon this picture, it's very easy to restore to a previous version.

- RAID 0 (striping), RAID 1 (mirroring), and RAID 5 (striping with parity) are supported by default.

- Distributed file services allow you to move and split volumes for easier management of storage growth.

- There is no limitation to the number of NSS volumes that can be stored on a partition.

- Data on the volumes can be encrypted (NetWare only) and other advanced features like data shredding are available as well.

- One NSS volume can span multiple storage devices for increased flexibility.

- Trillions of files can exist in one single directory.

- Lower memory requirements: there is no longer an ever-increasing Directory Entry Table that requires more and more memory; just 1MB of RAM is enough to mount any NSS volume, no matter what its size.

- NSS volumes can be shared to allow for cluster storage.

- CDs and DVDs are automatically mounted as NSS volumes.

- CD and DVD image files can be activated as NSS volumes.

- Recovery from crashes is very fast.

NSS Architecture

In the NSS architecture, storage devices, partitions, pools, and volumes allow for storage of files. The starting point of any volume is a partition on some device. On this partition, free space may be available. This free space is detected by the NSS storage provider and can be used to create an NSS pool. In an NSS pool, free space from different storage devices on a server can be put together. From the NSS pool, volumes can be created. This is outlined in Figure 11-1.

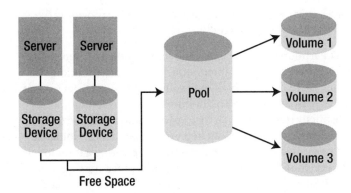

Figure 11-1. *The NSS architecture*

Upon installation of OES - NetWare, NSS volumes are automatically created. If you want NSS volumes on OES - Linux, you must create them manually after the initial installation is completed. By default on OES - NetWare, an NSS pool sys is created automatically with a volume named SYS: inside it. This volume does not have a fixed size, but can grow to the size of the pool, which is 4GB by default. This system pool and volume should only be used for your system files. Volumes to store data files must be created manually in other storage pools.

Within an NSS pool, NSS volumes must be created as logical volumes. You can add any number of volumes to a pool, and these volumes can be created with a fixed size. It's possible as well to create a volume that can grow dynamically to the size of the pool. In the latter scenario, only a maximum size has to be defined for the volume. When you're creating more than one NSS volume in a pool, the feature of overbooking can be used to allow for more flexibility. For example, imagine a 500GB NSS pool in which you want to create two volumes: one for applications and one for data files. If you wanted to create these volumes with a fixed size like you had to when using NetWare 4 traditional volumes, you would have made an estimate of the amount of disk space needed for each of these volumes. In this scenario, you could choose, for example, to create a data volume of 400 GB and an application volume of 100GB. If, however, the data volume was entirely filled up with no space left, but the applications volume had 80GB of disk space available, it would be very difficult to reallocate available disk space from the application volume to the data volume. This problem doesn't exist if you use the overbooking feature in NSS, where upon creation of the application volume and the data volume, you specify that the volumes are allowed to grow to a maximum of 500GB each (meaning that theoretically both can be 500GB). The advantage in this scenario is that it allows for maximum flexibility, since available storage space will be available automatically in the volume where you need it. On OES, overbooking is enabled by default for all new volumes.

Creating Traditional Volumes on OES - NetWare

Because it's very flexible, it's recommended you use NSS instead of traditional volumes. If, however, you're running an application on OES - NetWare that still needs a traditional volume, like Novell BorderManager for its cache, it's possible to create one. To create a traditional volume, Novell Remote Manager must be used (in iManager you'll only find options to create NSS volumes), as explained in the following steps.

1. Navigate to Remote Manager at https://yourserver:8009 and log in by providing the name of your admin user as well as your password.

2. From Manage Server, select Partition Disks to display the screen shown in Figure 11-2. This displays an overview of current storage adapters, attached devices, partitions, and existing NSS pools and volumes. To create a traditional volume, you need a device that still has unallocated disk space. In the overview of the current storage configuration of your devices, this will be distinctly marked as Free Disk Space. It's also possible that you may see a device where no storage has been configured yet. In that case, an Initialize Partition Table link should be available. In this scenario, you are creating a traditional volume on a device that has existing free disk space. To start this procedure, click the Create link next to "Free Disk Space." If the device hasn't been initialized yet, first click Initialize Partition Table.

3. On the next screen, select NetWare Traditional File System from the Partition Type drop-down list. Next, select Create A New Partition if you want to first create a new partition and then later create more than one new traditional volume. Or select Create a New Partition And Volume to create a new partition and a new volume at the same time. In this procedure, the latter is demonstrated. The next screen can be shown in Figure 11-3.

4. The available disk space will be displayed. By default, all available disk space will be claimed by the new partition, but it's easy to modify this by entering any amount of disk space you want to use for the new partition. Next, enter a name for the volume and the size of the volume you want to create. You can make the volume the same size as the partition, but it's possible as well to make it smaller. You do need to specify a fixed size for this volume, however; overbooking is only available for NSS volumes.

5. Specify the block size you want to use. In general, it's better to use big blocks since it makes the volume faster.

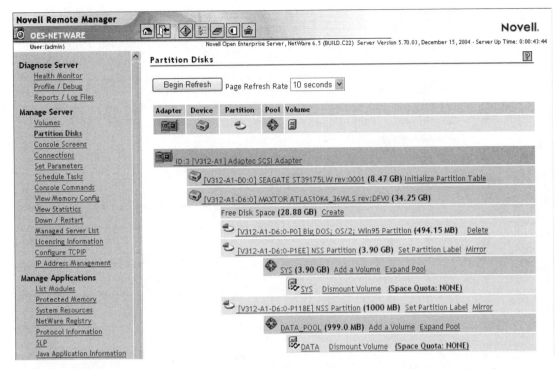

Figure 11-2. *Available free space can be displayed as Free Disk Space or be seen on a new device by using Initialize Partition Table.*

6. Now indicate which options you want to use. The following options are available:

   • *Compression*: This enables the compression of individual files on the volume. Since compression is a processor-intensive process and disk space is cheap nowadays, it's generally recommended that you don't use it. If you want to use disk compression anyway, several set parameters are available to tune the working of the compression process. With these parameters, it's possible to indicate exactly under what circumstances the compression engine may be started. You'll find an overview of these parameters later in this chapter in the section "Creating NSS Volumes." The compression engine used on traditional volumes is the same as the compression engine used on NSS volumes.

   • *Sub-allocation*: if you've chosen to work with 64K blocks on the volume, a minimum of 64K will be reserved for any file you write to the system. So if, for example, you write a 1-byte file to the system, a 64K block will be claimed anyway. In this scenario, you lose nearly 64K of available disk space. If sub-allocation is enabled, the default blocks on your system can be divided into sub-allocation units with a minimal size of 512 bytes. In this scenario, if sub-allocation is enabled, you no longer lose 65535 bytes of available disk space; this is cut down to just 511 bytes. In general, sub-allocation is a very useful feature, but it unfortunately can't work with some applications. In that case, you have to disable it.

- *Migration*: In a network environment where many files have to be available at all times, a near-line storage medium may be deployed. This can be, for example, a tape-robot that is connected directly to your server. If a file hasn't been touched for a long time, it can be migrated automatically to the near-line storage medium. When it's on this medium, users can still access the file, but it will take considerably longer to access it from a near-line storage medium as compared to a real hard drive. Select this option if near-line storage is available on your network. The advantage of using near-line storage solutions are that they allow you to store large amounts of files for direct access on the network.

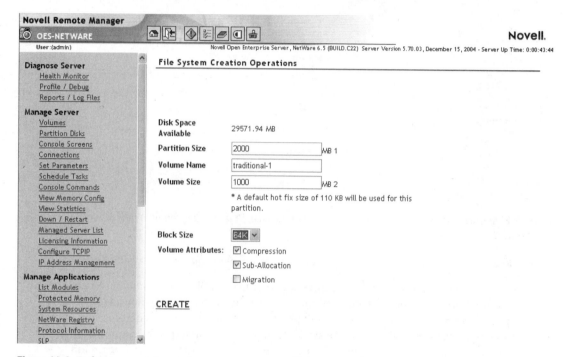

Figure 11-3. *Before you create a volume, you must specify its properties.*

7. After specifying all options for the new volume, select Create to create it. Click OK in the pop-up window to continue the creation of the volume. You'll see that it's added imme-diately to the list of available storage on your server. From this overview, click Mount Volume to mount the volume on your server. In Figure 11-4, you can see the new volume on the fourth line from the bottom. Available free space on the device where the new volume was created has also gone down given the size of the new volume.

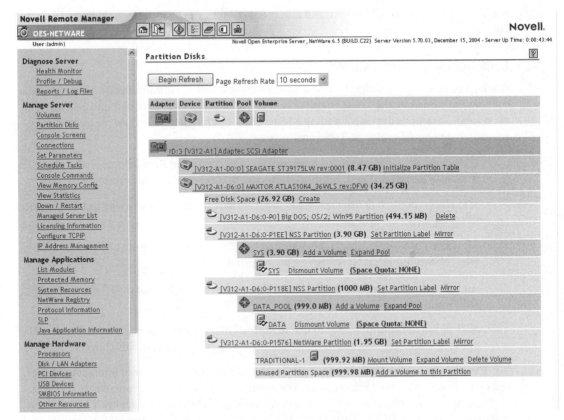

Figure 11-4. *Newly created volumes are immediately added to the list of available storage devices.*

Creating NSS Volumes

The procedure to create a traditional volume is rather straightforward: simply claim the available disk space and assign it to the traditional volume. It's more difficult to create an NSS volume, mainly because more components are involved and NSS allows for more different options, but that's not the only reason. If you want to enable NSS on Linux, you must have a disk available to be managed by EVMS, which is a non-default file system required to create NSS volumes. On OES - NetWare, the procedure is easier because you have to first create a partition, followed by an NSS pool and volume.

Working with NSS Volumes on OES - Linux

The major problem if you want to work with NSS volumes on OES - Linux is that you need a disk managed by EVMS. The boot partition /boot and the system partition / are by default managed by the Logical Volume Manager (LVM). If a disk is managed by LVM, it cannot be managed by EVMS, since only one device manager can manage the volume at a time. It's there-fore recommended you use a separate disk where no LVM volumes already exist to create your NSS volumes on OES - Linux. Although in this chapter I will also explain how to prepare a hard disk for EVMS if it is the only hard disk in your server, I strongly recommend using a separate disk for NSS.

Traditional Linux Volumes vs. NSS

When a Linux server is installed, some Linux volumes are added automatically. These Linux volumes are formatted in a native Linux file system like Reiser or ext3. Both of them are journaling file systems, so what's the use of adding NSS to OES - Linux? There are a few reasons why an administrator should prefer NSS volumes anyway:

- NSS allows an administrator to work with the advanced set of Novell rights on the volume instead of just basic Read, Write, and Execute that exist in the Linux universe.

- NSS is very robust: it doesn't use tables to access files, but is based on a very fast database to allow for faster file access.

- An NSS volume on Linux can be migrated to OES - NetWare without any problem. Likewise, NSS volumes on NetWare can be migrated to Linux.

- An NSS volume is present in eDirectory as well, but this is not the case for native Linux volumes.

- NSS allows the administrator to use advanced NSS features that don't exist on other file systems. More information on these features is discussed later in this chapter.

The presence of the NSS volume in eDirectory allows you to do a lot of interesting things you can't do with a native Linux volume. For example, it's possible to create user home directories on it, to map drives to it from a Novell client environment and to deploy it for services that depend on it like Novell Clustering Services (NCS). In short, if you use OES - Linux just for eDirectory and some services that don't rely heavily on a native Novell file system (like iFolder or iPrint), you can do perfectly well without NSS. If, however, you want to take advantage of the strong system of rights offered by NSS, or want to use Novell services that depend on NSS, you need NSS volumes on Linux as well.

■Tip If you just want to work with the enhanced set of Novell rights, just create an NCP-share on a Linux volume. This NCP share will be represented in eDirectory as a volume object as well, thus allowing you to put eDirectory related things like the user's home directory on it.

Preparing OES Linux for NSS upon Installation

The best way to install NSS volumes on OES - Linux is by using a separate hard drive for the NSS volumes. It is, however, also possible to use NSS volumes besides Reiser volumes if a server just has one hard disk. In such cases, when OES - Linux is installed, some additional steps must be performed.

Caution The procedure described next is not yet stable in OES in its first release. Future versions of OES will likely make the process easier, but for the present I can't guarantee your success in using it to create NSS volumes. Therefore, I strongly suggest you only create NSS volumes on a separate hard disk. Think of the following procedure as merely a workaround, not as something to be used on a production server.

By default, OES - Linux installs LVM as the volume manager on a server's hard drive by using the procedure described next, thus allowing EVMS to be configured as the volume manager for your hard drive. Since this is the only condition needed to configure an NSS volume, afterward you can create NSS volumes on OES - Linux on the same drive that the Linux file system is installed on.

Caution The following procedure will delete all data from your server's hard drive!

1. When installing OES - Linux from the Installation Settings screen, select Partitioning.

2. Choose Create Custom Partition Setup and then click Next.

3. Select Custom Partitioning—For Experts. Then, select Next.

4. Choose Expert ➤ Delete Partition Table and Disk Label.

5. Read the warning and click Yes twice. This deletes all data that currently exists on your server's hard drive.

6. Now that the old partitions on your server's hard drive have been deleted, you can create a boot partition and an EVMS partition. The boot partition cannot be an EVMS partition, so in this procedure you have to create it as a separate partition. To create the boot partition, select Create and then click Primary Partition. Click OK to continue. Use the following specifications to create the new partition and then click OK again.

   • From Format, select ext3.

   • In the Size box, click End and enter the value **250M**.

   • Set the mount point to /boot.

7. Now you can create an EVMS partition to create other volumes on your server's hard drive. Make sure you don't use all the available disk space on your server's hard drive, otherwise you won't have any free space to create NSS volumes. Select Create and then choose Primary Partition. Next, click OK to enter the screen where you can specify all the properties of the EVMS partition you want to use. Use the following specifications and then click OK to continue:

- Select Do Not Format.

- In the File System ID drop-down list, choose 0x8E Linux LVM.

- From the Size box, select End and specify the size of the partition you want to create. For example, if you want to create a 50GB partition, enter the value +50GB.

8. You have just created a partition that's ready for EVMS. Now it's time to create EVMS volumes on this partition. This is a two-step procedure. First, you have to create an NSS container, and then in the EVMS container you must create the EVMS volumes. As part of the first step, from the Expert Partitioner screen, select EVMS. This opens the EVMS Configurator screen, as shown in the illustration below. On this screen, click Create Container. You'll need this container to create EVMS volumes later. In the Device list you'll see one of two possible devices: the device sda (your SCSI hard disk) or the device hda (an IDE hard disk). You'll also see a device with a number added to it, like sda2. Select this device, verify that the container name is system, and then click Add Volume. Next, click OK to close the screen. This brings you back to the EVMS Configurator main screen.

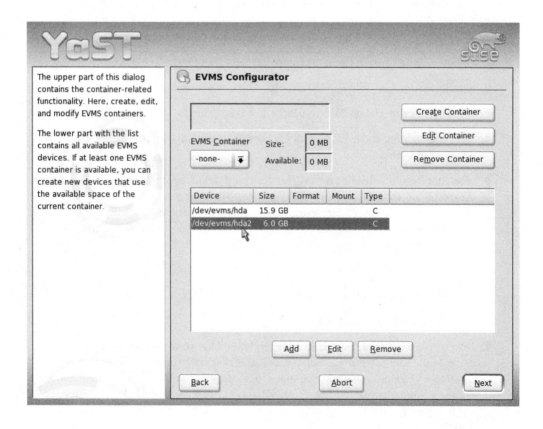

9. Now that you've created the EVMS container, it's time to generate the EVMS volumes for it. These EVMS volumes are similar to logical partitions that are created in an extended partition. Make at least a swap volume and a Linux root file system volume. Steps 10 and 11 show you how to create these volumes.

10. To create a swap volume, click the Add option. Make sure the lvm/system container is selected and then specify the properties of the swap volume. Be certain the file system type swap is selected, enter a volume name, and then specify the swap volume size. In most cases, 1GB is enough to create the swap volume.

11. Select Add Volume again and enter the properties to create a Linux root file system volume. After entering these properties, select OK and then click Next.

    • Select the ext3 file system type.

    • Enter a volume name, like sysvolume.

    • Create the volume with the remaining disk space by clicking the Max button.

    • Verify that the moint point is set to the root directory (/) of the file system.

12. After creating the volumes, click Next twice to continue. Read the warning, as shown in the illustration below, about EVMS and non-EVMS being on the same hard drive and accept it by clicking Yes. This step finalizes the preparation of your server's hard drive for the creation of NSS volumes.

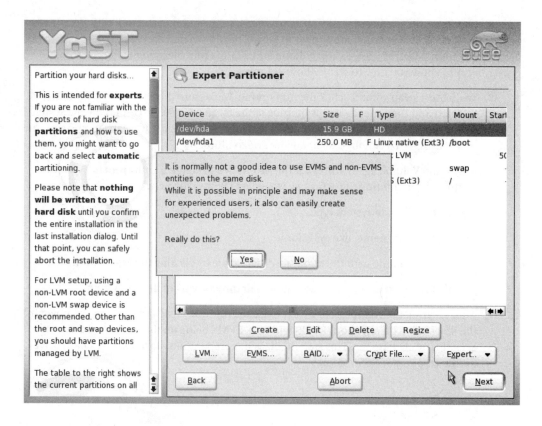

13. From the Installation Settings screen, select the software option and make sure Novell NSS is selected. Then, continue the installation procedure, as described in chapter 2 of this book.

When the installation is complete, you must perform some additional steps: the EVMS boot-script /etc/init.d/boot.evms has to be modified so the EVMS system can function properly. Next, you have to change the mount lines in /etc/fstab. You also have to modify the startup procedure to disable some services that are needed for LVM only on system boot. In the next procedure, you'll first disable these services and then modify the EVMS boot script.

1. From YaST, select System ➤ Runlevel Editor. In the runlevel editor, choose Expert Mode. This shows an overview of all services started automatically. Make the following modifications to the list. After making these changes, click Finish to save them.

   • Select runlevel B for boot.evms.

   • Deselect the B option for both boot.lvm and boot.md.

2. Open the configuration file /etc/fstab with an editor. Next, you have to change the mount lines for all EVMS-volumes. For example: /dev/hda2 must be changed to /dev/evms/hda2. Repeat this procedure for all EVMS volumes.

3. Open the file /etc/init.d/boot.evms in an editor and scroll down until you see a line with stop). Find the line echo -n *"Stopping EVMS"*: and add the following lines immediately under it.

```
mount -n -o remount,rw/
echo -en "\nDeleting devices nodes"
rm -rf/dev/evms
mount -n --o remount,ro/
```

4. Save the modified file and restart your server. When the server has restarted, you can continue and add NSS volumes to your server, as described in the section "Creating NSS Volumes on OES - Linux."

Creating NSS Volumes on OES - Linux

To create NSS volumes on OES - Linux, you need the EVMS volume manager. The problem is that, by default, SUSE Linux Enterprise Server 9 uses Linux Volume Management (LVM) and the kernel prevents multiple volume managers from managing the same device. As a result, EVMS may display free space that it cannot manage. To prevent display of space unavailable to EVMS, modify the /etc/evms.conf file to exclude a specific device for use by EVMS. If you don't want to convert LVM volumes to EVMS volumes, you need to do this for the drive that your Linux root-partition (/) is on. This implies that you have another disk available to be used by EVMS. To exclude device /dev/sda from usage by EVMS, edit /etc/evms.conf as follows:

```
sysfs_devices {
...
exclude = [sda]
}
```

Alternatively, it's possible to install EVMS as the default volume manager as described in the previous section or to convert LVM volumes to EVMS volumes after SLES installation, but this is a rather complicated procedure that this book doesn't recommend. Hopefully, it will get better when OES support packs are released.

After you've done all the necessary EVMS preparation, you can create NSS volumes on OES - Linux. iManager is the recommended tool for creating NSS volumes on OES - Linux. When creating NSS volumes, it's possible to create all necessary elements step by step. In this procedure, however, I'll explain the easiest way to do it, by creating an NSS volume and all other dependant objects automatically. In this procedure, a separate disk is used that's managed by EVMS.

■**Tip** If you're already experienced in managing NSS volumes on the NetWare platform, then I have good news for you! Good old NSSMU, which allows you to create NSS volumes on NetWare, is available on OES - Linux as well. Just enter the command **nssmu** from the shell and you'll be provided with a nice NSS Management Utility interface. Never worked with it? In the next section, which discusses how to create NSS volumes on OES - NetWare, you'll learn how to create NSS volumes from NSSMU.

---

1. Before you can configure NSS on OES - Linux, you must install it from YaST. On the OES - Linux console, launch YaST. Enter the administrator password and select System ➤ NSS. This launches the NSS configuration utility.

2. Follow the prompts to install the NSS files on your server. Insert the required CDs in the CD drive of your computer when asked for.

3. After installation of the NSS program files, you're prompted for the LDAP server configuration. Select Local System if eDirectory is running on this server, or choose Remote System if you need to contact eDirectory on another server. Next, enter the IP address, admin name, and password needed to write information in eDirectory.

4. Now enter the object name of the NSS admin volume that must be created for this server. In almost all situations, the default name is fine. Click Next to continue. The NSS settings are now written to your computer. You can proceed with managing NSS volumes from iManager now.

5. Start your browser and access iManager at https://yourserver/nps. Next, log in as a user with supervisory rights to the server and the container where you want to create the NSS objects.

6. From Roles And Tasks, select Storage Devices. Your browser window should now resemble Figure 11-5. Next, browse to your OES - Linux server and verify that the device in which you want to create the NSS volume is present. If you find that the device where you want to create the NSS volume is not present, make sure the settings in the configuration file /etc/evms.conf are as described in the introduction of this section.

Tip From iManager, only Novell volumes can be managed. If any non-Novell volumes exist on the hard disk that you want to use for your NSS volumes (like ext3 or Reiser), delete them first with YaST2. You'll find the Partitioner tool to modify the content of an existing hard drive in the YaST2 System menu.

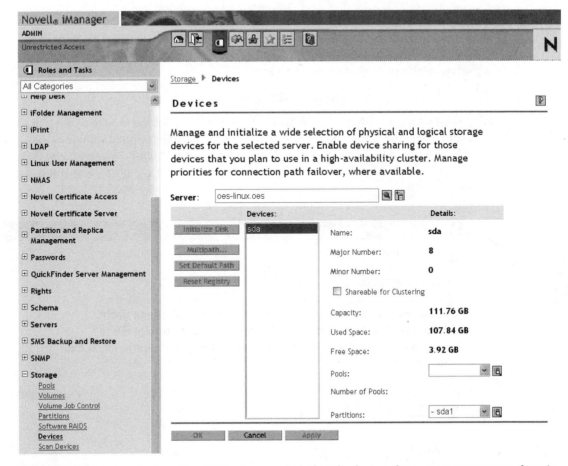

Figure 11-5. *Before you start making NSS volumes, verify that the device where you want to create them is recognized properly.*

7. Now, select Storage ➤ Volumes and browse to the OES - Linux server where you want to create the volume. Next, click New to specify the properties of the new volume. This starts a short wizard that helps you create the NSS volume.

8. Enter the name of the volume you want to create and click Next.

9. If there are already NSS pools present on your server, select a pool from the list of those available, and then create the volume inside it. If this is the first NSS volume on your server, click New Pool to create a new pool.

10. Enter a name for the new pool and click Next to continue.

11. A window appears where you can specify the size of the pool you want to create (see Figure 11-6). You can see how much space is available on the selected volume as well; select the amount of disk space you want to assign to this volume. Also make sure that the option Mount On Creation is selected and click Finish to complete the creation of your NSS pool.

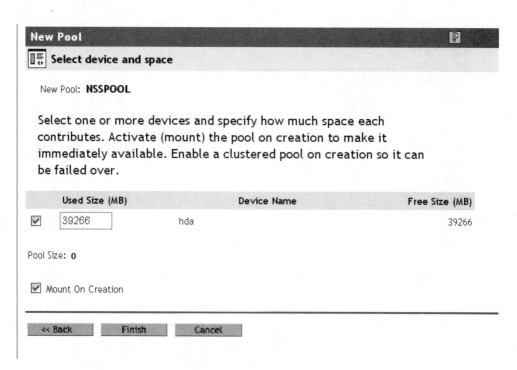

Figure 11-6. *All you have to do to create the NSS pool is select its size.*

12. Now that you've created the pool, you can create its volume as well. In order to create the volume, first select the pool where you want to create it. Since you've just created the pool, select it from the New Volume screen (as shown in Figure 11-7). Next, choose Allow Volume Quota To Grow To The Pool Size to automatically allocate as much space as needed to the volume. If more than one volume exists in a pool, specify the maximum size for the volume. To do that, deselect Allow Volume Quota To Grow To The Pool Size and select the volume quota you want to use. Click Next to continue.

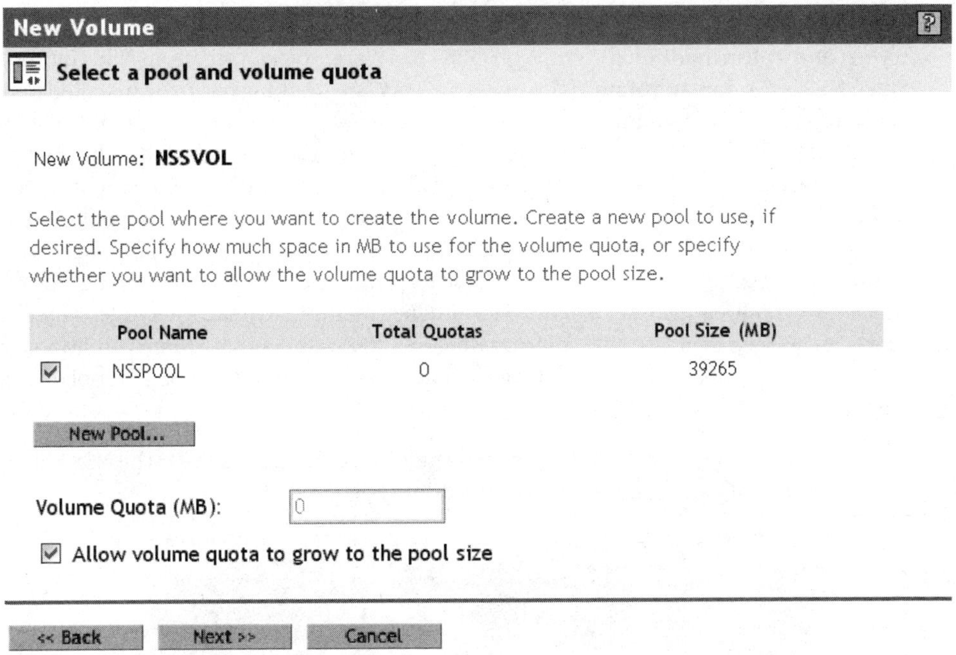

New Volume

Select a pool and volume quota

New Volume: **NSSVOL**

Select the pool where you want to create the volume. Create a new pool to use, if
desired. Specify how much space in MB to use for the volume quota, or specify
whether you want to allow the volume quota to grow to the pool size.

Pool Name	Total Quotas	Pool Size (MB)
☑ NSSPOOL	0	39265

New Pool...

Volume Quota (MB): `0`

☑ Allow volume quota to grow to the pool size

<< Back   Next >>   Cancel

Figure 11-7. *Specify which pool you want to create the volume in and how much space to
allocate to it.*

13. A list of attributes that can be assigned to the volume are displayed. (The following
    section offers an overview of these attributes and their use. Be aware that some attributes
    can only be set during volume creation.) Apart from the attributes, you can also specify
    whether the volumes must be activated and mounted on creation. Additionally, you
    can choose a mount point. This is a directory in the Linux file system where the volume
    will be mounted. From this mount point, the contents of the NSS volume can be accessed
    directly from the Linux server. As a user, however, you normally don't need this mount
    point, because you can access it from one of the shares that give access to the volume.
    The default mount point is set to /media/nss/NSSVOL (where NSSVOL is the name
    you've given to the volume). If you're happy with all the settings, click Finish to create
    the volume and mount it on the Linux server.

Note Since the NSS volume will be accessed from the OES - Linux console only by the administrator of
the OES - Linux server, it's not important to create a mount point that is easily accessible for users. Users only
access the NSS volume from their workstations. Therefore, the default mount point is good enough in most
scenarios.

14. The NSS volume is now created and you can use it like any other eDirectory volume.
    Select Roles and Tasks ➤ Volumes to verify its properties.

Creating NSS Volumes on OES - NetWare

If you can create a traditional volume on OES - NetWare, you can create an NSS volume as well. Since NSS is the default volume type on OES - NetWare, nothing has to be installed before you can start creating NSS volumes. You do, however, need to make a choice on how you want to install the NSS-volume. One possibility is to first create an NSS pool and after the pool has been added, create NSS volumes in it. This method allows for maximal flexibility. If however you want to start using an entire hard disk and dedicate the entire hard disk to a new NSS volume, you can choose to create the NSS Volume without first creating the NSS pool. In this scenario, a pool will be added automatically and will be the same size as the NSS volume. In the following procedure, you'll learn how to add the pool and the volume in two separate steps. Three different tools can be used to create NSS volumes on OES - NetWare: Remote Manager, iManager, and the server-based utility NSSMU. In this procedure, you'll deploy the NSSMU tool on the server to create the NSS pool and volume.

1. Access the console of your server and enter the command **NSSMU**. The NSS Management Utility will be started, as shown in Figure 11-8.

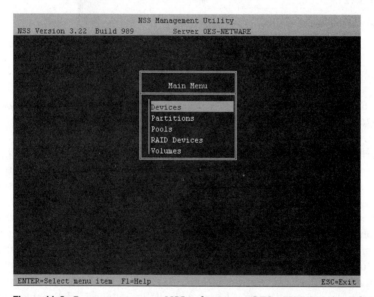

Figure 11-8. *One way to create NSS volumes on OES - NetWare is with NSSMU.NLM.*

2. From the NSS Management Utility interface, select Devices to display a list of all available devices. Verify that your device is listed here. If it's not listed, use the command **scan for new devices** on the OES - NetWare console to instruct the operating system to scan for new devices and then repeat this procedure.

3. Now select Partitions. A list of all currently existing partitions will be displayed. Select a partition to display its properties. To create a new partition, press the Insert key on your keyboard. You'll now get an overview of available free space. Select the free space where you want to create the partition used by NSS (see Figure 11-9) and press Enter to continue.

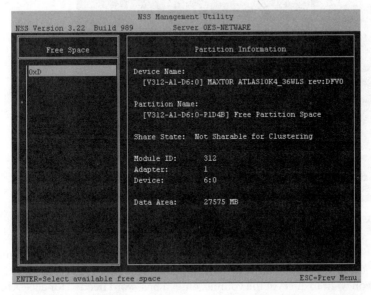

Figure 11-9. *To create a partition, you must select the free space that you want to create the partition in.*

4. Select the partition type you want to create. You can choose between iSCSI and NSS. Select NSS and press Enter to continue; you'll learn how to configure iSCSI later in this chapter. In New partition Size, specify the amount of disk space you want to reserve for the new partition; press Enter to continue. Next, select Create to create the partition and press Escape twice to return to the NSSMU main screen.

5. Now that you've created a partition for NSS, select Pools from the NSSMU main menu to start creating an NSS Pool. A list of NSS pools present will be displayed. Amongst these pools, you'll notice that a SYS pool is already present for the OES - NetWare system volume. Press the Insert key on your keyboard to create a new pool. Next, enter a name for the new pool and press Enter.

6. You'll now see an overview of all available free storage on your server (as shown in Figure 11-10). In this overview, you'll notice that the partition you've just created is listed, but all unpartitioned space on your hard drive will be listed as well. You can choose either the partition that is just created, or the unpartitioned disk space to create the NSS pool. Select the partition you've just created and press Enter to create the NSS pool. The new pool will be added to the overview immediately. You can activate it and press Enter to see its properties. Next, press Enter to return to the NSSMU main menu.

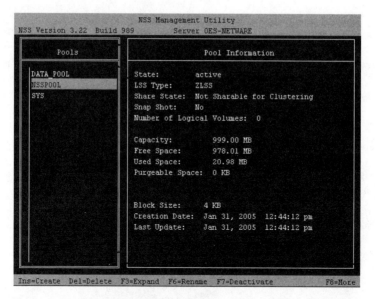

Figure 11-10. *Select the new pool and press Enter to see its properties.*

7. From the NSS main menu, select Volumes and press Insert to create a new volume. Next, enter the new volume name. You'll be asked if you want to encrypt the NSS volume. If you want to encrypt the volume, enter a password needed for access to the encrypted files and continue. If you don't want to encrypt the volume, from the list of NSS pools, select the NSS pool where you want to create the new volume. Next, specify some volume properties (see Figure 11-11). Most of these properties can only be set upon volume creation, so think carefully about what you want to do here. The following options are available:

• *Backup*: Use this option if data exists on the volume that you want to be able to back up.

• *Compression*: This attribute allows you to compress files on the volume. You can only set this attribute upon volume creation. The behavior of compression itself can be tuned with the compression-related set parameters.

• *Datashredding*: When data is deleted from a volume, it can still be accessed by someone using advanced tools like a disk editor. The data shredding attribute allows you to electronically overwrite deleted and purged data areas so that the data cannot be recovered. Data can be shredded a maximum of seven times, which guarantees the highest level of protection.

• *Directory Quotas*: If you want to be able to assign a maximum quota of space a directory can consume, you have to set the directory quotas option.

• *Modified File List*: The modified file list (MFL) is an alternative to the DOS archive attribute. It provides a list of all files modified since the last backup. The vendor of your backup software must implement this feature, otherwise it's useless.

- *Salvage Files*: If you specify that you want to use the salvage option, all deleted files are kept for recovery until the space where the deleted file is kept is needed for the storage of other data. If you want to be able to restore files with the salvage option, this option has to be enabled at the volume level. Later in this chapter in the section "Salvaging and Deleting Files," you'll learn how files can be salvaged and how deleted files can be purged.

- *Snapshot – File level*: Under normal circumstances, an open file cannot be backed up. The file-level snapshot attribute enables a backup utility to capture the last closed version of a file at the time when a backup is in progress.

- *User Space Restrictions*: Two ways exist to restrict available space on a volume: the directory space restriction and user space restriction. Use the user space restriction attribute to restrict space to specific users.

- *Flush Files Immediately*: Under normal circumstances, data written to the hard drive of your server must wait in the cache for the next write cycle of your hard drive before it's written to disk. This involves a certain amount of risk: if the server fails while this data is still in the cache, the data is lost forever. To prevent this, you can use the Flush Files Immediately attribute, with the cost of a small performance hit: all files on which this bit is marked are written to disk immediately without being cached first.

- *Migration*: Use this attribute to migrate to a near-line storage medium possible.

- *Read Ahead Count in Blocks*: To speed up searches on an NSS volume, a read ahead feature is enabled. This feature specifies that the server should always try to read the next two blocks of data, even if there is no specific request for these blocks. A limited read ahead will improve performance of your disk system.

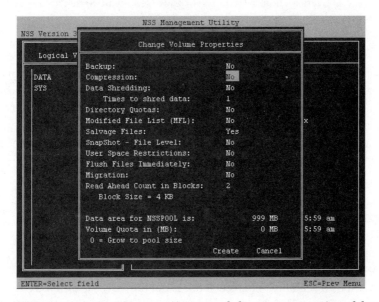

Figure 11-11. *Some NSS properties can only be set upon creation of the volume.*

8. After selecting all required attributes, select Create to create the volume. Next, press Alt+F8 to update eDirectory with the new volume to ensure that the volume is added to the directory. If you get an error message saying that there's already a volume with such a name at the specified context, cancel the action since the volume will have already been added successfully. You're ready to create the volume now, which is added to the eDirectory database.

Maintaining Volumes

Now that you have some NSS volumes in your tree, you'll have to start managing them! Some management tasks can be performed on NSS volumes. In this section, you'll find an overview of some of the most important tasks.

Activating and Deactivating Volumes

Before you can use an NSS volume, it has to be activated. Normally, this is done automatically when you boot up your server. There are, however, instances where you'll want to activate and deactivate an NSS volume manually (for example, because you have to perform some maintenance tasks on it). It's very easy to activate and deactivate NSS volumes from iManager:

1. Start iManager and select Roles and Tasks ➤ Storage ➤ Volumes.

2. Select the server on which you want to activate or deactivate a volume.

3. In the volumes list now displayed, select one or more volumes you want to make active or inactive.

4. Click Activate to activate an inactive volume or click Deactivate to deactivate a volume that is currently active.

■**Note** An NSS volume can be activated and it can be mounted. You can also deactivate it or dismount it. You're probably wondering what the difference is. Well, when a volume is deactivated, it's no longer accessible for users, but programs can still access it. If, however, a volume is dismounted, neither users nor programs can access the volume. For example, if you need to perform some management tasks on a volume, you should deactivate it, but you should not dismount it, because the management program will not have access to a dismounted volume.

Accessing CDs and DVDs on OES - NetWare

Normal volumes that exist on a hard drive of your server can be activated from iManager. If you're using OES - NetWare, this is not the case for CDs and DVDs you insert in the drive of your server. On OES - Linux, however, the Linux kernel automatically recognizes the new medium and mounts it if automount is enabled. If this is not the case, use the Linux **mount** command to activate a CD or DVD.

To support CDs and DVDs on OES - NetWare, a special module with the name cddvd.nss is needed. You can activate this module by just typing **cddvd.nss** on the server console (normally, it should be activated automatically when your server boots). If at that moment a CD or DVD is in the drive, it will automatically be mounted. If after loading cddvd.nss on your server you insert a new CD or DVD, it will automatically be mounted, with the disk's label as its volume name. If no label is available, cddvd.nss dynamically generates a volume name that looks like CD_*nnn* (where *n* is a number). This volume can be accessed like any other NetWare volume. If you also need to add the CD or DVD to eDirectory, use the command **nss /UpdateCDtoNDS=*cdname***.

Accessing CD and DVD Image Files on OES - NetWare

Since NetWare 6.5 Support Pack 2, the option has existed to mount CD and DVD image files as read-only volumes as well. This is also supported by cddvd.nss. To mount an image file, you must use the MountImageVolume switch with the **nss** command; to dismount it, use the RemoveImageVolume switch. There is one condition to mount CD or DVD image files this way: they have to be present on an NSS volume. For example, use the following command to mount an image file as an NSS volume: **nss /MountImageVolume=nssvol:\sles9_1.iso**.

Tip The **nss** command on the OES - NetWare server has many options. To get an overview of all available options, enter **nss /help**. This shows you a complete list of all available NSS options. On OES - Linux, use **nsscon** instead of the **nss** utility.

Accessing DOS Partitions as NSS Volumes

NSS is very flexible. The only thing you need is the right NSS module; NSS supports virtually all storage devices on OES - NetWare. One of these devices is the DOS partition used on your server to boot it. This partition can be mounted as an NSS volume as well, which is very useful because when the DOS partition is mounted as a volume, it's easy to copy files to and from it. In order to access files on the DOS partition, the NSS module dosfat.nss is needed. When you load this module, all available DOS partitions will be mounted automatically. You can then access them from eDirectory, map drives to them, and all OES - NetWare utilities can freely access them.

Exporting NSS Volumes with NFS on OES - Linux

NSS is the best way to work with NetWare files. If, however, you want to make an NSS volume on OES - Linux accessible to other Linux users, you can export it with the Linux Network File System (NFS). Every Linux or UNIX client natively supports this file system; an NFS-exported NSS volume will therefore be accessible natively for every Linux client. This client, however, will not be able to benefit from special features like the famous Novell rights, since to use them a Novell client is needed as well.

1. On your OES - Linux server, start YaST2 and select Network Services ➤ NFS Server.

2. Select Start NFS Server and click Next.

3. In the window Directories To Export To The Others, click the Add Directory selection. Next, enter the complete path to the mount point of your NSS volume for an NSS volume with the name NSSVOL; the default path will be /opt/novell/nss/mnt/volumes/ NSSVOL with the name of the volume in uppercase.

4. In the next screen, select the options rw, no_root_squash, sync, and fsid=value. The first three options are more or less defaults and specify that the volume will be mounted with read/write access, user root will have normal access, and file system writes are synchronized to disk immediately. The last option is used to specify a unique ID for all mounted NSS volumes. If this is your first NSS volume, just specify fsid=1.

Now that the NSS volume is exported, a Linux client can mount it with the **mount** command. For example, to connect the NSS volume to the local directory /mnt/nss, use **mount –t nfs servername:/sharename /mnt/nss**.

Applying User and Directory Quotas

On an NSS volume, user and directory quotas can be used to limit the amount of disk space that can be used by individual users or by directories. Use a user quota if you want to limit the amount of files a user can store on the server, no matter where they are stored. Use disk quota to limit the total size of a directory. This is an excellent way to control the total amount of files stored in a shared directory. In order to enable these disk limitations, it's necessary that you set the necessary NSS volume attributes. In the following procedure, you'll learn how to view and manage user space restrictions.

1. From iManager, select Roles and Tasks ➤ Storage ➤ Volumes. Choose the server where your NSS volume resides and next make sure your NSS volume is selected.

2. To set the user quota, click User Quotas and select the tab Users With Quotas, as shown in Figure 11-12. Normally, no users will be displayed on this tab.

3. Click New to open a window where you can browse to a user you want to assign a quota to. Use the magnifying glass to select one or more users and click OK. Next, specify the Quota in KB, MB, GB, or TB and click Finish. This adds the user with its current quota to the list. Repeat this procedure for all users you want to set a quota for.

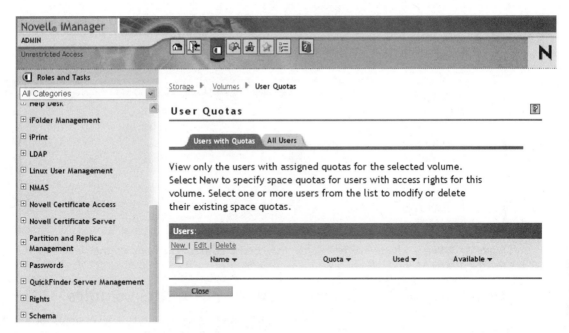

Figure 11-12. *In the overview of user quota, you'll see a list of all users that have a quota and the current amount of disk space in use for that user.*

Salvaging and Purging Files

If the Salvage attribute is enabled on an NSS volume, it's possible to recover deleted files. Alternatively, it's possible to purge the deleted files stored on your server that are still salvageable. The best tool to purge or salvage files is ConsoleOne.

1. Open ConsoleOne and browse to the container that the volume containing the deleted file resides within.

2. Using the right mouse button, click the volume object and from the menu select View ➤ Deleted File View, as shown in Figure 11-13. Browse to the directory where your deleted files were previously present in the file system. This shows you a list of all deleted files and directories.

3. Select the file you want to salvage or purge and click Salvage or Purge on the ConsoleOne toolbar.

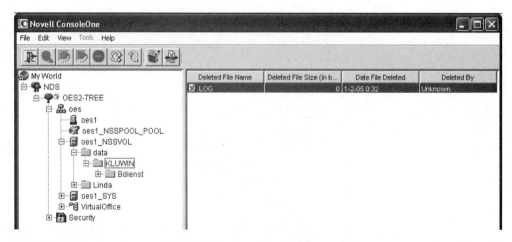

Figure 11-13. *You can browse to deleted files from ConsoleOne and salvage or purge them from the deleted files view.*

Using the File-Level Snapshot Attribute for NSS Volumes

Normally, an open file cannot be backed up. The solution for this is the file-level snapshot attribute. This attribute uses block-level copy-on-write technology, allowing capture of images of data as they're modified by applications. If backup software needs to make a backup of this data, the image file can be backed up. In order to enable file-level snapshot, a copy of the state of the file as it existed when it was opened by an application is saved to a virtual volume that is maintained especially for this purpose. Files in this virtual volume can only be accessed by backup software, but not all backup software is able to work with file-level snapshot. When the open file is closed, NSS updates the files metadata (owner, creation, date, and time and other information about the file) and erases the blocks of original data stored in the virtual volume.

In order to work with file-level snapshot, some disk space is needed for the virtual volume. Initially, the virtual volume will be empty, but as file system usage increases, files will be copied to the virtual volume. The virtual volume's size will be increased dynamically if needed. To ensure that there is always enough free space available for the virtual volume, it's recommended to set the physical volume's size to grow dynamically to the size of the pool. Otherwise, you must periodically monitor the volume size to make sure enough free space is available.

To enable file-level snapshot, the file snapshot attribute must be enabled at the volume level. You can enable this attribute upon creation of the new volume, but it's possible to set it for an existing volume as well. Deactivate the volume and activate the volume again after you've set the attribute to enable it:

1. In iManager, select Storage ➤ Volumes and browse to the volume where you want to set the file-level snapshot attribute.

2. Look at the details of the volume and make sure that it's currently mounted. You can verify this from the State item in the volume details. If it's not mounted yet, mount it by clicking the Mount button before continuing.

3. Click Properties and select the Attributes tab, as shown in Figure 11-14.

4. Select Snapshot – File Level and click Apply to save the changes.

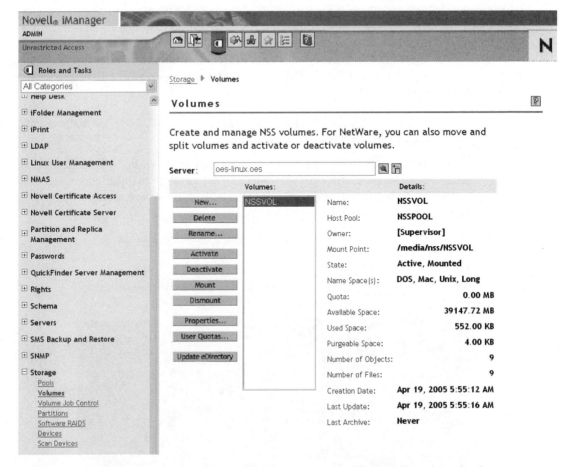

Figure 11-14. *File-level snapshot must be enabled by setting an attribute at the volume level.*

5. Click OK to return to the list of volumes and make sure your volume is selected.

6. Click Deactivate to deactivate the volume. Wait until the state of the volume has changed to deactive.

7. Select the volume again and click Activate. This applies the changes to the volume and makes sure the virtual volume is ready for file-snapshot.

Verifying and Repairing Pools and Volumes

When a server is not shut down properly, files, directories, volumes, and pools can become damaged. Novell provides tools to analyze and repair damaged volumes for traditional volumes as well as NSS volumes.

Troubleshooting Traditional Volumes

If you have problems with files on a traditional volume, you must use the classic tool VREPAIR. This tools runs as an NLM utility on the server console. You can start it manually, but you'll find that in many cases it will be started automatically if needed. This happens if a serious anomaly is detected in the volume structure on server startup. VREPAIR is thorough enough, but it has one major drawback: it's slow. Its slowness is due to the fact that VREPAIR can do just one thing: it checks all tables that are needed to access files and, if needed, tries to recover files from the volume. Because it needs to check all tables that exist on a volume, VREPAIR can take a very long time to complete. It's not difficult to run VREPAIR manually:

1. Access the OES - NetWare console and type **DISMOUNT** *YOURVOLUME* to dismount the volume you want to repair with VREPAIR.

2. Next, enter **VREPAIR** *YOURVOLUME*. VREPAIR.NLM will be started automatically and repair any errors present. It can take a long time for VREPAIR to finish: count on a minimum of about 15 minutes; on large volumes, it can take several hours. When it's finished, VREPAIR shows a screen like in that in Figure 11-15.

3. Enter **MOUNT** *YOURVOLUME* to mount the repaired volume again.

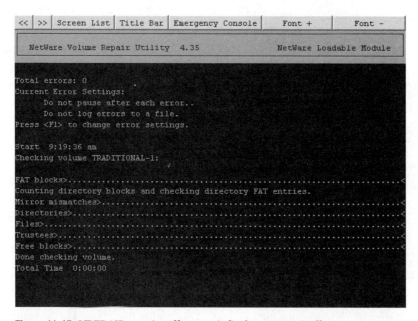

Figure 11-15. *VREPAIR repairs all errors it finds automatically.*

Troubleshooting NSS Volumes

VREPAIR is developed to work with traditional volumes and doesn't work on NSS volumes. In fact, if you have a problem with an NSS volume, you don't repair the volume itself, instead you repair the pool the volume was created in. Normally, any errors in the volume or pool are repaired automatically during volume mount. If errors persist, run the Verify and Rebuild utilities on the NSS pool to resolve them. Like VREPAIR, the Verify and Rebuild utilities can't be used on active pools, so you need to deactivate the pool before running any of them. If you suspect any errors on an NSS pool or volume, first run the Verify utility. This utility searches for inconsistent data blocks and other errors. If it finds serious problems, it notifies you and indicates that you need to run the Rebuild utility.

■Caution Because files could get lost if you run the Rebuild utility on a volume or pool that doesn't need it, you shouldn't run it if not indicated by the Verify utility. If the Verify utility finds critical errors, it will indicate that the Rebuild utility should be used.

After running the Verify and Rebuild utilities, a log file of errors and transactions is created with the name *yourvolume*.rlf. The error log *yourpool*.vlf contains information about the data that has been lost or recovered. Both files are created in /var/log. To verify an NSS pool, enter **nss /poolverify** on the server console. To rebuild a pool, enter **nss /poolrebuild=yourpool**. Be aware that it can take a long time to rebuild an entire volume.

■Note On OES - Linux, unlike OES - NetWare, the **nss** console command works with three different options that allow for generic management of your volumes. To get access to all available options as offered by the NSS command on OES - NetWare, on OES - Linux, start the **nsscon** utility as shown in Figure 11-16. This utility gives you access to all NSS to set parameters discussed in this chapter.

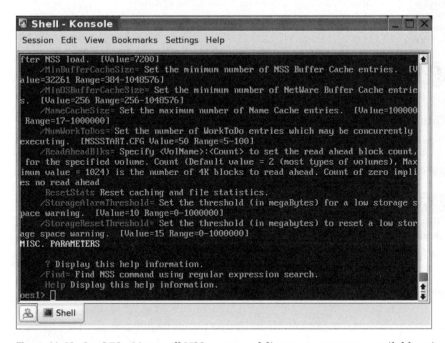

Figure 11-16. *On OES - Linux, all NSS command-line parameters are available using the* ***nsscon*** *utility.*

Implementing Advanced NSS Features

NSS is a very versatile file system and merits a book of its own given how many features it has. Just the PDF with the official NSS documentation alone boasts almost 200 pages! Apart from the features already discussed, NSS has many others as well. In this section, you'll learn about some of the most useful advanced features.

Configuring and Managing Encrypted Volumes

New NSS volumes can be created with Encrypted Volume Support (EVS). This makes data on the volume inaccessible to anyone other than the legal users of the data on the volume. EVS can be applied to all volumes, except for the volume SYS: since essential system files reside on this volume. Encryption can be enabled only when the volume is created and enabled, and can be used for the entire life span of the volume. EVS is transparent to the applications: your applications won't notice that encryption is used. There will, however, be some degradation in performance since files have to be encrypted and decrypted all the time. Currently encrypted volumes can be created only on OES - NetWare.

Novell has some guidelines for working with encrypted volumes:

- The SYS: volume cannot be encrypted.

- Avoid applying compression and encryption to the same volume.

- Encryption can only be enabled at volume creation time.

- When encryption is enabled, a password with a minimum of 6 and a maximum of 16 characters is applied.

- Backups of encrypted volumes are not encrypted.

- While working with files on an encrypted volume, the non-encrypted version of the file is stored in the NSS cache memory. Be sure to exclude this memory from any core dump you make, otherwise the data from the encrypted volume will be displayed in clear-text.

- Encrypted volumes cannot be moved across platforms.

- If you use Novell Archive and Version Services to create file versions of files on the encrypted volume, make sure to encrypt the archive volume as well. Otherwise, file versions are not secure. For more information about archiving and versioning, consult the online documentation at www.novell.com/documentation/oes.

In the following procedure you'll learn how to create an encrypted volume on OES - NetWare:

1. On the OES - NetWare console, run NSSMU, select Volumes and press Enter.

2. Press the Insert key to create a new volume and enter the name for the new volume. A pop-up appears that asks if you want to create an encrypted volume. Select Yes.

3. Type the password used for encryption. Use a password with a minimum of 6 and a maximum of 16 characters. This password will persist for the entire life of the volume (see Figure 11-17).

4. Click OK to continue and then enter the volume size and other attributes that are used on normal volumes as well.

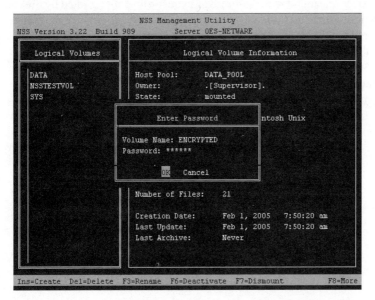

Figure 11-17. *Use NSSMU on the OES - NetWare console to create an encrypted volume.*

5. After creation, the volume will be activated and mounted automatically.

Note After a server restart, the encryption password must be entered. For security reasons, it's not recommended to provide the password automatically, so you should do that manually after each server restart. If you want the password to be supplied automatically, add the line **nss /activate=volumename:password** to the server's startup files.

Configuring and Managing Compression

If space on your hard drive is limited, you need to make use of it as efficiently as possible. Thankfully, compression can be used on NSS just as with traditional volumes. The price in performance for employing compression is rather high, so it should only be used as a last resort. That said, in some cases it can be a welcome solution for a shortage in available drive space. If you want to use compression, parameters must be set at three different levels:

- Use set parameters on the server to specify the configuration of the compression engine.

- Enable compression at the volume by selecting the compression attribute.

- Set compression parameters on specific files or directories to allow for immediate compression or no compression at all.

Normally, compression is scheduled at the server level to occur only during nonpeak hours. This is because the compression engine causes high CPU usage and you don't want that when a lot of users are working on your server. Based on file timestamps and other compression settings, the compression engine evaluates whether a file qualifies for compression. All files eligible for compression are added to the compression queue and are handled by the compression engine one by one. If there are too many files to process during one run of the compression engine, files remain in the queue until the next time the compression engine starts its work. By default, the convert to uncompressed set parameter is set to 1 so that a file will be uncompressed if it's touched twice within the given interval. This is, however, not possible if not enough storage space is available. In that case, the file that was just opened will remain stored in a compressed state on your volume.

If you want to use compression, first configure the compression settings for the server. Only when the proper server settings have been made can you enable compression on specific volumes and fine-tune its workings by using compression-related attributes. On OES - NetWare, three utilities can be used to specify compression settings on the server:

- Monitor

- Novell Remote Manager

- The **set** command

In the next procedure you'll learn how to manage compression with Remote Manager because it's the method that's most easily accessible. From MONITOR.NLM, use the option Server Parameters to set these options. If you want to use the **set** command on the command line, type **set** followed by the parameter as specified in the following.

1. Start your browser and access remote manager by entering the URL http:// yourserver:8008. Next, enter the name and password of your admin user.

Note On OES - NetWare, you can access Remote Manager directly on its secure port 8009. This does not work in OES - Linux, so it's better to use the insecure port 8008 on both versions of OES because it always works.

---

2. Select Manage Server ➤ Set Parameters. Next, choose Common File System to display a list of all available set parameters related to compression, as shown in Figure 11-18.

    - *Compression Daily Check Stop Hour*: Specifies the hour when you want the compression engine to stop. By default, the engine will stop at 6 a.m.

    - *Compression Daily Check Starting Hour*: Specifies the hour when the compression engine should start. By default, it will start at midnight every evening.

    - *Minimum Compression Percentage Gain*: Specifies the minimum percentage a file must compress to decide whether or not the file should be compressed. The default value is 20 percent, but you can set it to any value between 0 and 50 percent.

    - *Enable File Compression*: This option can be used to suspend compression at a given volume. It doesn't allow you to enable compression if it hasn't been enabled at volume level, however.

    - *Maximum Concurrent Compressions*: Specifies the maximum number of concurrent compressions. The default value for this parameter is 2. Be aware that setting this value too high may result in severe server performance degradation.

- *Convert Compressed to Uncompressed Option*: Specifies what the server must do with a compressed file after it has been opened and therefore decompressed. The default value of 1 specifies that the file must be left compressed if it's opened just once. Use 0 to always leave the file compressed, or use 2 to always leave the file decompressed. In that scenario, it's only compressed again if it hasn't been touched for the default period of 14 days.

- *Decompress Percent Disk Space Free To Allow Commit*: Specifies the percentage of disk space that must be available on a volume to permanently change compressed files to decompressed. By default, 10 percent of the volume space must be available.

- *Decompress Free Space Warning Interval*: Sets how often a warning must be issued if not enough space is available to save compressed files as decompressed files.

- *Deleted Files Compression Option*: Specifies what must happen to deleted files. The default value of 1 specifies that these files must be compressed the next day. Alternatively, you can use 0 (don't compress deleted files) or 2 (compress deleted files immediately).

- *Days Untouched Before Compression*: This is probably the most important setting for compression. It specifies when a file qualifies for compression. With the default value, a file only qualifies for compression if it hasn't been touched for 14 days. Don't set this parameter too low, because it will cause an enormous amount of work for the compression engine.

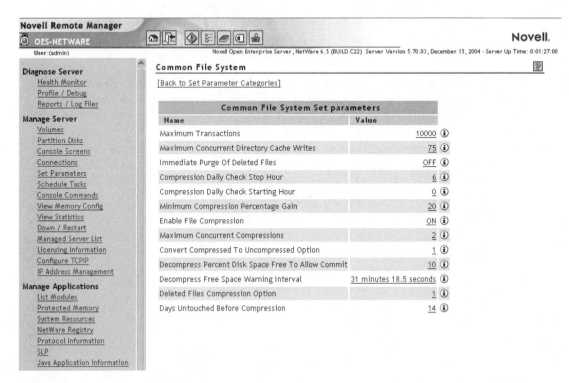

Figure 11-18. *Before you enable compression, make sure the compression engine is tuned by setting the proper set parameters.*

After setting the compression parameters at a server level, some settings can be done at a volume, directory, and file level as well. At the volume level, use the volume attribute to specify whether or not compression should be used on that volume. Next, at a directory or file level, specify how compression should be applied to that directory or file by using attributes like Immediate Compress (Ic) or Don't Compress (Dc). With these attributes you can specify at a directory or file level: Immediate Compress forces files to be compressed without the default delay of 14 days; Don't Compress tells the operating system never to compress these files.

Viewing and Salvaging Deleted Volumes in a Pool

If you have the salvage attribute enabled on an NSS volume, deleted files will not be deleted immediately, only when the space they occupy is needed for something else. Likewise, when you delete an NSS volume from a pool, during a specified amount of time you can still review and restore these volumes. This amount of time is specified by the Purge Delay Time settings. After this purge delay time elapses, NSS automatically removes deleted volumes from the system and you can no longer access them. By default, the purge delay time is set to four days after the volume is deleted. During this period, you can salvage the deleted volume, view its contents, or purge it manually if you wish. The following procedure explains how to manage deleted volumes in a pool:

1. In iManager, select Roles And Tasks ➤ Storage ➤ Pools.

2. Select the server you want to manage and then choose the pool to manage.

3. Select the Deleted Volumes option. This option is available only if there are deleted volumes in the selected pool. A list of deleted volumes is now displayed.

4. Select one or more of the deleted volumes and specify what action to perform on it. Click Purge to remove the volume permanently from your server; select Salvage if you wish to recover it.

It's a nice feature that accidentally deleted volumes can be recovered this easily. The drawback, however, is that valuable disk space is needed for it. To prevent deleted volumes from taking up too much space, you can configure the purge delay, low watermark, and high watermark areas for the salvage area. To change the Purge Delay time, enter the command **nss / LogicalVolumePurgeDelay=***seconds* at the server console.

■Note Not all of the features described here are available from OES - Linux. Some features, such as the recovery of deleted volumes are available from future versions of OES. If you're not sure whether an option can be used or not, activate the NSS Console on OES - Linux by entering the command **nsscon**. This opens an NSS prompt where NSS commands can be entered.

To store deleted volumes for the time specified, you must first have enough space in the NSS volume. To specify when automatic purging should start, the PoolHighWaterMark and PoolLowWaterMark parameters can be used. By default, the Low Watermark is set to 10 percent of available disk space and the High Watermark is set to 20 percent. The purging of deleted volumes begins when the Low Watermark is hit and stops when the High Watermark is reached. Both watermarks can be set on a pool level only. To set a low watermark of 5 percent and a high watermark of 10 percent for the NSS pool with the name "nsspool", add the following commands to be executed automatically upon system startup:

```
nss /PoolHighWaterMark=nsspool:5
nss /PoolLowWaterMark=nsspool:10
```

Configuring iSCSI on NSS

Ten years ago, storage was attached directly to the server. Today it's more and more common that storage is not attached to the server itself, but is instead somewhere on the network. For this purpose, a Network Attached Storage (NAS) device or a storage area network (SAN) can be used. In both cases, huge investments are required in hardware. As an alternative to expensive SAN solutions, iSCSI can be used to replace expensive proprietary SAN solutions. In an iSCSI environment, a SAN can be built based on traditional Ethernet hardware without needing to make a large investment in Fibre channel–based solutions typically used in a SAN environment.

The Novell iSCSI solution is based upon two parts: the iSCSI initiator and the iSCSI target. First, there is the iSCSI target that provides access to a shared disk based on the SCSI protocol. This shared disk can be on a specialized iSCSI target device, or it can be a partition on your server running the iSCSI target software. All servers that want to access such a shared disk must run the iSCSI initiator software. The iSCSI initiator could, for example, be a server operating as a node in a cluster environment. An example of a typical iSCSI environment can be seen in Figure 11-19.

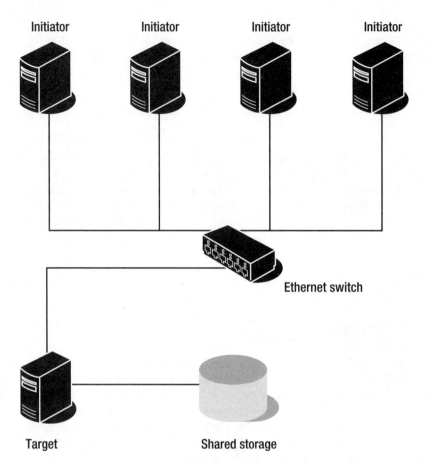

Figure 11-19. *An iSCSI solution is based purely upon Ethernet hardware and the SCSI protocol.*

Generally, there are three different ways to implement an iSCSI solution:

- *Non-dedicated Ethernet hardware*: In this solution, the iSCSI target is just another node on the network. The same network card is used for communication with the iSCSI target as for communication with all other servers and workstations in the network. This is the cheapest solution, but it doesn't provide the best possible performance and fault toler-ance, since iSCSI traffic is sent with the normal network traffic across the same network.

- *Dedicated Ethernet hardware*: In this configuration, all iSCSI initiators are connected to two networks. One of these networks is used for normal data communication, the other network is used as a storage area network. This solution is more expensive than the solution with non-dedicated Ethernet hardware, but it also offers much better performance. Another advantage is that in this case a special high-speed storage network can be built between iSCSI initiators and targets.

- *iSCSI Storage Router Configuration*: A iSCSI router can be used with non-dedicated Ethernet hardware as well as with dedicated Ethernet hardware. In this solution, the server running the iSCSI target software is replaced with a dedicated iSCSI router. This is the most expensive solution, but it also offers the best performance.

iSCSI in an OES Environment

iSCSI is fully implemented in OES - NetWare. For this reason, you can build an iSCSI solution with an OES - NetWare target and one or more OES - NetWare initiators. Be aware though that Novell Clustering Services must be installed if more than one iSCSI initiator is to attach to the shared storage. If you're running OES - Linux, the situation is different. This is because the Novell implementation of the iSCSI target and initiator is not present in OES - Linux. There is, however, Linux iSCSI initiator software present in OES - Linux that allows you to configure an OES - Linux server as an iSCSI initiator to an OES - NetWare iSCSI target. In this section, you'll first learn how iSCSI can be deployed on OES - NetWare and then learn about the possibilities offered by OES - Linux. Later, Chapter 19 of this book shows you how Novell Cluster Services (NCS) can take advantage of iSCSI.

Installing and Configuring iSCSI on OES - NetWare

During the installation of OES - NetWare, iSCSI initiator software is automatically copied to your server. If you want to use the iSCSI target software, it has to be installed separately. This can be done during a server installation or with the Install utility (see Chapter 13) on an existing server (see Figure 11-20). If you want to install Novell Cluster Services as well, you must do so after installing and configuring iSCSI initiator software and before partitioning the disks on the shared system.

■Note Normally you would only deploy iSCSI in a clustered environment. Since iSCSI is an NSS feature, I have chosen to discuss it in this chapter. You should, however, be aware that in this scenario the iSCSI configuration only works to create an NSS volume accessible on another server for one server. Normally, you wouldn't do that in an operational environment. In Chapter 19 of this book, you can read more about the deployment of iSCSI in a clustered environment.

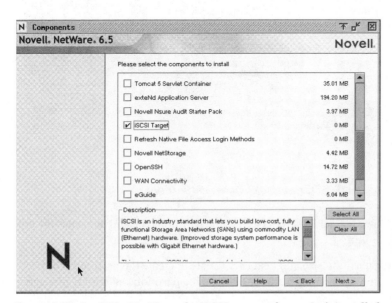

Figure 11-20. *On OES - NetWare, the iSCSI target software isn't installed automatically.*

The following procedure describes how to configure iSCSI. First, you'll read how to create an iSCSI target. Then the iSCSI partition is generated and you load the iSCSI target software. After that, NSS partitions, pools, and volumes are configured and access control to the iSCSI targets is arranged. Finally, you'll learn how to access the iSCSI partition on the iSCSI target by configuring the iSCSI initiator. In the configuration described next, one iSCSI target and one iSCSI initiator are configured. Several tools can be used for this purpose: the NSSMU tool at the server console, ConsoleOne, and Novell Remote Manager. The procedure shown next explains how to configure iSCSI with the Novell Remote Manager because it's the easiest tool to manage shared storage with.

1. Start your browser and access remote manager at http://yourserver:8008. Next, authenticate to the tree where the iSCSI target server resides.

2. Select Manage Server ➤ Partition Disks, as shown in Figure 11-21. You'll now see a screen with an overview of all storage adapters, devices, partitions, pools, and volumes in the server. Under the device where you want to create the iSCSI partition, select Create to open the dialogue to create a new partition.

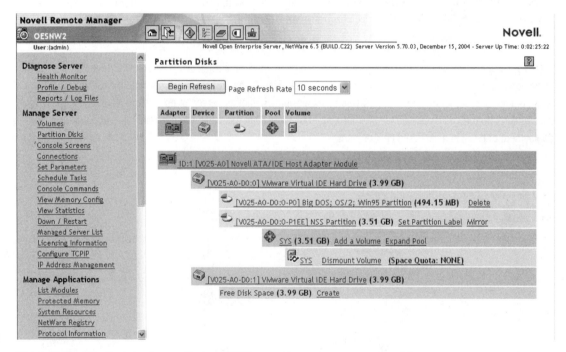

Figure 11-21. *The first step in creating an iSCSI target is to create a new partition.*

3. From the drop-down list, select Novell iSCSI as the partition type and then click the link Create A New Partition.

4. Select the desired partition size and next click Create to create the partition. The partition is immediately added to the overview of existing partitions in Remote Manager.

Now that you've configured an iSCSI target partition, you can go on and use it from the iSCSI initiator. Before continuing, make sure the iSCSI target software is installed on the server you want to use as the iSCSI target. If the software hasn't been installed already, you can install it now from the product installation program on the server. This is just a straight software installation procedure that doesn't require additional configuration. You can read more about the installation of software in general in Chapter 13 of this book. After successful installation, TON.NCF is added to your server's AUTOEXEC.NCF, so that the target software will be executed automatically when the server begins. From TON.NCF, all necessary iSCSI components are activated. The most important of them is ISCSITAR.NLM. This component is responsible for setting up the connection with an LDAP server. To read the exact configuration on which the LDAP server is connected, check out the encrypted file SYS:\ETC\ISCSI.LSS. It contains the admin name, password, and the name of the LDAP server that it's saved in. The iSCSI software will be loaded automatically on the server that is the target, you can also load and unload it manually:

- Use TON.NCF to load the target software manually.

- Use TOFF.NCF to unload the target software.

Before an iSCSI initiator can be allowed access to the iSCSI target machine, you need to configure access. By default, LDAP is used as the access mechanism, and is configured in a way that all iSCSI initiators that reside in the same eDirectory tree can access the iSCSI target software. The only alternative you have is to switch off the LDAP configuration, which will make the iSCSI target available for any iSCSI initiator. You can disable LDAP authentication by choosing Novell Remote Manager ➤ Storage Services ➤ iSCSI Services, shown in Figure 11-22.

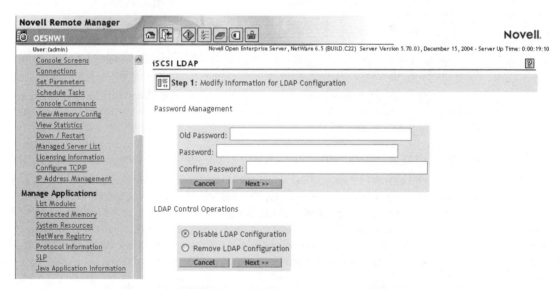

Figure 11-22. *If you switch off LDAP authentication from Remote Manager, you enable access to all initiators that want to configure an iSCSI volume on the iSCSI target server.*

If the iSCSI initiator resides in another tree, you have to create an iSCSI initiator object manually and add it as a trustee to the iSCSI target object, as discussed next. This procedure is best performed from ConsoleOne.

1. In ConsoleOne, create an iSCSI Initiator object in the same content that the iSCSI target object can be found in. Notice that you can only create an iSCSI initiator object as an unmanageable object in ConsoleOne. This doesn't matter, however, since you don't have to configure it; you just have to make it a trustee of the iSCSI target object.

2. Add the iSCSI initiator as a trustee of the iSCSI target object. This object will be created automatically when you run the iSCSI target software for the first time. Don't assign any specific rights; the default rights will work fine.

3. Now you must change the Internet Qualified Name (IQN) on the initiator server console to reflect the object you've just created. In order to do this, you first have to find out the current IQN in use by the remote server—use the command **ISCSI LIST** at the remote server console. In the first line displayed, you'll see the IQN of this server. This line may look like "InitiatorName"="iqn.1984-08.com.novell:.oes-netware.oes.oes-tree." If, for example, the name of the iSCSI Initiator object you've just created is OES-NETWARE.oes. iscsi-tree, you should set the new IQN of the iSCSI Initiator to the same name—in this case, the name would become "iqn.1984-08.com.novell:.OES-NETWARE.oes.iscsi-tree."

4. Set the new initiator name on the console of the iSCSI initiator server with **ISCSI SET**, for example:

```
ISCSI SET InitiatorName=iqn.1984-08.com.novell:.OES-NETWARE.oes.ISCSI-TREE
```

Setting the IQN of the iSCSI initiator allows LDAP authentication to take place properly. You've now configured all that's needed to provide access to the remote iSCSI server. If both servers are in the same tree, you must make the iSCSI initiator a trustee of the iSCSI target. You don't need to assign specific access rights, you just need to make each Initiator object a trustee of the Target object.

When iSCSI target software is first started on a server, an iSCSI target object for each iSCSI partition is automatically created in the same eDirectory context as the target server.

Now that you've configured all access control for the iSCSI initiator to the iSCSI target, you can configure the iSCSI initiator. For each server that you want to use as an iSCSI initiator, do the following:

1. Enter **ION** at the server console to load the iSCSI initiator software.

2. Enter **ISCSI CONNECT** *ip-address-of-target-server name-of-the-target-object*. You can find out the name of the target object that should be used by entering **ISCSINIT DISCOVER** *ip-address-of-target* at the initiator console, as shown in Figure 11-23. A really long name should display. Use the name of this target object to connect to the specific target. Alternatively, if just one target is configured at the target server, use **ISCSI CONNECT** *ip-address-of-target-server* to connect the initiator to the target server.

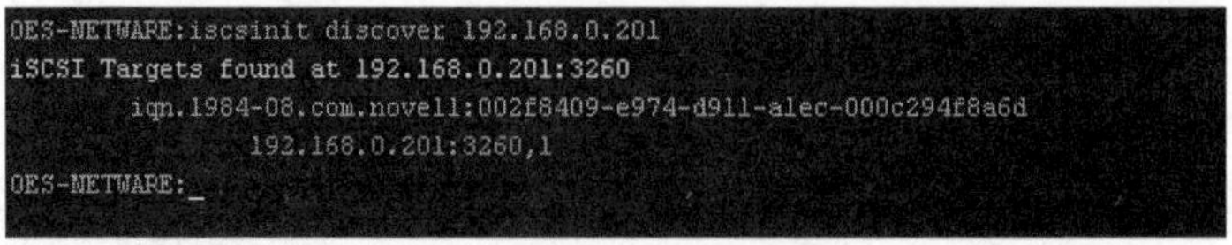

```
OES-NETWARE:iscsinit discover 192.168.0.201
iSCSI Targets found at 192.168.0.201:3260
        iqn.1984-08.com.novell:002f8409-e974-d911-alec-000c294f8a6d
             192.168.0.201:3260,1
OES-NETWARE:_
```

Figure 11-23. *The iSCSI target object usually has a long and cryptic name. The structure of this name is described in RFC 3720, which is about iSCSI.*

3. Now that you've successfully attached the iSCSI Initiator to the target, you'll also probably want to use it after rebooting your server. To ensure that the iSCSI initiator will still work after a server reboot, make sure the command **ION** and **ISCSI CONNECT** *target-server* are added to your autoexec.ncf on the server.

4. At the iSCSI Initiator console, use the command **list devices**. This command displays a list of all available storage devices. Notice that the iSCSI target is listed as a normal device which starts with the name Novell. You can use it just like any other SCSI device and create a partition on it.

■**Tip** Found the preceding three-step configuration complicated? Well, there's good news for you! This procedure can also be accomplished from Remote Manager. On the iSCSI Initiator, select Storage Services ➤ iSCSI Services (see Figure 11-24) and click Add Target. Enter the IP address of your iSCSI target and a list of all available targets will be displayed. Click Next to select the target and have it added to your iSCSI initiator. If you wish, you can even configure CHAP authentication from the Remote Manager interface.

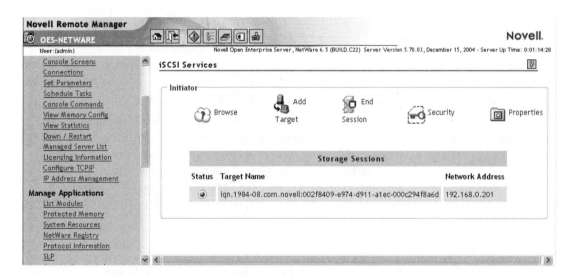

Figure 11-24. *Instead of working with complex commands at the OES - NetWare console, you can also configure an iSCSI initiator from Remote Manager.*

Now that you've configured both target and initiator, you can create an NSS volume on the iSCSI Target from the iSCSI initiator. If you're using iSCSI as shared storage in a clustered environment, you must install and configure the cluster first before making a volume on the iSCSI device. Because of your iSCSI configuration, the iSCSI initiator sees the iSCSI target as a local device. The iSCSI Target will be listed as an iSCSI HAM adapter (see Figure 11-25) and you can create an NSS volume on it, just like on any other device.

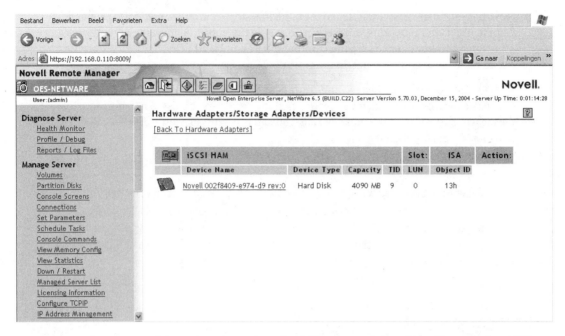

Figure 11-25. *After a successful iSCSI configuration, the iSCSI adapter is listed just like any other SCSI adapter from Remote Manager.*

Using OES - Linux as an iSCSI Target or Initiator

If you want to include an OES - Linux server in your iSCSI configuration, you might be disappointed to know that Novell hasn't written any software to support it. Fortunately, there is iSCSI software included with OES - Linux that comes from a Linux Open Source project. This software enables you to set up OES - Linux as an iSCSI initiator. There is also an open source project that allows you to set up OES - Linux as an iSCSI target, but this software hasn't been optimized for OES - Linux and is not supported. For this reason, I recommend not configuring OES - Linux as an iSCSI target. The following procedure explains how to set up OES - Linux as an iSCSI initiator.

1. On your OES - Linux server, start YaST and log in as user root. Select Software ➤ Install And Remove Software, and from the Filter drop-down list, select Search.

2. Enter **iscsi** as the keyword you want to search for and press search to start the search. Select the package Linux-iscsi, as shown in Figure 11-26, and click Accept to install it. Insert the CD the installer asks for and click OK to continue.

3. Use ConsoleOne to create the initiator object in eDirectory, as described earlier, and remember the name of this object. Don't forget to make this object a trustee of the iSCSI Target object.

4. Use an editor to open the file /etc/initiatorname.iscsi on your OES - Linux server. Despite the warnings, change the last line in this file to reflect the correct name of your initiator. This name should reflect the name of the initiator as configured in eDirectory. If, for example, the name of your initiator object in your tree is oes1.oes, change the last line in /etc/initiatorname.iscsi to **InitiatorName=iqn.1987-04.com.cisco:cn=oes1,o=oes.** (Do

not include the dot at the end of the line!) The name of your initiator should always start with **iqn.1987-04.com.cisco:** and must be followed by the LDAP name of the iSCSI Initiator object you created in the container where the iSCSI Target is configured as well. Notice that the name of the tree is not needed; it's only needed for NetWare initiators connecting to a target in a different tree.

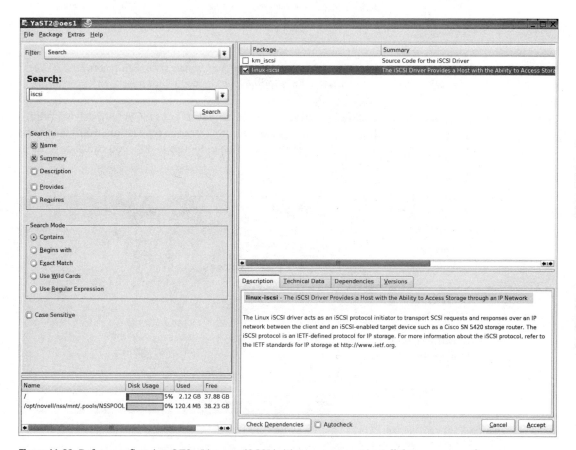

Figure 11-26. *Before configuring OES - Linux as iSCSI initiator, you must install the necessary software.*

5. Edit the configuration file /etc/iscsi.conf to enter the address where the iSCSI target can be reached. This line should read DiscoveryAddress=*ip-of-your-target*. Notice that this example file contains a lot of possible settings and documentation. These settings can be very useful in, say, situations where encryption is needed, and I recommend that you read the excellent documentation in the file if you want to make an advanced configuration. For the purposes of this procedure, it will be enough just to change the line with the DiscoveryAddress.

6. Start the iSCSI software components with **/etc/init.d/iscsi start**. If everything works the way it should, you'll immediately be prompted by the SUSE hardware detection program that a new disk was found (see Figure 11-27). Don't forget to change your runlevel configuration to make sure the iSCSI initiator software runs each time you start your server—for example, use **chkconfig iscsi 235** to start the services automatically in runlevels 2, 3, and 5.

Figure 11-27. *When the OES - Linux iSCSI initiator connects successfully with the iSCSI target, the SUSE hardware detection module lets you know that a new disk was found.*

You now have configured OES - Linux as an iSCSI initiator. Your iSCSI hard drive should, however, appear on OES - Linux as a local hard drive with a strange type (some weird hexadecimal number). From the YaST partitioner utility (as seen in Figure 11-28), you can access the drive and create partitions on it.

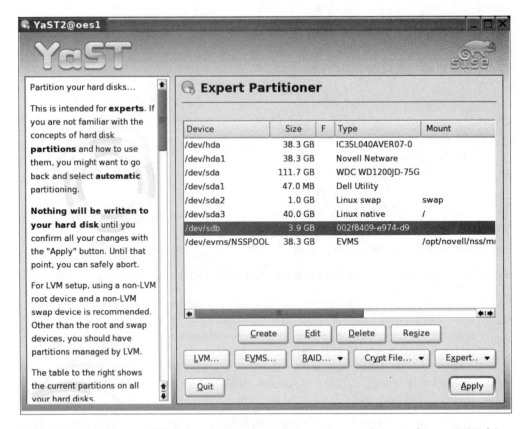

Figure 11-28. *Currently, on OES - Linux, only native Linux partitions can be created on an iSCSI drive.*

Summary

NSS is not just a file system. While most file systems offer limited abilities, NSS offers many advanced abilities. In this section, you learned about some of the most important of these possibilities. You should, however, realize that many options haven't been discussed at all. Some of these are distributed file services, moving and splitting NSS volumes, pool snapshot, and versioning. Each (as well as many others) is described extensively in the Novell documentation that can be found at www.novell.com/documentation. In the next chapter, you'll learn about configuration and management of security in Open Enterprise Server.

CHAPTER 12

■ ■ ■

Managing Security

One of the most important aspects of a network operating system is its security, so in this chapter I'll discuss security in Open Enterprise Server.

Security in an OES environment consists of various levels. First, there is login security. This is the security related to the use of an account. Login security determines when a user can log in to the network, from what network address he can log in, and it defines password policies. Login security is also known as authentication, which was covered in Chapter 9, so this chapter presents different techniques that can be used to authenticate securely to the network.

The next level of security is file system security. With file system security, the administrator determines to which files and directories on the server a user may get access, and what exactly he can do with these files. The administrator determines file system security with rights and attributes that are applied on these files and directories. Novell offers excellent options for file system security for both OES - Linux and OES - NetWare.

The third component of OES security is eDirectory security. By means of eDirectory rights, a user is granted rights to how he can access objects in eDirectory. eDirectory security is fine in most cases with its default settings, but for certain tasks, additional eDirectory security must be defined. Both file system and eDirectory security belong in the authorization category.

The fourth component in a secure network environment is the public/private key infrastructure. This component contains many elements that help you use encryption in your network. Of these, the certificate server regulates the use of public and private keys in the network. These keys are necessary in all situations where a user wants to make a secure connection to a server. You'll go quite far with the default settings, but sometimes it's necessary to perform some certificate server management. Managing encryption falls under the security category of confidentiality.

The last part of security concerns the server console itself. If a hacker can get access to the console of your server, he's basically in and can get access to all your server files, causing untold damage. Therefore, I'll take some time to discuss server console security as well. More details about securing the OES - Linux or OES - NetWare console can be found in Chapters 4 and 5 of this book.

Authentication

For most people, authentication equates to entering a username and password at the login prompt provided by Novell Client on their workstation—but there's often more to it than this. In a given environment, it might be necessary to use strong authentication where a user authenticates with a special token he's been given, or with a fingerprint reader. These features are not supported by default; to use them, you need the Novell Modular Authentication Services (NMAS). NMAS is a default part of Open Enterprise Server and is installed automatically because it's needed to support OES features like the simple password.

NMAS is a complex technology that enables different kinds of authentication to the network. One of the nicest features is that it doesn't just support strong authentication, but also works with graded authentication. In graded authentication, the permissions assigned to a user are determined by the login method employed by the user. If, for example, the user has just logged in with his username and password, he'll only have access to one part of the file system of his server, while authentication with his username, password, and RSA device grants him full access to the network. To use NMAS, a version of Novell Client with NMAS support must be installed on the workstation. NMAS is supported with the latest Novell Clients.

To enable NMAS for a user, a login sequence must be defined. You can do this from the NMAS section in iManager. After a login sequence is defined, it can be referred to from the NMAS Login Sequences tab on the user object. An example of this is shown in Figure 12-1. The login sequence defines how a user should authenticate to the network. Here, for example, you could determine that all authentication requires a smart card to be used. Next, the login sequence must be assigned to a user or a group of users; for these users, the login sequence automatically applies. To make management of login sequences easier, some default login sequences are provided with NMAS. So, if a user needs to authenticate with a Universal Smart Card device, the login sequence **Universal Smart Card** must be assigned to that user. It's also possible to assign more than one login sequence to a user. In such cases, the user can choose from the available login sequences: this is more useful for the user because he can choose to bypass strong ,authentication based on his smart card, but it makes the network less secure. For this reason, it's usually best to set a default login sequence and allow just that. You can manage login sequences for users from the NMAS Login Sequences tab on the user object. For more details on NMAS, visit www.novell.com/documentation.

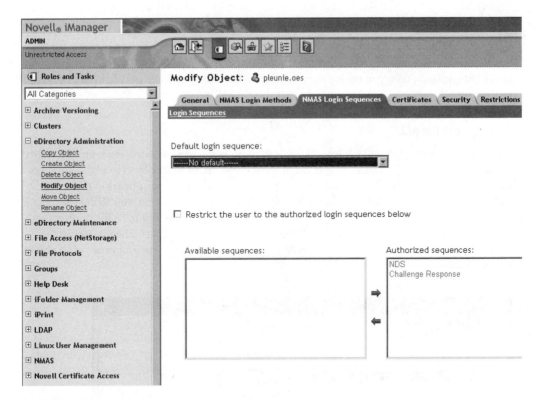

Figure 12-1. *By defining an NMAS login sequence, you can specify how the user logs in to the network.*

File System Security

On some network operating systems, everyone gets all rights to all files on the server. Novell isn't that generous though. After installation, users only get limited access to files on the server. If they need more access, the administrator can configure that manually. Novell has developed a strong system of file-system rights to determine exactly what a user can and can't do on the file system. As you've already learned in Chapters 10 and 11, these rights can be used on both NCP shares and NSS volumes. Before diving into file system rights though, let's discuss some general security concepts. Understanding these concepts is important because they also apply to eDirectory security, which is covered in the section that follows it.

General Security Concepts

If you're working with rights in a Novell environment, some general concepts always apply whether you're dealing with file-system rights or eDirectory rights. Before you can comprehend how rights work though, you must understand how these general concepts are used in a Novell environment.

Trustees and the ACL

The most important concept while working with rights is the trustee. A trustee is an eDirectory object that gets rights to a directory or file in the file system, or to an object in eDirectory. For example, if a user is added as a trustee to a directory, the user's name appears in the access control list (ACL) associated with that directory. In the access control list, you'll find the names of all eDirectory objects that have rights on the specific object, whether it's a file or directory, or an eDirectory object. A user is only allowed into the ACL of an object if he is specifically assigned to that object. Figure 12-2 shows an ACL as it's displayed in the properties of an object in ConsoleOne.

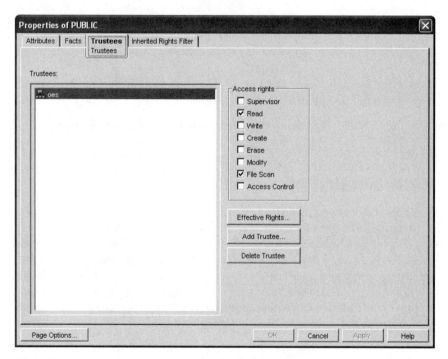

Figure 12-2. *In the ACL, you can see exactly who the trustees are of a specific object.*

Objects That Can Be Used As a Trustee

Different objects can be assigned as trustees. Before designing a security strategy, you must consider which object you want to use as a trustee. Table 12-1 offers an overview of the most common objects used as trustees and what should be considered when using these objects. In fact, other objects can also be used as trustees—for instance, if it exists in eDirectory, it can be a trustee. These other objects, however, are only used in special cases.

Table 12-1. *Overview of Objects That Can Be Used As Trustees*

Object	Consideration
[public]	The [public] trustee represents anyone who has a connection to the network. You don't have to be currently logged in to take advantage of rights granted to the public trustee. This trustee exists to make it easier to start using the network. The public trustee is granted some minimal rights that allow a user to choose the network resource she wants to work with before she logs in. For security reasons, you should avoid manually granting rights to the public trustee.
Tree	In some cases, it's necessary to grant rights to everyone who has logged in to the network. In such instances, the tree trustee can be used. Rights granted to the tree trustee are inherited to all objects in that tree.
Container objects	In many situations, it's necessary to grant rights to a limited group of users. Sometimes this group already exists as a container object in eDirectory. If it does, you can grant rights to these container objects.
Groups	Since the very first days of NetWare, it's been possible to work with group objects. A group can be used as a security entity, but the most important feature of a group is that you can grant rights to it. This has made groups a very popular way to grant rights in an eDirectory environment.
Organizational role	An organizational role is an eDirectory object that functions like an eDirectory group object. Instead of an Organizational Role object, you can also use a group object. The best aspect of the Organizational Role object, however, is that it's created to represent a function within an enterprise. One or more users can be assigned to this function as occupants, and these users inherit all rights granted to the organizational role.
User	If an individual rights assignment has to be made, you can assign the rights directly to a user object. It's best not to assign rights directly to a user object though since you could very easily lose track of who has rights over what objects.

Inheritance and Effective Rights

Earlier in this chapter, you learned about the concept of a trustee, a user object that has rights to a certain object. Imagine an example where user Alex is made a trustee of the directory SYS:\public. In this case, Alex would appear in the ACL of that directory. In a Novell rights environment, rights are inherited by default. This means that all rights that Alex has in the directory public also apply to all files in this directory and all subdirectories in public, including the files in these subdirectories.

The next question is: is Alex a trustee of the file \public\capture.exe? The answer is no. He's not a trustee, because his name doesn't occur in the ACL of this file. It would be a very inefficient system if a user had to be made a trustee of all files under a certain directory if he was made a trustee of that directory—after all, what if it contained 10,000+ files?! A better question is: does Alex have rights over the file \public\capture.exe? The answer is yes, he has effective rights, which he's gotten because of inheritance. Rights granted at a high level are always inherited at a sublevel of the level where the rights were granted—this is true for both the file system and the directory. You'll see some examples of this later in this chapter.

Remember, the default setting is that rights are inherited. But there are some exceptions to the default of inheritance, as shown next.

1. Inheritance stops if the same trustee gets a new rights assignment.

2. Inheritance can be stopped by means of an inheritance rights filter.

Later in this chapter in the section "Applied Inheritance," you'll learn how inheritance works in a real-life file system. In the section called "File System Rights," some extensive examples of inheritance are discussed. Here, you'll also find examples of how exceptions to the default of inheritance are used in practice.

Working with Group and Organizational Role Objects

As you learned earlier, groups are very often used to apply rights. If rights need to be granted to the file system, it's often logical to work with groups. Next up is an example showing how groups can be applied to a file system structure, then afterward you'll learn how to create group and organizational role objects.

Working with Organizational Roles and Groups: an Example

Imagine a very small company that has its own server. This server is used for storage of data files and for storage of application files. There's a directory, data:apps, with subdirectories db for the database program and wp for the word processor (see Figure 12-3). There's also a directory called data:groups, which is for data that has to be shared between workers at the different departments. Under data:groups exists data:groups\operations and data:groups\sales.

Figure 12-3. *A sample directory structure*

Our small imaginary company has only one organization object: o=small. All user objects exist directly under this organization object. Thus, in this instance it makes sense to create groups to work with these four directories. In fact, it would be quite practical to create a group for each of the following directories, wherein:

- db will be granted rights to the directory data:apps\db

- wp will be granted rights to the directory data:apps\wp

- operations will be granted rights to the directory data:groups\operations

- sales will be granted rights to the directory data:groups\sales

In this way, you create a very transparent structure in which it's immediately obvious why these groups exist. Besides, it would be easy if a new employee started work with the company. All you'd have to do is make him a member of all the necessary groups, and he'd have the rights he needs immediately.

In a small company, it can make sense to create a group for every single shared directory on the server. There are, however, some exceptions: imagine that in a somewhat bigger company there are already two containers called sales and operations in which all employees of these two departments reside. In that case, it doesn't make sense to create a group sales and also a group operations. In such a case, you'd just use the container object as a kind of natural group. The other exception to working with groups is occurs when you want to grant rights to everyone in the network. Here, you don't make a separate group to which you add all users as members, instead you just use the tree object or the organization object as a trustee to grant rights to everyone.

Now imagine that in our small company with the four groups there is also a person that works on the help desk. Since the users of our imaginary company are terrible, all helpdesk employees flee after a few weeks. For the system administrator, this causes a lot of work, because a lot of special rights are granted to the helpdesk employee, and they need to be redone every time a new person takes over the helpdesk role. In such a case, an organizational role can help: add the rights to the organizational role instead of the individual user and make the poor soul that occupies the role of help-desk employee at a given moment the occupant of this organizational role. That way, when the person at the help desk flees again, it's very easy to make a new user occupant of the help-desk role, which prevents you from having to grant all the rights again. Though this sounds nice, you're probably wondering if you could just use a group object for the same purpose. Well, you can! There's nothing an organizational role can't do that a group can. The only advantage of using an organizational role is that it's easier to recognize what a specific object is used for in your Directory tree.

Well, enough theory, let's look at some examples.

Creating Groups and Organizational Roles

The best program to manage groups and organizational roles is still iManager. The following procedure outlines how to create an eDirectory group object and add some members to it.

1. Start iManager, log in, and select Roles And Tasks ➤ Groups. Here, you'll find the options that can be used to create and manage group objects.

2. Select Create Group (this gives you the screen shown in Figure 12-4) and enter a name and context for the group object. If you want to specify a dynamic group, select the Dynamic Group option as well. You'll learn more about dynamic groups later in this procedure. Click OK twice to create the group.

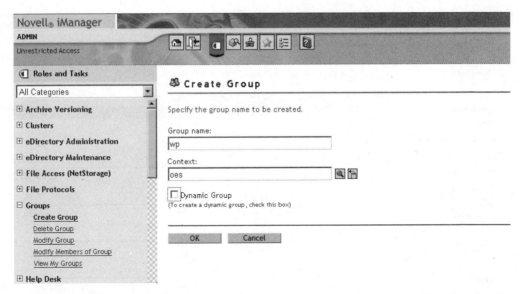

Figure 12-4. *To create a group, enter a name for the group and specify in what context the group must be created.*

3. If you want to make the group a LUM group as well, select the Linux Config Object or the Linux Workstation objects you want to associate the group to, otherwise click Cancel to cancel creation of the LUM group.

4. From iManager Roles And Tasks ➤ Groups, select Modify Group to modify the properties of the group you've just created (this screen's shown in Figure 12-5). Select your group and click OK to display the group's details.

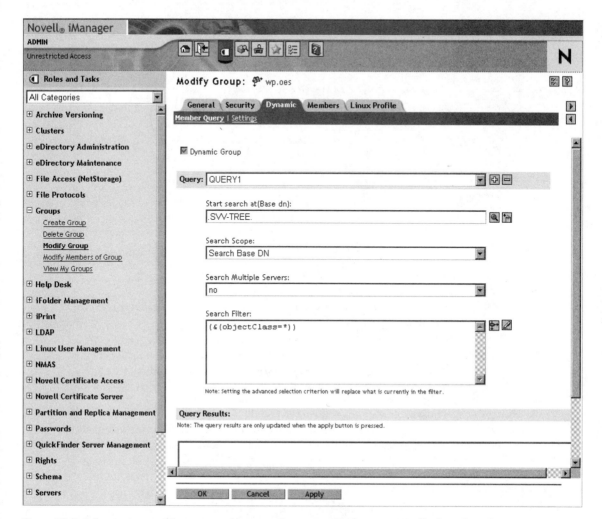

Figure 12-5. *A dynamic group is a group where members are added automatically, based on the presence of a specific attribute defined in a filter.*

5. The most important property of a group is its member list. Here you specify the names of all users that must be members of the group you just created. Select the Members tab and use the magnifying glass to choose all the users you want to add as a member to this group.

If you have specific functions in your organization that are occupied by different persons or by persons who won't work in that function for very long, you can create an organizational role:

1. From iManager, select Roles And Tasks ➤ eDirectory Administration ➤ Create Object.

2. From the list of objects, select Organizational Role and click OK.

3. Enter a name and a context for the organizational role and click OK.

4. Click Modify to modify the properties of the organizational role you just created.

5. On the General tab, click the Role Occupant link, as shown in Figure 12-6. Use the magnifying glass to browse for users you want to add as occupant to the role. These users automatically inherit all rights granted to the organizational role. Click OK when finished.

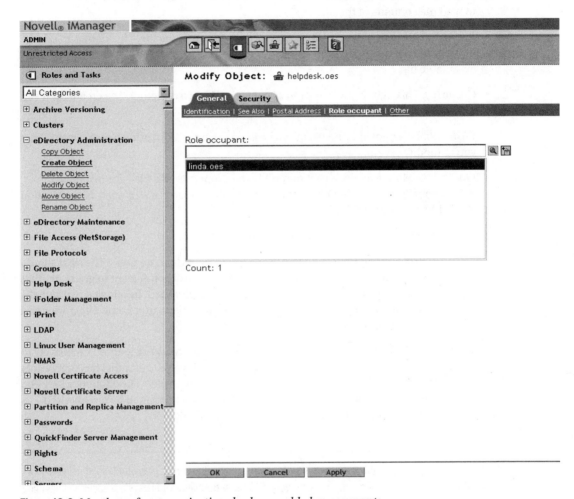

Figure 12-6. *Members of an organizational role are added as occupants.*

File System Rights

Now that you have a basic understanding of the background mechanisms used when working with rights, it's time to have a look at the real file system rights themselves. First, let's discuss the eight different rights that can be applied to the file system, followed by some examples of inheritance and the exceptions that can be made to file system inheritance. Lastly, I'll explain how an additional layer of security can be created for the file system by using file system attributes.

The Eight Rights

On a traditional NetWare volume or NSS volume, the following eight rights can be used to apply file system security:

- *File Scan (F)*: This right allows a user to see the name of a file, but doesn't allow the user to read the contents of the file.

- *Read (R)*: This right allows the user to read the content of the file. This right is needed in order to read a text file on your computer. You also need it to execute code in an executable file.

- *Create (C)*: This right allows a user to create new files in a directory. The create right can only be applied to directories, not to individual files.

- *Write (W)*: This right allows a user to write in an existing file. In other words, write allows you to modify existing files.

- *Modify (M)*: Modify allows a user to modify the properties of a file—for instance, the name or attributes of a file. Other properties can be changed as well, such as the creation or modification date of the file.

- *Erase (E)*: With this right, a user is allowed to delete a file.

- *Access Control (A)*: This right enables a user to grant rights to other users. The right should only be granted to network administrators. Access control is sufficient to grant all other rights; if a user only has access control and no other rights, he'll be allowed to grant all these other rights as well. Access control is used by default on user home directories so a user can grant rights to his files to other users.

- *Supervisory (S)*: The supervisory right is also a right that should be granted exclusively to system administrators. It implies all other rights. In other words, a user that has supervisory rights to the file system doesn't have any limitations to these files. The difference between access control and supervisory is that access control can be filtered by an inherited rights filter, whereas supervisory can never be filtered out.

■**Caution** Rights can be granted to directories, but also to individual files. It's recommended never to work with rights on individual files since this makes it very difficult to troubleshoot file system security if anything is wrong.

Because there are so many different rights that can be granted, network administrators sometimes find it difficult to grant the rights needed for specific tasks. Novell rights are a lot easier to understand if you divide them into different categories. According to the task that needs to be performed on the network, three different rights categories can be distinguished:

- *Application use*: If a user needs to be able to start an application, in most cases Read and File Scan are enough; the only thing the user has to do is load the program code in the memory of his workstation to be able to execute the file. If, however, an application needs to write a temporary file, more rights may be needed. In most cases, however, this problem can be solved in the applications environment. Most applications have the ability to define a working directory where temporary files can be created.

- *Working with data*: If a user needs to be able to work with data files, almost all tasks must be performed on files. For this reason, the user is granted read, file scan, create, modify, erase, and write rights.

- *System administration*: Only system administrators can grant rights to other users. For that reason, access control and supervisory are only granted to administrative users. You can grant just supervisory to an administrative user, or all eight rights explicitly; there's no difference because Supervisory implies all other rights. In a properly designed file system, there's no need to grant access control instead of supervisory to an administrative user.

In most cases, you can work with rights as defined in these three default scenarios. Only in special cases is it necessary to work with individual rights.

Applied Inheritance

One of the most difficult items to understand when working with file system rights is the way they are inherited. If no complications arise, then it's easy: rights granted at a certain level are inherited by all levels underneath it. If, however, inherited rights filters are used, rights are combined, or the same trustee gets new rights, the situation can get rather complicated. Let's look at some cases to help you understand more clearly how this works.

■**Note** The following examples were designed to help you understand the complex mechanism of inheritance. Essentially, they're examples of how NOT to apply trustee rights in an eDirectory environment.

The Same Trustee Gets New Rights

Exception number one to the basic rule of inheritance is when the same user gets new rights. Imagine a volume of data which has two directories: apps\wp and apps\db. User Alex gets RFCWEM on data:apps. Normally, these rights are inherited to the subdirectories, so Alex has the same rights in data:apps\wp and data:apps\db. If, however, the user is granted new rights at a lower level, only the rights granted at the lower level are effective. So if Alex is granted a trustee assignment at data:apps\db with just the RF rights, only these rights apply to the lower directory. (See Table 12-2.)

Table 12-2. *A New Trustee Assignment Overwrites Previously Assigned Rights*

Directory		User Alex
Apps	Inherited rights filter	
	Trustee assignment	RFCWEM
	Effective rights	RFCWEM
Apps\wp	Inherited rights filter	
	Trustee assignment	
	Effective rights	RFCWEM
Apps\db	Inherited rights filter	
	Trustee assignment	RF
	Effective rights	RF

Rights from Different Trustees Combined

The situation becomes a bit more complex if an eDirectory object gets its rights from more than one trustee assignment. This happens, for example, in the case where Alex is also a member of the group db. This group has a trustee assignment with the rights RFCW on the directory apps\db. In this case, the rights inherited from the different trustee assignments can be added to each other: as an individual, Alex had only left R and F on the directory apps\db, but now since he is a member of the group db, which has a trustee assignment of RCW in this directory, RCW is added to the user's individual rights. These rights are added to the rights he has from his trustee assignment as a user. The grant total of his rights to apps\db in this case is RFCW. (See Table 12-3.)

Table 12-3. *User Rights and Trustee Rights Combined*

Directory		User Alex	Group db	Sum of Effective Rights for User Alex
Apps	Inherited rights filter			
	Trustee assignment	RFCWEM		
	Effective rights	RFCWEM		
Apps\wp	Inherited rights filter			
	Trustee assignment			
	Effective rights	RFCWEM		

Directory		User Alex	Group db	Sum of Effective Rights for User Alex
Apps\db	Inherited rights filter			
	Trustee assignment	RF	RCW	
	Effective rights	RF	RCW	RFCW

The Inherited Rights Filter

To make the situation even more complex, an administrator can also choose to work with inherited rights filters. An inherited rights filter (IRF) is a filter that blocks inheritance of rights. In general, you should avoid using inherited rights filters because they make your network less transparent. In most cases, it isn't necessary to work with IRFs. In a properly designed network, only a few rights need to be granted high in the file system structure. More rights are granted low in the structure, so if your file system is properly designed, you don't need an inherited rights filter.

Up to now, I've discussed rights that are granted to a specific eDirectory trustee object. The special thing with inherited rights filters is that they just filter the inheritance of rights. An inherited rights filter that's applied to a directory determines effective rights for that directory. If, however, a user has a trustee assignment to the same directory, the trustee assignment won't be influenced by the inherited rights filter. Imagine that in this example inherited rights filters are applied to apps\db and apps\wp. The inherited rights filter to apps\wp filters the rights that are normally inherited by this directory. The IRF to apps\db does the same thing, but the direct trustee assignment that already exists for that directory isn't influenced by the IRF.

In an IRF, rights are specified that can be inherited. Every directory has a default IRF in which all rights are present, so by default all rights can be inherited. If you want to block the inheritance of a certain right, you must remove it from the IRF. But remember that on the file system the S right can never be blocked by an IRF; you therefore always see the S right in the IRF. Once you have the S right on the file system, you never lose it.

Tip Having trouble remembering how an IRF works? If so, just keep in mind that in the file system S right can never be filtered out by an IRF. Therefore, you'll always see an S in the IRF, as well as all other rights that aren't filtered out by the IRF.

Also remember that an IRF is a property of a directory, and that IRFs are the same for all users that have rights to a specific directory. Table 12-4 explores what happens to the inheritance of rights when IRFs are applied. To make the example more obvious, I've removed the specific trustee assignment for user Alex on the directory apps\db so you can see how the inheritance of his rights granted at the apps directory is influenced by the IRF.

Table 12-4. *The Effect of an IRF*

Directory		User Alex	Group db	Sum of Effective Rights for User Alex
Apps	Inherited rights filter	FRWCEMAS	FRWCEMAS	
	Trustee assignment	RFCWEM		
	Effective rights	RFCWEM		
Apps\wp	Inherited rights filter	FRS	FRS	
	Trustee assignment			
	Effective rights	FR		FR
Apps\db	Inherited rights filter	WCS	WCS	
	Trustee assignment		RFCW	
	Effective rights	WC	RFCW	RFCW

Granting File System Rights

File system rights can be granted in many ways, although iManager cannot be used to manage file system rights. The best tools to set them are Novell Remote Manager, ConsoleOne, and Windows Explorer if Novell Client is installed. If NSS is installed on OES - Linux, you can use the rights utility as well, but this utility has a rather complex syntax so consult its man page for more details. The following procedure shows you how to set file system rights with ConsoleOne, because this is the only tool that can be used to manage file system rights on both OES - Linux and OES - NetWare.

■**Note** You can start ConsoleOne from the directory SYS:public\mgmt\consoleone if you're using OES - NetWare. However, if you're using OES - Linux, ConsoleOne is not installed. In that case, both a Windows and Linux version of ConsoleOne can be downloaded for free from http://download.novell.com. If so required, download this version and install it. The installation procedure is very straightforward: upon installation, select all default values to install the software. Next, start it from your local workstation (which is a lot faster than starting it from the server).

---

1. Start ConsoleOne from your server or from your workstation. In this procedure, I assume that ConsoleOne is installed locally at the workstation.

2. The ConsoleOne startup screen appears, as shown in Figure 12-7. If you're using ConsoleOne on a Linux workstation where Novell Client isn't installed, from the file menu you must select Authenticate to authenticate yourself to the network before you can use it. On a Windows workstation, you don't have to authenticate if you're already logged in via Novell Client.

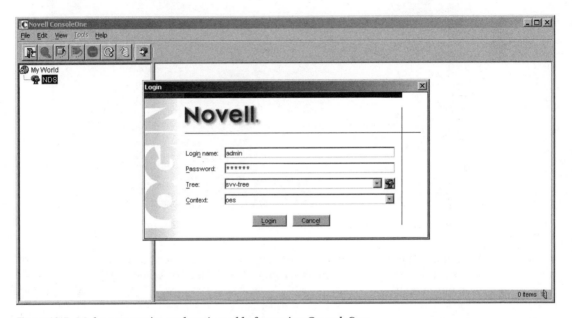

Figure 12-7. *Make sure you're authenticated before using ConsoleOne.*

3. Click the NDS symbol and browse to the volume object that has the directory you want to set rights for. Click that directory with the right mouse button, and from the menu, select Properties. Next, activate the Trustees tab to select a trustee and grant Novell rights to it (see Figure 12-8 for an example).

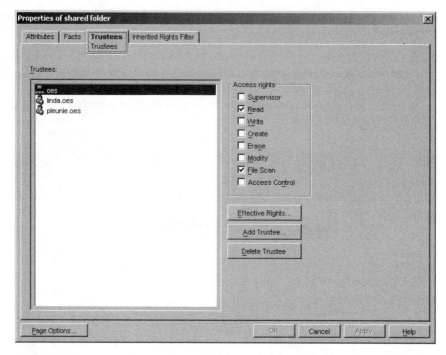

Figure 12-8. *To grant rights, you must first select a trustee to grant those rights to.*

4. To grant rights to a new trustee, click the Add Trustee button and browse eDirectory for the trustee you want to assign (see Figure 12-9). When you've located the trustee, select it and click OK.

Figure 12-9. *Use the eDirectory browser to locate the trustee you want to assign.*

5. Now you can specify the rights you want to assign to the selected trustee. By default, Read and File Scan are selected. Assign any other rights you want to grant and click OK to save them.

6. To change the IRF for the selected directory, click the Inherited Rights Filter tab (shown in Figure 12-10). This displays an inherited rights filter where, by default, all rights are selected: this indicates that there's no blocking of any rights. In the overview, remove all the rights you don't want inherited. By default, all rights can be inherited; deselect all rights for which you want to disable inheritance. Notice that only normal rights can be deselected; the supervisory right is not present in this list.

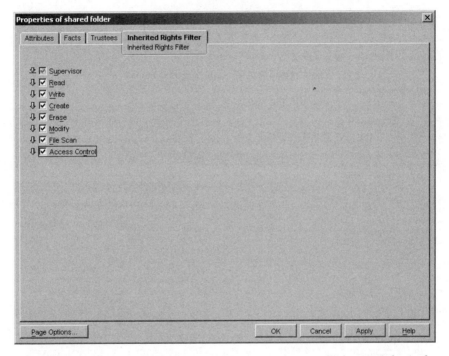

Figure 12-10. *To create an IRF, simply deselect the rights you don't want inherited.*

Tip If you're using OES - NetWare, you can manage Novell rights from Remote Manager as well. To do so, click the Info icon that appears before all the files and directories displayed when you click a volume object in Remote Manager. This icon gives you access to a web page where you can set rights. An example of this page is shown in Figure 12-11.

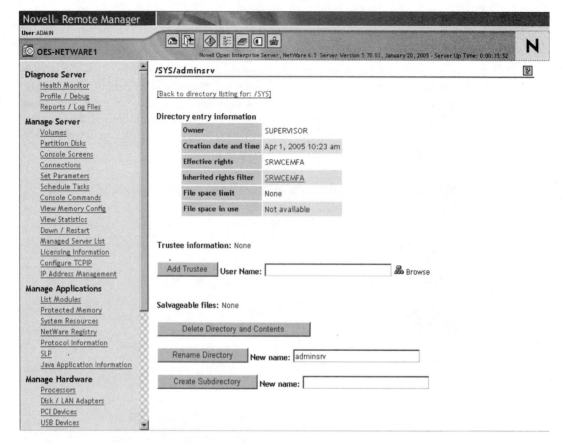

Figure 12-11. *From Remote Manager, you can set file system rights as well.*

Monitoring Effective Rights

Determining the effective rights of a user can be complicated, but Novell provides efficient tools to determine the rights of eDirectory objects in a given location in the file system. In ConsoleOne, you can find one of these tools by performing the following steps.

1. Start ConsoleOne and log in (if necessary).

2. To find out the effective rights given to a user for a particular directory or file, browse to the file/directory and click it with the right mouse button.

3. From the menu, select Properties and then click the Trustees tab.

4. Click the Effective Rights button and browse to the eDirectory object you want to determine the effective rights for. Click OK to select this object.

5. In the Effective Rights window, all rights that the selected user has on the given directory are highlighted in black. If a right isn't effective for the selected eDirectory object at that position in the tree, it's greyed out.

Traditional Linux rights

Earlier, you read about Novell rights that can be applied to a traditional Novell volume or an NSS volume. On OES - Linux, you can also have Linux volumes, which are often of the Reiser file system type, but other Linux file system types exist—for example, ext3 and its predecessor, ext2. On these volumes, the Novell rights discussed earlier can only be used if an NCP share is created (see Chapter 10 for more details). Even then, you must deal with the traditional Linux rights read, write, and execute (rwx), even if Novell rights are applied. (See Chapter 4 for more on these rights.) For file usage by users that access NCP shares or NSS volumes, they aren't important since users access files on an OES server by means of the NSS volume on that server and don't communicate directly with traditional Linux volumes.

■Note When working with NSS or NCP, a user using Novell Client is granted access based upon her Novell rights, not upon the Linux rights always present on the underlying file system. Therefore, Novell hasn't even attempted to work out a proper mapping mechanism between the two permission systems. If an eDirectory user that has rights on an NSS or NCP volume on an OES - Linux server also exists as a LUM user, she'll be the owner of the file with full access on the Linux rights level. If, however, the user is not a LUM user, at the Linux permission level, both user and group root are made owner of the file and the permission mode is set to 777.

File System Attributes

File system rights are just one part of the story. The other part is file system attributes. With file system attributes, an extra level of protection can be added to the individual files and directories in the file system. File system attributes are user independent. It doesn't matter who you are— an attribute applied to a file or directory applies to all users that try to use the file. If, however, a user has the modify right on the file in question, this right allows him to remove the file system attribute and do with the file as he likes anyway. So the modify right can be used to overrule file system attributes. There's no file system attribute that can be used to overrule the workings of file system rights.

A lot of attributes are available for the file system on an OES volume. Some attributes can only be applied to files, some can only be applied to directories, and some can be applied to both files and directories. Table 12-5 offers an overview of all available attributes, where they can be applied to (F stands for file and D stands for directory), and a short description.

As you've seen, many attributes can be used to protect your network environment. There are, however, only a few attributes that are really important from a security perspective. These are *Read Only* and *Sharable*. The *Read Only* attribute is significant because it prevents a file from being deleted by accident. The *Sharable* attribute is important because it allows an application file to be opened by more than one user at a time. The following procedure outlines how attributes can be set with ConsoleOne. Be aware that ConsoleOne isn't the only tool that can be used to set attributes. Remote Manager, Windows Explorer (if you have Novell Client installed), and the command-line utility flag can be used as well.

Table 12-5. *File and Directory Attributes*

Attribute	Applies to	Description
System	FD	Indicates a system file or folder. System files are hidden by default.
Hidden	FD	If active, this file is excluded from normal directory searches.
Archive	FD	If checked, the file has changed since the last backup and needs to be archived in the next backup.
Immediate Purge	FD	If active, this attribute indicates that when this file or directory or directory contents are deleted, they are unrecoverable with the salvage utility (see Chapter 10).
Don't Compress	FD	Indicates that the file or folder cannot be compressed by the OES compression engine.
Don't Migrate	FD	Indicates that this file or folder cannot be migrated to a near line storage device.
Delete Inhibit	FD	Indicates that the file or folder cannot be deleted.
Rename Inhibit	FD	Indicates that the file or folder cannot be renamed.
Immediate compress	FD	If checked, this attribute indicates that the file or folder is scheduled for compression the next time the compression engine is activated.
Read Only	F	The file cannot be deleted or modified.
Shareable	F	Indicates that the file may be used by multiple users at the same time. This is a very important attribute for application files in a network environment.
Don't Suballoc	F	Indicates that this file won't use block suballocation (see Chapter 11) to save space.
Execute Only	F	The file may only be executed as a program; no modifications to the program file are allowed. This attribute is only effective for Apple Macintosh clients.
Transactional	F	Indicates that the legacy Transaction Tracking System will be enabled for this file.
Copy Inhibited	F	Indicates that the file cannot be copied. This attribute is only effective for Apple Macintosh clients.

1. Start ConsoleOne and log in (if necessary).

2. Browse to the volume object containing the file whose attributes you want to modify and then double-click the volume to display its directories.

3. Browse to the file or directory whose attributes you wish to modify and click it with the right mouse button. From the menu, select Properties to display its properties.

4. Select the Attributes tab (see Figure 12-12) and specify the attributes you want to set for the selected item. When finished, click OK to save your changes.

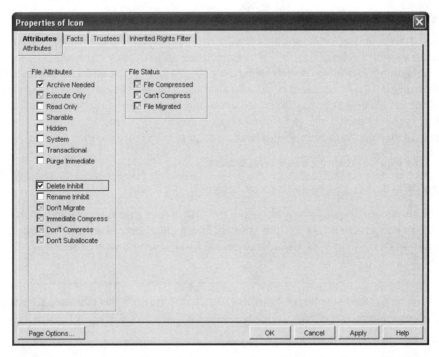

Figure 12-12. *ConsoleOne is one of the many tools you can use to change the attributes of a file or directory.*

■**Tip** Ever wondered what happens when file system rights conflict with attributes? It's really very simple. The most restrictive item takes precedence. So, if you don't have any attributes on a file, but you only have the read and file scan rights granted, you won't be able to modify the file. The same is true if you have the write right, which allows you to modify the content of the file, but the file is flagged read only. The only exception occurs when you have the modify permission right, in which case you can change attributes.

eDirectory Security

Most network administrators know exactly how to handle file system security. The reason for this is obvious: if you haven't set file system security, the user can't do his work. The situation is entirely different for eDirectory rights, however: without doing anything, users are perfectly able to use eDirectory objects. In this section, you'll learn when to apply eDirectory security and read about the difference between entry rights and attribute rights since eDirectory can be applied to eDirectory objects (entries) as well as to attributes (their properties). You'll also learn how entry rights and attribute rights relate to each other. The end of this section covers how inheritance can be applied in eDirectory security, and how it can cause serious problems on your network!

The Need for eDirectory Security

You can have a perfectly functioning network without having ever done anything about eDirectory security. The reason for this is simple: default eDirectory rights allow a user to do almost anything he needs to do with eDirectory objects. In only a few cases must the administrator configure eDirectory security to make an object usable. In Chapter 9, you read about the Profile object which can be used to create some kind of a group login script. Before a user can effectively use the profile login script, additional eDirectory rights must be granted. A few more cases exist in which the administrator has to configure eDirectory security:

- You want to create a back up admin user.

- A help desk employee needs specific rights.

   In specific situations, some other needs can also make it necessary to apply eDirectory rights. The bottom line is that you don't need to do anything about eDirectory security to make your network usable since the default rights work just fine in almost all cases.

Note General concepts like trustee, inheritance, and the inherited rights filter (discussed at the beginning of this chapter) also apply to eDirectory security.

Entry vs. Attribute Rights

The purpose of eDirectory rights is to make eDirectory objects manageable and usable. To do this, rights can be granted to the entire object (the entry rights), but it's also possible to grant rights to all or some attributes of that object. In general, entry rights do not influence attribute rights. For instance, if a user has the browse right, which allows him to see if an object exists in eDirectory, it doesn't automatically give him read rights to all attributes of that object as well. Compare this to real life: if you're able to look at a closet, it doesn't give you the automatic ability to look at what's inside as well. The closet may be locked, for example. There are a few exceptions, however, of which the most obvious is the supervisor right. Supervisor rights to the object grant you supervisor rights to its properties, and when you have supervisory rights to all properties, you can effectively give yourself more object rights because you then also have the supervisory right to the access control list attribute.

   In addition to the relationship that exists between entry rights and attribute rights, there's also a relationship between rights granted to all attributes and rights granted to a single attribute: the right granted to the single attribute always overrules the rights granted to all attributes. If, for example, an administrator has granted read and write rights to all attributes of a certain object, but just read rights to the ACL property of that object, the trustee will just have read rights to that single attribute—a good idea indeed, because the write right on the ACL property would make a trustee supervisor for that object. That's because the ACL is the property in which all trustees are recorded; if someone has rights to write in that list, he can effectively do anything to that object.

Note Basically, there's no relation between file system security and eDirectory security; a user can have all rights on the file system of a server without having any rights in the eDirectory container in which the server is installed. There is, however, one exception and that's the ACL property of the server object. If a user has write rights to this property, it gives her effective supervisory rights at the file system level. From this, it follows that a user who has Supervisory rights to the server object automatically has supervisory rights to all files on that server.

Entry Rights

In eDirectory security, the following entry rights can be granted:

- *Supervisor*: This entry right gives the trustee all eDirectory rights to the given object. If a user has supervisor rights on an eDirectory object, she automatically has supervisor rights to all attributes as well.

- *Browse*: The browse right allows a user to see that an object exists in eDirectory. Browse is the most basic eDirectory right and as such it's granted to the [Public] trustee (see Figure 12-13) so that all users who are attached to the network but not yet logged in can browse their client to the container they want to set as their context.

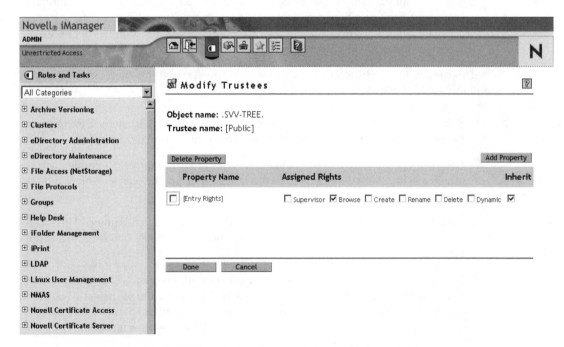

Figure 12-13. *By default, the [Public] trustee has browse rights to all objects in the tree.*

■**Caution** In an eDirectory environment, the whole world has browse rights to your entire tree. If security is a hot issue for your company, you might not be happy with that, because it provides a lot of information to hackers. For this reason, some administrators prefer to take away the browse right from the [Public] trustee. The downside is that a user is no longer able to browse to the container he wants to use while logging in, but instead has to know exactly where to go. This problem, however, can be easily resolved by having a network administrator set a default container for his users or implement LDAP contextless login.

- *Create*: The create right allows a user to create objects in a container where he has the create right. This right does not apply to leaf objects since it's not possible to create an object in a leaf object.

- *Rename*: The rename right allows a user to rename the object.

- *Delete*: The delete right allows a trustee to delete the object.

- *Inheritable*: The inheritable right is not a real right, but is instead more like a property of the rights granted to an object. In fact, it could be considered as a reverse inherited rights filter. If the inheritable right is selected, the rights will be inherited to objects that occur under the selected objects (these are called child objects). If, for example, a user Linda has supervisor rights at the tree level, and inheritable is selected as well for this trustee assignment, she'll also have this right for all underlying objects. The inheritable right is especially important when working with attribute rights. Some examples of this are discussed later in this chapter in the section "Inheritance and eDirectory Security."

eDirectory rights can be granted from iManager. The next example shows how a backup admin user can be created.

1. Start iManager and select Roles And Tasks ➤ Rights ➤ Modify Trustees. This opens a dialogue where you can select which object you want to grant rights to.

2. Use the magnifying glass to select an object you want to grant rights to for the backup admin and then click OK when finished. A list of trustees of the selected object appears, as shown in Figure 12-14.

3. Click Add Trustee and browse to the trustee you want to add to this object. This will be your backup admin. Click OK when finished. The trustee should now be added to the list of existing trustees.

4. Next, click Assigned Rights to modify the rights currently assigned to this trustee. Notice that eDirectory has automatically granted some default rights to the new trustee. In the row Entry Rights, select Supervisor to make this user a supervisor for the selected object. Make sure that Inherit is also selected, and then click Done when finished.

5. The new trustee has been added. Click OK to save your changes.

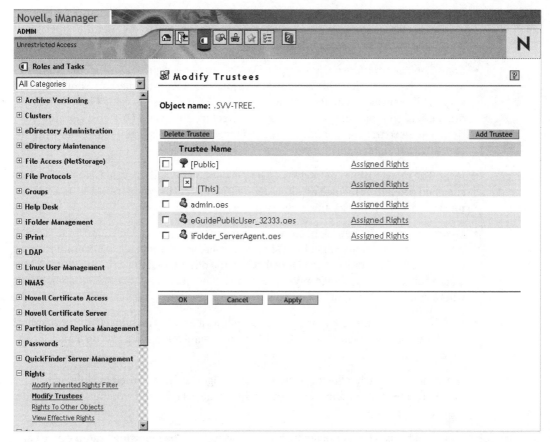

Figure 12-14. *When adding trustees to an object, you'll see all the trustees already present in its ACL.*

Note There are several different ways of creating a backup admin user. More about these options can be found later in this chapter in the section "Creating a Backup Admin."

Attribute Rights

In addition to entry rights, attribute rights can also be granted to eDirectory objects. The following attribute rights are available:

- *Supervisor*: Grants all rights to all attributes. Since under most circumstances this also implies the write right to the ACL attribute, it effectively makes the user the supervisor for the object. Even so, he still must change the ACL first before the rights become effective.

- *Compare*: The compare attribute right gives a trustee the right to compare the value of an entered query to the value assigned to a property. If, for example, you want to display a list of all users for whom the attribute *account disabled* has the value Locked (or any other query you want to use to search for eDirectory objects that match a certain criterion), you need this right. In most circumstances, this right is granted together with the read attribute right.

- *Read*: The read attribute right gives a user permission to read the value assigned to the specified property. The read attribute right also implies the compare attribute right. In most situations, you'll see these two rights occur together.

- *Write*: The write attribute right allows a trustee to write to the selected attribute. This right can be very useful—imagine a situation where you want to allow HR employees to write address data for users to eDirectory. On the other hand, the write attribute right can be very dangerous, especially if applied to the ACL property, so think carefully about where you apply this right.

- *Self*: This right, formerly known as add self, allows a user to add himself to the member list of the selected object. This right is especially useful for mailing lists on a mail server. In other situations, it's hardly ever used.

- *Inheritable*: This right allows selected attribute rights to be inherited to child objects. The following example shows how this right can be useful when working with attribute rights.

Attribute rights can be granted with iManager as well. In the following example, you can see how a selected user, who works in the HR department, can be granted read, compare, and write rights to all attributes of all users in the tree.

1. In iManager, select Roles And Tasks ➤ Rights ➤ Modify Trustees.

2. Browse to the tree object, select it, and click OK. The list of current trustees for the tree object displays. Since in this example you're granting rights to attributes of all users in the tree, you must specify them at the tree level.

3. Click Add Trustee, browse to your HR user, select it, and click OK. This adds the user to the list of trustees.

4. Click Assigned Rights to modify the default rights assigned to this user. In the list of currently assigned rights, select Write in the row [All Attribute Rights]. Make sure the option Inherit is selected as well. This gives the selected user write rights to all attributes of all objects in the entire tree.

5. Granting the write right to all attributes of all objects in the entire tree effectively makes your user a supervisor, so you must now limit this. Click Add Property and select ACL from the pop-up window. A new row is added to the list of currently assigned rights for your user. Make sure that only compare and read are selected for the ACL property, and also choose the option Inherit. This removes the write right to the ACL property of all users in the tree from your user.

Implementing eDirectory Security

As mentioned before, eDirectory security only needs to be managed in certain circumstances. The most common of these is when you create a backup user, when you want to assign rights to a special help-desk user, and when working with special objects like the Profile login script. You learned in Chapter 9 how to set the proper rights for the Profile object. Two other cases where you want to apply eDirectory security to get things working are for the backup admin user and the help-desk user. These examples are discussed next.

Creating a Backup Admin User

There are many different ways to create a backup admin user, or a delegated admin user. Backup admin users are normally granted supervisory entry rights to the tree object, whereas delegated administrative users only get supervisory rights to a specific branch of the Directory tree.

Granting Rights to a Help-Desk User

A more complex case is that of a help-desk employee. Creating a proper profile for a help-desk employee is complicated because rights must be granted only to some very specific attributes. If you want to allow the help-desk employee to do work on the entire tree, the rights must be granted at the tree level. If the help desk employee only needs to administer a specific branch of the tree, you grant the rights somewhere at a container level. Let's look at how you would go about granting these rights:

1. Start iManager and select Roles And Tasks ➤ Rights ➤ Modify Trustees to display an object selection screen. Select the tree object you want the help desk employee to work on and click OK. This displays a list of trustees currently assigned to the tree object.

2. Select Add Trustee and browse to your help-desk user to add him as a trustee. Select the user and click OK. This adds him to the list of trustees.

3. Click the Assigned Rights link next to the user and then click Add Property to add some new property rights.

4. A list of all properties of the tree object are now displayed. However, all properties needed to manage user objects in the tree aren't displayed by default. Select the option Show All Properties In The Schema to display all available properties from the schema (see Figure 12-15).

Figure 12-15. *Mark the Show All Properties In Schema check box to display a list of all available properties.*

5. Now, you must select all properties relevant to someone working on the help desk and add them to the list of current rights. The following list shows the most important things such an employee needs to get you started; obviously, exact needs can differ from organization to organization.

   • *Locked by Intruder*: The property needed to reset an account locked by intruder detection.

   • *Group Membership*: In this property is stored a list of groups which the user is a member of.

   • *Login Disabled*: Needed to reset an account that has been disabled.

   • *Login Maximum Simultaneous*: Needed to modify the number of times a user can be logged in simultaneously.

   • *Network Address Restriction*: Needed to set or modify a network address restriction for a user.

   • *Password Management*: Allows for all password management tasks.

6. After you've selected the required properties, make sure the rights compare, read, and write are set for each of these properties. Don't forget to select Inherit as well, or else the property right only applies to the tree object.

7. Click Done when finished. This adds the new rights assignments to the list and grants all rights needed to do work as a help-desk employee to your user.

■**Tip** The help-desk employee example was created to help you understand what's needed to set eDirectory attribute rights. Be aware though that there's an easier way to set someone up as a help-desk employee: a default role is available for this in iManager. You can find the role in the options in the left bar of the iManager interface.

Inheritance and eDirectory Security

In the section "File System Security" at the beginning of the chapter, you read about inheritance and inherited rights filters that can be used to block inheritance. If you understand how the file system works, you should also understand how it works with eDirectory rights as well since they're very similar. There are two differences, however. First, in an eDirectory IRF you must distinguish between two filters: one for properties and one for objects. Second, in an eDirectory IRF it's possible to filter the supervisor right. In some scenarios this can be useful—for example, when an enterprise admin needs supervisory rights to maintain his tree, but doesn't need the rights to manage objects in the leaf containers. For everything else, eDirectory security works the same way as file system security.

Filtering the supervisory right in an eDirectory IRF can be useful when creating a container in the tree in which the enterprise-level administrator doesn't have administrative rights. This way, the sensitive properties of objects in these containers can't be managed by the enterprise admin. This is helpful for a division that works with highly sensitive data. If you ever filter the supervisor right on a container level, you must always have a user object that has the supervisor right specifically assigned to that container; otherwise, the container would become unmanageable. By filtering eDirectory rights, it's even possible to create a hidden object in eDirectory: if all rights are filtered out by accident or on purpose and no object has explicit rights to the object, the object cannot be seen in the Directory. For a hacker, such a hidden object can be a useful back door to the network. Therefore, as an administrator you should watch out for hidden objects in your tree. The hidden object locator (see support.novell.com) can help you find hidden objects.

Modify an IRF

Modifying an eDirectory IRF isn't difficult, especially if you know how to do it on the file system. In the next procedure, you'll learn how to create a container with an exclusive container administrator. In the scenario, supervisor right is filtered out and a specific user is made trustee of the container.

■**Tip** In some situations, it may be necessary to create a container in which the corporate network administrator doesn't have any rights. It's best to always create a back door in such a situation; however, imagine if the administrator lost his password! In that case, it would be very handy if another administrator was capable of resetting it. To facilitate this, make the other administrator trustee of the container administrator with enough rights to manage the container administrator account before you create the IRF that filters out all other rights.

1. Start iManager, log in as an administrative user, and select Roles And Tasks ➤ Modify Trustees.

2. Browse to the container on which you want to create the IRF and select it. Add the user account that's going to be administrator for this container and grant her supervisor entry rights to the container. Click OK to save the changes to the Directory.

3. From iManager Roles And Tasks ➤ Rights, select Modify Inherited Rights Filter. Next, choose the container on which you want to create the IRF and click OK.

4. Click Add Property to add the filter (even if you want to create a filter that applies to entry rights only) and select [Entry Rights]. You'll now see a default IRF in which all rights are selected; by default, no rights are filtered out in the IRF on eDirectory objects (see Figure 12-16).

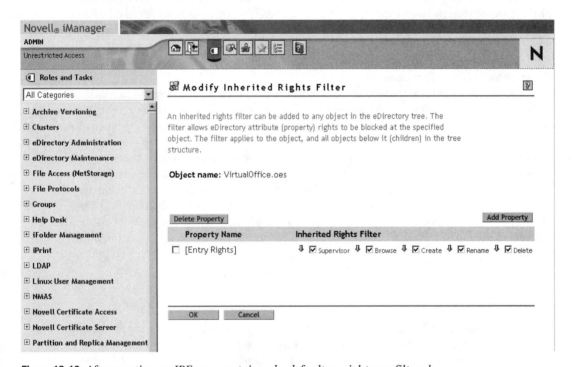

Figure 12-16. *After creating an IRF on a container, by default no rights are filtered.*

5. Deselect the Supervisor right from the inherited rights filter. If you really want to block all administration tasks on the container, deselect Create, Rename, and Delete as well. If you want to make the container a hidden container, you can even remove the Browse right; the container will no longer be seen in the tree by any users that don't have specific rights to the container.

6. You've now created a filter on the entry rights. If you really want to exclude all inheritance of management tasks, you must create an attribute filter as well. Click Add Property and from the list select All Attribute Rights. From the list that appears, remove Supervisor, Write, and Self, as shown in Figure 12-17. Click OK to save and apply the IRF. Now your corporate administrator no longer has administration rights to this container.

Figure 12-17. *To really filter out inheritance of management tasks to a container, you should create an All Attribute Rights filter and an Entry Rights filter.*

Viewing Effective Rights

Since an object can get rights to eDirectory objects in many different ways, it may be difficult to calculate the effective rights of a trustee on a certain object. For eDirectory rights, however, there's an option to see effective rights, just like there is for file system rights.

1. From iManager, select Roles And Tasks ➤ Rights ➤ View Effective Rights.

2. Select the name of the trustee whose effective rights you want to view and click OK. You'll now be presented with the screen shown in Figure 12-18.

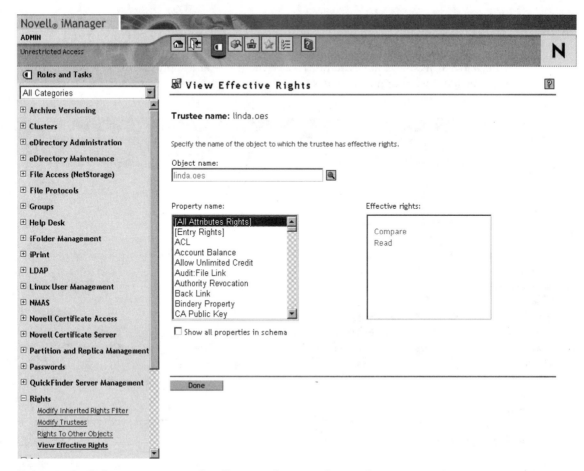

Figure 12-18. *Click a property to see the effective rights a user has on that property.*

3. Select the name of an object to which the trustee has effective rights to see a list of all properties of that object on which rights can be granted. Click a property to see the effective rights your user has on that property.

Cryptography Services

Security in eDirectory is not just about rights. An important component in the security structure of your server is the Certificate Authority (CA). This CA is the main component behind the public/private key infrastructure used in your network. Normally, there's just one CA in the entire network that signs all cryptographic keys used for secure communications in the network. The CA is a part of the entire infrastructure of Novell Cryptographic Services on the network. The other important part of Novell Cryptographic Services is NICI (Novell International Cryptographic Infrastructure). Novell provides all services related to cryptography to eDirectory and its related services.

NICI

In an eDirectory environment, many applications are used that relate to cryptography. One solution to provide cryptography to these applications might be to build all the necessary cryptographic modules directly into the applications that need it. There are, however, some problems with working that way:

- When the security of a given cryptographic module is compromised, a new version of all applications that use this type of cryptography must then be written.

- Because of national security regulations existing in many countries, localized versions of all these modules should be written.

NICI is Novell's solution to both problems. Since NICI provides all cryptographic modules, replacement of one or more modules is not too difficult: only the module needs to be replaced and not all applications that use the module. The same applies to the problem of national regulations: by using different versions of the NICI modules, it's rather easy to create localized NICI installations. Not all applications need to be written in a localized version, just the NICI modules. By using NICI, cryptography is implemented in a modular way.

In OES, NICI consists of a server component and a client component that both decide the level of cryptography used on the network. Both components are present by default. The server component provides all necessary modules to the applications that need it, and the NICI client component determines the level of security needed by an application. All this doesn't need any configuration, but is configured automatically upon installation. The only thing the network administrator has to do is make sure all recent patches are installed so that NICI is at the latest patch level, and is, above all, secure.

Public Key Infrastructure

In an Open Enterprise Server environment, cryptography is extensively used. Generally speaking, there are two ways to apply cryptography in a network: systems that work with symmetric keys and systems that work with asymmetric keys. In a symmetric key system, there's just one key that's used for encryption as well as decryption, and in an asymmetric key system different keys are used for encryption and decryption of messages. In Open Enterprise Server, the latter is implemented in Novell's public key infrastructures (PKIs).

In a public key infrastructure, two different keys are used: the public key and the private key. These are referred to as the public/private key-pair. Both are mathematically related; the public key is calculated from the private key. The nice thing is that the public key is related to the private key, but it's mathematically impossible to calculate the private key if you only have the public key. Public/private keys are used in three major situations:

- *Encryption of data*: Data encryption is commonly used when one user wants to send an encrypted message to another user, but the message contains sensitive data that they want to protect. Let's say user Frank is the sender and he wants to write an encrypted message to Audrey. For encryption of the message, Frank needs Audrey's public key. With this public key, the message is encrypted and sent to Audrey. Audrey then decrypts the message with her private key, which is very secretly stored and only available to her. In a typical system, all users on a network are able to get access to public keys since they're only used to encrypt data. To decrypt data encrypted with the public key, the private key related to that public key is needed; therefore, the private key is stored secretly.

- *Non-repudiation*: This is used when you want to prove that a message has not been tampered with during the transfer from sender to recipient. It's very simple: a checksum is sent with the message that's calculated using the entire content of the message. If the message is changed in any way, the checksum no longer matches the message, proving it was tampered with. This checksum is encrypted with the private key of the sender, so it can't be changed by any other user.

- *Proof of identity*: The third application of PKI is as a proof of identity. Imagine that Audrey is sending a message to Frank and wants to give him proof that it's really her who's sending the message. In that case, she can sign the message with her private key. If Frank uses Audrey's public key to decrypt this signature, he can get proof that she sent the message.

The Certificate Authority

Maybe you've noticed that in all the different ways encryption can be used, that there's one weak point: how do you guarantee that the public key you think is Audrey's is really hers? That's where the Certificate Authority (CA) comes in. The CA is a trusted entity that signs user's public keys with a public key certificate. Because everyone knows that the CA is trustworthy, if a user receives a certificate signed by the certificate authority, he's assured that the public key in that certificate is really from the party he thinks it came from. Normally, this process is entirely transparent: your client software knows the trusted CAs that can be used and when a certificate is received that's signed by a familiar CA, it's accepted automatically and the end user sees nothing. If, however, a CA is used that isn't known by your client software, you'll see a warning, as shown in Figure 12-19. Thus, you can decide for yourself whether you wish to trust the message you've received or not.

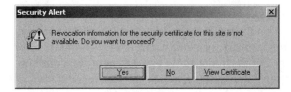

Figure 12-19. *If there's something wrong with a certificate that's received, the client gets a warning.*

There are two different kinds of CA that can be used in a network. If you need secure communication with an external party, it's recommended you use one of the commercially available CAs like Verisign. The procedure is simple: you prove that you really are who you say you are, you pay an amount of money, and the commercial CA grants you a PKI certificate. The advantage of using a commercial CA is that this CA is known by the application used by your customer and he won't get a warning that there's something wrong with the certificate. If, on the other hand, you need the services of a CA exclusively in your own private network, a private CA can be used. This is what happens in an OES environment. The advantage is that for use in your own network, you can create as many certificates as you like and you don't have to pay anything for it. The disadvantage is that this private CA is not known by your client applications, so the clients see a message indicating that something is wrong with the certificate when they use it for the first time. This is, however, an issue the administrator can easily address by distributing the software to the workstations, using ZENworks or some other software distribution software. (Chapter 13 has more on ZENworks.)

In an OES environment, certificates may be used in the following situations:

- A user wants to send an encrypted e-mail message to another user;

- A user wants to set up a secure connection to a server,

- A server needs to establish a secure connection to another server.

In all cases, PKI certificates are needed. You'll learn in the next sections how these PKI certificates can be created.

Creating Server Certificates

After installation of OES, two certificates per server are automatically created: SSL CertificateDNS and SSL CertificateIP. These certificates are automatically used by services that need a certificate for service-to-service communication. If needed, you can create your own server certificates as well, as the following shows.

1. From iManager, select Roles And Tasks ➤ Novell Certificate Server ➤ Create Server Certificate.

2. Select the server that owns the certificate and specify a certificate nickname. This is the object name the certificate gets in eDirectory. Next, select a creation method. In most situations, the Standard creation method provides everything you need. If specific parameters are required, use the Custom installation method. The Import option lets you import a certificate in PKCS12 format to eDirectory. This procedure covers the options in creating a custom certificate. Click Next to continue.

3. Specify which certificate authority will sign the certificate. For internal use only, you can use the Organizational Certificate Authority; if the certificate must also be used by external parties, it might be better to use an external Certificate Authority. In this procedure, I've chosen to work with an Organizational Certificate Authority.

4. Next, the properties of the certificate must be specified, as shown in Figure 12-20. One important part is the key size you want to use: for security, the maximum key size of 2048 bits is best. Local regulations, however, may prevent you from using this key size. In such cases, choose a smaller key. Also specify where you want to use the certificate. You can choose from unspecified, encryption, signature, SSL or TLS, and Custom. Selecting one of these options automatically lets you pick from three types of key usage:

   • *Data encipherment*: This is encryption of messages.

   • *Key encipherment*: This is encryption of keys as used in non-repudiation.

   • *Digital signature*: This is the digital signature that can be used as a proof of identity.

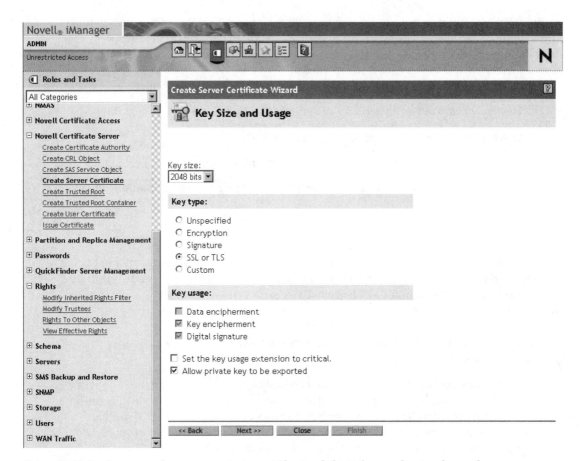

Figure 12-20. *In the custom key setup, you can specify exactly how the new key can be used.*

Two other options are available as well. The first is Set The Key Usage Extension To Critical. This forces an application to use any extension made to the key. This is more secure, but it does pose some risk because not all applications may be capable of using the key extensions and therefore can't use the key at all. It's best to select this option and only deselect it if it poses any problems. The second option is Allow Private Key To Be Exported. This option should be selected if you need to export the private key for use in some specific applications. When finished, click Next to continue.

5. On the next screen, more parameters for the key may be specified. The most important parameters are the algorithm used by the key, and the validity period. The maximum validity period is ten years. Because it's unlikely that the encryption algorithm won't be compromised in this ten-year period, it's better to take a shorter period such as two years for maximum validity. This way, you're sure all certificates are re-created after two years with fresh encryption algorithms. As for the algorithm, in most cases the default of SHA1-RSA can be used since it's very secure. Only if an application has a particular need for another algorithm is it necessary to specify it here. Click Next to continue.

6. Next, specify the trusted root used by the certificate. The trusted root is the company that guarantees the authenticity of the CA. In most cases, you can accept the default of your organization's certificate. In this instance, a "self-signed" certificate is used. This is fine for use in your internal network, but if a certificate is also needed for services used by external customers, it's recommended to use a trusted root that's generally accepted for this purpose. Click Next to continue.

7. A summary screen for the certificate now appears, as shown in Figure 12-21. If everything is configured the way you wish, click Finish to create the certificate in eDirectory.

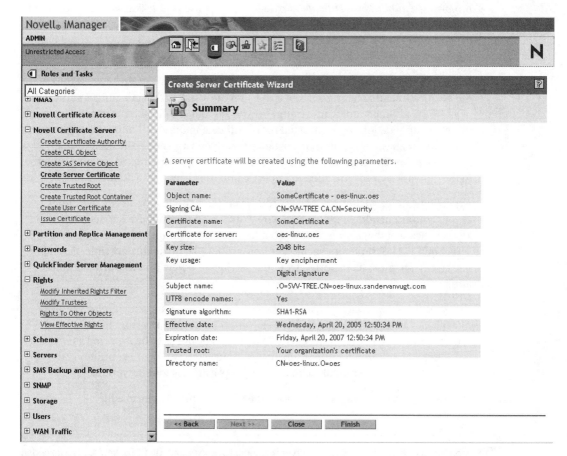

Figure 12-21. *If everything is configured the way you want it, click Finish to create the certificate.*

Exporting Server Certificates

If an application that needs a certificate is completely eDirectory-aware, you don't need to export anything. From the application itself, you can indicate directly what eDirectory certificate must be used. However, in other cases it may be necessary to export a certificate. Perhaps you need to export the private key in the certificate for use by your application, or it might be necessary to export the public key—it all depends on whether your application is the secure service you want to use on the network, or the client that needs to use the secure service. The following provides an overview of the most common scenarios where keys are imported and exported:

- *Exporting a CAs self-signed certificate*: If an internal Certificate Authority is used in a company, this CA has to be known by all clients that use certificates signed by the CA. This way, the client can verify that the certificate of some application that is signed by this CA is valid. For internal use, it's okay when the CA uses a self-signed certificate. You would export this self-signed certificate to import it in a client application so that the client application can verify the certificate's authenticity.

- *Importing a public key certificate into a server certificate object*: This is what you would do after issuing a certificate signing request where the certificate is sent to some certification for signing. After the signed public key certificate comes back, you would import it in the server certificate object to provide it with a valid and signed public key.

- *Exporting and importing a trusted root certificate*: A trusted root certificate is the end of the certificate chain. The trusted root is the ultimate instance that guarantees authenticity of a key. An administrator would export the trusted root certificate, so it can be important in a client application. With a trusted root certificate in the client application, the client application can verify the ultimate instance that signed a given certificate. Normally, this is not necessary if a common trusted root is used, but if instead a trusted root that's internal to the network is used, you need to import it into the client application.

- *Exporting and importing a public key certificate*: If an application needs to establish secure communication with a server, you would need to configure it to use the public key certificate of that server. This is what happens, for example, if you configure a web server or an LDAP server for secure communication. To make this possible, the public key certificate must be exported from the certificate object and imported into the application.

- *Exporting a user private key*: If a user wants to use his key pair in an application—for instance, in an e-mail client—he needs to export his private key from his eDirectory object to import it in the e-mail client. The public key needs to be exported as well since it has to be distributed to other users that want to establish secure communication. Once this is done, the e-mail client can use his private key for encryption.

The following procedure explains how to export a public or private key to a file.

▪Tip Upon installation, the public key of a server is automatically exported. On OES - NetWare, it's exported to sys:\public\rootcert.der. On OES - Linux, you can find it in /etc/opt/novell.

---

1. From iManager, select Roles And Tasks ➤ eDirectory Administration ➤ Modify Object and browse to the certificate from which you want to export a key.

2. From the properties of the certificate, select the Certificates tab and next Public Key Certificate. Click Export to start exporting the certificate. A wizard starts. In some cases, you need to export the trusted root certificate as well. Consult the documentation of your application to find out which certificate you need.

3. Indicate if the private key must be exported (as shown in Figure 12-22) or not and click Next to continue. If you choose to export the private key, it will be exported to a file in the PKCS12 format. This file is password protected. In the next screen, you can specify the password you want to protect the file with. Click Save The Exported Certificate To A File to write the certificate to a file that can be imported into the application.

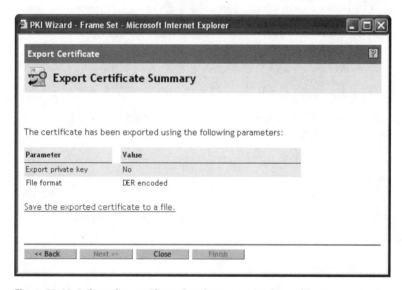

Figure 12-22. *When the certificate has been exported to a file, it can also be used by applications that can't communicate with eDirectory.*

4. If you just want to export the public key, select No when asked if you want to export the private key with the certificate. Then, click Next to continue. In the screen that appears, you must indicate in what output format you need to export the file. Consult the documentation of your application for more information about the output format; not all applications support all output formats. Click Next to continue and then click Save The Exported Certificate To A File to export your certificate.

Creating User Certificates

PKI also offers the functionality to create user certificates for use in mail applications or other applications that offer the possibility to work with certificates. Using iManager, users can create certificates for themselves, while administrators can create certificates themselves or other users on the network. Let's have a look at how that is done.

1. To create a user certificate, from iManager select Roles And Tasks ➤ Novell Certificate Access. If a user needs to create a certificate for himself, he can select View My Certificates, while an administrator can create certificates for other users with the option View User Certificates, which brings up the interface shown in Figure 12-23. In both cases, the same procedure can be followed.

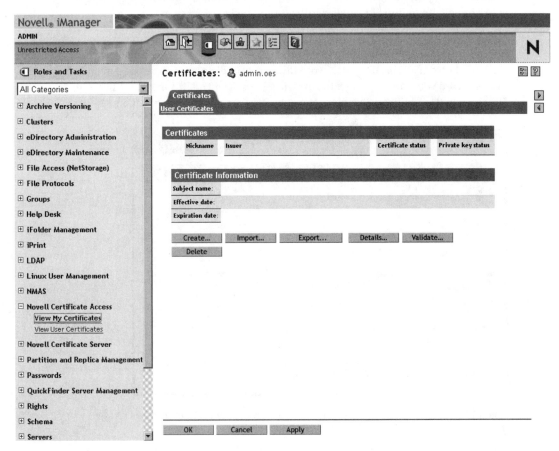

Figure 12-23. *From the certificate management interface, a user can perform basic management tasks on his certificate.*

2. Select Create to start the wizard to create a user certificate.

3. Select the server that will generate the key pair and the name you want to give to the certificate. In the Creation Method field, specify whether you want to create a certificate with standard parameters, or a certificate with custom parameters. Click Next to continue. If you chose to create a certificate with custom parameters, specify the parameters you want to use.

4. In the summary screen, click Finish to create the certificate. This creates the certificate as a property of the selected user. From the interface, the user can now choose to perform some basic management tasks on his certificate, like exporting it to a file so it can be used in an external application.

Securing the Server Console

You can secure everything you want on the network, but if you forget to secure access to the physical console of the server, everything else you've done will be worthless. If a hacker manages to get access to the console, he can get access to all files on the server as well. Therefore, the best form of server console security is to lock the physical server machine in a place where only authorized people can access it. But even that might not be enough, therefore some tips are presented next to make it as difficult as possible to get access to the console of the server. Remember, no security system is infallible, but you should still give it your best shot.

The console of OES - Linux is relatively secure because you have to log in before you can get access to it and enter commands on a shell prompt. There is, however, no default screensaver when login security is active on OES - Linux. Thus, the best thing to do is always log out when you leave your OES - Linux server alone. As an extra aid, the KDE screensaver can be activated: right-click anywhere on the desktop of the server and from the menu that appears select Configure Desktop. Next, select Screensaver and choose the option Require Password To Stop Screen Saver.

After a successful server startup, anyone sitting behind your OES - NetWare server can enter commands on the OES - NetWare console. This is bad. The minimum required in order to prevent this is SCRSAVER.NLM—the OES - NetWare screensaver. It automatically activates when no one is working at the server console, and requires a login with a valid eDirectory account before the screensaver can be disabled.

SCRSAVER.NLM is a nice start for OES - NetWare console security, but there's more. At least as useful and important is the console command **secure console**. This limits the things a user working from the server console can do:

- Time cannot be changed.

- NLMs can only be loaded from SYS:SYSTEM and C:\NWSERVER, and not, for example, from a user's home directory where he may have a copy of a malicious NLM.

- When the server is brought down, it has to be restarted manually.

- All functionalities in the bash shell and other shell environments on the server console are disabled.

Remember, the best way to secure your server is to lock it up in a room which can't be accessed by unauthorized personnel. It also helps if you take away the keyboard and monitor, thus only permitting access to your server remotely.

■Tip Do you own one of the new KVM switches that work via the network? Or does your server have a lights-out management board? Make sure to secure communications to those devices as well, and don't forget to change the default manufacturer's password.

Summary

In this chapter, you learned about the security of OES, which is applied at many levels. The first level is the way authentication is handled. In OES, this is defined by Novell Modular Authentication Services (NMAS). NMAS makes it possible to use all kinds of strong authentication as well as, or as a replacement for, the traditional way of logging in with a username and password.

The next level of security is general login security. This type of security allows an administrator to manage the usability of accounts—for example, when a user can log in, what machines he can log in from, and how he's forced to work only with secure passwords.

After the user has gotten access to the server, he wants to access files and directories. In file system security, you can define how these files and directories are accessed. To secure file system access, eight rights can be used, as well as file system attributes.

Following that, eDirectory security was discussed. In eDirectory security, you can grant management rights to other users. In a few cases, eDirectory security is also necessary to make usage of an object possible. In most situations, however, the default eDirectory security is sufficient.

Another level of security is PKI cryptography, which allows users and services to communicate securely on the network by using public/private key algorithms. These are enforced by the Certificate Authority that exists in every eDirectory tree.

The last level of security covered had to do with securing the server itself. If the server isn't secure, then the rest of your security efforts are all for nought, because an intruder could access all files and eDirectory objects on your network.

In the next chapter, OES software management is discussed.

CHAPTER 13

■■■

OES Software Management

Like on any other server system, the administrator can install new software on OES. Since OES can run on either Linux or NetWare, there are some platform-specific options for software installation on both platforms. Software management on OES - Linux is based in all cases on the RPM package format. On OES - Netware, software can be installed according to the RPM standard, but it's possible to use the NetWare install utility as well to install software in the native NetWare package format. On both platforms, ZENworks Linux Management can be used as well. This chapter provides an overview of all of the three methods of installing new software components on OES just mentioned. The following subjects are covered in this chapter:

- The Red Hat Package Manager standard

- Installing software from tarballs

- Installing software in OES - Linux with YaST

- Installing software in OES - NetWare

- Managing software installations centrally with ZENworks Linux management

- Using ZENworks Desktop Management to manage Windows workstations.

The Red Hat Package Manager Standard

On most Linux distributions, the Red Hat Package Manager (RPM) is the most important way to install software packages. RPM provides a standard way to package software that has to be installed: software in an RPM package is bundled in a special way, and after installation, information about the installed software is maintained in the RPM database. This database is used to store all relevant data about installed packages. For example, a description of RPM packages is stored in the database, as well as a list of all files installed from a package. This last point is an important feature, because it allows an administrator to easily uninstall software.

Despite its name, RPM is not Red Hat–specific, but since it offers an excellent way to manage software packages on Linux, it's become the de facto standard used on many distributions. A second important package manager that can be used on the Linux platform is the Debian Package Manager, which creates software installation packages in the DEB format. This package manager, however, can only be used on the Debian platform and is therefore ineffectual in an OES environment.

Another RPM feature is its ability to track dependencies—that is, other files that need to be present for the software to function correctly. The programmer of new software can decide to use generic libraries when programming his software. In this case, the installer of the program often installs the specific program file he has written, but not the required libraries or components. This relationship between software parts is called a dependency. Upon installation of new software, all required dependencies are checked and if some dependency is missing, the RPM installer utility complains. This dependency check also works when you try to uninstall software: before uninstalling, a dependency check is performed and if the software you're trying to uninstall is still needed by some other software, the RPM tool will refuse to uninstall it. A good package manager like SUSE YaST is able to list all the software that still uses the packages you want to remove, allowing you to remove these software applications as well.

A last benefit I'll mention here is the ability to query the RPM database for information about installed software. Some examples of this query functionality are shown next, where the **rpm** command is used to query the database. Be aware that the **rpm** command is not the only possible way to work with software packages: all major Linux distributions provide good proprietary tools, such as Novell's YaST, which can be used for advanced RPM management.

- *rpm -qa*: Generates a list of all software packages currently installed.

- *rpm -qf /usr/bin/passwd*: Can be used to find out which package a given file belongs to. Be aware that not all files are a part of an RPM package: there are other ways of installing software on Linux. On a default-installed OES - Linux system, however, all files on the system belong to an RPM package.

- rpm -qi *SomePackage*: Displays information about the selected package. This option is useful for finding out what the purpose of a given package is.

- *rpm -q SomePackage*: Can be used to display the version number of a given package.

- *rpm -qpl SomePackage-5.i386.rpm*: Shows you what files will be installed when installing the selected package.

Installing Software from Tarballs

For Linux systems in general, other ways exist to install new software. The most important alternative is to use tarballs, which are archives of files that can be installed. These archives are created with the **tar** command and are thereafter compressed by utilities such as gzip or bzip2. They can be recognized by their extension, which is .tar.gz or .tgz. Chapter 4 has more information on these commands. The great disadvantage to using such archives is that no information about the installed files is retained after installing the files from the archive. The files are simply installed somewhere, leaving the administrator to track them down once they require removal.

■**Caution** Novell Open Enterprise Server is a carefully balanced server product where all software included has been tested thoroughly. You should take care not to install just anything on your server. Server security and stability can be easily undermined if dubious or unstable software is installed.

Most software from a trusted source, and which is tailor-made for use in an OES - Linux environment, is delivered in the RPM format. However, if you want to install a utility not in this format, it will be delivered as a tarball, containing source files that still have to be compiled, or binary files you can run immediately after extracting them. In most scenarios, source files can be installed using the following procedure:

1. Make sure the GNU C-compiler is installed. You'll really need it; otherwise, you won't be able to compile software from source files. On OES, the GNU C compiler isn't installed by default because you don't need it in most situations. You should carefully consider whether you really want a C compiler on your system. For security reasons, it may be better not to have it at all since an installed C compiler can make it a lot easier for a hacker to compile a malicious program on your server. Use the command **find / -name "gcc"** to find out if a C compiler has been installed. If it hasn't, you can install it with YaST. The next section provides more information about this procedure.

2. Unpack the tarball. Most tarballs are delivered as tar archived and gzip compressed archives. Copy them to some temporary directory and from there, extract the files with the command **tar xvf archivename.tar.gz**. Alternatively, if you're in the destination directory already, you can also provide the complete path and file name to the tarball to unpack its contents in the current directory. In most cases, this creates a subdirectory that normally has the same name and version number as the archive you just extracted. In some cases, however, the contents of the tarball can be created directly in the current directory, without the use of any subdirectory. If a subdirectory is created, use **cd** to activate the directory.

3. In the directory that was created upon extraction of the tarball, you'll almost always find a file with the name README. Most system administrators don't seem to understand that the meaning of this is that you must *read* it. In some cases, this file contains precious information about how the software package should be installed. Look to see if there is a file called INSTALL as well—sometimes it's used to include information on how installation of the software should happen. Be aware that there's nothing that obliges the programmer to create these files in this way. It may also happen that you simply find a bunch of .c source files and .h header files which you must compile all by yourself.

4. After reading the install, in most cases you can use **./configure** to prepare the compilation and installation of the source files in the tarball. With ./configure, the installer verifies that all conditions are met to install the package. For example, it will check if a C compiler can be found, and will also find out if some libraries necessary to install and use the software on your server are present. If some condition is not met, the ./configure script will stop with an error. In such cases, you should read the error code to find out what went wrong, correct the condition, and try again.

5. Once the ./configure script has completed without errors, it's time to perform the next step: the source files must be compiled. In most cases, you can use the **make** command for this. The command checks for a file that often has the name Makefile, and which exists in the current directory. In this file, all instructions are included that allow you to compile all program source files automatically. The compilation of source files involves lots of work: it may take a few minutes before the entire process completes. If it works without error, you're ready for the last step.

6. After compiling software from the source files, the program binaries have to be copied to the right location. You can attempt this manually, but it makes no sense because in most cases the programmer has included all the necessary information to do this automatically in the Makefile of the program directory. To install all binaries to the correct location automatically, use the **make install** command, employing the directory containing the extracted files as the active directory. This command extracts all software and copies it to the proper location. The software should be ready for use now.

■**Note** Programming is the work of humans, and there is nothing that obliges a programmer to follow a certain method. You'll find there are so many ways to make software available for Linux that it's impossible to describe all the methods in this book. The best advice I can give is to pore over the README files included in most packages. They should contain the information necessary to install the software. Sometimes, however, only one file may be available from a software package. If this is the case, it often helps to execute it by using **bash** *somefile*. Many times, if just one file is present, it will be a binary you can install easily on your computer using this method.

Installing Software on OES - Linux with YaST

Since the early days of SUSE Linux, YaST (Yet Another Setup Tool) has been used to install RPM packages. YaST is much more than a tool to install software packages; it can be used for general management of a SUSE Linux computer. More information about the general possibilities of YaST is provided in Chapter 4 of this book. One of the major advantages of using YaST to install software is that it automatically tries to resolve dependencies. Another useful component included with YaST is YaST Online Update (YOU), a system component configured to download updates automatically.

Using YaST to Install OES Software Components

I explained earlier how to use Red Hat Package Manager (RPM) to install software in Linux. Although you could use the **rpm** command to install software on OES - Linux, it's better to use YaST instead. The main reason is that YaST automatically tries to resolve dependencies: the utility knows the contents of the OES - Linux install CDs and will prompt you to insert a new CD to continue the installation.

■**Note** The following paragraphs explain how to install software from the installation CDs with YaST. You can also install software that's not on one of the installation CDs with YaST: From the file manager in the graphical user interface of your OES server, just click the RPM you want to install. A pop-up will appear, asking you if you want to install the selected package with YaST. Select Yes to activate YaST and install the package on your server. The advantage of this method is that YaST checks if there are required dependencies or conflicting packages that will prevent you from installing the package correctly. Another way to install RPMs with YaST is by modifying the YaST Installation Source. You can do this with the option Software ➤ Change Source of Installation in YaST. By default, the medium you used to install OES - Linux will be selected as the installation source. Choose Add ➤ Local Directory to add a local directory on the Linux file system which will be searched for software that should be installed automatically.

Several methods can be applied when installing software with YaST. It's possible to select packages from categories like Development, or to search for the names of specific software packages. The following steps outline what needs to be done.

1. From the OES - Linux desktop, click the YaST icon to start the program. A dialog box appears (as shown in Figure 13-1). Enter the password of the user root to continue. You can select the Keep Password option to enter the password automatically the next time YaST is started, but for security reasons this is not recommended. After entering the password of the user root, click OK to continue.

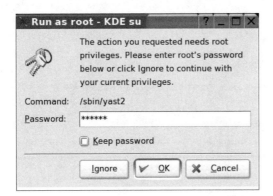

Figure 13-1. *You must enter the password of user root before you can install software with YaST.*

2. From the YaST main screen, select Software ➤ Install And Remove Software. This activates the software installation module. The most important part of this module is the
Filter portion in the upper-left corner of the screen. Here, you can select three different
modes to install:

- *Search*: Enter the name of the software package you want to install and then click
  Search, as shown in Figure 13-2. This automatically starts a search for packages
  containing the search string in their name or description. Some advanced options can
  be used as well to modify the way YaST tries to locate the package. When the search
  completes, in the package part of the screen you'll see the packets that were found;
  the current install status of the package is displayed as well. If the checkbox is empty,
  the package is not installed. Click the check box and then click Accept to install the
  selected package.

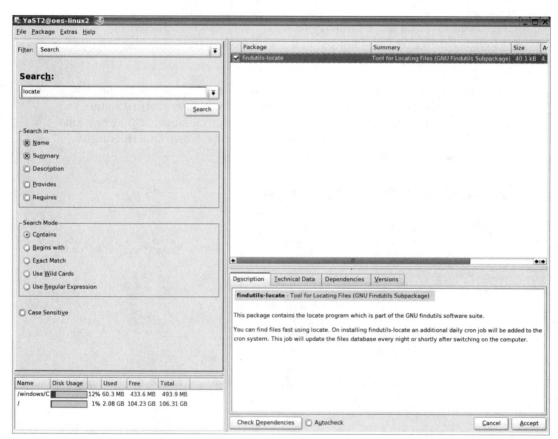

Figure 13-2. *Enter the name of the package you want to install in the Search field and click Search. YaST
then tries to locate the package on one of the installation CDs.*

• *Selections*: One of the easiest ways to install new software is from the Selections filter, shown in Figure 13-3. This option displays a list of all the so-called "selections" of software that can be installed. For example, there's a selection for the OES component iFolder 2, and a selection titled DHCP And DNS Server. In the latter, all the related packages needed for the selected functionality are listed. From this list, choose the packages you want to install and click Accept to continue the software installation.

■**Tip** YaST will always search a specific default location for any software that should be installed. Normally, this will be the same medium as the one used to install OES - Linux. You can change this default location by selecting the Change Source Of Installation option from the Software screen in YaST.

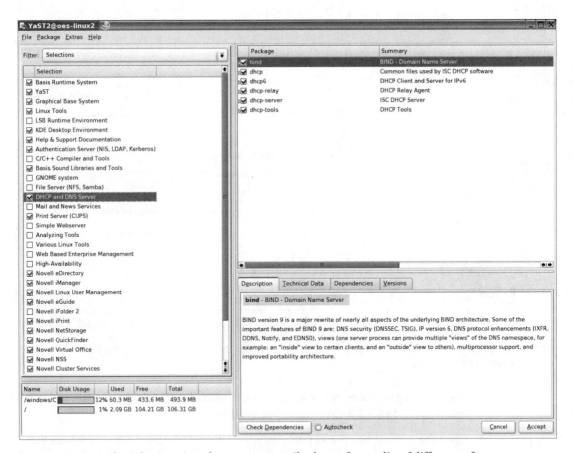

Figure 13-3. *From the Selections interface, you can easily choose from a list of different software categories.*

- *Package Groups*: When you're looking for software in a certain category, it can be useful to work with the software selections, but some people prefer working with software package groups. In this interface, shown in Figure 13-4, the software packages are subdivided into different categories like Applications ➤ Auditing where all packages of this software category are listed. From this list, select one or more packages and click Accept to continue.

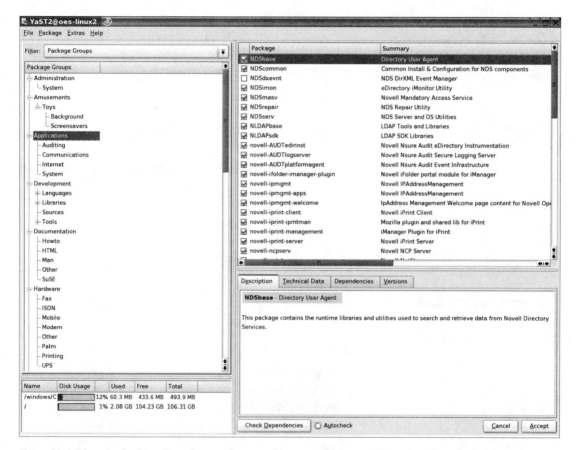

Figure 13-4. *If you're looking for software that provides a certain type of functionality, the Package Groups interface can help.*

3. After selecting the software to install, YaST will prompt for the media it needs. Insert the proper CD and click OK to continue the installation.

4. When the software installation successfully completes, the system configuration files will be updated and you'll return automatically to the software installation interface. From this interface, click Close to close YaST.

■Tip Dependencies can be hell. To prevent problems when installing new software, always make sure that a dependency check has been performed. Normally, this happens automatically, but if for any reason it doesn't, do it manually, otherwise the software may not function properly after installation.

Managing Installed Software with YaST

YaST also features the capability to manage installed software. This management consists of updating and removing packages as well as installing them. To remove an installed package is simple: from the YaST Install And Remove Software interface, select the Search filter to locate the package you want to remove. You'll see that the software package is currently installed, because the check box is selected. If you click the check box again, you can change its status to Update or Remove. Click Accept next to start updating or removing your selection.

Another option to manage your package selection is from the Installation Summary screen, shown in Figure 13-5. This is not the most practical interface to change the current status of a package, but it's very useful for seeing exactly what will happen if a certain software package is added or removed. From this filter, you can select packages based upon their current status. The following status indicators are available:

- *Delete*: The package is selected for deletion.

- *Install*: The package is selected to be installed.

- *Update*: The package is selected to be updated.

- *Autodelete*: The package is selected for automatic deletion. This occurs when some other package is selected for deletion and the package is no longer needed.

- *Autoinstall*: The package is selected for automatic installation. This occurs with packages that are dependent on something else.

- *Autoupdate*: This package is dependent upon a package that's selected for update and thus is updated automatically.

- *Taboo*: The package cannot be managed from this interface.

- *Protected*: The package is protected because either it's a dependency, or another tool is needed to uninstall the product safely.

- *Keep*: The package is currently installed and its status will not be changed.

- *Do not install*: The package is on the installation medium, but is currently not selected for installation.

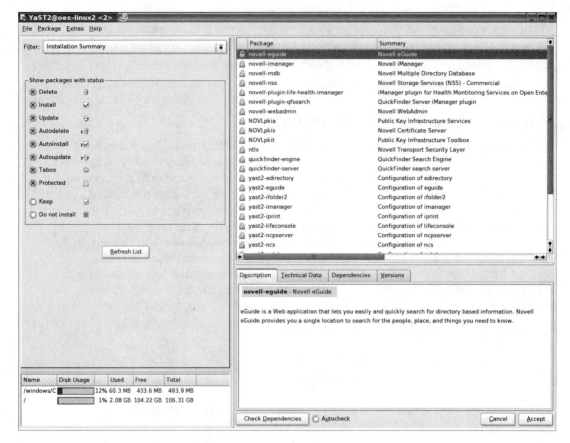

Figure 13-5. *From the Installation Summary screen, you can get a perfect overview of what will happen when you choose to install or remove a software package.*

Using YaST Online Update

On an OES - Linux system, two different methods can be deployed to install patches and updates automatically. The first of these is YaST Online Update (YOU). With this method, a YaST Online Update server is contacted periodically to see if new patches and updates are available. As an alternative, the Red Carpet daemons can be used. On OES - Linux, however, YOU is the preferred method. This section explains how this service can be used by registered OES users that own a valid license key. If you use OES in a test environment where no valid license key is entered, the feature of online updates is not available.

For deployment in a large network environment, OES - Linux can also be installed as a YOU server. This can be useful in a highly protected environment where not all servers are allowed to go on the Internet to fetch updates for themselves.

■Note Although in this version of OES, YaST Online Update can be used to perform updates of your server's software, in future versions ZENworks Linux Management will be used for that. If you need to set up an infrastructure for the automatic download of updates, I recommend using ZENworks Linux Management instead of YOU since it will be discontinued in the future. You'll learn more about ZENworks Linux Management later in the section "Managing Software Installations Centrally with ZENworks Linux Management."

Using YOU for Automatic System Updates

To use YOU to update packages on your server automatically, use Online Update from the Software panel in YaST, as shown in Figure 13-6. On this screen, all the information can be configured to allow for automatic updates of your server. The following steps explain how.

Figure 13-6. *Using YaST Online Update, all patches and updates can be installed automatically.*

1. From the Software panel in YaST, select Online Update.

2. In the Update Configuration panel, choose the server you want to fetch the updates from. If you want to acquire updates from the default YOU server at the Novell site, select the installation source http://update.novell.com/YOU. If you've built your own YOU server, click New Server and enter all the properties for the server you want to use. (See Figure 13-7.)

Figure 13-7. *If you're using your own YOU server, you must specify how this server can be contacted.*

3. Specify how the patches should be fetched. In the default configuration, a list of all available patches is displayed, from which the administrator can select for himself which ones to install. If you want patches to install automatically, deselect the option Manually Select Patches. On another front, if the Reload All Patches from Server option is checked, all patches will be fetched from the YOU server even if they are already available from a previous download. In general, it makes no sense to use this option.

4. To install patches automatically, click the Configure Fully Automatic Update button to display the dialog box shown in Figure 13-8. This allows you to create a cron job to install patches automatically. To enable this feature, first select the option Enable Automatic Update, and then specify the time of day you want the update performed.

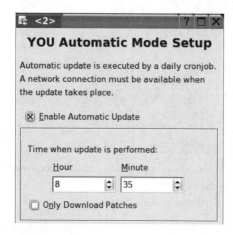

Figure 13-8. *The administrator can configure a cron job to download and install patches automatically.*

5. After configuring all settings properly, click Next to continue and download the patches. In most cases, a list of all patches that were found will be displayed. Select the patches you want to install and click Accept to install them. Your server will now be updated.

Configuring OES - Linux As a YOU Server

In the default configuration, your server will fetch patches automatically from an update server at Novell. In some networks, however, security policies don't allow servers to contact other servers on the Internet directly. In such scenarios, the administrator can choose to configure his own YOU server and download patches there so they can then be installed to other servers on the network. The setup of your own YOU server can be handled easily. To do so, start the service and simply synchronize your server with an Internet YOU server—*et voilà!* the server is ready for use. The interface to configure a YOU server is available from the YaST software panel.

1. In YaST, select the Software panel and click YOU Server Configuration. This displays the interface where you can configure the local YOU mirror server (shown in Figure 13-9).

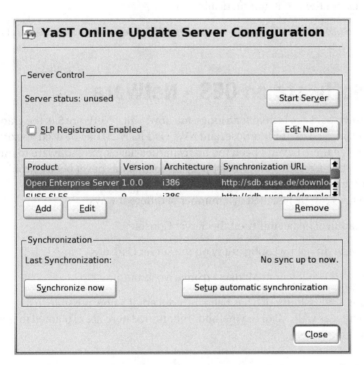

Figure 13-9. *As an alternative to connecting to a YOU server on the Internet directly, you can configure your own local YOU mirror server.*

2. Before your local YOU server can be of any use, it must be synchronized to an Internet YOU server. From the panel Synchronization, click Setup Automatic Synchronization to create a cron job that will synchronize your server with the Internet server once a day.

3. Click Synchronize Now to download the latest updates from the Internet to your local server. This will contact all servers displayed in the list of default servers.

4. To add another specific server to the list of YOU servers, click Add and specify the name of the server and the location where packages can be loaded from.

5. Click Start Server. This activates the YOU server on top of your current Apache web server. If the Apache packages have not been installed yet, you'll be prompted to install them before you can continue.

6. Now that the server is running, YOU clients can contact it directly by entering its name. It's also possible to enable the Service Location Protocol so that the availability of services will be known on the clients automatically. This removes the need to enter the name of the YOU server manually on the YOU client, which is useful if you want the flexibility to switch to a backup YOU server without having to change the names that are configured on all the clients. To use SLP for registration of the YOU server, select the SLP Registration Enabled option. Next, make sure that the parameter SLP_ENABLED in the configuration file /etc/sysconfig/onlineupdate on the YOU client is set to Yes. This adds the YOU server to the server list on the client automatically.

7. Click Close to close the configuration screen. Your YOU server is now added and ready for use.

Installing Software on OES - NetWare

NetWare has had its own package format for a long time now. Since NetWare 5.0, the graphical installation utility can be used for this purpose, and NWCONFIG.NLM can be used for software installation as well. Since there haven't been too many parties developing software to run on the NetWare platform, the use of this proprietary package format has never been a problem (to use software on NetWare, it would have needed to be developed for NetWare anyway). These native NetWare packages can be installed in a number of different ways:

- By using the graphical install utility on the Server Console

- By using the menu driven nwconfig utility on the Server Console

- By using the Novell Deployment Manager from a workstation

In OES - NetWare, a new alternative has been introduced. It's now possible to install software from RPM packages as well. All of the methods mentioned here are explained in more detail in the following paragraphs.

█Note On OES - NetWare, you should distinguish between two different ways of installing software. First, there is the method of installing server-based software on an OES - NetWare server. Examples of this include Apache web server, the Nsure Identity Manager server, and many more. To install these, you need to use the procedure discussed in this chapter. Next, there is the possibility of installing client-based applications on the server. For instance, think about a text-processing application that's installed on the server for clients. To load the application, an administrator would use a mapped or mounted drive to the server to make sure the application is installed in such a way that it can be accessed by all the users that need it. These kinds of installations are not discussed in this chapter for the simple reason that in such cases the server is transparent to the user that installs the application. Instead, the user just works from a connected drive on the server, which functions like an extension of the user's workstation.

Using the Install Utility on the Server Console

The most common way to install software on OES - NetWare is through the graphical install utility that runs from the graphical environment on the server. Many Novell products like Nsure Identity Manager and various support packs are installed from the graphical installer. This is primarily because installing software with this utility is simple. The following procedure describes how to use it to install some common OES - NetWare components. (Chapter 19 explains how to install Nsure Identity Manager with this utility.)

1. Activate the graphical console on your OES - NetWare server. Use Alt+Esc to activate its screen if it's already active, or use the **startx** command to start it.

2. Make sure the CD or DVD with the software you want to install is inserted in the CD or DVD drive of your server, or that the installation files are available from the server's file system. In this procedure, you can read how to install additional products from the OES - NetWare products CD. To follow this procedure, make sure the CD is inserted.

3. From the GUI on the server, click the Novell menu and select the Install option. This loads the Java-based installer utility. Don't worry if it takes a while, the Java-based installer is not the fastest component you can imagine on your server. When the utility is loaded, it displays a list of installed products, as shown in Figure 13-10.

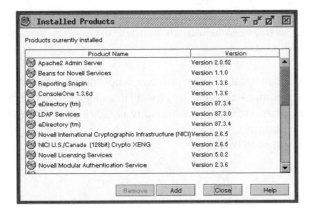

Figure 13-10. *The graphical installer utility offers an overview of all the software currently installed on your server.*

4. Click Add from the Installed Products window to start the installation of a new product. This opens the Source Path window shown in Figure 13-11. From this window, select the location where the response file resides that can be used to install selected software. Click the browse button on the right to navigate to that location.

5. From the browser window, browse to the CD inserted in your server, or navigate to any other location where an installable application resides. It's easy to recognize files that can be used to start the installation. They're the only files that will be displayed by the installer utility. If you want to select additional products to be installed from the OES - NetWare installation CDs, make sure to select the file Postinst.ni and click OK to continue. On the Source Path window displayed next, click OK again to start the installation of the software.

6. What happens next is entirely dependent on the product you want to install. In some cases, a file copy will begin automatically. In others, a new window opens where the administrator can select the components she wants to install. For the remainder of this procedure, as an example, you can read how to install additional products from the OES - NetWare install CDs.

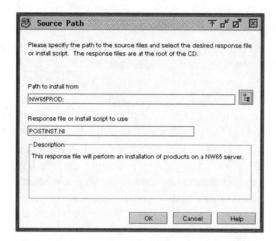

Figure 13-11. *From the Source Path window you can browse to the medium that contains the installation files for your product.*

7. A list of components that can be installed on your server is now displayed, as shown in Figure 13-12. In this list, the components that are already installed are not selected; instead, some default components (that also are probably already installed) are chosen. Before installing anything, make sure to click Clear All. Now, select the product or products you want to install and click Next to continue.

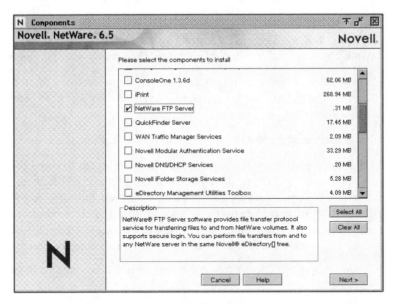

Figure 13-12. *Before installing anything, make sure to deselect all products currently selected.*

8. Some product-dependent additional screens may pop up, asking you to specify more information in order to install the particular product. Provide the information and click Next to continue.

9. When all the required information to install your selection is entered, you'll see an overview window displaying all the products selected for installation. Click Copy files to start the installation.

10. Wait while the files are copied. After successful installation, you'll see a message indicating what to do next. Follow these directions to finish the installation.

In the preceding procedure, you read how to install new software products on your OES - NetWare server. From the Installed Products window, it's also possible to remove products. Just select the name of the product you want to remove and then click the Remove button. Click OK when asked if you're sure you want to remove the product and it will be removed.

Using nwconfig to Install Applications

Some product installations need the graphical installer that was discussed in the preceding section. In many cases, though, it's still possible to use the NWCONFIG.NLM utility to install software products. In fact, if this method works for the product you want to install, you're advised to use it, because it's much faster than performing the product installation from the GUI interface.

1. From your server's console, type **nwconfig** to start NWCONFIG.NLM.

2. In the main menu, shown in Figure 13-13, select Product Options to enter the product installation module. From the screen displayed next, two options are of interest:

   • Use the View/Configure/Remove Installed Products option to remove or modify products currently installed. Also use this option to get an overview of all products installed on your server.

   • Choose the Install A Product Not Listed option to install a new product.

3. When installing a new product, a message will appear indicating that the new product will be installed from A:\, your floppy drive. Since very few products still fit on one floppy disk, press the F3 key to open a dialog to specify a different path. Enter, for example, NW65PROD: to install software from the OES - NetWare products CD. You must enter the exact line where the product installation file can be found on the CD. The file has the extension .IPS. Alternatively, the file PINSTALL.NLM can be called from this screen.

4. To complete the product installation, follow the directions that accompany the product you selected to install.

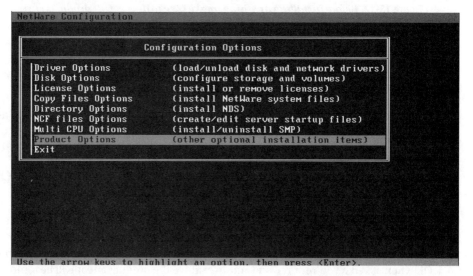

Figure 13-13. *In many cases, additional products can be installed from NWCONFIG.*

Using RPM on OES - NetWare

One of the new additions to the NetWare platform in OES - NetWare is the ability to install RPM packages on the NetWare server. This doesn't mean just any RPM can be installed on NetWare. The RPM still needs to install software that can run on the NetWare platform, which won't be the case with some random Linux program you downloaded from sourceforge.net. If you have an RPM that contains software for the OES - NetWare platform, the rpm utility on the NetWare server can be used. You should use this utility from the bash shell. For example, use **rpm -i SomePackage.rpm** to install new packages on OES - NetWare, or **rpm -e SomePackage** to remove it from your server.

Using the Novell Deployment Manager to Install Software from a Workstation

Another way of installing additional software on your server is through the Novell Deployment Manager utility on a workstation. To use this utility, use a Windows workstation that has the Novell client installed. After logging in successfully, insert the OES - NetWare installation CD in the workstation. This starts the deployment manager utility automatically. If it doesn't start automatically, you can start it by hand by double-clicking the file Nwdeploy in the root of the OES - Netware installation CD. From the deployment manager interface, select Install NetWare 6.5 Products. Next, click the link behind OES For NetWare to start the installation interface. This takes you to the interface where additional products can be selected from a list. The procedure is similar to installing software from the console of your server, so I'll skip over it here.

Managing Software Installations Centrally with ZENworks Linux Management

YaST Online Update offers limited possibilities for managing software on computers in the network from a central location, but Novell's ZENworks Linux Management (available as a separate purchase) offers much more. For this reason, this section is dedicated to ZENworks Linux Management (ZLM), even if it's not a part of OES. A quick start guide is given later. For an overview of complete functionality, you can consult the online documentation at www.novell.com/documentation.

■**Tip** Although ZENworks Linux Management is not included with OES, there's a way to try it anyway. A free download for evaluation is available from www.novell.com/products/zenworks. This evaluation version is limited to the support of two workstations only, but shows you all the options available to distribute software to Linux workstations and servers centrally in your network.

ZLM offers the administrator the option of managing an unlimited number of Linux workstations from one central ZLM server in the network. Of course, it's also possible to use ZLM in a distributed architecture in large network environments. ZLM supports virtually all Linux distributions; even OES - NetWare is supported. In short, if a platform offers support for RPM, ZLM can be used to manage it. Even if a distribution is not supported explicitly, you can add a definition for it yourself so it can be used anyway.

The basis of ZLM management, as illustrated in Figure 13-14, is an environment where groups of computers in the network are assigned to channels. Each of these channels is used to distribute particular software packages that can be pushed to groups of computers. For the distribution of software, ZLM uses RPM. Any RPM packaged software can be distributed to the client computers. A computer can be a member of more than one group, thus with ZLM an administrator can keep Linux workstations up-to-date with minimal effort.

The core component of ZLM is the Red Carpet infrastructure. This consists of two parts: the Red Carpet Enterprise server and the client components. The Red Carpet Enterprise server is the same as the ZENworks Linux Management server—ZLM is just a new Novell branded name for an old Ximian product. On the client, the most important component is the Red Carpet daemon rcd, which can be configured to fetch updates automatically from the ZLM server.

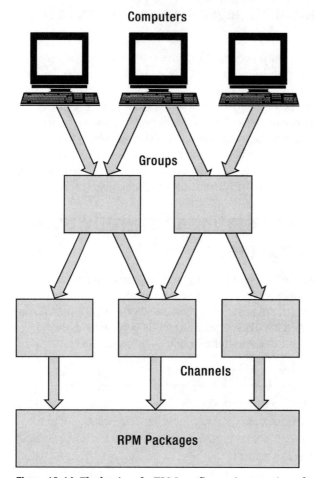

Figure 13-14. *The basics of a ZLM configuration consists of computers that are members of groups assigned to channels.*

ZENworks Linux Management Installation

To install ZLM, you need a supported Linux server. This can be one of the following:

- An OES - Linux server

- A Red Hat Enterprise Linux 3 server

- A SUSE Linux Enterprise Server 9 server

The requirements for the hardware are reasonable as well. A small to medium environment can run on a 1GHz CPU, 512MB of available disk space and a minimum of 15GB of available disk space. This 15GB of available disk space includes the space needed for the software packages that will be stored in a PostgreSQL database installed automatically with ZLM. Other databases are supported as well, but they require more configuration.

The following procedure describes the steps needed to install ZLM.

1. Mount the ZLM installation CD on your Linux server and activate the directory where the CD is mounted. If you're working with the ZENworks Linux Management ISO-file, you can use the command **mount -t iso9660 -o loop ZEN65_LinuxMgmt.iso /somewhere**.

2. Activate the directory where the ZLM installation CD is mounted, and use the command **./rce-install** to start the installation.

3. Accept the license agreement by clicking Yes.

4. When asked if you want to use Red Carpet Express to install, select No. Only if you have a purchased version of ZLM (rather than the evaluation version downloaded from the Internet), should you click Yes. This will allow you to download updates from the ZLM server on the Internet.

5. In the next step, the installer asks if you want to keep the rcd and rug client components after the installation. These are required to perform the installation. You wouldn't need them normally if you were using a standalone server. If, however, your server is part of a multitiered architecture or needs to fetch updates from the Red Carpet server at the Novell site, select Yes to keep these components.

6. After successful installation, the ZLM server must be initialized. As user root, you can do this with the command **/usr/sbin/rce-init**. This is a one-time only command that creates the PostgreSQL database and all required database tables. After initialization, the database is ready for use.

Now that the ZLM server is installed, all client systems can be installed. Be aware that in a ZLM environment, a server can also be configured as a client (any system that fetches software from a ZLM server is considered a client).

1. Mount the ZLM CD on the client system and become root by using the **su** command.

2. Install all required packages on the client by using **rpm -Uvh rug && rpm -Uvh rcd && rpm -Uvh rcd-modules**.

3. Start the Red Carpet Daemon with the command **/etc/init.d/rcd start**.

4. After installation, the ZLM client is required to use digital certificates for secured communication with the server. After the initial installation, however, these digital certificates won't yet be available. Therefore, it's recommended you use the command **rug set require-verified-certificates false**. This writes a setting to the configuration file /etc/ximian/rcd.conf indicating that no certificates are required.

5. Contact the ZLM server. You can do this by using the command **rug service-add https:// yourserver/data**.

Client Activation

The client is ready for use now. Before you can really start using it, you must perform one more step: the client needs to be activated. You can do this by generating an activation key at the server, or by working with a token that is placed in the configuration file /etc/ximian/rcd.conf on each client computer. This client activation is nothing like the typical software activation required by some vendors; it's a means to identify the client at the ZLM server.

If activation keys are used, the administrator can choose between a single use activation key and a multiuse key. The single-use key is used in an environment where every client really requires its own configuration. In most enterprise environments, this will not be the case. The multiuse key can be used to give more clients access to settings in a given channel. It's possible as well to use multiple activation keys for one client. This way, the client can be given access to several channels at the same time.

While working with channels and activation keys, you should be aware that the client only scans the settings in a channel when it's activated. If settings in the channel are changed, the client has to be activated again. Since this can be a very tedious job, it's recommended to create a cron-script in which the command **rug-activate**, used to activate clients, is performed automatically on a regular basis. Although it's possible to work with activation tokens as well, I recommend working with client-based activation keys. Activation keys are much more flexible than tokens and are easier to deploy.

The following procedure describes how to generate an activation key for the clients in the network:

1. Start a browser and access the ZLM management interface on https://yourZLMserver. You're now required to enter the login data for the administrator user. This user doesn't exist yet, so you must create it by entering a name, an e-mail address, and a password for that user. Next, click Initialize Database. This creates all the required data in the database and sets your administrative user as its manager. When these tasks have been performed successfully, the main ZLM screen will be displayed, as shown in Figure 13-15.

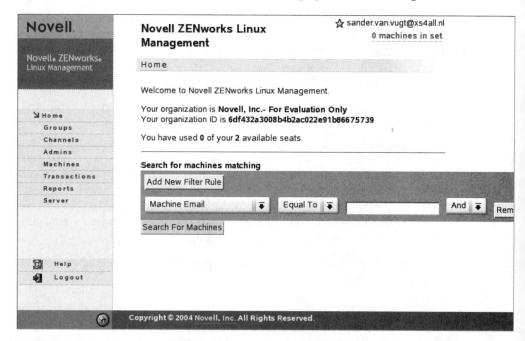

Figure 13-15. *After the administrative user is created and the database is initialized, the ZLM server can be managed from the web interface.*

2. In the menu bar on the left side of the screen (shown in Figure 13-15), select the Server option and click Activations. Then select Create New Reusable Activations to create a key that can be used by multiple clients.

3. Enter a name and a description for the key. Be sure to remember this name; you'll need it later to import your Linux workstations.

4. Now you must define the properties for the key, as shown in Figure 13-16. The most important properties are the group membership and the assignment to certain channels. There are other options which you can use to fine-tune the configuration, but you don't need them for an initial configuration. At this moment, however, you cannot define these properties because no groups and channels have been defined yet.

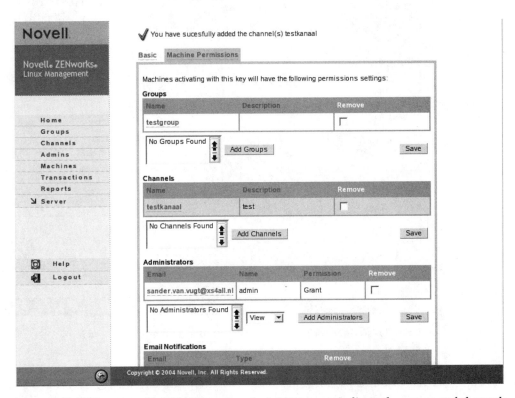

Figure 13-16. *When generating a new key, the administrator can indicate the groups and channels to which the key gives access.*

5. Now that the activation key has been created, you need it to activate the workstation. To activate a workstation, you must associate it with a given service. The service is the name of the ZLM server. You can get an overview of all servers currently known to the client with the command **rug-services list**. In most cases, you'll see just one service, but if the Novell Linux Desktop is used, a Novell update server will be listed as well. If there is more than one service available at the client, remember the number of the service you want to activate your client to. You'll need it for the activation command.

6. Now that all preparation is done, you can activate the client. Use the command **rug activate --service=2 nameoftheregistrationkey your.mail@some.address**.

Distributing Software with ZLM Channels

Now that the database is initialized and the workstations are activated, it's time to specify how software distribution should be performed. To do this, you first have to create a channel. A channel is a list of all software a client can install.

1. From the ZLM management interface, select the Channels option and click Create New Channel. This opens the screen shown in Figure 13-17. Enter a name, a description, and an alias for the channel you want to create, and then click Save to save the channel based upon this information.

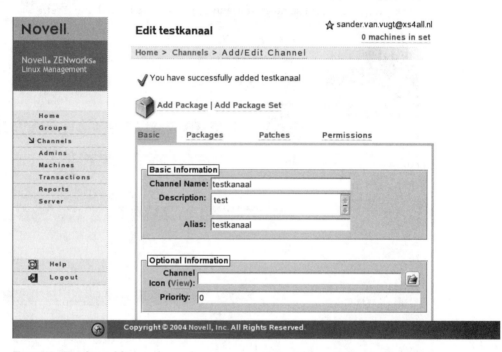

Figure 13-17. *After adding a channel, you can associate software to it.*

2. Before you can do anything to the channel, you must create a group as well. Red Carpet clients can subscribe to this group. This group is next granted access to the channel and is therefore a key component in the ZLM infrastructure. To create a group, click Groups and select Create New Group. In the screen that appears, enter a name and a description for the group you want to create. Click Add to define the group on the system. On the following screen, use the Add Machines button to add computers that have been activated successfully to the group (see Figure 13-18).

Figure 13-18. *A computer that has been registered successfully can be added to a group as a member.*

3. Now that all the required components are there, it's time to define the channel some more. The most important task is to add software packages to the channel. To do this, click the link Channels and next select Add Packages. You'll be presented with a screen (shown in Figure 13-19) showing a list of all known platforms. From this list, select the distribution type to which the software must be distributed. Add these to the list by clicking the Add button. Note that not only are Linux distributions listed, but OES - NetWare is also available. In addition, you can use ZENworks Linux Management to install software on OES - NetWare.

4. Now that you've specified which distributions will see the software in the channel, it's time to add the software. Click the Browse button behind the File Name option. Next, browse to the RPM package you want to distribute with ZLM. Click Save to save your changes.

5. Select the Groups link. The channel you just created must be associated to a group, otherwise no one can download the software associated to the channel. From the Groups interface, click Permissions and select the new channel. Next, click Add Channel to add the channel to the group.

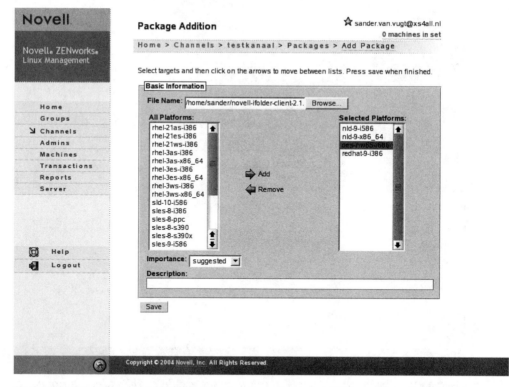

Figure 13-19. *Specify to which distributions each package should be made available.*

Installing Software from a Workstation

You now have configured the ZLM server with a channel containing various packages that can be imported by users. Having done this, you can use a Linux workstation to install this software automatically. In the following procedure, the commands mentioned must be used to perform the software update. I recommend entering these commands in a cron file so they can be executed on a regular basis.

1. On the Linux workstation, use **rug ch** to get an overview of all available channels. If you see nothing, double check that your distribution is associated to the channel. It's a very common error that the administrator forgets this step in the configuration.

2. Now sign in to the channel by using the command **rug sub channelname**. If after signing in you use the command **rug lu**, a list will be generated with all the software in the channel. If nothing is displayed, use **rug refresh** to re-read the information from the channels. To install software from the channel automatically, use the **rug update** command.

This section described a basic setup of a ZLM server. Besides the options mentioned here, many more exist. You can read about them in the ZLM documentation on www.novell.com/documentation. Alternatively, the man pages of rcd and rug provide some excellent information as well.

Using ZENworks Desktop Management to Manage Windows Workstations

To manage Linux workstations, use ZENworks Linux Management, and to manage Windows workstations, use ZENworks for Desktops. ZENworks for Desktops deserves a book of its own, so I won't cover everything here. To give you an idea of just how much it entails, this section offers a short overview of the different components used in ZENworks for Desktops. ZENworks for Desktops is part of the ZENworks Suite, which contains several products for use in managing your network.

- *Desktop Management*: Known as ZENworks for Desktops, Desktop Management is used to automate the setup, patching, healing, and migration of desktops throughout the life cycle of the device. Two of its components are Network Application Launcher, which can be used to deliver access to applications and install applications automatically, and policy management, which allows you to manage the complete user environment on a workstation with settings distributed from eDirectory.

- *Patch Management*: ZENworks Patch Management helps you roll out patches over the network with minimal effort.

- *Linux Management*: As described earlier in this chapter, ZENworks Linux Management helps you manage Linux desktops in your network. Not only can this product help you roll out software to the workstation, but it also offers options for policy-enabled management of users' workstations.

- *Server Management*: ZENworks for Server can be used to distribute configurations, software installations, and patches to servers automatically. It also comes in handy for server inventory and for monitoring the health of servers on an existing network.

- *Handheld Management*: More and more, handheld devices are being used in network environments. ZENworks Handheld Management helps the administrator with the policy-enabled management of these devices.

- *Data Management*: This feature helps you automate synchronization, backup, and the accessing of data anytime and anywhere.

For management of corporate Windows desktops, the most important product in the ZENworks suite is ZENworks Desktop Management. This product contains several products on its own that help you manage Windows workstations in a network. For software management, Network Application Launcher (NAL) is the most important of all. With NAL, an administrator can give access to applications that are installed on the network. It's also possible to distribute applications to workstations that meet certain criteria, as described earlier in this chapter in the sections about ZENworks Linux Management. This software distribution is based upon snapshot technology—that is, the network administrator makes a model installation of the application he wants to distribute. Before he installs anything, a picture (snapshot) of the entire state of the computer is made. In this snapshot, configuration files, registry keys, and existing files and directories are recorded. After installation of the software, another snapshot is made. Next, these two snapshots are compared to one another and from the difference between the two snapshots, a calculation can be made of all files and settings that were modified upon installation of the software.

Besides policy-based management of workstations and NAL, ZENworks for Desktops offers more interesting items, amongst which are a complete inventory solution and an imaging product that allows you to enroll workstation images automatically over the network.

■Tip ZENworks suite is a separate product and is not included with OES. There are, however, evaluation versions available for trial. You can download a complete evaluation version of ZENworks suite from download.novell.com. More information about the product can be found at www.novell.com/products/zenworks.

Summary

In this chapter, you learned how to install software in an OES environment. To install software on OES - Linux, the RPM package format is the most important installation source, although software from tarballs can be installed as well. The recommended method to install RPM packages on OES - Linux is by using YaST. This is because YaST automatically checks for dependencies and installs these automatically if needed. To query the RPM database where information about installed RPM packages is stored, the **rpm** command is very useful.

Three methods exist for installing software on OES - NetWare. Of these methods, the install utility, which can be activated from the GUI on your server, is the most common. In addition, if the application supports it, it's possible to install software packages with the NWCONFIG utility on the server console. You can also install software by using the Novell Deployment Manager utility from a workstation.

Lastly, this chapter covered ZENworks. In OES, ZENworks Linux Management (ZLM) is a very flexible way of installing software on Linux clients in the network and can even be used to enroll software to NetWare servers. To enable this installation, the Linux workstation must be activated. Once this is done, it can be assigned to a ZLM group. In turn, this ZLM group can be made a member of a ZLM channel to which software packages are assigned. ZENworks can also manage Windows environments. In this arena, the ZENworks Desktop Management software is of particular interest.

The next chapter discusses networking options in OES, explains how to manage installed protocols, and covers how name resolving can be configured with SLP or DNS in an Open Enterprise Server environment.

CHAPTER 14

■ ■ ■

Networking Open Enterprise Server

Open Enterprise Server offers a lot of options to help you manage your everyday user environment and provide applications to users. It also offers some network functionality related to IP address management and name resolving. In this chapter, you'll learn about all of the networking capabilities Open Enterprise Server has to offer. The following subjects will be covered:

- The IPX protocol and IPX/IP compatibility

- The IP Address Management tool and managing protocols in OES

- The Service Location Protocol

- DNS

- DHCP

Protocol Support

In the past, Novell had its own layer-3 and layer-4 protocols that were provided by the IPX/SPX protocol suite. With the coming of NetWare 5 in 1998, Novell made the switch to IP. Since NetWare 5 used IP as its native protocol, the phasing out of IPX began. In fact, on OES - NetWare, IPX can still be configured. On OES - Linux, IPX is not needed and is not an option in the default installation. In OES, IPv4 is the default protocol and support for IPv6 is implemented as well.

IPX

The Internetwork Packet Exchange (IPX) protocol is a proprietary protocol developed by Novell for network communications. You may need to implement OES in an environment where IPX is still in use. This is not really an ideal situation. For instance, if you run both IPX and IP, you must maintain both of them as well. Not only your servers, but also routers, switches, and other hardware components need to be configured to handle both protocols the right way. If IPX still needs to be deployed, the Compatibility mode and Migration Agent can be used to make cooperation of IPX and IP as easy as possible. Besides these two methods, which have been developed for use during a migration from IPX to IP, it's also possible to simply use both protocols separately, with all the related overhead (if IPX is still needed for a long time, this might be the best solution). You should, however, be aware of one important limitation to the IPX protocol in an OES environment: it's only supported on OES - NetWare, not on OES - Linux. On OES Linux, IP is the only protocol that can be used.

IPX Addressing

In an IPX address, three different kinds of information are included. The first part (before the first colon) is the network address. Like in an IP network, every network needs an address of its own. This network address is configured by the network administrator when installing a server with support for IPX. The second part (between the first and the second colon) is the MAC address of the network interface card on which this address is used, and the third part is the socket address. This socket address can be compared to a port address in the IP stack: it's a unique identifier for each process on the server. You can see these three parts in a complete IPX address, which looks like this: DFFABA12:00B012BB5656:0453. Together, they help make a unique identifier for a particular service that is available on a particular node in the network.

Compatibility Mode

If in a given environment, IPX is still needed occasionally, the Compatibility Mode Driver (CMD) can be used (see Figure 14-1). Since, however, IPX is only fully supported on OES - NetWare, the Compatibility Mode Driver can only be configured on OES - NetWare as well. The CMD functions like a network driver, allowing IPX packets to be communicated across the network. The major advantage of using the CMD is that no IPX is seen or needed on the network because all IPX packets are tunneled through IP. An IPX application makes an IPX packet, which is handed to the CMD, which in turn tunnels it in an IP packet across the network. To find the ultimate destination of the packet, the Service Location Protocol (SLP) discussed later in the section "Service Location Protocol," is used. SLP allows one server running the CMD to find other servers with the CMD available and then transports the packet across the network to the proper destination. This is a transparent process—all the administrator has to do for this to work is enable both SLP and the CMD. The CMD is only active when needed—if it's not needed, it sleeps, reducing unnecessary traffic on the network.

■**Tip** The client can offer CMD support as well. If you need support for an IPX stack on a client computer, then install IP with backward compatibility on the client. See Chapter 6 for more information.

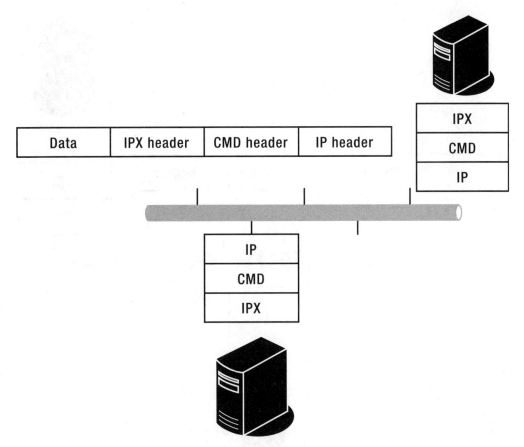

Figure 14-1. *If the Compatibility Mode Driver is used, just IP packets are seen on the network.*

Migration Agent

In a network where both IP-based and IPX-based systems are constantly utilized, the Migration Agent (MA) can be employed, as shown in Figure 14-2. The MA routes CMD tunneled IPX packets to a network card where IPX is physically bound. When an IP node generates an IPX packet, it uses the CMD to transport this packet across the network. The packet is sent to a node running both the CMD and a complete IPX stack. In fact, this node functions as an IPX router. The migration agent on this node routes the IPX packet from the CMD network to the network interface where IPX is bound to the network interface. This technique can be used if a network still has some nodes present that need IPX. These nodes can be old client computers, NetWare 4.X servers, or legacy printers. The migration agent can also be used to tunnel IPX packets across an IP-only network segment. In a default installation, the Migration Agent also needs SLP in order to discover other Migration Agents on the network.

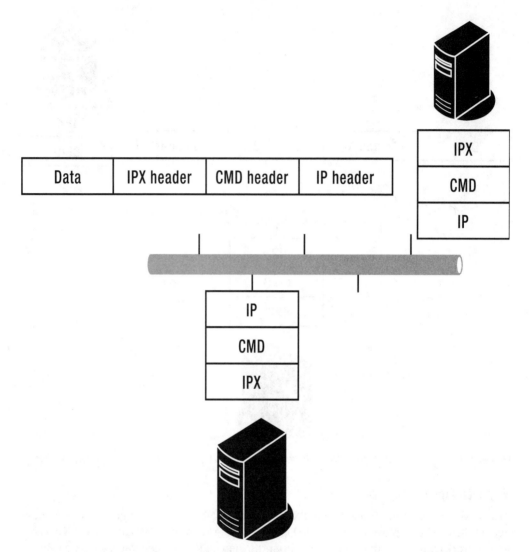

Figure 14-2. *The Migration Agent routes packets from the CMD network to the IPX network.*

Installing Compatibility Mode and Migration Agent

Compatibility Mode and the Migration Agent are only supported on OES - NetWare. Before an OES - NetWare server can be configured as a CMD node, it needs a server ID. This server ID can be entered in AUTOEXEC.NCF and is required because it provides a basic IPX address configuration to the server. After the server ID has been provided, the administrator can start the CMD by loading SCMD.NLM. This NLM provides the CMD network address on the server. The Service Location Protocol makes sure all other servers can find this CMD server so that packets can be sent the correct way to this server.

■**Caution** To work with the CMD, or to configure a Migration Agent on your OES - NetWare server, your server needs a server ID. This server ID is an eight-digit hexadecimal number used to identify the server on the IPX network. This server ID is not set by default in an OES environment so make sure it exists before trying to configure a migration agent or CMD.

Using the migration agent requires a bit more work. This is because the Migration Agent can only be active on a server where both IPX and IP are active. The next procedure shows you how to enable a server as a migration agent. The procedure includes the configuration of the IPX protocol with INETCFG.NLM. It requires a server that has two network cards, because packets must be routed between two networks by the Migration Agent. Perform the following steps to use the Migration Agent.

1. Start INETCFG.NLM on the OES - NetWare server used as the Migration Agent. When asked if you want to transfer LAN driver, protocol, and remote access commands, select Yes.

2. Now the configuration program asks if you want to restart your server. Select No; you can restart the server when the initial configuration completes.

3. When asked if you want to use the fast setup method, choose No, Use The Standard method.

4. From the Inetcfg main screen, select Protocols ➤ IPX. This sets the IPX status to Enabled automatically, as shown in Figure 14-3.

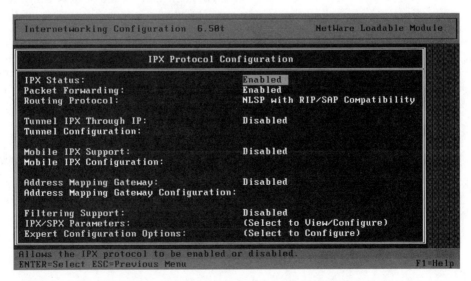

Figure 14-3. *The first step in using the Migration Agent is to enable IPX on the server where the Migration Agent is loaded.*

5. Press Esc twice to return to the INETCFG main menu. Select Reinitialize System. By selecting this option, you cause all settings you've just made from INETCFG to be applied immediately, saving you from having to restart your server. Press Enter twice to continue. The IPX stack is now active on your computer.

6. Now that the IPX protocol has been enabled, you can activate the Migration Agent by issuing the command **SCMD /MA** on the Server Console. This enables the migration agent and allows the server to route IPX packets between the CMD segment and the IPX segment.

The Internet Protocol

The Internet Protocol (IP) is the default layer-3 network protocol used on Open Enterprise Server. All services rely on it and you can't install a server without it. Later in this chapter, you can read how to manage IP with the IP Address Management interface. Both OES - Linux and OES - NetWare have their own interface to configure IP. On OES - NetWare you can use the multiprotocol router configuration interface INETCFG, while on OES - Linux you can configure IP from YaST.

Configuring IP on OES - Linux

The following steps lead you through how IP is configured on OES - Linux.

1. In YaST, select Network Devices and then click Network Card. This starts the interface where you can configure your network card (shown in Figure 14-4).

2. Normally, your network card will already be configured. To modify its settings, from the Already Configured Devices window, select Change to change the settings of this network card.

3. Click the network card you want to change settings for and then click Edit. An interface appears where you can change the IP address of your network card, as well as the default router and the DNS name server that should be used. Make all required modifications and click Next to continue.

■Tip Need to set advanced settings like the MTU, DHCP client options, or virtual aliases? Click the Advanced button for options with which to modify them.

---

4. Click Finish to finalize the new settings and apply them to the selected network card.

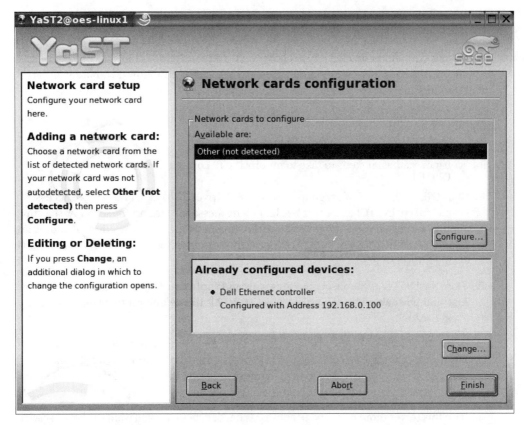

Figure 14-4. *In OES - Linux, use YaST to change settings for a network card.*

Adding a Secondary IP Address to OES - Linux

In some situations, it's necessary to configure more than one IP address on a server. These extra IP addresses are referred to as secondary IP addresses. For instance, a secondary IP address is needed if an Apache web server offers more than one service, and you want each of these services to be available on its own IP address. iFolder, which is discussed in Chapter 10, is an example of such a service. The number of secondary IP addresses that can be assigned is virtually unlimited. But there is one condition: all secondary IP addresses must be defined in the same IP subnet as the primary IP address of the server.

1. Start YaST and log in with the root password of your machine.

2. Select Network Devices ➤ Network Card.

3. From the screen section with the title Already Configured Devices, select Change. Choose the device you want to add a secondary IP address to and click Edit.

4. Choose Advanced ➤ Virtual Aliases and click Add. Now enter a name for the device, the IP address you want to assign, and its netmask. Click OK to add the secondary IP address.

5. To save your changes, click OK ➤ OK ➤ Next, and then choose Finish. The network configuration is now written and your network card is configured with a secondary IP address.

Configuring IP on OES - NetWare

To configure IP on OES - NetWare, use the INETCFG tool from the Server Console. In this section, you can read what steps to take to modify the IP configuration of your server:

1. Start INETCFG.NLM. If asked to transfer LAN driver, protocol, and remote access commands to INETCFG, answer Yes. Ignore the message to restart the server by selecting No. You can restart your server when you've finished the entire procedure of adding an IP address. Next, select the option No, Use The Standard Method to enter the INETCFG configuration screen.

2. From the INETCFG menu, choose Protocols and verify that TCP/IP is enabled. Normally, it should be enabled by default, because TCP/IP is the default protocol used by OES. Press Escape.

3. Select the Bindings option from the INETCFG main menu. This displays an overview of all current bindings. Select a binding and press Enter. In the option Local IP Address, you have the option to change the IP address in use on the local interface. Make sure you choose a corresponding subnet mask as well.

4. If on this server more than one IP address is needed, because you want to allow a service to be reachable on its own IP address, you can enable Secondary IP Address Support as well. This is needed, for example, when iFolder is used on your server, because iFolder by default needs its own IP address when other Apache-based services are running on your server. To enable a secondary IP address, from the Binding TCP/IP To A LAN Interface menu, select Secondary IP Address Support.

5. Make sure the Secondary IP Address Status field is set to Enabled. Next, the option Secondary IP Address List On This Interface is selected automatically. Press Enter to access the list of secondary IP addresses currently assigned. This list, of course, is empty since you just enabled the feature. Now press Insert to enter the secondary IP address you want to use. Make sure this address is on the same IP subnet as the primary IP address in use on your server. It's recommended to set the Arpable option to Yes for any secondary IP address you add to your server. This allows clients to use the Address Resolution Protocol to get the MAC address belonging to this IP address. Repeat this procedure for any secondary IP address you want to add. There is no limitation to the number of secondary IP addresses that can be assigned to a server.

6. Press Escape four times. When asked if you want to update the TCP/IP configuration, select Yes. Press Escape once more and from the INETCFG main menu, select Reinitialize System. This applies the newly made settings to your server. Next, close INETCFG. If this is your first time using INETCFG, you must reboot your server before these settings can be applied properly.

IPv6

On the Internet, the current version of the IP protocol in use is IPv4. There is, however, a shortage in IPv4 addresses, and for that reason a few years ago the next version of the IP protocol was specified. Because the draft of IP version 5 never made it, this new IP version is known as IPv6. In IPv6, 128 bits are used for addressing nodes. IPv6 offers some really flexible options to assign addresses to nodes automatically. This is because the entire MAC address of a node can be included automatically in an IPv6 address. That way, the node only needs to know the address of the network it's configured on in order to be set up. Although demand for IPv6 isn't really huge, OES offers support for it on both the Linux and NetWare versions. Since almost no one uses IPv6, this subject is not discussed in this chapter. For more information about IPv6 address management, refer to the online documentation at http://www.novell.com/documentation/oes.

IP Address Management

On both OES - NetWare and OES - Linux servers, IP addresses are stored in many places. In the past, this made changing an IP address a tedious task. Not only did the administrator have to change the main address configuration, but a lot of other configuration files where the IP address was used had to be changed as well. In OES - NetWare, IP Address Management is used as a centralized framework where IP addresses and port configurations are stored on a server. This way you can be assured that changing the IP address at one location always results in a change of address at all the required locations. In addition, port conflicts are prevented as well. IP address management is available on OES - NetWare only. To manage IP address changes on OES - Linux, YaST can be deployed. Because of the way YaST writes IP address changes to the operating system, the changes are automatically available at all places where the IP address is needed.

IP address management is implemented with two modules:

- IPMGMT.NLM can be loaded with IPMINIT.NCF to provide the basic framework to handle an application's IP address and port configurations.

- IPMCFG.NLM can be loaded with INETSTRT.NCF to provide Novell Remote Manager with the user interface for IP address management.

Managing IP Addresses from Novell Remote Manager

When these two modules are loaded, the complete management of IP addresses can be performed on OES - NetWare from the Novell Remote Manager, as shown in the following steps.

1. Activate Remote Manager on https://*yourserver*:8009 and authenticate as the admin user.

2. From Manage Server, select Configure TCP/IP and click Start TCP/IP Configuration. This displays a window (shown in Figure 14-5) with a menu structure that's a lot like the INETCFG interface.

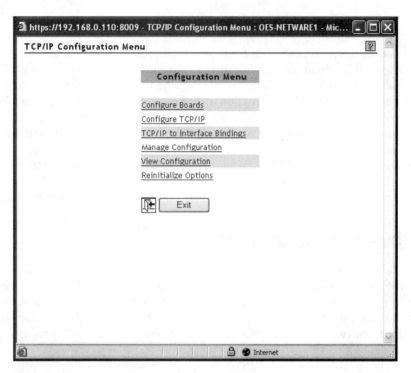

Figure 14-5. *The web-based TCP/IP Configuration Menu offers many options in common with INETCFG.NLM.*

3. Click Configure TCP/IP. This displays a window where all generic TCP/IP options can be set (as shown in Figure 14-6). The options are divided into two categories: Generic Configuration and Expert Configuration. I'll only discuss the Generic Configuration here since in most scenarios the Expert options are good with their default value. Consult the documentation at www.novell.com/documentation/oes for more information about the expert options. Modify these options as needed and click Save to apply them.

- *TCP/IP Status*: Use this option to enable or disable TCP/IP.

- *IP Packet Forwarding*: Set this to Enabled to make the server a router, or leave it at Disabled to configure the server as an end-node.

- *DNS Resolver Configuration*: Use this option to specify the DNS nameserver(s) you want to use.

- *RIP*: Set this to Enabled to make the server a RIP router. A RIP (Routing Information Protocol) router multicasts its routing table once every 30 seconds to all other RIP routers in the network. You should only enable this option if your server is used as a router and it needs to communicate with other RIP routers in the network.

- *OSPF*: Set this to Yes to make the server an OSPF (open shortest path first) router. This only makes sense if there are other routers in this network that use the OSPF protocol to exchange routing information and if your server routes packets between two IP networks. If you enable a server to be an OSPF router, some additional options must be specified as well via the OSPF Configuration option. I don't cover these options in the book, because the required OSPF configuration is dependent on the configuration of other OSPF routers in the same network.

- *LAN Static Routing*: This option is set to Enabled in most situations. This is because static routing is configured if you've specified a default gateway for this server, which is the case on most servers. The use of LAN Static Routing is also recommended in small networks where few changes occur. This way you can avoid routing protocols to send updates over the network at all times.

- *LAN Static Routing Table*: Use this option to enter the static routing table.

- *Default IP Address*: This option shows the IP address of the default route. Normally, it displays the value 0.0.0.0 to refer to all networks.

4. After configuring the generic options, bind TCP/IP to one or more network interfaces. From the main menu, click TCP/IP To Interface Bindings. This presents an overview of all interfaces whether or not they are already configured with TCP/IP.

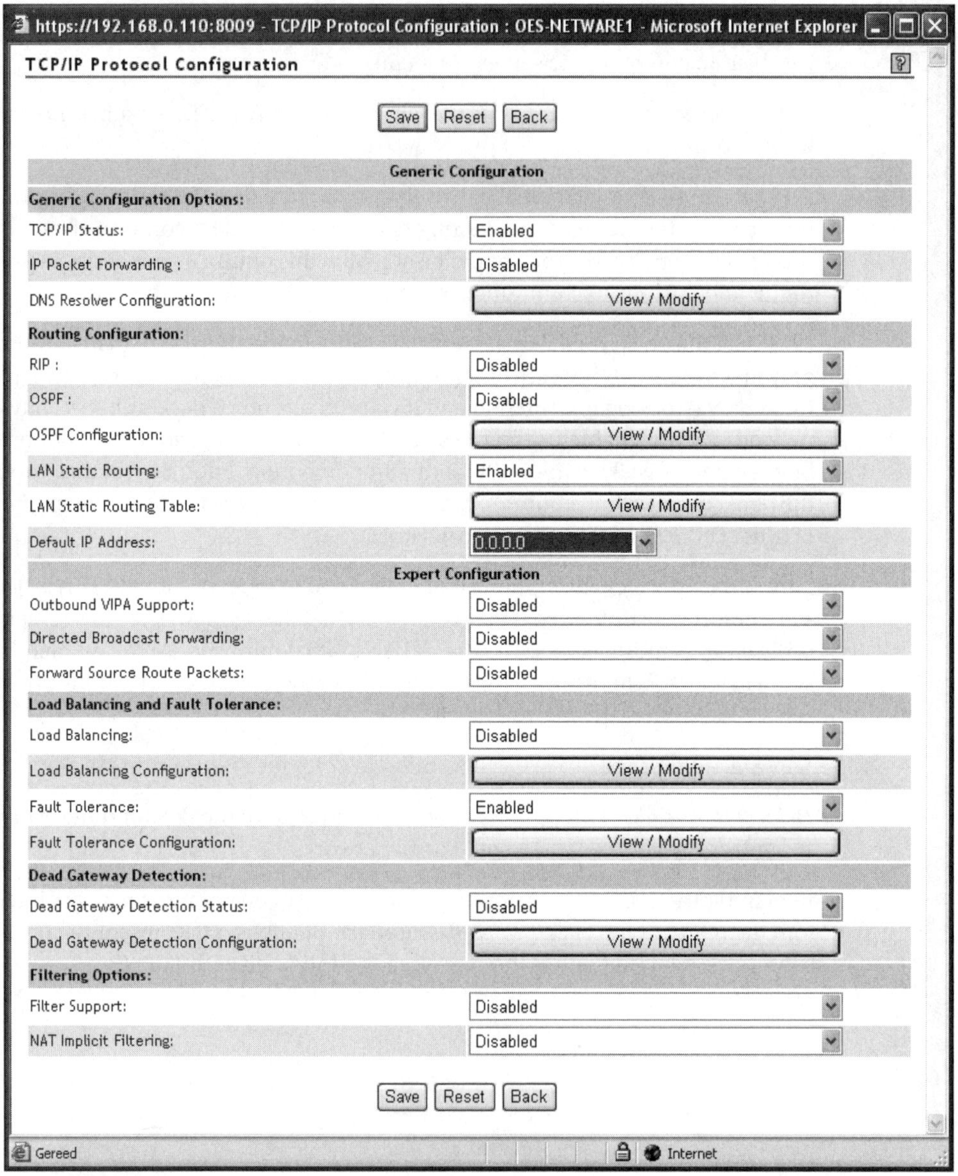

Figure 14-6. *The most important of the generic TCP/IP options is the option to configure your server with a static routing table.*

5. Click an interface to change its settings. This shows the current address configuration. From here, enter a secondary IP address, which is useful if your server is, say, hosting virtual web servers that are configured on their own IP addresses. The option Configure TCP/IP Bind Options is not needed often. The most important reason to use it is to configure Network Address Translation on the server. To do so, click View/Modify and then click View/Modify at the Expert TCP/IP Bind Options (see Figure 14-7). Then, click

View/Modify again to change the current Network Address Translation configuration. Now you can select the type of NAT you want to use. For example, choose Dynamic Only to allow all workstations on your private network to access computers on the Internet by using the registered IP address of your server. The Static Only option is used to allow access to one or more computers on the private network from the Internet. To use this option, you must configure secondary IP addresses on your server.

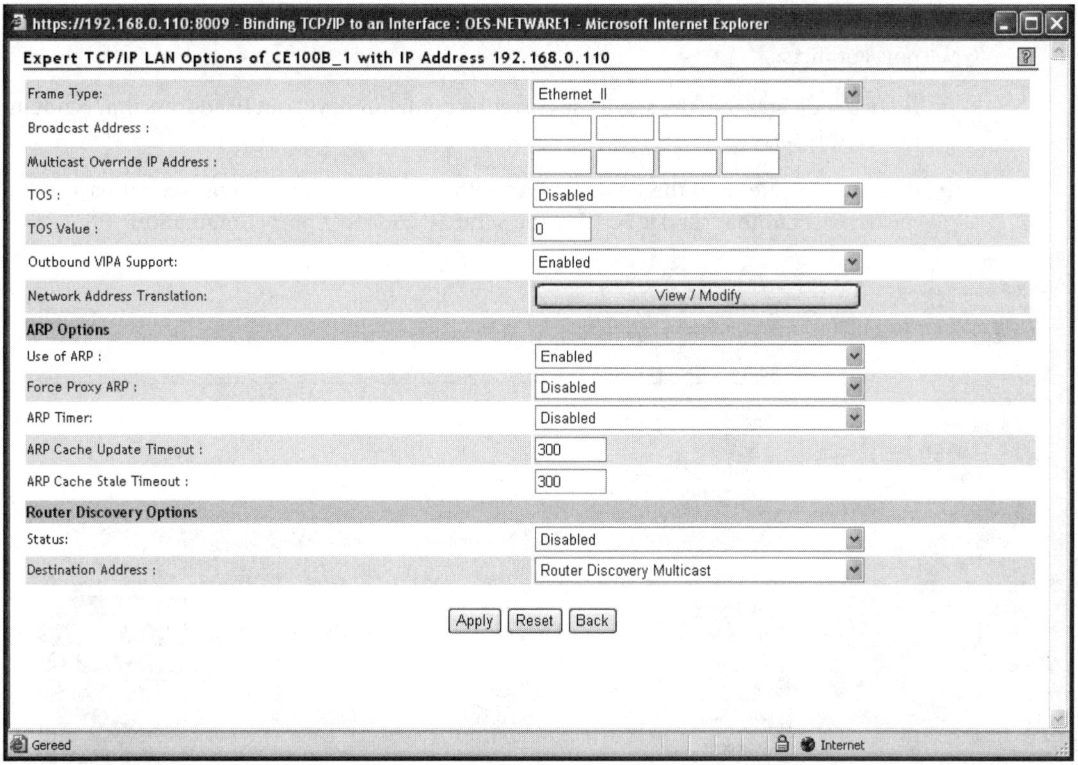

Figure 14-7. *The most important option you'll find under the expert TCP/IP options is the NAT configuration.*

6. When you've entered all required changes for your network interface, click Save and then select Back to return to the main configuration screen. To apply the changes, click Reinitialize Options and then choose Reinitialize System. This saves and applies all modifications you've applied. If new IP addresses have been entered, PKI certificates are automatically created to allow secure communications on the new addresses.

Managing IP Addresses and Ports from IP Address Management

After entering all required IP address configurations, you can make changes to these addresses from the IP Address Management interface, shown in Figure 14-8. In Remote Manager, select Manage Server ➤ IP Address Management to access this screen. This interface shows a list of all services on your server that are currently using the TCP/IP stack. For each of these servers, you can see on which IP address they are listening. In many cases, you'll see that the service is listening on the IP address 0.0.0.0, which means that it's not bound to a specific network board but is listening on all available network interfaces. In some cases, the service listens at the IP address of a specific network interface, or the default IP address, which is the first IP address configured for the server. You can also tell on which port the services are listening and find information about the current status of the service. This last part of the overview screen is particularly important since it shows you whether a service is currently available or not. The following status indicators are available:

- *Valid* indicates that the application is configured with a valid IP address and there are no port conflicts.

- *Invalid* indicates that the service is currently configured with an IP address that is not in use on this server.

- *Conflict* indicates that there is a conflict with another service. In most scenarios, this means that another service is using the same IP address / port combination.

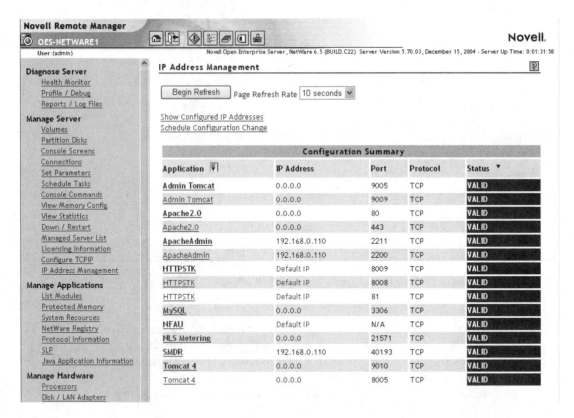

Figure 14-8. *From the IP Address Management interface, you can see immediately if all applications are functioning properly with regards to the configured IP addresses and ports.*

From the IP Address Management interface, it's easy to change the configuration for a given application:

1. From Novell Remote Manager, select Manage Server ➤ IP Address Management.

2. Click the link of the application you want to change the configuration for. This shows you the current configuration for the selected application (see Figure 14-9).

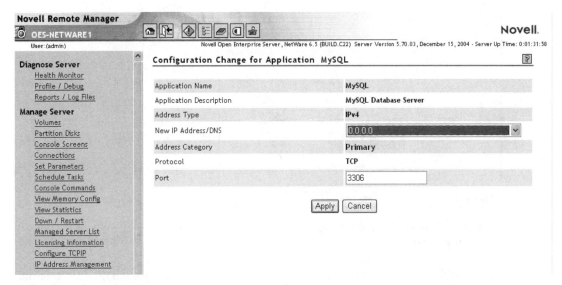

Figure 14-9. *When you click an application, you gain access to all the application parameters that can be changed.*

3. From the drop-down list, select a new IP address for the selected application. Only IP addresses that are currently configured are available. To change the default port for a service, enter the new port address directly in the interface.

4. Click Apply to save and apply the changes.

From the IP Address Management interface, it's possible to schedule a configuration change as well. This is useful because normally you don't want the entire IP configuration changed on an operational system that lots of users are connected to. To schedule a change of IP address, click Schedule Configuration Change (this presents the screen shown in Figure 14-10) and select the date, time, and the new IP address you want to start using. Next, click Apply. This creates a cron job to change the IP address at the given date and time.

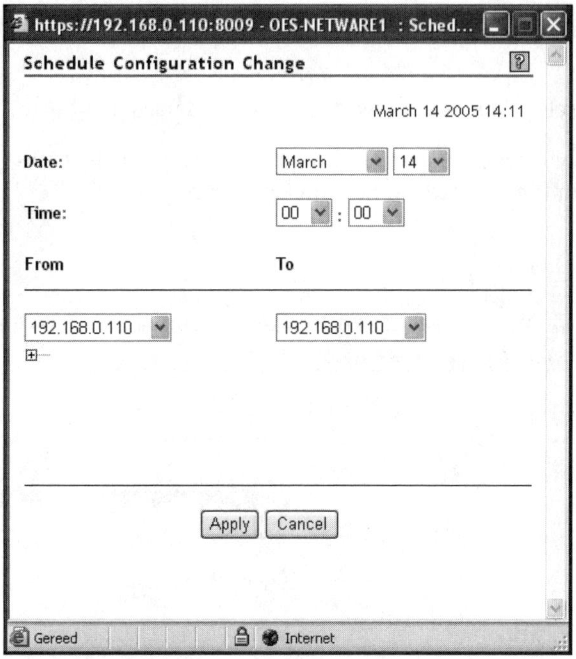

Figure 14-10. *To allow for the ultimate flexibility, it's possible to schedule a change of IP address at a future point of time.*

IP Address Management provides a great interface to manage ports and IP addresses from one central location on the network. You do, however, need to use applications that are supported by the IP Address Management interface (not all applications are supported yet). The following shows a list of applications currently supported.

- Admin Tomcat

- Apache 2.0

- Apache Admin

- exteNdAppServer

- DNS Server

- FTP

- HTTPSTK

- iManager 2.0

- MySQL

- NDPS Broker

- Native File Access for UNIX

- NLS License metering

- RSync NRM Management Utility

- SMS - Storage Data Requestor

- SSH Server

- Tomcat User instance

- NetWare Web Search Server 3.0.0

Resolving Names

On networks, IP addresses are used to enable communications between two hosts. For computers, this works fine; for humans, however, working with IP addresses is hard because they are so difficult to remember. Therefore, a system is needed that can translate an IP address to a name a human can remember and vice versa. Two of these systems are the Service Location Protocol (SLP) and Domain Name System (DNS).

SLP and DNS go beyond simply translating IP addresses into easy-to-remember names and vice versa. Both systems can also be used to locate services on the network. A classic example of this is the MX resource record in the DNS database that helps any application find the responsible mail server for a given DNS domain. In Open Enterprise Server, SLP plays an important role in finding services on the network. Configuration of both of these protocols is discussed next.

Service Location Protocol

In the IPX epoch, Novell used Service Advertising Protocol (SAP) to advertise the availability of services on the network. This was a rather noisy protocol where each server in the network would broadcast its table of registered services once every minute. No one shed any tears when SAP was finally phased out when IP became the native protocol used by NetWare. As a result, SAP was replaced by SLP, an RFC standard that allows for the location of services. To use this protocol in an OES environment, you should be aware of how it's deployed in large network environments.

SLP Architecture

In an SLP environment, three different kinds of agents communicate to exchange information about available network services. First, there is the SLP Service Agent (SA). This is a registration point where services can register their availability. Typically, an SLP SA is present on all servers in the network. The second part is the SLP User Agent (UA), which is present on all nodes that have some kind of client software available. Notice that it exists on most servers as well because they need it to request services from each other. The third part is the Directory Agent. This component can be used on a large network as a registration point where all SAs send information regarding the services they have available. The DA is discussed later in this chapter in the section "Creating the Directory Agent."

In the simplest configuration, the SLP SA and UA communicate about which services must be used. In this system, a service is never advertised. Instead, the UA sends a multicast to all SAs on the network to get a complete list of the services available. The process is as follows:

1. If a service becomes available, it registers with an SLP service agent.

2. All servers in the network have a list of services that are available locally on that server. A client that needs access to a given service sends a multicast on the network to all available SLP SAs.

3. The SLP SAs send unicast replies with a list of available services from which the client can choose.

This procedure is rather primitive, but it works in small- to medium-sized networks. If, however, the network becomes too large, the system earlier described runs into some problems. For instance, the UAs are multicasting across the network to build their list of available services. When there are too many services, or when the network is just too large because many routers are available, you may want to reduce multicast traffic as much as possible. Also, you should be aware that multicast doesn't work through most routers. This prevents workstations on remote sites from seeing central servers. Even some switches block multicast by default nowadays. You can view these other servers by creating an SLP Directory Agent (DA). If an SLP DA is used, all SAs on the network update the DA about services they have available. This prevents the client from multicasting to all SAs on the network. Instead, it can send a unicast to the SLP DA.

If an SLP DA is used, some method has to be used on the SLP SA and SLP UA to find out where the DA is available. Almost all methods you can imagine come into play.

- A DHCP server can be used to get information about available DAs to the client.

- A client computer can be configured manually with the IP address of an SLP DA.

- The client computer can multicast to find out if an SLP DA is available.

- On a server, a configuration file can be used to include the IP address of the SLP DA.

- The SLP DA can multicast its presence on the network.

On a very large network, it may not be enough that just one DA is available. Imagine a multinational company with sites in every country on the planet; it doesn't make sense to have all clients at every location send SLP packets to an SLP DA that only exists in San Francisco. In such a scenario, it's recommended you work with multiple scopes. In fact, SLP always uses at least one scope and the DA services all requests for that scope. In a large network environment, multiple scopes can be created and multiple SLP DAs used to service these scopes. In this scenario, the administrator has to specify the scope a computer belongs to on all computers on the network. This default scope can be assigned to an SLP client by using a DHCP server. Alternatively, it's also possible to specify for each individual client what scope should be used.

Using hosts.nds to Bypass SLP

SLP is a rather dynamic protocol. If you don't want this on your network, a configuration file called /etc/hosts.nds can be configured to bypass SLP. If this configuration file is created, a static reference to all services available on the network can be made. In this file, you can refer to the following elements:

- *TREENAME.*: Use this to reference the IP address of a server that has a replica of the root partition of the eDirectory tree that's referred to. Don't forget the dot after the treename, it's mandatory. More than one line TREENAME can be included in hosts.nds.

- *partition.TREENAME.*: Use this to refer to the IP address of a server that has a replica of the given partition. More than one of these partition.TREENAME lines can be used.

- *server*: A server can be referred to just by pointing to its IP address.

An example hosts.nds is shown next:

```
OES-TREE.      192.168.0.1
OES-TREE       192.168.0.2
SFO.OES-TREE.  192.168.0.10
SFO.OES-TREE.  192.168.0.11
server1        192.168.0.1
server2        192.168.0.2
server10       192.168.0.10
server11       192.168.0.11
```

SLP Deployment

The configuration of an SLP environment consists of the following three parts:

- The client must be configured with specific SLP parameters.

- The SA must be configured with options that determine how to communicate with other SAs or DAs.

- If required, a Directory Agent must be configured.

Configuring an SLP User Agent

There are two methods for configuring SLP settings on an end-user's PC: you can use the Novell DHCP server to configure required parameters on the client, or specify the required parameters in the Novell client software. The section "OES As a DHCP Server" later in this chapter explains how to configure the DHCP server to distribute SLP-related settings. The procedure for setting up the client is described next.

1. On a client computer where the Novell client is installed, right-click the red N in the task bar and from the menu select Novell Client Properties to bring up the dialog box shown in Figure 14-11.

2. Select the Service Location tab. This displays all settings related to the SLP configuration of the client. The following options are available:

- *Scope List*: Use this option to enter scopes where the client should look for available services manually.

- *Static*: Select this check box if you don't want the client to multicast for available scopes, but just to work with the scopes entered in the scope list.

- *Filters*: Use this to set a filter on the scopes that can be used by the client. The option prevents certain scopes from being contacted on the client.

- *Directory Agent List*: Use this option to enter the IP addresses of one or more Directory Agents manually.

- *Static*: Use this option (in the Directory Agent List section) to prevent a client from dynamically updating the list of available Directory Agents.

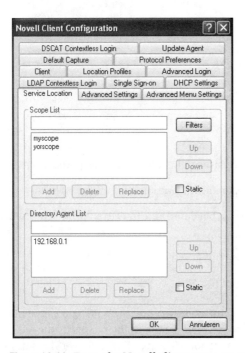

Figure 14-11. *From the Novell client, you can specify exactly how SLP should be used.*

Configuring SLP Parameters for the Service Agent

The way SLP parameters for the Service Agent are configured depends on the version of OES you're using. If you're using OES - Linux, all settings must be entered in the configuration file slp.conf. If you're on OES - NetWare, you can use set parameters from the Novell Remote Manager to specify the behavior of the SLP SA on your server.

To use SLP on OES - Linux, install the product with YaST. In a default installation, SLP is not installed automatically. After installation, the SLP daemon can be started with the command **/etc/init.d/slpd start.** If the service is installed, it should be restarted automatically each time you restart your server. All related configurations are in the configuration file /etc/slp.conf. This file can be used to configure the SLP daemon both as an SA and as a DA. For the configuration of an SLP SA, the following parameters are important:

```
net.slp.useScopes = <comma delimited scope list>
net.slp.DAAddresses = <comma delimited address list>
net.slp.passiveDADetection = <"true" or "false">
net.slp.activeDADetection = <"true" or "false">
net.slp.DAActiveDiscoveryInterval = <0, 1, or a number of seconds>
```

Of these parameters, the useScopes option indicates in which scopes the SA advertises its services. The DAAddresses option is used to specify a comma-separated list of preferred DAs. If this list does not support the list of scopes as in useScopes, the SA starts multicasting to find the DAs responsible for the specified scopes. The passiveDADetection option specifies that the SA listens to the periodic broadcasts by the DA on a specific port. This parameter is set to true by default. The parameter activeDADetection, which is also true by default, specifies that the SA is allowed to send a broadcast periodically to find an active DA. With the last option of DAActiveDiscoveryInterval, the default value of 1 specifies that the SA should send out just one DA discovery packet upon activation. A value of 0 disables the sending of DA discovery packets. Alternatively, a number of seconds can be specified. This is the number of seconds between discovery broadcasts.

To set up SLP SA parameters on an OES - NetWare server, use Remote Manager, as shown in Figure 14-12. To configure OpenSLP on OES - Linux, the only available method is by manually configuring the configuration file slp.conf as described earlier.

1. Activate Remote Manager on https://*yourserver*:8009.

2. Select Manage Server ➤ Set Parameters and click Service Location Protocol. This displays a list of all available parameters needed to configure SLP on your server. For the SLP SA, the following options are important:

   - *SLP Scope List*: This parameter is used to specify a comma-delimited string specifying the Scope List.

   - *SLP Static Scope List*: This specifies whether or not scopes that are not in the SLP Scope list are accepted. The default value for this parameter is ON. If set to OFF, the SLP SA also uses scopes from the configuration file slp.cfg.

   - *SLP Retry Count*: This specifies the maximum number of retries the SLP SA uses before abandoning the effort.

- *SLP Rediscover Inactive Directory Agents*: This specifies the minimum amount of time the SLP SA waits before attempting to contact an inactive DA again. The default value for this parameter is set to 60 seconds.

- *SLP DA Discovery Options*: This parameter is used to specify how a DA should be located. The argument of this parameter is a hexadecimal number. The possible options are 1: dynamic discovery via multicast, 2: DHCP discovery, 4: by using the static file /etc/slp.cfg, 8: never do dynamic discovery when the DHCP or static file options are set. Bits may be added to use several options. The default value of 15 specifies that the SLP SA tries all available methods to contact a DA.

- *SLP Broadcast*: This parameter designates that broadcast packets instead of multicast packets can be used for DA discovery.

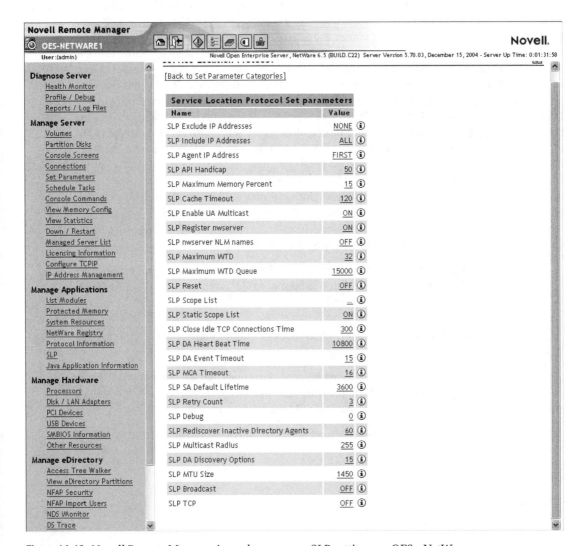

Figure 14-12. *Novell Remote Manager is used to manage SLP settings on OES - NetWare.*

Note On OES - Linux, the RFC standard for SLP configuration is used. According to this standard, all configuration settings are in the ASCII text file slp.conf. On OES - NetWare, the Novell-adapted version of SLP is used. Both versions are compatible with each other, but in the Novell-adapted version some additional methods have been implemented to allow for easier management of SLP. An example of this easier management is the way that SLP parameters can be set by using Novell Remote Manager. However, for RFC SLP compatibility on OES - NetWare, it's also possible to specify SLP settings in the configuration file /etc/slp.cfg, but it's not recommended.

Creating a Directory Agent

In large network environments, you may want to install an SLP Directory Agent. On OES - Linux, this is relatively easy: the SLP daemon slpd can be used both as an SLP SA or an SLP DA. The difference is made in the configuration file slp.conf. In OES - NetWare, it's a different story. Here you must load SLPDA.NLM and provide all required parameters from the Remote Manager interface.

As said before, on OES Linux you must modify the configuration file /etc/slp.conf to make it a Directory Agent. In this file, you can find specific parameters related to the SLP directory agent. An overview of these parameters is provided next:

```
net.slp.isDA = true
net.slp.DAHeartBeat = 10800
```

The parameters are not hard to understand. The first of them makes your slpd an SLP DA if set to true. With the second, you specify how often the DA should notify servers and nodes of its presence on the network by sending a heartbeat. The default value for this parameter is set to 10800 seconds, which equals three hours. Currently, OpenSLP version 2 does not offer any options to configure scopes for use by the Directory Agent. This may be resolved in a future version, however. For more information about the OpenSLP implementation used on OES, consult http://www.openslp.org.

To configure an SLP DA on OES - NetWare, run the command **SLPDA /A** on the OES - NetWare server. This automatically creates an SLP DA and a default scope object in the directory. A container with the name SLPDEFAULT is created in eDirectory automatically. In this container, the SLP scope object Default is created. Within this scope object, all SLP services register automatically, as shown in Figure 14-13.

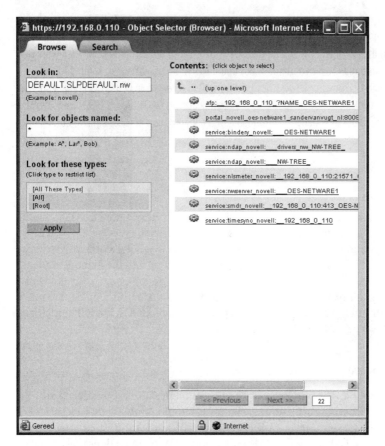

Figure 14-13. *When the SLP DA object is created, a default scope object is created automatically, and it's in this container object that all the SLP services start registering.*

Displaying SLP Services

As an administrator, you want to be able to check the availability of SLP services. Two commands are available to do this. On OES NetWare, use the command **DISPLAY SLP SERVICES** to display a list of all SLP services currently known to this server (see Figure 14-14). On OES - Linux, you can use **slptool** for this purpose. For example, use **slptool findsrvs service:service-agent** to display all SLP SAs currently known on the network. The former is a generic command that presents a list of all the SLP registered services it finds; the latter is more specific and can be used to query SLP for specific information about services.

```
Searching Network . . .
  service:ndap.novell:///ISCSI-TREE.
  service:ndap.novell:///SVU-TREE.
  service:portal.novell://oesnw1.sandervanvugt.nl:8008/OESNW1
  service:portal.novell://oesnw2.sandervanvugt.nl:8008/OESNW2
  service:afp://10.0.0.1/?NAME=OESNW1
  afp://10.0.0.1/?NAME=OESNW1
  service:afp://192.168.0.201/?NAME=OESNW2
  afp://192.168.0.201/?NAME=OESNW2
  service:smdr.novell://10.0.0.1:413/OESNW1
  service:smdr.novell://192.168.0.201:413/OESNW2
  service:bindery.novell:///OESNW1
  service:bindery.novell:///cluster251
  service:bindery.novell:///OESNW2
  service:bindery.novell:///oes-linux10
  service:nwserver.novell:///OESNW1
  service:nwserver.novell:///OESNW2
  service:nlsmeter.novell://10.0.0.1:21571/OESNW1
  service:nlsmeter.novell://192.168.0.201:21571/OESNW2
  service:ntp://oes-linux10.sandervanvugt.nl:123
  service:ssh://oes-linux10.sandervanvugt.nl:22
  service:fish://oes-linux10.sandervanvugt.nl:22
  service:smb://oes-linux10.sandervanvugt.nl
<Press ESC to terminate or any other key to continue>_
```

Figure 14-14. *On OES - NetWare, use DISPLAY SLP SERVICES to show a list of all SLP services currently known on the network.*

■**Note** SLP was once thought of as the successor to SAP. However, currently the tasks that SLP is capable of are more often performed by DNS. Thus you'll find that SLP on OES is not as fully developed as it once was on NetWare 5 and 6. If you need it anyway, I'd recommend configuring it on OES - NetWare. This is because on OES - NetWare, the Novell-adapted version of SLP is used, while on OES - Linux the more limited open-source version is used.

On OES - Linux, another easy way to display information about SLP services is through the YaST SLP browser, as described in the following steps:

1. Start YaST, provide the root password and click Network Services.

2. From the Network Services interface, select SLP Browser to get to the screen shown in Figure 14-15.

3. A tree view is displayed where all available SLP categories are listed. The category bindery.novell, for example, is used to display information about NCP servers present on the network, while ndap.novell is used to refer to eDirectory services.

4. Click the category for which you want to see SLP services. A list of all services available in this category is displayed next.

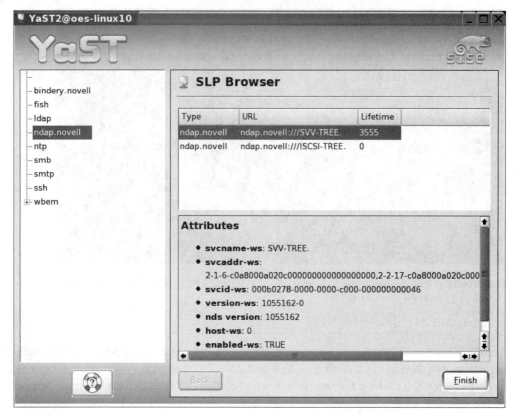

Figure 14-15. *YaST on OES - Linux contains a perfect tool to search for available SLP services: the SLP browser.*

Domain Name System

To be able to judge what service should be used for name resolving on the network, you should know in what order eDirectory uses discovery protocols to locate services on the network. This search is conducted in the following order:

1. Domain Name System (DNS)

2. Service Location Protocol (SLP)

3. Service Advertising Protocol (SAP)

Currently, DNS is particularly important for locating services on the network. It's therefore recommended that you create a resource record in the DNS domain that allows clients to find all important services. For example, use an A record to indicate the servername where eDirectory can be found, or even better, use the SRV record, because it allows you to specify the IP address as well as the port address of services in the network.

The way that DNS is configured is dependent on the OES platform you're using. On OES - Linux, the DNS server is configured from YaST and its configuration is stored in local text files.

On OES - NetWare, the DNS database is stored in eDirectory. I cover both in the following section. The advantage of this is that the resource records are replicated with eDirectory and it's therefore much easier to provide an up-to-date DNS configuration. As an administrator, you should be aware that the service is completely different on both platforms and you should choose between them before you start configuring it. If you're using a mixed environment, I recommend you configure DNS on OES - NetWare for the simple reason that it provides a much better integration with eDirectory.

Configuring DNS on OES - NetWare

Since DNS on OES - NetWare is integrated completely into eDirectory, it must be managed from iManager. In this procedure, I'll describe how to set up a simple DNS configuration. It's assumed that the reader has a basic understanding of the DNS protocol.

■**Caution** Before you can configure DNS on OES - NetWare, the eDirectory schema must be extended and some basic objects (for example, the DNS/DHCP Locator object) must be created. If you find that in the next procedure, the DNS Locator object is not present in your tree, the eDirectory schema has not been extended yet. In that case, from the OES - NetWare console, run the DNIPINST utility. This utility asks you to log in as administrator and then creates all the required objects in eDirectory. After an initial schema extension, the utility asks for the eDirectory context where the three required objects (the Locator Object, the Group Object, and the RootSrvrInfo Zone object) are created. Specify a context for each of these objects and press Enter to continue. This creates the required objects in eDirectory and allows you to continue with the procedure described next.

---

1. From iManager, select DNS ➤ DNS/DHCP Scope Settings. Before each session in which you manage DNS or DHCP on OES - NetWare from iManager, you must specify the DNS/DHCP scope. If you do not configure the DNS/DHCP scope setting for a session, you'll receive a warning before every task you perform. You can, however, still continue with the task. To set the scope, specify the context of the DNS/DHCP Locator object and the context where the administrative scope object can be created dynamically. Take notice that you don't have to point to the actual objects; it's enough if you just specify their contexts.

2. Select DNS ➤ DNS Server Management and from the drop-down list, select Create Server. Click OK to continue.

3. To create the DNS Server, enter the name of the NCP server object you want to create the DNS server on and enter both its DNS Host Name and Domain Name. Next, click Create to create the server object.

4. Now that the DNS server is created, you can start managing the DNS Zone this server is created in. In iManager, click DNS ➤ DNS Zone Management and from the drop-down list, select Create Zone to create a new DNS Zone. Click OK to continue.

5. Now you must create two DNS Zones. One is a normal zone that allows names in your DNS zone to be resolved to IP addresses. The other is the IN-ADDR.ARPA zone that allows IP addresses to be resolved to DNS names. Let's first learn how to create a normal zone, though. Select Create New Zone, and then specify the eDirectory context in which you want to create the zone. This is the context where the zone object is stored for automatic replication of all DNS data. Next, enter the Zone Domain Name. This is the DNS domain name your DNS server will serve.

6. Now specify if this is going to be a primary zone or a secondary zone. If this is a primary zone, the DNS name server is authoritative for the zone. If it's a secondary zone, the DNS server functions as a slave to an existing master DNS server for the zone. In the latter case, you must specify the name of this master DNS server before continuing. Next, specify the hostname of the DNS server you created in step 3 of this procedure. In the Create Domain field, enter the name of the top-level domain in this zone. Your DNS zone is now created. Click OK to finish this procedure.

7. Now that the normal DNS zone is created, you must also create the reverse DNS zone as well. From iManager, select DNS ➤ DNS Zone Management and choose Create IN-ADDR.ARPA. Next, enter all required data for the IN.ADDR-ARPA zone. These are

   • *eDirectory Context*: The context in eDirectory in which you want to create the zone object.

   • *Network Address*: The address of the network this IN-ADDR.ARPA zone will service.

   • *Zone Type*: Select Primary if there is no master nameserver for this zone, or select Secondary if the server is synchronizing with an existing name server.

   • *Name Server Host Name*: The hostname of the nameserver that will service this zone.

   • *Domain*: The name of the domain that this name server will service.

8. When finished making selections, click Create to create the zone in eDirectory. Next, click OK to finish the procedure.

9. Now that the zones have been created, data must be added to the DNS databases. From iManager, select DNS ➤ Resource Record Management and from the drop-down list, select Create Resource Record and click OK.

10. From the drop-down list, select the domain name you want to create the resource records for.

11. Specify the owner name under which you want to create the resource record. This is the zone you're going to create the resource record in.

12. From the other drop-down menu, select the resource record type and specify all appropriate parameters. Next, click Create, OK, and then Done to finish creating the resource record and complete the task.

Note Many options can be used to configure DNS. A complete overview of all available options is provided in the Novell DNS/DHCP Services for NetWare administration guide. You can find this guide on the Novell documentation web site at www.novell.com/documentation.

Configuring DNS on OES - Linux

The big difference between the DNS server on OES - NetWare and the DNS server on OES - Linux is that the former is integrated in eDirectory, while the latter is not. Configuration of DNS on OES - Linux is simple and straightforward, especially because the entire DNS configuration can be managed with YaST.

1. Click the YaST icon on the OES - Linux desktop to start YaST. Enter the password of the user root and click OK to proceed.

2. From the left panel, select Network Services, and then click DNS Server, as shown in Figure 14-16.

Figure 14-16. *On OES - Linux, the DNS server can be managed from YaST.*

3. On the first screen that YaST offers, you can specify a forwarder to be used. This is a DNS server that your server forwards requests to that it cannot resolve itself. If no forwarders are defined, all requests that your DNS server cannot resolve are forwarded directly to one of the servers of the DNS root domain. Enter the IP address of a forwarder or click Next to continue without a forwarder.

4. Enter the name of the zone you want to create and specify its zone type. Use Master if this server is authoritative for this zone, or use Slave if you want it to communicate with a master server somewhere in the network. Next, click Add to add the zone to your configuration. The zone is now added to the list of available zones.

5. Select the zone and click Edit Zone to modify its properties using the screen shown in Figure 14-17. You should now see a window with five different tabs where you can specify the properties of the zone and create resource records for it. In the next step, I explain the most important options. Details about the options not discussed here can be found on the Novell documentation web site at www.novell.com/documentation.

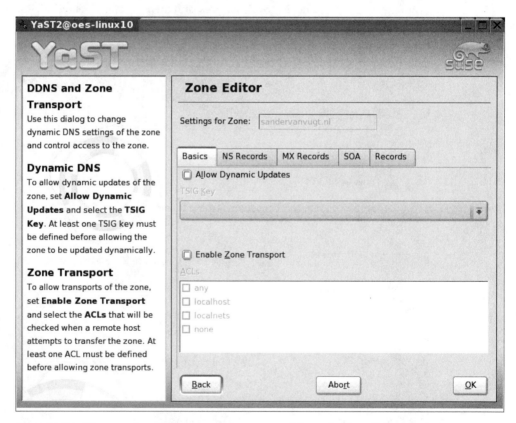

Figure 14-17. *All properties of the zone can be managed from the Zone Editor.*

6. On the Basics tab, select the option Allow Dynamic Updates. This allows the DNS zone to be updated by Dynamic DNS updates from the DHCP server on your network.

7. On the NS Records tab, enter the name of all master and slave name servers servicing this zone, including the name of your current server. Then, enter the addresses and click Add to add them to the list. Don't forget you must create an A resource record for all these servers. If you forget it, the names you use cannot be resolved.

8. Select the MX Records tab to specify the name of the mailserver for your domain. Besides the name, you must also specify a priority where 0 is the highest priority and where normal priorities are incremented by ten. This is not an absolute requirement, however. In fact, a mailserver with a priority of, say, 2 should work fine as well.

9. Specify the SOA properties using the options available on the SOA tab, shown in Figure 14-18. These are the properties for the authoritative DNS server in your network. The following properties can be set:

   • *Serial*: The serial number used by slave servers to determine if a change has occurred to the database of the master server.

   • *TTL*: The time to live. This is the time that a dynamic resource record is maintained in the database without being updated. The default value is set to two days.

   • *Refresh*: Specifies how often the zone should be synchronized from the master to the slave servers.

   • *Retry*: Sets how often a slave server should retry synchronization with the master if it fails on the first attempt.

   • *Expiry*: Specifies the period after which the zone information expires at the slave server when no successful synchronization has occurred.

   • *Minimum*: The amount of time a slave server should spend caching a negative answer when name resolution has failed.

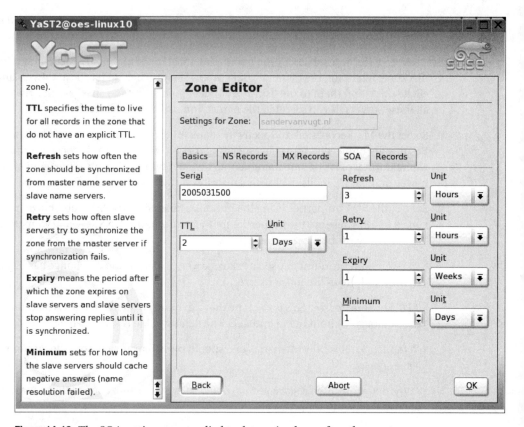

Figure 14-18. *The SOA settings are applied to determine how often the master nameserver should synchronize with the slaves.*

10. Now that all the basic configuration is done, it's time to create the resource records in the DNS database. Take special care that at least one A resource record is created for all nameservers. To create an A resource record, click the Records tab and enter the name of the host in the Record Key field, as shown in Figure 14-19. This can be a complete hostname that's ended by a dot (linux.oes.com., for instance) or a hostname relative to the current zone (for example, Linux if the current zone is set to oes.com.). Continue this procedure until resource records have been added for all hosts and then click OK to finish configuring the zone. Click Next to continue.

11. In the booting section of the next screen, select On -- Start DNS Server Now And When Booting. This activates the DNS server immediately after you click Finish to close the window. It starts the DNS Server.

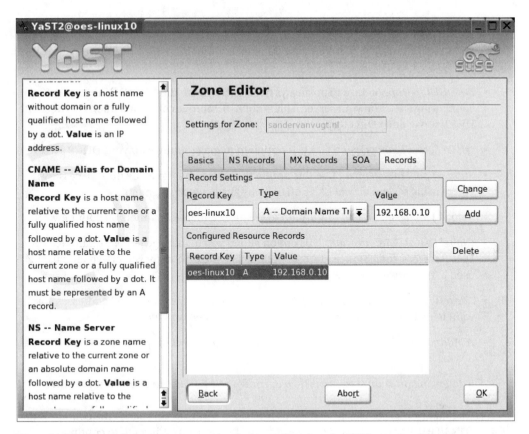

Figure 14-19. *One of the most important tasks in configuring the DNS zone is adding the proper resource records.*

Tip Although you've configured it with YaST, this is still Linux. Thus, the configuration has been written to some configuration files on your server. The main configuration file is /etc/named.conf, and it's from this configuration file that the zone-specific configuration files are called. If, for example, you've created your DNS server as master server, the zone file is created in /var/lib/named/master. All other configuration files are in the /var/lib/named directory.

OES As a DHCP Server

The last network related kind of functionality discussed in this chapter is OES as a DHCP server. The configuration of this type of server also depends on the version of OES you're using. In OES - NetWare, the DHCP server stores its information in eDirectory and you need iManager to configure it. In OES - Linux, use YaST to configure the DHCP server.

Configuring DHCP on OES - NetWare

To configure DHCP on OES - NetWare, use iManager. From iManager, the following DHCP-related options are available:

- *DNS/DHCP Scope Settings*: You always need to configure the DNS/DHCP scope before configuring DHCP on your server. This is done to improve communications between the DHCP server and eDirectory.

- *DHCP Server Management*: Use this option to manage settings for your DHCP server.

- *Subnet Pool Management*: Use this option to create subnet pools. This is necessary if you're using several virtual LANs on one physical network segment.

- *Subnet Management*: Use this option to create and manage subnets on your network.

- *Global DHCP Configuration*: This option allows you to manage global settings for your DHCP server—for instance, think of options like the DNS nameserver, which must be used in the network segment.

- *Address Range Management*: Use this option to specify the range of IP addresses you want to distribute on the network, including all related options.

- *IP Address Management*: Use this option to determine specific parameters for particular hosts.

The following procedure explains how to configure a DHCP server on your network.

1. In iManager, select DHCP ➤ DNS/DHCP Scope Settings and specify the context of the DNS/DHCP Locator object and the Administrative scope. Click OK to continue.

2. Select DHCP Server Management, and from the drop-down list choose Create Server and click OK.

3. Enter the name of the server object as it exists in eDirectory and click Create. This creates the DHCP server in your network.

4. Click Subnet Management from the drop-down list, and then select Create Subnet. Click OK to continue. You should now be looking at the screen shown in Figure 14-20.

5. Enter the following information to create the subnet in eDirectory:

    - *Subnet Name*: The name the subnet object will get in eDirectory.

    - *eDirectory Context*: The location in eDirectory where the subnet is created.

    - *Subnet IP Address*: The network IP address of the subnet.

    - *Subnet Mask*: The subnet mask of the subnet.

    - *Default DHCP Server*: The default DHCP server you want to assign to the subnet.

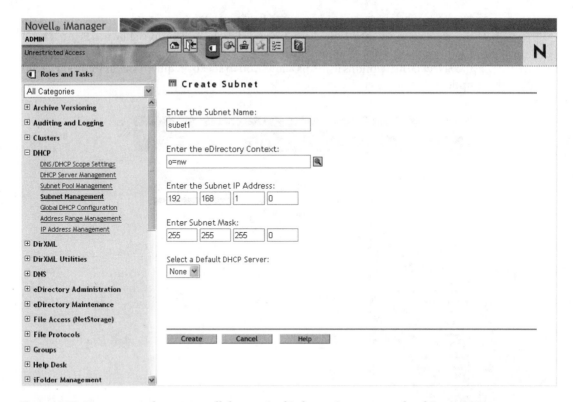

Figure 14-20. *To create a subnet, enter all the required information to create the object in eDirectory.*

6. Click Create to create the subnet.

7. Click Global DHCP Configuration and from the drop-down list, select View/Set Global Preferences. Click OK to continue. You'll now see a list of all DHCP options currently available (there probably won't be any so far since nothing has been configured yet). This is an important screen, because you can choose from a large list of protocol-related options which can be distributed to client computers this way. Some of these are common RFC standards, like Time Offset, Router, Time Server, and Name Server. Some Novell-specific options are also available as well. Of these, the most interesting are listed next:

- *SLP Directory Agent*: Allows you to distribute the IP address of an SLP directory agent from a central location in the network.

- *SLP Service Scope*: Use this option to define a scope for the workstations.

- *NDS Servers*: This option can be used to set a default server for a client.

- *NDS Tree Name*: Use this option to specify the eDirectory tree the client should contact.

- *NDS Context*: With this option, the administrator can set a default context for client computers.

8. To add any of these DHCP options, click the Modify button and a new screen appears. In this window, select the required options and click the Add button (shown in Figure 14-21) to add them to the list of configured options. Choose the options you've just added from the Select DHCP Options list. This allows you to specify required values for the selected options. When finished, click Done.

Figure 14-21. *From the Global DHCP Options screen, you can add options that are distributed to all DHCP clients.*

9. Back on the list of global DHCP options that are configured for your server, click Next to continue. You now have the opportunity to exclude MAC addresses from being served by the DHCP server. If this is required, click Add, enter the MAC addresses you want to exclude, click Done to return to the main screen with DHCP options, and then click Next to continue.

10. The next option allows you to include the top-priority hardware addresses that your DHCP server will serve. Click Add to add them, and when finished, select Done and then click Next to continue. You'll now return to the list of Global DHCP Preferences, where an overview of all available options is given. Click Done to finish this procedure and proceed to the next step.

11. Click Address Range Management to define a range of addresses that can be distributed by the DHCP server. From the drop-down list, select Create Address Range and click OK to continue.

12. In the Create Address Range screen, select the subnet where you want to create the address range and enter a name, a start address, and an end address for the address range. These addresses must always fall within the range specified in the subnet you've selected. Click Create to create the range.

13. Now, if required, you can specify the settings for specific nodes with the option IP Address Management. This option allows you to specify an IP address and specify whether you want to exclude the address from the subnet address range or assign a specific MAC address to it (see Figure 14-22). Enter your options and click Create when finished. This defines the exception to the address range.

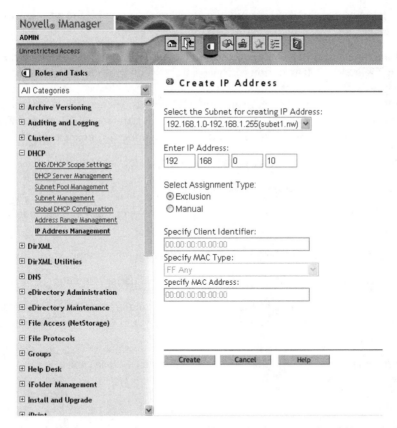

Figure 14-22. *If required, you can specify IP addresses that should be excluded.*

14. Now that all options have been specified, it's time for the last step: activating the DHCP server. You can do so by issuing the command DHCPSRVR on the OES - NetWare console, or by selecting Start Server from the drop-down list in the iManager option DHCP Server Management.

Configuring DHCP on OES - Linux

The configuration of a DHCP server on OES - Linux is much more straightforward than it is on OES - NetWare. The main reason for this is that no information is written to eDirectory. You can use YaST to configure an OES - Linux DHCP server. This sets all required options and writes them to the configuration file /etc/dhcpd.conf, which can also be edited by hand. The following procedure describes how a DHCP server can be configured on OES - Linux.

1. From the OES - Linux console, start YaST and select Network Services ➤ DHCP Server.

2. If more than one network card is configured on your server, select the interface the DHCP server should use and click Next to continue.

3. Now you can specify the most important global options for this server in the screen shown in Figure 14-23. If an option you need isn't listed on this screen, you can add it by hand to the dhcpd.conf configuration file. From the options listed, specify at least the Primary/Secondary Name Server IP and Default Gateway, because these options are needed if you want your computer to communicate with the rest of the world. When done, click Next to continue. The following lists those options that are available.

    - *Domain Name*: The DNS domain you want to specify for the clients.

    - *Time Server*: The IP address of a server that can be used as a time server.

    - *Primary/Secondary Name Server IP*: The IP address of the primary and secondary DNS name server.

    - *Print Server*: The IP address of a server that is used to send print jobs to.

    - *WINS Server*: The IP address of a server used for WINS name resolving.

    - *Default Gateway*: This is the default gateway that should be used for your clients. Be aware that you can't specify this as a global option of your DHCP server if it's servicing multiple subnets.

    - *Default Lease Time*: The default time after which a DHCP lease expires.

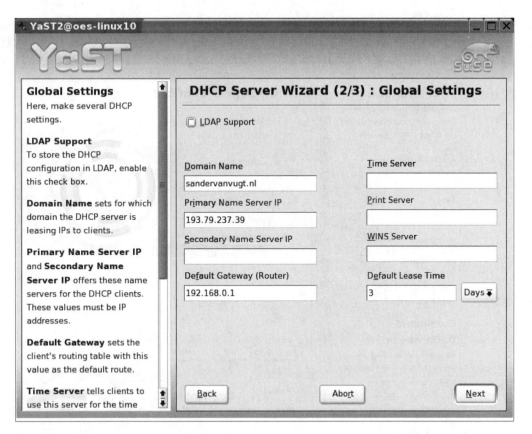

Figure 14-23. *In the YaST Configuration Wizard, only the most common options for the DHCP server can be set.*

4. Now that the generic options are specified, you can define a range of IP addresses to be serviced by this server. Enter the first and last IP address of this range, and if required, enter a lease time and a maximum lease time specific to this range. Click Next to continue.

5. Select On -- Start DHCP Server During Boot. If you're happy with the settings you've made, click Finish to save the settings and start the DHCP server. If you need to configure advanced settings, select Expert Settings to reach the screen shown in Figure 14-24. Ignore the warning and specify the advanced settings you want to use. This option is particularly useful if you need support for more than one subnet, or if you want to make arrangements for specific hosts in your network. When you've finished entering the advanced options, click Finish to stop the configuration and start the DHCP server.

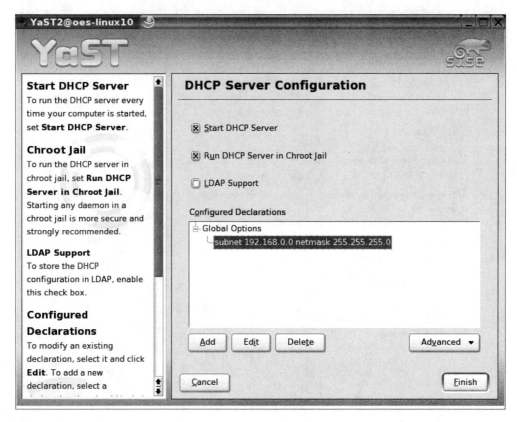

Figure 14-24. *If your network must support more than one subnet, you can specify the various subnets to be serviced on this screen.*

Summary

In this chapter, you learned how to configure generic network services on OES. The configuration of IP addresses, name services, and DHCP was also covered. With regard to these subjects, some important differences exist between OES - NetWare and OES - Linux. In OES - NetWare, most elements are perfectly integrated into eDirectory. On OES - Linux, however, the old-fashioned Linux method is used, meaning some text configuration files need to be created, but the advantage here is that these files can be configured from the YaST configuration utility.

The next chapter will teach you about how to set up printing in an OES environment.

## CHAPTER 15

Managing iPrint

IPrint is the latest Novell printing solution and is entirely compatible with the Internet Printing Protocol, making it an extremely flexible solution for printing over the Internet. It includes advanced features, like printer selection based on maps and automatic printer driver downloads when a printer is selected. It can also work with any client; client software is available for Windows, Linux, and Macintosh. In this chapter, you'll learn how to configure the iPrint environment for easy access to all printers in the network.

iPrint Components

To understand how iPrint works, you need to be familiar with all its necessary components. In each iPrint environment, the following components are used:

- iPrint Manager
- iPrint Driver Store
- iPrint printer objects
- iPrint Client
- iPrint Map Designer

The iPrint Manager

The iPrint Manager is responsible for forwarding print jobs to the printer. It exists as an object in eDirectory, but also exists as a process running on your server. In functionality, it can be compared to the Print Server used in a legacy NetWare queue-based printing environment, or to the LPD process that on a Linux system listens for incoming print jobs.

Only one iPrint Manager is needed in a network since it can serve multiple printers. If, however, you've remote locations in your network, additional iPrint Managers can be created. Be warned though that it's not possible to run more than one iPrint Manager on a server.

The iPrint Manager works with printer agents. These entities represent the printers in your network's iPrint Manager database. A print agent is created automatically when you create a printer object in eDirectory. The printer agent is the final component integral to your printer's operation: it manages the processing of print jobs and communicates with the clients on the network about the status of the print job.

Another important component of the iPrint Manager is the IPP server. This is the interface between the web server and the iPrint Manager that processes incoming IPP and IPPS (IPP Secure) requests from clients.

Internet Printing Protocol (IPP) is the standard on which iPrint is based. It's an Internet standard that can be used on all platforms for increased interoperability between different kinds of clients. It also supports data encryption through the use of SSL or TLS for a more secure printing environment.

The iPrint Driver Store

The iPrint Driver Store is a repository of printer drivers for your print system. When a user installs a printer on his workstation, the iPrint Manager requests the associated printer driver from the iPrint Driver Store. As an administrator for the printing environment, it's your responsibility to manage the iPrint Driver Store and provide all necessary drivers. If no drivers for a new printer are available, you have to install them there. In the section "Adding Printers to the Driver Store" later in this chapter, you'll learn how to do this. In some cases, you may need to upgrade existing drivers in the iPrint Driver Store.

Normally, just one iPrint Driver Store is needed in the network, but if your network has remote locations, it's useful to create more iPrint Driver Stores to avoid downloading printer drivers across slow WAN connections. If, however, you work with more than one iPrint Driver Store, these different driver stores need to be synchronized: if a new driver is added to one, you have to synchronize it to all the other Driver Stores in the network to avoid problems.

■**Note** Think this all looks like good old-fashioned NDPS printing? You're right! iPrint is an extension of the NDPS print environment that was introduced with NetWare 5.0. The management of it has changed a bit, but basically it's still the NDPS system that's being used in the background. There are, however, some NDPS features that have disappeared. For example, it's no longer possible to work with plug and print in the same manner as before.

---

iPrint Printer Objects

In order to work with an iPrint printer, you need a printer object. All printers in the network have a printer object; the difference between a public access printer and a private printer as it existed before, is no longer valid. iPrint printer objects are managed by an iPrint Manager and associated with a driver for the printer that is configured in the iPrint Driver Store. If a user installs a printer on his workstation, he communicates directly with the iPrint printer object.

iPrint Client

To use iPrint printers on the network, the user needs an iPrint client. This is composed of a browser plug-in and some shared library files that need to be installed on the client. This software allows a user to install printers and download printer drivers to their workstation. When a user tries to install an iPrint printer, iPrint checks if the iPrint client is already installed on the user's workstation. If it's not installed, the user is prompted to install it before continuing. This is an easy procedure that can be performed by anyone with sufficient rights on the workstation.

After installation of the iPrint client, several components are added to the user's workstation:

- A browser plug-in that allows you to access iPrint printers from your browser

- Client configuration options that allow sophisticated communications with the iPrint printers

- Command-line utilities for advanced management of iPrint printers

- The iPrint Map Designer, which allows you to build customized maps of the iPrint printer environment

iPrint Map Designer

One of the coolest features of iPrint is that you can choose printers from a map instead of a list. Imagine that you're visiting a conference, and during the boring keynote session you want to use the Internet to check the information for your flight the following day. After verifying flight times, you want to print your boarding pass. If the conference center uses iPrint, access the portal site provided by the conference to connect to the iPrint printers available in the center. Next, you'll see a map where you can immediately locate the printer nearest you. From this map, without even knowing what brand and type of printer it is, just click to configure everything on your workstation that's needed to print a job on the selected printer. Also, you don't need to install any client, because this is done automatically from the printer link you selected from the map.

iPrint Installation and Configuration

The iPrint installation can be performed as part of the server installation. It's also possible to install iPrint later by using the install utility on the server console or Deployment Manager. In order for iPrint to work, the following products have to be present:

- The Apache web server

- The Java Virtual Machine

- Tomcat

- eDirectory

- iManager 2.02 or later

After the initial product install, you're ready to configure iPrint. This configuration consists of several steps:

1. Create and activate a Driver Store.

2. Add printer drivers to the Driver Store.

3. Create and start the iPrint Manager.

4. Create printer objects.

5. Configure workstation or users' printers.

6. Create printer maps.

7. Apply advanced options if needed.

Configuring the Driver Store

The first part of iPrint that has to be configured is the iPrint Driver Store. You must create this object in eDirectory, and after configuring it, printers must be added to the Driver Store. The following procedure explains how these tasks can be performed.

1. Open iManager from https://yourserver/nps. Enter your username, password, and tree, and then click Login to authenticate.

2. From Roles and Tasks, select iPrint, and then choose Create Driver Store (see Figure 15-1).

3. Enter a name for the Driver Store and the default container where the object will be created. In the Target Server field, enter the IP address or DNS name of the server that will host the driver store. In the eDir Server field, specify the name of the eDirectory server object that will host the driver store.

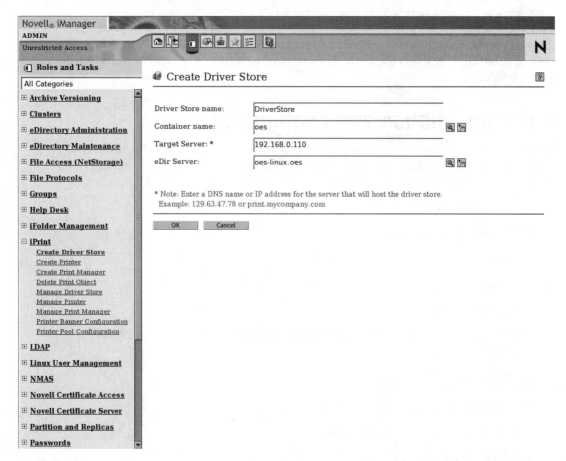

Figure 15-1. *To create an iPrint Driver Store, enter the IP address of the target server as well as its eDirectory object name.*

4. Click OK to finish creating the Driver Store.

You've now created an iPrint Driver Store. On OES - Linux, the configuration related to this driver store is stored in several configuration files. Apart from the configuration files, there is also the script **/etc/init.d/novell-ipsmd**, which can be used to stop and start the iPrint daemons on OES - Linux. Enter **/etc/init.d/novell-ipsmd start** to start the service and **/etc/init.d/novell-ipsmd stop** to stop it. After the iPrint environment is configured on your server, the server has to be started with this command.

Some configuration files are also involved in iPrint management, the first of which is the file /etc/opt/novell/iprint/conf/idsd.conf. (See Figure 15-2.) In this file, a list of iPrint Driver Stores and their assignment to the server is maintained. For the creation of this file, the file /etc/opt/novell/iprint/idsd-template.conf is used. If you ever need to change the default eDirectory server on which iPrint is installed, you can modify the parameter DSServer1 from idsd.conf.

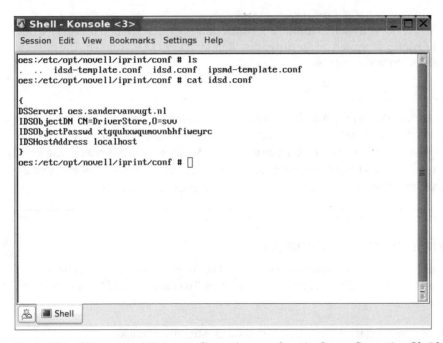

Figure 15-2. *All important iPrint configurations are kept in the configuration file idsd.conf.*

Adding Printers to the Driver Store

After the driver store has been created, drivers can be uploaded to the driver store. You can do this with the .INF file that contains the drivers for your printer. It's also possible to upload printer drivers currently in use on your workstation. To make starting easier, some drivers are already included in the Driver Store. If you want to upload printer drivers, you need Internet Explorer running on a Windows workstation that already has the iPrint client installed. Later sections in this chapter explain how to install the iPrint client. Perform the following steps to add printer drivers to the Driver Store:

1. In iManager select iPrint and choose Manage Driver Store.

2. Browse to the iPrint Driver Store object in eDirectory and click OK to continue.

3. Select Drivers and next select the operating system you want to install drivers for. You can install drivers for Windows, Linux, and Macintosh.

4. Click Add From File to add drivers from the driver installation CD that comes with your printer, or select Add From System to add a driver for a printer that's already installed on your local workstation.

■**Note** If you choose Add From System, you can only upload drivers to the same platform as the workstation you're currently using.

---

5. Select the driver you want to install. If it's a Windows driver, you'll find it in the INF file for your Windows version on the driver installation CD. Click OK to add it. The driver is now added to the driver store.

■**Caution** Some conditions have to be met before you can successfully add drivers to the iPrint driver store. First, you need DNS. iPrint works only with DNS names and if a DNS name cannot be resolved, you'll only get a cryptic error message. So make sure that DNS is configured or add your server's DNS name to your local hosts file if you're not running internal DNS services. Next, you need a supported browser. The latest versions of Internet Explorer and Mozilla will work, but other browsers aren't guaranteed to function.

Configuring the iPrint Manager

All iPrint printers in the network require the services of the iPrint Manager. It must be created before you can continue installing printers to the network. To create a Print Manager, perform the following steps.

1. From iManager, select iPrint and then choose Create Print Manager.

2. Enter the name for the Print Manager. Next, specify the name of the container where you want to create the Print Manager object. (See Figure 15-3.) Also choose the name of the eDirectory object for your server and the eDirectory name of the Driver store. Next, specify the DNS name or IP address of the server where iPrint can be reached. It's recommended to use a DNS name instead of an IP address. This allows users to continue using a printer when the IP address is changed.

3. Make sure the Start Print Manager After Creation option is selected and click OK to create the Print Manager object in eDirectory.

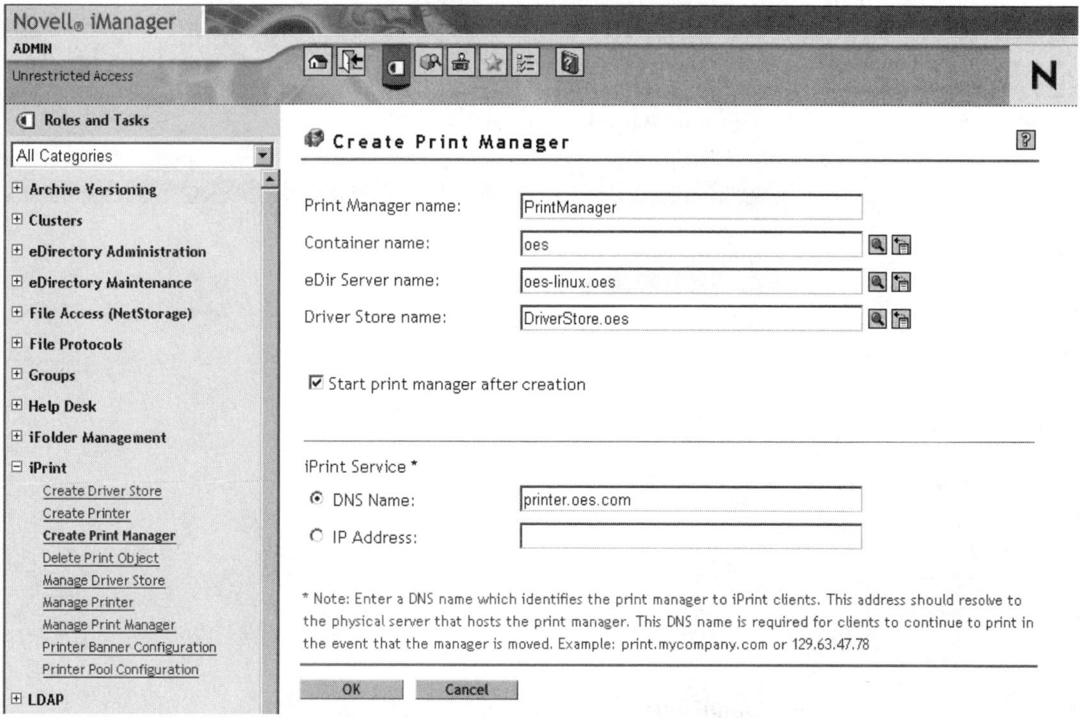

Figure 15-3. *The Print Manager must work closely with the Driver Store.*

■**Caution** If the certificate used for secure connection to the iPrint server is not currently trusted by your browser, you'll get an error message that creation of the print manager has failed. In the error, you'll see a link to start the iPrint Certificate Manager. Clicking this link shows you the Certificate Manager interface. From this interface, you'll see all the conditions that caused your browser to issue the warning. Select all options that indicate you want to trust this certificate and click OK to continue. Unfortunately, you'll have to specify all options to create the Print Manager again.

The Print manager is the object that manages all printers in the network. On the object itself, not much has to be configured. One of the most interesting configuration options can be found on the Access Control tab (see Figure 15-4). Here, you can specify the name of eDirectory objects that have administrative rights to the iPrint Manager. By default, your admin user will be the only manager, but if needed, you can add other users as well.

■**Tip** The iPrint Manager is also responsible for spooling print jobs. On OES - Linux, this happens in the directory /var/opt/novell/iprint/PrintManager.oes.psm. Since print jobs can be huge, it's recommended to put the directory /var on a separate partition when installing OES - Linux. This way, you can make sure that the spooling of print jobs never claims all the available disk space on your server.

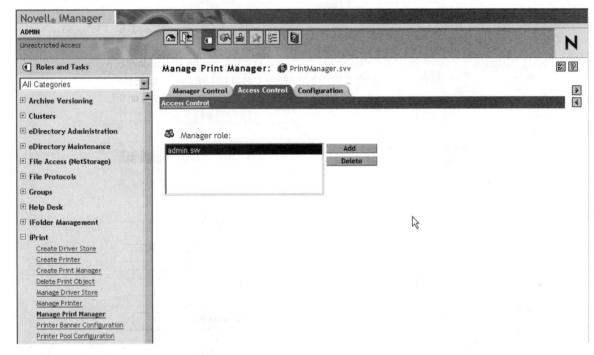

Figure 15-4. *You can define additional administrators for the Print Manager.*

Configuring Printers

If the Driver Store and the iPrint Manager have both been configured, you can start creating printer objects. These represent the physical printers you actually work with.

■Note In NDPS printing, there was the possibility to work with public access printers. These were printers that existed as a property of the Print Manager, not as separate objects. In iPrint, this concept is no longer used. In fact, all printers are public access, by default, and can be used by anyone. Only when you enable access security can access to the printer be limited to valid users.

---

1. In iManager, select iPrint and then choose Create Printer (see Figure 15-5). Next, enter the printer name, the name of the print manager that this printer will use, and the DNS name or IP address of this printer. For the last value, a DNS name is preferred. This allows users to continue using the printer even if it's physically moved to another subnet. If your printer is attached to a server or workstation, use the DNS name or IP address of this computer.

Tip iPrint does not care about how the printer is connected to the network. All iPrint needs is a DNS name or an IP address. In most cases, this will be the name or the address of the printer itself because most printers are connected to the network with their own network card. It can, however, also be the IP address of the host on which the printer is configured. For example, if on a small network the printer is directly attached to an OES - Linux server, the printer has to be shared with the local CUPS system before it can be accessed on the network.

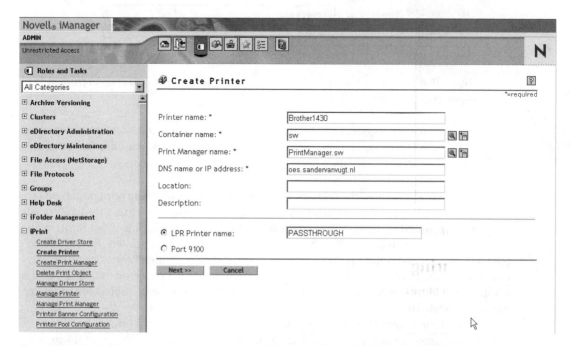

Figure 15-5. *To define a printer, you need to specify a name for it, the names of the Print Manager and the Container, and the address where the printer can be reached.*

2. If desired, a location and a description can be specified for the printer. Next, you must define an LPR printer name for the printer, or specify that the printer should use port 9100. Some printers can only be reached on port 9100. For these printers, select Port 9100. For all other printers, accept the default LPR Printer name PASSTHROUGH. Click Next to continue.

3. Select the printer drivers you want to use (see Figure 15-6). If no drivers are available from the drop-down lists, add them to the Driver Store object in eDirectory. Click Next to continue after installing the drivers.

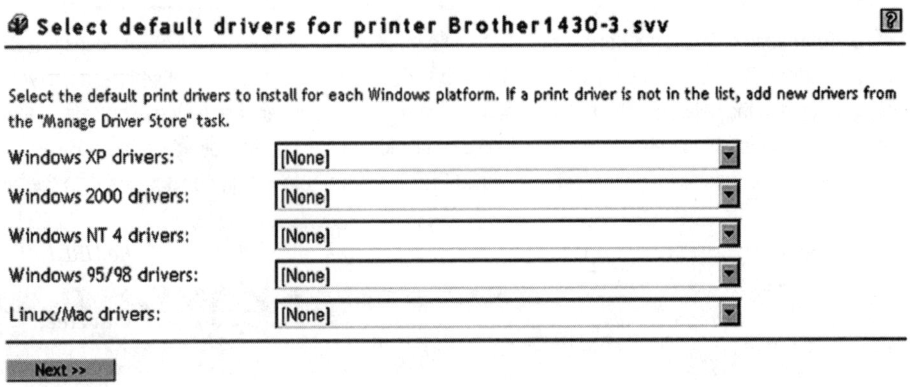

⚔ Select default drivers for printer Brother1430-3.svv [?]

Select the default print drivers to install for each Windows platform. If a print driver is not in the list, add new drivers from the "Manage Driver Store" task.

Windows XP drivers:	[None] ▼
Windows 2000 drivers:	[None] ▼
Windows NT 4 drivers:	[None] ▼
Windows 95/98 drivers:	[None] ▼
Linux/Mac drivers:	[None] ▼

Next >>

Figure 15-6. *If no drivers are available from the drop-down lists, select them from the Manage Driver Store task.*

4. A screen will be displayed in which you can see if the printer has been created successfully. Click OK to stop creating printers, choose Repeat Task to create another printer or select Modify to change the printer's current setup.

Now that you've created the printers, you must determine how these printers can be installed on the workstations. This is because, in order to create a printer a user normally needs administrative permissions to the workstation she is currently working on. iPrint resolves this issue with the option to work with either workstation printers or user printers. A workstation printer is a printer that is available to all users on the workstation. To install a workstation printer, users need administrative permissions to the workstation. A user printer, on the other hand, is a printer that's saved to the local user's profile. No administrative permissions are needed to install user printers.

As the administrator of the iPrint environment, you can define how printer creation is handled. On OES - Linux, this is determined by the iPrint configuration file, iprint.ini, in /srv/www/htdocs/ippdocs. Open this file with an editor, and select the AllowUserPrinters option. This option can have three different parameters:

- *0*: Only users with administrative rights can install a printer to the desktop. In all cases, the printer will be installed as a workstation printer.

- *1*: If the current user doesn't have enough rights, the printer will be added as a user printer.

- *2*: Regardless of the users' rights, the printers will always be added as user printers.

Creating Printer Maps

There are two ways to select a printer from a workstation. The first method is to select it from a list that can be found at http://yourserver/ipp (as shown in Figure 15-7). Then just click the name of the printer you want to install. The other method is to create a map in which all available printers can be selected. The advantage of using a map is that the user will always be able to select the nearest printer without even knowing its name. The user simply clicks the printer's name which automatically installs it to the user's desktop, provided that the correct drivers for their local workstation are installed.

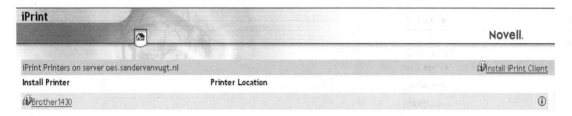

Figure 15-7. *Users can choose from the available printers on the iPrint server at the URL http://yourserver/ipp.*

As an alternative to selecting the printer from a list, the administrator can create printer maps from which the printers can be selected:

1. Copy all maps you want to use to the directory ippdocs/images/maps in the document root of your Apache web server.

2. Open a web browser and go to the http://yourserver/ippdocs/maptool.htm address to access the screen shown in Figure 15-8. If on the workstation the iPrint client hasn't already been installed, the user will be prompted to install it before continuing.

Figure 15-8. *Use the map tool to create a map from which the user can select a printer.*

3. From the drop-down list Background at the bottom left of the Map Designer window, select a background image you want to use for the printer map.

Tip You can use any type of bitmap. It doesn't have to be a real map. A photo of your company's building is fine as well. You can also organize your printers with their icons into a matrix or into categorized sets of pages with color printers, plotters, and so on.

4. In the Printer icon drop-down list, select an image of a printer that best represents the printer you're using.

5. Drag the printer icon to the location in the map where you want it (see Figure 15-9 for an example).

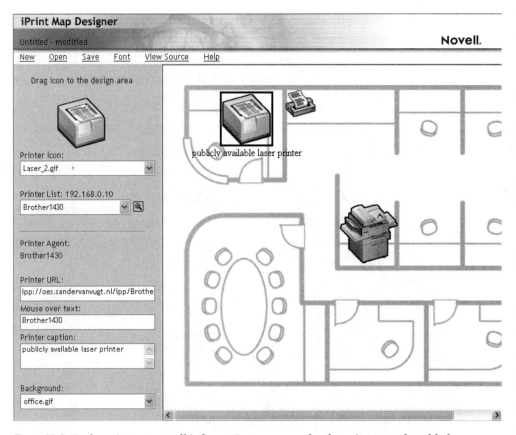

Figure 15-9. *In the printer map, all information necessary for the printer can be added.*

6. Select the printer you've just dragged to the map. Next, from the Printer List select the printer defined in iPrint that you want to assign to this printer icon. This automatically enters a value for the printer URL and the mouse-over text. Mouse-over text is text that appears if a user moves her mouse cursor over the printer icon. You can change this as needed.

7. Enter a printer caption. This is the text displayed below the printer in the map.

8. Click Save to save your map as it is so far. Save the file to the folder ippdocs in your web server's document root. This makes the file instantly available to users and makes sure no changes you've made so far are lost when you go on. To finish the map configuration, change the default font for the printer. Click Font in the upper portion of the map tool screen and choose the base font you want to use for the selected printer.

Accessing Printers from Workstations

To access printers from a Workstation, the iPrint client must be installed. After successfully installing this component, you can access printers from the printer maps available on your network. The iPrint client will be installed automatically when the user wants to perform a task in which this client is needed.

Accessing Printers from a Windows Workstation

Before printers can be accessed from a Windows workstation, the iPrint client needs to be installed. The installation procedure starts automatically when the user wants to access an iPrint printer. (See Figure 15-10.)

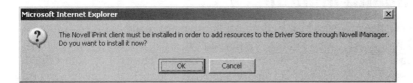

Figure 15-10. *The system will prompt you to install the iPrint client when needed.*

1. If a pop-up appears, prompting you to install the iPrint client, click OK.

2. Click Open to start the installation procedure immediately after downloading the file.

3. Click Next on the iPrint Client Setup screen. All necessary components are installed to the local workstation now.

4. Click Finish to finish the installation procedure. The iPrint client is now installed and ready for use.

Now that the iPrint client software has been installed locally on the workstation, the user can start using the printer. To do this, one of the maps the administrator has configured can be used. Alternatively, the user can choose from a list of available printers from the URL http://servername/ipp.

Accessing Printers from a Linux Workstation

Besides Windows workstations, Linux workstations are supported as well. The necessary iPrint client will be installed when a user tries to access one of the iPrint printers. It can also be installed from the iPrint page at http://server-address/ipp. Click Install iPrint Client and the client software installation will start. Then perform the following steps.

> **Tip** To install the iPrint client automatically, it's best to use Konqueror as a browser because it will automatically recognize the RPM file to install. If you prefer another browser, first save the file to the location of your choice and then install it by double-clicking the filename from the file browser on your Linux desktop.

1. Your browser will recognize the iPrint installation file as an RPM file and will ask if you want to open it. Select Open.

2. Select Install package With YaST to automatically install the iPrint client with YaST.

3. Enter your root password to install all the necessary files to your system and then click OK.

4. YaST starts and installs the iPrint client. This can take a minute, after which you can return to the original page at http://server-address/ipp to select a printer from the list.

5. Select the printer you want to use. It's then installed locally.

The iPrint Health Monitor

The Health Monitor can be employed by the administrator to manage the iPrint environment (see Figure 15-11). This is a web-based interface from which all aspects of the iPrint environment can be monitored. From the Health Monitor, you can also configure the error threshold, customize print system settings, and generate reports about the system. In the opening page of the Health Monitor, you'll see all your printers, their current state, and general statistics about the number of jobs processed in the last hour or last day since the iPrint Manager was started. The Health Monitor can be accessed from https://server-address/psmstatus. In this URL, the server address is the address of the server on which the iPrint Manager is activated.

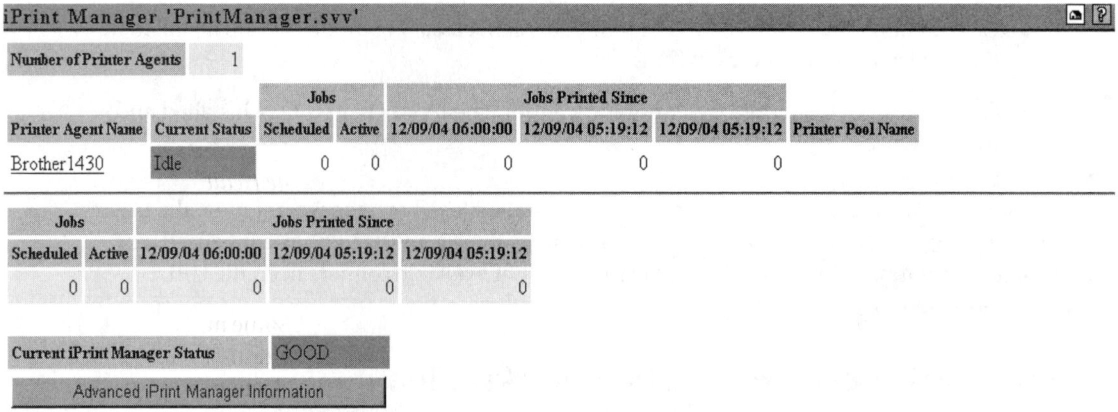

iPrint Manager 'PrintManager.svv'

Number of Printer Agents   1

Printer Agent Name	Current Status	Jobs		Jobs Printed Since			Printer Pool Name
		Scheduled	Active	12/09/04 06:00:00	12/09/04 05:19:12	12/09/04 05:19:12	
Brother1430	Idle	0	0	0	0	0	

Jobs		Jobs Printed Since		
Scheduled	Active	12/09/04 06:00:00	12/09/04 05:19:12	12/09/04 05:19:12
0	0	0	0	0

| Current iPrint Manager Status | GOOD |

Advanced iPrint Manager Information

Figure 15-11. *From the iPrint Health Monitor, you can see immediately if there are severe problems with regards to printing on your network.*

After activating the iPrint Health Monitor, you'll have access to lots of information about the printer. By clicking the link for one of the printers, detailed statistics about it will be displayed. Not only will you see a detailed list of all jobs processed, but an extensive summary of the configuration of this printer is also provided. From this information, for example, you can tell from which URL the printer can be reached and what directory in the file system it uses for spooling.

One of the most interesting things about iPrint Health Monitor is that it's possible to perform some printer management from this utility (see Figure 15-12). Some tasks like Shutdown Printer, Pause Output, and Pause Input are available from the drop-down list. Some basic configuration options are also available from this interface.

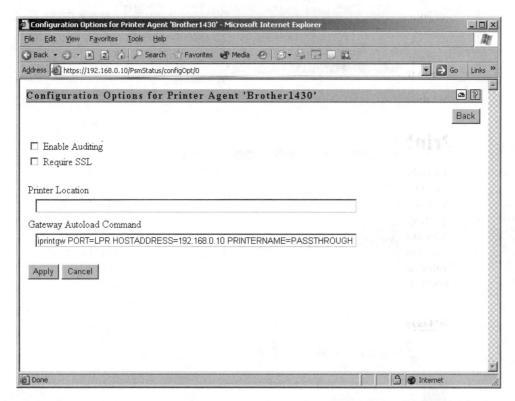

Figure 15-12. *Some basic printer management tasks can be performed from the Health Monitor.*

Managing Printers from iManager

The iPrint Health Monitor is not the only tool available to manage printers. Some management tasks can be performed from iManager as well, and because it offers more options, iManager is still the most important interface from which to manage your printers. After selecting the printer you want to manage, choose the basic printer control options available on the Printer Control tab. From this tab, you can also manage jobs that are currently waiting for the printer. It's possible to delete or pause a job, or promote it so it's completed before other jobs.

Another important feature of iManager is the ability to control access to the printer. In fact, this option exists on all objects related to printing in eDirectory, but the Access Control tab for the printers offers the most possibilities (see Figure 15-13). You can differentiate between those users allowed to access printers, operators, and managers.

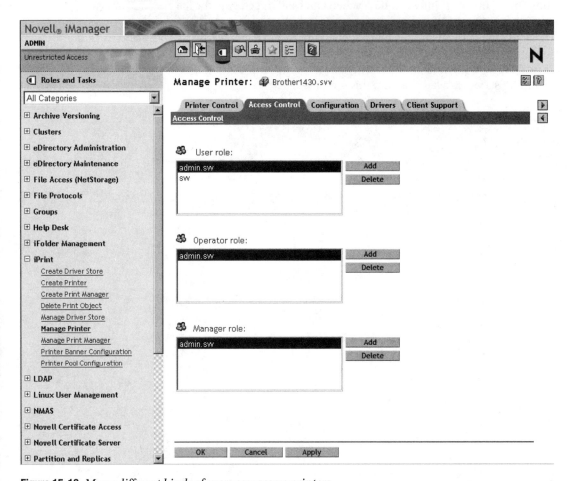

Figure 15-13. *Many different kinds of users can access printers.*

A manager is typically the eDirectory object that can do anything he wants with the chosen printer. If you're the manager for a printer object, you can delete it or add and remove other operators and managers from the printer. Operators for a printer object are only able to perform the daily management tasks on that printer, like pausing, restarting, or reinitializing printers, removing jobs from the print queues, and so on. An operator can never delete the printer object itself from the Directory.

The last tab of interest available on the printer object is Client Support (see Figure 15-14). On this tab, you can specify what kind of clients can access the printer. There are two different kinds of client. The first is the iPrint client. This is a client computer on which the iPrint client software is installed. As an administrator, you can specify for these clients whether access to the printer is secure or not. If you want printers to be accessed securely, select the Enable Secure

Printing option. With this option selected, user authentication and SSL/TLS are required to print—before a user can access a secure printer, she'll be prompted to enter her username and password.

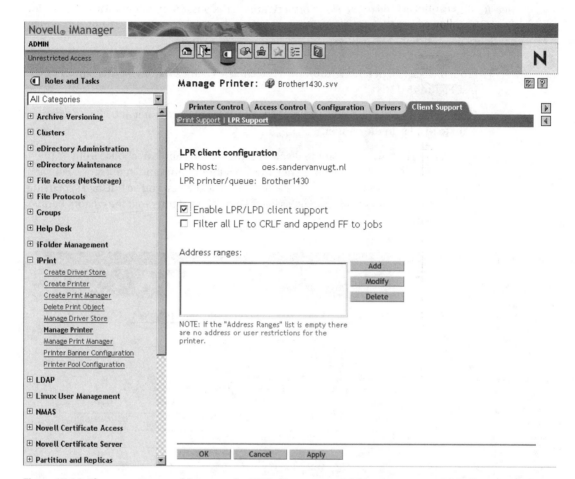

Figure 15-14. *If you want to enable access for LPR clients to your IPP printer, some LPR client options can be specified.*

The second kind of supported client is the LPR client. An LPR client is a traditional UNIX client that uses the LPD printing system to access a printer. If you want these clients to be able to access your printer, you should activate the Enable LPR/LPD Client Support option. Depending on the type of printer you're using, it may be necessary to select the Filter All LF to CRLF and Append FF to Jobs option as well. In normal English, this option stands for "Filter all line feed to carriage return / Line feed and append form feed to jobs." This option may be necessary to translate a print job in a proper way for some types of printers.

In an LPD/LPR environment, it is possible to work with address restrictions. If you only want to allow a limited amount of workstations access to your printers, you can specify an address range for the IP addresses that you want to allow. If no address range is specified, there is no restriction on the usage of this printer.

Working with Banners

New for iPrint (but very old in the world of NetWare), is the possibility to work with banners for your print jobs. From iManager, select iPrint, and then choose Printer Banner Configuration to configure banners for your printers:

1. From the Select Operation drop-down list, choose Create Custom Banner, and click OK (see Figure 15-15).

2. From the form, specify a banner name, the location of the banner and all items you want to display in the banner.

3. Select all the options you want to display on the banner. You can choose from 12 pre-configured options, like the Job Owner, the Job Submit Time, and many more. For each of these options, a font size can be selected. Click Next when you've finished specifying what to display on the banner. A message then displays stating that the custom banner was created.

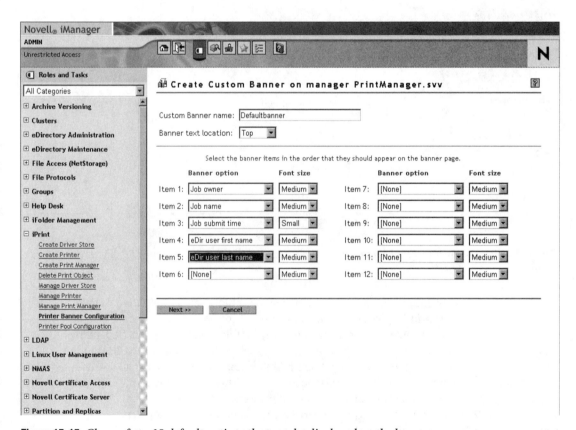

Figure 15-15. *Choose from 12 default options that can be displayed on the banner.*

Working with Printer Pools

If a high volume of printing is required, one printer often just isn't enough. In such cases, it's recommended to work with printer pools. A printer pool is a collection of printers that are all of the same type. When a job is submitted to a printer pool, it can be handled by any printer defined in that pool. This is why all printers in a pool need to be of the exact same type. Since they'll be offered jobs formatted by just one driver, the formatted text has to be printed the right way. To create a printer pool, apply the following procedure:

1. From iManager, select iPrint, and then choose Printer Pool Configuration.

2. Specify the name of the Print Manager and next select Create Printer Pool from the Select Operation drop-down list.

3. Specify a name for the printer pool, and from the list of available printers select all the printers you want to add to the printer pool (see Figure 15-16). Click Next to continue. The printer pool is created.

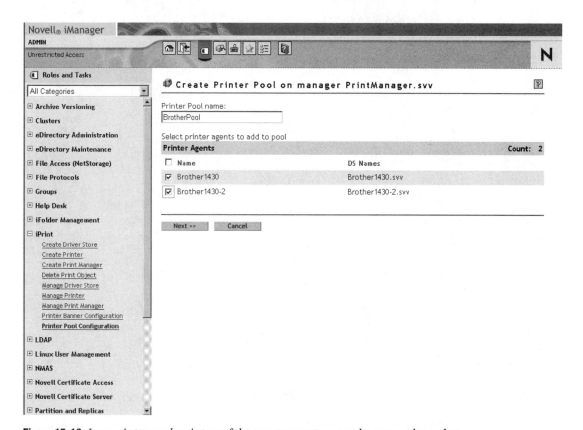

Figure 15-16. *In a printer pool, printers of the exact same type can be grouped together.*

Summary

In this chapter, you learned how to offer network printers in an OES environment. iPrint is the solution to all your printing needs. One of its major benefits is that it's based on the Internet Printing Protocol, which allows users to access printers from a browser. To configure iPrint, you've to add printer drivers to an iPrint Driver Store, create an iPrint Manager, and then configure your printer objects. For easier access to the printers, create a map so that the user can select her printer by just clicking its icon in a map. This installs the required iPrint client utility automatically on the user's workstation, no matter whether it's a Linux, Macintosh, or Windows workstation. In the next chapter, you'll learn how to manage Apache and Tomcat in an OES environment.

PART 3

■■■

Open Enterprise Server Web-Based Services

When NetWare 6.0 first appeared, it brought with it an important new way of working: NetWare 6.0 was the first version of NetWare where Novell properly "went Internet." This is still the case in Open Enterprise Server. In an Open Enterprise Server environment, a traditional Novell client is hardly needed anymore; all important services can be used from a browser. This part of the book teaches you how to configure some of the most important components behind this browser-based Novell world: the Apache web server and Virtual Office.

## CHAPTER 16

The Apache Web Server

Novell has a rich history of web servers. The very first web server came into existence with NetWare 4.11, which was called Intra NetWare. This web server's capabilities were woefully limited, however. In NetWare 5, Novell came up with the NetScape Enterprise web server, which was tailor-made for Novell environments by a company called Novonyx, a joint effort of Novell and Netscape. This was the first serious web server to come with NetWare, offering, for example, advanced possibilities for integration of the web server with eDirectory. Since NetWare 6.0, however, its Internet capabilities have taken great leaps forward, with Apache being included as NetWare's default web server.

Apache is by far the most widely used web server on the Internet, and one of the most powerful. Almost anything is possible using the Apache web server, thanks to its capability to extend its functionality using different modules. To make it easier for OES administrators, management of the Apache web server can be performed using eDirectory objects rather than having to go into the Apache httpd.conf configuration file and mess around with code lines. Most of this chapter is, in fact, dedicated to the Apache web server, but other important open-source services that work closely with the Apache web server are discussed as well, such as the Tomcat Servlet Engine, which is used by important services like iManager, the QuickFinder Web Search Server, and the MySQL database server.

Managing the Apache Web Server

The Apache web server is a very powerful web server. Indeed, it has so much functionality it can't all be possibly covered in this book. This chapter offers an overview of the most important aspects of Apache web server management. To start with, the tools used to manage the Apache Web Server are discussed—for instance, it's possible to access the configuration file httpd.conf directly, but in an OES environment, Apache Manager can also be used to manage multiple instances of the Apache web server from one browser-based interface. This section teaches you how to manage Apache Web Server parameters, content, modules, and security.

Apache Installation and Configuration

In all default installations for OES - NetWare and OES - Linux, the Apache server is installed by default. Only in customized installations is it possible not to select the Apache server for installation. This isn't necessarily a good idea, however, since you'll need it for many of the services running on OES - NetWare. Therefore, make sure the Apache server is always listed when performing an installation. After installation of OES, you'll find yourself with a brand new copy of Apache 2.0 on your server as well, which is used by many services on OES. For instance, iFolder and iPrint won't operate without it. In rare cases where the Apache web server isn't installed by default, it's possible to install the Apache web server from the Product installation option on the OES - NetWare console, or with YaST on OES - Linux. Chapter 13 has more on this procedure.

After installation, it's possible to fine-tune your Apache web server. The central configuration of this web server is stored in a configuration file called httpd.conf. If you're a long-term Apache administrator, you've probably already started worrying about httpd.conf and directives. Never fear! It's possible to change this file directly on both editions of OES. If, however, several Apache web servers in your network must be managed this way, Apache configuration can become cumbersome very fast. As an alternative, use the Apache Manager. This web-based interface can be used to manage the Apache configuration as it's stored in eDirectory. From the Apache Manager, use the Single Server Administration Interface to manage parameters on one single server, or use the Multiple Server Administration interface to manage multiple servers from one interface.

Installing Apache Manager on NetWare

Apache Manager is not installed by default on the OES - Linux platform. On OES - NetWare, it's installed when you select Apache for installation and you can access it on port 2200 (see Figure 16-1).

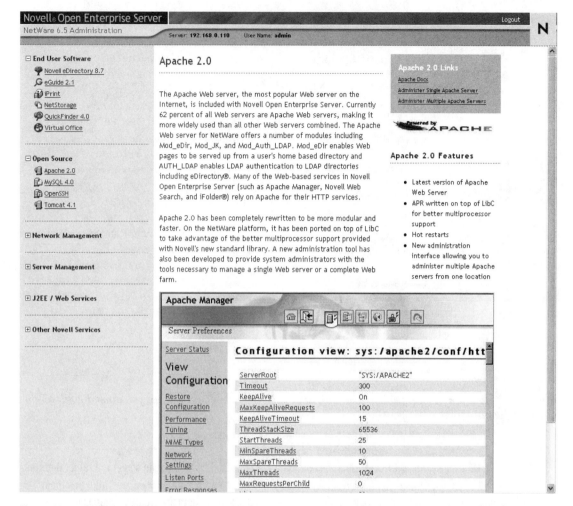

Figure 16-1. *On OES - NetWare, the generic management program that can be reached on HTTPS port 2200 also gives access to Apache Manager.*

Installing Apache Manager on Linux

Apache Manager is not installed by default on OES - Linux. If you want to use it, you can download and install the Apache Manager daemon from the Novell Forge Web site. Visit http://forge.novell.com/modules/xfmod/project/?apache_manager (see Figure 16-2) to download the file apacheadmin.tar to the computer where you want to run the daemon. You must meet the following minimum requirements to install the Apache Administration module:

- Java 2 version 1.3.1 or later must already be installed.

- The LDAP server must be running and accepting connections.

- Apache web server 2.0 or later is installed and running.

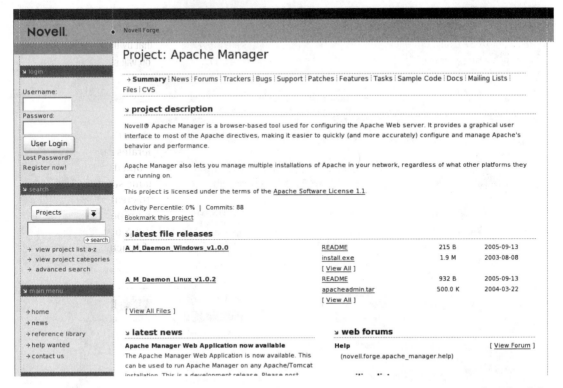

Figure 16-2. *Before you can manage Apache with Apache Manager on OES - Linux, you must download the program file from forge.novell.com.*

■Tip On OES - Linux, the structure of the configuration files used by the Apache server are rather different than other Linux distributions. A main configuration file, default-server.conf, is used, and from this main configuration file a lot of other configuration files are called. Some of them are created dynamically when the Apache server is started. This structure is not developed to be managed by hand. Thus, it's best you also use Apache Manager for management of Apache on OES - Linux. Limited management of the Apache web server can be performed from YaST as well.

---

1. Click the file apacheadmin.tar and download it. After downloading, copy the file to the directory where the Apache web server is installed. Normally, this is /usr/share/apache2.

■Note The procedure described here is based on an open-source project to implement an Apache Manager daemon for OES - Linux. Currently, people are still working on this project. It could be that by the time you read this, the procedure will have already changed. Most likely, though, the configuration will still be stored in the file startup.properties.

2. As root, run the command **tar xvf apacheadmin.tar** to extract the tarball. ("Tarball" is Linux slang for an archive that's created with the tar utility.) This generates a subdirectory apacheadmin in the Apache program directory where you've copied the tarball. In this directory, under the subdirectory conf, create a file with the name startup.properties. By default, this file already exists, but is empty. An easy way to create a new startup.properties file is to copy the entire contents of the file startup.properties.back to startup.properties. After that, you can modify the contents of startup.properties (see Figure 16-3). On several lines in this file, you can define the workings of Apache Manager using parameters shown in Table 16-1.

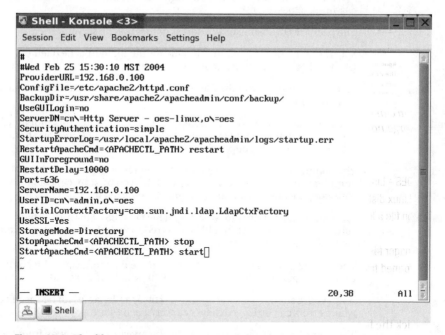

Figure 16-3. *The file startup.properties is used to specify how Apache Manager should work*

Table 16-1. *Parameters in /usr/share/apache2/apacheadmin/conf/startup.properties*

Parameter	Used For
InitialContextFactory	Specifies the name of the Java class used to generate the initial LDAP context. This line should read `InitialContextFactory = com.sun.kndi.ldap.LdapCtxFactory`.
ProviderURL	The DNS name or IP address of the LDAP server
Port	The listen port for the LDAP server. Use 636 for secure communications.
UseSSL	Specifies whether or not to use SSL for the LDAP connection. Select yes to use it.
SecurityAuthentication	The Authentication type for the LDAP connection. Default is `simple` and this is fine.
UserID	The user used for LDAP authentication by the daemon. This user must be a member of the eDirectory group apchadmn-Administrators. It's sufficient if you create a dummy user with no rights for this purpose.
ServerDN	The LDAP distinguished name for the Apache server object associated with this instance of the daemon. This should be a name like cn=Https Server – oes-linux,o=oes.
ServerName	The primary DNS name or IP address of the Apache server.
ConfigFile	Specifies the Apache configuration file for the main Apache daemon. Usually this is the httpd.conf file on your server.
BackupDir	An optional directory in the file system used by the daemon to save backup configurations.
StartApacheCmd	The command required to start Apache. On OES - Linux, this should refer to the apachectl script followed by start. On OES - NetWare, this should refer to the file ap2webup.ncf.
StopApacheCmd	The command required to stop Apache. On Linux this would be the complete name of the apachectl script, followed by stop. On OES - NetWare, the file ap2webdn.ncf should be referred to.
RestartApacheCmd	The command required to restart Apache. On OES - Linux, the Apache startup script apachectl should be referred to with the parameter restart. On OES - NetWare, refer to ap2webrs.ncf
RestartDelay	The polling delay that specifies how often the daemon checks for configuration changes. The default value is 10000, which is 10 seconds.
StartupErrorLog	If Apache is started with the option –E <file>, a filename can be specified where errors can be logged that occur on Apache startup.
StorageMode	This parameter specifies whether to get the Apache configuration from the configuration file as listed in the `ConfigFile` property, or from LDAP by connecting to the object listed in the ServerDN property. For daemon configuration, this property is always set to Directory.
UseGUILogin	Tells the daemon whether to prompt for the password using a command-line prompt or a GUI prompt. Can have the values yes and no.
GUIInForeground	Specifies whether the GUI should run in the foreground, or disappear after getting the password.

3. To start the Apache Manager daemon, run the file daemoninstall.bat from the directory /usr/share/apache2/apacheadmin.

■**Caution** It sometimes happens that the daemon refuses to start. This is because in the script daemoninstall.bat where the Java code is executed to start the script, there is a reference that starts with <PATH>. Replace <PATH> with the directory where the Apache2 binaries are installed (/usr/share/apache2 on OES - Linux) and execute the file again. You should now be able to run the installation script.

---

4. Fill in the `Enter The Base Path For The apacheadmin Directory` field with the name of the directory **/usr/share/apache2**. Press Enter to continue.

5. Now you're asked what password to use. Use a blank password, otherwise the script will always ask for a password when you start it. After entering the password, start the Apache Manager daemon by executing the script **ap2webman.bat**. Before you can execute it, use the command **chmod +x ap2webman.bat** to make the script executable.

■**Tip** It's possible to start, stop, and restart the Apache server from the Apache Manager interface. You can also start and stop it from your server's console by doing the following:

- Use **AP2WEBUP** from the OES - NetWare console to start Apache.

- Use **AP2WEBDN** from the OES - NetWare console to stop Apache.

- Use **/etc/init.d/apache2 start** from the OES - Linux console to start Apache.

- Use **/etc/init.d/apache2 stop** from the OES - Linux console to stop Apache.

Managing Apache Configuration

After a successful installation, you can access Apache Manager on HTTPS port 2200 of your server. From the general web administration interface, select Open Source, Apache 2.0. This will bring you to a page where you can find a general description of Apache web server management. From this page, select the Administer Single Apache Server link to manage one Apache web server, or choose the Administer Multiple Apache Servers link to manage a group of Apache web servers. In the Single Apache Server administration, you can manage one Apache web server at a time. The web interface in this case is a remote control for the settings of the httpd. conf configuration file of the Apache server you've chosen to manage. In Single Administration mode, you can choose to save your settings to the httpd.conf file. You can also choose to save them in eDirectory as well, as shown in Figure 16-4. The former is called file mode, the latter is directory mode. For fault tolerance, it's better to store the configuration in eDirectory. The single administration interface gives an intuitive graphical interface to manage Apache parameters.

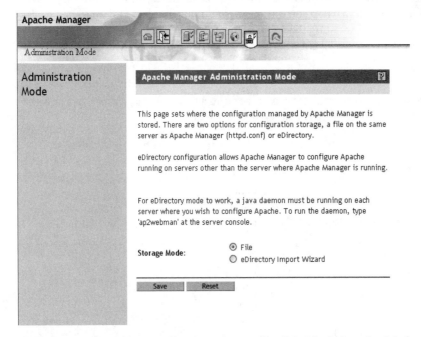

Figure 16-4. *In Single Server Administration mode, click Administration Mode to access the eDirectory Import Wizard that can be used to import an Apache configuration into eDirectory.*

In Multiple Server Administration mode (as shown in Figure 16-5), you can manage all Apache web servers in an Apache group. All Apache directives are managed from your server's interface. You need a good understanding of these directives, since you must enter them directly into the system. There's no choice between file and directory mode in Mul le Server Administration mode; all settings are saved in eDirectory by default.

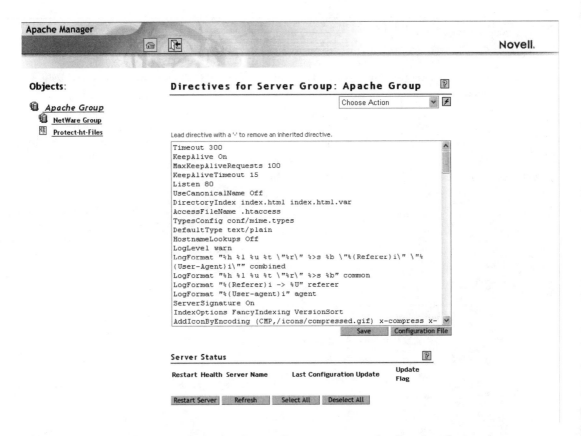

Figure 16-5. *In Multiple Server Administration mode, you can access the directives that apply to all Apache servers and that are members of an Apache server group by clicking the Apache Group link.*

Managing Apache Web Server Parameters

The most important screen in the Apache Manager's Single Server Administration interface is View Configuration, as shown in Figure 16-6. Here you have access to all parameters from the Apache configuration file httpd.conf. The advantage of this interface is that parameters of the Apache web server are also accessible for administrators who do not have a lot of experience working with Apache directives. All directives are changed from the web-based interface, so there is little risk of making mistakes. You can click all hyperlinked directives and modify them as necessary. To make you a good Apache administrator, however, you should be aware of the proper use of these settings: it's still very easy to destroy an Apache web server that's properly working by entering the wrong values for some settings. Imagine, for example, what could happen if an administrator accidentally sets the MaxThreads parameter to 1. This would allow just one user at the same time to be connected to the Apache web server!

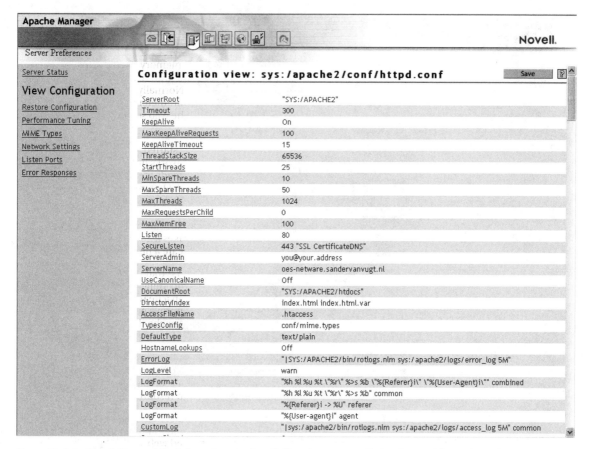

Figure 16-6. *In Single Server Administration mode, all directives can easily be changed from the web interface.*

In the left bar of the Apache Manager in Single Server Administration mode, you'll see an overview of all available settings that can be used to tune the Apache server. These settings are divided into different groups. The most important of these groups is the Performance Tuning link. Here you'll find all the settings related to the performance of your Apache server. An overview of these performance-related parameters is shown in Table 16-2.

More settings for your web server are available from the Server Preferences page. These include the following:

- Click MIME Types to define file associations that your server can work with. These associations allow the Apache server to open the right application when a file with a given extension is accessed. Use the New button found under this link to define a new default type of file and extension used for that file.

Table 16-2. *Performance-Related Apache Parameters*

Parameter	Default value	Use
Thread stack size	65536	Defines the amount of memory available for the thread stack. This is RAM that's available to run processes. Normally, the default value is fine, but this parameter may be increased if your Apache web server works with a lot of modules.
Start threads	25	The amount of threads started automatically. The default of 25 works fine for most environments. New threads are allocated automatically if needed. On a very busy server, it can be useful to increment the default number of threads started automatically in order to increase Apache web server performance since it takes a good deal of performance to allocate a new thread.
Minimum spare threads	10	A spare thread is a thread that is allocated automatically for new incoming connections. Increase this number on a heavily used Apache web server to improve performance. This number of spare Apache threads will always be available for new client connections.
Maximum spare threads	50	The maximum amount of spare threads. Don't make this number too big because all threads allocate system resources.
Maximum total threads	1024	The maximum amount of active threads on this server. This parameter only needs to be changed on heavily used web servers.
Enable keep alive	Yes	Allows a virtual connection to remain open if a user hasn't sent data for some time. This is good because it prevents your server from establishing a new connection every time a user has been disconnected for a short period.
Maximum keep alive requests	100	The maximum number of keep alive requests that can be handled. For almost any circumstances, the default of 100 is good.
Keep alive timeout	15	Number of seconds that a keep alive connection remains open. 15 seconds is reasonable—if a user doesn't send new data for longer than 15 seconds, he is probably gone anyway.
Enable DNS Lookups	No	Do you want Apache to do a reverse DNS lookup for logging-in purposes so that the DNS name of a client can be logged instead of the IP-address (which is meaningless in most cases)? Only enable this parameter if you really need it for troubleshooting purposes since your server will take a large performance hit as a result.

- Click Network Settings to specify the mail address of the administrator. Here, you can also decide if you want to use server-side includes (SSI) to update information on a web page based upon information queried from the server. On this page, you can also specify the name of the extension to use when working with SSI. By default, server-side includes are not allowed because they pose a limited security risk.

- On the Listen Ports link, you can specify the ports on which your web server listens for incoming connections. Here you can also enable or disable the use of encryption. By default, the web server is configured to listen for incoming connections on port 80 (non-secure) and on port 443 for secured incoming connections.

Managing Web Server Content

All documents offered by the Apache web server are created in the Apache web server document root. This is a directory specified in the Apache configuration file that can be used to store all documents offered by the Apache web server. This document root is also the default directory that will be presented to all users accessing the Apache web server. All other directories where content is stored on the Apache web server are related to this document root as well. In the Apache configuration, you'll only see the partial name of such a directory, as in `TypesConfig = conf/mime.types`. On OES - NetWare, this document root is on the SYS volume, by default. Since it's a very bad idea to put documents on the SYS volume, you might want to change that, as listed in the following procedure. Before you apply these steps, make sure you've created the new documentroot and that you've copied all files from the old document root to the new one.

1. Start the Apache Single Server Manager interface.

2. Select View Configuration and then DocumentRoot. This opens a pop-up window.

3. In this pop-up window, enter the name of the directory in quotes that you want to use as the new document root. Click Save to save your changes.

4. In the left column of the Apache Manager interface, select Server Status. From the Server Status interface, choose Restart Server. The Apache web server will not detect changes made to the configuration automatically; you must restart it to apply all changes.

■**Note** On SUSE Linux, the Apache configuration is stored in many files. The file /etc/apache2/default-server.conf is used as the main configuration file, and from this file other configuration files are included using include directives. If you want to change the default DocumentRoot directive on OES - Linux by editing the Apache configuration files manually, you must edit the file default-server.conf.

If you want to include additional document directories, activate the Content Management interface by clicking the Content Management button in the button bar. From this interface, you can change several parameters, like those listed next.

- The location of the primary document directory.

- *The location of additional document directories.* These are other directories on the Apache web server where HTML documents can be stored. These directories can be located anywhere in your server and can be reached at their own URL. While creating these additional document directories, specify the URL prefix and the location in the file system where the directory is created.

- *Whether or not you want to allow users to create their own home directories.* You can also define the name of a default directory that must be created in the user's home directory for the user to store his HTML documents inside.

- *Document preferences.* With this option, you can specify the name of the default index file names (normally index.html or home.html).

- *URL-forwarding.* Use this option to define a URL that can be used on your local web server to forward to a location on another web server.

- *Virtual hosts.* Use this option to define virtual hosts hosted by your Apache web server. A virtual host is a web server that can be reached at its own name and IP address.

Extending Apache Functionality with Modules

The Apache server itself only provides basic functionality, but this functionality can be extended through the use of modules. If, for example, your Apache server must be able to handle PHP-scripts, you can install PHP as a module to provide this functionality. These modules can be included with the LoadModule directive in the Apache configuration. Some of these modules, and the directives that point to them, are already present in the default configuration. You can view them from the View Configuration option in the Single Server Management interface. Some modules can also be managed from the Modules interface. You can activate this interface from the Modules button at the top of the screen (shown in Figure 16-7). In an OES environment, some specific modules are used to enhance the Apache capabilities, including the following:

- *mod_jk*: Provides access to the Tomcat servlet container (see the section "Managing the Tomcat Servlet Engine" later in this chapter for more on this).

- *mod_auth_ldap*: Enables the Apache server to communicate with an LDAP server for user authentication.

- *mod_edir*: Allows the Apache server to work with information from eDirectory.

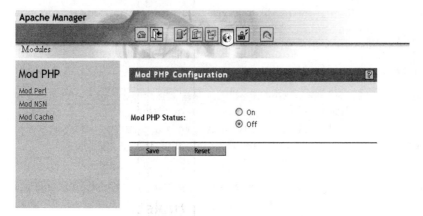

Figure 16-7. *Some modules can be activated from the special modules interface.*

Enabling Directory Mode

As stated before, there are two different modes in which the Apache web server can be managed if you work from the Single Server Administration module. If you choose to work in File mode, all modifications are stored in the default Apache configuration files. If you specify to work in Directory mode, all changes are stored in eDirectory. You can use the Administration Mode button from the button bar to specify which of these modes must be deployed—by default, your Apache server will work in file mode. There are, however, some advantages if you store the information in eDirectory. The most important being that the data is stored in a fault-tolerant database and is no longer in one single file. To store the information in eDirectory, perform the following steps.

1. To activate Directory mode storage, from the Administration Mode interface select the eDirectory Import Wizard option and click Save to start the wizard (this sounds illogical, but it's really the way it works).

2. On the next screen, click Next to continue.

3. Now select the option Create A New Server Object and click Next to continue. This creates a new server object in eDirectory.

4. If there is more than one Apache group object in eDirectory, you can specify the group to which your server must become a member. Also enter the server eDirectory object name and server DNS name for your Apache web server. Click Next to continue.

5. Now, specify how directives on your newly created Apache server object in eDirectory must be managed. There are two options: the first is to import the current settings from httpd.conf on your Apache web server. You can also choose to work with an inherited eDirectory configuration. If your Apache server is imported in eDirectory, you can specify properties for the server to be used at the Apache group level. These properties can be inherited by all Apache server objects that are members of this group. If you already have an Apache group object that is completely configured, choose Use Inherited eDirectory Configuration (as shown in Figure 16-8) and click Next to continue.

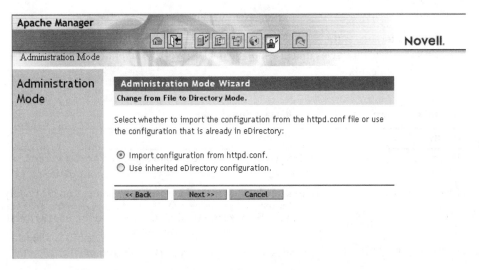

Figure 16-8. *If an Apache configuration is already present in eDirectory, new Apache servers can inherit its properties from this configuration.*

6. All information needed to create the Apache server object in eDirectory is now present. Review it, and if you're happy with it, click Finish to close the wizard and create the eDirectory object.

7. You'll now see a message that the Apache configuration has been changed in eDirectory. Click Refresh to change the appearance of Apache manager. A screen appears in which you see a list of all available Apache servers stored in eDirectory. From this screen, select the server you want to manage.

Connecting Apache to eDirectory Users

Since the Apache server is used in OES on an eDirectory platform, it might as well use information *from* eDirectory. Two kinds of information are especially important. First, there are the home directories of eDirectory users. If users have permission to create a personal web page in their home directory, the Apache web server must be able to read the eDirectory property homedirectory for the users. Second, eDirectory information can be used to restrict access to certain directories. On a normal Apache web server, a specific Apache user database must be created for this purpose with the command **htpasswd**. However, since Apache can get information from eDirectory, eDirectory users can be utilized for this purpose in an Apache OES environment. To do all this, the following two Apache modules must be loaded:

- mod_edir

- mod_auth_ldap

Use the LoadModule directive to include these modules in the Apache configuration. You can input these lines directly into the Apache configuration file. If you're using mod_edir, always make sure that mod_auth_ldap is also used, since mod_edir depends on it, as shown in the following:

```
LoadModule mod_auth_ldap
LoadModule mod_edir
```

Once a reference to the mod_edir module is included in the Apache configuration file, you can add some new directives that are specific to eDirectory. You'll find an overview of these directives in Table 6-3.

Table 16-3. *Directives Made Available from mod_edir*

Directive	Description
eDirServer	Specifies the server to be used to log in and extract information from eDirectory.
eDirUserAccount	This directive can be used to specify the name of an eDirectory user for use as a proxy-user for the LDAP process. This user object has the right to get information from eDirectory, such as the Home Directory attribute of each user object.
eDirPassword	Specifies the password of the eDirUserAccount.
eDirCacheTimeout	Used to specify the number of seconds that information from eDirectory remains stored in cache. The default value for this parameter is 300 seconds.
hDirUserTag	This directive specifies the character that should be used to determine that what follows is a username. It's recommended to stay with the default value of the tilde character (~).
hDirUserSubDirectory	Specifies the name of the default subdirectory where mod_edir attempts to access a web page stored in a user's home directory. By default, the directory public_html in the user's home directory is used.
hDirSearchContexts	Use this important directive to specify the list of contexts to search when attempting to find a user's home directory. By default, each context and all its subcontexts are searched until a matching user ID is found.
HomeDirEnabled	Use this directive to specify whether or not home directories can be used to store personal web pages. It has two different values: On and Off.
RemoteDirEnabled	In an OES Apache environment, sometimes a user's home directory won't be stored on the server designated as eDirServer. In that case, the user's home directory can be accessed as a so-called Remote Directory. With this directive, support for remote directories is enabled by default. Use the parameter Off to switch it off if so desired.
Require edir-user	This directive specifies that in order to access a certain directory, a user has to be authenticated first as an eDirectory user. You also need the directives AuthName, AuthType, and AuthLDAPURL from mod_auth_ldap to be able to use this directive. The following lines of code show how these directives can be used. For more information, see the mod_auth_ldap documentation on the Apache.org web site.

In the following code sample from SYS:\APACHE2\CONF\HTTPD.CONF on OES - NetWare, notice how the directives from mod_edir can be used to limit access to a given directory only to users defined in eDirectory in the container o=oes or below.

```
LoadModule ldap_module
<IfModule util_ldap.c>
                LoadModule auth_ldap_module
                LoadModule edir_module
                Alias /secure /srv/www/htdocs/Corpdata
                <Directory secure>
                        Order deny,allow
                        Allow from all
                        AuthType Basic
                        AuthName LDAP_Protected_Site
                        AuthLDAPURL ldap://oes-netware.oes.com/o=oes
                        require edir-user
                </Directory>
</IfModule>
```

Managing the Tomcat Servlet Engine

The Tomcat Servlet Engine is one of the most important services running on top of the Apache server. Tomcat is needed to access and administer many of the Java-based components running on OES. Without Tomcat, it's impossible to access or manage typical OES services like iFolder or iPrint, for example.

Tomcat Servlet Container Overview

Tomcat is a servlet container. This is a runtime shell that runs on top of a web server and manages and invokes servlets when they are requested by any kind of client. As such, the Tomcat servlet container is, in fact, a small application server. It's also a part of Jakarta, an open-source project in which different people work together to make a Java-based application server. You can find more information about this project at jakarta.apache.org/tomcat/index.html.

On your server, two different instances of Tomcat are configured: an administration server and a public server. Both use the same configuration, which is in the default Tomcat directory: sys:tomcat on OES - NetWare or /srv/www/tomcat on OES - Linux. The administration instance of the Tomcat servlet container is always installed on OES - NetWare, if OES services are used on OES - Linux, it's installed by default as well. The public instance is only installed if you choose to install it during installation. Both instances are started from the same script: autoexec.ncf on OES - NetWare and /etc/init.d/tomcat on OES - Linux. In the following listing, you can see how both instances are started from autoexec.ncf on OES - NetWare:

```
#tc4admin begin
SEARCH ADD SYS:/tomcat/4/bin
tcadmup.ncf
# tc4admin end
# tomcat 4 begin
sys:/tomcat/4/bin/tomcat4.ncf
# tomcat 4 end
```

The Administrative instance of the Tomcat Servlet Container is used by OES to host and manage typical Novell services such as iManager, Apache Manager, and the OES welcome screen. Requests to these specific products are passed through the Apache module mod_jk to the Tomcat server. Tomcat processes the request and forms a response in HTTP which is passed back to the Apache server.

The public instance of Tomcat functions as your own application server, which can be used to work with servlet applications. Tomcat, however, is developed only to work with very basic Java servlets and JSPs. If you don't need to implement a complete application server, it's a good choice. If, however, you need Java API support beyond servlets and other advanced Java features, the Novell exteNd Application Server may be a better choice. To manage the extend application server properly, however, you need experience with Java programming as well.

Tomcat Configuration

Two web-based tools can be used to manage Tomcat:

- The Tomcat Administration Tool, also known as Tomcat Admin

- Tomcat Web Application Manager, also known as Tomcat Manager

The difference between the two is that the Tomcat Manager is used to manage the Tomcat content: the servlets and applications offered by the Tomcat server. The Tomcat Administration Tool is used to manage the Tomcat environment itself. Both tools run perfectly on OES - NetWare and OES - Linux.

Using the Tomcat Administration Tool

You can start the Tomcat Web Server Administration tool at the URL https://yourserver/tomcat/admin/index.jsp (see Figure 16-9). After logging in with your eDirectory credentials, you'll be able to manage all aspects of the Tomcat environment. You can find extensive documentation on this tool at Sun's web site: http://java.sun.com/webservices/docs/1.0/tutorial/doc/Admintool.html. I recommend using this excellent administration tool if you need to change anything on your Tomcat environment. It can save you the hassle of manually editing the XML configuration files used by the Tomcat server. However, you'll find that it's not really necessary to work with this tool if you're only running Tomcat to provide access to the OES tools using it. The default configuration is fine since it's designed for this purpose. In this regard, only the following two parameters are important to a network administrator:

- On the Tomcat Server page, you can enter the default port number for the Tomcat server. Here, you can also specify the debug level. By default, debug level 0 is used for a minimum amount of debugging information. You can set this as high as 9 for the maximum amount of debugging information.

- Select Tomcat Server ➤ Service to specify the default hostname that Tomcat uses. This is important on a server that can be reached on multiple names to specify the name of the host that Tomcat should bind to.

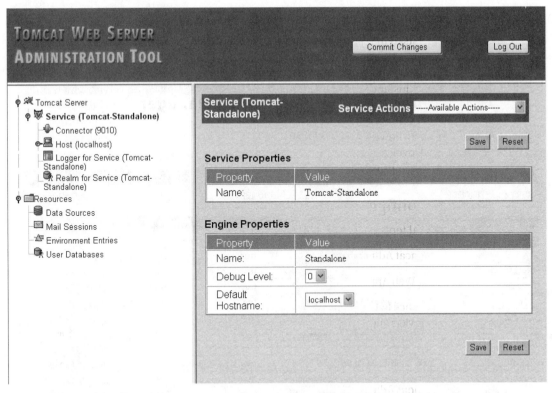

Figure 16-9. *You can manage all aspects of thse Tomcat environment from the Tomcat Administration Tool.*

Using the Tomcat Web Application Manager

To start the Tomcat Web Application Manager, you can access it from your browser at the URL https://yourserver/tomcat/manager/html (see Figure 16-10). After logging in to the application, the Tomcat Manager allows you to add and remove Java components that should be made accessible by the Tomcat servlet container. This tool is really useful to manage applications currently running on your server. Imagine, for example, a situation where eGuide is not performing well and you consider it necessary to restart just eGuide. Without this tool, the only way to do so is by restarting the entire Tomcat servlet container. With Tomcat Manager, you can select the service you want to restart and click Reload from the web-based interface. The Tomcat Web Application Manager offers other useful functions as well, like the following:

- It allows you to see if an application is running or not.

- It allows you to monitor the current number of sessions that are open to a given application.

- It allows you to install new applications that use the Tomcat servlet container. All you need is a WAR file that's provided with the application to install it.

- By clicking the links for the applications that are currently active, you can get easy access to all the applications.

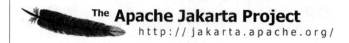

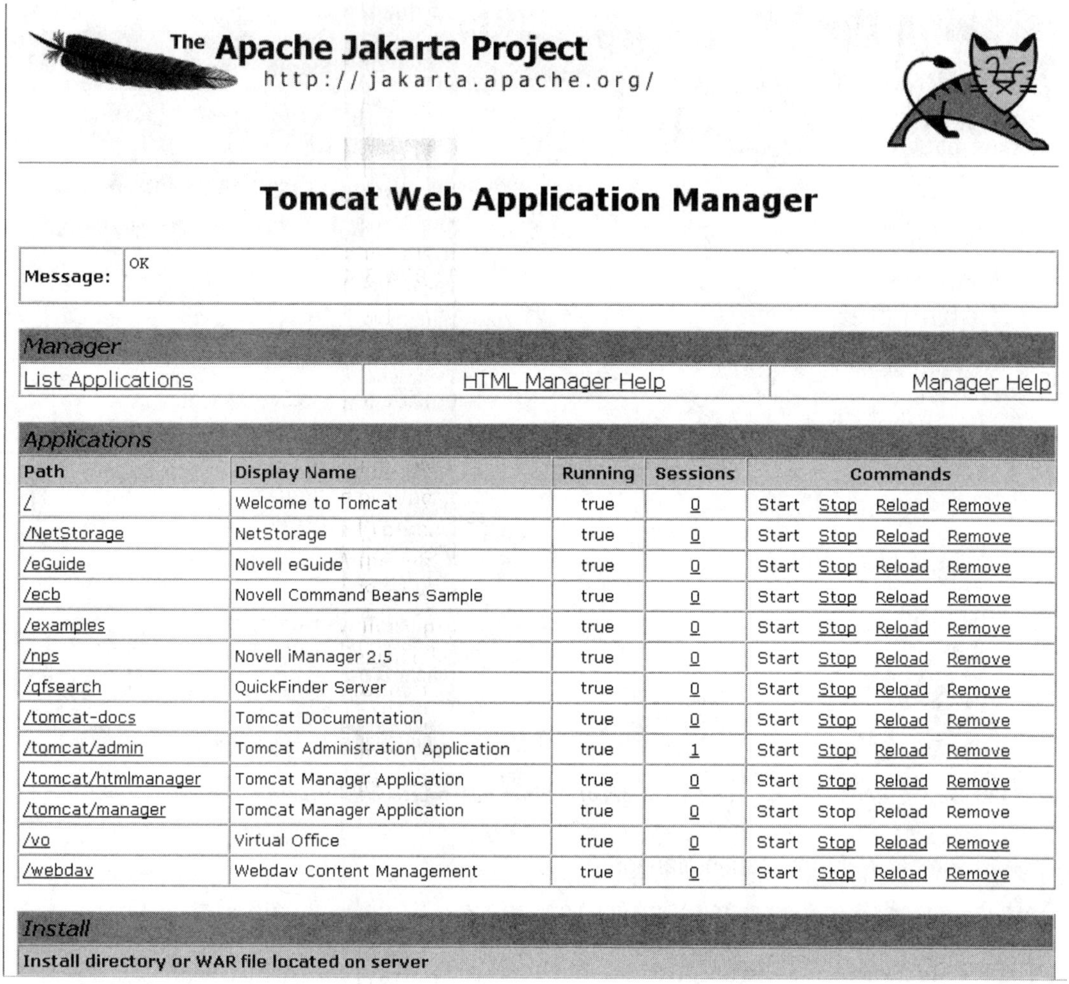

The Apache Jakarta Project
http://jakarta.apache.org/
Tomcat Web Application Manager
Message: OK
Manager
List Applications
HTML Manager Help
Manager Help
Applications
Path
Display Name
Running
Sessions
Commands
/ Welcome to Tomcat true 0 Start Stop Reload Remove
/NetStorage NetStorage true 0 Start Stop Reload Remove
/eGuide Novell eGuide true 0 Start Stop Reload Remove
/ecb Novell Command Beans Sample true 0 Start Stop Reload Remove
/examples true 0 Start Stop Reload Remove
/nps Novell iManager 2.5 true 0 Start Stop Reload Remove
/qfsearch QuickFinder Server true 0 Start Stop Reload Remove
/tomcat-docs Tomcat Documentation true 0 Start Stop Reload Remove
/tomcat/admin Tomcat Administration Application true 1 Start Stop Reload Remove
/tomcat/htmlmanager Tomcat Manager Application true 0 Start Stop Reload Remove
/tomcat/manager Tomcat Manager Application true 0 Start Stop Reload Remove
/vo Virtual Office true 0 Start Stop Reload Remove
/webdav Webdav Content Management true 0 Start Stop Reload Remove
Install
Install directory or WAR file located on server

Figure 16-10. *The Tomcat Manager provides some management possibilities for applications that use Tomcat.*

■ **Note** If for any reason you have problems accessing the Tomcat server, first make sure that it's started. On OES - NetWare, type **tomcat4** at the console to start the server and **tcadmdn** to stop it. On OES - Linux, use **/etc/init.d/tomcat start** to start the server and **/etc/init.d/tomcat stop** to stop it. After a default installation, Tomcat will be started automatically on OES - NetWare. You might be required to use the runlevel editor to start it automatically on OES - Linux as well. Use **/etc/init.d/tomcat status** to check the status of your Tomcat server after system initialization. If it appears that the Tomcat server has not started automatically, use **chkconfig tomcat 235** to add it to all important runlevels on your server.

Searching the Web with QuickFinder

The QuickFinder server (formerly known as NetWare Web Search) allows you to create your own web search server—very useful if you're hosting a large web site. QuickFinder can be used to find information on public or private web sites and any attached file systems or servers. It works on the basis of indexes. These indexes can be made of HTML, XML, PDF, Word, and OpenOffice.org documents, and you can manage them from the QuickFinder's web-based administration module.

QuickFinder Benefits

Generic search engines such as Google are able to locate some of the information on your site, but a much better result can be reached if you maintain your own web search server.

The use of the QuickFinder server offers many beneficial features, some of which are mentioned next:

- Hosting search services for more than one organization

- Defining as many indexes as you like to increase search performance

- Working with access restrictions so that only authorized people can work with sensitive documents

- Adjusting the relevance of documents to ensure a user gets the best possible results

- Generating reports of all search activity so you can learn what your customers are looking for and optimize the web search server as a result

- Looking up information within your own organization

- Customizing the look and feel of the QuickFinder server

QuickFinder's Architecture

The QuickFinder server is composed of four major components:

- Virtual search servers

- Indexes

- Templates

- Configuration settings

To manage the QuickFinder server efficiently, you need to know how these four components are deployed.

Virtual Search Servers

A virtual search server is a collection of one or more indexes and their related configuration files that allows you to search for information within a specific context. It's common that several virtual search servers are hosted on a dedicated QuickFinder server. You can install, for example, a virtual search server for the Sales department of your company and another one for its IT support branch. There's no limitation to the number of virtual search servers hosted on a QuickFinder server.

Every virtual search server works with its own environment, which consists of a name, a set of indexes, scheduled indexing events, log files, configuration settings, reports, and an administration interface. Although all virtual search servers work with their own environment, it's possible to share resources between virtual search servers. For instance, you can create an index that's used by more than one virtual search server. If you want to do that, you must create a duplicate index on each of the virtual search servers that points to the same shared index directory.

Indexes

The index is more or less the key component that QuickFinder works with. It's a file generated by the QuickFinder server that contains keywords and matching URLs. Every virtual search server has at least one index. Two different types of indexes can be created: the file system index and the crawled index. If you want to index the contents of a file server, you need a file system index. When you want to index the contents of a web server, a crawled index is needed.

Templates

The QuickFinder server uses templates as interfaces to communicate with users. A template generates a search form, prints results, and allows users to provide feedback. Essentially, it's an HTML document that contains one or more QuickFinder server variables. With these variables, a dynamic result can be created. It's possible to provide each virtual search server with its own templates, but it's also possible to share templates across the network. Some default templates are included with QuickFinder.

Configuration Settings

Finally, each QuickFinder server has its own set of configuration settings. These settings define how the QuickFinder server will perform and what virtual servers, indexes, and templates are used by this server. Configuration settings exist that apply to all virtual servers defined on your QuickFinder server—you configure them on the QuickFinder server from the Global Settings page of the QuickFinder Server Manager. You'll read more about configuring QuickFinder in the following sections.

Managing QuickFinder

To manage all virtual servers and their indexes on your QuickFinder server, the QuickFinder Server Manager is used. It can create default settings that are applied to all the virtual servers you later generate. In order to use QuickFinder Server Manager, start the browser-based interface, and log in as a user that has enough rights to access the QuickFinder directory: /var/lib/qfsearch on Linux and /qfsearch on NetWare. If you're using QuickFinder server on OES - Linux, use LUM so you can log in as an eDirectory user with enough rights to manage files in the directory /var/lib/qfsearch on the local Linux file system. (Chapter 9 has more on the configuration of LUM.) If LUM is not configured, log in to the QuickFinder Server Manager as a local Linux user with enough rights. To start the QuickFinder Server Manager, browse to http://yourserver/qfsearch/admin to get to the screen shown in Figure 16-11.

Tip In most situations, eDirectory rights are needed to administer the different components of OES. With QuickFinder, you just need rights to the local file system. This means that in many cases you must log in as root (not as your eDirectory admin user) to be able to administer the QuickFinder server. All you're doing as a QuickFinder administrator is creating an index file.

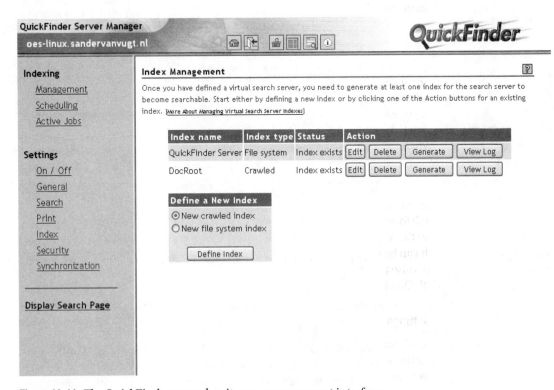

Figure 16-11. *The QuickFinder server has its own management interface.*

Immediately after installation, users can start using the QuickFinder server. Some of your server's content is automatically indexed and appears on the default search form. If you want to create your own indexes and virtual search servers, it's best to read the online documentation of the QuickFinder server at http://www.novell.com/documentation.

Without even configuring anything, it's possible to get a quick impression of how the QuickFinder server can be used:

1. Access the main web page of your OES server at http://yourserver:2200.

2. From End User Software in the left column on your screen, select QuickFinder 4.0. This opens a default QuickFinder page where you can find specific items on your server (as shown in Figure 16-12).

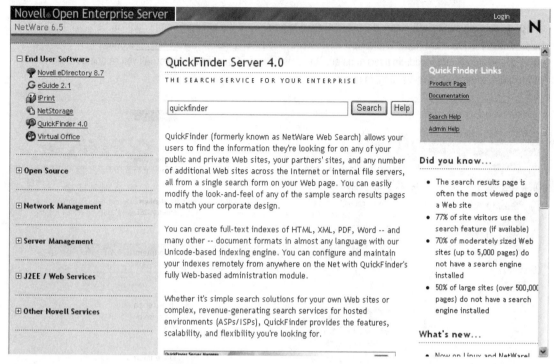

Figure 16-12. *Without any configuration, you can start using the QuickFinder server immediately after installation.*

3. In the search bar, enter the word you want to search for (QuickFinder, for example) and click Search.

4. A list of all search hits will be displayed (see Figure 16-13 for an example). The most relevant hits displayed at the top of the list. It's possible, however, to modify the way the results window is displayed. You can search results by Relevance (default), Title, or Date.

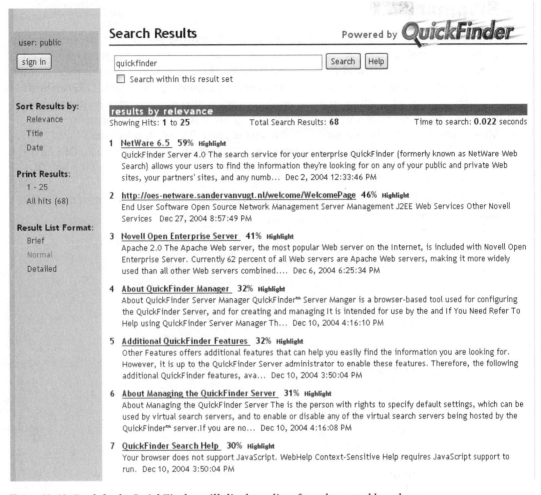

Figure 16-13. *By default, QuickFinder will display a list of results sorted by relevance.*

MySQL

An important component used with OES web services is the MySQL server. MySQL is an open-source SQL database server that can be deployed on NetWare as well as Linux. To effectively use it, a basic knowledge of the Structured Query Language (SQL) is needed. MySQL is often used as the database back-end of a web application. Using a scripting language such as PHP or Perl, you can create a web application that gets its data from a MySQL database. The scripting language issues commands to the MySQL server which runs constantly, listening for commands and then manipulating the database accordingly. Together, the Apache web server, the MySQL database server, and a scripting language such as PHP or Perl are a powerful combination for creating web applications. Since this is an entirely different subject (and a science all its own), I won't cover MySQL, PHP, and Perl administration here. For more information on these subjects, check out the following books: *Beginning PHP 5 and MySQL: From Novice to Professional* by W. Jason Gilmore (Apress, 2004) and *Pro Perl* by Peter Wainwright (Apress, 2005).

Summary

There are two sides to the Web components of Open Enterprise Server. First, the combination of the Apache web server and the Tomcat servlet engine is essential to run most web-based administration tools and products provided by Open Enterprise Server. For this reason, you'll find that both Apache and Tomcat are part of any installation of OES. Second, OES can be used as a web server as well. Although this is not the primary purpose, some rather advanced possibilities are available in OES, of which the most important is the combination of Apache, MySQL, and PHP/Perl, which can be used to create powerful web applications.

In this chapter, you learned how Apache and Tomcat can be managed in an OES environment. You also got an introduction to the QuickFinder Web Search Server and the MySQL database server.

In the next chapter you'll read about an end-user product that runs on top of the OES web infrastructure: Virtual Office.

CHAPTER 17

■■■

Using Virtual Office

In the past, the only way a user could connect to services offered on the network was by using a network client. Nowadays, most services OES offers can be accessed from a browser. For these services, a dedicated software client on a user's workstation is no longer needed. Most of the web-based services, such as iFolder, iPrint, and NetStorage can be accessed from Virtual Office. In this chapter, you'll learn how to configure, access, and optimize Virtual Office. You'll also learn how to configure eGuide, an application that can be accessed from Virtual Office, in order to look up information about users.

Configuring Virtual Office

Before Virtual Office can be used, the administrator must install it and perform some basic configuration options. This configuration consists of two parts, the first of which is performed from the software installation utility. When the initial configuration is entered from this utility, the administrator is then able to manage Virtual Office settings from the Virtual Office administration interface.

Configuring Virtual Office from the Software Installation Utility

To make sure that Virtual Office is installed, in YaST on OES - Linux select Virtual Office from Network Services. This option checks if Virtual Office has already been installed on your server. If it is installed, you'll get a message indicating as such. If you click Yes on this message, the software is installed and configured again. If Virtual Office hasn't been installed yet, you'll be prompted for installation CDs to install the required software from CD. After the software has been installed, you can enter configuration details:

1. In the first configuration screen, specify whether eDirectory is installed locally on this server, or remotely on another server, as shown in Figure 17-1. You must connect to eDirectory, because Virtual Office gets a lot of data from eDirectory. If choosing the latter, specify the IP address of the eDirectory server, the admin name, and the password you need to connect to this server. If eDirectory is reachable at a different port than the default port, specify the port details and click Next to continue. If you're configuring Virtual Office on a machine where eDirectory is installed locally, select Local System, and specify the required login data. Then, click Next to continue.

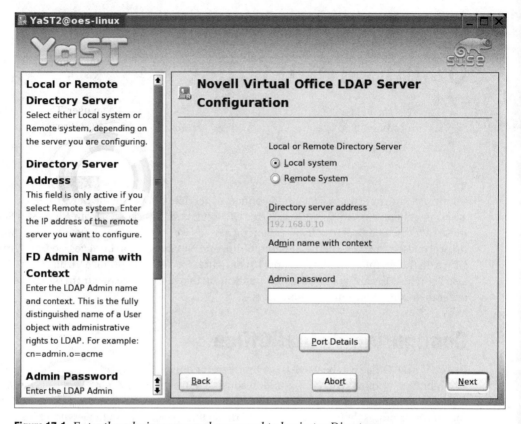

Figure 17-1. *Enter the admin name and password to log in to eDirectory.*

2. Enter the IP address of the server where Virtual Office software is installed and specify the context where Virtual Office starts looking for user objects. Normally, this would be the organization object in your tree, since from there Virtual Office can find additional user accounts in subcontainers. After entering the required information, click Next to continue.

3. The information is now written to your server. When this process is finished, you'll see a message indicating that the Apache and Tomcat server need to be restarted. Click Yes to restart them. After restarting these servers, Virtual Office can be reached from http://*yourserver*/vo.

To install Virtual Office from OES - NetWare, a similar procedure must be performed from the installation utility on the OES - NetWare console. Follow these steps:

1. From the Graphical User Interface on the OES - NetWare server, click the Novell menu and select Install.

2. Click Add. Insert the OES - NetWare Products CD and make sure the path to install from is set to NW65PROD:.

3. Click OK. From the list that's now displayed, select Virtual Office, and complete the installation procedure.

Configuring Virtual Office from the Virtual Office Administration Interface

When all required software components have been installed, Virtual Office can be configured from the Virtual Office administration interface.

1. Access Virtual Office at http://*yourserver*/vo and log in as admin user. This brings you to your personal Virtual Office home page, as shown in Figure 17-2. From this home page, various administration utilities are available.

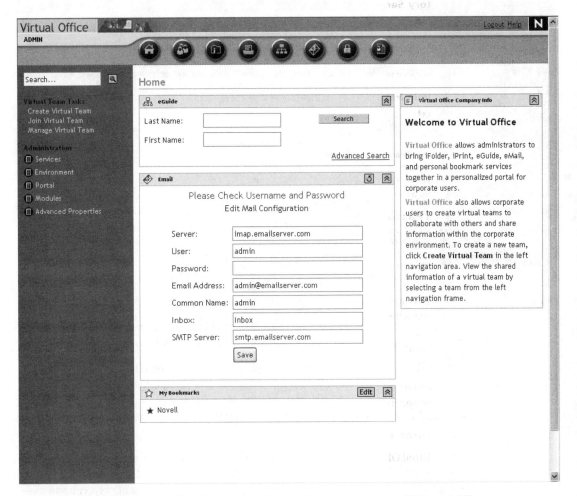

Figure 17-2. *From the Virtual Office home page, the admin user can access all Virtual Office administration utilities.*

2. The most important administration utility is under the Services link, which leads you to the screen shown in Figure 17-3. Here you can configure what type of access the user has to web-based components available in Virtual Office. If you don't configure these options, only some services will work, so you must configure them in order to specify where all required services can be found. The following services can be configured from this link:

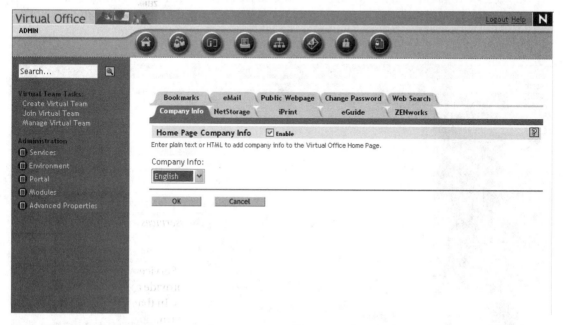

Figure 17-3. *The administrator can configure access to all services offered by Virtual Office from the services link.*

- *Company Info*: On this tab, you can enable or disable access to company info that will be displayed on Virtual Office home page. You can also select the language it's displayed in.

- *Netstorage*: Here the administrator specifies whether or not a link to the NetStorage application must be displayed on the home pages. By default, access to this service is enabled and it's assumed that this information can be accessed from NetStorage as installed on this server. If NetStorage is installed on another server, you must enter the URL to NetStorage here.

- *iPrint*: As shown in Figure 17-4, here you specify whether you want to display an iPrint link on users' Virtual Office home pages and to what URL this link should refer. By default, the link refers to the iPrint web page on this server. Alternatively, you can have it point to a custom URL if iPrint isn't installed on this server.

- *eGuide*: Specify here whether or not you want to display a link to the eGuide utility. This is a white pages solution that helps you locate information about users. There's more on this utility later in the chapter in the section "Viewing User Information with eGuide." If you want to enable eGuide, select the Enable option on this page and specify where the eGuide installation can be accessed.

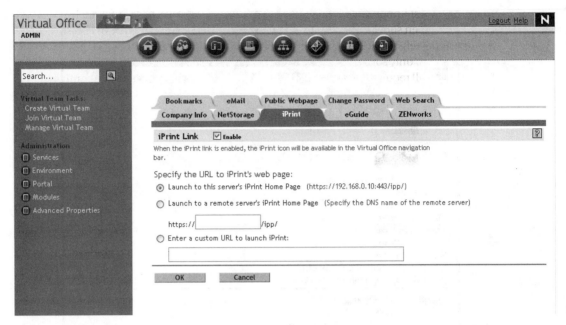

Figure 17-4. *For all services, you must indicate whether you want those services enabled and on what URL the service can be found.*

- *ZENworks*: If ZENworks Desktop Management and Web Self-Service components are installed in your network, you can use the ZENworks link to provide access to applications that are delivered with ZENworks to Virtual Office users. In that case, you need to specify the URL to the ZENworks' web page. For more information about this option, consult http://www.novell.com/documentation/lg/zenworks65/index.html.

- *Bookmarks*: Virtual Office offers an option to display bookmarks on users' Virtual Office home pages. By default, a bookmark to the Novell web site is provided. Use the Add button on this page to create other bookmarks that are displayed on the users' Virtual Office home pages. Creating a bookmark is simple: just enter the name of the bookmark and the associated URL.

- *eMail*: Users can also access their e-mail from their Virtual Office home page. To enable this, as an administrator you must specify what kind of e-mail server is used. Almost every kind of e-mail server is supported—for example, generic IMAP/POP3, Lotus Notes, GroupWise, and even Exchange. To specify where the e-mail server can be found, first select the type of mailserver used, then click Edit, and enter information about where the e-mail server is located, as shown in Figure 17-5. Here you enter the DNS names of the mailservers needed. If the user credentials to get access to the e-mail server are in the eDirectory tree where Virtual Office is installed, select the option User Credentials Are Synchronized With Virtual Office Tree. If the e-mail server has its own user database, select Different Than Virtual Office Tree and then click OK.

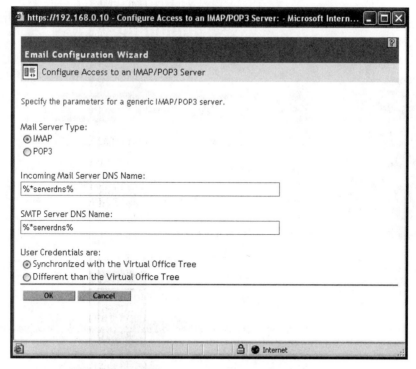

Figure 17-5. *If from Virtual Office you want to give access to users' e-mail, you must indicate where and how the e-mail server can be contacted.*

- *Public Webpage*: On this page, you can enable the Public Webpage link. Once enabled, a Public Webpage icon appears in the Virtual Office navigation bar.

- *Change Password*: Here, you can specify options that allow users to change their password. By default, a link shows where the user can change his eDirectory password. You can change that to None (no link to change the password is displayed) or Change Universal Password Link if Universal Passwords are enabled in your network.

- *Web Search*: Enable this link if you want users to access the server formerly known as the Novell Web Search server in order to search for information. In OES, this server is called the QuickFinder server. If it's installed on your network, use this page to indicate where it can be accessed.

3. After configuring access to Virtual Office services, on the Environment link specify the configuration of virtual teams and any generic portal information, and then set up logging for your virtual office server using the various tabs listed next.

   - Click Team Configuration to change settings for virtual teams on your network, as shown in Figure 17-6. By default, the virtual team feature is enabled and users have full access to all teams. If you work with virtual teams, you can also give access to a team file share—as administrator of the Virtual Office environment, you can create a Samba/CIFS share where members of the team may store their files for common use. An address of an SMTP server and the IP address for the chat server can be entered as well.

Figure 17-6. *A Virtual Office administrator can specify under exactly what conditions virtual teams can be used.*

- On the Portal tab, you can specify in which eDirectory container the portal used by Virtual Office can be found. Normally, the default value is fine, which refers to the portal configuration that was entered when the Virtual Office environment was installed.

- The Logging tab is the last important tab to consider (see Figure 17-7). It's found under the Environment link on the left side of the screen. Here, you can enable logging for Virtual Office. By default, logging is off, and it's best to leave it off, unless you need to troubleshoot problems using Virtual Office. If instead it's enabled, the administrator can specify what exactly must be logged and where the information should be logged. There's also an option to view or clear log files from this page.

4. Be aware that it's possible to configure the portal used by the Virtual Office environment. However, since it requires an in-depth knowledge of the portal environment, this subject isn't covered here. Consult the documentation at www.novell.com/documentation for more information. The default configuration is fine in almost all situations and requires no modifications.

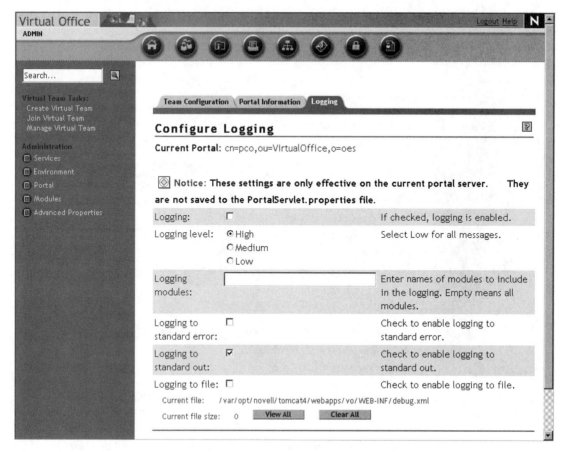

Figure 17-7. *By default, no logging is enabled for Virtual Office.*

5. On the Modules tab, notice what modules are enabled in the portal to provide a Virtual Office environment. By default, four modules are available to build the entire Virtual Office environment: the Administration module, the Community Services module, the Forgotten Password module, and the Virtual Office module. All are installed, by default. If new modules for Virtual Office are released in the future, you can enter them here by using the Install button.

6. Finally, on the Advanced Properties link you can modify the eDirectory objects that were created when Virtual Office was installed. These objects have been added to the PCO object container in eDirectory. It's best not to touch these, however, unless you have in-depth knowledge of their workings. In almost all situations, the default values work fine.

Using Virtual Office

For a user, Virtual Office is a very accessible environment. It displays URLs to access web-based components of Open Enterprise Server. Almost all of these components have been discussed somewhere else in this book, except for eGuide and virtual teams, which are described in the remainder of this chapter. Here, you can learn how to work with teams in a Virtual Office environment. To be able to work with virtual teams, you must understand how to do the following:

- Create virtual teams

- Join virtual teams

- Manage virtual teams

Creating Virtual Teams

Every user can create a virtual team. All available virtual teams are displayed in the virtual team list. Any user can create new virtual teams, and the user that creates a virtual team automatically becomes its owner. As the owner of a team, you can invite new users to join the team and grant access to users that want to join the team. To create a virtual team, perform the following steps.

1. On the Virtual Office home page, click Create Virtual Team.

2. Enter the name and a description for the virtual team, as shown in Figure 17-8.

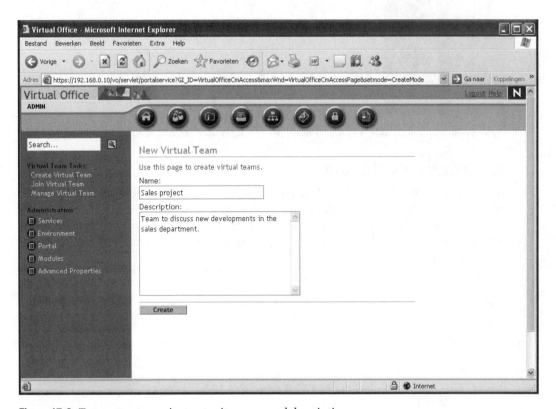

Figure 17-8. *To create a team, just enter its name and description.*

3. Click Create to create the team.

Joining Virtual Teams

Joining a virtual team is easy. From the Teams button on his Virtual Office home page, a user can see all existing virtual teams. To join a team, the user clicks the Join Virtual Team link. Next, she selects the team she wants to join from the list and then clicks the Join button. This sends a join request to the owner of the team. Figure 17-9 shows the result of sending a join request. If the owner of the team is willing to let you in as a new user, you can join the team, otherwise you can't. This isn't the only option for a user to join a team. Users can also be invited to join a team, you can read more about this in the next section.

Figure 17-9. *A user that wants to join a team must send a request to join to the owner of the team.*

Managing Virtual Teams

The owner of a virtual team can manage the properties of the team. By default, the creator of the team automatically becomes the owner. To manage a virtual team, from My Virtual Teams select the team you want to manage. As shown in Figure 17-10, this displays all the properties of the team on the main page and, in the side bar, lists all the tasks you can perform as manager of the team. The latter are discussed next.

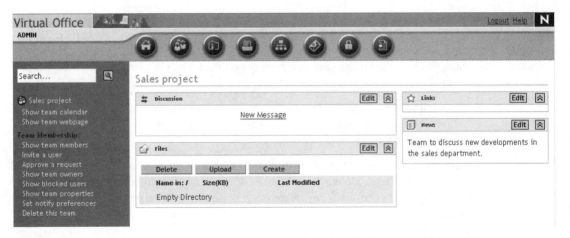

Figure 17-10. *The owner of a virtual team sees all available tasks to help manage the team's settings.*

1. Click Show Team Members. This displays a list of all the virtual team's members. From this list, you can remove current members or click Properties to see details about them.

2. Click Invite A User to ask a user to join the team. Use the Add button to browse for the user account in eDirectory.

3. Click Approve A Request to see a list of all users that have requested team membership. From this list, select one and click Approve to grant access or click Deny to deny access to that user. If you first want more details on the user before allowing him access, click the Properties button.

4. Select Show Team Owners for a list of current owners of the team. You'll probably just see your own account, since as the creator of a team you're initially its only owner. To add other users as team owner: click the Add button and then choose Search to display a list of all users available from eDirectory. This list is sorted by the user's last name, so make sure your users have clear last names so you can select them! Select the user, click OK, and the user is added to the list of team owners.

5. If the owner of a team has denied access to a user, he's added to the list of blocked users. If you later change your mind about a user and want to make him a team member anyway, select the user from this list and click Add to add him as a member. If you're sure you never want this user as a member on the team, click Remove to remove him from the list permanently.

6. On the link Show Team Properties, you can see current information about the team. This is the information you entered when creating the team. If required, change the information and click Save to save it.

7. A very useful option is Set Notify Preferences, which brings you to the screen shown in Figure 17-11. Here, you can have Virtual Office send an e-mail if something important happens. Four events can be selected to initiate an e-mail whenever they occur. They include

   • New Discussion Posts

   • New Discussion Posts from threads I'm in

   • Events are created

   • Files are uploaded

8. For all of these events, you can set your personal preferences, and as the team owner you can set the team defaults as well. The only requirement for this to work is that all users have an e-mail address setting in eDirectory.

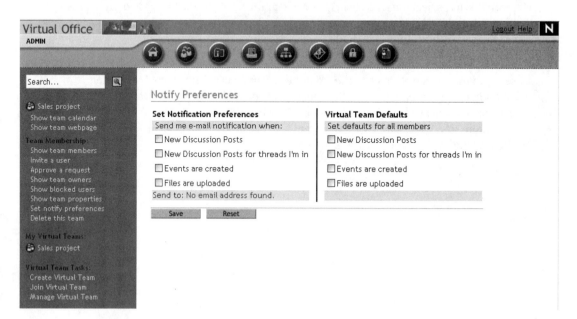

Figure 17-11. *From this list, you can select events for e-mail notification.*

9. In a project-based environment, there comes a time when you no longer want to work with a team. If this is the case, click Delete This Team to delete it. The team is removed, along with all associated settings from your current configuration.

Using Virtual Teams

The purpose of virtual teams is to allow users to work together on a task. To this end, the team home page offers various options. From My Virtual Teams, you can select the team you wish to work in. This displays the team home page, which offers four different options. You'll also find two more options on the sidebar, again enabling you to collaborate with other members of the team.

1. Click Show Team Calendar from the sidebar to display a calendar, as shown in Figure 17-12. This calendar can help manage time for all members of the team. If you want to schedule a meeting with the other team members, select the day you want to meet and then click New. Next, enter any details you want to share with the team members. After inputting the details, it's a good idea to select the option Notify All Members before clicking Save to schedule the meeting. This option makes sure all members of the team get an e-mail invitation to join the meeting.

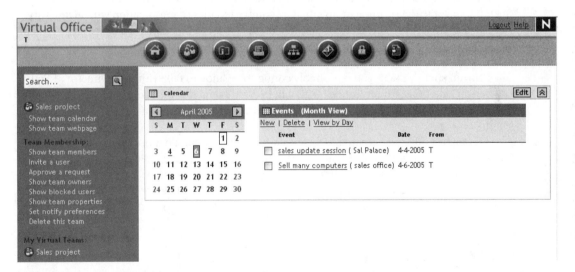

Figure 17-12. *From the team Calendar page, team members can schedule meetings.*

2. From the Team Webpage link it's possible to customize the web page for the team. Click Edit to create the web page. On this web page you can publish links that are relevant for other members of the team and add files you want to make accessible for other team members.

3. Select Discussion ➤ New to enter a new message for all members of the team. This item allows team members to use the team server as a type of news server where discussion threads can be created.

4. In the files section of the team web page, you can create new files or upload them from your computer. These files are automatically shared with all other members of the team. If as a team member you want to use one of these files, click the link of the file and download it.

5. In the Links section, click Add to add a new link to a web page that's relevant for all the members of the team. You'll see a list of links added there by other members of the team. Click a link to access the associated web site.

6. In the new section, click Edit to modify the message displayed here by default. With this option, you can add one message that's displayed at a prominent position on the team web page.

Viewing User Information with eGuide

eGuide is a useful utility that can be used as part of a Virtual Office environment to search for, say, more information about co-workers on eDirectory. Although its primary purpose is to look up user information, it can also display other information as well. The most common place to access eGuide is from the Virtual Office environment, but it can be configured as a standalone utility, too. To work with eGuide, the administrator must perform some configuration tasks beforehand since the eGuide utility must be configured for communication with eDirectory. Once this is done, users can access it as a standalone utility or from the Virtual Office environment.

Essentially, eGuide is nothing more than an LDAP client with a nice browser interface. As such, you can use it to look up information about any LDAP data source it communicates with. In a Novell environment, you'd probably configure eGuide to talk with the eDirectory LDAP servers or other LDAP data sources. This can be very useful during a company merger where eGuide can be used as the uniform utility to look up information from the LDAP directories of both companies.

Though eGuide was created to look up information, it can do more than that. It's capable of displaying organizational charts as well. This only works though if all required information is entered into eDirectory. In addition, it can be configured to work with permissions as well. For instance, you can configure it to display only limited properties when a search is performed by anonymous users, while if used by an authenticated user it can display reams of detailed information.

Configuring eGuide

Since it's an LDAP client, the most important part of the eGuide configuration is linking it to an LDAP server. To get information from the LDAP server, eGuide needs to know how it can access this server. This is because in an LDAP server such as eDirectory, rights are used to determine what information is accessible. Three methods exist to establish a connection between eGuide and the LDAP server:

- Anonymous bind

- eGuide proxy user

- Transport Layer Security

Understanding Communication Between the LDAP Server and eGuide

The easiest, but also the most limited, way to get information from an LDAP server is to use an anonymous bind. In this kind of communication, the client does not authenticate to the LDAP server and instead gets all information that's available for reading by everyone on the network. By default, when using an anonymous bind, the eGuide utility has the same rights as the eDirectory [Public] object—the browse right to all objects in the tree. The public trustee, however, does not have any rights to see attributes of these objects, so its use is rather limited.

A much better way is to configure eGuide with an eGuide proxy user. In this scenario, the administrator creates a special user account for eGuide use and configures this account with all eDirectory rights required to see the considered information. This eGuide proxy user can be compared to an LDAP proxy user, the difference being that the LDAP proxy user applies to all LDAP anonymous binds, whereas the eGuide proxy user is unique to the eGuide application. If you want to keep it simple, you can use the LDAP proxy user. For better security, however, it's advised to create the eGuide proxy user.

The anonymous bind and the eGuide proxy user determine what rights eGuide has when searching eDirectory for information. Another issue that must be handled is how eGuide should communicate with the LDAP server. Should it be done by using Transport Layer Security (TLS) or without it? The former is preferred, since on a TLS connection, data is encrypted for better protection. You can enable TLS by selecting the SSL option in the eGuide Quick Setup Wizard. To use TLS in communications with the LDAP server, you must configure TLS on the LDAP server as well. The LDAP server can be configured through two options:

- *TLS for Simple Binds with Password*: This is the default setting in an eDirectory 8.7 environment. It ensures that passwords used to bind to the LDAP server are encrypted.

- *Require TLS for All Operations*: This is the more secure option on the LDAP server object, and thus the one that's recommended. If it's selected, all communications with the LDAP server are secured with TLS. Since this is by far the most secure option, it's recommended to use this option. If, however, a client tries to bind to the LDAP server without any TLS configuration, it receives the error "Invalid authentication proxy credentials, could not authenticate to the server." To use this option in the communication between eGuide and the LDAP server, select the Enable SSL check box in the eGuide Quick Setup Wizard.

■Note Using TLS seriously impacts your server's performance. If eGuide and eDirectory are running on the same server, it's best not to use any TLS option for performance reasons.

Running the eGuide Administration Utility

Before configuring and using eGuide, you must run the eGuide Administration Utility. To do so, perform the following steps.

1. From your browser, access the URL http://*yourserver*/eGuide/admin/index.html.

2. Enter the username and password of an administrative user and click Login to log in to the eGuide Administration Wizard. This displays the eGuide administration interface, shown in Figure 17-13.

Figure 17-13. *From the eGuide administration interface, you can set all parameters required for eGuide to communicate with the LDAP data source, and to display all required information.*

3. Select Configuration ➤ LDAP Data Sources. Click New to add a new LDAP data source on which the eGuide application can search for information. A page with three different tabs is displayed, as shown in Figure 17-14. On the tab LDAP Settings, enter all parameters needed to communicate with the LDAP server. Notice that, by default, parameters are displayed to communicate with the LDAP server running on the same server as the eGuide application. Change these parameters as needed.

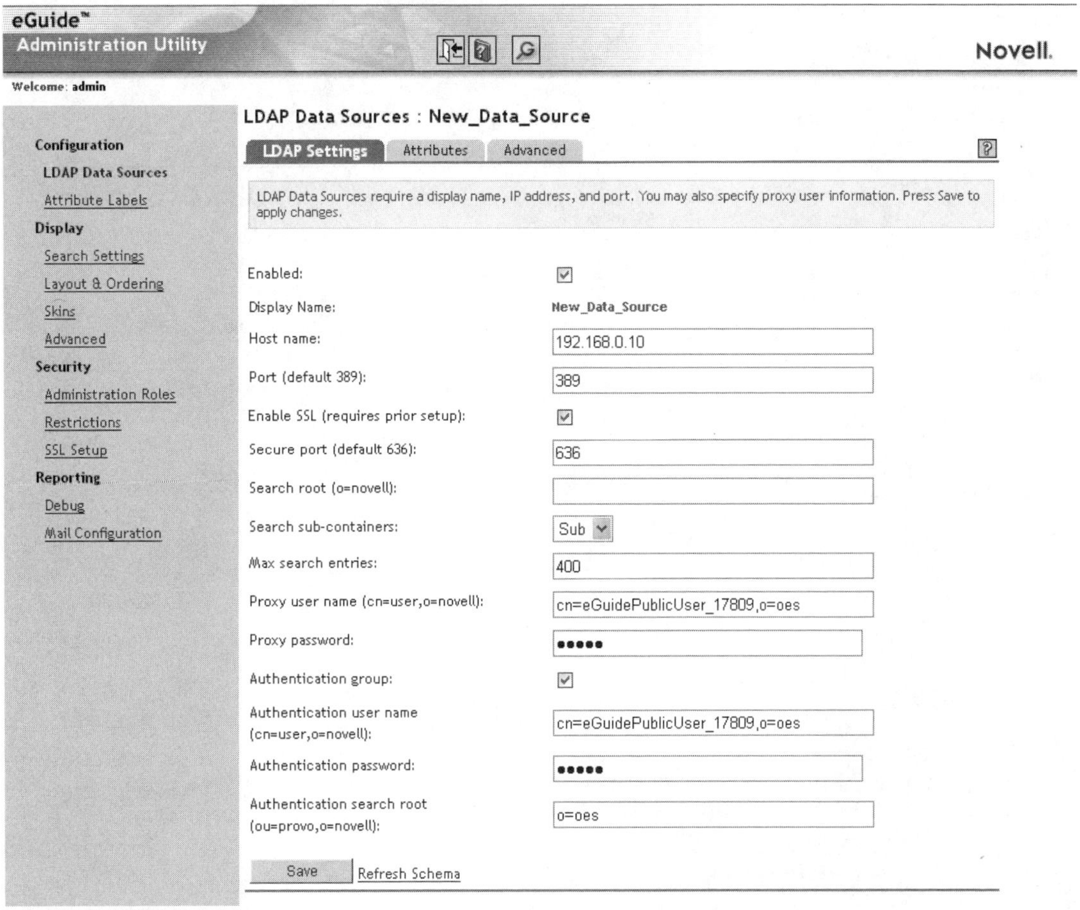

eGuide™
Administration Utility   **Novell.**

Welcome: admin

Configuration
  LDAP Data Sources
  Attribute Labels
Display
  Search Settings
  Layout & Ordering
  Skins
  Advanced
Security
  Administration Roles
  Restrictions
  SSL Setup
Reporting
  Debug
  Mail Configuration

LDAP Data Sources : New_Data_Source

| LDAP Settings | Attributes | Advanced |

LDAP Data Sources require a display name, IP address, and port. You may also specify proxy user information. Press Save to apply changes.

Enabled:	☑
Display Name:	**New_Data_Source**
Host name:	192.168.0.10
Port (default 389):	389
Enable SSL (requires prior setup):	☑
Secure port (default 636):	636
Search root (o=novell):	
Search sub-containers:	Sub ▾
Max search entries:	400
Proxy user name (cn=user,o=novell):	cn=eGuidePublicUser_17809,o=oes
Proxy password:	•••••
Authentication group:	☑
Authentication user name (cn=user,o=novell):	cn=eGuidePublicUser_17809,o=oes
Authentication password:	•••••
Authentication search root (ou=provo,o=novell):	o=oes

| Save | Refresh Schema |

Figure 17-14. *By default, the LDAP server on the server that's local to the eGuide client is searched.*

4. On the next tab, Attributes (see Figure 17-15), you can specify with which attributes eGuide will work. All available attributes are listed on this screen. Before eGuide can do anything with an attribute, enable it by selecting the Enable check box. Then check Searchable to allow eGuide to search for this attribute and then Editable to allow eGuide to edit this attribute.

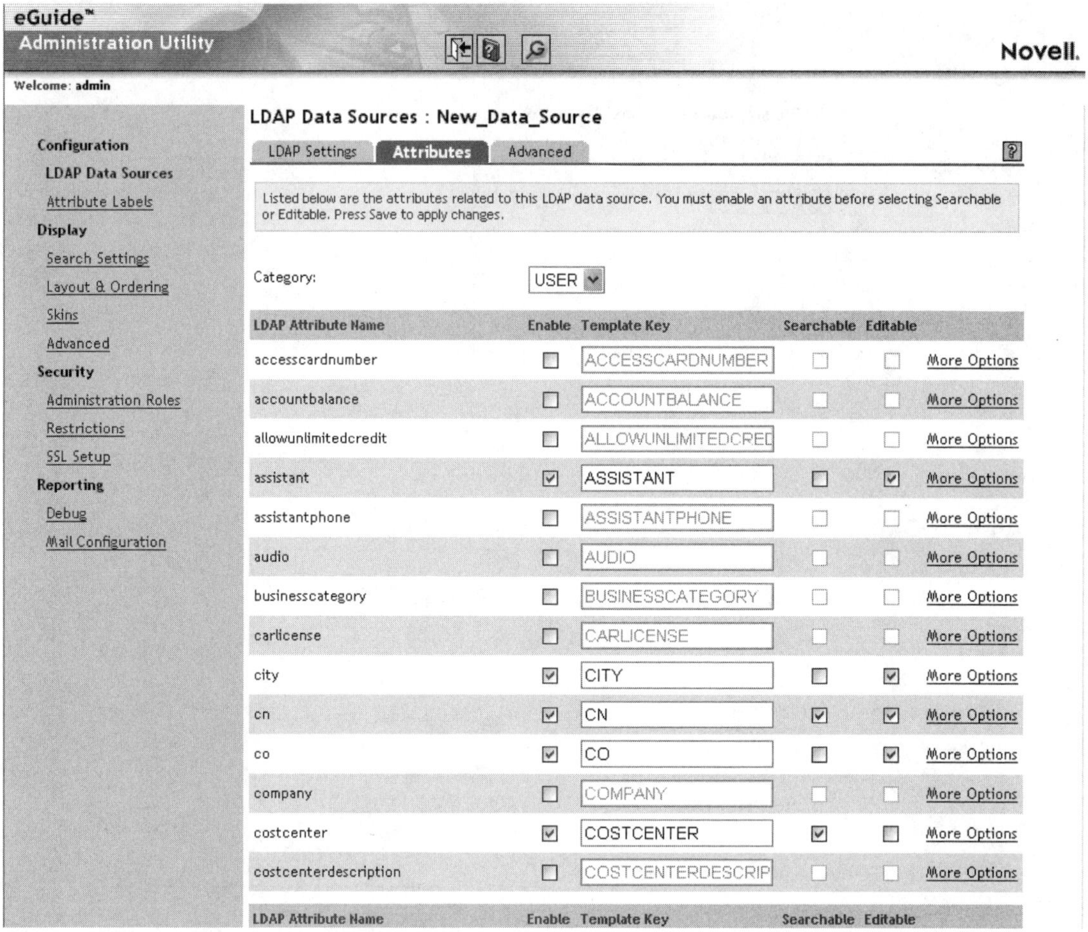

Figure 17-15. *On the Attributes tab, you configure the attributes that can be displayed by eGuide.*

5. The next important options needed to configure eGuide are under the Security header in the sidebar. Click Administrative Roles to define eGuide administrators. Here you'll see three different security roles. The User Administrator is a user account that has rights to modify users' information in eGuide. The eGuide administrator is a user account that has rights to modify eGuide settings, and, finally, there is the option Role Based Services, which can be used to create iManager RBS objects that allow you to manage eGuide from iManager. Consult Chapter 7 of this book for more information about iManager RBS.

6. By clicking Security ➤ Restrictions you can find the following settings related to restrictions. Modify them as needed and then make sure to click Save before continuing.

   • Select Allow Save Credentials to let a user save her login information in a cookie on her computer.

   • Use Cookie Expiration to specify the number of seconds after which such a cookie is removed automatically.

   • Choose Force User To Authenticate to force a user to authenticate before he can use eGuide.

   • Enable Allow Self Administration to permit users to change various settings related to their user account in eGuide.

7. The last interesting option you'll find from the eGuide administration interface is the link SSL Setup. On the SSL Certificates tab found under this link, you can view properties of currently existing SSL certificates, or click the New button to see important new SSL certificates. You'll need to perform this task to establish a TLS secured connection with an LDAP server if the certificates of this server are not known.

In the foregoing procedure I have discussed the most important options to configure eGuide. Some options were not discussed, such as the ability to choose an eGuide skin or format the default layout that eGuide uses to display its results. I recommend you get used to the eGuide interface before changing these settings: if afterward you don't like the default interface, you can fine-tune it using the settings.

Using eGuide

To use eGuide, you can launch it as a standalone client on the link http://*yourserver*/eGuide, or from Virtual Office. After launching, it will show you a simple search interface where you can search for users. These searches focus on the user's Last Name by default, but you can choose other attributes to search for as well. For example, there's a default option to search for objects based on their cell phone number. If one line isn't enough to define the search query, you can click the plus sign (+) to tune the query more by adding another line.

If this is your first eGuide experience, it's a good idea to start your search for users by just entering an asterisk in the search field. This asterisk functions as a wild card character, allowing you to search for all users. Next, choose Search. This displays a list of all users currently created in your eDirectory tree. When you select a user, details about them appear (see Figure 17-16) based upon the properties defined in eDirectory and marked in the eGuide administration utility. You'll also see that some of these details are clickable, such as the e-mail address. If you click it, your e-mail program launches so you can send an e-mail to the user. Alternatively, you can click the magnifying glass next to the user's department name to find other users in their department.

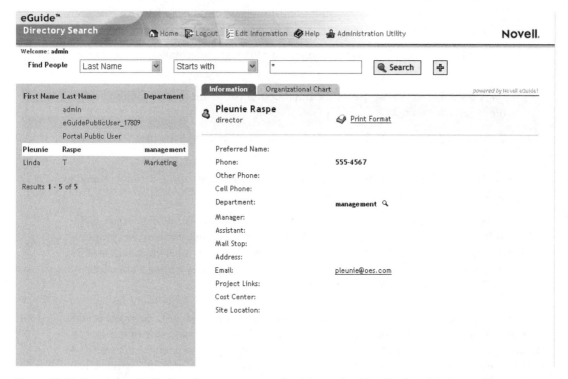

Figure 17-16. *From the eGuide interface, you can work with much of the displayed information.*

Optimizing Virtual Office

Just out of the box, Virtual Office works fine. But there are some issues you should be aware of. The following are tips to help you optimize Virtual Office (which become more important in a heavy-use environment).

- By default, Virtual Office configuration is stored in the Apache document directory. This is something you should be aware of, especially on OES - Netware, because the default location of this directory is on the SYS: volume. All the data that members of your virtual teams add to the Virtual Office web site are stored in this directory as well. You should be aware that this can fill up your SYS: volume very fast. To avoid problems from this, you should move the directory to another location. For more information on the subject, read TID 10092335 on the Novell support web site at support.novell.com.

- In large trees, team membership searches can be sluggish. You can improve them by creating an index for the bhCmAcceptList attribute. You can read more about creating eDirectory indexes in Chapter 8.

- By default, Virtual Office is configured not to be a memory hog, but instead to run efficiently on a server that functions primarily as a file server. As a result, Virtual Office starts quickly running out of memory—this can occur even after only ten users have simultaneous connections to the Virtual Office. To resolve this problem, you must adjust memory settings for Virtual Office. Since Virtual Office is running on Tomcat, these settings must be adjusted in the Tomcat configuration file. On OES - NetWare, you can find this file in SYS:tomcat\4\bin\tomcat4.ncf; on OES - Linux, it's /etc/opt/novell/tomcat4/tomcat4.conf. Two settings must be adjusted. The first defines the minimum amount of memory the server must allocate when started. Next, you must specify the maximum amount of memory that can be allocated by the Tomcat server. The former can be set with `initial Java heapsize -Xms128m`. To define the maximum amount of memory that can be allocated, set `maximum Java heap size -Xmx2048m` in the Tomcat configuration file. These parameters, however, only work if you turn down the amount of memory allocated for NSS, by default. Initially, NSS eats up almost all its memory when it starts so it can be a good fileserver. You can adjust the amount of memory NSS claims on startup with `nss /MinOsBufferCacheSize=XX` or `SET NSS CACHE BALANCE PERCENT=XX`, where XX refers to the percentage of memory that NSS can claim. To co-exist with Virtual office, using 30 percent of the memory is good enough for the NSS server.

Summary

In this chapter, you learned how to deliver access to all web-based components of OES with Virtual Office. This is a very easy-to-use portal page offered by the Tomcat server. Virtual Office can be used as a portal to all web-based user components of OES, including eGuide, which is an LDAP interface that allows users to get information from any LDAP Directory server. Another asset of Virtual Office is the possibility to work with virtual teams. Each user can create a team on Virtual Office server and other users can subscribe to these teams to become a member of it.

In the last section of this chapter, you discovered that Virtual Office offers excellent functionality, but that its performance must be tuned after installation. If you configure a server as a heavy-use Virtual Office server, it's best to set some parameters in order to dramatically improve the performance of Virtual Office. In the next chapter, you'll read how you can use clustering in OES for high availability of services.

PART 4

■■■

Advanced Services

So far in this book, you've learned about normal services that can be deployed in an OES environment. Most of these services are essential for everyday use, but some advanced services offering optional extras are provided as well. The first product discussed in this book's final part is Nsure Identity Manager, which is covered in Chapter 18. This optional install allows you to synchronize identities from one identity store to another. In chapter 19, you'll find out how Novell Clustering Services can be deployed in an OES environment to ensure the high availability of network resources like applications and shared storage devices. In the final chapter, Chapter 20, you will explore how the new management standards OpenWBEM and CIMOM are used in the Server Health manager.

CHAPTER 18

■ ■ ■

Nsure Identity Manager

In the Novell strategy, two products are very important. The first is Linux, because Novell considers Linux to be one of the most important operating systems in the future. This is also one of the main reasons that Novell made OES available in two flavors: one for NetWare and one for Linux. (You learned a lot about combining Novell products with the Linux server platform in the preceding chapters of this book.)

The second actually isn't a single product—it's Novell's line of identity management software, which enables an administrator to manage identities in a network environment. You're already familiar with the most important member of Novell's identity management line: eDirectory. This is the central repository in your network where identities are stored. eDirectory as a Directory Service allows you to connect users to the network resources.

Although eDirectory is probably the most powerful Directory Service on the planet, there aren't many companies that just use one Directory Service to store all their company information. For example, a PeopleSoft database can be used to manage a company's employees, or Microsoft's Active Directory may be used because a vendor of a mission-critical application forces you to deploy it. This is the point where Nsure Identity Manager can be very useful to your network. Nsure Identity Manager allows you to connect different identity stores so all identities in your network can be managed from one interface: eDirectory. In this scenario, eDirectory is used as an Identity Vault (also called a meta Directory) from which changes are synchronized to the rest of the network.

Open Enterprise Server comes with a free version of Nsure Identity Manager that includes functionality to connect to some of the most common identity stores available. To connect to less common identity stores, separate drivers are available for purchase. Identity Manager offers lots of possibilities. In this chapter, you'll learn about the basic Identity Manager configuration, including how to set up a connection between two instances of eDirectory as well as a connection between eDirectory and Active Directory.

■**Caution** The Identity Manager starting pack that comes with Open Enterprise Server provides you with temporary licenses. To be able to continue the use of Identity Manager services, the administrator must register the Identity Manager drivers within 90 days.

What Is Identity Manager?

Most companies have different applications that require some kind of identity management. For example, a telephony system could be running on the PBX, ERP applications, database applications, your e-mail system, and so on, and all of these could be running beside a Directory Service that's already deployed in a network for user management. All these applications would therefore require separate administration, translating to a lot of time and money.

Instead, it's better to use one centralized Directory in the network where all the information is stored. There are, however, some disadvantages to just using one Directory Service:

- A general-purpose Directory Service can't be tuned for specific needs.

- There's no way to choose which of the object's attributes are presented to the customer: it's either all or nothing.

- The overheads for partitioning and replication may be heavy since there's a lot of information to deal with.

Although eDirectory (or even LDAP as an open standard) is a perfect solution to store all corporate information, in many cases it's better to work with several smaller Directory Services. This is especially true since some applications don't have an interface to a generic directory service, but need to work with their own Directory Service instead.

If you're trying to use several Directories in the same network, you'll discover a management problem: all these applications must be managed—and that can be a real pain in the neck for the administrator. Nsure Identity Manager can solve this problem. Installing it allows eDirectory to be used as an Identity Vault, which hangs like an umbrella over all these other applications that have to deal with identities. Because eDirectory functions over the other Directories in this manner, it essentially acts as a meta Directory. In such a solution, an administrator could create user objects anywhere on the system (including the Identity Vault) and, from there, only information that's specifically selected would be synchronized to those applications linked to this centralized Directory. Thus, eDirectory is all that's required to deploy Nsure Identity Manager in your network.

The Nsure Identity Manager Architecture

The purpose of Nsure Identity Manager is to connect disparate identity management systems to each other. In this connection of different systems, the DirXML Engine plays a centralized role. The DirXML engine translates code from an application's own proprietary format to XML (which eDirectory can use,) and back again when it returns to the application. This is where the name comes from: DirXML is XML code that's used to connect different Directories. Originally, the entire product was known as DirXML, but today the name Nsure Identity Manager is used because it's more descriptive.

■**Note** Although the official name of the product is now Nsure Identity Manager, you'll find that most of its components are still referred to by the ancient name of the product. Thus, you may hear people talk about the DirXML engine and the DirXML driver.

To have a DirXML engine is one thing, but if you want to be able to do something useful with it, you must connect it to an application as well. On one side, the DirXML engine must be connected to eDirectory. For this, use a generic eDirectory interface that's included with the DirXML engine. On the other side, DirXML must also talk to your application, which is the most challenging part. The scenario's general architecture is illustrated in Figure 18-1. You need an application that translates code generated by the application to the XML language used in the DirXML engine. This is the task of the DirXML Driver. Several drivers are available for applications to synchronize their data with Nsure Identity Manager. In this chapter, the following drivers are discussed in the upcoming section titled "Drivers."

- The clear-text driver

- The eDirectory driver

- The Active Directory driver

Many other drivers are available. Currently, about 60 applications are supported and the number is growing.

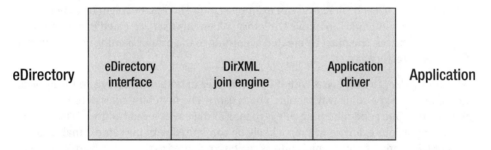

Figure 18-1. *The DirXML join engine makes communication between eDirectory and the application possible.*

DirXML Driver

The driver consists of two components—the first being the shim, which is a program that interfaces with the application. This program is written to understand everything that happens in the application. On the other side of the shim, events from the application are written as XML events that can be understood by the DirXML engine. The second component is a configuration file that determines what exactly should happen in the DirXML driver.

There is one other important component connected to the DirXML driver: the Remote Loader. This component takes care that the driver running on a remote machine is able to communicate with eDirectory, even if eDirectory or the Novell client aren't present locally on that machine.

Subscriber and Publisher Channels

Now that you know how eDirectory and the other applications communicate, you may suspect that problems sometimes arise when data is synchronized between eDirectory and the application. One particular problem concerns questions of authority over the data. Normally, with DirXML you can create a situation where both the application and eDirectory can modify the data. In some situations, however, you just want the specific application (or eDirectory) to modify the data. Someone who works in Human Resources, for example, would not be pleased if a network administrator were able to change the personal data of an employee. The authoritative instance over the data can be configured in the publisher and subscriber channels. The publisher channel is the channel used by the application to communicate data to eDirectory, while the subscriber channel is the method eDirectory uses to communicate changes to the application. In the following listing, you'll find an overview of some of the most common issues that must be addressed by the publisher and subscriber channels.

- *Schema mapping*: The schemas of the application and eDirectory may be incompatible. Thus, it's the job of the publisher and subscriber channels to make sure that proper translation takes place.

- *Data authority*: When two applications are synchronizing data, one of them must have authority over it. With this authority, you define which of the applications has permissions to modify data. This is especially important when a contradiction arises due to modifications that both applications are trying to make to a particular data set.

- *Object naming*: If a user exists in two applications simultaneously, they might have a different name in each Directory—for example, Linda Thomassen might be LThomassen in eDirectory and LindaT in Active Directory. When this user is created in either of the Directory Services, she must be created according to the proper naming conventions in the other Directory as well.

- *Matching rules*: If a user exists with different names in both eDirectory and the application, there must be some way to match both users. The matching rules determine how this is done. One good matching rule is to look at the user's e-mail address. User Linda from the previous example will most likely be configured with the same e-mail address in both Directories, so this e-mail address can be configured as the matching rule criterion.

- *Placement rules*: If a user object is synchronized from one hierarchical Directory Service to the other, somewhere a decision must be made as to where the user object will be created. For this purpose, placement rules are created.

In the publisher and subscriber channels, the rules previously discussed are applied to the DirXML engine, as illustrated in Figure 18-2. Some basic rules are present by default, depending on the application driver you want to conure with DirXML. For complex tasks, however, basic rules may not be enough. In such cases, policies and stylesheets can be deployed. A policy is a complex rule that can be created fairly easily with the Policy Creation Wizard. By creating a policy, you ensure that information is transformed the way you want, even if no default solution is available. If the tasks become really complex, you may need to write your own code to assure that proper transformation takes place. This is where stylesheets come in. A DirXML stylesheet is a complex policy used to perform a very specific task. Be aware, however, that it requires very advanced skills to implement a stylesheet; this is definitely not a task for your average network administrator. Due to the advanced nature of stylesheets, they won't be discussed in this chapter. You can find more information about them on the Novell documentation web site at www.novell.com/documentation.

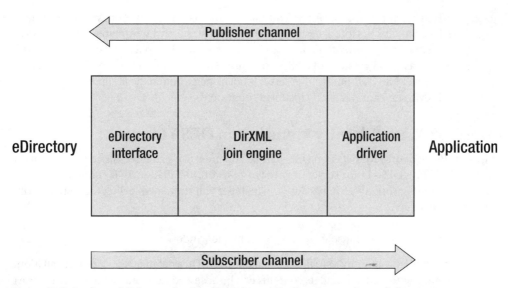

Figure 18-2. *In the publisher and subscriber channels, data is transformed the proper way.*

You've now learned about the most important Nsure Identity Manager components. Later sections of this chapter explain, via various examples, how these components can be deployed in real-life scenarios.

Installing Nsure Identity Manager

Nsure Identity Manager is not installed by default on Open Enterprise Server, but it's available as a separate installation that can be used on OES - Linux and OES - NetWare. In this section, you'll learn how to install it on both. To perform the installation, you need the Nsure Identity Manager 2 installation CD. Before starting the Identity Manager installation, however, you must decide exactly what you want to install. Three different system components can be installed.

- *DirXML Server*: This is the complete product. It consists of a DirXML engine, the Nsure Audit agent, DirXML service drivers, and NMAS components that allow for proper authentication. You can install the DirXML server on most platforms, as long as eDirectory is present. You must use at least eDirectory version 8.6.2, but it's recommended you use 8.7.3 or higher. On OES, this isn't a problem since eDirectory 8.7.3 is installed by default.

- *Connected System Server*: A connected system server is one in which the application you want to synchronize with Identity Manager runs if eDirectory is not present on the system. The Connected System Server provides the DirXML Remote Loader service, which allows the server to connect with the DirXML server. A Windows-only Remote Loader configuration tool is provided as well, as is the Nsure Audit agent, which is an auditing tool that allows for advanced reporting of Identity Manager components on the connected system server.

- *Web-Based Administration Server*: This allows you to manage the DirXML environment as well. It contains the interfaces needed for administrators who want to manage DirXML from iManager, but also offers the end-user password self-service and eGuide applications. It runs on all versions of OES, and requires a running copy of Novell iManager as well. The web-based administration server is not installed automatically upon installation of the DirXML server and must be installed separately.

Installing Nsure Identity Manager on OES - Linux

To install Nsure Identity Manager on OES - Linux, you must use a console-based shell script on the console of your OES - Linux server. Before you start the installation, make sure there aren't any users currently working on it, because the installer will shut down eDirectory temporarily to install the product.

1. On the OES - Linux console, open a root console window.

2. Insert the Nsure Identity Manager 2 installation CD. On a default OES - Linux installation, it mounts automatically and its contents can be accessed from one of the subdirectories in /media. The exact name of the subdirectory depends on the type of drive you're using, as shown in the following list.

   • If you're using a CD-ROM drive, access mounted CDs at /media/cdrom.

   • If you're using a DVD drive, access mounted CDs at /media/dvd.

   • If you're using a CD or DVD writer, access mounted CDs at /media/cdrecorder.

3. In the directory where your Nsure Identity Manager CD is mounted, open the directory linux/setup. Here, you'll find the installation program dirxml_linux.bin. Activate it by issuing the command **./dirxml_linux.bin**. This starts the Linux installer.

4. Read the message in the welcome screen and press Enter to continue. Next, read the license agreement and enter Y to continue.

5. Select the install set that's to be loaded, as shown in Figure 18-3. If the server you're installing to already has eDirectory loaded and you want to make it a DirXML server and thus manage the product from this server, select both the DirXML server component and the web-based administrative server. Keep in mind that you can't install both at the same time. You must start by installing the DirXML server, running the installation program again, and then selecting option 3 to install the web-based administrative server (see the following). Make sure that the DirXML Server option is selected and press Enter to continue.

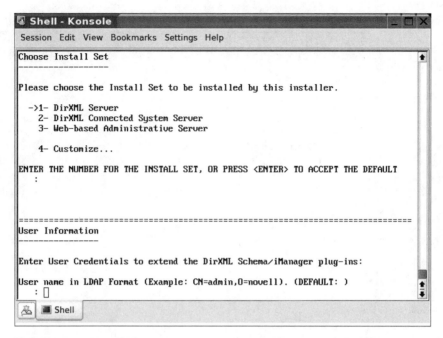

Figure 18-3. *To install Identity Manager on OES - Linux, you need to run a console-based installation script.*

6. Enter the user credentials needed to extend the eDirectory schema. You'll need your admin user for that. Enter its complete LDAP name—for example, cn=admin,o=oes. In the next screen, enter the password of your Admin user and press Enter to continue.

7. Review the pre-installation summary. If everything looks okay, press Enter to continue and start the product installation. Press Enter again to exit the installer once the Installation Complete message appears. Now start the installation program again and from the installation menu, select the option Web-Based Administrative Server to install all components required to manage DirXML from iManager.

8. Enter the name of the admin user in its LDAP-format and press Enter to continue. Enter the user's password next, then review the Pre-Installation Summary and press Enter to continue.

9. When all necessary components are installed, press Enter to exit the installer. Restart your Tomcat server to make sure the newly installed iManager snap-ins can be used. You can restart the Tomcat server with the command **rctomcat4 restart**. DirXML should be installed now, so start iManager and verify that you can see the DirXML management snap-ins, as shown in Figure 18-4.

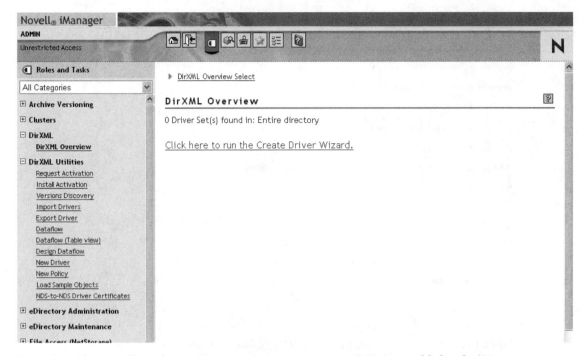

Figure 18-4. *After installing Identity Manager, options to manage DirXML are added to the iManager interface.*

Installing Nsure Identity Manager on OES - NetWare

Installation of the Nsure Identity Manager software on OES - NetWare is simple and straight-forward. It can be installed like any other additional product on OES - NetWare.

1. Insert the Identity Manager installation CD in the CD drive of your server.

2. From the graphical console, select Novell ➤ Install. This starts the install utility.

3. Click Add to install a product that's not listed and then select the file browser to browse to the Identity Manager installation CD. On this CD, select the subdirectory NW and from this directory, select the Product.ni file. Click OK. Click OK once more to start the product installation.

4. Wait a few moments until the Java tool comes up. Once it appears, read the Welcome message and click Next to continue.

5. Read the license agreement and click I Accept to continue the product installation.

6. Read the overview about the kinds of installations you can perform and then click Next twice.

7. From the components to install window (see Figure 18-5), make sure all the components are selected. You'll notice two differences between the installation on OES - Linux and OES - NetWare. Here, there's no option to install the Connected System Server. This is

because you're running on NetWare, and therefore you're automatically working with eDirectory. It's not possible to configure NetWare as a connected system. Even if you want to use the eDirectory driver to synchronize eDirectory to eDirectory on the server where the DirXML Identity Vault is created, you need the complete product. The second difference is that, with the OES - NetWare install, the Utilities are selected as well. The most important component added with these utilities is the Nsure Audit tool that can be used to monitor the Identity Manager environment. After making a selection, click Next to continue.

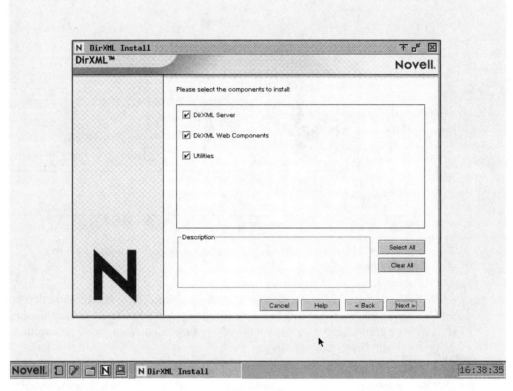

Figure 18-5. *From OES - NetWare, you can also install the DirXML utilities.*

8. Now specify which components to install (see Figure 18-6). Because this is an Identity Manager server, the DirXML engine is always installed. All supported drivers are installed as well. Notice that other drivers are also available, like the Active Directory driver. These aren't selected by default since it doesn't make sense to run them on NetWare: Active Directory needs Windows to run. Later in this section, you'll find more information on how to install and configure the Active Directory driver—for now, though, leave it unselected. You can choose to skip other drivers as well, but be sure that at least the eDirectory and the Delimited Text Drivers are selected. Click Next to continue.

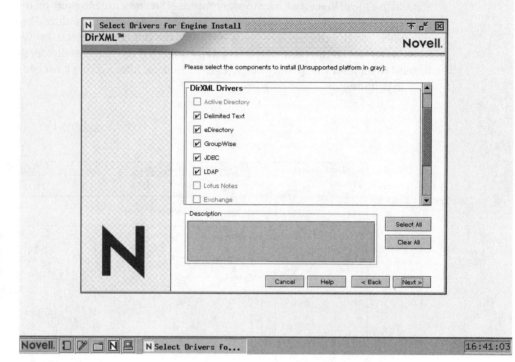

Figure 18-6. *You need to install drivers for all applications with which you wish to synchronize.*

9. Before the product is installed, you'll see a warning. This warning states that you must activate the Nsure Identity Manager components if you want to continue using them after a period of 90 days. After this period, the configuration stops synchronizing automatically. Click OK to continue.

10. Enter the admin name in its LDAP format (so use **cn=admin,o=oes** instead of cn=admin.o=oes) and enter the user's password as well. Click Next to continue.

11. Review the screen with all selected components. These are the components that will be installed. If you're happy with it, click Next to start the installation.

12. In the next screen, select still more components to be installed. Notice that the Nsure Audit System Components aren't selected by default. This is because an Nsure Audit logging server must be installed in the tree before installing these components. More information on Nsure Audit can be found later in this chapter in the section "Logging and Reporting with Nsure Audit." Leave the default selection for now, and click Next to continue.

13. Depending on the drivers you've selected to install, in the next window you'll be able to select more components to install. Normally, all supported components for the drivers you've installed are selected automatically, so typically you don't have to change anything in this window. Click Next to continue.

14. In the Summary window, click Finish to start the installation. Wait a few moments for the installation to finish. When the installation has completed, reboot the server. After rebooting on a workstation, start iManager to verify that all the plug-ins needed for Identity Manager management have been installed properly.

Drivers

The most important part of an Nsure Identity Manager configuration is its drivers. The drivers allow data coming from an application to be translated to XML and vice versa. Without DirXML drivers, no synchronization can take place. Many drivers are currently available. In this section, the most commonly used drivers are discussed. These are

- The Delimited Text driver

- The eDirectory driver

- The Active Directory driver

Configuring the Delimited Text Driver

Sure, there's a lot you can say about Identity Manager, but if you want to know how to configure it properly, you have to play with it. For that reason, this and the following two sections explore how to configure various driver sets. I start with a description of the Delimited Text Driver, for the simple reason that it's the easiest driver to understand and there's no difficult application behind it. Apart from that, it's very useful. Almost all applications have an option to export data to a delimited text file. Therefore, by using the Delimited Text Driver, you're able to export data in the form of delimited text files from almost any application, import it into eDirectory, and vice versa. So, without further ado, let's find out how to use this driver.

1. Start iManager, log in as admin and select DirXML Utilities. Next, click New Driver to start the Create Driver Wizard.

2. When you're creating a driver, a lot of objects are generated automatically in eDirectory. To make it clear which objects belong to which DirXML driver configuration, it's a good idea to create a new driver set for all the drivers you install on your system. On the welcome screen of the Create Driver Wizard, select In A New Driver Set to create this driver set automatically, and then click Next to continue.

3. Enter the properties for the new driver set, as shown in Figure 18-7. You must enter a name, a context, and the name of the server where you've installed the Identity Manager software. Optionally, you can specify whether or not to create a new eDirectory partition for this driver set. This is an important option, because in an Nsure Identity Manager environment, relations are server to server. If your main Identity Manager server crashes, it will make all Identity Manager data unavailable. In order to troubleshoot this in an easy way, it's recommended you create a new partition for all driver sets and

replicate it strategically. This makes it a lot easier to configure another Identity Manager that can work with the same data after your main Identity Manager server has crashed. Make your choice and click Next to continue. The driver set and partition are now created. This can take a few moments.

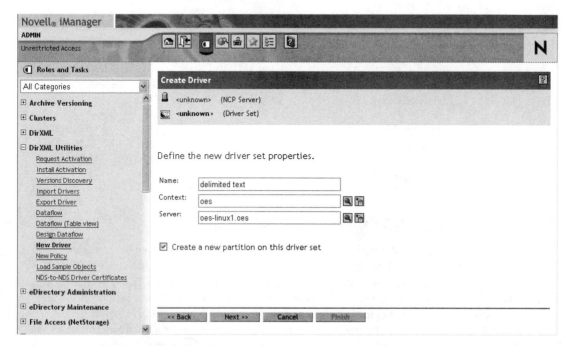

Figure 18-7. *DirXML drivers are stored in a driver set. It's recommended you create a new eDirectory partition for all driver sets you use.*

4. Now that the driver set has been created, you can create the application driver for this set. Select Import A Driver Configuration From The Server and from the drop-down list, choose the DelimitedTextCSVSample.xml driver. Click Next to continue.

Note There are two ways to create drivers in a driver set. You can use one of the drivers provided with the product, or you can write your own driver, as indicated in Figure 18-8. If you want to work with a driver that's provided with the product, import it from either the server or the workstation. Only if you're really skilled (and patient) should you attempt to write your own drivers. In most situations it's much easier to import one of the preconfigured drivers.

```
Shell - Konsole                                              _ □ X
Session  Edit  View  Bookmarks  Settings  Help
<?xml version="1.0" encoding="UTF-8"?>
<driver-configuration
        description="xlfid(DriverDescr)Delimited Text - CSV"
        dn="Delimited Text.DriverSet.Services.YourOrganization"
        driver-set-dn="DriverSet.Services.YourOrganization"
        name="Delimited Text">

        <variable-decl>

                <text-var var-name="DT.DestPath"
                        description="xlfid(DestPathDescr)Enter the platform spec
ific path to the local directory where output files should be created. (Example
text is for Windows platform)"
                        highlight="()"
                        prompt="xlfid(DestPathPrompt)Output File Path:">c:\csvsa
mple\output</text-var>

                <text-var var-name="DT.DestExt"
                        description="xlfid(DestExtDescr)Enter the extension to a
ppend to output files when created."
                        prompt="xlfid(DestExtPrompt)Output File Extension:">.csv
</text-var>

                <text-var var-name="DT.SrcPath"
                        description="xlfid(SrcPathDescr)Enter the platform speci
fic path to the local directory where input files will be found. (Example text i
s for Windows platform)"
                        highlight="()"
                        prompt="xlfid(SrcPathPrompt)Input File Path:">c:\csvsamp
le\input</text-var>

                <text-var var-name="DT.SrcExt"
                        description="xlfid(SrcExtDescr)Enter the extension used
to designate input files."
                        prompt="xlfid(SrcExtPrompt)Input File Extension:">.csv</
text-var>

                <text-var var-name="DT.RenameExt"
                        description="xlfid(RenameExtDescr)Enter the extension to
 rename an input file with, after it has been processed.  Leave this field blank
 if you want the file to be deleted."
                        prompt="xlfid(RenameExtPrompt)Rename File Extension:">.b
ak</text-var>

                <text-var var-name="DT.UserContainer"
                        browse="yes"
r/lib/dirxml/rules/DirXML.Drivers/DelimitedTextCSVSample.xml lines 1-33/862 3%
       Shell
```

Figure 18-8. *If you're good at XML, you can write all the Identity Manager drivers yourself, but it's not recommended.*

5. In the next screen (see Figure 18-9), you must specify all properties for the delimited text driver. The available options are listed next. Make your choice and press Next to continue.

- *Driver name*: The name you want to give to the driver. By default, the driver name for the delimited text driver is "Delimited Text."

- *Output File Path*: When synchronizing data between the eDirectory driver vault and a delimited text file, the driver must be able to create output files somewhere in the file system. For this, you need to specify an output path. For example, on OES - Linux, you could create a directory /idm/output for this purpose.

- *Output File Extension*: The extension that's given to files that are created with the delimited text driver. By default, the value .csv is used.

- *Input File Path*: The path upon which the driver looks for input files. These are the delimited text files that contain information which should be synchronized to eDirectory.

- *Rename File Extension*: The extension automatically given to an input file so the administrator can see that the delimited text driver has handled it. By default, the extension .bak is used.

- *New User Container*: The container in eDirectory where new users are automatically added.

- *Configure Data Flow*: With this option, you specify which data source is authoritative. With the default value of Bi-Directional, you specify that both eDirectory and the delimited text file are considered authoritative. If you choose this option, new information will synchronize from eDirectory to the delimited text file and from the delimited text file to eDirectory. Alternatively, you can choose the DT To eDirectory option, where the delimited text file is authoritative, or eDirectory To DT, where eDirectory is authoritative.

- *Password Failure Notification User*: This feature is used to specify which user should get an e-mail if password synchronization fails. Since password synchronization is not typically a feature of the delimited text driver, you can ignore this option.

- *Driver Is Local/Remote*: Specifies whether the driver is installed locally or remotely (and used with the remote load service). By default, the driver is installed locally. If you choose to work with a remote driver, in the next screen you can provide the contact details for the remote server where the Remote Loader service is active.

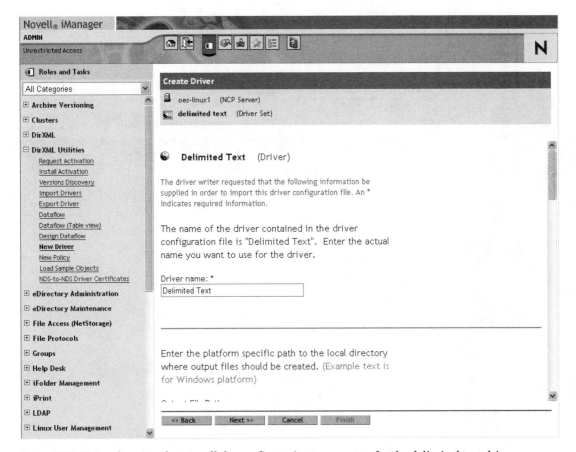

Figure 18-9. *Using the wizard, enter all the configuration parameters for the delimited text driver.*

6. In the next screen, you must define some security settings. First, Security Equivalences must be defined. With this setting, you make the driver security equivalent to a user in eDirectory. You can use the admin user for this purpose, but be aware that that gives unlimited rights to the driver, which may be a security problem. Thus, it's better to create a special-purpose user that only has the rights it needs to perform its tasks on limited parts of eDirectory. Another benefit is that if there is a problem with the admin account, it doesn't affect the DirXML environment. Next, you must exclude administrative roles. With this function, you specify the name of administrator accounts that must be excluded from synchronization. This is to help prevent disasters in which your admin account suddenly disappears. You should always specify your admin account here. Click Next when finished.

7. You'll now see a list of all the objects created in eDirectory (see Figure 18-10). The good news is that you don't have to manage these eDirectory objects directly. Click Finish With Overview to get a more workable view of your driver's configuration.

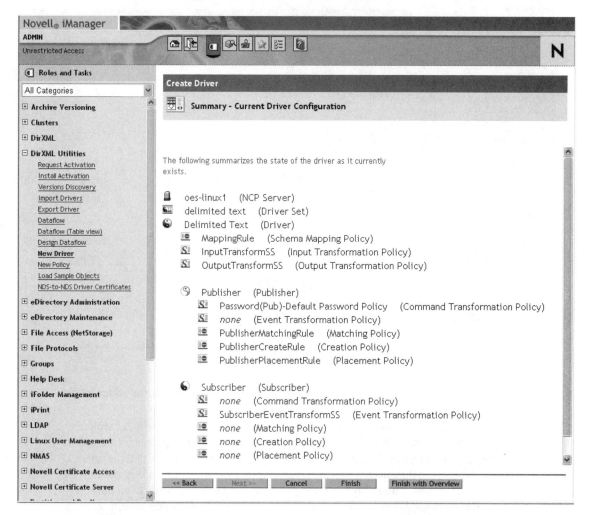

Figure 18-10. *After successfully creating the driver, an overview appears of all the objects that have been created for it in eDirectory.*

8. You'll now see a graphical overview of the current driver configuration (see Figure 18-11.) Notice in the middle the Identity Vault, with the driver you've just created connected to it. The next section teaches you how to configure it from there.

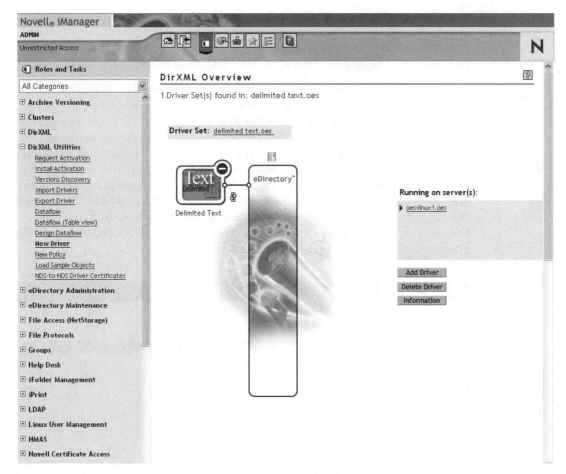

Figure 18-11. *The driver and its communication with the Identity Vault can be managed from the overview screen.*

Tuning Your Driver

In the steps just described, you learned how to install a driver. Basically, this is enough to get a working configuration, and chances are, when it comes to the configuration of the delimited text driver, you won't have to do anything else. If you do need to do more for the configuration, start with the DirXML Overview screen. From here, you can manage the elements of all components of the driver configuration; you can even use it to create some new XML code if you want to! The next procedure offers a guided tour through all the elements found on the DirXML Overview screen. Be aware that on this tour you'll only see elements specific to the Delimited Text driver. The available elements will be different if you've configured another driver, such as the eDirectory or the Active Directory driver (discussed later in this chapter).

1. From iManager, select DirXML ➤ DirXML Overview. You'll now be given an option to search for the driver configuration you want to manage. Select Search Entire Tree and then click Search to locate all available DirXML configurations in your tree. If there's only one driver configuration available, it is shown automatically.

2. In the upper part of the screen, you'll see a link with the name of the driver set. In this case, its name is delimited text.oes (but only because oes is used as the name of the container). Click this link to get more details about the driver set. You'll now see a window with two tabs in it: the first tab is called DirXML and is used for various purposes, the most important of which is the option to specify the log level. Another interesting link found here (shown in Figure 18-12) is Status Log, which allows you to look into the status log of a specific server. The other options are rather advanced. There is, for example, the link Global Config Values, which can be used to enter new XML code to modify the configuration of the driver. On the General tab is information about the driver's configuration and synchronization in eDirectory. Make your modifications as required on this screen and then click OK to return to the main screen.

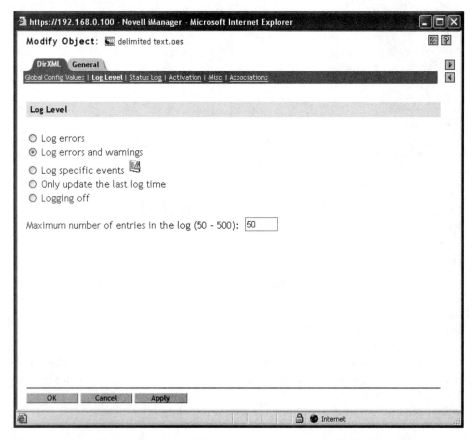

Figure 18-12. *On the property page of the DirXML driver set, you'll find an option to modify the default log level.*

3. The next important option is the symbol for the driver itself. On this symbol, you can see a sign that's used to indicate whether the driver is working properly or not. Do you see a Yin/Yang sign? If so, then everything is fine and the driver is working properly. If, however, you see a stop sign, the driver hasn't been started yet. Modify the driver's current state by clicking this sign. A menu then appears, as shown in Figure 18-13, showing options that allow you to start or stop the driver, restart it, get its current status, or edit its properties.

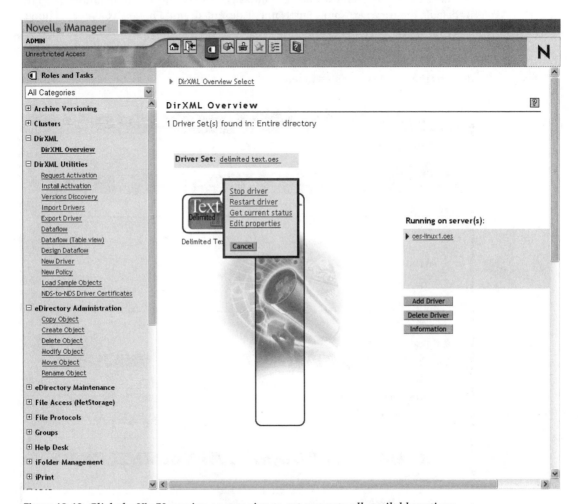

Figure 18-13. *Click the Yin/Yang sign or stop sign to get access to all available options.*

4. Click the Yin/Yang or Stop sign and from the menu that's displayed, select Edit Properties. This gives you access to all the properties of the selected driver, and as you'll see, there are quite a lot. Not all of them are important though. I'll only explain the two most important links shown in this window, because it would require a separate book to cover them all! For more details, consult the Identity Manager manual at www.novell.com/documentation/oes.

5. On the DirXML tab (see Figure 18-14), make sure the Driver Configuration link is selected. This shows the current configuration of your driver. On this page, you'll find some useful options. First, there's the Startup Option. Here, your Delimited Text driver only starts up manually, which makes sense in most cases. If, however, you want the driver started automatically, specify it here by selecting Auto Start. Next on this tab are the driver parameters, which show where the exact syntax your driver file uses is determined. In the Field Delimiter field, specify the field delimiter character, which is a comma by default. Next, in Field Names, note the names of the fields used in the delimited text file. By default, these are LastName, FirstName, Title, Email, WorkPhone, Fax, WirelessPhone, and Description. In addition, the object class name that the driver is used for is displayed, which is the user object class in this scenario. This tab is an excellent place to do some troubleshooting if the driver isn't working properly, because everything that should be done by the driver is specified here.

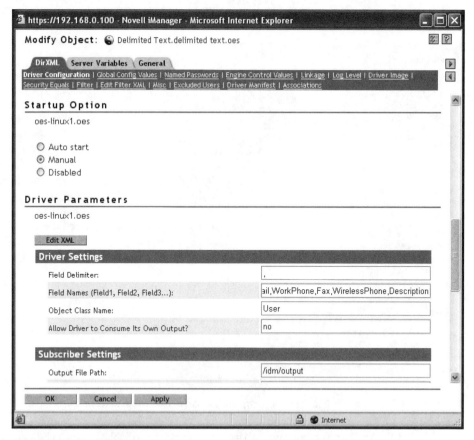

Figure 18-14. *On the Driver Configuration tab, you'll find an exact description of what should be in the delimited text files.*

6. The next useful link under the driver properties (shown in Figure 18-15) is Filter. On this page, you'll see an overview of the objects synchronized by this driver and all their properties. The interesting thing about this tab is that you can specify at a property level how it should be handled. If, for example, you need a property to be synchronized on the publisher channel, but not on the subscriber channel, specify it here. You can also specify which is the merge authority in case of conflicting settings: the application or eDirectory. You can even specify that for users that are new in eDirectory, a home directory should be created automatically.

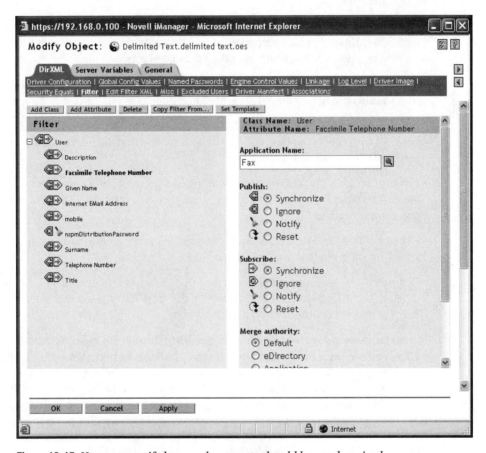

Figure 18-15. *You can specify how each property should be synchronized.*

7. More interesting information can be found by clicking the driver itself on the DirXML Overview screen. This shows all the details of the entire Identity Manager synchronization that takes place between the driver and the application shim, as shown in Figure 18-16. From the application to the Identity vault that's used as the meta Directory, you can see the publisher channel and all its details; from the eDirectory to the application vault, the subscriber channel details will be visible. The small pages that are displayed are the log files attached to all the different components. In the channels themselves, you can see the different policies deployed in this scenario. The most important of these elements include the following:

- *Schema Mapping Policies*: Defines how incompatible schemas should be mapped to each other. This policy is important if the application that synchronizes with the Identity Vault uses a schema that is different than the eDirectory schema.

- *Driver Filter*: Specifies what objects and attributes should be synchronized and how they should be synchronized. This is the same filter as in Figure 18-15.

- *Matching Policies*: This policy is used to determine upon what criterion a match between two objects can be made. The default value is that the match should be based on the user's e-mail address.

- *Creation Policies*: These specify what criteria must be met before an object can be created. For example, use this to specify what properties should be present before an object can be created.

- *Placement Policies*: These policies can be used to specify where in the application or Directory Vault new users should be created.

- *Command Transformation Policies*: If the application and the Directory Vault use different commands to get things done, you can translate these commands with the aid of command transformation policies.

8. In general, it's very easy to modify the properties of the policies in both channels. If you click it, you can see a list of all the policies that the selected policy consists of. The terminology is confusing here: the software states that the policy you click consists of several policies. To modify a policy from this screen, click Edit. In general, this displays three links. On the first link are the rules the selected policy consists of. You can add new rules to that by using the Append New Rule button, or just view the properties of the current rule by clicking its link (this gives you access to the rule builder utility). Using the second link, you can view the XML code and edit it if you wish to optimize it. The last link gives you access to a short description of the selected policy.

■Tip All drivers come with a set of default policies, but it's possible to build your own policies if you wish. Identity Manager has a very powerful policy builder for just such occasions.

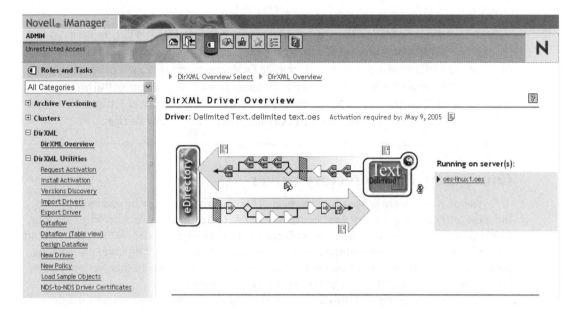

Figure 18-16. *Click the driver to get a detailed overview of how it synchronizes with the Directory Vault.*

Now that you have some basic knowledge of the working of all Identity Manager components, it's time to test your delimited text driver. You must know the following four things in order to test it.

- What is the input directory for delimited text files?

- What is the output directory for delimited text files?

- Is any extension required for input files?

- What container in eDirectory are your users synchronized to?

If, for example, your text files use the default extension of .csv, input files are placed in /idm/input, output files are placed in /idm/output, and the contents of these files are synchronized with the eDirectory container users.oes, all you need to do is create a text file in the proper format to synchronize a user from the text file to eDirectory, or create a user in eDirectory to synchronize it to an output text file. For instance, if you create the input file /idm/input/users.csv with the contents of Thomassen,Linda,,lindat@oes.com,12345,54321,67890,none, you'll find that the new user is created automatically in eDirectory within seconds. And if you create new users in the eDirectory container that's synchronized with the Delimited Text File driver, you'll find that all users created there are synchronized to a delimited text file created in your output directory almost instantly.

■**Note** Think this Delimited Text File driver sounds useless? Well, it isn't at all! In fact, the Delimited Text File driver is the most flexible driver of all since almost every application supports delimited text files. You could, for example, use it to export users from, or to, an Excel spreadsheet, or to a proprietary datastore of new students in a school that has been entered into the school administration system but that isn't supported by any Identity Manager driver. From the application where you want to import data to, just import all the new students to a huge delimited text file and import that into eDirectory with Identity Manager.

Configuring the eDirectory Driver

At first sight, it may seem senseless to connect eDirectory to eDirectory by means of Identity Manager. After all, why not just use one tree? Actually, there are many reasons why someone would choose to connect one instance of eDirectory to another instance of eDirectory, without creating one large tree—for example, imagine a situation where two companies are working closely together, but not closely enough to integrate all user accounts. In this section, you'll learn what to do to connect two instances of eDirectory to each other.

Before you start configuring this driver, you should be aware that it behaves a bit differently than other drivers. First, in order to use the eDirectory driver, you must install Identity Manager on both servers. The eDirectory driver can't work with a Remote Loader service because the driver in one tree communicates directly with the driver in another tree. Next, you'll also need the Novell Certificate Server and a Certificate Authority to ensure SSL-secured communication between the two trees. Last up, be aware that in Identity Manager communication between two trees, there is no normal publisher/subscriber hierarchy. Both drivers have a subscriber channel going that communicates with the publisher channel on the other tree, as shown in Figure 18-17. In the configuration, you'll normally want to place the rules on the publisher channel, not on the subscriber channel.

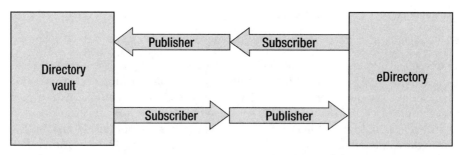

Figure 18-17. *In an eDirectory-eDirectory configuration, the publisher channel of one driver communicates with the subscriber channel of the other driver and vice versa.*

The following procedure explains how to configure the eDirectory driver. First, you'll learn how to create a working connection between two trees based upon the sample eDirectory driver. Then, once the connection is established, you'll find out how to secure and modify it so that eDirectory passwords can be synchronized as well. Notice that this procedure must be applied on both servers.

1. From iManager, select DirXML Drivers ➤ New Driver. If you have an existing driver set, you can install the driver there; otherwise, create a new driver set. Consult the preceding section for more information about the creation of a new driver set. After specifying what to do with the driver set, proceed to the next screen in the wizard.

2. Select Import A Driver Configuration From The Server and choose the driver eDirectory.xml. Click Next to continue.

▪**Tip** Know someone who's configured the perfect driver which matches your needs exactly? If so, ask her for the XML file, copy it from her server, and put it somewhere on your workstation. Use the option Import A Driver Configuration From The Client and refer to the exact location of the XML file to import the driver.

---

3. Enter all the details for the driver. After filling in all the details listed in the following, click Next to proceed.

   • *Driver name*: Specify the name you want to assign to your driver. It's recommended you select a different name than the default name of "eDirectory Driver." This way, a new XML file will be created for your driver.

▪**Caution** Only use alphanumeric characters in the drivername, otherwise you'll have a problem setting up the NDS-to-NDS driver certificates.

   • *Remote Tree Address and Port*: Specify the IP address or DNS hostname of the remote server you want to connect with. Leave the default port setting (8916) as is.

   • *Configure Data Flow*: With this option, you specify which tree is the authoritative tree. The default setting, Bi-directional, allows changes made in both trees to be synchronized to the other tree. Alternatively, select Authoritative to make this tree the authoritative tree or Subordinate to make the other tree the authoritative tree.

- *Configuration Option*: Here you specify how data should be synchronized between two trees. The default option, Mirrored, mirrors the entire container structure of this tree to the other tree so two identical trees are created. Select Flat to synchronize users between specified containers, or choose Department to synchronize users with some specific department.

- *Base Container*: Here you can specify the base container for synchronization in the local tree. If you chose Mirror in the preceding option, this should be the local base container you want to mirror. For Flat, this is the container in which you want to place users, while for Department, this is the parent of the departmental containers.

- *Password Sync Version*: Specifies how passwords should be synchronized. Select version 1.0 to sync eDirectory passwords using their public/private keys or select 2.0 if you want to synchronize Universal Passwords. You'll find more information about password synchronization later in this chapter.

- *Password Failure Notification User*: If you're using version 2.0 of the password sync program, you have the option to send e-mail alerts to a user when password updates fail. Select the name of a suitable help desk/administration person or leave this field blank if you don't want any alerts to be sent automatically.

4. Enter the name of the container in the other Directory tree you want to synchronize to, and then click Next to continue.

5. Define the security equivalences for this driver, and exclude the administrative roles. Click Next to proceed.

6. In the summary screen, review all objects created in eDirectory and click Finish With Overview to complete the configuration of this driver. This shows you a display of your eDirectory Identity Vault and all drivers currently connected to it, as shown in Figure 18-18. Notice that the eDirectory driver is not started yet. Before starting it, you must perform the exact same procedure on the server you want to synchronize with in order to configure its driver.

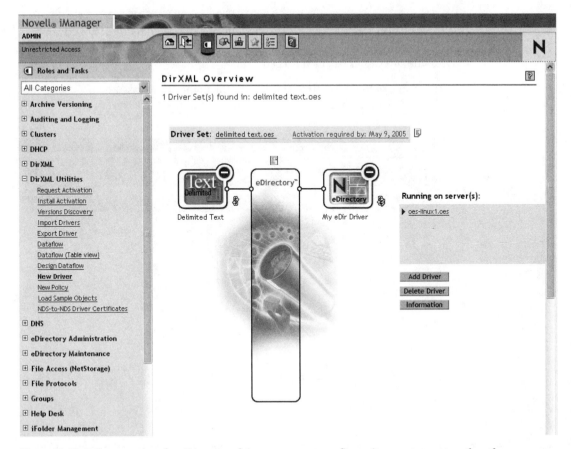

Figure 18-18. *Before starting the eDirectory driver, you must configure its counterpart on the other server as well.*

Establishing Secure Communications

Congratulations! Your eDirectory driver should work now, and even some simple password synchronization is provided. There are some limitations, however. For instance, there's no support for the Universal Password and there are no NDS-to-NDS driver certificates configured that allow for a really secure communication between the two trees. The best available method for securing communication between the two drivers is PKI certificates, which is what I'll cover in this section. For more details about the synchronization of Universal Password, consult the Identity Manager documentation at http://www.novell.com/documentation/oes. Information about the Universal Password is also provided in Chapter 9.

1. From iManager, on either tree, select DirXML Utilities ➤ NDS-to-NDS Driver Certificates (see Figure 18-19). On the first screen, enter the distinguished name of the driver, the name of the local tree, and the username, password, and context you used to authenticate to that tree. Click Next to proceed.

2. Enter the name of the driver in the other tree, the name of the tree, and the username, password, and context needed to authenticate to that tree. Click Next to continue.

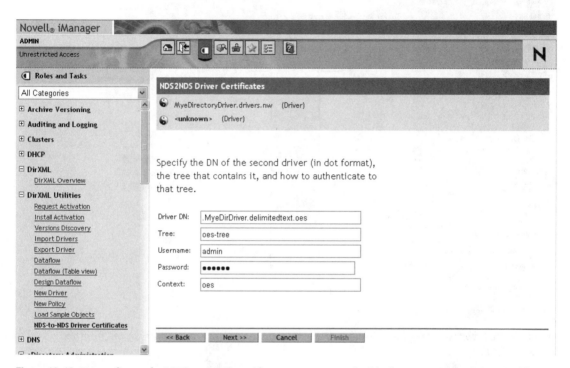

Figure 18-19. *To configure the NDS-to-NDS certificates, you must provide the name of the driver and login credentials of your admin user for both trees.*

3. Based upon the information you entered, the parameters for your server certificates are set automatically. Review their default values (see Figure 18-20) and click Finish to complete the Driver Certificates Wizard. This creates the certificates and automatically enables them so a secure communications channel can be established between the two servers.

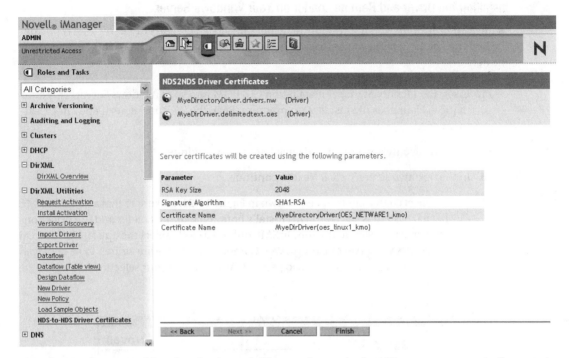

Figure 18-20. *After successful authentication on both trees, the required certificates are automatically created.*

Configuring the Active Directory Driver

In many networks, Active Directory is used in addition to an eDirectory installation. Often, this involves two network administrators making accounts for the same users. With Identity Manager, this waste of time and effort can be stopped: the Active Directory driver allows you to send data from eDirectory to Active Directory and vice versa. When you configure the Active Directory driver, you typically need to configure the Remote Loader as well since it's required to execute the driver on the Windows server. The Remote Loader is a service that executes the driver shim and passes information between the shim and the DirXML engine. When using the Remote Loader, install the driver on the server where the Remote Loader is running, not on the server where the DirXML engine is active.

To install the Active Directory driver, the following requirements must be met:

- You need Windows 2000 Server with Service Pack 2 or later or Windows Server 2003.

- Internet Explorer 5.5 or later must be installed on both the server running the Active Directory driver and on the target domain controller.

- The server hosting the Active Directory driver should be a member of the Active Directory domain. This is also a requirement when using password synchronization.

Installing the Driver and Remote Loader on Your Windows Server

In the next procedure, you'll learn how to install the Active Directory driver on a server using the Remote Loader. This assumes that the Identity Vault is running on some other server in the network.

1. Insert the Identity Manager installation CD-ROM into your Windows Server. This automatically launches the installation program. Read the Welcome screen and click Next to proceed.

2. Read the license agreement and click I Accept to continue.

3. In the next two screens, click Next to continue.

4. On the select components screen, shown in Figure 18-21, make sure that at least DirXML Connected System is selected. This installs both the Remote Loader and the driver on your server. If you want to use the DirXML utilities as well, select the option Utilities. Do not select DirXML Server or DirXML Web Components. These are written to be deployed on a server where eDirectory is also present. After making your selection, click Next to continue.

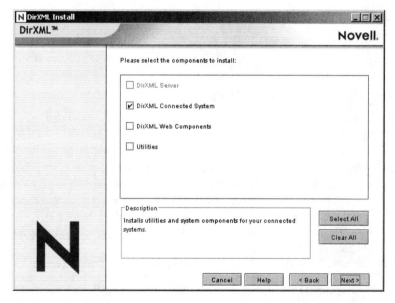

Figure 18-21. *To install just the driver and the Remote Loader on your Windows server, select DirXML Connected System.*

5. Select the installation path and click Next to continue. Now, select all the components you want to install, as shown in Figure 18-22. Make sure at least the Active Directory driver and the Remote Loader Service are selected before clicking Next to continue. All the other drivers can be deselected since you don't need them to synchronize data between eDirectory and Active Directory.

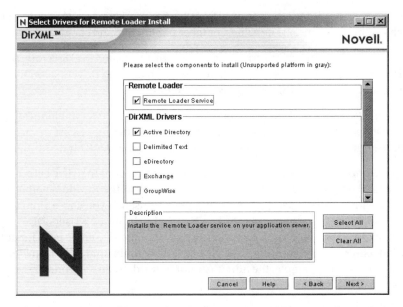

Figure 18-22. *To synchronize data between Active Directory and eDirectory, simply select the Remote Loader Service and the Active Directory driver.*

6. Click OK twice to continue.

7. From the Products To Be Installed screen, click Finish to start the product installation. Notice that the PasswordSync Agent is installed automatically. This is good because it allows you to synchronize passwords between eDirectory and Active Directory. More details about eDirectory—Active Directory password synchronization is provided later in this chapter.

8. Specify whether you would like a shortcut on the desktop for the Remote Loader Console. Next, click OK to close the Installation Completed screen and finish the installation.

Configuring Your Driver

Now that you've installed the driver on the Windows machine, you must create and configure all the required driver objects in eDirectory. This task must be performed in iManager, as shown in the following steps.

1. Start iManager and log in to the server hosting the Identity Vault.

2. Select DirXML Utilities ➤ New Driver to start the creation of a new driver.

3. Specify if you want to create a new driver set or add the driver to an existing driver set and click Next to continue.

4. Select Import A Driver Configuration From The Server and make sure the driver ActiveDirectory.xml is selected. Click Next to continue.

5. Enter all the properties for your driver. The following configuration parameters are available. Enter the appropriate values for these parameters and click Next to continue.

- *Driver name*: The name of the driver object that will be created in eDirectory. If you're updating from a previous version of this driver, from Existing Drivers select the driver that exists in the same driver set you want to update.

- *Authentication Method*: Here you can select the method used for authenticating on Active Directory. The default selection, Negotiate, provides the easiest way to authenticate. Alternatively, you can select Simple to use a simple LDAP bind to authenticate.

- *Authentication Id*: Here you enter the name of a user account in Active Directory that can be used by your DirXML driver. Depending on the authentication method you selected earlier, several naming conventions can be used. If you chose Simple LDAP authentication, enter a name like CN=Administrator,CN=Users,DC= yourdomain,DC=com. If you've specified that Negotiate should be used for authentication, enter a plain Windows NT–style name like Administrator, or Domain/ Administrator. For example, the Administrator in the domain ad.sandervanvugt.nl would use ad/Administrator.

- *Authentication Password*: Here you specify the password for the user you configured in the previous step. Notice that this password is not synchronized automatically: if you change the password in Active Directory, you need to manually enter a new password for the eDirectory driver as well.

- *Authentication Server*: Here you enter the name of your domain controller. Only if simple authentication is used can you specify an IP address. If negotiation is used, you must use the server's DNS name, which requires a working DNS configuration for name resolving. You can arrange for proper name resolving as well by editing the local hosts file on the server where the DirXML engine is running; just enter all IP addresses and names that are needed in /etc/hosts to configure a simple way of host resolving.

- *Domain Name*: Here you must enter the LDAP name of the domain. This will be a name like dc=ad,dc=sandervanvugt,dc=nl.

- *Domain DNS Name*: This is where you provide the DNS name of the Active Directory domain.

- *Driver Polling Interval*: This is the time interval (in minutes) that the driver delays before querying Active Directory for changes. A high number implicates a low performance load but slow synchronization of changes made in Active Directory, while a low number implies fast response but a higher load on Active Directory.

- *Password Sync Timeout*: The amount of time that the driver will try to synchronize a password change. It's recommended to set this parameter at least three times as high as the polling interval.

- *Base Container in eDirectory*: The container in eDirectory where new objects must be created. This value will be written in the publisher channel policies.

- *Base Container in Active Directory*: The container in Active Directory where new objects can be created. Enter a name like CN=users,DC=ad,DC=oes,dc=com.

- *Configure Data Flow*: Here you specify which Directory Service is authoritative. The default value of this parameter is Bi-Directional, which allows changes made in both directories to be synchronized to the other side. Alternatively, choose AD to eDirectory if Active Directory is the authoritative database, or eDirectory to AD if eDirectory is authoritative.

- *Publisher Placement*: Choose mirrored if you want Active Directory to create new objects with the exact same hierarchy under the base container, or select Flat to place objects strictly within the base container, without any hierarchy being applied.

- *Subscriber Placement*: Same as the previous parameter, but for the subscriber channel.

- *Password Failure Notification User*: The name of a suitable administration/help desk user account to be notified when password updates fail. Leave this field empty if you don't want password update failures to be reported by e-mail.

- *Support Exchange*: Here you specify whether you want support for Exchange 2000 or 2003.

- *Driver Is Local/Remote*: Specifies whether the driver is running on the same system as the DirXML engine, or remotely with the Remote Loader service. In most situations, you'll specify that the driver is running remotely.

6. If you've indicated that the Remote Loader service should be used to contact the driver, in the next screen (see Figure 18-23) you must specify how this service can be located. Enter the DNS name or IP address of the server where the Remote Loader has been installed, its port (8090 if you're using the default), and the passwords you entered upon installation for the Remote Loader and the driver. After entering all the required information, click Next to continue.

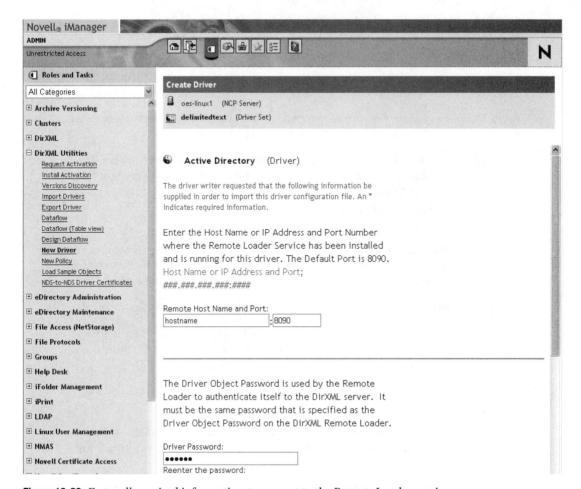

Figure 18-23. *Enter all required information to connect to the Remote Loader service.*

7. Enter the eDirectory security equivalences for the driver, which are needed to create new objects in eDirectory. Then, choose to exclude Administrative roles. When finished, click Next to continue.

8. You'll now get an overview of all objects created in eDirectory for this driver configuration. Click Finish With Overview to verify that the driver has been installed properly. (The resulting overview is shown in Figure 18-24.) You can also start it now, but be aware that it won't be able to synchronize anything yet because the Remote Loader service still has to be configured. This is your very next task, incidentally.

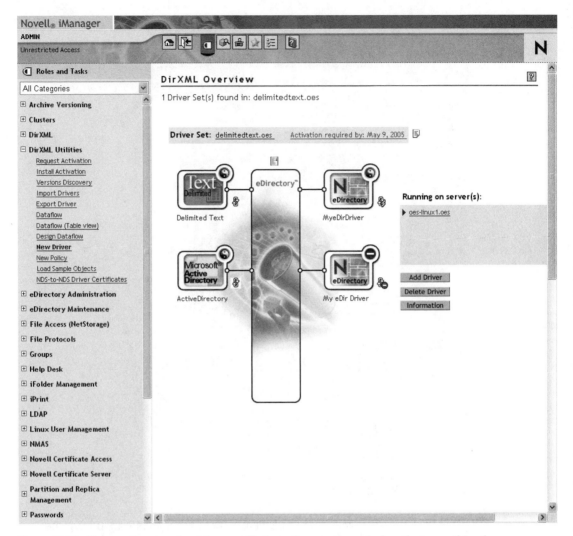

Figure 18-24. *After configuring the driver, verify from the overview window that everything has been configured properly.*

9. On the Windows server where the driver is installed, select Start ➤ DirXML Remote Loader Console and click Add to configure the Remote Loader, as shown in Figure 18-25.

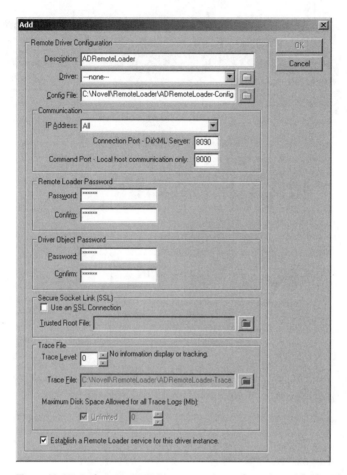

Figure 18-25. *Before Active Directory can synchronize with the Identity Vault, you must configure the Remote Loader.*

10. In the Remote Loader configuration screen, enter all required information for the Remote Loader service. The minimum you must enter is a description, the Remote Loader password, and the Driver Object password. All other information is optional. When finished, click OK to save your settings.

■**Tip** By default, the Remote Loader contacts the DirXML engine over a non-secured connection. It's not difficult to secure this connection in the Remote Loader configuration screen: first, you must export a Trusted Root file from the Certificate Authority in the eDirectory directory tree to the server where the Remote Loader is configured. Next, select the Use An SSL Connection option from the Remote Loader configuration screen and browse to the location where you saved the trusted root file. Click OK and the Remote Loader service sets up an encrypted connection.

---

11. The configuration program now asks if you want to start the DirXML Remote Loader service. Click Yes to start it. You'll now see that the Remote Loader is active in the Remote Loader Console. If you want to view more detailed information on what's happening, click Trace On to open a DSTRACE screen on the Windows Server Console so you can see more precisely how objects are being synchronized between both Directories (see Figure 18-26).

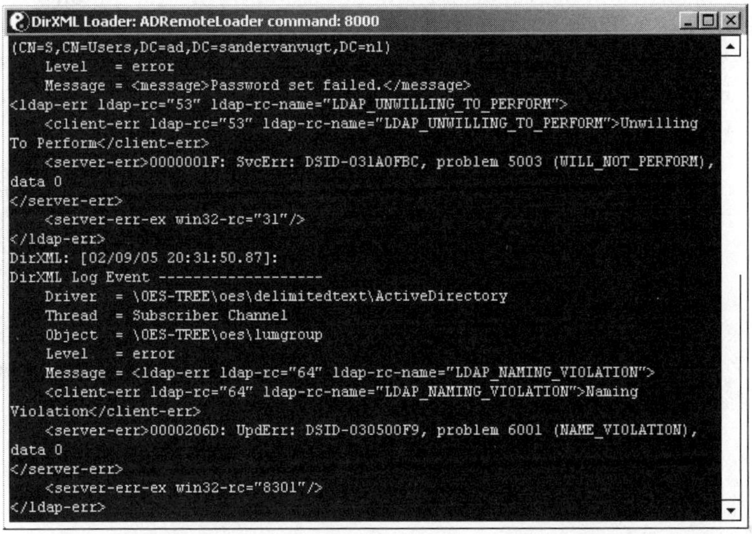

```
DirXML Loader: ADRemoteLoader command: 8000                        _ □ ×
(CN=S,CN=Users,DC=ad,DC=sandervanvugt,DC=nl)
    Level   = error
    Message = <message>Password set failed.</message>
<ldap-err ldap-rc="53" ldap-rc-name="LDAP_UNWILLING_TO_PERFORM">
    <client-err ldap-rc="53" ldap-rc-name="LDAP_UNWILLING_TO_PERFORM">Unwilling
To Perform</client-err>
    <server-err>0000001F: SvcErr: DSID-031A0FBC, problem 5003 (WILL_NOT_PERFORM),
data 0
</server-err>
    <server-err-ex win32-rc="31"/>
</ldap-err>
DirXML: [02/09/05 20:31:50.87]:
DirXML Log Event ------------------
    Driver  = \OES-TREE\oes\delimitedtext\ActiveDirectory
    Thread  = Subscriber Channel
    Object  = \OES-TREE\oes\lumgroup
    Level   = error
    Message = <ldap-err ldap-rc="64" ldap-rc-name="LDAP_NAMING_VIOLATION">
    <client-err ldap-rc="64" ldap-rc-name="LDAP_NAMING_VIOLATION">Naming
Violation</client-err>
    <server-err>0000206D: UpdErr: DSID-030500F9, problem 6001 (NAME_VIOLATION),
data 0
</server-err>
    <server-err-ex win32-rc="8301"/>
</ldap-err>
```

Figure 18-26. *The Trace screen displays all synchronization activity. This is especially useful if you're having trouble setting up a proper connection.*

Enabling Password Synchronization Between the Identity Vault and Active Directory

One of the most difficult parts of Identity Manager configuration is password synchronization. This is difficult because not all connected systems are supported. Currently, you can only synchronize passwords with the following drivers:

- NIS

- NT Domain

- eDirectory

- Active Directory

To use password synchronization, several elements must be configured. First, you must enable usage of Universal Password. In this Universal Password configuration, you need a DirXML password policy, which is added by default upon installation of Identity Manager. This password policy allows the eDirectory password to be synchronized with passwords coming in through the driver. You also need another password policy that allows usage of Universal Password for all users in your tree. You can create this policy in iManager by selecting Passwords ➤ Password Policies. Here, make sure the following are selected:

- Enable Universal Password.

- Synchronize NDS Password when setting Universal Password.

- Synchronize Distribution Password when setting Universal Password.

Next, you must enable Password Synchronization. You can find this feature by going to iManager ➤ Passwords ➤ Password Synchronization. This option displays an overview of all drivers currently enabled on your system and how the password synchronization policy is set for these drivers (see Figure 18-27). You can also set the properties of the current password synchronization status for your driver by clicking its link. Here, it's important to make sure the option Use Distribution Password For Password Synchronization is chosen on your Active Directory driver (it's not selected by default).

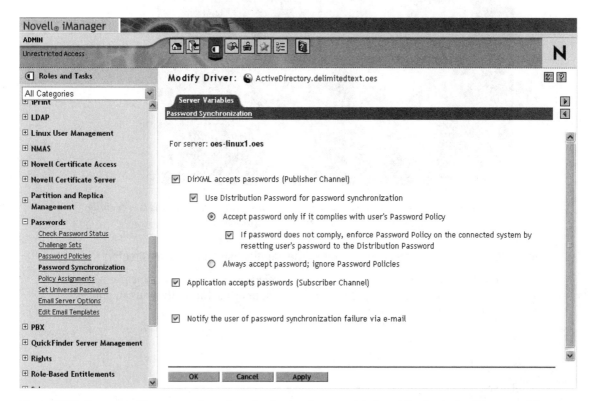

Figure 18-27. *Some specific password synchronization options need to be set for the Active Directory driver.*

In addition to the configuration you must do in the iManager Password options, you also must enable a password filter on the Active Directory server as well. With the installation of the DirXML driver on that server, the PassSync utility is installed as well. This utility allows passwords to be captured and to be synchronized to the Identity Vault.

1. On the server where the DirXML driver and Remote Loader are installed, open the Control Panel and select the DirXML PassSync program.

2. When asked if this is the machine where the DirXML driver is configured to run, click Yes.

3. You'll now see an overview of all the Active Directory domains that passwords are currently synchronized for (see Figure 18-28). Since you haven't configured anything yet, this list will be empty. Click Add to add all the domains you want to synchronize passwords with automatically.

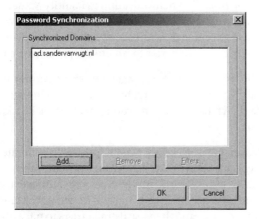

Figure 18-28. *Before passwords can be synchronized from a domain to eDirectory, you must configure the Password Sync utility on that domain.*

4. Select the name of the domain to configure password synchronization on. Optionally, you can also enter the name of a computer that's a member of the specified domain, but since in this example you're working directly on the domain controller, this isn't necessary. Click OK to add the domain. When asked if you want to use the DNS name for the domain, click Yes. Repeat this procedure for all domains for which you want to synchronize passwords to DirXML.

5. Reboot all the domain controllers. When the status for all the domain controllers once again reads Running, confirm that password synchronization is properly working.

You've now connected Active Directory to eDirectory and it should all be working fine. This doesn't mean, however, that you've implemented Identity Manager yet. In fact, your work is really only just beginning. After the installation of Identity Manager (which is relatively easy) you must fine-tune it. This is a delicate job where you have to apply the wishes of the customer or your organization to the Identity Manager configuration. To get it all going, carefully tune all policies on both the subscriber and the publisher channel. I can't teach you how to do all that in one small chapter, but I hope this section about DirXML driver synchronization has provided a good introduction to the subject and will help you set up your own environment.

A Quick Guide to Troubleshooting Identity Manager

Note that if you're encountering problems with Nsure Identity Manager, sometimes it can be very difficult to find their cause. For those times when you run into trouble, follow the next steps.

1. *Identify general issues.* Before you start troubleshooting, you must identify what's really wrong with your system. Identity Manager consists of many components and it can be hard uncovering just what's going on.

2. *Understand your Identity Manager in general.* Synchronization in Identity Manager is a flow of events in which different steps can be distinguished. Try to understand what happens to your data and which actions unfold at which locations in the publisher and the subscriber channel. That way it will be a lot easier to isolate the problem area.

3. *Understand general driver functionality.* In Identity Manager, no two drivers are equal. A general understanding of Identity Manager isn't enough; you need to understand what a specific driver is doing as well. A fault in your environment may well be a known issue for the driver you're trying to use.

4. *Generate a trace file.* In a trace file, you can see exactly what happens. To generate the trace file, you need three **dstrace** commands. On OES - NetWare, just enter these commands at the prompt; on OES - Linux, enter them from the Ndstrace interface that appears after you issue the command **ndstrace**. To get a complete overview of all Identity Manager errors, first switch off all other traces and then use **dstrace +dvrs** to trace driver errors, **dstrace +dxml** to trace errors generated by the DirXML engine, and finish with **dstrace screen on** to make sure the errors are logged to the screen. If in your configuration a Remote Loader is used, don't forget to run a trace file on the Remote Loader as well.

5. *Identify the error and its cause.* In all cases, you'll end up with a specific error code. Write it down, because this is what you're going to resolve.

6. *Identify possible solutions.* Using documentation found online, you must identify possible solutions for the error, choose the best solution, and implement it. Hopefully, this will help in resolving the error.

Logging and Reporting with Nsure Audit

After installation and configuration of Identity Manager, you also need a way to monitor its performance. Of course, there are the default log files that offer information on how the system is working, but in most cases that's not enough. To perform extensive event management, set up an Nsure Audit system. This is the ideal tool for logging and reporting. Nsure Audit provides a set of preconfigured reports, notification services, and user-defined data logging. You can also monitor real-time Identity Manager events, send e-mail notifications, and generate advanced reports.

Nsure Audit is a centralized logging service that can work with multiple applications to log data into a centralized data store. It can be used with a lot more applications than just Identity Manager. For each of the applications you want to use with Nsure Audit, you need a platform agent that reports events to the Nsure Audit Secure Login Server.

■**Note** Although Nsure Audit provides great services to your Identity Manager environment, the product is not a part of Open Enterprise Server. It's only available as a separate purchase.

Setting Up the Secure Logging Server

The core component of Nsure Audit is the Secure Logging Server, which can log events to several locations. MySQL, Oracle, Microsoft SQL, Java Applications, SNMP, SMTP, Syslog, and even clear-text files are supported. The Secure Logging Server can run on multiple platforms such as NetWare, Linux, Windows, and Solaris. To get information from this Secure Logging Server, the Nsure Audit Report tool is used. This is a custom application to query these databases for events. An Nsure Audit solution can be designed in many ways. One of the most common is to use a MySQL database. The following sections explain how to configure the Secure Logging Server on top of MySQL.

Installing MySQL

The key component of the Nsure Audit Secure Logging Server is the event repository. This section of the book explores how to set up MySQL as an event repository. MySQL can be installed both on Linux and NetWare, and the installation is quite straightforward.

To install MySQL on OES - Linux, use the YaST software installation tool, as explained in the following steps.

1. Start YaST2, enter your root password, and from the Filter dialogue, select Search. In the search bar, enter **mysql**. This displays a list of all available MySQL packages. Make sure the following packages are selected.

    • mysql

    • mysql-client

    • mysql-shared

2. Click Accept to start installation. A pop-up window will probably now appear indicating that other packages must also be installed to resolve dependencies. Click Continue to proceed. This automatically installs all the required dependencies.

3. Enter all required CDs and press OK to continue. When the installation has completed, the system configuration is written and the software install module is closed automatically.

4. Now, from a terminal window on the OES - Linux server, enter **/etc/init.d/mysql start** to start the MySQL database. Run the command **chkconfig mysql 235** as well to make sure the database will be started automatically when you reboot your server.

5. Before using the MySQL database, you must set the password for the MySQL root user. To do so, issue the command **mysqladmin –u root password** *new-password*. Your MySQL database is now ready for use.

To install MySQL on OES - NetWare, use the software install feature from the Server Console, as described in the following steps.

1. From the GUI console on your OES - NetWare server, select Install ➤ Add.

2. Insert the OES - NetWare products CD in your CD-drive and click the Browse button. Browse to the file Postinst.ni on the root of this CD, select it, and click OK twice to continue.

3. From the Components screen, select MySQL and click Next to continue. On the next screen, click Copy Files to copy all required files to your server.

4. When the file copy has completed, enter the MySQL data directory. Its default location is on the volume SYS:. This may not be a good idea, however, if you anticipate intensive use of the MySQL database. To avoid this, select another directory if you want. Next, enter the password for the user root twice and click Next. This password is for the administrator of the MySQL database, whose default name is root. Don't confuse it with the user root on your Linux server! Next, make sure the option Secure Installation is selected and click Next to continue.

5. Click Close to finish the installation. MySQL is now ready for use.

Creating a MySQL Database for Nsure Audit

Now that the MySQL database has been created, you must create an Nsure Audit database and user in it. The following procedure can be used both on NetWare and on Linux.

1. Enter the command **mysql –u root –p** to launch the MySQL monitor and then log in as root (see Figure 18-29 for a console listing of all commands entered in this section). You'll be prompted for a password before access is granted to the MySQL monitor. You'll recognize it because it has its own prompt: mysql>.

2. Enter the command **CREATE DATABASE naudit;** to create an Nsure Audit database. The command must be input exactly as displayed here because it's case-sensitive.

3. Create an Nsure Audit user and grant it some rights. You can do so by issuing the command **GRANT ALL PRIVILEGES ON naudit.* TO auditusr@'%' IDENTIFIED BY 'auditpwd' WITH GRANT OPTION;**. This creates a user with the name auditusr. The construction @'%' after the name of the user in the command allows the user to log in remotely. This is only needed when the Secure Logging server is on a server other than the MySQL database. You should also notice that a default password of 'auditpw' is used. Thus, it's best to change this to something else.

4. Enter **FLUSH PRIVILEGES;** to flush the MySQL privileges.

5. Exit MySQL monitor by issuing the command **exit**.

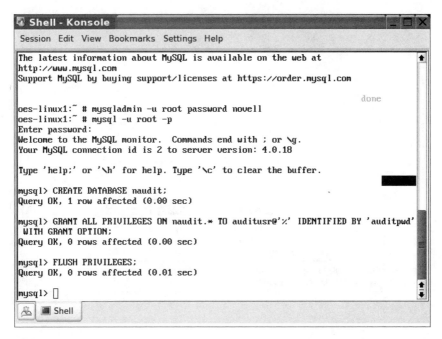

Figure 18-29. *Before configuring the Secure Logging Server, you must create the MySQL database.*

Installing Novell Nsure Audit on Linux

On OES - NetWare, an Nsure Audit starter pack is available for installation. On OES - Linux, this is not the case and so you must install the software manually from the Nsure Audit installation CD using the following steps.

1. Log in as root on your Linux host, insert the Nsure Audit CD, and wait until the CD is mounted.

2. Activate the directory on the CD with the Linux installation files, and enter the command **./pinstall.lin** from this directory. This installs the installation script.

3. Select All to install all required components and then press Enter to continue.

4. Enter your admin name and password and press Enter to continue.

5. Select Add Schema Extensions and press Enter to accept (see Figure 18-30). This extends the schema of your Directory to prepare it for Nsure Audit.

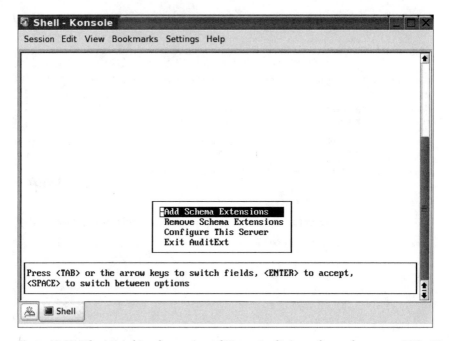

Figure 18-30. *The initial configuration of Nsure Audit is performed on your OES - Linux server.*

6. After extension of the schema, select Configure This Server. Enter a name for the Log Server or accept its default name and press Enter to continue. This creates all the objects in eDirectory and makes a link to the NCP server object.

7. Select Exit AuditExt to close the configuration program. Nsure Audit will now be started. Continue its configuration from iManager after installing the iManager plug-in.

Installing the iManager Plug-In

Now that you've installed the Nsure Audit software, you must make it manageable as well. To do this, you need to install the iManager plug-in.

1. On the workstation where you start your browser to access iManager, insert the Nsure Audit installation CD.

2. Start iManager, log in, and click Configure.

3. Select Module Installation ➤ Available Novell Plug-in Modules (see Figure 18-31) and click New to install a new module.

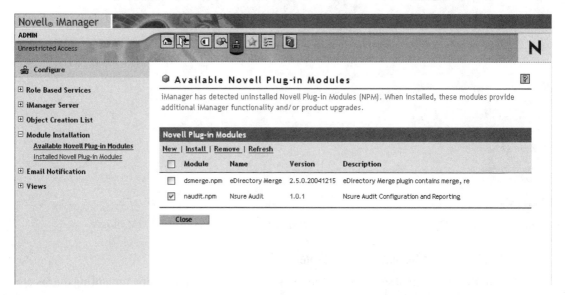

Figure 18-31. *Before managing the Secure Logging Server, you need to install the iManager plug-in.*

4. Browse to the Nsure Audit plug-in module, naudit.npm, which you can find in the directory add_ons file on the Nsure Audit installation CD. Select it and click OK to install it. The module will now be added to the list of iManager modules available, but it won't be installed yet. Select it and click Install to add it to your iManager configuration.

5. You'll now see a message that the module has been installed successfully. Click Close to close the module installation screen.

6. Before using the new iManager plug-in, you must restart Tomcat. On OES - NetWare, enter **TC4STOP** at the NetWare prompt. On OES - Linux, enter **rcnovell-tomcat stop**. Wait one minute before continuing, and then enter **rcnovell-tomcat start** on OES - Linux or **TOMCAT4** on OES - NetWare. It can take a few minutes before Tomcat fully initializes. Wait five minutes and then log in to iManager again. The Nsure Audit Role should now be displayed in the available options (as shown in Figure 18-32).

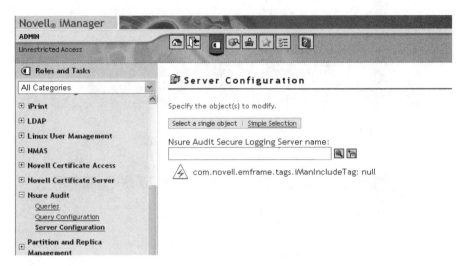

Figure 18-32. *After installation of the plug-in, you can manage Nsure Audit from iManager.*

Configuring the Secure Logging Server

Now that all required software components are installed, you can start configuring the Secure Logging Server from iManager by using these steps.

1. From iManager, select Nsure Audit ➤ Server Configuration.

2. Select the Nsure Audit Secure Logging Server. You'll find its object in the container Logging Services, which is created directly under the root of your tree (as shown in Figure 18-33). Click Apply to continue.

3. On the General tab, make sure the server that the Nsure Audit software is running on is selected. Next, specify the directory on the server where the Nsure Audit drivers are located. For OES - NetWare, this is sys:\system, for OES - Linux, you should indicate /usr/local/naudit as the default directory. On this tab, you also must create a log channel. This is the location where messages are logged to. In the default configuration, messages are logged to a file. In this example, however, you're configuring the Secure Logging Server to log to the MySQL database you created a few steps earlier. Before indicating that this database should be used, you must create a channel for it.

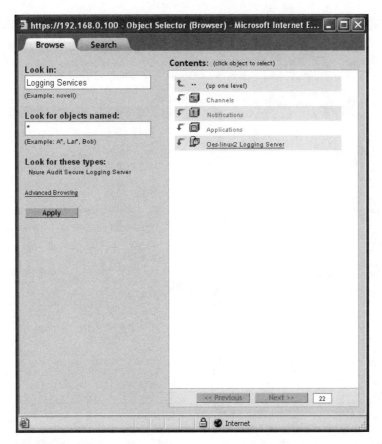

Figure 18-33. *The Secure Logging server and all related objects are created in a special container directly under the root of your tree.*

4. Click Channels and check the box next to the default channel container with the name Channels. Next, click New Channel to create a new channel. Click OK in the pop-up to continue.

5. In the New Channel window, enter a name for the channel, select MySQL Channel, and click OK to continue. This adds the MySQL channel to the list of channels currently available (as shown in Figure 18-34).

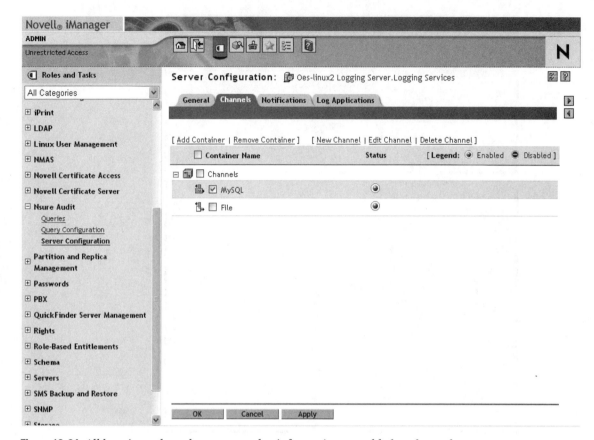

Figure 18-34. *All locations where the server can log information are added as channels.*

6. In the channel list, select the channel you've just added and click Edit Channel to modify its properties. On the Configuration tab (see Figure 18-35) you must specify all the information that's required to contact the MySQL server. The following information must be provided. After specifying all options for the channel, click OK to save it and then continue.

• *Address*: The address of the server where MySQL is configured.

• *User*: The name of the MySQL user.

• *Password*: The password of the MySQL user.

• *Database Name*: The name of the MySQL database you've created.

• *Table*: The table to be created in the MySQL database for adding information from the Secure Logging Server.

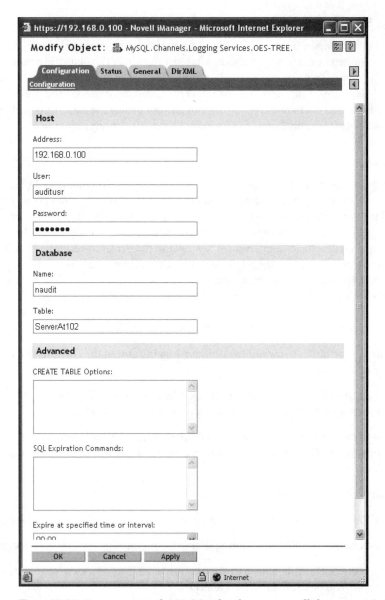

Figure 18-35. *To connect to the MySQL database, enter all the contact information.*

7. Now go back to the Configuration link on the General tab and at Log Channel make sure that the MySQL channel you just created is selected. You don't have to specify any value for the Secure Logging Certificate File and the Secure Logging PrivateKey file; the software automatically uses the keys that are present internally in the system.

This is enough configuration for now. Save all changes to the Directory by clicking OK. You now must restart the Secure Logging Server using the commands **/etc/init.d/novell-naudit stop** and **/etc/init.d/rcnovell-naudit start**.

Configuring the DirXML Agent

When the Secure Logging server has been configured, you must next configure the DirXML Agent, which is also known as the platform agent. After installation of the platform agent, open the configuration file to specify where the Secure Logging Server can be found. On OES - NetWare, the name of this file is sys:\etc\logevent.cfg; on OES - Linux, you must modify the file /etc/logevent.conf. In this file, edit the parameter LogHost and give as its value the name or IP address of the host where the Secure Logging Server can be found. Next, restart Identity Manager.

Logging Configuration

By default, only critical events and user-defined events generated by the Identity Manager driver are logged. However, in Identity Manager you can configure exactly when an event should be logged using several predefined levels, or by individually selecting each event you want to log. There are two places where you can set how logging should happen: on the driver set and on the individual drivers in the driver set. By default, the driver inherits settings from the driver set. If you access the log settings from an individual driver, you can see that, by default, it will inherit settings from the driver set. You can choose to set individual settings for the driver as well. The following procedure outlines how this can be configured.

1. In iManager, select DirXML ➤ DirXML Overview.

2. Click the driver for which you want to configure logging and in the DirXML Driver Overview window, click it again.

3. Select the Log Level link on the DirXML tab. Deselect the option Use Log Settings From The DriverSet to make settings for the individual drivers you've selected.

4. If you want to modify the log settings for the driver set, make sure the option Use Log Settings From The DriverSet is selected and click the link Click Here to make your modifications.

5. Select what exactly should be logged from the following list:

   • *Log errors*: This is the default log level. Only errors and user-defined events will be logged.

   • *Log errors and warnings*: With this setting selected, both warnings and errors are logged.

   • *Log specific events*: Use this option to choose from specific events; only the selected specific events will be logged in this scenario.

   • *Only update the last log time*: This will log only user-defined events. If the same event is logged again, only the last log time of the last logged instance of that event is updated. Thus, you can only see when it last happened.

   • *Logging off*: Only logs user-defined events.

   • *Maximum number of entries in the log*: Specifies the maximum number of entries that's logged.

6. If you don't want to be overwhelmed by logged events (a wise decision), select the option Log Specific Events. Click the icon next to it and from the Events window (see Figure 18-36) define what exactly should be logged. This allows you to make logs only for information you really need to know about. For example, you could select the Password Sync check box under the Transformation Events heading to only display information about the synchronization of passwords.

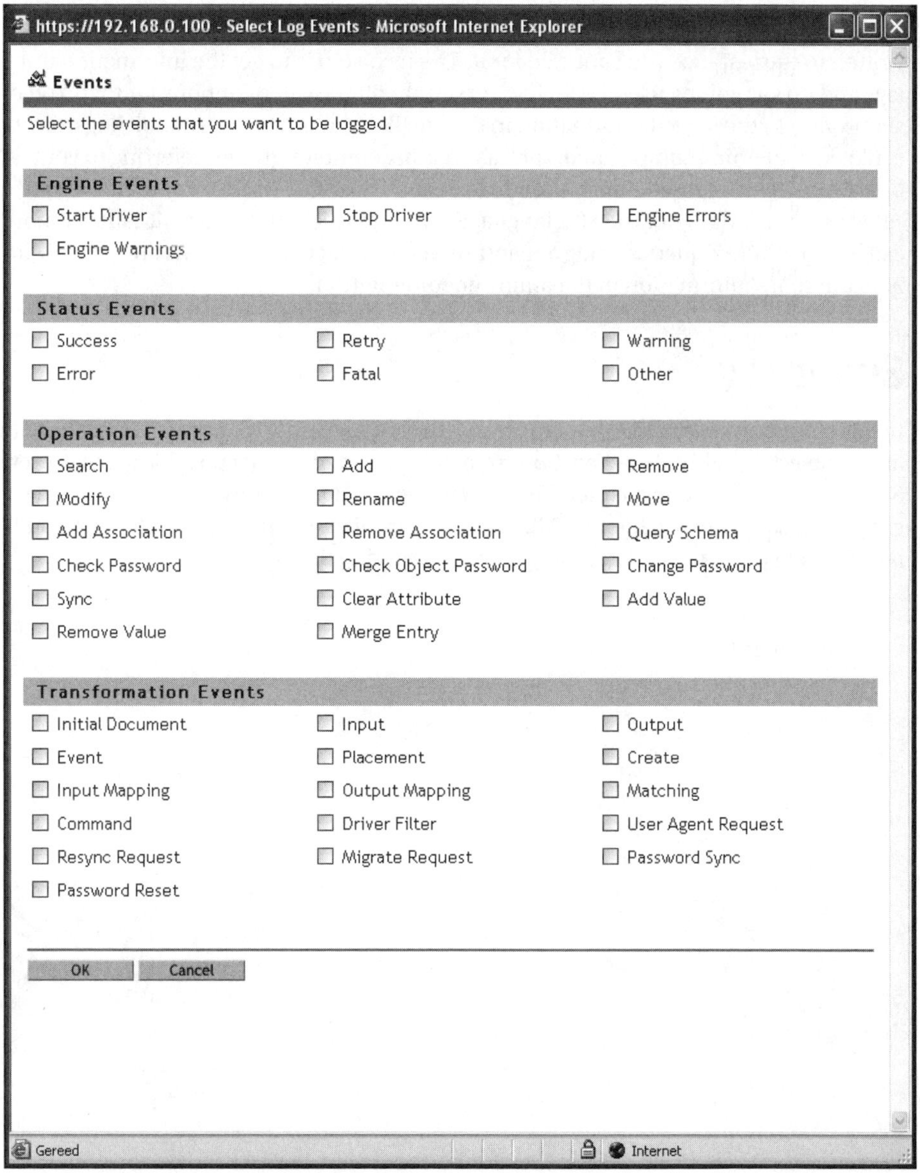

Figure 18-36. *It can be useful to specify your own events. In such cases, you can ensure you're only offered the information you really need.*

The preceding section explored how to enable logging on the driver or driver set. It's possible to do a lot more customization, however. For instance, use the DirXML: Policy Builder to specify exactly when an event should be logged and what severity is associated to a given event. Consult the online documentation at www.novell.com/documentation/oes for more information about this procedure.

Working with Nsure Audit Queries, Reports, Notifications, and Data Logs

You've now configured a basic Nsure Audit environment. In this environment, logs will be written to the instance you specified for it. The next step is to get the information out of these logs and do something useful with it. Nsure Audit offers a lot of options for that. You could simply access the logged information in the log file /var/opt/nove//naudit/logs/log, or you could do something complicated, such as creating complex queries referring to your SQL database if you've configured Nsure Audit to log data to MySQL. If you want to make good queries, some basic knowledge of the SQL language is required. There's also an iManager module that can help you make queries using a menu-driven interface. The options are virtually limitless. Find out more information in the online documentation.

Summary

In this chapter, you learned about the basics of Nsure Identity Manager. Due to the complexity of the subject, I could only explain how to get things started. It's not possible to cover everything Nsure can do in just one chapter. I hope, however, that this information gives you a solid grounding in how to use Identity Manager synchronization. In the next chapter, you'll learn how to set up a cluster on OES using Novell Clustering Services.

■ ■ ■

Introduction to Novell Clustering Services

Novell Clustering Services (NCS) is a server clustering system that ensures the high availability and manageability of network resources such as data volumes, applications, and services. Novell Clustering Services is a multinode clustering solution that can be deployed on OES - NetWare as well as OES - Linux; it even supports mixed environments where Linux and NetWare are used together to provide high-availability for clustered resources! It supports failover, failback, and the load balancing of individually managed cluster resources. NCS exists in two versions, and included with OES is a license for a two-node cluster. You can also buy additional node licenses and have up to 32 nodes in the same cluster. This chapter teaches you how to set up NCS on both OES - Linux and OES - NetWare.

Introduction to Clustering

The main purpose of a clustering service is to ensure the high availability of resources. In a clustered environment, resources aren't physically attached to one server, but to the cluster. Since a cluster consists of two servers or more (called nodes), one of the nodes can take over if the other node fails. The cluster provides failback as well. For instance, when the node that crashed comes back online, the resource originally attached to that node can automatically return to the node again.

NCS doesn't just offer high-availability features, it offers load balancing as well. Since normally on a cluster many services are deployed, an administrator can manually load-balance these services between the nodes in the cluster so that a situation doesn't occur where one server is running all services while the other server is doing nothing.

A Novell clustering environment is extremely flexible. As an administrator, you can configure everything you want, managing the cluster in a way that best fits your organization.

Major Components in a Cluster

Before you can decide how to install the cluster, you must be familiar with its major components. To make it clear what we're talking about, in this section the most important clustering terminology is introduced. First, there is the cluster itself: this is a group of servers linked together that monitor each other and hosts the services provided by the cluster. A server in the cluster is known as a cluster node. All that the cluster is created for are the cluster resources. These are the network services, applications, and other resources that you created the cluster for. A cluster resource is assigned dynamically to one of the cluster nodes. These are the nodes the administrator assigned the resource to.

Another important part of the cluster is the shared storage device. Since cluster resources are moved dynamically from one cluster node to another, it makes no sense to store the cluster resource files on one specific node in the cluster. If that node should go down, the resource wouldn't be able to store its data, rendering it useless. Therefore, in order to configure a cluster, you need shared storage for the cluster resource's data. Different kinds of shared storage can be used, such as those following.

- *A Storage Area Network*: This is the most expensive kind of shared storage, but it's also the storage method with the best performance. In a SAN environment, a server is attached to two networks simultaneously. One of these is the normal data network; the other is the storage network. Normally, cluster nodes are attached to this network by means of fibre channel, which connects them to the storage devices on the SAN.

- *A shared SCSI device*: This solution can only be used in a two-node cluster. A shared SCSI device is a SCSI hard disk connected to two servers at the same time. It's not the most flexible solution, but it's rather cheap and therefore quite popular.

- *iSCSI*: iSCSI is a protocol that makes storage space on another device available. This other device can be an OES server configured as the iSCSI target, but it can be a dedicated iSCSI target device as well. You can read more about the configuration of iSCSI in Chapter 11 of this book.

All the cluster is concerned with are the cluster resources. These are dynamically allocated to cluster nodes. Different things can happen to the resources in a cluster:

- *Failover*: This is what happens when one of the nodes in the cluster goes down and the cluster resource was assigned to that node. Failover is the process of restarting the cluster resource on another node in the cluster. Fan-out failover can be used as well: this means that the cluster administrator determines in advance on what node a resource is going to be activated in case its primary node crashes. In order to create an optimized load-balanced solution, fan-out failover should be configured.

- *Failback*: This is the process of returning the failed node's resources to their original node when the node comes back into operation on the cluster. This can be a manual process, or automated. Normally, it's recommended to only use manual failback because an administrator should analyze why a node in a cluster became unavailable before running vital services on it again.

- *Migration*: Migration is the process where an administrator manually migrates a cluster's resources from one server to another without waiting for its cluster nodes to fail.

Designing a Clustered Solution

Before implementing a cluster, you must design a proper cluster solution for a business scenario. In order to design the cluster, you should know how nodes communicate with each other in the cluster and what happens when one of the nodes fails. These points are discussed next.

In a clustered environment, the cluster exists as some kind of virtual server that has its own IP address. The first node that comes up in the NCS cluster gets the cluster IP address and is called the master node. All other nodes in the cluster are referred to as slave nodes. The master node has some important tasks: it updates information transmitted between the cluster and eDirectory and monitors the availability of other cluster nodes. These are vital features; therefore, your cluster cannot exist without a master node. If the master node fails, one of the other servers in the cluster automatically becomes the master node.

One other thing that's needed in the cluster in most situations is the shared storage device, as you can see in Figure 19-1. This is your SAN, your iSCSI device, or your shared SCSI device. The shared storage device is the location where the cluster resources store their data and where cluster users access their data. On the shared storage device, the administrator creates cluster-enabled NSS volumes. These volumes are in NSS pools that can be reached at a unique IP address. This IP address is attached to the virtual server object created for the cluster. In a properly designed cluster, all storage can be moved from the cluster nodes to the shared storage device. If you configure this shared storage on a SAN for optimized fault tolerance, it allows for the highest possible availability.

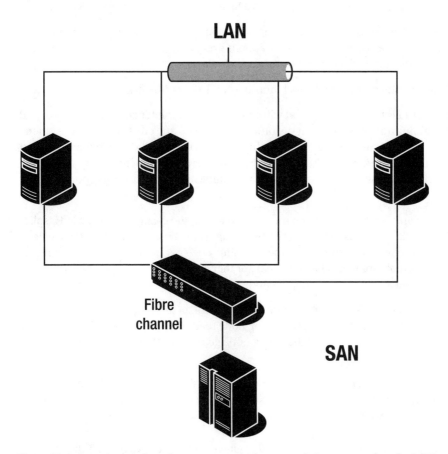

Figure 19-1. *In a clustered environment, each cluster node is connected to the LAN and to the shared storage device.*

The shared storage device is also important for the split brain detector that's used to detect if all nodes in the cluster are still there. This feature is especially important if the cluster consists of more than two nodes. For detection of availability of other nodes, the cluster master node sends heartbeat packages on the LAN. These are multicasts, sent to all slave nodes in the cluster. Normally, the slave node replies to these multicasts with unicast packages to the master node, so that the master node knows the slave node is still there. The administrator of the cluster has configured a tolerance rate. This is the amount of time a node in the cluster waits for heartbeats from other nodes in the cluster before taking action. This action consists of stopping the failed node. If a heartbeat isn't received from a node within the tolerance rate, this other node is considered a failing node. It thus receives a poison pill and stops with an abend.

Apart from the heartbeats on the LAN, each node also periodically writes an epoch number to the Split Brain Detection partition on the SAN. Each time a node leaves or joins the cluster, the epoch number is increased by one. This procedure of heartbeats and epoch numbers allows the cluster to automatically cast out a failed node. The following steps outline how a failing slave node is cast out from the cluster.

1. By default, each node in the cluster sends a heartbeat over the LAN every second.

2. Each node also writes an epoch number to the split brain detection partition on the shared storage device. By default, this happens every four seconds. This epoch number represents the nodes view on the state of the cluster.

3. The master node monitors all epoch numbers and all heartbeats.

4. If one node fails to send a heartbeat within the 8-second tolerance rate, the master and the remaining nodes assume that the other node is dead and create a new cluster membership view. This new cluster membership view does not include the node that failed to send the heartbeat within 8 seconds. Since this new cluster membership view represents a change in the state of the cluster, all remaining nodes increase their epoch number by one.

5. Now there are two different epoch numbers in use on the cluster. This is called a split brain. This situation has to be resolved by voting. There are now two different cluster membership views, and the cluster membership view that has the most votes wins. If the vote is evenly split, the side of the cluster that has the master node wins. In the special case of a two-node cluster, the node that still has LAN connectivity wins.

6. The nodes that win the voting now write a special token to the Split Brain Detection partition on the shared storage. The losing node reads this token and quits by taking a poison pill. This termination of the losing node guarantees that the failing node can't corrupt the new cluster.

7. After casting out the failing node, the resources that were running on that node are migrated to other nodes in the cluster. Normally, the only thing a user using one of these resources will notice is a short interruption of service availability.

Though the preceding procedure explained dealt with a failing slave node, if the master fails, something similar happens. In the new cluster membership view, only slave nodes are present. Each of the slave nodes updates its epoch number by one and since the master node is the only node in the cluster that still has the old epoch number, it loses the vote, eats the poison pill, and dies. The new master node is now selected randomly.

When a node in the cluster fails, the cluster-enabled volumes and resources assigned to that node migrate to other nodes in the cluster. As an administrator, you can design and configure where each of the cluster resources migrate to. This redistribution of clustered resources is known as the fan-out of the resources. This configuration allows you to create some basic load balancing on the cluster.

Installing the Cluster Software

Upon installation of OES, the cluster software is not installed automatically. The following sections explore how to install it on both OES - Linux and OES - NetWare. In these sections, it's assumed that a shared disk system is already present. If needed, in Chapter 11 of this book you can find more information on the setup of iSCSI as a shared disk system. If you want to use iSCSI as the shared disk system, first configure and initiate the iSCSI initiator before installing the NCS software.

Installing NCS on OES - Linux

On OES - Linux, YaST can be used to install NCS after initial installation, as shown in the following steps.

▉**Note** It's possible to select NCS to be installed upon initial server installation, but if you're working with an iSCSI shared device, you can't configure it at that time because you first have to configure the iSCSI device. In such cases, select Configure Later when installing the server. After installation, you can configure NCS from the YaST System tab.

---

1. From the OES - Linux console, start YaST and enter the password of the user root as requested.

2. Select Software ➤ Install And Remove Software. In the filter, select Selections and next, select Novell Cluster Services. Make sure that Novell NSS is selected as well and click Accept to continue. If a message about automatic changes is displayed, click Continue to continue installation of the software.

3. Enter the requested OES CD and click OK to continue.

4. Before you can configure NCS, you must specify where the LDAP server can be found, as shown in Figure 19-2. If on your local server, a replica of eDirectory is present, select Local System. If no replica is present, select Remote System and enter the IP address of this server. In both cases, enter the typefully distinguished admin name and password and click Next.

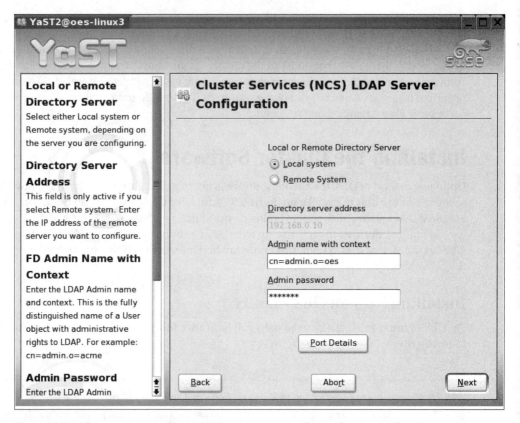

Figure 19-2. *Before you can configure NCS, you must specify on what server the eDirectory information can be found.*

5. Select New Cluster to configure a new cluster, as shown in Figure 19-3. Now, enter the name you want to give to your cluster and enter a unique IP address for use by the cluster. Enter the name of the external device where you want to create the SBD partition as well. The installer says it's optional to specify the name of the external device, but you do need a Split Brain Detector (SBD) partition somewhere on the network, and for that reason you need this optional device. If necessary, start the YaST partitioner tool to look up the name of the external device. If you're using an iSCSI device and the initiator is already configured (this is required), the iSCSI device will be accessible as a local SCSI device, like /dev/sdb. This does make sense, because iSCSI is a native SCSI protocol and your server can't differentiate between directly attached SCSI and SCSI that's somewhere on the network. Click Next when finished.

6. Confirm the name of the node where you're currently installing NCS and click Next. The initial configuration is written to your server now. Start the same procedure on the next node you want to add to the cluster, but instead of choosing to configure a new cluster, specify that you want to configure an existing cluster there and enter the typeful distinguished name of the cluster. This also adds any other nodes to the cluster.

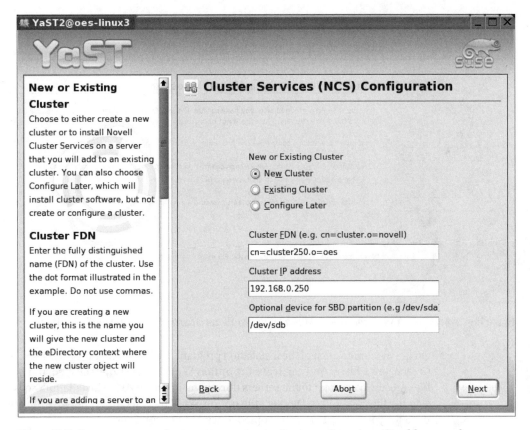

Figure 19-3. *To create a new cluster, you must enter its name, its unique IP address, and the name of the device where you want to create the SBD partition.*

7. The cluster software is now installed, but it isn't activated automatically. Use **/etc/init.d/novell-ncs** on all nodes to join the cluster. You'll see a message after the node has successfully joined the cluster. If you want to start the cluster automatically when your server boots, use **chkconfig novell-ncs 35** to add it to your runlevel configuration.

Installing NCS on OES - NetWare

To install cluster services on OES - NetWare, you need the Novell Deployment Manager, nwdeploy. You can find this utility on your OES - NetWare installation CD. This utility has to be started from a Windows workstation, which needs to have an authenticated client connection to the tree where you want to install the cluster software.

1. On the Windows workstation, insert your OES - NetWare installation CD. The Novell Deployment Manager starts automatically.

2. From the bar on the left of the screen, select Post-Install Tasks ➤ Install/Upgrade Cluster. Read the text displayed and click Install Or Upgrade A Cluster, as shown in Figure 19-4. This starts the Java tool that helps you install NCD on OES - NetWare.

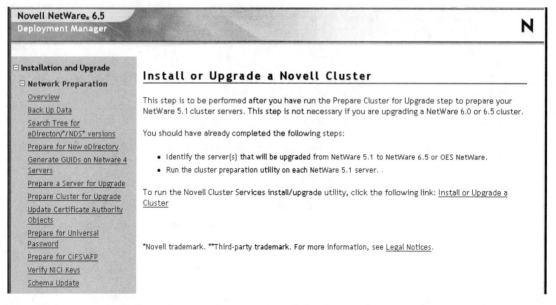

Figure 19-4. *You need Novell Deployment Manager to install the cluster software on OES - NetWare.*

3. On the welcome screen of the installation program, click Next. On the next screen, select Create New Cluster. You can leave the option Skip The File Copy selected; the needed files are always copied to the servers during the initial NetWare installation, so you can skip the file copy safely. Deselect the option Skip The File Copy, otherwise the files you need for your cluster won't be copied. Click Next to continue.

4. Enter a name for the cluster object and select the Directory tree and context where you want to create the cluster object (see Figure 19-5). Click Next to continue.

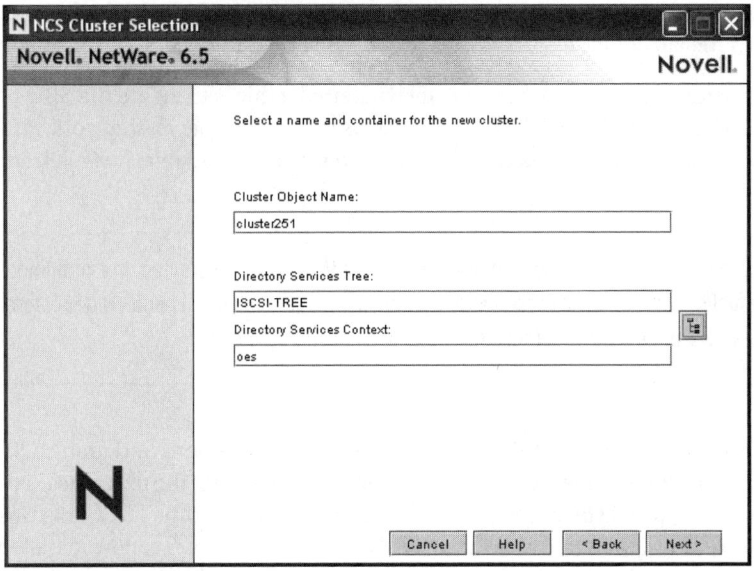

Figure 19-5. *To create the cluster, enter its name and eDirectory context.*

5. Now, select all OES - NetWare servers that will participate in the cluster and click Next to continue (see Figure 19-6). With the Novell Deployment Manager tool, you just need to configure the cluster once, and all servers in your network are automatically provided with the software they need.

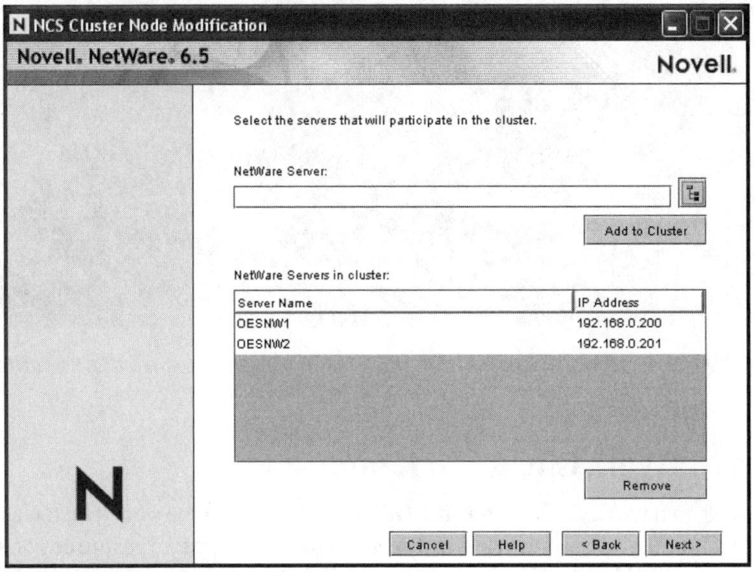

Figure 19-6. *Add all the servers you want to the cluster.*

6. Enter an IP address for the cluster. Be sure it's a unique IP address that exists in the same subnet as the cluster nodes.

7. If your cluster has shared media, specify what media this is to create the SBD partition and then click Next. If the shared media allows it, you can specify that you want to mirror the cluster partition as well. If no shared media is available, just click Next.

▪**Note** If no shared media is present, no split brain detector partition can be created. In a multimode cluster this can be problematic, if, however, you're clustering a resource that doesn't depend on data stored locally on some partition, a two-node cluster suffices perfectly without shared media.

---

8. Select Yes to automatically start the cluster on each of its servers, and then click Next to continue. The files will now be copied to the cluster nodes. After the file copies, a message appears asking you if you're interested in poring over the readme file. Click Close to close this window, or read the readme file. Your cluster software is now installed and should automatically be started on both servers, as you can see in Figure 19-7.

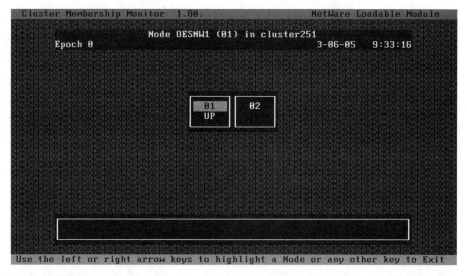

Figure 19-7. *After a successful installation, the cluster software is started automatically on all nodes.*

Migrating a NetWare Cluster to Linux

It's perfectly possible to have OES - NetWare and OES - Linux nodes in the same cluster, although the administrator should be aware that the scripts used to load clustered resources on OES - NetWare must be modified before they can run on OES - Linux. This functionality helps you migrate NetWare cluster servers to OES - Linux. One of the major challenges is the configuration of the load scripts used to load cluster resources: a NetWare load script uses other commands than an OES - Linux load script. In fact, it's rather easy to migrate a NetWare cluster node to

Linux: just bring down the NetWare server, which automatically migrates all cluster resources to other nodes in the cluster, and install the OES - Linux server that is going to replace the NetWare node in the cluster. Once this OES - Linux server is installed, it's automatically available as a cluster node; however, if it's hosting resources that were formerly running on NetWare, the load scripts of these resources are in the wrong syntax. After you have converted all nodes in the former NetWare cluster to OES - Linux, you must finalize the conversion with the **cluster convert** command on one of the Linux nodes. Enter the command **cluster convert commit** to convert all NetWare-based load scripts to the proper Linux syntax. You can read more details about this procedure in the OES documentation at www.novell.com/documentation/oes.

Setting Up Novell Cluster Services

Now that all the preliminary work has been done, you can start setting up the cluster services. In most scenarios, you'll set up both clustered volumes on the shared storage device as clustered resources, but it's not absolutely necessary to always work with shared storage. If for example you're running a service like DNS that doesn't need to write any data to disk, or works with data replicated in eDirectory, you can do perfectly without. Although not common, you can even do without an SBD partition on a shared storage device. In most scenarios, however, you'll find yourself setting up shared storage as well as clustered resources.

Creating Shared Disk Partitions and Pools

If you set up your shared storage device before installing the NCS software, you're now ready to create some shared partitions. If your cluster consists of only OES - Linux nodes, you can use your Linux partitioner to create any kind of file system on the shared storage device you like—for instance, it's perfectly possible to set up a shared storage device with ext3, ext2, or Reiser. If, however, you're working in a mixed environment where both OES - Linux and OES - NetWare are used, you're required to use NSS for your shared storage device.

Creating Cluster-Enabled NSS Volumes

To create a cluster-enabled NSS volume, use the tools you normally do to create an NSS volume. It's possible to use iManager, but you can enter **nssmu** from the Linux console as well. The following procedure shows you how to create a cluster-enabled NSS volume with **nssmu**.

Caution You can only create cluster shared volumes if the cluster software has been installed and the initial configuration has been done. If you haven't performed the basic configuration of the cluster so far, do it before you continue.

---

1. On the server that you want to assign the shared volume to, open a console and enter the command **nssmu** to start the NSS Management Utility.

2. From the main menu, select **Devices** and press **Enter**. Select the device where you want to create the cluster-enabled NSS volume, as shown in Figure 19-8, and press F6 to make this device sharable for clustering.

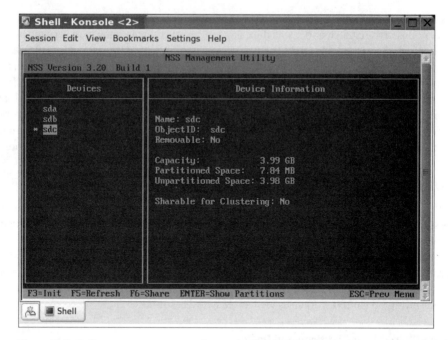

Figure 19-8. *Before you can create a cluster-enabled NSS volume, you must mark the device where you want to create it as sharable for clustering.*

■**Caution** You have now marked a device as sharable for clustering. Be aware that the device isn't locked for other servers that aren't part of your clustering configuration. Never attach a non-clustered server to a shared device because it can destroy everything on the device. In fact, since NetWare 6.5, NSS uses Pool Multiple Server Activation Prevention to avert these kinds of mistakes. It's still good practice though to prevent errors and to not attach non-cluster nodes to shared storage devices.

---

3. Press Escape to return to the NSS Management Utility main screen, and from there select Pools. Press Insert to add a new pool and enter its new name. Next, browse to the shared storage device to specify where the new pool should be created (see Figure 19-9).

4. Enter the size you want to use for the shared pool and press Enter to continue. Make sure both the options Activate On Creation and Cluster Enable On Creation are set. Specify other parameters for the shared pool as well: you need to at least specify its Virtual Server Name (this is the name of the virtual cluster server object in eDirectory that was created when clustering was installed) and the IP address of the pool. Be aware that in a clustered environment, each pool needs its own IP address. You can select all advertising protocols you want enabled. NCP is selected by default, but if needed, select CIFS and AFP as well. After that, choose Create to create the new pool.

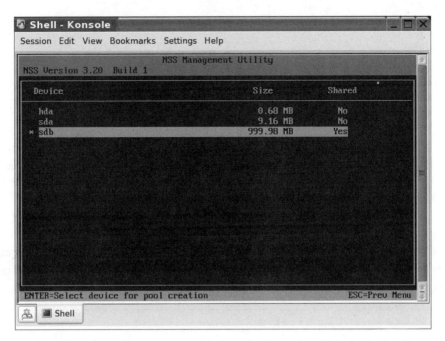

Figure 19-9. *Select the shared storage device to create a pool used for clustering volumes.*

5. After you've created the cluster-enabled pool, you can generate NSS volumes in it. The procedure to create NSS volumes in a clustered pool is exactly of the same as creating normal NSS volumes except for one small difference: after creating the volume, you must cluster-enable it. You can do this from the volumes properties.

■**Note** If you're connecting to an iSCSI target that already has NSS partitions and pools created on it, you may not be able to access them until you reboot the Linux initiator server. Alternatively, you can run the **evms_activate** command at the Linux server console. This is required for each Linux initiator server that will access the iSCSI target.

Creating Cluster Resources

The purpose of a cluster is to make a resource always available. To make this happen, cluster resources have to be created. One cluster resource is needed for every resource or application you run on servers in the cluster. Virtually all applications can be configured as a cluster resource, the only thing you must do is configure the right cluster resource load script. Creating cluster resource load scripts is beyond the scope of this book, so I'll explain how to configure clustered resources by using the templates provided with OES. Currently, the following templates are provided:

- DHCP

- iPrint

- iFolder

- Samba

- Generic IP SERVICE

These templates can be modified to create cluster resources for applications running on your cluster. The commands in the load scripts are very similar to the commands you can use in the Linux bash shell environment or on the OES - NetWare console. By using these load scripts, you tell the resource exactly how to initialize on your OES server.

■Note Not just services are configured as a cluster resource. If you want to allow a volume to migrate to another node in the cluster when there is a failure, you must make a cluster resource object for that node as well.

The following procedure outlines how to create a cluster resource for the monitor application. This may not be the most realistic application to cluster, but it shows very clearly how an existing template can be modified for use with a new clustered object. Consult the online documentation for information about other cluster objects and the load commands used to create them.

1. Start iManager and authenticate as the admin user.

2. From the panel on the left, select Clusters ➤ Cluster Options. Use the magnifying glass to select the cluster you want to view options for. You'll now see a list of all objects that currently exist in the cluster (see Figure 19-10).

3. Click New and next select the type of resource you want to create. To make a resource for the OES - NetWare MONITOR application, select Resource and click Next to continue.

4. Provide a name for the resource and use the magnifying glass to select an application that the clustered application can inherit from. Since MONITOR.NLM has the same load behavior as the OES - NetWare DHCP server DHCPSRVR.NLM, choose the DHCP Server template to inherit settings from. Make sure the Define Additional Properties option and the Online Resource After Create option are selected and then click Next to continue.

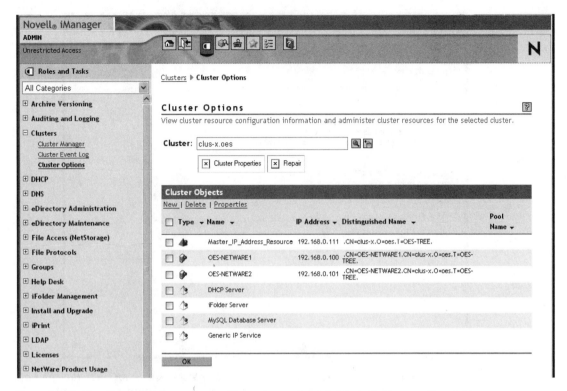

Figure 19-10. *The Cluster Options screen offers an overview of objects that currently exist in the cluster.*

5. On the next screen is the script associated with the template you chose to inherit from. Edit this script to load the MONITOR.NLM service properly, as shown in Figure 19-11. Since MONITOR.NLM is very basic, you don't have to do anything complicated: just enter the name of the module to load. All other lines are preceded by a comment mark and are not interpreted, you don't need them to load a simple application like monitor. While modifying the load script, you must specify a timeout value as well. This value specifies how long the script may take to load completely. The default setting is ten minutes. If the resource can't be loaded in these ten minutes, it becomes comatose. A state of comatose indicates that the cluster resource could not be loaded in a reasonable amount of time and is therefore not available. Modify this parameter as needed and then click Next to continue.

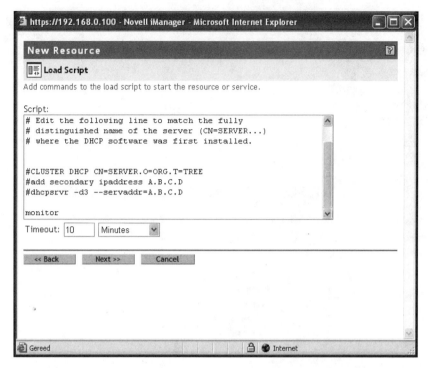

Figure 19-11. *It's very easy to create a script for a simple service like MONITOR.NLM, but for more complex services the load scripts can become quite complex.*

6. Now create the unload script. In this script, you'll specify everything that has to happen when the resource terminates. In this particular case, the unload script can be very simple: just include the line unload monitor to properly unload the monitor application. Not every resource needs an unload script, but if your resource has used a secondary IP address, for example, you should use the **unload** script to remove this secondary IP address after the resource has been terminated. Click Next to continue.

7. Next, specify how the resource must be started, and what should happen if a node in the cluster fails (see Figure 19-12). First, choose whether or not the resource should be automatically started when the cluster comes up. If you don't want that, at Start Mode select the radio button Manual. Next, you must decide how the failover mode and the failback mode should work. In most scenarios, it's preferred to set Failover Mode to Auto. This automatically starts a resource on the next node assigned to the resource in case of a failure. If you select Manual, you'll have to intervene manually when a cluster node goes down. Then there is the Failback Mode as well. This can be set as Auto, Disable, and Manual. By default, Disable is selected. This means that nothing happens if the failed node comes back, and in most cases this is a good setting: normally an administrator likes to know why a node has failed before a resource is failed back to it. Select Manual if you want an administrator to decide manually what happens when the failed node comes back, and then select Auto if you want a resource to fail back to the failed node automatically when it comes back.

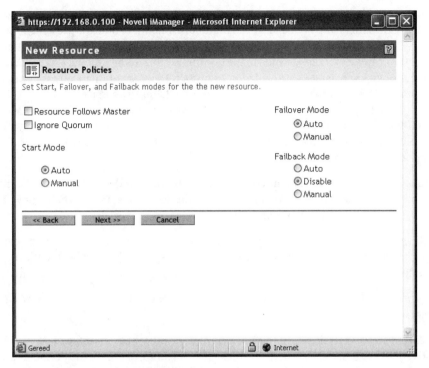

Figure 19-12. *For each node in the cluster, you can define how it should be started by modifying the parameter Start Mode, and what should happen when a node in the cluster fails or comes back by modifying the failover mode and the failback mode.*

8. On this screen, you have two more options: select Resource Follows Master if you want the resource to always run on the master node. If you want a resource to be activated immediately when a resource comes online without waiting for the timeout defined in the quorum, select Ignore Quorum as well. Click Next to continue.

9. In the last step, you must assign nodes to the resource. A minimum of two nodes should always be assigned. The resource runs automatically on the first node in the list. Click Finish after you have assigned all the nodes you want to assign. The resource is then created and brought online automatically.

Tip Want to make sure it all works? Take out the network cable from the node where at least one clustered resource is active. If everything is configured the way it should be, the resource must be started automatically on the next node that's assigned.

Tuning the Cluster Environment

You've learned how to install a cluster resource—a very important step to master—but that's just the beginning. Equally important is editing the configuration settings of the cluster itself. First, there are the timeout and quorum settings. The quorum specifies the minimum amount of nodes that should be running in the cluster before resources start loading. The quorum is specified in the membership field. Before the minimum amount of nodes is present, no services will run in the cluster. Next is the timeout value. This parameter specifies the amount of time to wait for the number of nodes defined in the quorum setting. If the timeout expires before the quorum membership reaches its specified minimum, resources automatically start on the nodes that are present anyway. This is to assure the availability of services.

The next set of general properties are the cluster protocol properties. Here, you specify the transmit frequency and tolerance settings for all nodes in the cluster. You can modify these settings, but they become effective only after you've restarted all nodes in the cluster. The following settings are available.

- *Heartbeat*: Specifies the amount of time in seconds that nodes which aren't the master should send a heartbeat packet to all other nodes in the cluster to let them know they're still alive. The default value is one second.

- *Tolerance*: The amount of time the master node gives all other nodes to send heartbeat packages. The default value is 4. If a slave node fails to send a heartbeat to the master node within the specified tolerance period, it is cast off the cluster automatically.

- *Master Watchdog*: Specifies how often the master node of the cluster should transmit a signal indicating that it's still alive.

- *Slave Watchdog*: Indicates how often a slave node must hear from the master node that it's still alive. If the master node hasn't sent a watchdog packet in the period indicated here, it is cast off from the cluster automatically.

Through the following steps, you can use iManager to configure these settings.

1. From iManager, select Clusters ➤ Cluster Options.

2. Use the magnifying glass to select your cluster object in eDirectory. Next, click Cluster Properties to modify its properties, as shown in Figure 19-13.

3. On the General tab under Quorum Triggers, select the cluster timeout and the number of nodes installed in the cluster. On this tab, you can specify notification as well: select Enable Cluster Notification Events and specify the mail address of the cluster administrator. This way, alerts are sent by e-mail in case of a critical event. If you prefer to know about everything that happens on the cluster, select Verbose Messages to specify that all kinds of information should be sent by e-mail. Be aware, however, that in this case, the flow of information can be quite overwhelming.

4. Normally, you specify the cluster IP address when you install the first node in the cluster. If you need to, this address can later be changed on the General tab of the Cluster Properties. You can also change its default port assignment.

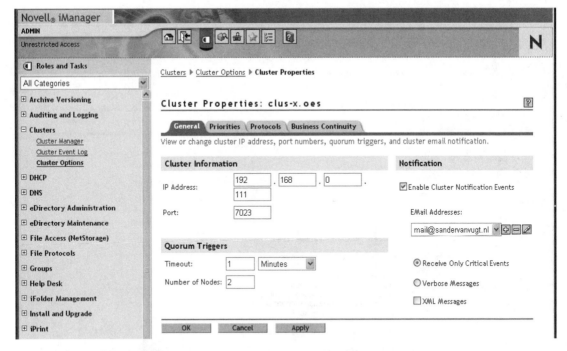

Figure 19-13. *In the cluster options, you can specify the quorum triggers and the minimum amount of nodes required in the cluster.*

5. On the Priorities tab, you can specify cluster resource priorities. If more resources are configured in the cluster, here you can make sure the most important resource is listed first, making it the first resource loaded when the cluster comes up.

6. The last important tab is the Protocols tab, shown in Figure 19-14. Here, you can specify the heartbeat, tolerance, master watchdog, and slave watchdog settings. The maximum number of retransmits can also be set to specify how often a packet should be re-sent if there's an error on the network that prevents it from reaching its destination. All these settings are then automatically applied through the cluster protocol parameters script (also shown on the tab).

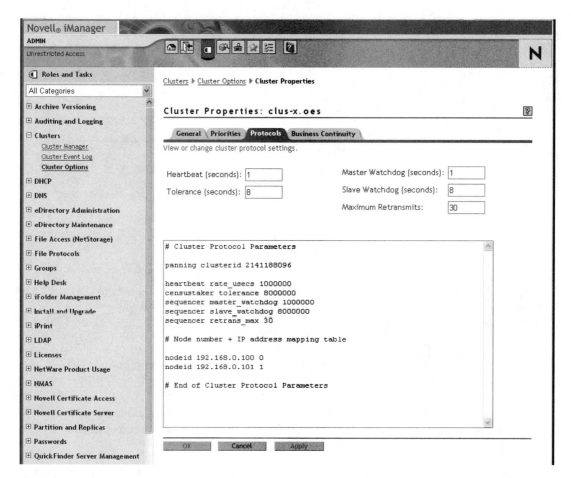

Figure 19-14. *On the Protocols tab, you can specify how often the nodes in the cluster should send packets to each other to verify they're still alive.*

7. The Business Continuity tab has an advanced clustering feature that's available as a separate purchase and thus isn't installed on OES by default. Novell Business Continuity Cluster software creates a cluster of clusters, allowing for the highest possible fault tolerance. This product, which is relatively new, is mostly used for a cluster of clusters on two different locations. For more information, check out the products page at www.novell.com.

There are still some other general settings related to the cluster that you might want to change occasionally, such as the cluster node settings. If you change the IP address of a server that's a node in the cluster, this change won't be applied automatically to the cluster node object. You must modify it manually instead through the following steps.

1. In iManager, select Cluster ➤ Cluster Options.

2. In the list of cluster objects, check the box next to the node whose properties you want to modify, and then click the Properties link.

3. You can now edit the node's IP address (see Figure 19-15). Click OK to save and apply your changes to eDirectory.

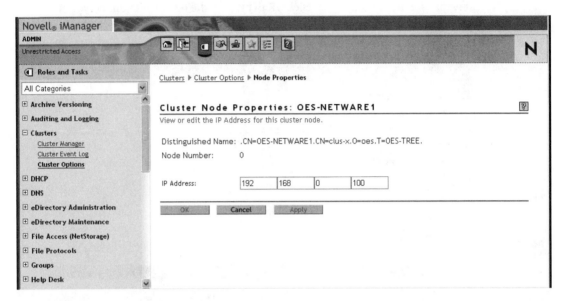

Figure 19-15. *If you change the IP address on the server, you must apply the change to the cluster node as well.*

Managing Novell Clustering Services

You now know how to install and configure the NCS Cluster—fantastic! Now that you have some clustered resources active in the cluster, they need to be managed. Cluster management basically consists of migrating resources from one node to another, migrating them back to their primary node if it comes back after a failure, and monitoring cluster and resource states.

Migrating Resources

If one of the nodes in the cluster is failing, resources are migrated automatically to other nodes in the cluster. Occasionally, you might want to migrate resources manually. This could be used for manual load balancing, or to prepare a server before bringing it down for scheduled maintenance. Migrating resources in a cluster is easy and straightforward, as shown in the following steps.

1. In iManager, select Clusters ➤ Cluster Manager.

2. Enter the name of the cluster you want to manage. A list of all clustered resources is then displayed, as shown in Figure 19-16.

3. Click the box next to the resource you want to migrate and click the Migrate link.

4. A list appears showing all the servers to where you can migrate the resource. Select a server from this list, and then click OK to migrate the resource to this server.

Figure 19-16. *From the Cluster Manager page, it's easy to migrate resources from one node to another.*

Monitoring Cluster and Resource States

Since a clustered environment is a dynamic environment where servers come up and go down occasionally, the state of resources in the cluster changes from time to time. Normally, all resources exist in the Running state. This is typical and so no action is required. There are, however, other states in which you may find a resource, as shown in Table 19-1.

Table 19-1. *Cluster Resource States*

Resource State	Description
Alert	The resource is waiting to start, fail over, or fail back. This can't happen automatically since the administrator has specified it to start, failover, or failback manually. Click the alert status indicator to find out what's wrong. You'll automatically be prompted to take the appropriate action.
Comatose	The resource is not running properly and requires intervention. To resolve this state, click the comatose state indicator and bring the resource offline. Resolve the problems and then bring it back online again.
Loading	The resource is in the process of loading on the server. This state should automatically change to Running.
NDS_Sync	Changes to the resource are synchronized to eDirectory. This state should change automatically to Running.
Offline	The resource is currently not available. This may have a very plausible reason—for instance, the administrator may have recently shut down the resource. Click the offline state indicator and take the proper action.
Quorum Wait	The resource is waiting for the minimum amount of nodes in the quorum before it can begin loading. This state should automatically change to running after the quorum has been established.
Running	The resource is in the running state, everything is perfect, and the sun is shining.
Unassigned	The cluster is assigned to nodes that currently aren't available in the cluster. Assign the resource to some other nodes as well, or wait until at least one of its assigned nodes comes back.
Unloading	The resource is currently unloading from the server it was running on.

The Cluster Manager main screen also contains important information about the state of all nodes in the cluster. Each node has a symbol with a certain color attached to it (listed next), indicating its current state.

- *Yellow*: The node is the master server in the cluster and is performing well.

- *Green*: The node is a slave node and is performing well.

- *Red with a break in the icon*: The node has failed.

- *Red*: The node is waiting for administrator intervention.

- *Gray*: The node is currently not a member of the cluster or its state is unknown.

- *Blank*: The node is unassigned, offline, changing states, or is in the process of loading or unloading.

Cluster Console Commands

The main part of NCS management is performed from iManager. There are other ways to manage NCS from the server console. To execute a cluster console command, enter **cluster** followed by the command. You can also use **cluster help** to get an overview of all cluster console commands available. Table 19-2 offers an overview of the most important cluster console commands.

Table 19-2. *NCS Console Commands*

Command	Description
alert {resource} {yes|no}	The resource is waiting for manual start, failover, or failback. Specify the name of the resource and the argument yes or no to indicate whether this action can be taken or not.
convert {preview,commit} {resource}	This command can only be used on OES - Linux nodes and is employed to finalize the conversion of cluster scripts written for OES - NetWare. For a preview of the work to do, enter **cluster convert preview resourcename**; to convert all scripts to the proper Linux syntax, use **cluster convert commit**.
down	Removes all nodes from the cluster, which effectively brings the cluster down.
info	Can be used to display information about the cluster. This command can work with many options: **all** displays as much information as possible, **basic** displays IP address, port, and quorum settings, **notification** shows e-mail notification settings, **priority** displays the resource priority list, **protocol** displays the cluster protocol settings, and **summary** shows the cluster protocol summary. Use, for example, **cluster info all** to display all information about the cluster.
join	Adds a node to the cluster. You can only do this on a node that already has the NCS software installed.
leave	Removes the node from the cluster.
maintenance {on|off}	Temporarily suspends the heartbeat. This is useful if you want to switch off or reset the LAN switch without bringing down all nodes in the cluster.
migrate {resource} {node name}	Migrates a resource from one node to another.

Table 19-2. *NCS Console Commands (Continued)*

Command	Description
offline {resource}	Unloads the resource from the node where it's currently active.
online {resource} {node name}	Starts the resource. If you don't specify the node name, it starts on its most preferred node; otherwise, specify a node name where to start the resource.
pools	Displays a list of NSS pools on the shared disk system that are accessible by Novell Cluster Services.
resource	Lists all resources that currently exist in the cluster.
restart {seconds}	Restarts NCS on all nodes in the cluster.
set {parameter} {value}	Can be used to set generic cluster protocol settings. The available parameters are ipaddress, port, quorumwait, quorum, heartbeat, tolerance, masterwatchdog, slavewatchdog, maxretransmits, enableemail, emailaddresses, and email-options. These are exactly the same parameters as those that can be set from the iManager interface. A description of these parameters was given earlier in this chapter.
stats {display, clear}	Reports the node number, node name, and heart beat information.
status {resource}	Reports the status of the specified resource.
view	Displays the node name, cluster epoch number, master node name, and a list of all nodes that are currently members of the cluster.

Displaying Cluster Reports and Event Logs

The NCS software also comes with options for viewing what has happened on the cluster. First, there's the possibility of running a report from the cluster interface. Next is an event log that displays all events that have occurred in the cluster. You can access the report from iManager by performing the following steps.

1. In iManager, select Clusters ➤ Cluster Manager.

2. Browse to the cluster you want to manage and click Run Report. A report of the current cluster state is displayed immediately, as shown in Figure 19-17. This report also includes all load scripts used by the resources in your cluster, and is an excellent way to produce cluster documentation.

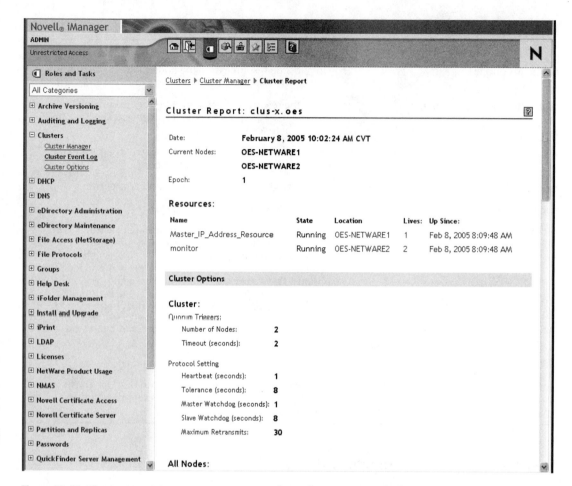

Figure 19-17. *The report option generates a report about the current state of the cluster.*

Next, there is the cluster event log, which displays a list of all events that have occurred in your cluster environment. You can access this list from iManager by choosing Clusters ➤ Cluster Event Log. The list can be rather extensive; therefore, it's best to work with filters, which allow you to display only events of a certain severity that have occurred on certain cluster nodes, and with certain cluster resources. You can also specify a start date and time in the event log filter. To create a filter, click the Filter button from the cluster event log overview and a screen like that in Figure 19-18 appears.

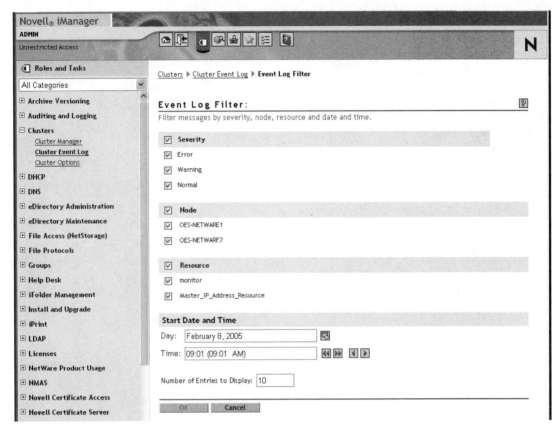

Figure 19-18. *The event log filter allows you to filter only the information you really need.*

Summary

In this chapter, you learned how to install and configure a cluster on OES - NetWare and OES - Linux. Based upon the information provided in this chapter, you're now able to configure NSS pools as cluster resources and to create cluster resources for applications running on your network. There are, however, a lot of possibilities to make complex applications run on the cluster. These options have not been covered in this chapter. Consult the online documentation at www.novell.com/documentation/oes to find out more about these possibilities.

CHAPTER 20

■■■

Using OpenWBEM for Server Health Monitoring

For a very long time, the Simple Network Management Protocol (SNMP) has been the default for managing and monitoring the diverse components of a network. In Open Enterprise Server, however, SNMP is replaced by an entirely new infrastructure based upon CIMOM and OpenWBEM. The first service that runs on top of this infrastructure is Server Health Monitoring, which can be accessed from iManager. This chapter explores how both OpenWBEM and CIMOM can be used to make monitoring of server health possible, and how the Server Health Monitoring utility takes advantage of this infrastructure.

A New Management Infrastructure

In Open Enterprise Server, Novell has implemented the new standard of Web-Based Enterprise Management (WBEM), proposed by the Distributed Management Task Force. The goal of this task force is to simplify management of disparate systems in a network. One component that relies heavily on these standards is Server Health Monitoring, which is discussed in this chapter.

The OpenWBEM standard consists of different mechanisms which together allow for easier management of any system in a network.

- WBEM is a set of standard technologies that are developed to unify management of computing systems. In these technologies, three components stand out: the data model, which is the Common Information Model (CIM) standard, CIM-XML, which is used as an encoding mechanism, and CIM over HTTP, which is used as a transport mechanism.

- The CIM is used to communicate information between different parts of a management infrastructure. In this infrastructure, agents, which are written for network devices, and managers (which manage these devices) work together to communicate information. The format of the data communicated by CIM is defined by the CIM schema.

- The CIM Object Manager (CIMOM) is an application that's used to manage objects according to the CIM standard. In OES, for example, this application is integrated into the iManager environment.

Managing OpenWBEM in OES

In most cases, OpenWBEM is installed and works fine, but in some scenarios it may be have to manage various OpenWBEM components. This is discussed in following pages.

Installing OpenWBEM

Installation of OpenWBEM is a non-issue on OES - Linux and OES - NetWare since it's installed by default. Only if NetWare 6.5 SP 3 is used is a separate installation of OpenWBEM is necessary. To install OpenWBEM, perform the following steps.

1. Insert the NetWare 6.5 Products CD into the CD drive.

2. Locate the cimom.zip file in the directory NW65PROD:\Products\OpenWBEM and unzip it to the root of the SYS: volume of your server.

3. Generate a certificate that can be used by OpenWBEM. To do this, as an administrator, you need to enter the command **/system/cimom/etc/openwbem/owgencert** from a Bash console shell; the bash shell can be started with the **bash** command.

4. From the NetWare console prompt, enter the command **openwbem** to call the openwbem.ncf configuration file.

5. Include openwbem.ncf in the autoexec.ncf of your server to ensure it starts automatically when your server reboots.

Starting and Stopping OpenWBEM

The OpenWBEM and CIMOM functionality are implemented on both OES - Linux and OES - NetWare. As an administrator, occasionally you may need to restart them. On OES - Linux, use the **owcimomd** script that's installed in the directory /etc/init.d. An easy way to start or stop it is by using the **rcowcimomd** command. This command listens to the arguments **start**, **stop**, and **status** to start it, stop it, or display its status. To start OpenWBEM on OES - NetWare, call **openwbem.ncf**. To unload it, use the command **unload owcimomd**.

Managing the OpenWBEM Configuration

If you need to tune the OpenWBEM CIMOM configuration on either OES - NetWare or OES - Linux, you can modify the openwbem.conf configuration file. On OES - NetWare, you can find this file as sys:\system\cimom\etc\openwbem\openwbem.conf; on OES - Linux, it's stored as /etc/openwbem/openwbem.conf. Some elements of the OpenWBEM configuration can be changed from this file, as described in the following bullet points.

- *Authentication configuration*: Use this option to specify how users should authenticate to the CIMOM configuration. By default, on OES - Linux local users authenticate to CIMOM with their local credentials using PAM. On OES - NetWare, local authentication is enabled by default.

- *Certificate configuration*: After installation, OpenWBEM has a self-signed certificate generated for it. If desired, you can replace the path for the default certificate with a path to a commercial certificate that you've purchased. This is done by changing the `http_server.SSL_cert` parameter.

- *Port configuration*: By default, OpenWBEM listens on the secure port 5989. The unsecure port 5988 is available as well, but disabled by default. It's strongly recommended not to use the unsecure port since all communications between CIMOM and client applications will be open for review by anyone who captures the data. It's only recommended to use the unsecure port for debugging purposes. To change the ports where OpenWBEM is listening, the parameters `http_server.http_port` and `http_server.https_port` can be changed. To disable a port, give the option `-1` to any of these parameters—for example, the unsecure port can be disabled by default with the parameter `http_server.http_port = -1`.

- *Logging configuration*: The owcimomd.conf file offers advanced options to configure where and how much logging occurs, what type of errors are logged, and the log size, filename, and format. For a complete list of these, consult the documentation at http://www.novell.com/documentation/oes.

- *Debug logging configuration*: In addition to the normal logging configuration, additional debug logging configuration can be specified as well. For instance, the options used to configure debug logging can be configured to use different colors for different kinds of log messages. For a complete overview of the available options, consult the documentation at http://www.novell.com/documentation/oes.

- *Additional logs*: If the default logging configuration is still not enough, additional logs can also be created so that specific types of information are logged in a certain way. More information about these additional logs can be found in the documentation at http://www.novell.com/documentation/oes.

To modify the configuration file, I recommend you read it thoroughly: there are lots of comments explaining what happens in the file (as shown in Figure 20-1). Be aware, however, that in most situations, the default values work perfectly well, and you almost never need to change these settings if you just want to get Health Monitoring Services running.

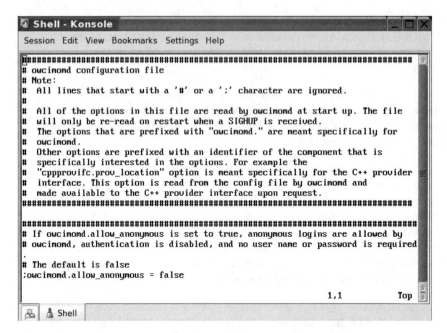

Figure 20-1. *The configuration file for OpenWBEM is well documented. In most cases, you never need to change its settings.*

Health Monitoring

One of the most important services in OES that uses OpenWBEM to communicate with devices in the network is Health Monitoring Services. It instantly reveals the status of a monitored network server.

This section explains how to work with Health Monitoring Services.

Types of Monitoring

Health Monitoring Services offers two monitoring types: Robust Health Monitoring and the Simple Server Status. In robust health monitoring, several server parameters can be managed, including the following:

- Memory usage

- Type of operating system

- Processes and threads

- Network

- CPU utilization

Robust Health Monitoring is only available when the owcimomd module is running on the server you want to monitor. By default, this module is started as a part of the OpenWBEM architecture on both versions of OES. You must be authenticated to the server you wish to monitor in order to see its health status, or if you want to modify settings on the server.

The second option is Simple Server Status Monitoring. With this option, the monitoring utility checks whether the server is up and running, based upon a connection attempt on a number of standard ports. If a server can be reached on any of these ports, the server is considered to be up. In the current release, these ports are hard-coded and cannot be modified. The way these ports are used by the Server Health Monitoring utility is covered in the section "Server Health Monitoring" later in this chapter. The following ports are monitored:

- 7 (Echo)
- 13 (Time)
- 20 (FTP)
- 22 (SSH)
- 23 (Telnet)
- 80 (HTTP)
- 135 (DCE endpoint resolution)
- 443 (Secure HTTP)
- 445 (Microsoft Directory Services)
- 524 (NCP, eDirectory)

In order to perform simple monitoring, you should take care that no firewall is currently blocking these ports.

Setting Up Servers for Health Monitoring

Before Health Monitoring can be used, you must set it up. This setup assumes that a number of eDirectory objects are created and that you specify a location in eDirectory where the monitoring list can be stored. This monitoring list is (just as it sounds) a list of servers that are monitored. To set up Health Monitoring, apply the steps in the following procedure.

1. From your browser, access iManager at http://*yourserver*/nps and log in as an admin user. Next, select Servers ➤ Monitor Servers. This displays an empty list of servers, as shown in Figure 20-2.

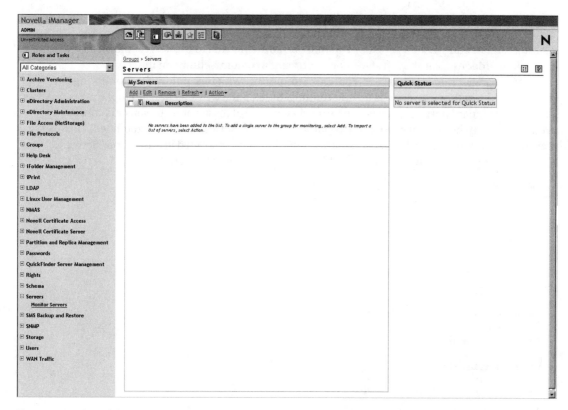

Figure 20-2. *If Health Monitoring has not been set up yet, all you'll see is an empty list of servers.*

2. To add a single server to the monitoring group, click Add. If you've already defined a list of servers that you want to import, select Action and then click Import Server List.

3. Click Add to add a server. Specify a name for the server you want to monitor. This doesn't have to be a real name; any name that's descriptive is good enough. Next, specify the server's IP address or DNS name. Optionally, you can enter a description as well. Next, select the monitoring type you want to use. If OpenWBEM is active on the server, select Robust Health, if OpenWBEM is not active, select Simple Server Status. Next, click OK to add the server to the monitoring list. If necessary, repeat this procedure to add more servers to the list. When finished, you'll see a list of servers with a status indicator for each of these services (see Figure 20-3). This list is refreshed periodically to monitor a change of status.

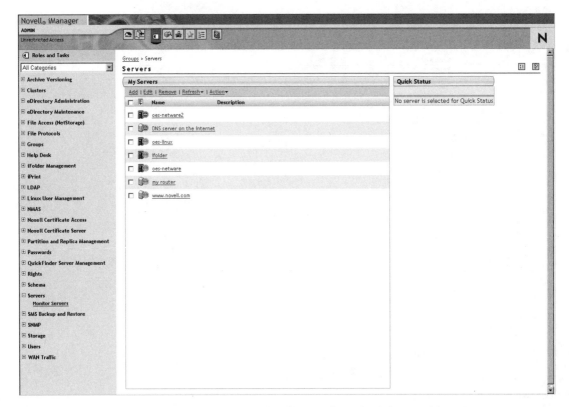

Figure 20-3. *All monitored servers in the list are polled frequently to check for any change in status.*

■**Tip** To make it easier for you to use the same list of servers from another configuration, export the server list. To do this, select Action ➤ Export Server List. Next, enter the name of a Comma Separated Value file where you want to store the list of servers. From the Action menu, you can import this list of servers very easily if you're working on another management interface.

In a small to medium network, it's no problem if all the servers are displayed in the same list. In a large network where hundreds of servers are used, this isn't a very practical situation, however. Therefore, you can create groups of servers, which makes the monitoring of servers in a specific category easier. To do so, perform the following steps:

1. From the Servers screen (where you can add individual servers to the list), click Action and then select Manage Groups. As shown in Figure 20-4, just one group does exist by default and all servers are members of it.

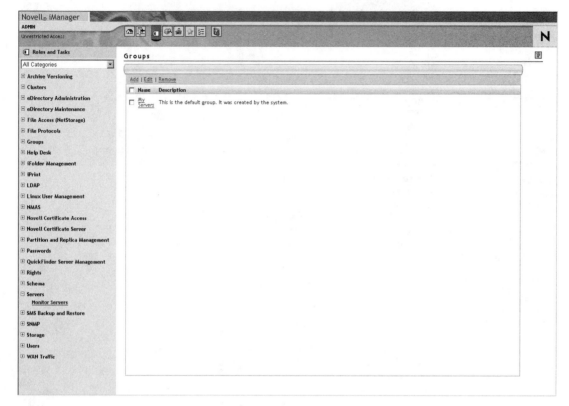

Figure 20-4. *By default, just one group of servers exists.*

2. Click Add and enter the name of the group and a description for it.

3. Click the name of the new group. This brings you to the Servers screen again. From this screen, you can add servers to the group by applying the steps in the previous walkthrough.

Tip If you need to add a large list of servers, you can do so from a CSV-file. In this file, four columns are defined: Name, IP address or DNS name, Description, and Port. For the port number, use port 5989 if you want to do robust server monitoring. Otherwise, enter the port you want to monitor. The beginning of such a file could look like the following:

- server1,192.168.0.1,My Router,5989

- server2,192.168.0.2,My backup router,5989

After creating this CSV file, import it to the list of monitored servers by selecting Import Server List from the Action menu.

Monitoring Server Health

From the list of servers, you can monitor the health of all servers in different ways. For instance, at a glance you can see the current status of a server. It's also possible to select a server and get detailed status information about its current situation. Of course, the level of detail depends on the type of monitoring you do on that server.

From the list of servers in the server's Health Monitor, there are two ways to get more information about the status of a server. The first is via a quick status overview, as shown in Figure 20-5. To get this overview, click the row of the server for which you want to see a quick status overview. This row will then be marked blue, with a blue arrow pointing to the status overview on the right part of the screen.

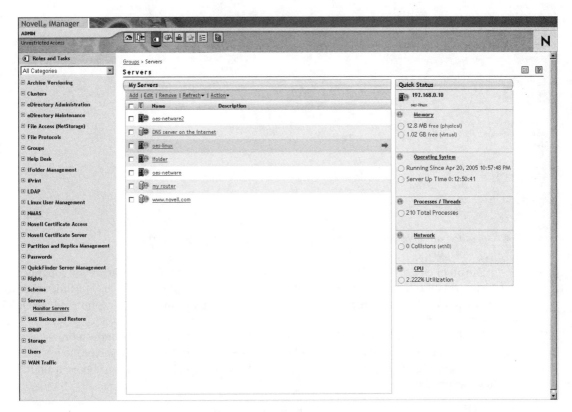

Figure 20-5. *The Quick Status overview shows a summary of the health of a server that's monitored by robust monitoring.*

From the quick status view, you can get access to detailed information easily. This is useful if a server indicates a problem in a certain category of monitored items. For example, click the Memory link to get a detailed overview of all memory in use on your server. This allows you to see immediately, and in detail, what portion of memory usage may pose a problem. An example of this is shown in Figure 20-6.

Figure 20-6. *The quick status view offers details of what's happening on your server.*

The other way to view the status of a server is by clicking its link. This shows you roughly the same information as the Quick Status view, but it takes up the entire screen, leaving little space for other servers to be displayed. Since this option much in the way of extras, I recommend the Quick Status view instead.

One last item that's useful when using the server Health Monitor is the refresh time. By default, each server in the list is polled every 15 seconds, but this setting can be changed. To do so, click the Refresh menu and select the refresh rate you wish. You can choose from the following options:

- Off
- Immediately
- Every 5 seconds
- Every 15 seconds
- Every 60 seconds
- Every 5 minutes
- Every 15 minutes

This way, you can apply the refresh rate best suited for your network bandwidth usage.

Summary

Server Health manager is a new management module in Open Enterprise Server that allows you to get a quick overview of the health of servers in your network. Two types of monitoring are currently supported—of which, the most interesting is the Robust Health status of a server. This view is only supported if on the server the OpenWBEM modules are active. OpenWBEM is the underlying architecture that allows Health Monitor to do its work. As a standalone module to monitor the health of a server, the server Health Monitor isn't that impressive; Remote Manager currently offers more options and extras. As an open standard for network management, however, OpenWBEM probably has a great future since it allows any device to be managed this way. The Health Monitoring Services in Open Enterprise Server are just a proof-of-concept of something that's going to be used much more often in future versions of OES.

INDEX

forums.apress.com

FOR PROFESSIONALS BY PROFESSIONALS™

JOIN THE APRESS FORUMS AND BE PART OF OUR COMMUNITY. You'll find discussions that cover topics of interest to IT professionals, programmers, and enthusiasts just like you. If you post a query to one of our forums, you can expect that some of the best minds in the business—especially Apress authors, who all write with *The Expert's Voice*™—will chime in to help you. Why not aim to become one of our most valuable participants (MVPs) and win cool stuff? Here's a sampling of what you'll find:

DATABASES
Data drives everything.

Share information, exchange ideas, and discuss any database programming or administration issues.

PROGRAMMING/BUSINESS
Unfortunately, it is.

Talk about the Apress line of books that cover software methodology, best practices, and how programmers interact with the "suits."

INTERNET TECHNOLOGIES AND NETWORKING
Try living without plumbing (and eventually IPv6).

Talk about networking topics including protocols, design, administration, wireless, wired, storage, backup, certifications, trends, and new technologies.

WEB DEVELOPMENT/DESIGN
Ugly doesn't cut it anymore, and CGI is absurd.

Help is in sight for your site. Find design solutions for your projects and get ideas for building an interactive Web site.

JAVA
We've come a long way from the old Oak tree.

Hang out and discuss Java in whatever flavor you choose: J2SE, J2EE, J2ME, Jakarta, and so on.

SECURITY
Lots of bad guys out there—the good guys need help.

Discuss computer and network security issues here. Just don't let anyone else know the answers!

MAC OS X
All about the Zen of OS X.

OS X is both the present and the future for Mac apps. Make suggestions, offer up ideas, or boast about your new hardware.

TECHNOLOGY IN ACTION
Cool things. Fun things.

It's after hours. It's time to play. Whether you're into LEGO® MINDSTORMS™ or turning an old PC into a DVR, this is where technology turns into fun.

OPEN SOURCE
Source code is good; understanding (open) source is better.

Discuss open source technologies and related topics such as PHP, MySQL, Linux, Perl, Apache, Python, and more.

WINDOWS
No defenestration here.

Ask questions about all aspects of Windows programming, get help on Microsoft technologies covered in Apress books, or provide feedback on any Apress Windows book.

HOW TO PARTICIPATE:

Go to the Apress Forums site at **http://forums.apress.com/**.

Click the New User link.